[a canadian focus]

introduction to sociology

edited by | ninth edition

w.e. hewitt
UNIVERSITY OF WESTERN ONTARIO

jerry white
UNIVERSITY OF WESTERN ONTARIO

james j. teevan
UNIVERSITY OF WESTERN ONTARIO (EMERITUS)

PEARSON

Prentice
Hall

Toronto

Library and Archives Canada Cataloguing in Publication

Introduction to sociology : a Canadian focus / edited by W.E. Hewitt,
Jerry White, James J. Teevan. — 9th ed.

Includes bibliographical references and index.
ISBN-13: 978-0-13-175178-1

    1. Sociology — Textbooks.   2. Canada — Social conditions — Textbooks.
I. Hewitt, W. E. (Warren Edward), 1954–   II. White, Jerry Patrick, 1951–
III. Teevan, James J., 1942–

HM586.I57 2008   301   C2006-906971-9

ISBN-13: 978-0-13-175178-1
ISBN-10: 0-13-175178-6

Editor-in-Chief, Vice-President of Sales: Kelly Shaw
Acquisitions Editors: Ky Pruesse, Laura Forbes
Executive Marketing Manager: Judith Allen
Senior Developmental Editor: Jennifer Murray
Production Editors: Tara Tovell, Richard di Santo
Copy Editor: Gail Copeland
Proofreader: Tara Tovell
Production Coordinators: Sharlene Ross, Avinash Chandra
Composition: Integra
Art Director: Julia Hall
Interior and Cover Design: Opus House Inc. / Sonya Thursby
Cover Image: Jupiter Images

1 2 3 4 5   12 11 10 09 08

Dedicated to our students—past, present, and future

Table of Contents

Preface

In this ninth edition of *Introduction to Sociology: A Canadian Focus,* we have added new content reflecting changing interests and concerns within the field of sociology. Given expanding interest in issues related to human capital, we have added a new chapter on education (Chapter 13). The deviance chapter (Chapter 5) has also been completely rewritten to reflect a more contemporary focus of high relevance to Canadian students. All the chapters have been updated with timely material that will engage our readers and several have contributions from new authors. These changes have been made while generally keeping true to our original concept: having specialists in touch with the most recent research in their respective areas contribute a part of the text. As editors, our job has been to integrate this material into an accessible resource that will inform and interest beginning students in the sociological enterprise.

This edition is divided into five parts. Part 1 introduces the field of sociology and its major variants, and includes a brief history of the discipline in Canada. It then discusses the research methods or strategies sociologists use to collect the data for their analyses. Part 2 focuses on society and the individual—the core of sociological thought—and includes discussions about culture, the shared way of life that is passed from generation to generation; the learning of culture through a process called socialization; and deviant behaviour (such as crime or mental illness), which some sociologists believe is due to failed attempts at socialization. Part 3 considers social differentiation and inequality in Canada. Here, the text examines social inequality, briefly defined as the relatively enduring differences in resources existing between social groups; gender roles, a major form of social differentiation and a source of considerable current interest in sociology; Canada's racial and ethnic groups; and our aging society. Part 4 looks at social institutions, and contains chapters on the major structures of society: families, religion, and the media. Social organization is examined in Part 5, with discussions of education, formal organizations and work, social movements, demography and urbanization, and social change.

As you will see, there is more than one sociological perspective on these various topics. The variety of sociologies is demonstrated throughout this volume, as the authors analyze their subjects and apply these various perspectives to the study of past and present Canadian society.

Acknowledgments

We would like to take this opportunity to express our appreciation to the various authors included in this text for their cooperation, hard work, and patience. We also gratefully acknowledge the many friends and colleagues who assisted our authors and us in putting the volume together, as well as the University of Western Ontario's Department of Sociology for its support. Many thanks as well to Rob Downie for his superb organizational and editing skills.

We would also like to thank the reviewers, who offered many helpful suggestions: Marlilynn Belle-McQuillan, University of Western Ontario; Howard Doughty, Seneca College; Augie Fleras, University of Waterloo; Kim Luton, University of Western Ontario; Elinor Malus, Champlain College; Barry McClinchey, University of Waterloo; Daniel Popowich, Mohawk College; Sharon Roberts, University of Western Ontario.

Finally, we would like to acknowledge the professional help from the staff at Pearson Education Canada. Our thanks to Ky Pruesse, Jennifer Murray, Tara Tovell, and Gail Copeland for assisting us in developing this fine volume.

Contributors

Tracey Adams

Carol Agòcs

Roderic Beaujot

Danièle Bélanger

Edward Bell

Marion Blute

Michael P. Carroll

Samuel Clark

Ingrid Arnet Connidis

James Côté

Lorne Dawson

Edward Grabb

Kevin D. Haggerty

Wolfgang Lehmann

Kevin McQuillan

James J. Teevan

Jerry P. White

Andrea E. Willson

Nick Dyer-Witheford

For the Instructor

The contributions of our constituent authors, combined with an editorial emphasis on clear language and minimal overlap, have resulted in an instructive text, consistently praised for its uniformity in level and consistent writing style. In this latest edition, significant updating, rewriting, and the addition of new sections covering a range of current topics in sociology make this ninth edition tighter, smoother, and more current than ever.

Features of This Edition

1. **New chapter and sections:** A new chapter on education (Chapter 13) has been developed, and Chapter 5, on deviance, has been entirely rewritten and updated. The chapters on aging and work have had input from new authors and all the chapters have been updated to include current data and concepts.

2. **Balanced approach to theoretical perspectives:** In this edition we have continued our efforts to provide a solid balance between theoretical and empirical discussion, and to illustrate concepts with Canadian examples relevant to students.

3. **Feminist theory:** Wherever possible, coverage of gender issues has been enhanced and integrated throughout the text.

4. **Up-to-date research:** The multi-author approach offers a degree of accuracy and a wealth of information attainable only through specialization. As in the past, this edition cites the most recent studies from Statistics Canada and other sources.

5. **Improved readability:** Throughout the book, passages previously identified as difficult by students and expert reviewers have been rewritten to produce a clear, concise, and comprehensive text.

Established Features

1. **Multi-author perspective:** This text combines the expertise and research base of specialists in the various subfields of sociology with a strong editorial focus to create the best of both worlds: the most up-to-date and accurate information—in a dynamic world and ever-developing discipline—explained by experts in each area, and presented in an integrated and consistent way.

2. **Accessible writing style:** The editorial team has always exercised strong control to produce an attractive and complete text with a focus on clear language and uncluttered phraseology. The result is a text that engages and motivates students to read on.

3. **Thought-provoking boxed inserts:** Boxes now include discussion questions to promote student debate. All boxes are categorized—as Applied Sociology, Debate, Research Focus, or Social Trends—to organize and facilitate classroom discussion.

4. **Canadian perspective:** Through the use of distinctly Canadian examples and applications familiar to students, this volume brings students a view of their own sociological environment and culturally relevant issues.

5. **Content coverage:** The volume covers the full spectrum of sociological theory, providing an excellent, balanced view of the major paradigms of the discipline. Core subject areas covered include: research methods, culture, socialization, deviant behaviour, social inequality, gender relations, race and ethnic relations, aging, families, religion, media, social organization and work, social movements, demography and urbanization, and social change.

6. **Introductions:** The editors have included an introduction at the beginning of each major part of the book, designed to help students tie individual chapter topics together by providing context and perspective, and suggesting a focus and emphasis to guide student learning. Students develop an understanding of the general picture and of the relationships between separate subfields in an overall sociological context.

7. **Pedagogical aids:** This text is designed to provide a firm informational base while capturing the excitement of sociology. Photos, tables, figures, charts, and extensive use of boxed articles make the book visually stimulating while supplementing written information. The boxed articles present a number of special-interest items and commentary, allowing real-world applications of theoretical perspectives through in-depth discussion of topical cases and viewpoints. Each chapter ends with a summary, a list of key terms, a series of critical-thinking exercises designed to spark student interest and debate, a list of suggested readings, and websites for further

exploration. Key terms appear in bold print in the text for easy identification and reference. A full glossary appears at the end of the volume, with page numbers to guide readers to the place in the text where the term is first discussed.

8. **Predictive focus:** All chapters include an important discussion regarding future trends and developments on the topic in question. Not only are students made aware of past and present tendencies in sociology, they are encouraged to think about what might come next, reinforcing the predictive dimension of the discipline.

Supplements for the Instructor

This edition is accompanied by a range of instructional aids, designed to meet student and instructor needs.

1. **Instructor's Manual:** This instructor's manual has been designed to ensure maximum utility to the intro-level teacher. The introduction includes general tips on teaching introductory-level sociology, especially in large-class format—now a fact of life on most university and college campuses. Chapter sections comprise: (1) a list of chapter headings; (2) a summary of *Introduction to Sociology* chapter contents; (3) a list of learning objectives; (4) a summary of key terms and concepts; (5) issues for class discussion; and (6) a list of NFB videos relevant to the topic.

2. **PowerPoint Presentation:** The PowerPoint Presentation provides graphic and text images for complete multimedia presentations in the classroom.

3. **Test Item File:** Questions in the Test Item File include: (1) fill-in-the-blank; (2) multiple choice; (3) short essay; and (4) true-false. Answers, page numbers, and difficulty level are appended to each question for easy reference to the text.

4. **MyTest:** A special computerized version of the Test Item File, this powerful assessment generation program helps instructors easily create and print quizzes, tests, exams, as well as homework or practice handouts. Questions and tests can all be authored online, allowing instructors ultimate flexibility and the ability to efficiently manage assessments at anytime, from anywhere. Issued on the Instructor's Resource CD-ROM, the MyTest is compatible with Windows and Macintosh systems.

5. **Instructor's Resource CD-ROM:** This CD-ROM contains text graphics (figures and tables); the PowerPoint Presentation, Instructor's Manual, and Test Item File for the ninth edition; as well as the MyTest.

Supplements for the Student

1. **Study Guide:** Prepared by co-editor James Teevan, this guide provides students with a study aid designed to complement the text. Chapter sections comprise: (1) a summary of objectives; (2) a summary of key terms and definitions; (3) self-quiz multiple-choice questions; (4) fill-in-the-blank questions; and (5) answers. Students can pinpoint areas of weakness and return to the text for review, as necessary.

2. **Companion Website:** A website has been developed for this text, at **www.pearsoned.ca/hewitt**. Features of the website include chapter outlines, learning objectives, key points, key terms, practice tests, web destinations and an index of names referenced in the text.

part one

Introduction

The first section of this book provides an overview of sociology as a discipline. In Chapter 1 we examine its origins and varieties, as well as a brief history of sociology in Canada. Chapter 2 describes how sociologists conduct research. Although the process generally involves the collection of data to describe or explain social phenomena, there are many specific research strategies from which to choose. Each strategy is explained in a general way, followed by a discussion of its actual practice. An assessment of the relative strengths and weaknesses of the various research methods is also presented. Read each option carefully, and then, as the various topics in need of research are suggested in the text, think about the option you might choose.

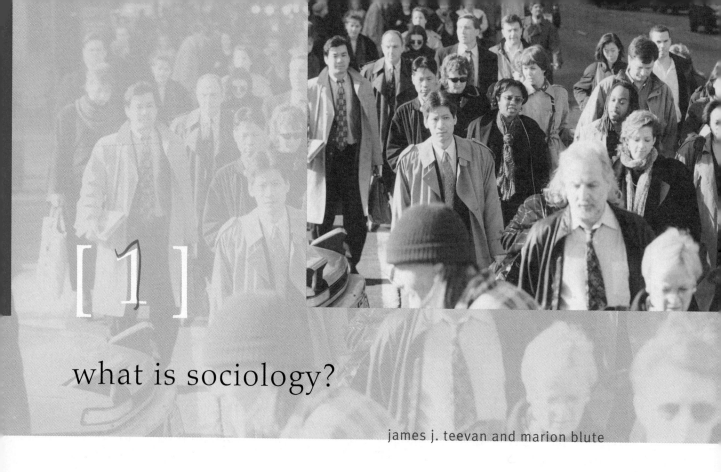

[1]

what is sociology?

james j. teevan and marion blute

Introduction

Probably the major concern of sociology is to explain why members of some groups behave differently than members of other groups. The groups can include whole societies that share a common territory and way of life, such as Canada and the U.S.; smaller groups that share the same status, such as trade unionists, doctors, or right-to-life advocates; and even social categories, individuals who may not see themselves as forming social groups at all, but who possess some social characteristic in common, such as having no children, being over six feet tall, or living in the same province. Thus, sociology attempts to answer such questions as why the U.S. has more crime than Canada (see Chapter 3, Culture), why the crime rate in B.C. is higher than in Newfoundland (see Chapter 5, Deviance), why fewer women than men are in certain professions (see Chapter 7, Gender Relations), how cohabiting couples differ from those who are married (see Chapter 10, Families), or why some Quebecers are attracted to separatism (see Chapter 15, Social Movements).

In seeking to explain such differences, many sociologists adopt a viewpoint developed over a century ago by the French sociologist Émile Durkheim (1858–1917)

in his investigation of suicide. Many of Durkheim's contemporaries thought that mental illness, inherited tendencies, or unhappiness were causes of suicide. Although each of these explanations had merit, Durkheim believed that they focused too much on the person as an isolated individual. Durkheim argued that social factors—factors pertaining either to group structure or to the relationships between individuals in groups—also affect suicide.

Durkheim called these social sources of behaviour social facts. **Social facts** point to social or group-level explanations of behaviour, such as ethnicity, gender, place of residence, and marital status. They are shared and thus unlike psychological factors, which emphasize individual, internal processes, such as drives and motives. (For a comparison of sociology, psychology, and other social sciences, see Chart 1.1.

In his classic study of nineteenth-century suicide, Durkheim uncovered variations that pointed to social causes of suicide: men had higher suicide rates than women, Protestants higher rates than Catholics and Jews, older people higher rates than the young, and single people higher rates than the married (Durkheim, 1897). Durkheim saw the greater frequency of suicide among

Chart 1.1	Sociology and the Social Sciences: A Comparison
Sociology	The study of social behaviour and relationships, it examines the effects of society and group membership on human behaviour, as well as people's perceptions of their social environment, and the effects of these perceptions on social interaction. There is much overlap between sociology and the other social sciences described below.
Psychology	Primarily the study of individual sources of behaviour, its emphasis is on processes internal to the individual, such as motivation, cognition, perception, and personality.
Social and cultural anthropology	Traditionally the study of small, nonindustrial societies, it has been extended to communities in industrial societies. This discipline tends to study these groups in totality, from their organization and culture, to specific institutions, including their economic, familial, religious, and legal systems. Sociologists attempt to achieve a more detailed view of a more limited subject area.
Political science	This discipline looks at government and political life, including the exercise of power and voting. Political sociologists study these issues as well, but usually examine them as they affect and are affected by selected aspects of the broader social context.
Economics	This discipline studies the production, distribution, and consumption of goods and services. As with political sociology, sociologists interested in the economy study these issues in a wider social context.
History	History includes both careful description of past human behaviour and examination of causal processes, usually in narrative form. Although some historians seek generalizations that hold across several specific historical instances, much historical analysis is of individual events or sequences. Sociologists generally prefer newly collected data to historical data.

men, Protestants (see van Poppel and Day, 1996), the older, and the unmarried as due in part to the relative social isolation they experienced. As a group, men were more independent than women; Protestants on average were less integrated into religious communities than Catholics and Jews; the older and the unmarried generally had fewer ties to friends and family than the young and the married. Durkheim argued that these social links, found more frequently in some groups than in others, act as buffers against suicide. He called the suicides that occur because of the lack of such social ties *egoistic suicides*.

Excessively strong social ties, claimed Durkheim, can also lead to higher suicide rates. This kind of suicide, called *altruistic suicide*, is exemplified by suicide bombers and by members of the Branch Davidian religious sect, who committed suicide in Waco, Texas, in 1993. Durkheim identified other types of suicide, also with social origins. *Anomic* suicides are found in societies marked by insufficient regulations, a condition that might arise in times of extensive or rapid social change. In anomic societies individuals experience feelings of unpredictability or being without limits, and are thus

prone to suicide. *Fatalistic* suicides occur in societies having too many rules and too few options. Individuals may feel trapped, with suicide the only way out.

The degree of regulation in society, like the strength of the ties in social groups, is a social and not an individual variable. (Indeed, individuals may be little aware of these conditions.) Thus, in his explanation of suicide, Durkheim demonstrated how social conditions affect human behaviour. Note how sociologists are concerned with *rates* of behaviour—for example, suicides among men, and not the suicide of any one man—and with group differences, comparing, for example, the suicide rates of married versus single adults (Trovato, 1991).

We should add here that sociologists never argue that behaviour is fully determined by the common experiences that may arise from group membership. Sociologists accept that people can and do make choices. But social environments, which may be different in different groups, cannot be ignored. Thus, rates of behaviour (e.g., of suicide, divorce, or alcoholism) in various groups (e.g., men and women, Canadians and Americans) may differ according to these differing circumstances.

Test Your Powers of Prediction

One of the simplest groups to consider is a cohort (a group of people with a shared, identifiable characteristic), for example, Canadians born between 1973 and 1985, who were adults aged 18 to 30 in 2003. The *Globe and Mail* (June 7, 2003) reported various cohort differences between these young adults and those born earlier. Some differences are expected, such as the better education level (especially for females) and lower religious commitment of the younger group. Can you predict other differences among these cohorts with respect to the following areas?

The answers are printed at the very end of the chapter.

- Less likely to vote
- More faith in the courts and less in Parliament
- More in favour of the government providing daycare
- Proud of the Charter of Rights and Freedoms
- More likely to call themselves Canadian
- Think Canada should be more like the U.S.
- Proud that Canada helped the commercial U.S. planes on 9/11

Suicide is obviously only one of the topics examined by sociologists. In later chapters, additional social facts are examined in depth. But first let us briefly discuss the historical forces that led to the development of sociology and take a look at its theoretical approaches.

Sociology: Its Modern Origins and Varieties

Although some sociology existed prior to the eighteenth century, the French and Industrial Revolutions kindled its modern development. Each caused upheavals in traditional European life: the French Revolution expanded the potential for democracy; the Industrial Revolution led to a new economy, the further growth of trade and cities, and a radically new organization of work. One result of these two upheavals was that relatively small, simple, rural societies—based on family and tradition, an accepted hierarchy of authority, and at least an outward appearance of consensus—gave way to more urbanized, heterogeneous, dynamic societies, marked by increasing conflict and growing social problems.

At about the same time as these social changes were occurring, science and scientific explanations, products of the Enlightenment, were increasingly supplanting religion and theological explanations of natural phenomena.

Where earlier explanations were rooted in religious dogma based on authority and faith, scientific explanations were based on observation and on reason. (For one view of science, see Chart 1.2.) Many people hoped that, just as science had revolutionized industrial production, a science of society, applied to its social ills and growing pains, could bring societies to new heights of cooperation, good will, and orderly growth. Credited by some as its founder, Auguste Comte (1798–1857) saw sociology as both a religion and a science. Sociologists would be its "priests" who would guide societies through turbulent times and heal their social problems. The decline of traditional religion, which tended to see society as divinely fixed and unchangeable and social ills as part of God's will, made possible this new discipline. The excesses of the French Revolution—exemplified by the reign of terror and mass executions—and of the Industrial Revolution—as seen in the conditions of early factories—made the development of this new discipline seem mandatory. Thus was born the modern science of sociology (see Curtis, 1992).

Almost immediately after its birth, disagreements arose concerning the approach to research that sociology should take. (This topic is discussed more fully in Chapter 2, Research Methods.) There were also disputes over the extent to which group membership affects behaviour and how societies are structured. We shall discuss this last topic first.

[Research Focus]

Sociology—A Very Broad Field

Sociologists can, and do, study just about all aspects of human behaviour. Their research topics range from differences between birthday cards intended for women and those intended for men (Brabant and Mooney, 1989) to such crucial issues as the relationship between race and disease (see Clarke, 1990). This text will offer you many sociological insights, including how watching television affects people, the myths and reality of gender differences, how wealth is distributed in our country, the changing face of immigration, the effects of divorce on children, New Age religion, First Nations' protest movements, and forms of work organization. Below is a selection of other discoveries taken from papers presented at recent conferences of sociologists.

- Infants born to women with higher education, economic status, and autonomy are more likely to survive their first year of life.

- Parents in Korea prefer the birth of a son, while those in Jamaica prefer the birth of a daughter.

- Self-identified lesbians are no more likely than other women in the population to have suffered childhood or sexual abuse, suggesting that such mistreatment is not a cause of lesbianism.

- People who feel that they are worse off than others have a greater tendency to exhibit negative attitudes toward new immigrants.

- Regardless of academic ability, children born closely spaced together in time are less likely to pursue higher education than those children born at longer intervals.

- Gossip is a weapon likely to emerge where the principals to the conflict are equals, intimate, and socially homogeneous and where there is no formalized authority structure.

Source: Adapted from various recent *Sociological Abstracts*, San Diego, CA: Sociological Abstracts Inc.

How do these discoveries reflect Durkheim's belief that social structure and group membership affect behaviour?

Some early sociologists, among them Durkheim, argued that society is based on consensus and cooperation. A modern society is structured like a human body: a collection of organs, each performing a necessary function. Implicit in this view was the idea that the various segments of society (organs) work for the benefit of society as a whole (the body) and, hence, that social ills are temporary phenomena curable by appropriate "medicines" and "repairs."

Others, such as Karl Marx (1818–1883), rejected this analogy and saw society as made up of individuals and groups held together by the strongest members, who use their power to coerce the weaker members into submission. In this account, social ills are chronic and serious, built into the very structure of society. Cures can only come from radical social change in which the powerful are forcibly overthrown and a more cooperative society established.

Put more simply, some believe societies to be founded upon consensus and cooperation, while others assert that power, coercion, and conflict mark their existence. Proponents of these two alternatives, historically known as **functionalism** (or structural-functionalism) and **conflict theory**, respectively, became major protagonists, each fighting to make their perspective dominant in the new science of society. Later, a third ("micro") approach emerged, called **symbolic interactionism**, followed by a range of feminist approaches. In the sections that follow, we examine each in turn.

Functionalism

Functionalism borrowed three major concepts from biology and medicine: function, equilibrium, and development. The term *function*, first of all, means that social arrangements exist because they somehow benefit society,

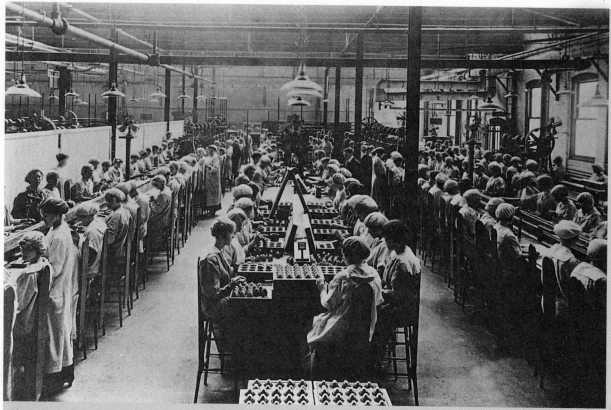

The Industrial Revolution heralded a new economy and a radically new organization of work.

and points to the importance of each part of society for the functioning and health of the whole. (Note the biological analogy with the parts of the body working together for the benefit of the whole organism.) Following this logic, functionalists could even argue, for example, that female prostitution (male prostitution was generally ignored) is beneficial and functional for society (see Davis, 1937). The general functionalist position is that if something persists in society, especially, as in the case of prostitution, in spite of widespread disapproval, then it must serve a function. If it served no function it would disappear. More specifically, prostitution is seen as an outlet for attached males' excess sexual energy but in a business arrangement, quickly concluded, and demanding little or no emotional involvement. Affairs with single women or women married to other men, on the other hand, while satisfying sexual needs, would generally require greater emotional attachment and last longer. As such they pose a greater threat to family stability. Therefore, prostitution is beneficial or functional for a society in that it decreases the potential for family disruption and divorce. We return in a few paragraphs to a viewpoint that soundly rejects these arguments. A functionalist explanation of sexual jealousy among males is examined in Chapter 3, Culture.

In the functionalist perspective, **equilibrium**, a stability based on a balance among parts and consensus, is seen as the natural state of a society. A society will return to equilibrium after it adapts to the inevitable occasional, temporary, and minor problems, called **dysfunctions**, that occur from time to time. Equilibrium also means that a change in any one part of society will be felt in other parts of society. For example, eliminating prostitution might lead not only to more family disruption, but also, according to functionalist logic, to greater premarital sexual activity and even to increased rates of sexual assault.

Finally, the concept of development or progress is often, although not always, implied in functionalist thought. Social change is seen as gradual and usually in the direction of both greater *differentiation*, the development of new social forms, and functional integration.

Chart 1.2   Characteristics of Science[1]

Empirical	Science is empirical—that is, based on observation and experience. Faith, intuition, and common sense may be sources of ideas, but science demands that such insights be subjected to empirical testing.
Explanatory	Science not only describes empirical reality but also uses laws and theories to explain why events occur, and in so doing, follows the rules of logic. For example, if groups with few social ties have relatively higher suicide rates, and if Protestants are such a group, then it is predicted that Protestants will experience higher suicide rates. This is sometimes called the "covering law" model of scientific explanation.
Simple, parsimonious, and elegant	Science prefers simple to complex explanations and seeks to explain the largest number of diverse kinds of observations with the fewest possible laws and theories. Hence Durkheim explained higher suicide rates among very diverse groups—men, Protestants, the elderly, and singles—with a single theory. Simple, parsimonious explanations are often said to be elegant and are admired by scientists as a work of art is admired.
Predictive	Science generally involves stating with a certain degree of probability that if a certain event occurs, another will follow. In sociology these predictions focus on rates of behaviour in groups—for example, on suicide rates among Protestants—and not on individual behaviour.
Pure versus applied	Science ranges from pure, seeking knowledge for its own sake, to applied, concerned with putting that knowledge to use. Sociologists do not fully agree on this issue: some seek only descriptions and explanations; others use sociological insights in their attempts to solve social problems.

[1]The above description is only one view, not a universal description of scientific practice. When historians and sociologists compare this ideal with actual scientific practice, significant discrepancies are revealed (see Ziman, 2000).

Through time, society adapts to its problems and is improved in the process. Thus, to return to our prostitution example, excess sexual energy is a dysfunction; society differentiates (creates) the occupation of prostitute to provide for a return to equilibrium and the family remains intact. Should prostitution become widely seen as dysfunctional (a view held by both the Canadian legal system and many feminists), it would disappear.

Conflict theory

In contrast to functionalism, conflict theory suggests that power, not functional interdependence, holds a society together; that conflict, not harmony, is society's natural state; and that revolutions and radical upheavals, not gradual development, fuel social change and improvement. According to this view, the major source of social conflict is inequality, something that must be eradicated, not applauded (as in the functionalist argument) as a way to ensure that society's difficult jobs will be filled (see Chapter 6, Social Inequality). Society is viewed as composed of groups acting competitively rather than cooperatively,

exploiting and being exploited rather than each fulfilling a function for the whole.

"Functional for whom?" is the common question of conflict sociologists who believe that existing social arrangements benefit the powerful—such as capitalists and religious or political leaders, more often men, struggling among themselves for dominance—certainly not all of society. Whatever the split, whether it be environmentalists and loggers, anglophone and francophone Canadians, or students and teachers, there is division and conflict. At the same time, conflict theorists generally admit to some degree of consensus and cooperation—otherwise society would fall apart—but then suggest that this agreement results from coercion and domination.

In perhaps the best-known example of conflict theory—and it should be emphasized that Marxism is only one of several conflict perspectives—Marx argued that contemporary society is held together by capitalist domination, which pits the proletariat (workers) against the bourgeoisie (owners of capital) in a constant struggle for the profit from labour. He saw the relative calm of such societies as based not on consensus or

Conflict theory suggests that conflict is society's natural state and that it fuels social improvement.

functional interdependence, as functionalists might argue, but on the capitalists' coercion of the proletariat and the workers' lack of awareness of their own exploitation. Only through revolution, Marx argued, can workers ever hope to change the capitalist-dominated structure of society. (These themes are explored further in Chapter 6, Social Inequality.)

Going back to the female prostitution example, a conflict view would see prostitution not as serving a social need but as marked by power and coercion. Prostitutes are victims forced to work under degrading and dangerous conditions, competing for clients. They are paid as little as possible by their male customers, and much of that is taken by male pimps. Male police officers arrest female prostitutes more often than their male clients. Thus, from a conflict perspective, prostitutes are best viewed as another example of females exploited by males (cf. Lowman, 1992). A radical overhaul of sex roles in society is required to modify the traditionally male-dominated arrangement of prostitution and lead, if not

to an end to sexual exploitation, then at least to more equal treatment, by the police and judiciary, of prostitutes and their customers.

Symbolic interactionism and the micro perspective

Despite their different views of society, one emphasizing cooperation, the other conflict, both functionalists and conflict theorists share a tendency to downplay the influence of individual actors in their analyses. These theorists have a "macro" focus, concerned more with groups or societies and their interrelationships. Moreover, both functionalists and conflict theorists generally see individuals as shaped by the groups and societies to which they belong, rather than the other way around.

There is much truth to the macro point of view. After all, each of us is born into a pre-existing society with its own way of life, and into particular groups such

Symbolic interactionism focuses on individuals and the autonomy of their behaviour.

as families, ethnic/linguistic communities, social classes, and even nations that shape us. At the same time, we know that individual actions can and do affect the larger group. Compare the leadership provided by Nelson Mandela in urging South Africans to overcome racial divisions with that provided by Slobodan Milosevic in exploiting ethnic divisions in Yugoslavia. Obviously we are dealing here with a "chicken and egg" situation; societies and cultures make individuals who make societies and cultures that make individuals, and so on. Unlike most functionalists and conflict theorists, however, some microsociologists prefer to begin their analyses with individuals and their interactions.

Rather than viewing individuals in terms of a mechanical analogy in which they are pushed and pulled around by social forces, as did Durkheim in his work on suicide, microsociologists view individuals as active *agents*. Individuals have goals, objectives, purposes, intentions, motives, or utility functions (the precise terminology hardly matters) as well as knowledge and

expectations about which kinds of behaviours are most likely to achieve them. As a much-quoted aphorism puts it, "People act from reasons not causes."

In conducting their research, many microsociologists emphasize the subjective over the objective. If we were in a room together looking at the furniture, we probably would not have much difficulty in agreeing that X is a table and Y is a chair. Variation in these observations (table versus chair) would be largely attributable to differences in what is being observed rather than differences among observers. In other instances, however, the reverse is the case. The same falling snow can be seen happily by groups of skiers, fearfully by others who have to drive in it, romantically by still others who watch it coating the trees, and resentfully by those who must shovel it. Behaviour and attitudes therefore can depend upon how individuals *perceive, define*, or *construct* their social world. While to some, all this may simply suggest popular ideas about "free will," a variety of schools of microsociology have explored more sophisticated understandings of the nature of individual-level processes and interaction, including their subjective aspects. One of the earliest and still influential schools of microsociology, symbolic interactionism, was founded by George Herbert Mead (1934). Symbolic interactionists claim that, unlike other animals, humans think and interact on the basis of information encoded in strings of symbols, such as sentences in a language like French or American Sign Language. A symbol is something that stands for or represents something else and in which there is no intrinsic connection between the symbol and what it signifies. Hence, while a red light means stop and a green light means go, it could conceivably have been the reverse; the connection is an accident of history. According to Blumer's (1969) view of symbolic interactionism, humans act toward things on the basis of the meanings that the things have for them, meanings that arise out of social interaction with others and are modified through an interpretive process.

Later, other microsociologists such as Homans (1950) took their cue about the nature of individual-level processes and interaction from the psychology of *learning*. According to **learning theory**, individuals learn in a variety of ways—for example, by association, or through reward and punishment. Such individual-level learning processes can explain social life by noting that, beyond the physical environment, those with whom they interact are the source of most of the rewards and punishments that people experience. They mutually shape each other's behaviour; through these means people are socialized, acquiring a variety of social identities. Add to that the observation of models and direct instruction as in school, additional forms of social learning, and you get a social theory of behaviour.

Still more recently, other microsociologists such as Coleman (1990) took their cue about the nature of social interaction from microeconomists. According to **rational choice theory**, the principles of microeconomics are applicable whatever the objective, including explaining social behaviour. At issue may not be money, but power, prestige, even motherhood or a reputation for saintliness. Among these principles, the most important is the *marginal value theorem*, that a rational actor will allocate energy, time, or other resources among alternative courses of action in such a way that the satisfaction received from the last (i.e., marginal, or least desirable) unit (course of action) allocated is equal to the others. Typically, although the satisfaction received per unit allocated to any one course of action may increase initially, sooner or later it tends to decline (think of how the amount of satisfaction you receive from eating an ice cream cone declines with each additional cone eaten and may even become negative, i.e., make you sick).

If, in addition, the outcome for any one individual depends upon what others choose, a more complicated theory called *game theory* is required to predict behaviour. For example, if professors tend to teach more successfully or give higher marks in smaller classes, then your choice of a psychology or a sociology course might be influenced not only by the relative costs (e.g., how much work is required) and the relative marginal utility (e.g., how much more knowledge or contribution to your academic record would be gained from an additional course in one or the other), but also by what others are choosing, opting for what is least popular to get a higher grade.

In their analyses, microsociologists are as interested in cooperation and conflict as are macrosociologists. Rational actors may choose to cooperate with other actors, working together or engaging in exchanges of various kinds, or they may choose to exploit others, depending upon the conditions. But the rational choice approach, like the individual learning approach, presents yet another chicken-and-egg situation. What we want influences what we learn, which influences what we want, and so forth.

Elements of various sociologies (such as symbolic interactionism, learning theory, and rational choice theory) are present in the work of some classical nineteenth-century social theorists. Gabriel Tarde (1903), a French sociologist and contemporary of Durkheim, opposed Durkheim's rather mechanical conception of social forces in his work on suicide. Instead, Tarde argued that *imitation*—what today we would call social learning—is the basic *social fact*. Tarde was a judge for many years and became convinced that criminals learn to be criminals from other criminals—that being a criminal is a profession. The German sociologist Max Weber believed that sociologists must be able to empathize (to put themselves in the place of those they study) and attempt to understand, given the actor's goals and interpretations of their situation, the reasons for their actions. For example, in his classic study of the origins of capitalism, *The Protestant Ethic and the Spirit of Capitalism* (1904–1905), Weber argued not only from a societal or macro perspective that the doctrine of Protestantism was associated with capitalism (in the same sense that Durkheim argued that Protestantism was associated with suicide) but also from a micro perspective that the link between the two was subjectively understandable and traceable to Protestants' interpretation of their worldly role.

While elements of various micro theories were present in the nineteenth century, these were more fully developed in the twentieth century. In recent years sociologists have become very interested in whether and how macrosociological approaches dealing with groups and entire societies and microsociological approaches dealing with individuals and their interactions can be integrated with, or at least used to inform, each other. Much remains to be accomplished in this respect, as the two choose to begin the story at different points.

Feminist theories

As you will read in Chapter 7, Gender Relations, there is no one "feminism." While all feminists would agree that gender inequality exists, they may disagree on its causes and thus on any "solutions." Some seek radical measures, others pursue more minor adjustments to current arrangements. Correspondingly, there is also no single feminist sociology. Still, it is the most important of the recent perspectives in sociology. Feminist sociology may be broadly defined as one "of" women from their standpoint and "for" women in the political sense of change (cf. Madoo-Lengermann-Brantley and Niebrugge, 2004). It asks: "And what about the women?"; "Why is women's situation as it is?"; "How can we change and improve the social world?"; and "What about differences among women?" which points to variations in inequality and oppression by other characteristics such as race, social class, age, and sexual orientation, among others. Feminist sociology also does not treat gender as one variable among many, as for example Durkheim did in his study of suicide. Instead, the main focus is directly on gender, because gender crosscuts all aspects of social life.

Along with its focus on women, there is within feminist sociology a general consensus in at least four other areas. First, it tends to be more activist than other types of sociology; for example, it has been successful in raising public consciousness. Certainly everyone is more aware of spousal violence, date rape, and stalking, with growing numbers aware of societies where genital mutilation of women takes place.

Second, because gender is important in all fields, including economics, history, anthropology, literature, science, and art, feminist sociology is more interdisciplinary, with feminist sociologists more linked to scholars in these and other fields, than is the case for other sociologists. (According to Eichler and Tite [1990], they also tend to be the leaders in these interdisciplinary approaches.)

Third, feminist sociology is more accepting of a broader range of approaches to research. (For more on female-friendly science, see Chapter 2, Research Methods.) Practitioners see knowledge as partial and incomplete and not strictly disinterested, affected by power relations and discovered from a point of view, not "objective." Thus it would be phrased as "I learned" rather than "the data revealed."

Finally, feminist approaches often mix different sociological perspectives, with the exception of functionalism—no feminist would defend a division of labour based upon gender as a consensual and mutually beneficial arrangement. Many sociologists, however, are comfortable with some aspects of both symbolic interactionism and the various conflict approaches. Using the former, some might be concerned with how women and men learn to be feminine and masculine. But there are important disagreements too. Symbolic interactionism is not political enough for many and, worse, it may distort the experience of women when it assumes that male perceptions of reality are the "norm."

From conflict theory, some feminist scholars focus on political economy and capitalism, as did Marx, and others on the system of male dominance or patriarchy; still others look to both as sources (both topics are further discussed in Chapter 7, Gender Relations). But compared to other conflict theorists, feminist sociologists examine the oppression of women more than the oppression of class and include unpaid labour ignored by traditional Marxists, like housework, mothering, and "invisible" work—those informal, hidden, and often devalued aspects of social life more often assigned to women.

All four models—functionalism, conflict theory, micro sociologies like symbolic interactionism, and feminism—are popular in sociology today. A sociologist's specific choice of model depends in part on the phenomenon being examined. A conflict approach may best explain far-reaching and rapid social change, while functionalism may be used to understand long-lasting, stable, and widespread phenomena. The area of study is important too. Symbolic interactionism is frequently applied to the subject of learning (see Chapter 4, Socialization) while conflict theory is generally not stressed, although it could be. In the case of inequality (see Chapter 6, Social Inequality; Chapter 7, Gender Relations; and Chapter 8, Race and Ethnic Relations) the position is generally reversed. Feminist perspectives are appearing more frequently in all areas of sociology. Generally speaking, however, most sociologists can be said to be "postmodern" (a term borrowed from the humanities) in that they reject the exclusive correctness of any single theoretical approach ("grand narrative") in favour of an eclectic mix, choosing what is suitable for the problem at hand.

Sociology in Canada

In its earliest phase, sociology in both English and French Canada scarcely existed as a discipline. While in American universities, under the influence of the Protestant-based "social gospel" movement for social reform, sociology was widely established by the turn of the century, the same movement in English Canada initially produced only a few courses in some Baptist colleges, along with some Methodist- and Presbyterian-sponsored social research (Campbell, 1983). Similarly, in French Canada, although the French Catholic sociologist and social reformer Frédéric LePlay gained an audience among some French Canadian intellectuals interested in Catholic social doctrines, the church-controlled educational institutions in Quebec were hostile to Durkheimian-style sociology (Rocher, 1977).

Eventually, however, sociology took hold in both English and French Canada. Both communities were influenced by the "human ecology" approach of Robert Park at the University of Chicago in the 1920s and his student Roderick McKenzie, eventually at the University of Michigan (Shore, 1987). The human ecology approach studies the geographical distribution or zones and natural history (succession and change) of the components of communities. With reference to our earlier discussion, the Chicago approach to sociology is a mixture of conflict and functional approaches. Change begins with an "invasion" from one zone to another—for example, when a shopping mall is built in a residential neighbourhood. Competition ensues between developers and residents (both conflict phenomena), but eventually an accommodation is reached. This accommodation could involve a buffer zone—for example, the planting of trees and the construction of small hills to separate the two areas. A symbiotic (mutually beneficial) relationship and equilibrium are then restored, both functional phenomena (see Shore, 1987: 109–12).

The first sociology department in Canada was established at McGill University in 1925 under Charles A. Dawson, trained at the University of Chicago and co-author of the first Canadian sociology textbook (Helmes-Hayes, 1994; Palantzas, 1991). It was not until some years later that a group of francophone social scientists assembled at Laval, where a department encompassing ethics and sociology was founded in 1943 (becoming a sociology department in 1951). In the 1940s the Laval group came under the leadership of Jean-Charles Falardeau, the first professionally trained sociologist in francophone Canada. From McGill and Laval the first

classics of Canadian sociology emerged. The departments examined a range of national issues including, for example, Dawson's studies of the settlement process in western Canadian communities, and the work of Everett Hughes (first affiliated with McGill and later with Laval as well) on modernization and ethnic relations in "Cantonville" (Drummondville), a textile town in Quebec. Hughes came to be known as one of the great sociologists of his time, and his *French Canada in Transition* (1943) remains an international classic in the discipline.

Not surprisingly, like other aspects of Canadian history, society, and culture, there was also a British influence. In addition to Dawson and Hughes, the McGill department in its early years included Leonard Marsh, educated at the London School of Economics, which was founded to conduct empirical social research in the service of socialism. Marsh's early research at McGill, on Canadians "in and out of work" during the Great Depression, had a lasting impact on Canadian society (Helmes-Hayes and Wilcox-Magill, 1993). In 1932 he helped found The League for Social Reconstruction, a forerunner of the CCF, which itself was the forerunner of the New Democratic Party. The recommendations of his *Report on Social Security for Canada* (1943) for the federal government laid the foundation for the Canadian social security system, including family allowances and employment insurance.

In 1949, John Porter returned from the London School of Economics to Carleton College (now Carleton University) in Ottawa. Sixteen years later he produced *The Vertical Mosaic: An Analysis of Social Class and Power in Canada* (1965), which became another international classic of Canadian sociology. In it, Porter argued that although Canada may be an ethnic and cultural mosaic (a picture made up of small pieces), it is an unequal or vertically stratified one —hence the "vertical mosaic" of the title, a phrase that Marsh had used many years before. These topics are discussed further in Chapter 6, Social Inequality, and Chapter 8, Race and Ethnic Relations.

A second legacy of the British influence on Canadian sociology was to slow its spread beyond Quebec. In Britain, sociology was commonly viewed as an ahistorical and "shallow American discipline" (Hiller, 1982: 3). Thus, although from the 1930s through the 1950s research that can be viewed as sociological was performed in anglophone Canada, it was usually conducted in history, political economy, and even humanities departments; sociology departments just did not exist. The most important stream of this research, and one usually considered native to Canada, was

Innis argued that Canada's economic, political, and social organization were shaped by a dependence on staple products.

performed at the University of Toronto by Harold Innis and later by S.D. Clark and Marshall McLuhan. Even there, however, the Chicago connection was stronger than has sometimes been supposed (Shore, 1987).

Harold Innis, a historical and institutional economist whom you will encounter in Chapter 17, Social Change, was trained at the University of Chicago economics department and influenced by Chicago-style sociological theory. In a trilogy of monographs on mining, the fur trade, and the cod fishery published after 1930, Innis argued that changes in demand for staple products (such as fur, fish, timber, iron ore, and wheat), the physical properties of the staples themselves, the technological means by which they are processed, and their geographical locations relative to transportation and markets shape not only economic but also political and social organization. For example, Innis maintained that the political boundaries of Canada were created by the demand for furs in Europe, the ease with which they were over-exploited in any

particular area, the geography of the pre-Cambrian shield and river systems, and the canoe as a means of transportation. He also argued that the perishability of cod, the coastal location of the resource, and the technology for curing it created the characteristic geographical distribution and social organization of Canada's east coast, with its numerous, small, scattered fishing villages.

Late in his life, Innis turned from the study of the transportation of goods to the communication of information. He concluded that the physical properties of media, like those of staple goods, had enormous consequences. He contrasted, for example, the relative permanence but unportability of stone and clay tablets with the relative portability but impermanence of papyrus and paper. Innis's work on communications media then influenced a fellow University of Toronto professor, an English professor, who became (along with Northrop Frye, the literary critic) Canada's most internationally celebrated scholar—Marshall McLuhan.

In *The Gutenberg Galaxy: The Making of Typographic Man* (1962) and *Understanding Media: The Extensions of Man* (1964), McLuhan argued that the dominant force in political, social, and cultural change in human history had been changes in the dominant medium of communication—from oral to written to electronic (see Chapter 12, Media). Various media are extensions of specific human senses; whatever medium predominates distorts perceptions in favour of a specific sense, the radio for hearing, and television for seeing. Consequently, media shape not only the economic, political, social, and cultural environment but also the very nature of human consciousness.

McLuhan's thesis was almost instantly recognized as the most original idea since Marx's attempt to explain all of human history with the concept of class conflict. "The medium is the message" briefly and clearly stated its central thesis, while phrases such as "the Gutenberg galaxy" and "the global village" succinctly communicated McLuhan's view that those steeped in a print rather than an electronic culture to all intents and purposes inhabit different universes (see Marchand, 1989). Although McLuhan himself always maintained a rich network of multidisciplinary contacts, friends, and associates, the fairly rapid creation of separate communications departments within universities caused the study of communications to have less influence on sociology and the other social sciences than it might otherwise have had.

Meanwhile, a student of Innis's, Samuel D. Clark, led a small group of sociologists out of the department of political economy at the University of Toronto to establish the first department of sociology in Canada outside of Quebec. For many years, Clark was Canada's best-known sociologist (Magill and Michelson, 1999). Educated first at the University of Saskatchewan, then at the London School of Economics, McGill's sociology department, and finally under Innis in political economy at Toronto, Clark owed something to all of these influences. *Church and Sect in Canada* (1948) and *Movements of Political Protest in Canada* (1959), for example, include an Innis-style setting of new areas of economic exploitation (in the Canadian west), social disorganization (religious sects and political protest), and a Chicago-style focus on restoration of equilibrium in social organization.

By the early 1960s, sociology was tenuously established in Canada. Institutionally it was still limited to Quebec and Toronto. Intellectually it had inherited an interest in the structure of entire communities from the Chicago-style sociology of the 1920s. Yet it often combined this focus with an historical approach, to examine long-term change in greater depth than was common in Chicago-style sociology.

In the 1960s, the baby-boom generation came of age and, simultaneously, governments decided that continued economic prosperity depended on a having more university-educated people. As a consequence new universities, including new sociology departments, sprang up around the country, creating an unprecedented demand for university teachers of sociology. Large numbers of foreign sociologists, primarily American, immigrated to Canada to take up the newly created positions. By 1970–71, 60 percent of sociology and anthropology professors in Canada were not Canadian citizens (Hiller, 1982: 25). Such mass immigration could not fail to be disruptive, as any community- and ecology-minded sociologist would predict. Conflicts were initiated, some of which were never resolved entirely.

In English-speaking Canada, the new faculty members came into conflict with those already there, and not infrequently with each other, as the American imports were not a homogeneous group but reflected the many sociologies being practised in the United States. While Harvard graduates emulated the European classics (Parsons, 1937, 1951) and "grand theory," a whole technology of polling and survey research had spread outward from Columbia University to many other American universities. If some Canadian sociologists thought Chicago-style studies of communities were too ahistorical, one can imagine what they thought of New York's Columbia-trained sociologists whose idea of research was almost exclusively to administer surveys of attitudes and beliefs! (This and other research options will be discussed in Chapter 2, Research Methods.) Political conflicts, too, were not uncommon. For some of the newcomers, the move to Canada was a straightforward professional one. For others it was an abandonment of a society they viewed as hopelessly racist and war-mongering (this was the period of America's involvement in Vietnam). For still others it was an escape from the protesting students on American campuses. One can imagine the sparks that flew when protesters and the protested-against sometimes found themselves colleagues in the same department. And last but not least, both the old and the newly arrived professors often came into conflict with their students—the old because the sociology of communities did not seem to address the conflict-ridden times adequately, and the new because their knowledge of, and sometimes even interest in, Canadian society was often elementary at best, at least initially (Hiller, 1979).

As a result of some of these problems, the Association of Universities and Colleges of Canada established a commission on Canadian Studies in 1975. Their report, *To Know Ourselves*, stated "a curriculum in this country that does not help Canadians in some way to understand the physical and social environment that they live and work in . . . cannot be justified" (Symons, 1976: 13). This in turn led to federal attempts to place limits on the hiring of foreign academics by Canadian universities. To this day the 1970s movement to "Canadianize" university curricula and personnel remains contentious—viewed as a success by some (Cormier, 2004) and a failure by others (Ogmundson, 2006).

In Quebec the changes and conflicts were different, but equally dramatic. Those same demographic and economic forces at work led to the "Quiet Revolution" (see Chapter 15, Social Movements) in which the state took over responsibility for education from the Catholic Church. As a result, the number of sociologists increased and departments were added—first at the Université de Montréal and later elsewhere. Because of the language difference, however, Quebec imported fewer Americans and relied more on people without doctorates and on French Canadians trained in France or the United States. Conflict in Quebec was often associated with the addition of new departments, which tended to put forth, in their early days, different interpretations of Quebec society (Renaud et al., 1989). The earlier "modernizing" view, which had predominated at Laval, was displaced by various Marxist interpretations and by an analysis of Quebec as at once a distinct ("global") society and an "ethnic class" within Canada (Dumas, 1987).

Until about the mid-1960s the two coexisted. There was a sense of belonging to a Canadian Sociology and a wish to establish ties with anglophone colleagues in other provinces, to share with them the fruits of Quebec research (Rocher, 1992: 66). Gradually, however, English-language and Quebec sociology in Canada went their own ways, with different journals, professional associations, and intellectual concerns. Rocher (1992) documented this decline in interaction and related it to a growing preoccupation by Quebec sociologists with changes within Quebec society, their increasing interaction with francophones beyond Canada, and the increasing anglophone unilingualism of Canadian professional meetings (although Canadian Sociology and Anthropology Association [CSAA] publications remain bilingual). Today there exist major differences between the two sociologies. For example, sociology proper in Quebec has remained concerned almost exclusively with macrosociological questions (Breton, 1989: 563). Associated with this

emphasis, according to Béland and Blais (1989), is the infrequent use of quantitative methods in sociology in Quebec. Morris (1991) also found in Quebec sociology a greater emphasis on social policy and on applied rather than pure sociology. For a final example, perhaps because of the greater availability of funding for social research at the provincial level in Quebec, sub-specialties of sociology (such as criminology, demography, and urban and regional studies) have tended to become independently institutionalized there (Juteau and Maheu, 1989: 371).

Future Challenges

French Canada in Transition, The Vertical Mosaic, and *Understanding Media,* among others, are classics of social scientific and sociological scholarship, each contributing in its time to our understanding of ourselves. The Association of Universities and Colleges of Canada (2005) estimates that 40 000 faculty members will have to be hired by Canadian universities over the next decade due to retirements, enrolment growth, and quality improvement demands. Many of these are again being hired from abroad. It remains to be seen whether the next generation of sociologists, Canadian or otherwise, will provide insights into such issues as

- the consequences of accelerating globalization in a world with one superpower and the continuing gap between rich and poor countries;

- the weakening of existing nation-states, combined with a resurgence of conflict among ethnic/linguistic groups in Europe, the former Soviet Union, and Africa;

- the future of Canadian federalism and other integration issues in a country with the highest per-capita immigration rate in the world;

- the continued existence of discrimination based on race, gender, age, and sexual orientation; and

- last but not least, the fate of human societies (and of other species) given current and projected levels of resource depletion and environmental degradation including global warming brought about by the size of the human population and its way of life (see Wright, 2004; Diamond 2005).

As you read in later chapters about the social facts that sociologists have already uncovered, and the theories offered to explain these facts, perhaps you will make your own tentative judgments.

[Applied Sociology]

Careers in Sociology

Later in this book you will read about postsecondary education. For now, let us assume that you are attending school not only for the enjoyment of learning and to gain the credentials necessary to validate your claim to be an educated person, but also as an avenue to an interesting, well-paying job, one that will give you freedom to express your creative talents.

Sociology graduates work in a wide variety of occupations, especially in education, social service agencies, and other government departments. They apply the critical and creative thinking skills they developed in sociology to teaching and research, helping to explain social phenomena; to social welfare programs, seeking to improve people's lives; to the criminal justice system; and to social movements and private organizations working for a better society. Whether as personnel or communications managers, as designers or analysts of opinion polls, they generally share an appreciation for the social factors that affect individual behaviour and an optimism for the possibility of social change.

Source: Adapted from Scott Davies, Clayton Mosher, and Bill O'Grady, 1992. "Canadian sociology and anthropology graduates in the 1980s labour market." *Society,* 16: 39–46.

While the value of sociology is apparent within the public sector, can you think of important contributions that sociology can make to business?

Questions for Review and Critical Thinking

1. To what extent should sociology be used to ameliorate the problems of society, rather than simply "study" them?

2. In the study of social phenomena, how much objectivity is possible? What are some examples of how subjective experience may bias a sociologist's observations?

3. How would a conflict explanation of divorce differ from a functionalist one?

4. Ask your instructors how they became sociologists. Where were they educated? In what kinds of sociology were they trained? What kinds of sociology do they prefer now?

Key Terms

conflict theory, p. 5
dysfunctions, p. 6
equilibrium, p. 6
functionalism, p. 5
learning theory, p. 10
rational choice theory, p. 10
social facts, p. 2
symbolic interactionism, p. 5

Suggested Readings

Carroll, William K., Linda Christiansen-Ruffman, Raymond Currie, and Deborah Harrison (eds.)
1992 *Fragile Truths: 25 Years of Sociology and Anthropology in Canada.* Ottawa: Carleton University Press.
This work has articles on sociology in Canada, including its relationship to social change, how sociological knowledge is made (including a look at feminist alternatives and the differences between English and French Canadian sociologies), its academic milieu, and finally its professional association.

Hoecker-Drysdale, Susan
1990 "Women sociologists in Canada: the careers of Helen MacGill Hughes, Aileen Dansken Ross, and Jean Robertson Burnett." Pp. 152–76 in

Marianne G. Ainley (ed.), *Despite the Odds: Essays on Canadian Women and Science.* Montreal: Véhicule Press.

The lives and careers of three early Canadian women sociologists reveal a familiar story of obstacles, frustrations, and finally accomplishments made but then not fully or only belatedly recognized.

Ritzer, George and Douglas J. Goodman

2004 *Sociological Theory.* (6th ed.) New York: McGraw-Hill, Inc.

This theory text, although a bit advanced, describes the major early sociologists as well as perspectives in contemporary sociology including functionalist, conflict, symbolic interactionist, and feminist views.

Websites

www.sosig.ac.uk/welcome.html
Social Science Information Gateway
This page provides links to dozens of sites of interest and potential use to students of sociology, from sociology associations, to electronic journals, to information on famous sociologists such as Durkheim.

http://socserv.mcmaster.ca/sociology/resources.htm
Sociology and Anthropology Organizations and Departments
At this site, you will find a complete listing of and links to sociology departments at postsecondary institutions in Canada, Canadian sociology journals online, and the Canadian Sociology and Anthropology Association.

Key Search Terms

Functionalism
Conflict theory
Feminist theory
Symbolic interactionism
Sociology in Canada

For more study tools to help you with your next exam, be sure to check out the Companion Website at **www.pearsoned.ca/hewitt**, as well as Chapter 1 in your Study Guide.

Answers to "Test Your Powers of Prediction"

• Less likely to vote	Younger cohort
• More faith in the courts and less in Parliament • More in favour of the government providing daycare • Proud of the Charter of Rights and Freedoms	Younger cohort—This group has less faith in government per se, but still expects the government to provide basic social services, and is proud of Canada's written laws and how the courts interpret them.
• More likely to call themselves Canadian	Younger cohort— Intermarriage and a longer time away from "the old country" also make them more likely to call themselves Canadian.
• Think Canada should be more like the U.S. • Proud that Canada helped the commercial U.S. planes on 9/11	Older cohort

[2]

research methods

Introduction

Suppose you wanted to know if Canada's divorce rate is changing, whether husbands or wives remarry more quickly, or what happens to children after their parents get a divorce. One way to answer these questions would be to look to your personal experiences (or to those of your friends) or to ask authorities such as your parents or religious leaders.

Sociologists are reluctant to use such strategies because of their potential for distortion. For example, though there may have been fewer divorces recently in your family, it does not mean the national rate is going down. Because your cousins seemed happier once away from the constant fighting of their parents does not mean that most children feel better after divorce. The fact that Aunt Liz remarried quickly does not mean that women remarry more quickly than men (the opposite is true). Personal experience is usually not general enough (and, worse, may be based on selective perception—seeing what you want to see) to produce accurate statements about the larger society. Even authorities can give incomplete answers or favour one interpretation over another equally compelling one. And finally, what

happens when one person's experience or authorities contradict those of another? How is that resolved?

Sociologists argue that questions about divorce, and social life in general, require a research project of some sort. They want to collect and analyze data from a wide variety of settings before drawing any conclusions. The different ways sociologists conduct their research is the topic of this chapter. It begins with an overview of two basic approaches and then presents a more in-depth example of each, examining their relationship to theory, model, forms of measurement, sampling, and data analysis—terms that will be defined below. An evaluation of the advantages and disadvantages of each approach ends the chapter.

Quantitative and Qualitative Methods

In Chapter 1 you read that Durkheim and Weber had quite different ideas on how to conduct research. Durkheim adopted a position called **positivism**, meaning that he wanted to use the research methods of the natural sciences, appropriately adapted, for the social

[Debate]

Is Science Gendered?

Although there is still much disagreement among feminists about both the existence of "women's ways of knowing" and of a single feminist research perspective, there is more agreement that in many instances women conduct science differently than do men (Hesse-Bieber and Yaiser, 2004). Early on, in fact, Rosser (1990) concluded that a less andro-centric (male-centred) more "female-friendly science" would affect research methods including topics we have already mentioned here: theory, observation, data-collection techniques, and analysis.

In the first instance, the literature surveyed under a more female-friendly approach is more interdisciplinary, breaking down (artificial) disciplinary barriers to cooperative research and at the same time expanding the context to encompass a more holistic, global scope. Still, gender is always a crucial part of the questions being asked and more females are the subjects in research. Regarding data gathering, an increase in the number of observations and a lengthier observational stage is common, along with combinations of qualitative and quantitative methods, including oral history and *focus groups*, group interviews with an emphasis on group interaction and the joint construction of meaning. These are accompanied by more methods that shorten the distance between the observer and her subjects. The key is less hierarchy, and a construction of knowledge that includes those being studied and less positivistic so-called "objectivity."

Finally, female-friendly science tends to be less competitive, making the role of scientist only one facet to be integrated with other aspects of life, including family life. A greater emphasis on strategies such as teaching and communicating with non-scientists to break down the barriers between science and the layperson is also apparent, along with a greater awareness of other sources of bias in research such as race, class, sexual orientation, and religion.

For more on this and related topics, see work by Canadians such as Reinharz (1992).

Identify a specific example of how traditional "male" science tends to reflect a male, as opposed to a female, perspective on social life. Can science ever be gender neutral?

sciences. Durkheim's followers favour what we today call *quantitative* methods. Counting and precise measurement of *observable* behaviour, a limited number of variables, and *prediction* are hallmarks of a quantitative approach. In an example of quantitative research, Cook and Beaujot (1996) found that, while having young children tends to reduce the probability of fathers leaving the workforce, the presence of children increases the chances of work interruptions for mothers, especially those who are single. As in that instance, most quantitative sociologists never directly observe actual behaviour. Survey researchers, for example, take verbal reports from those they study. Even experimenters, another quantitative type, observe laboratory instead of real-world behaviour (see the box "Does Drinking Lead to Date-Related Sexual Assault?").

Weber argued that the social sciences should not copy the research methods and experimental designs of the natural sciences. Human behaviour, he argued, is unique, because of the subjective meanings and motivations attached to it. Human beings are complex and make choices based on these meanings, making any discussion of gender, parenthood, and work more involved than described above. Moreover, sociologists need to *understand* behaviour, not just predict it. Do more men stay employed because they hate housework? Do women more dislike leaving infants at home? Is it because men make more money than women and thus it is economically rational for them to be the one who works? Because humans give meanings to their behaviour, because they engage in what Weber called *social action* (meaningful goal-directed behaviour), the predictions would be incomplete without some understanding and explanation of the behaviour from the actors' point of view.

To get at these meanings, *qualitative* methods had to be developed. Weber thought empathy might be a tool— imagining yourself in the shoes of those whose behaviour you want to understand. Today, in a method called **participant observation**, researchers observe actual behaviour, talk at length and in depth with those being observed and ask them the meaning of their behaviour. Now, having introduced quantitative and qualitative approaches generally, let us turn to one specific quantitative approach.

A quantitative option: Survey research

Survey research is the most common type of research undertaken today and is familiar to most of you in the form of interviews or questionnaires. (See the box "What's in a Word? Analyzing Media Content" for another quantitative option.) It involves asking people questions, either in written or oral form, and recording their answers. Let us now examine its relationship to theory, its model, and strategies for measurement, sampling, and analysis in survey research.

Theories and hypotheses

At its most general level, theory refers to the basic, but often abstract, approach to subject matter, for example, a conflict approach, mentioned in the last chapter. At a middle level, **theory** gets more specific and refers to a set of interrelated statements that organize and summarize knowledge about some part of the social world. There could, for example, be a theory of crime or a theory of prejudice. The statements found in these theories are often taken from the conclusions of prior research on the topic in which variables are linked to one another. A **variable** for sociologists is something (like income or religion) that takes on different values (i.e., it varies) in different groups. A relationship between two variables means that they go together in some way—changes in one accompany changes in the other. For example, level of integration and suicide rates are related, as pointed out in the last chapter, with the over- and under-integrated more prone to suicide. Integration and suicide are the variables, and the relationship is that extremes in integration may encourage suicide.

From these theories a testable **hypothesis** can logically be derived. An hypothesis is a statement of a *presumed* relationship between two or more variables, usually stated in the form, "Other things being equal, if A, then B." If the A variable occurs, then the B variable also

occurs. We might hypothesize that, other things being equal, gender (A) is related to a choice of research methods (B), with men more often favouring a quantitative approach and women more often a qualitative one (see Oakley, 1998). The B variable is the one being explained, the A variable the explanation. In causal statements, A is the cause or **independent variable**, B the effect or **dependent variable**.

The first type of logic used in this hypothesis derivation is **axiomatic logic**, making connecting links between related theoretical statements, as in, "If A → B and B → C, then A → C." For example:

Theoretical statements (known to be true):

1. Birth order (A) is related to closeness to parents (B) (first-born children more closely tied to their parents than later-born).
2. Closeness to parents (B) encourages conservative values (C).

Axiomatic logic:

3. Therefore, birth order (A) is related to conservative values (C) (first-born children more conservative than later-born).

Deductive logic involves deriving a specific statement from a more general statement. Thus, given the general statement that birth order (A) is related to conservative values (C), we can hypothesize that it is related to number of sexual partners (C_1) or instances of marijuana use (C_2), with first-borns more likely to have fewer of each.

But remember that hypotheses include the phrase *other things being equal*. That means that, at least *collectively*, the groups compared should be similar in other social characteristics. In the current example, first- and later-born children should be the same in terms of age and sex. To compare a group of first-borns marked by a preponderance of 14-year-old girls to a group of second-borns overpopulated by 20-year-old young men would be an unfair test of the effect of birth order on number of sexual partners, with age and gender the real reasons. The ideal of "other things being equal" may be difficult to achieve, but must be attempted because these variables are also related to sexual permissiveness.

Model

Models are built by combining two or more "if A, then B" statements to fill in or extend the explanation chain.

For example, one could develop the following model to explain the relationship between social class and adult crime: Social class (A) is related to (B) age of parents at birth of first child (poorer parents have children at a younger age); age of parents (B) is related to (C) family breakup (the earlier the onset of family responsibilities, the higher the separation rate); broken families (C) are related to (D) children's school difficulties, especially to failing grade one; early school failure (D) is related to (E) delinquency; and finally, delinquency (E) is related to (F) adult criminality. For any two variables in this chain, let us axiomatically link family breakup (C) and (E) delinquency (broken homes produce more delinquents, via C→D→E). The variable that occurs first here (C) is generally assumed to be an independent variable, the later one (E) a dependent variable, and the others, including D, the control variables. We shall explain control variables more fully later.

Measurement

Measuring variables is probably the most difficult task survey researchers have to perform. Generally it involves transforming the *theoretical* language of the hypothesis into the *operational* language of measurement. **Operational definitions** describe the actual procedures used to measure theoretical concepts. For example, an I.Q. score is an operational definition of the theoretical concept of intelligence; counting the number of times per month people attend religious services can be an operational definition of religiosity. The general strategy in operationalizing variables is to devise simple, directly observable or *empirical* measures of things that may be complex, difficult to measure directly, and hard to observe. Operational definitions, therefore, are what researchers *look for* or *listen to* in order to measure their variables.

How would you operationalize prejudice? Would watching to see if people do not like certain groups be an operational definition? No, because you still would not know what to look for. How do you see "not liking"? Would laughing at jokes that make fun of certain groups be an operational definition of prejudice? Yes it would, because it is observable and relatively clear—both major requirements of an operational definition. It is an empirical measure that can be heard. Alternatively, you could ask: "Are you prejudiced against (insert name of group), yes or no?" That question is also an operational definition, providing an empirical indicator: the "yes" or "no" response.

Some of you probably do not like either of these operational definitions, the first because unprejudiced people may laugh at these jokes, and the second because people may be evasive in their answers or even lie. These objections raise the issue of the **validity** of operational definitions—the degree to which they actually measure what they claim to measure, always an issue in constructing operational definitions.

Besides being valid, operational definitions must also be reliable. **Reliability** means that measures of a variable should be consistent and not fluctuate over time or with the person using them. Thermometers, for example, are generally reliable. Operational definitions, however, may lack reliability, as when respondents (1) admit to certain attitudes early in a questionnaire but later on, perhaps because they are growing tired, deny the same attitudes; or (2) tailor their responses to the person asking the questions, for example when female interviewers get different answers than male interviewers. If a measure is unreliable, yielding inconsistent results, it cannot be valid. One of the differing results might represent a valid measure, but researchers could not specify which one. Would it be the first? The last? The one given to a male or the one given to a female interviewer? On the other hand, although reliability is necessary for validity, it cannot guarantee it. Even fairly reliable measures such as income may not be valid measures of lifestyle or social class.

Sampling

No survey researcher has the time or resources to study everyone. For this reason they usually draw a *sample*, selecting a subset of individuals from the population they wish to study. There are really only two rules of sampling. First, a sample should be *representative* of the population from which it is drawn. Second, conclusions should not be *generalized* beyond the group from which the sample is drawn.

The second rule is simpler, so we shall discuss it first. It means that if researchers fail to sample from some groups, they cannot say their findings hold for them. For example, if researchers ask a sample of sociology students at the University of Alberta to fill out a questionnaire about Quebec separatism, they cannot then discuss the attitudes of *all* students at the University of Alberta on this topic because the views of non-sociology students were never measured. Non-sociology students may be unlike sociology students in many ways,

Researchers usually draw a sample of individuals from the group they wish to examine.

including their attitudes about Quebec separatism. Similarly, the researchers cannot generalize from Alberta sociology students to all sociology students. York and Dalhousie sociology students, among others, may be quite different from Alberta sociology students in their feelings about Quebec.

The goal of representativeness involves drawing a sample that "looks like" and thus can represent the total population. To accomplish this, researchers could take, for example, a **random sample**. In simple random sampling, all individuals are listed (the result is called a *sampling frame*) and then some are selected purely by chance, just like names from a hat or numbered balls from the cages on television lottery shows. For an alternative to this listing, see the box "Hello, I Am Calling to Ask Your Opinion."

Although preferred in theory, because every individual has an equal chance of being selected, random samples in practice are often difficult to achieve. Listing all of the individuals from whom the sample will be drawn—for example, all Canadians—is time consuming, often difficult, even impossible. Therefore, researchers

may opt for cluster sampling or multistage random sampling, to simplify the task.

In **cluster sampling**, researchers first sample large units, then medium units within the large units, and finally, even smaller units within the medium units, each time randomly. For example, they could list the geographical areas (tracts) used by the census to facilitate enumeration in Canada, and select 100 at random. Then they could list all streets in these census tracts and randomly select 500 of them, and finally, list all residents who live on those streets and randomly select 1000 for interviewing.

Both simple random sampling and cluster sampling permit generalizations to the population—a major goal of researchers. Anyone can be chosen and thus the samples should be representative, reflecting the population from which they are drawn. But, in reality, researchers using random sampling techniques often cannot generalize to the total population because many of the randomly chosen individuals refuse to be interviewed. For this and other reasons, some researchers turn to also imperfect, but easier to execute, quota samples.

"Hello, I Am Calling to Ask Your Opinion . . . ." Sound Familiar?

Telephone interviews have unique advantages over other types of interviews: lower cost, better response rate than mailed questionnaires, easier access (many people will not admit interviewers into their homes and many interviewers do not feel safe entering the homes of strangers), and reduced lying because respondents feel a greater anonymity. On the down side, people can easily hang up on the interviewer, and the overall response rate is lower than for personal interviews. Nevertheless, the disadvantages are seen as acceptable costs in this increasingly popular survey research technique (for a discussion see Bryman and Teevan, 2005).

Most researchers used to use Random Digit Dialling (RDD), a sampling technique that used computers to randomly dial enough phone numbers to constitute a sample. This method was considered better than using a phone directory because it got around unlisted and newly listed numbers. But today increasing numbers of individuals (young people especially) do not own a hard-wired phone number and rely on a cellphone or BlackBerry device with charges for incoming calls. They will not pay for a phone interview and thus RDD is being modified to draw the sample from only listed numbers thus excluding cellphone numbers.

What types of individuals or groups might be missed using telephone interviews?

Quota sampling is a less expensive alternative to random sampling and involves a conscious, as opposed to chance, matching of the sample to certain proportions in the population. For example, if researchers know that 35 percent of a population are women in the labour force, 19 percent women at home, 40 percent men in the workforce, and 6 percent men at home, they interview people in exactly those same proportions, thus ensuring that the sample is "representative" of the population. The actual respondents are generally chosen by availability—that is, from those who are close by and/or willing to be interviewed, until the final list of respondents conforms to the 35, 19, 40, and 6 percent figures. The major drawback to quota sampling is that those who are nearby and cooperative may be quite different from the further-away and/or uncooperative segments of the population.

Quota sampling is really a sophisticated version of *accidental sampling*, in which researchers talk to anyone at a selected location, regardless of social characteristics. Shoppers in a mall and students in introductory sociology classes are frequent accidental samples. This type of sampling is relatively inexpensive, making it a popular choice; its drawback is the inability to generalize to the larger unsampled population.

In conclusion, limited resources mean that not everyone can be studied. If researchers have substantial

University students often form accidental samples. Their drawback is the inability to generalize to the larger population.

funds, they will draw simple random or cluster samples; if less money, quota samples; and with little money, accidental samples. The ability to generalize the findings to the population decreases in the same order, due to increasing doubts concerning representativeness.

Analysis

After collecting their data, researchers must analyze the data to look for relationships among the variables. The exact type of analysis depends on the complexity of the hypotheses being studied, but the basic process in survey research involves an examination of relationships between independent and dependent variables. For example, suppose a researcher collected data (see Table 2.1) on perception of punishment and shoplifting among adolescents. Recall that the B variable is the one being explained, the A variable the explanation.

The independent variable (here placed at the top of the table) might be the expected severity of punishment, the dependent variable frequency of shoplifting, and the hypothesized relationship that those who expect severe punishment are less likely to shoplift than those who

Table 2.1	Relationship between Perception of Punishment and Shoplifting

Categories of the independent variable

Categories of the dependent variable	Expect severe punishment	Expect light punishment
Shoplift	36% (21)	78% (38)
Do not shoplift	64% (37)	22% (11)
N	100% (58)	100% (49)

expect only light punishment. N refers to the number of individuals in each category of the independent variable: 58 who expect severe punishment and 49 who expect light punishment, called *marginals* because they fall outside of the actual table. Of the 58 who expect severe punishment, 21 shoplift and 37 do not. Of the 49 who expect light punishment, 38 shoplift and 11 do not. These numbers appear in the *cells* where the independent and dependent variables meet. As a general practice, researchers do not

[Research Focus]

What's in a Word? Analyzing Media Content

Content analysis involves the examination (analysis) of themes (content) from communications such as conversations, letters, newspapers, books, or movies. It is often like survey research in its assumptions and practices. It tends to use deductive logic to derive hypotheses, and to focus on a limited number of variables.

Because it generally uses operational definitions, content analysis also resembles survey research in its measurement, leading to quantifiability, reliability, and replicability. But the method is less strong on validity. Researchers can only assume that they have uncovered the actual values and meanings of the original communicators who are never contacted, and may even be dead, and that the audiences understood these values and meanings. Subtle, hidden, or between-the-lines

meanings, known perhaps only to the communicators and their audiences, are especially problematic for content analysts. Finally, researchers cannot tell if the people actually acted in the ways their communications would suggest.

As for sampling, content analysis generally involves some form of random sampling procedure, allowing generalizability at least to the sampling frame. Authors, their books, and then certain pages may be cluster-sampled, for just one example. The analysis tends to be quantitative and statistical, much like survey research analysis.

The great strengths of content analysis are (1) it is inexpensive; (2) it lends itself to historical and cross-cultural analyses, and (3) someone else can easily recheck the study because the data are inanimate and unlike humans unaffected by the research process.

What are some of the potential weaknesses of this approach?

examine these numbers, called the *raw* data, in their analysis. Percentages allow for better comparisons. The only rule to remember about these percentages is that *each category of the independent variable must add up to 100 percent*. To calculate a percentage, divide the number in any cell by its corresponding column marginal (or N) and multiply the result by 100; e.g., $37 \div 58 \times 100 = 64$ percent. Here it can be seen that those who expect a more severe punishment are less likely to shoplift (36 percent) than those who expect only a light punishment (78 percent). Again, notice that *each* of the categories of the independent variable adds up to 100 percent.

On the basis of these data, it can be concluded that there is a relationship between perception of severity of punishment and shoplifting. Note, however, that the relationship is not perfect. Some who expect light punishment do not shoplift, while some who expect severe punishment do. Most sociological relationships are like this, incomplete and imperfect. Sociological research usually finds that two variables *tend* to be related under *certain* conditions for *some* people. Collectively, human beings are too complex, have too many pressures acting upon them, and possess too many options to exhibit the simpler relationships more characteristic of the natural sciences.

The conditions and kinds of people are the "other things being equal" of the hypothesis. As mentioned, sociologists call these "other things" **control variables**, and survey researchers take them into account *statistically*. To do so, they take the original data and divide them into additional tables, one table for each category of the control variable. Suppose we think that threats of punishment work more for girls than for boys, who more often allow peer pressure to make them ignore such consequences. When researchers "control" for sex, they make two identical tables, one for boys and one for girls. The new tables look exactly like the original, with the same headings and the same categories, and all categories of the independent variable still add up to 100 percent, but in each table the control variable is constant, the same for everyone in the table, all boys or all girls, allowing examination of the sexes separately. Examining these tables could show that the predicted relationship between severity of punishment and shoplifting holds better among girls and less well among boys.

This examination of control variables still does not complete the analysis stage. Sociologists must attempt to explain why, for example, some boys who expect light punishment still do not shoplift. Perhaps it is because they are very religious. Why do some girls who expect

[Applied Sociology]

The Art and Craft of Predicting Election Results

All of us have seen polls reported in the media, and what is noteworthy is how different, even contradictory, some seem—especially at election time. How can the Liberals and the Conservatives both be leading by 10 percentage points? One quick answer is that polls never claim to be exact. That is indicated in the phrase "+/–" so many percentage points. So a 55 percent is really between 51 percent and 59 percent. Sometimes a result may even be completely off; the "19 times in 20" figure means there is a 5 percent chance they are even beyond 51 and 59 percent.

But what else happens? First, and very rarely, outright fraud may be operating. More likely, however, a more subtle bias may be in evidence. This may occur, for example, in how "not at homes" are treated. Replacing these respondents by others who are at home means that those more likely to be out (and thus employed?) may be under-represented. Or suppose the first question in one survey asks about the burden of high taxes while in another it asks about overcrowded hospitals. Which do you think would lead to more and which to less support in a later question on voter opinions on candidates who support cost cutting? And finally, recall that many polls talk about decided voters. There is always some chance that a 40/40 dead heat with 20 percent still undecided, could become a 60/40 landslide.

In your experience, how accurate are public opinion polls? How might polls affect election results?

Does Drinking Lead to Date-Related Sexual Assault?

Experiments are better than survey research in demonstrating cause. In the simplest social science experiment (Neuman, 2003 describes more complex designs), subjects are divided by chance into two groups—for example, by the flipping of a coin, with heads to one group and tails to the other. Once the subjects are in separate groups, a cause (independent variable) is introduced into one, called the **experimental group**. Since the cause is introduced to it only, any effect (dependent variable) should be found in that group only and not in the second or **control group**, which does not experience the cause.

Suppose researchers were interested in the relationship between alcohol and the sexual assault that can occur in dating. After random assignment of dating males to either group, alcoholic beverages would be served to the experimental group and soft drinks to the control group. Then both groups could be given a series of hypothetical situations to examine their dating behaviour. They could be asked, "Your date has just said 'no' to sexual intercourse. Would you: (a) respect her wishes, (b) ask again, (c) pressure her to change her mind, (d) continue a bit further to see how serious she is, (e) ignore her and go ahead?" If alcohol reduces inhibitions, the males in the experimental group should more often choose the latter options (c, d, or e) than the males in the control group. If alcohol were not a factor, there would be no difference in answers between the two groups.

It is in their models that a crucial difference between survey research and experiments occurs. The effects of all potential control variables are supposed to be eliminated through the random assignment of subjects to the experimental or control conditions, making true the statement "other things being equal." For example, there should be approximately similar numbers of the very religious, the going-steady, and children of professional parents in each group.

Even variables in which the experimenters are not interested, like dancing ability, should be approximately the same as a result of this chance assignment. With these "other things being equal," their influence on the dependent variable can be ignored and the model quite simple, involving only the independent variable, here

alcohol, and the dependent variable, response to a date's "no." Recall that in survey research, other variables must be included in the model because they may affect any relationship between the independent and dependent variables, and thus must be statistically controlled.

Analysis in experiments involves comparing the experimental and control groups on the dependent variable. But what if, by chance, the random assignment did not make the two groups equal? To examine this possibility, most experimenters take two measures of their dependent variable (here, dating behaviour) although perhaps with slightly different but equivalent questions. The first is called a *pre-test*, which comes before the introduction of the independent variable (here, alcohol). The second is a *post-test*, since it comes after. Analysis looks for changes in predicted dating behaviour between the pre- and post-test in both groups. Any difference in the control group could have been caused by many factors, such as boredom or greater familiarity with the questions on dating, but should not have been caused by alcohol, which its members did not drink. The difference between the experimental group's pre- and post-test, minus any difference in the control group, thus represents the net effects of the independent variable. As in survey research, however, the relationship will not be perfect, and additional causes of sexual assault on dates can be examined in additional experiments to explain why this is so.

While experiments are good in demonstrating cause and effect, they have their downsides. First, ethical considerations make many experiments impossible. Researchers cannot, for example, force people to attend religious services to examine the effects of such attendance on racial prejudice. They have no control over whether a person is born male or female, to a large or small or rich or poor family—all key variables in social research. Turning to measurement, merely being in an experiment can alter people's behaviour as they try to please the experimenters, doing things they think the experimenters want. This is sometimes called the *Hawthorne effect* (see Chapter 14, Organizations and Work). So experimental measures are sometimes even more removed from real behaviour than the measures used in survey research, and thus they have the potential for even greater invalidity. In fact, **external validity** refers to how well experimenters can generalize from the lab to the real world, from hypothetical questions to actual behaviour.

Finally, with respect to sampling, experimenters generally need more cooperation than do survey researchers, because subjects in experiments have something done to them, even returning for several sessions of such manipulation. Because of these greater costs in time and effort, subjects for experiments tend to be drawn from accidental samples, with paid volunteers and university students being frequent choices. Generalizing experimental results to non-volunteers and to non-university populations should therefore be done only with caution.

Should participants in these types of studies be paid for their time? How might remuneration affect research results?

severe punishment still shoplift? Perhaps boyfriends are a factor in these instances. These findings must also be added to any conclusions drawn.

The list of control variables that serve to qualify the generalizations suggested by the original analysis can be lengthy. Researchers, however, ordinarily collect and analyze data on only those variables logically and closely connected with their independent and dependent variables, and use their knowledge of the field to decide which variables are relevant. The purpose of these controls is to approximate the conditions of the natural science controlled experiment, a basic goal of positivism, to make all other things equal except for variations in the independent and dependent variables. A quite different approach marks the qualitative alternative of participant observation, to which we now turn.

A qualitative strategy: Participant observation

Direct observation of real-life behaviour is rare in quantitative research. Qualitative researchers, in contrast, generally make such observation a central requirement in their research strategies. For example, in participant observation a researcher asks permission to join and observe a group and to question its members about the meanings of their behaviour. It is this strategy we shall describe in the next section, examining theory, models, measurement, sampling, and analysis, as we did for quantitative research.

Theories and hypotheses

Many qualitative sociologists feel that because most theories about social life are incomplete, *perspective* is a better word than theory, because it is more tentative and flexible. This also fits in with their ideal of beginning a study with minimal preconceptions and then to allow the data whenever possible to speak for themselves. Perspectives, then, are sensitizing devices, showing researchers where to look but not limiting their investigations.

Many participant observers thus refuse to derive hypotheses, as survey researchers do, but instead use inductive logic, allowing the facts they observe eventually to lead to theoretical generalizations. As deductive logic goes from the general to the specific, **inductive logic** goes from specific facts to general statements. Thus, participant observers tend to collect their data first and conclude with what they call **grounded theory**, theory rooted in and arising from their data. For example, researchers might note that women seem to ask more questions and try to extend rather than limit social conversations compared to men. If the rest of their data support this conclusion they can then conclude with a generalization about how gender affects conversation. Thus the theory comes after examining the data, not before as in most quantitative approaches. (In practice in both qualitative and quantitative methods the relationship between data and theory is more like a circle, with data forcing revisions of theory and theory affecting the type of data collected, in a continuous loop.)

Model

Participant observers never deal in simple, one independent and one dependent variable, models. Instead, models involve many variables acting at once, as happens in the real world. One common strategy in participant observation is to look initially at many things and over time to focus on fewer variables, thereby simplifying the model as the research progresses. Even with such simplification, however, participant observation ordinarily involves more complicated models than either experiments or survey research. Variables are not isolated, either artificially, as in laboratory experiments, or statistically, as in the control tables of survey research, and thus the models are correspondingly more complex. In addition, the models of participant observers are often more general than specific, in the form of themes and motifs, and arise as the researchers are immersed in the data. Another difference concerns cause. Participant observers are satisfied in many instances with *associations* between variables without any idea of cause or talk of independent and dependent variables. When they do look at cause, multiple causes and longer causal chains (A→ B→ C→ D→ E) are stressed.

Measurement

The most important difference in measurement between quantitative methods and participant observation is that participant observers view real behaviour, going beyond survey research's verbal reports of that behaviour and the artificial behaviour of laboratory experiments. They can also see behaviour the actors are unaware of, behaviour the actors might be unable to describe adequately on a questionnaire, and even behaviour the actors might not admit to in an interview. If clarification is needed to interpret these observations, explanations from the actors themselves can supplement researcher interpretations. The researcher-controlled "objective" measures and operational definitions more typical of quantitative researchers are replaced by the subjective definitions of the actors. Indeed, in their reports, participant observers often allow the actors to explain their behaviour as it makes sense to them.

Sampling

Obviously, if researchers live with a group of people to observe them, they cannot study a large number of such groups. The time, money, and effort required would be

Teaching Qualitative Methods at University

Qualitative methods are generally based on Weber's notion that understanding, or **verstehen**, should be the goal of sociology. They became popular in the 1920s when they were borrowed from anthropologists by sociologists to study urban life in Chicago. The 1940s then marked a return to positivist research but the 1960s gave new life to qualitative, also called humanistic, methods. Today many sociology departments offer courses in qualitative methods, which differ from quantitative courses by:

Involvement means that researchers interact with those they study, usually face-to-face and for a sustained period of time. There is less distance between the observer and the observed, a tenet of feminist research mentioned earlier. A qualitative researcher must "take the role of the other," attempting to see the world through the eyes of the observed. This in turn may lead to a rejection of the positivist's ideal of detachment and to the researcher

taking a stand on the problems of the subjects, especially any oppression they suffer. More specifically, *participatory action researchers* (Whyte, 1991) deliberately use their high status as professionals to advance the political claims of the less powerful groups they study.

Interpretation means that objectivity is an illusion, that all knowledge inevitably involves the researchers' perspectives and thus interpretations. Indeed many investigators today state their standpoint (e.g., Tastsoglou and Miedema 2003) before presenting their research findings. Gender, race, class, age, and sexual orientation are but a few of the researchers' traits that could affect findings and are therefore revealed. A few, usually postmodernists, have gone so far as to say that the researchers' position of privilege takes away the authority of those studied to tell their story, in effect questioning whether even well-meaning qualitative research is acceptable.

It is sometimes said that qualitative methods provide for very "rich" data. In what ways might this be true?

too costly. Thus, participant observation usually involves only a small number or even just one case, generally chosen because of availability. But sampling considerations extend beyond the choice of group to be studied. Inside the group there is much sampling involved; observers cannot be everywhere at all times, or watch all things even in one place. Thus, they must sample times, places, people, and behaviours, sometimes randomly or perhaps on a quota basis. Often they are not methodical, however, and instead are determined by chance, by the unpredictable flow of the interaction. Still, deliberate bias, including choosing data to support preconceived notions, must be avoided whatever the sampling procedure.

Analysis

As previously stated, participant observers often let the actors explain their own behaviour. Some of the actors' explanations may be rationalizations, and in fact their subjective perceptions may be objectively inaccurate, but the explanations still are recorded as motivations behind the actors' behaviours. The participant observers can then add their explanations to those of their informants.

Analysis in participant-observation research is often descriptive, attempting to make a coherent portrait of a complex social reality. Numbers are less apparent and words more so. Causal relationships may or may not be specified, but if they are they must be fitted into a larger overall description of the subject matter. In fact, one problem that arises with participant observation is the researchers' inability to describe all that is going on, to complete the picture fully. This occurs because there are just too many facts and too much data to include. Thus, inevitably, participant observers must be selective and edit the information with which they attempt to describe their subject matter. Such decisions are based on their familiarity with the topic, logic, guidance from both colleagues and the actors themselves, and the feelings and intuitions of the researchers. Such a process is hard to plan fully in advance, and must be partly determined in the field.

One common analytical strategy is to examine the data while still in the field, while the research is still going on, with the early analysis rather unfocused and the later increasingly limited. In this way, models and hypotheses that become apparent in those earlier stages can be tested in later ones. This sequential practice is a good way to test grounded theory. *Negative case analysis*, examining those cases that fail to support the generalizations drawn, can

Public behaviour is most amenable to secret observation by a researcher who takes the role of outsider.

then force their revision. Thus, like most social scientists, participant observers use both inductive and deductive logic in examining social reality.

This concludes our brief description of participant observation. More unstructured and flexible than survey research, its exact operations are harder to specify. Still, after reading this section, you should at least be familiar with its logic and rationale. The next section compares participant observation with the previously discussed survey-research approach.

The Methods Compared

Survey research and participant observation can be compared in many ways. Each has both strong and weak points. Thus, let us compare them on the same criteria: validity—whether their measures are accurate reflections of social reality; generalizability—whether their conclusions hold beyond the actual group studied; and ability to identify causes of behaviour.

The issues of validity and generalizability are related and are at the heart of the debate between quantitative and qualitative researchers. Participant observers argue that much survey research is invalid, because survey researchers often examine *attitudes* instead of *behaviour*, and people often do not act as their attitudes would predict (explaining why husbands think they *should* share more household tasks than they actually *do*). Even if they do examine behaviour they get only verbal reports of that behaviour and respondents may slant their answers to what they think the interviewers want to hear. They may even lie, giving socially approved answers that reflect well on them and avoiding responses that place them in an unfavourable light. Finally, in quantitative research, operationalization lets the researcher rather than the actor measure and explain behaviour, again raising validity issues.

Survey researchers counter these claims by arguing that a careful research design can reduce validity problems. Self-administered (and cheaper) anonymous questionnaires, as opposed to interviews, for example, decrease lying and the effects of respondent–researcher interactions. To increase validity, interviewers can be trained to detect misunderstandings and resistance and to encourage candour and honesty. Survey researchers suggest, moreover, that participant observation also yields invalid data, first, because people, even those who fully trust the observer, will not act totally naturally while being observed. Second, quantitative researchers believe that participant observation data are too vulnerable to potential biases, needs, and unconscious distortions of the observers themselves. Thus different observers will "see" different things, making the measures unreliable. And while a need for validity checks is all the more important in such instances, the flexibility of the method (seen as a strength by its practitioners) makes **replication**, or the repeating of a study, difficult in participant observation. Thus invalidity is harder to uncover than it is for quantitative researchers, who can more easily replicate their studies.

A difficulty in making generalizations is another significant criticism survey researchers make of participant observation. With few groups (or sometimes only one group) studied, the chance that the observations may not be representative of other groups is increased. Thus generalizations from participant-observation data to the wider but unstudied population should be made only with caution.

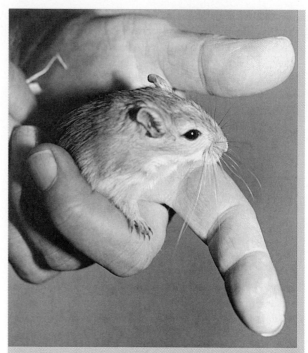

Many social scientists would prefer to apply the methods of natural scientists to their data.

Needless to say, this participant-observation/survey-research debate continues. Qualitative participant observers, while admitting that their small non-representative samples may permit only limited generalization, still lay claim to greater validity, because they observe actual behaviour, over time, and in a natural setting. Moreover, given a choice between validity and generalizability, participant observers feel that validity is the more important criterion to satisfy. A valid picture of even a non-representative sample is preferable to an invalid description of a perfectly random sample. Survey researchers, on their part, point to their improvements in validity and reject this argument.

Turning to cause, to demonstrate that A causes B, researchers must show not only a logical connection between them, but that A is prior to B and that A and B are not connected only through C, a variable causing both A and B. The random assignment in experiments attempts to rule out all such C variables by making all of them equal, thus ensuring that A is the only cause operating. Survey research and participant observation cannot rule out other causes as easily.

In most survey research, data on independent and dependent variables are collected at the same time, a procedure called **cross-sectional research**. This is quite cost-efficient, but it means that researchers often cannot demonstrate which variables come first, which are causes, and which are effects. For example, as will be discussed more fully in Chapter 12, Media, does exposure to television violence cause violent behaviour? Or do violent people choose to watch violent television? Or is it both?

Survey research is forced to deal in **correlations**, demonstrations that changes in one variable go with changes in another. But variables may "go together" without any causal link. Survey researchers must be especially careful about inferring **spurious relationships** from these correlations—assuming that a relationship is causal when it is really only through a third variable, C, that A and B are linked. For example, there is a correlation between the amount of money spent in dating relationships, A, and sexual activity, B. Survey research data would reveal that other things being equal, the more money spent, the greater the sexual activity. Is money, an independent variable, causing sexual activity, a dependent variable? No—the real relationships are between involvement, C, and money spent, A, and between involvement, C, and sexual activity, B. The greater the involvement, the more money is spent and also the more sexual activity. Interpreting the correlation to mean that money leads to sexual activity is spurious. A discussion of how survey researchers see through such spurious relationships is beyond the scope of this text, but generally involves examining the effects of control variables on the original relationship. Spuriousness is not an insurmountable problem, but it is an issue that must be dealt with by survey researchers.

Participant observers, because their research is done over time (called **longitudinal research**), may be better able to see which variable comes first, but they have a problem in that many variables happen at once; their full, rich picture may make it difficult to isolate a specific cause of behaviour. This is one reason some participant observers choose not to focus on cause and instead deal mainly with descriptions.

In sum, validity is potentially stronger in participant observation than in survey research. For generalizability, survey research may be better. Each has difficulty in demonstrating cause and effect. Because no method is without flaws, some researchers engage in **triangulation**,

the application of several research methods to the same topic, hoping that the weaknesses of one method will be balanced by strengths of the others. For example, the findings of a participant-observation study may be confirmed by survey research or vice versa. Quite often the subject of inquiry will point to a choice. National voting studies generally require survey research and much of the research in stratification and religion reported in this book used survey research. On the other hand, participant observation, because of its flexibility, is often used to examine culture, social movements, and emerging topics on which there is little prior research.

A common omission: Historical and comparative issues

The qualitative and quantitative research techniques described so far collect data over a short period of time, making it difficult to examine long-term trends. In addition, most researchers confine their work to their own society. *Historical* and *comparative analysis* of different societies attempts to fill these gaps. Both allow a special type of replication, a retesting of hypotheses in new settings, leading researchers either to greater confidence if similar results appear, or to reformulations if conflicting data are uncovered. Because of these strengths, let us examine these methods more closely.

Since it is undertaken after the fact and must rely on whatever data were collected at the time, historical analysis actually entails a variety of research methods. Thus, researchers can perform a qualitative study of diaries or letters written a hundred years ago or can do a statistical quantitative analysis of census data originally collected through survey research, or of official data. For example, one study of medical payments found that requiring pregnant adolescents to inform their parents and get their consent before having an abortion did not, as predicted, reduce the number of girls having an abortion rate in six states passing such legislation (*NY Times* 6/3/2006, p. 1). In comparative research too, any method can be used, with the one chosen used repeatedly across cultures.

As a by-product of the versatility of their methods, historical and comparative analysts can use deductive and/or grounded theory. Their models can be simple or complex. Still, it would probably be fair to say that historical analysis is especially attractive to conflict theorists because it best allows a focus on change. We know also

Following Their Own Path: Marxist Research Methods

There are several research strategies that appeal to conflict sociologists, reflecting the diversity of conflict approaches outlined in Chapter 1. As a group they may have little in common except for a rejection of Durkheim's positivist stance—that natural sciences methods should be used to study social reality. Here we focus on a Marxist conflict model.

Generally those who adopt a Marxist approach are critical of subjective perspectives on social life, such as that of symbolic interactionism (see Chapter 1, What Is Sociology?). Marxists argue that people are constrained by (and are not the makers of) social reality. But they could be free if someone, perhaps social scientists, would reveal to them their oppression. People have potential but they are deceived and exploited, and have lost control over their own destiny.

Marxists find theory useful to the extent that it reveals the causes of oppression and helps its victims to see a path to an improved life. The model used in Marxist research concentrates on the potential for change and generally sees the amount of power and resources held, especially economic power and resources, as the major independent variable affecting all other aspects of life. Attention to history, something missing in much functionalist research, is especially important to Marxists because change, which results from the conflict over

resource ownership, rather than stability, is the focus. A *dialectical* approach, which sees history as a series of conflicts over existing material arrangements, is also attractive to Marxists. This approach maintains that the seeds for transformation exist in every society, and the new societies that emerge, in turn, contain the seeds for their transformation.

Measurement and sampling are of less concern to Marxists. They prefer a critical approach: to ask embarrassing questions, to uncover exploitation, and to expose hypocrisy. Marxists look for the conflicts surrounding the unequal distribution of resources, in the hope of encouraging large-scale changes to the status quo. And they prefer to do this in the real world, as opposed to the laboratory.

Nor is analysis, at least in the form of hypothesis testing, so important. Marxists generally "know" what is going on. Instead their role is to act upon their research, a strategy they call **praxis**. They reject Weber's recommendation, that a scientist should be detached, as too passive. Instead they see the role of social scientific analysis specifically as one of unmasking the unjust conditions in the world in order to help the downtrodden see the sources of their ills. Thus research should be action-oriented, a step taken to empower the weak. Smashing myths and uncovering contradictions are just the first part of that process (see Neuman, 2003).

What topics are likely to be of interest to Marxist researchers? What topics might they avoid? Why?

that positivists, especially survey researchers, tend to avoid historical sociology. The more problematic issues for historical and comparative analysis relate to measurement and sampling. We shall discuss each in turn.

In collecting their data, historians distinguish between primary and secondary sources. **Primary sources** are records produced at the time, described by a contemporary of the event, including eyewitness accounts, diaries, and official records. **Secondary sources** are created when individuals report what a primary source said. The potential problems surrounding the validity of secondary sources are readily apparent. The greater the

distance in time, in space, and in perspective between the primary and secondary sources, the greater is the chance for misinterpretation. But the primary source may be invalid as well. Who wrote it down and why? Did the person deliberately or unwittingly distort the data to tell a certain story? And worse, while the validity of current data can be checked against other current or new data, historical data often cannot be. Thus, validity is always an issue in historical analysis.

Cross-cultural researchers can collect new data or use available data. One excellent source of existing, generally participant observation, data is the anthropological reports found in the *Encyclopedia of World Cultures*, summaries of over 1500 ethnographies of societies around the world. One of the problems with using someone else's data, a procedure called **secondary analysis**, however, is that they may be incomplete, since the original collectors were not aware of the information later researchers would need.

Sampling remains the final stumbling block in historical and comparative research. In the latter, how many societies are to be included? Costs multiply quickly. Inside the countries chosen, a national random sample might be impossible, leading to questionable generalizability. The preference in historical analysis for a complex picture also generally results in a small number of cases and a limited time frame. (Historical studies using census or other official data—see for example Chapter 16, Demography and Urbanization—are an obvious exception to this generalization.) The problems of missing or incomplete data may then further reduce the sample size, again reducing generalizability.

Summary

The discussions of Durkheim and Weber begun in the Introduction were continued in this chapter, this time with respect to their different research strategies. Durkheim was associated with quantitative research and specifically survey research, Weber with qualitative research and participant observation. The place of theory and hypotheses, types of models, measurement issues, sampling, and simple analysis were presented for both, and their strengths and weaknesses compared. Included in boxes in the chapter were alternative strategies such as content analysis and experiments, along with Marxist and feminist comments on methods, and a further elaboration of qualitative methods.

If you decide to become a sociologist and to conduct research, you thus have many options open to you. Whatever method you choose, the most anyone can reasonably ask of you is honesty, competence, and a healthy scepticism. You should never deliberately choose one method over others because its data will most likely support your own biases; you should be willing to undergo the training that will allow expertise in whatever method you choose; and you should be aware of the weaknesses, especially concerning validity and generalizability, of your method. This is a big order, one best saved for an advanced course in research methods.

Before continuing to the next general topic of the book, Culture, read the following section on writing library research papers. If a research paper is required in an introductory sociology course, it will probably involve library research rather than the collection of new data.

Writing a Sociology Library Research Paper

When writing research papers, students should choose a topic in which they are interested and initially should define the subject quite broadly. The second step involves a review of the literature—an examination of existing studies on the chosen topic, let's say homosexuality. In our example, recent books can be found by looking up "homosexuality" in the library's subject catalogue. The locations of scholarly articles on homosexuality can be found by using databases like *Sociological Abstracts*, saving you much time. For popular articles in print, *The Reader's Guide to Periodical Literature* is useful.

The amount of information available will probably be overwhelming. (In the rare instances when little is written on a topic, introductory students should probably choose a new topic.) Restricting the search to the last five years can make a review more manageable and make the paper more current as well. But there probably will still be too much to read. To narrow the subject down further choose a smaller focus—for example, the difference between gay and lesbian lifestyles, the extent of hidden homosexuality, or how the role is learned. Each of these topics might come out of the next few chapters of this book. What about the discrimination and prejudice homosexuals face, what about homosexual families, how does religion treat homosexuality? The possibilities are endless, and the earlier stages of even this narrowed review will probably reveal the need for an even more restricted focus.

The next step is to decide the *type* of research review to be written. Choices here include an integrative review that summarizes what is known on a topic, showing points of agreement and disagreement and issues needing further research; a historical review tracing what has been learned about a topic over time; a cross-cultural review comparing the subject in different societies. For all relevant articles, the author, title, date, name of journal, volume number, and pages should be recorded. DO THIS FIRST. These will later become the bibliography. Then in a second file, for each source consulted, write up your relevant notes on the chosen topic, with the author's name and enough of the title to definitively identify the source recorded in its own section at the very top of the page. Specific page numbers for all quotes and for any specific ideas borrowed should also be clearly recorded there for later documentation. For long quotes or whole sections, cutting and pasting each into it own file may be appropriate, again *with the page number prominently recorded*. It is always wise (and highly recommended) to print a hard copy of the information as a backup.

As the notes accumulate, patterns begin to emerge. There seems to be agreement on some matters, disagreement on others. Links between certain aspects of the general topic become clearer, and an order becomes apparent. Sorting the entries into categories is the final step before the actual writing. The categories become the basis for an outline of the paper. Avoid the error of poor organization by outlining carefully, re-outlining, and using subtitles freely, according to the information found. Proper organization allows movement from point to point in a systematic and nonrepetitive way. It also helps improves focus. Students who do not have a specific objective in mind may end up merely citing scattered findings, or they may include irrelevant facts, perhaps in the hope that including every fact possible will impress their instructors. The opposite is more often true; students should include only the material directly relevant to the focus of the paper.

The following suggestions for structuring a report are not rigid rules, but general guidelines.

1. *Introduction.* The introduction to a paper should indicate why the paper is being written. Why is the topic important—is there a need to solve a problem in society, to test a theoretical position, to reveal or discuss a contradiction? The introduction should begin with the most general rationale for the paper and logically proceed to a more specific problem. The last paragraph of this section should indicate what the paper will accomplish, giving a very brief outline of the contents.

2. *Results of literature review organized according to purpose of review.* Students should decide which sections of the works reviewed they are going to use, adding their own analysis and summaries as appropriate. Findings should be clearly presented, supported when necessary with tables, charts, and graphs (with proper

credit given). Each finding should be explored within the framework of the arguments developed in the introduction. Failure to reveal sources and omitting quotation marks are forms of *plagiarism*.

3. *Discussion.* In this section, the student must discuss the meaning and importance of the points made in the previous section and show how they relate to the purpose of the investigation as stated in the introduction. In many ways, the discussion is the most important part of the paper as it represents the student's original thoughts, not an organization of the insights of others. Thus, a great deal of thought and care is required for this section. It should make sense out of the sometime disparate information included in the previous section. To make linkages between ideas, transitional phrases such as "thus," "moreover," "however," "nevertheless," and "on the other hand" make the writing smoother, although they will not suffice unless the connections are also apparent in the text itself.

4. *Summary and Conclusion.* Students should briefly summarize the paper here, in so doing showing the progress in knowledge made since the introduction. Suggestions for research that would provide answers to unanswered questions raised in the paper may be included here.

Finally, about the writing itself, consistency is important. Choose a tense and stick to it—for example, "Mundy *says* that homosexuals *are* . . . " Also choose a person. In general, it is best to write in an impersonal style (avoiding "I," "me," "my," etc.), keeping some distance between author and topic. Plurals ("they," "their") help to avoid the awkward "he/she" construction and the sexism of relying on the singular pronouns of "he" or "she." On the other hand, particularly in discussion sections, students should not be afraid of an occasional "I think" or "I believe." Writing should also be somewhat formal; some students become so informal that rigour and organization suffer. A thesaurus and dictionary are useful to help avoid repetition. Finally, the pages must be numbered, and proper footnoting and referencing used. Scholarly journals—for example, the *Canadian Journal of Sociology* or *The Canadian Review of Sociology and Anthropology*—provide good examples of proper reference style. The purpose of references is to enable readers who want to know more on a topic to find the sources used. It is not useful to list everything you even thought of looking at. Be selective here.

Several revisions are usually necessary. Showing a draft to someone who has experience with this type of assignment can help. A spell check function catches obvious errors, but can miss such things as confusing *their* for *there*, and *too* for *to*. A friend can help with such proofreading. Finally, keep a hard copy of the final product.

Writing papers is always hard. We hope these suggestions will make the process a bit easier.

Questions for Review and Critical Thinking

1. What problems would have to be overcome if you wanted to conduct an experiment to test the advantages and disadvantages of assigning qualified minority teachers to teach children of their own ethnic group, as opposed to having any qualified teacher instruct them?

2. Which research strategy would be most useful in studying why some of your friends continued their education after high school while others did not? Defend your choice.

3. Design a questionnaire to examine both the extent of and reasons for drug use among students.

4. What topics would *you* like to study in sociology? Do personal values affect your choice? Will you be value-neutral or an activist, using research as a tool to improve the world?

Key Terms

axiomatic logic, p. 20
cluster sampling, p. 22
content analysis, p. 24
control group, p. 26
control variables, p. 25
correlation, p. 31
cross-sectional research, p. 31
deductive logic, p. 20
dependent variable, p. 20
experimental group, p. 26
external validity, p. 27
grounded theory, p. 27
hypothesis, p. 20
independent variable, p. 20
inductive logic, p. 27

longitudinal research, p. 31
operational definition, p. 21
participant observation, p. 20
positivism, p. 18
praxis, p. 32
primary versus secondary sources, p. 32
quota sample, p. 23
random sample, p. 22
reliability, p. 21
replication, p. 30
secondary analysis, p. 33
spurious relationship, p. 31
theory, p. 20
triangulation, p. 31
validity, p. 21
variable, p. 20
verstehen, p. 28

Suggested Readings

Bryman, Alan and James J. Teevan
2005 *Social Research Methods*. Toronto: Oxford University Press.
This text includes Canadian examples and provides a thorough overview of the research methods discussed in this chapter.

Eichler, Margrit
2002 "The impact of feminism on Canadian sociology." *The American Sociologist* 33: 27–41.
This article examines how Canadian sociology by the end of the last century became the leading feminist discipline. Introductory textbooks including this one were examined.

McLaughlin, Neil
2005 "Canada's impossible science: Historical and institutional origins of the coming crisis in Anglo-Canadian Sociology." *Canadian Journal of Sociology* 30: 1–40.
This article examines the potential for Anglo-Canadian sociology to become a unique, multi-method, and critical discipline and what may happen if it does not.

Silverman, David
2005 *Doing Qualitative Research: A Practical Handbook*. London: Sage.
This readable text shows, step by step, how to conduct qualitative research from selecting a topic, to using theories, data analysis, and the final chapter.

Websites

www.lib.uwaterloo.ca/discipline/sociology/doing_research _guides.html
Doing Research in Sociology
Learn how to search for research material in periodicals, newspapers, and social science databases, as well as how to prepare your research report.

www.statscan.ca
Statistics Canada
Interested in doing quantitative research on Canadian subjects? At the Statistics Canada website, you can find the most recent census data on various aspects of life in Canada.

Key Search Terms

Qualitative methods
Quantitative methods
Validity
Sampling
Data analysis

For more study tools to help you with your next exam, be sure to check out the Companion Website at **www.pearsoned.ca/hewitt**, as well as Chapter 2 in your Study Guide.

part two

Society and the Individual

In this section of the book, our central concern is to expand and illustrate Durkheim's claim that social structure and membership in social groups are important determinants of human behaviour. In Chapter 3, culture is defined as the way of life shared by a group of people. It is passed on to later generations, and affects their behaviour and perceptions in some way. Culture includes the values and norms that shape social conduct, the rules and conventions of everyday social life. Culture also includes the social roles that people play, and the variety of social conditions under which people live. Values, norms, and roles vary from one society to another. Even within a society, cultural features vary. For instance, the social unit called Canada is composed today of various subgroups whose different racial and ethnic origins and regional locations have given rise to correspondingly different *sub*cultures.

Cultures may be analyzed from various viewpoints. To a functionalist, cultural elements help to make society stable and viable. On the other hand, conflict sociologists analyze culture with reference to power differences in society. Research here focuses on questions such as which groups benefit from the way of life that is adopted and who determines the norms and values. As you read the chapter, try to think of alternative explanations that could be substituted for some of the arguments offered.

For culture to affect behaviour it must be learned; such internalization may occur when members learn to play roles—for example, the roles of teacher, farmer, or daughter. The acquisition of culture is the focus of Chapter 4, Socialization. Chapter 4 points to biological, social, and environmental influences on human learning and examines socialization agents and contexts from a historical perspective. Social factors are especially important in shaping identity, or a sense of self, which is in turn an important determinant of behaviour. While symbolic interactionism and conflict theory are discussed, the chapter does make a number of assumptions about human adaptation drawn from the functionalist perspective. Who benefits and gains from the socialization experience should be a constant question in your reading of the chapter.

The failure of some individuals to internalize the norms, values, and "appropriate" social roles contained in their culture is discussed in Chapter 5, Deviance. The chapter examines the social origins of definitions of deviance, including functional and conflict explanations, and shows how these definitions vary across cultures. The roles of power and societal reaction are also discussed as factors in the labelling of acts as deviant. The general sociological perspective again is applied: social structure and group membership affect types and rates of behaviour, this time deviant behaviour.

[3]

culture

michael p. carroll

Introduction

In observing individuals in a social group—whether a nation, a family, or a classroom—it soon becomes clear that their behaviour is not random but patterned. Not all behaviours that are possible actually occur, and if you were to observe the group long enough, you would notice that certain behaviours tend to happen with a great deal of regularity. Obviously, there is something that produces such order in social life.

Much of that "something" is what sociologists call *culture*. The use of this particular word is a bit confusing, because culture also has a perfectly legitimate everyday meaning that has nothing to do with the orderliness of social life. In everyday language, people are "cultured" if they have sophisticated or refined tastes. What this usually means in actual practice is that they enjoy those activities favoured by the educated elite but not by the general public. Hence, drinking expensive wine is a mark of culture, drinking domestic beer is not; watching a ballet is cultured, watching stock car racing is not.

Social scientists, however, use the word culture in quite a different sense. The most common definition found in sociology texts is one constructed by a nineteenth-century anthropologist named Edward Tylor. For Tylor, culture included "knowledge, belief, art, morals, law, custom, and any other capabilities and habits acquired by man as a member of society" (1871: 1). Notice that this definition gives no clue as to what the things listed (knowledge, belief, art, etc.) have in common. Upon reflection, though, it turns out that each of them is something that (1) is shared by all or almost all the members of some social group; (2) the older members of the group try to pass on to the younger members; and (3) shapes behaviour (as in the case of morals, laws, and custom), or at least structures perceptions of the world (as in the case of the other items listed in Tylor's definition). If we call anything that meets these three criteria a **cultural element**, then we can define the **culture** of a given group very simply as the sum total of all the cultural elements associated with that group.

Sociologists consider certain elements of culture to be particularly important. They are values, norms, and roles.

Some Basic Concepts
Values and norms

Values are shared, relatively general beliefs that define what is desirable and what is undesirable; they specify general preferences. The view that divorce should be only the last resort for unhappy couples and a preference for abstract art are both values. **Norms**, on the other hand, are relatively precise rules specifying which behaviours are permitted and which prohibited for group members. Note that in everyday usage, norm has quite a different meaning—it means average. Here, again, sociology has constructed its own vocabulary by attaching a new meaning to a familiar word. When a member of a group breaks a group norm by engaging in a prohibited behaviour, other group members will typically *sanction* the deviant member. To sanction is to communicate, in some way, disapproval to the deviant member (a topic to which we shall return in Chapter 5, Deviance).

Because values are relatively general, there is usually no one-to-one relationship between a particular value and a particular behavior. Phrased differently, different individuals holding the same set of cultural values can express those values differently in their day-to-day life. Michael Atkinson's (2004) study of tattooing provides a good example of what's involved here. Atkinson starts by noting that although tattoos have traditionally been associated with deviant groups (like youth gangs and prisoners), there has been a "tattoo renaissance" in both Canada and the United States over the last decade or so that has made tattoos more mainstream. To find out why this has happened, Atkinson did a participant observation study of tattoo artists and their clients in two Canadian cities (Calgary and Toronto). What he found is that for most of the individuals in his study, getting a tattoo was simply an atypical way of expressing cultural values they shared in common with society at large.

For example, ours is a culture in which a great many people would endorse the suggestion—really a value—that it is both appropriate and desirable to "improve" our bodies in order to make ourselves more attractive and appealing to others. For many people, this might lead them to work out at the gym or go jogging; for others it might mean getting a tan; for still others it might mean plastic surgery. For the people in Atkinson's study, however, it meant getting a tattoo. What Atkinson found, in other words, is that the people in his study saw getting a tattoo as a way of "improving" their bodies. But this was not the only cultural value being expressed. Ours is also a culture that values individuality, and the people in Atkinson's study also saw tattoos as a way of expressing this cultural value—that is, of expressing their individuality in a way that met with the approval of their friends. Finally, Atkinson found that for many women getting and displaying a tattoo was a form of active sexual empowerment and so very much in keeping, Atkinson suggests, with broader cultural values suggesting that the empowerment of women is desirable. In all three ways, in other words, "getting a tattoo" was for the people involved a behaviour that they saw as linked to values they shared in common with other Canadians.

Norms, unlike values, tend to be more tightly linked to particular behaviours. When asked to give examples of a norm in our society, most students tend to think of laws, such as those against murder and physical assault. Most laws in a society are indeed social norms. The more important point, however, is that your life is governed by many norms that are not laws.

A good example of a set of non-legal norms in our daily life are the norms regulating the physical distance that we maintain (or at least, want to maintain) between ourselves and other people. The general patterns here were documented some time ago by Edward Hall (1981) and remain valid today. The first thing that Hall discovered was that personal space norms vary by context. Generally, for example, the norm in Canada and the U.S. is that people should not speak to us at a distance of less than 30 centimetres or so unless something confidential is being communicated or unless the relationship is of a sexual and/or emotionally intimate nature. When someone violates this rule (by literally "getting in our face"), we get uncomfortable or angry or both. When we're talking with someone in public in order to exchange information of a non-personal nature (as when, for example, you are talking to a clerk in store) Hall found that most people prefer a distance of something like 120 centimetres, and that discomfort levels increase as the distance here decreases.

Hall found other patterns as well. For example, few of us are bothered (too much) if we're on a bus and the number of people makes crowding inevitable. If we're the only person on the bus, however, and a stranger enters and sits next to us, most of us would be upset. Why? Because obviously there's an implicit norm suggesting that in this situation people should distribute themselves as evenly as space permits. Finally, Hall found that personal space norms vary greatly by culture, and that, generally, in any given context, the minimum distances maintained by English-speaking North Americans tend to be greater than the minimum distances maintained, say, in Middle Eastern and Latin American cultures.

[Debate]

"Society": Defining an Important Term

Society is probably one of the most commonly used words in all of sociology. Despite that (or more likely because of that), there is no single definition found in all sociology textbooks. Generally, however, sociologists apply the term to any fairly large group of people who: (1) share a common culture, (2) think of themselves as having inherited a common set of historical traditions, (3) interact with other group members frequently, and (4) see themselves as being associated with a particular geographic area. The term society is often applied to nations (Canadian society, U.S. society). It can, however, be applied to subgroups within nations (French Canadian society), or to groups that cut across national boundaries (Western society).

How far can this be taken? Can the City of Toronto be a society?

As soon as you begin to list the norms that regulate your behaviour, it becomes clear that some are more important than others. For sociologists, the crucial difference between important and less-important norms lies in the nature of the reaction of other group members to a norm violation by an individual member. Sumner (1940) long ago introduced two terms, folkways and mores, to capture this distinction. **Folkways** are those norms that do not evoke severe moral condemnation when violated. The requirement to wear clothes is probably a folkway for most people.

If you saw someone running around campus naked, you might feel embarrassed, amused, or titillated, but not morally outraged. **Mores** are those norms whose violation does provoke strong moral condemnation. Our strong moral condemnation of sexual assault, arson, and murder, for instance, suggests that the norms prohibiting these behaviours are mores.

It must be emphasized that the difference between mores and folkways lies in the nature of the *reaction* produced by the violation of the norm, and not in the *content* of the rule. For instance, one of the norms in our society is that dogs should not be eaten, while one of the norms in contemporary Hindu society is that beef should not be eaten. These two norms are similar in content, but one is a folkway, the other a *mos* (singular of *mores*). You may be very upset if you hear that someone has eaten a dog, but you are unlikely to be morally outraged. Yet that sense of moral outrage is exactly what would be evoked among Hindus were someone to openly slaughter, cook, and eat a cow. We shall have much more to say about the importance of audience reactions to norm violations in Chapter 5, Deviance.

Social roles

A **role** is a cluster of behavioural expectations associated with a particular social position within a group or society. For instance, "teacher" and "student" are social positions of importance in most classrooms. Most of us expect that a teacher will come to class prepared, will not assign grades arbitrarily, will not show up to class drunk, etc., and so these expectations, taken as a sum,

A social role is a cluster of expectations about the behaviour that is appropriate for a given individual in a given situation.

define the teacher role. (As an exercise, you might try to think of the expectations that define the student role.)

A moment's reflection will indicate that one person can occupy several different roles at once. What roles have you occupied during the past week? Brother? Sister? Student? Friend? Enemy? Assuming multiple roles opens the door to **role conflicts**—that is, situations in which the behavioural expectations associated with one role are inconsistent with those associated with another concurrent role. Some of the clearest examples of role conflict involve the parent role. The need to care for children—physically, emotionally, and otherwise, or even to arrange for others to care for them on a regular basis—quite often interferes with the demands of a full-time occupation. Thus, there is the potential for conflict between the parent role and the full-time worker role, a role conflict that perhaps falls more frequently upon women. (We shall have more to say on this topic in Chapters 7, Gender Relations, and 10, Families.)

In studying roles we must always keep in mind that, without exception, they are social constructions, and thus, to a certain extent arbitrary. This means that roles we take for granted in our own culture may not exist in the same form in other cultures. The "mother" role is a particularly good example for making this point.

In our culture, the traditional definition of the mother role suggests that mothers are supposed to provide their children with emotional support, especially when the children are hurt and frightened, to nurse them when they are first born (with either breast or bottle), and to provide them with guidance as they grow. Some members of our society might even regard these behaviours as natural, but the evidence suggests otherwise. For example, in many European societies prior to the nineteenth century, it was common for biological mothers to send their newborns for care and feeding to a "wet nurse" and her family for a period of one to two years. When the wet nurse returned these children,

[Social Trends]

On Defining the "Mother" Role

A social role is a cluster of expectations about the behaviour that is appropriate for a given individual in a given situation.

Ask yourself the following question: "Is the increase in the number of married women with families, working outside the home, having a harmful effect on family life?" The odds are that you have a definite opinion on this subject. When a recent Gallup poll asked a similar question of a national sample of Canadians, 53 percent said that a woman working outside the home did have a harmful effect on family life, 43 percent said it did not, and only 4 percent expressed no opinion at all (Bozinoff and Turcotte, 1993).

Now suppose I asked you a second question: "Does the large number of married men with families in the working world have a harmful effect on family life?" Likely you would be taken aback. In this case, the odds are that you do not have a definite opinion on the subject, if only because it's a question you've never asked yourself. In fact, it's a question that sociologists themselves almost never ask. While there have been hundreds, possibly thousands, of studies on the effects of maternal employment outside

the home on children, there have been few on the effects of paternal employment outside the home.

But why does changing "married women, with families" to "married men, with families" convert the question from one on which you have a firm opinion (one way or another) and which has been well studied by sociologists, into one that is puzzling, about which you do not have a firm opinion, and which has not been particularly well studied? The answer, presumably, is that you, along with most sociologists, still see the raising of children as primarily a mother's responsibility—that is, as an expectation that is part of the definition of the "mother" role.

Consequently it "makes sense" to you to think about the possible "harmful effects" of something (like working outside the home) that might diminish the amount of time that a mother devotes to her children. Because "primary responsibility for raising children" is not an expectation that you have for the role "father," it does not occur to you to think about the "harmful effects" of a father working outside the home.

Would asking one question like, "Does having both parents work full-time harm family life?" get around the problem?

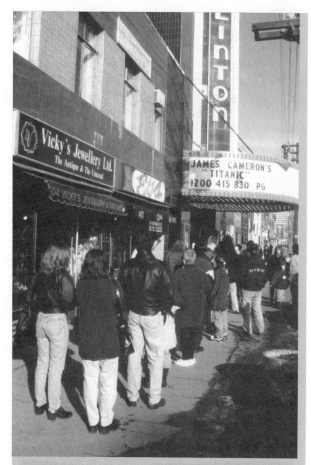

Popular culture refers to those preferences and objects that are widely spread across all the social classes in a society.

they were often cared for by older siblings or by other relatives, and not by the biological mother. In the case of peasant families, in which the mother had to work alongside the father in the fields, a pattern like this might reflect only economic necessity. It happens, however, that this same pattern was especially strong among the middle and upper classes in traditional Europe. But obviously, if the behaviours that for us are all associated with the single role we think of as "mother" were split up and allocated to a range of different people, then in these societies there was no role that can be said to correspond precisely to the mother role in our own society.

The general point to be made here is that every role is a cluster of expectations about behaviour, but this clustering varies from culture to culture. That our own culture bundles together certain behavioural expectations to form a particular role does not guarantee that other cultures will group those same expectations together in the same way to form the same role.

Some additional terms

At this point, it will be useful to introduce a few additional terms. The first of these is **subculture**, a group of people within a single society who possess, in addition to the cultural elements they share with the other members of their society, certain distinctive cultural elements that set them apart. Thus, Chinese, Ukrainians, Jews, Italians, or Iranians residing in Canada are often called subcultures because they share among themselves certain religious or ethnic beliefs and customs that are not characteristic of the Canadian population as a whole. Canadian subcultures will be discussed more fully in Chapter 8, Race and Ethnic Relations.

When the members of a society or a subculture agree that a specific set of norms and values should regulate some broad area of social life, such as the economy, family life, religion, or politics, then that set of norms and values is called an **institution**. Institutions are discussed in Part IV of this text.

The term **popular culture** refers to those cultural objects and beliefs that are widely distributed across all social classes in a society, such as comic books and horror films. Needing a wide distribution, larger societies do not usually develop a full popular culture until they develop mass media, including print, radio, and television (see Chapter 12, Media). Also, since relatively expensive things are unlikely to be widely afforded, the elements of popular culture are relatively inexpensive. For instance, the relatively low cost of comic books partly accounts for their popularity, just as it did in the nineteenth century for the dime novel. For sociologists, the study of popular culture can provide insights into societal values and norms that structure thinking and behaviour, their content so ubiquitous that they are not thought about in any precise way (see the boxes "Urban Legends" and "More Than Just a Toy").

Aspects of Culture

Ever since the nineteenth century, three observations have consistently forced themselves upon virtually every student of culture: (1) cultures exhibit enormous variation with regard to their values, norms, and roles; (2) few cultural elements are common to all known societies; and (3) the elements of culture in a given society are often interrelated.

Cultural variation

If we take an overview of the hundreds of societies in the world, past or present, the first thing that strikes us is the tremendous variation in their cultural elements. In fact, the values and norms of many societies are directly opposite to those we take for granted in North America.

Some of this cultural variation was apparent in our discussion of the mother role, and other examples are not difficult to discover. In our society, for example, many believe in one god, responsible for all of creation, and they typically describe this god using male imagery. A great many of the non-industrial societies in the world also believe in a single god, responsible for creation, but that god is not always male, or even human. Among the Iroquois, for instance, god was female, and among the South American Lengua, a beetle. But there also societies whose members believe in many gods, no one of which is responsible for all creation, or who do not believe in personalized gods of any sort (see Chapter 11, Religion).

Documenting cultural variation has always been a special concern of anthropologists, and one of the most famous of all these studies of cultural variation is still Margaret Mead's *Sex and Temperament in Three Primitive Societies* (1935). In this book, Mead described three societies in New Guinea (a large island just to the north of Australia) that she studied in the early 1930s. Mead focused on gender roles, and in the first of her societies, the Arapesh, she found both the males and females cooperative, mild-mannered, gentle, and very concerned with helping their young. Among the Arapesh, in other words, both males and females seemed to embody the traits that Western societies associate with females. Mead's second society, the Mundugumor, was quite different: both males and females were aggressive (and that included being sexually aggressive), uncooperative, jealous, hostile, and relatively unconcerned with parental tasks. To Mead it seemed as if both males and females among the Mundugumor conformed to the gender stereotype associated with males in Western societies. But, for Mead, her third society, the Tchambuli, was the most important. Among the Tchambuli, women were confident and efficient, very much involved in economic

activities, cooperative (as least with other women), and central to the organization of the household. Tchambuli men, by contrast, seemed relatively passive and peripheral. They concerned themselves mainly with artistic activities of one sort or another, argued among themselves, and—to Mead—seemed maladjusted. Among the Tchambuli, Mead claimed, the gender roles associated with males and females in our own society had been reversed.

Something that we can learn about ourselves in studying other cultures is that many of the behaviours we consider to be deviant (deviance will be considered at length in Chapter 5) are normative elsewhere. For instance, in the late 1800s an anthropologist studying a Native society in New Mexico, the Zuni, brought a Zuni woman to Washington, DC. The woman, whose name was We'wha, was quickly dubbed a "princess," and soon became the toast of Washington society. There was just one thing: her physical appearance seemed a bit unusual. One newspaper account of the time suggested that We'wha had a relatively broad face, a massive body, and parted her hair strangely (Ward and Edelstein, 2006). In fact, We'wha was a biological male who had adopted the behaviours and dress more usually associated with females in Zuni society. The Zuni, like many indigenous societies in North America, recognized that some biological males had an affinity for the female role and encouraged such individuals to take on traits normally associated with females. Sometimes as well, biological females took on male roles. Early anthropologists used the term *berdache* to describe these individuals and the roles they occupied. More recently, Native scholars have suggested that such people be called "two-spirited." Whatever the term used, these individuals were behaving in perfect accord with Zuni norms. In our own society, by contrast, "two-spirited" individuals would almost certainly be labelled as transvestites, and their behaviour would be seen as deviant—that is, inconsistent with prevailing cultural norms.

Is globalization reducing cultural variation?

Sociologists are increasingly concerned with globalization. Within the cultural realm, much of this concern is focused on whether globalization is eroding cultural differences and promoting a homogeneous, largely American, global culture. Certainly more and

Urban Legends

Urban legends are stories with the following characteristics: (1) they are passed along mainly by word of mouth; (2) the people who repeat them believe them to be literally true; (3) the stories are set in the recent past and associated with some nearby geographical location; and, most importantly, (4) the stories are almost always completely false. Some of the best-known urban legends include stories about albino alligators in New York sewers, young boys found castrated in shopping centres, pets put into microwaves, corpses that are mislaid, Mexican dogs that turn out to be rats, etc.

Such stories can tell us something about the fears that characterize urban societies. For instance, the story about the boy found castrated (recorded at hundreds of locations all over North America) usually includes racial overtones, with the alleged perpetrators often said to be black. Attributing such an act to a minority group is by no means something new. During the Middle Ages, for instance, Jews were regularly accused of ritualistic castration and killing of Christian boys, just as, during the early days of the Roman Empire, Christians were regularly accused of the same thing. It seems obvious that the popularity of this modern version of the castrated boy story, and a story well known to my students, says something about the fears of the dominant white population in North America.

Often urban legends reflect more than one cultural attitude simultaneously. For instance, in the 1990s there were a number of urban legends about AIDS. In one a man meets an attractive woman in a bar, they go to his hotel room, and they have sexual intercourse. The next morning, when he awakes, the man finds the woman gone and a message scrawled in lipstick on the bathroom mirror: "Welcome to the wonderful world of AIDS." At one level, the story can be seen as reflecting very real worries about this disease. But notice in the story that the disease is knowingly spread by *a woman to a man*. While this pattern of transmission is possible, it is far more common—in the real world—for a man to spread the disease to a

woman or another man. Furthermore, of those people with AIDS who knowingly spread the disease, most are males, not females. The fact that the urban legend reverses the observed pattern to make a woman the source of danger says something, it has been argued, about cultural attitudes toward women in our society. Eve, not Adam, is still to blame.

Another common sort of urban legend involves what Fine (1992) called "redemption rumours." The core of this story is a large company redeeming tokens from one of its products to make a donation to a medical charity. In the two most common versions of this urban legend, the tokens are (1) pop-can tabs or (2) the foil inside cigarette packages. When these legends began circulating several decades ago, they suggested that the charitable donation would be used to purchase wheelchairs, iron lungs, and guide dogs; more recent versions suggest the purchase of kidney dialysis machines. Quite often the stories include the name of a particular person, usually a child, who will benefit when the tokens are redeemed. Despite such detail, the stories are generally false. Yet, as Fine pointed out, they persist and many people continue collecting, even when both the companies and the charities deny their participation. What accounts for the popularity of these stories?

Fine suggested two possibilities here. First, the fact that redemption rumours attach themselves to things like cigarettes and soft drinks may mean that people are simply trying to rationalize their continued use of products otherwise perceived as unhealthy. Second, and more important, redemption rumours may be attempts to re-establish a "folk community," a society in which everyone is honestly concerned with the well-being of everyone else and works together to ease human suffering. On the other hand, the need to manufacture stories to recapture such a folk society implies a widespread sense that our society has become something else, one in which individuals and groups are generally concerned with their own special interests and not with the interests and well-being of the whole.

Describe another urban legend you have heard. What fear might it represent?

more people throughout the world are purchasing food at McDonald's, Kentucky Fried Chicken, or Pizza Hut; getting copies made at Kinko's; watching reruns of American TV shows; accessing their e-mail using a Hotmail account—and so on. Is all this causing distinctively American norms and values to spread throughout the world? For many sociologists, the answer is "yes."

Ritzer (1996) argued that the principles that guide the U.S. fast-food industry increasingly dominate all aspects of life in all parts of the world—a process that he calls the "McDonaldization of society." These principles include an emphasis on predictability, on quantity over quality, and on control (by which he meant that behaviour is shaped more by the organizations with which people interact than by their own values). Evidence of McDonaldization, he argued, can be seen in contexts as diverse as the way university courses are taught, the way funerals are organized, and the way people receive medical care. Because American corporations have long promoted these same emphases in other nations, Ritzer predicted a net result of a homogenous global culture. The immense popularity of Ritzer's book, especially with university students, suggests that he is clearly tapping into something that is widely experienced.

Work by other investigators, however, suggests that things are more complicated than Ritzer's analysis indicates. Watson (2000), for example, has looked at the cultural effect of McDonald's in China (where the fast-food outlet has proven enormously popular). He noted that the McDonald's experience *did* promote some norms that were distinctively American. Chinese customers, for example, quickly learned to "line up" rather than mob the cash register (the traditional practice) and the chain's obsession with cleanliness, especially as regards toilets, seems to have affected expectations regarding urban middle-class life in Chinese cities. But McDonald's has adapted too. Students and retirees in China quickly came to regard McDonald's outlets as one of the few public places where they could gather and interact for long periods throughout the day in pleasant (and air-conditioned) surroundings. In effect, Watson argued, McDonald's outlets have become something like unofficial "community centres" in many Chinese cities. McDonald's tolerates this practice in China. In Canada, where there is greater emphasis on processing large numbers of customers and minimizing the amount of time that a given customer spends in an outlet, this would not be tolerated.

Canadians and Americans: Are we the same or different?

Long before "globalization" became a buzzword in sociology, any number of Canadian commentators grappled (and still grapple) with the issue of preserving a distinctively Canadian identity in the face of American influence. Much of this discussion has taken it for granted that Canada's cultural traditions are fundamentally different from those in the United States. But is that true? Some time ago Seymour Martin Lipset (1990), an American sociologist, suggested that it was. Lipset argued that American cultural traditions have given greater emphasis to rebellion against authority, individualism, and egalitarianism while Canadian cultural traditions have emphasized respect for authority, collectivism (e.g., groups are more important than individuals), and elitism. The net result, Lipset argued, is that U.S. society is more committed to change and Canadian society is more conservative.

For Lipset, these cultural differences explained other differences. The greater respect for authority and conservatism in Canada, for example, explained why rates of violent crime are lower in Canada. Similarly, the emphasis on collectivism in Canada explains why Canadians have long been more receptive to social welfare policies (like publicly funded medical insurance) designed to ensure that all members of society have access to basic services. These cultural differences also explain, Lipset argued, why so many Canadian writers emphasize "survival" (something that Lipset interprets as reflecting a conservative orientation) while American writers emphasize rebellion against authority.

For Lipset, the origin of these cultural differences lies in the fact that the U.S. experienced a revolution and Canada did not. In the United States, he argued, the Revolution bred a basic distrust of government and a strong emphasis on individualism. Canada, by contrast, underwent no such revolution. Just as important, Canada became a haven for Americans who rejected the Revolution (usually called the United Empire Loyalists). The result in Canada was a greater trust in government and a greater emphasis on the group and maintaining harmony within it.

These cultural differences were reinforced by institutional differences between the two countries. Lipset noted, for example, that throughout most of the nineteenth century the two dominant religious organizations in Canada were the Anglican Church in English Canada and the Roman Catholic Church in Quebec. Each was hierarchically arranged and had a long history (especially in Europe) of close cooperation with the state. These historical ties made it even more likely that Canadians would have a greater trust in their government and be less individualistic. The dominant religions of the United States, in contrast, were Protestant sects that stressed the separation of church and state and promoted religious individualism.

Lipset's theory has been criticized by a number of sociologists (see for example, Grabb and Curtis, 2005). Generally, their criticisms fall into three categories. First, they suggest that Lipset's account of history is flawed. For example, they suggest that the United Empire Loyalists came to Canada for a variety of reasons having little to do with core values and that their core values were not that different from the Americans who supported the Revolution. Second, Lipset's critics point out that if we take Quebecers (who, these days at least, tend to be "liberal" on most issues) and people living in the U.S. South (who tend to be conservative) out of the analysis, most surveys find no significant differences between Canadians and Americans on things like individualism and respect for authority. Finally, they argue that the existing differences between Canada and the U.S. can be explained without invoking culture. For example, although rates of violent crime *are* higher in the U.S., this is more likely due to the greater gap between the rich and the poor in the U.S. than to differing cultural traditions.

Lipset (2001), for his part, has found flaws in the work of his (mainly Canadian) critics, as have others (Carroll, 2006). The result is that the debate over differences in Canadian and American values continues and shows no signs of being resolved in the near future.

Cultural universals

So far, we have been concerned with cultural diversity. But among all the diversity, are there any **cultural universals**, any elements of culture found in every single, known society? There do seem to be a few. Every society, for instance, has rules limiting sexual behaviour, though the content and number of these rules vary greatly from society to society. In every known society,

there is a division of labour by sex, with certain tasks allocated to females and others to males, although the task assignments to either men or women vary among societies.

Some students might think that an incest *taboo*, a norm prohibiting sexual intercourse between parents and children and between siblings, is universal, and they would be right—almost. It turns out that there are about six known societies in which incestuous relationships were permitted, even encouraged, for members of the royal family. For instance, between 325 B.C. and 50 B.C., Egypt was ruled by the Ptolemies, a royal dynasty founded by Ptolemy I, one of Alexander the Great's generals, and eleven of the thirteen Ptolemaic kings married either a half- or full sister. There is also evidence that brother/sister marriage was widely practised among commoners in ancient Egypt. One estimate (Roscoe, 1996) suggests that in certain Egyptian communities at least one-sixth of all marriages were between full siblings. The incest taboo, then, is only a near universal.

One of the most important cultural universals concerns the relative status of men and women. There are many societies in which men, on average, have more political power and more social prestige than women; these are usually called *patriarchies*. Then there are a fair number of known societies in which men and women are roughly equal in social status, either because one group does not, on the average, have more power and prestige than the other, or because greater male power and prestige in certain areas of social life are balanced by greater female power and prestige in other areas. The existence of a true *matriarchy*, a society in which women have more political power and social prestige than men has, however, not yet been proven. The Amazons of myth and legend are just that: myth and legend. What we have, then, is a negative universal: matriarchy is universally absent from all known societies.

The most important point to make in connection with cultural universals, however, is that the number of such universals is relatively small, at least as compared with the number of ways in which cultures vary.

Cultural integration

Before closing this section, it is necessary to point out that many of the elements that comprise a given culture are interrelated, so a change in one element can produce

Anthropologists often attempt to detect cultural values that are strongly held but not consciously conceptualized.

changes—often quite unintended changes—in other elements. This interrelationship is known as **cultural integration**. The best way to illustrate this process is to consider the extreme case, in which a single cultural change, made with the best of intentions, had ramifications that were massive and disastrous.

An Aboriginal society in Australia, the Yir Yoront, traditionally travelled throughout various regions of Australia in small bands, each band a cooperative unit that gathered plants for food and hunted animals. In the early twentieth century, the Anglican Church set up a mission to convert the Yir Yoront to Christianity. To reward those who came to the mission and took instruction, the missionaries passed out something they thought would be useful: axes with steel heads. Before that time, the Yir Yoront used stone-headed axes they made themselves. A few years after the advent of the Anglican mission, many Yir Yoront bands had ceased to function as cohesive social units,

their members dependent upon handouts from the mission. What happened? For Sharp (1952), the key lay in the impact of those steel axes upon Yir Yoront culture; but to understand this impact you need to know more about that culture.

Most of us probably formed our initial impression of life in a non-literate culture from movies, and in most movies tribal societies have a single leader or chief of some sort, a notion that seems to most of us as perfectly natural and obvious. But, in fact, the Yir Yoront did not have chiefs. In this society, any two individuals would determine who had authority over the other with a system of rules. Basically, these rules specified that older people had authority over younger, men over women, and some blood relatives over other blood relatives. Though the rules tended to concentrate authority in the hands of older males within a given kinship group, the system was complicated enough that the lines of authority were not always clear. To solve this problem, the Yir Yoront had devised a very concrete procedure for constantly reinforcing these lines of authority; this procedure involved their traditional stone-headed axes. These axes were used for a variety of tasks and while everybody might need an axe, the axes were the property of the older males within each kinship group. This meant that anyone needing an axe would have to go to one of these individuals. In effect, asking one of these older males to borrow his axe became a way of acknowledging that male's authority.

Now enter the missionaries, filled with the typically Western attitude that superior technology (steel axe-heads rather than stone, for instance) is always a good thing. They distributed axes with steel heads to the Yir Yoront who came to the mission—as it turned out, these were mainly women or young men. Having their own axes meant, of course, that they no longer had to go to the older males for the use of an axe. While this might seem very fair and egalitarian to us, lacking the concrete procedure to reinforce the lines of authority in the society (asking for permission to use an axe), the authority system fell apart, and no other system arose to take its place. Without an authority system, it then became difficult to maintain the cooperation among band members necessary for successful hunting and gathering activities. Consequently, the bands ceased to function as independent social groups, all because some missionaries gave axes to a category of individuals (young men and women) who, under their culture's prevailing social norms, should not have owned them.

The point concerning cultural integration should not be overemphasized. Cultures are never so tightly integrated that any change will have widespread effects. Whether a particular cultural change introduced within a group will have further cultural ramifications depends upon the particular pattern of interrelationships among the cultural traits found in that group. Tracing out the relationships linking the cultural traits in various groups is one of the primary tasks of the sociologist and the social anthropologist.

Studying Culture

There are several conceptual dangers in the study of culture. One of the most obvious is ethnocentrism. In its most general sense, **ethnocentrism** refers to the tendency to see things from the point of view of the observer's culture rather than from that of the observed. In its most extreme form, ethnocentrism leads investigators to view other cultures as inferior rather than just different. This type of ethnocentrism was especially prevalent during the nineteenth century. For instance, most social anthropologists of the time accepted a view of social evolution that saw societies as passing through three stages: savagery, barbarism, and civilization. They also believed that most non-industrial cultures were stuck at the levels of savagery or barbarism, indicating the low esteem in which they held these cultures.

Though far less common today, ethnocentrism of this sort still crops up occasionally. For instance, someone who uses the term "primitive society" to refer to what is really a non-industrial society might be accused of ethnocentrism, since "primitive" now carries negative connotations that go far beyond a simple consideration of the type of economy found in a society. Another form of this bias occurs when investigators systematically associate people from other cultures with child-like traits, a process called **infantilization** (which happens more often than you might think). A content analysis (Zavitz-Gocan, 2003) of Canadian newspapers, for example, showed that stories describing disputes between First Nations groups and the federal government routinely depict Aboriginals as disruptive, out of control, and irresponsible (traits we associate with children), while simultaneously suggesting that federal officials are reasonable, responsible, and sometimes tough, but only because officials know what is best for Aboriginal populations and therefore, better able to determine what has to be done for them (traits we associate with parents).

More subtle forms of ethnocentrism, harder to spot but nevertheless very common, are *Eurocentrism* and *androcentrism*.

Eurocentrism is a bit of a misnomer, since it refers to a bias that goes beyond the borders of modern Europe. Basically, a theoretical perspective is said to be Eurocentric when it has been shaped by the values and experiences of the white, middle class in Western industrialized societies. In the simplest case, Eurocentrism means assuming that these values and experiences are universally shared. This happens more often (and more easily) than you might expect.

In the early part of the twentieth century, archaeologists investigating the Ice Age in Europe began discovering female figurines carved out of stone, found

Orientalism

Orientalism is a form of ethnocentrism identified some time ago by Palestinian-born Edward Said, who taught at Columbia University. For him, Orientalism meant the sum total of all the theories, analyses, and interpretations developed in the nineteenth century by Western scholars to understand "Oriental" societies (by which he meant mainly Arab societies in the Middle East). Said's overall point was that the theories owed less to what was actually happening in those societies than to the West's need to feel superior.

This is why, he suggested, Western scholars followed a fairly standard procedure in studying Oriental cultures. First, they focused on those things that Western audiences would find most exotic (e.g., "strange" clothing and ceremonies) to create the impression that people living in the Orient were *different* in some fundamental way. Second, people living in Oriental cultures were depicted as being driven primarily by *emotion*: by violent men driven by age-old hatreds and sensuous women driven by sexual desire. Third, Oriental societies were depicted as timeless and unchanging despite, as Said pointed out, evidence to the contrary. Finally, accounts of the Orient featured females,

some in veils or in harems, others as belly dancers. The resulting Western view of oriental cultures—as exotic, sensuous, unchanging, and "feminine"—ensured that these cultures were seen as inferior to the West, which was by implication associated with rationality, progress, and a range of political and technological innovations associated mainly with men.

Said's argument has been extended to cultures closer to home. Several commentators, for instance, have suggested that the Pueblo Indian cultures of the American Southwest have been "Orientalized," explaining why pictures of Pueblo women carrying a water jug (something that establishes Pueblo culture as both different and feminine) appear more frequently in accounts of Pueblo culture than any other type of picture. It also explains why the Pueblo art that strikes English speakers as traditional (i.e., as supposedly reflecting age-old and timeless traditions), is eagerly purchased at high prices by collectors while art that does not seem traditional (e.g., Pueblo figurines depicting white people, a type of art that Pueblo artists have been producing for over a century) is not valued.

Sources: Adapted from Said (1978); Babcock (1997); Seidman (1996).

While Said's work has been subjected to criticism, there is no denying that it has forced Western scholars to look far more carefully than before at the ways in which their accounts of other cultures may have been shaped by an implicit Western bias. Can you think of other examples of Orientalism?

---

over a wide area, from France to the Ural Mountains. In the majority of cases, the breasts, hips, and buttocks of the woman depicted seemed especially large, something which suggested to the (mainly male) archaeologists that the figurines were associated with fertility. The figurines were promptly dubbed "prehistoric Venuses" (after the Roman goddess of beauty) and accepted as evidence of fertility goddess worship in prehistoric Europe.

Over the past few decades, archaeologists, including most feminist archaeologists, have challenged the fertility-goddess interpretation of these figurines. Rice (1981), for instance, demonstrated that the figurines display the same

diversity with regard to physical traits (some are pregnant, some are not; some are young, some are old, etc.) that you would expect to find among a living population of prehistoric women. This would suggest that the figurines are more likely representations of individual women. But more importantly, nothing in the archaeological record itself suggests that the figurines were used for a religious purpose. Indeed, other possible explanations exist.

Townsend (1990) pointed out, for example, that human figurines have been used for a variety of purposes in non-Western societies. In certain First Nation societies in Alaska, shamans had dolls that were thought to travel

The idea of a "fertility goddess" conforms to a Eurocentric gender stereotype of women as nurturing beings.

to another world to retrieve lost souls. Tanzanian women attempted healing by driving their illnesses into a figurine. In other societies, human figures are used in magical procedures designed to harm somebody. In short, there is a range of meanings that the Venus figurines could have had for prehistoric peoples in Europe.

So why had the interpretation of Venus figurines as prehistoric goddesses become so popular with Western audiences? Most likely because part of the traditional gender stereotype associated with women in the Western tradition is that women are most of all supposed to be mothers, whose primary goal is to bear and nurture children. The idea of a nurturing "mother goddess" responsible for fertility is consistent with this Western stereotype and so makes sense to us. Earlier commentators simply assumed that what makes sense to us would have made sense as well to prehistoric peoples. That is Eurocentric thinking.

Androcentrism means "male-centredness." It is a bias that involves seeing things from a male point of view or in a way that reinforces male privilege in society. One form of androcentric bias, for example, is to develop cultural interpretations that see men as active and women as passive. This particular bias is especially easy to document in those cases where investigators create "precise" accounts of situations in which precision is impossible. For example, while we know very little about day-to-day "social life" in prehistoric groups if only because "social life" leaves little or no trace in the archaeological record, some commentators and many anthropology textbooks describe prehistoric life in great detail.

One analysis (Gifford-Gonzales, 1993) of a fairly large sample of these depictions found that males usually outnumber females in these scenes by a ratio of 2:1; that males are far more likely than females to be shown constructing tools, conducting religious rituals, or simply walking and running; that females are more likely to be shown in association with children, to be depicted low to the ground, and to be engaged in activities that do not involve moving around. In short, these depictions (which are based, remember, on nothing that appears in the archaeological record) reinforce modern stereotypes about males and females (i.e., males are dominant, active, and creative while females are subordinate, passive, and suited for routine tasks). Just as important, by projecting these modern gender stereotypes on the past, these depictions "naturalize" those stereotypes. In other words, they suggest that these gender stereotypes are part of an evolutionary heritage—something that (according to a number of feminist critics) has the effect of undermining present efforts to erode those stereotypes.

Androcentric bias also leads us to choose the male experience over the female experience for study. Traditional anthropological accounts of hunting and gathering societies, for example, devoted far more space to describing hunting activities (usually done by males) than to gathering activities (usually done by females) even when gathering provided most of the food consumed in a society. The simple fact that we call these societies "hunting and gathering societies" rather than "gathering and hunting societies" is for some feminist anthropologists an indication of androcentric bias.

When cultures collide: Studying First Nations communities

Sometimes cultures vary not just with respect to the content of particular norms and values but also with respect to what might be called "ways of thinking about the world." Increasingly, sociologists and other

More Than Just a Toy: Barbie As Cultural Icon

In Greek mythology, Athena sprang fully grown from the head of Zeus and went on to acquire a reputation for cleverness. In 1959, Barbie emerged as a fully formed teenager from somewhere within the Mattel Corporation to become the best-selling toy in the world. Athena was born wearing a suit of armour; Barbie came equipped with a hard plastic body. Athena was virginal but worked with males on a number of difficult tasks; Barbie is virginal (at least semi-virginal) and paired with Ken. But Barbie and Athena differ dramatically in at least two ways: Barbie has lots more stuff and a whole lot more fun!

Barbie's success is phenomenal. In the United States and Canada, the vast majority of girls under the age of twelve have at least one Barbie, and it's common for a girl to have several Barbies. What accounts for Barbie's popularity? Partly, it's because Barbie, and the merchandising package that surrounds her, meshes so well with the dominant culture in most capitalistic societies. Barbie, after all, is the quintessential consumer and young girls learn to become consumers in a never-ending task of acquiring for Barbie her own special cars, horses, furniture, jewellery, and clothing. Barbie also embodies qualities that have long been favoured in middle-class families: she's pretty, neat, always anxious to have the proper outfit for the occasion, and (it goes without saying) intensely heterosexual. Finally, Barbie works to reinforce the traditional gender roles that so many members of the middle class now see as under attack by feminists. She is concerned with her appearance (her hair in particular), likes nice clothes, and gravitates toward occupations traditionally associated with women (e.g., flight attendant, teacher, hospital volunteer, perfume designer). When she broke away from traditional gender stereotypes in the early 1970s and became a medical doctor, she did not sell very well (Urla and Swedlund, 1995: 283).

As a cultural icon, however, Barbie is most distinctive for her impossible body. Even with the many transformations over the last few decades and the variety of Barbies that differ in skin colour and facial features, two things have remained constant: her elongated body and her large breasts. Urla and Swedlund (1996) compared the measurements from a sample of different Barbies with the measurements of the statistically "average" female in the United

States. Needless to say, they discovered that if Barbie were scaled to the height of the average female, and her bodily proportions remained constant, then she would be clinically anorexic to an extreme degree—albeit unusually buxom. These same authors did a similar study with Barbie's friend Ken. They found that Ken's proportions were also unrealistic when compared with the statistically average male, but (and this, they argued, is the important point here) far less so than Barbie's. To the extent that Barbie's body sets a standard impossible for real-life girls to meet, she reinforces a cultural climate in which women must inevitably be considered inferior. Moreover, Urla and Swedlund pointed out, a slender body is something that can be achieved only through self-discipline and control; Barbie's hyper-slender body therefore suggests that females are in special need of control and discipline and this, too, may reinforce male domination or patriarchy (see Chapter 7, Gender Relations).

But nothing is ever simple, and Urla and Swedlund went on to suggest further that we should also pay attention to what Barbie is not. For instance, although Barbie has many accessories, a husband and (her own) children are not among them. Barbie is not, in other words, a wife and mother. Nor is she, like so many other dolls, a child to be cared for as a child. On the contrary, Barbie is a strongly sexualized female who conveys an aura of independence. In short, there is little about Barbie or Barbie's merchandising that can be seen as socializing young girls for a traditional role as mother and wife. To paraphrase the authors: Barbie owns an expensive car and isn't married; she can't be doing everything wrong!

Finally, we must not fall into the trap of regarding young girls as purely passive consumers of what confronts them. Whatever Mattel may intend Barbie to be, young girls are capable of associating their Barbie dolls with a range of roles and personalities. What is needed, these authors suggested, is more research into just what these different roles and personalities are.

In the end, then, Barbie turns out to be surrounded by a fairly complex set of cultural values. These values may not all be consistent, but they all reflect the cultural milieu from which Barbie sprang and in which she flourishes.

Is Barbie still popular with the young girls that you know? If so, how do you think they themselves would explain this? If not, what does that say about the analysis given above?

academics are coming to realize that this fact raises a number of ethical issues about what is and what is not appropriate when sociologists from a European background study people and communities whose culture is non-European. In recent decades, at least in Canada, this issue has come up most often in connection with the study of First Nations communities.

Canadian museums, for example, like the Canadian Museum of Civilization in Ottawa, are full of objects that were collected—usually a long time ago—from First Nations communities. Sometimes Aboriginal groups have requested, often successfully, to have these objects returned. What is often more problematic, however, is how to treat the objects that for one reason or another remain in the custody of a museum. For example, although Western museum curators might take note of a connection between an object and some particular ritual in the past, their main concern has often been to treat First Nations artifacts as examples of "art" that can be appreciated in and of themselves (i.e., without regard to the role that the objects played in First Nations culture). Moreover, it has also been taken for granted in most Western museums that the objects in their collection should be seen by the public. First Nations peoples, by contrast, often reject both attitudes here on the grounds that (1) there is an intimate and ongoing connection between certain rituals and certain objects that should not be broken and (2) some objects are meant to be seen and handled only by certain groups. One result is that some Canadian museums (but only some) have now accommodated First Nations traditions by withdrawing certain objects from public view; by suggesting that certain objects not be handled by female museum staff if they are objects meant to be handled only by men; and by lending out objects in their collections for use in First Nations rituals (Phillips and Johnson, 2003).

Sociologists studying First Nations communities face ethical issues that are even more complex than those facing museum curators. Sociologists, for example, have a long-standing disciplinary interest in studying the causes and consequences of social and economic inequality (see Chapter 6, Social Inequality). Given that the conditions prevailing in many First Nations communities are far worse than the national average with respect to things like infant mortality, average income, access to clean water, etc. (Cooke, Beavon, and McHardy, 2004), it is hardly surprising that Canadian sociologists have often taken First Nations communities as an object of study. Unfortunately, all too often the members of First Nations communities themselves have felt that the "explanations" developed by

sociological investigators often proceed from a Eurocentric stance that fails to capture the mix of conditions that define life in these communities.

To address the concerns raised by First Nations communities, the three most important federal granting agencies in Canada have developed a special set of ethical guidelines that sociologists must observe if they want federal money to finance studies of Aboriginal communities. Those guidelines (which are available at the website listed at the end of this chapter) take explicit note of the fact that in many cases in the past inaccurate and/or insensitive sociological research has promoted a negative view of Aboriginal peoples among the general public. The guidelines also point out very explicitly that a part of the problem here is that members of First Nations communities often hold views that are quite different from those held by non-Aboriginal investigators (e.g, the distinction between what is private and what is public, and what is or is not "property"). The granting agencies go on to recommend a number of "good practices" that sociologists and other investigators should observe. Such good practices include (1) involving the Aboriginal group being studied in the design of the project, (2) providing a preliminary report of findings to members of the Aboriginal group for comment, and (3) taking note in scholarly publications of any disagreements that Aboriginal communities might have with the research findings being reported.

Theoretical Perspectives on Culture

Sociologists who study culture have used a range of theoretical perspectives. The most important and best-known analyses of culture, however, have each drawn upon one of four quite different perspectives. These are: (1) functionalism, (2) conflict theory, (3) cultural materialism, and (4) feminism.

Functionalism

You encountered **functionalism** in the introductory chapter, and you will it see again many times throughout this book. The essence of functionalist explanation, when applied to culture, is that a given norm or value or cultural practice is explained by showing how it contributes to the overall stability or survival of the society in which it is found. The explanation offered for the collapse of Yir Yoront society, for example, can be viewed as an example of functionalist explanation since a concern was to show how the "asking for an axe" ritual had contributed to social stability.

But some of the clearest examples of functionalist explanation, and certainly the best known, were offered some time ago by a social anthropologist named Bronislaw Malinowski. His work, even today, provides some of the clearest examples of functionalist explanation. Malinowski (1954 [1925]) studied a society located among the Trobriand Islands in the South Pacific. The Trobrianders derived much of their food from fishing in the ocean waters surrounding their islands. What Malinowski found was that every aspect of such ocean fishing was surrounded by an elaborate system of magic. But why did they use magic? At first glance the answer might seem obvious: the Trobrianders used magic because they believed it would help them catch more fish. But, Malinowski argued, if magic is used simply to ensure success, then every society should use magic extensively to ensure success at whatever activity is important to its members. Such widespread use of magic, however, is simply not the case. Some societies, like the Trobrianders, make extensive use of magic; others do not. What accounts for this cultural difference?

In beginning his explanation, Malinowski noted that ocean fishing is an extremely uncertain activity. The Trobrianders had no control over the weather or over the locations at which fish might be caught. Added to this, of course, was the fact that taking a canoe onto the ocean was a relatively dangerous activity. How would you feel if you had to engage in a dangerous and uncertain activity day after day? You would probably feel quite anxious, and Malinowski assumed that the Trobrianders felt the same way. This anxiety would be reduced if you felt, however incorrectly, that you could control your environment, a feeling that magic can provide. The use of magic allowed the Trobrianders to believe that they could control both the weather and the locations at which fish were to be found. Malinowski's conclusion, then, is that magic is likely to be used whenever people face dangerous and uncertain environments. The Trobrianders faced such an environment, and therefore used magic. Other societies face relatively safe, certain environments, and therefore do not use magic.

Malinowski had one final bit of data that provided an especially convincing conclusion to his argument. Besides fishing on the open ocean, the Trobrianders also fished in a sheltered lagoon. Unlike ocean fishing, fishing in the lagoon was relatively safe, and since the lagoon was a relatively small place, finding the right place to fish was less of a problem. Given Malinowski's argument, one would expect that magic would not be associated with lagoon fishing, which was exactly what he found. Although the Trobrianders surrounded ocean fishing with much magic, none was associated with lagoon fishing.

Notice how Malinowski's explanation fits the basic functionalist pattern. He explained a given cultural element, in this case the use of magic, by showing how it contributes to the overall stability of the society: magic reduces the anxiety produced by the dangers and uncertainties associated with ocean fishing.

The functionalist perspective used by Malinowski influenced not only social anthropologists but sociologists as well. Perhaps the best examples of functionalist explanation in sociology are contained in a book entitled *Human Society*, written by Kingsley Davis (1949) and reprinted many times. *Human Society* was intended to be an introductory text, though one that explicitly adopted a functionalist perspective. As a result, most of Davis's discussion is devoted to those fairly standard topics, such as socialization, religious institutions, and marriage and the family, that tend to be covered in every introductory textbook. But Davis also devoted an entire chapter to something that would strike many as an unlikely candidate for functionalist explanation: sexual jealousy among males.

Most people probably regard such jealousy as somehow pathological, as resulting from, say, the basic insecurity of males concerning sexual matters. Nevertheless, sexual jealousy among males is found in every known society, and for the functionalist, like Davis, that means that it probably contributes to social stability. But how?

Davis started off by making a very crucial assumption, crucial in the sense that if it were false, his entire argument would fall apart. He assumed that, unless a society placed some restrictions upon sexual intercourse, most males would be constantly competing with other males for sexual access, producing much conflict. The conflict, in turn, would prevent the cooperation that must be maintained if society is to survive. This assumption led Davis to conclude that every society must have norms of some sort regulating sexual intercourse. But how are these norms enforced? That is, what ensures that most members of society obey most of the norms most of the time? There has to be some type of deterrent. That is where sexual jealousy comes in.

[Debate]

Rereading Mother Teresa: A Conflict Approach?

If I asked most of you to list ten public figures you admire and respect, Mother Teresa would probably appear on a great many lists. Born in 1910 in the former Yugoslavia to Albanian parents, Mother Teresa founded an order of Roman Catholic sisters who today minister to the poor in over eighty countries. From the early 1950s until her retirement for reasons of health in 1990, she personally gathered the dying from the streets of Calcutta, India, and brought them to her hospital where they could die with dignity. As a result, Mother Teresa was often called a "living saint," and in 1979 was awarded the Nobel Prize for Peace.

Although it rarely makes the news, Mother Teresa also was criticized by a number of Roman Catholic activists, in India and elsewhere. In an interview published in an Italian magazine (*L'Expresso*, 9 September 1990), a Catholic theologian who teaches near Calcutta suggested that it was the Western media that "created"

Mother Teresa. He meant that it was the Western media—not the media in India or the rest of the Third World—that first raised her to mythic status. Certainly, it was a Western agency that granted her the Nobel Peace Prize.

Why the criticism? It relates to Mother Teresa's approach to poverty. For her, poverty was something to be alleviated by good works. In her many speeches, she never attacked the root causes of poverty, those social conditions that ensure that the mass of people in the Third World remain poor while relatively few remain rich. Her approach to poverty, in other words, did not threaten entrenched privilege. The conflict approach to religion, to be discussed in Chapter 11, Religion, makes the same point, that religion is a conservative force, one that can be used as a means to calm the masses, a flower on the chain of oppression. In applying a conflict perspective, surprising issues can be raised, even about Mother Teresa.

How much of the West's regard for Mother Teresa is due to a sincere appreciation of her selflessness (and certainly no one doubts that as an individual she was selfless) and how much to the fact that the West controls and consumes most of the world's resources and finds in Mother Teresa someone whose approach to poverty does not threaten that pattern of control and consumption?

Jealousy is an emotional response that fosters aggression. Specifically, it fosters aggression against people who have given others a reason to be jealous. Given this, Davis argued that a community would encourage its members to be jealous whenever their sexual rights guaranteed under the prevailing sexual norms have been violated. The fact that the community encourages people to be jealous whenever their sexual rights have been violated will deter individuals who might think of violating those rights. For instance, suppose that one of the sexual norms in a society is that the only person who has a right to sexual intercourse with a married woman is her husband. The foreknowledge that a husband will be jealous (and aggressive) if another male has intercourse with his wife and the foreknowledge that this jealousy will be encouraged by the community at large would,

according to Davis, deter to some degree both the wife and any potential lover from violating that norm. To convince yourself of the reasonableness of the Davis argument, you might think about things the other way around. If it were absolutely certain that people in this society would not be jealous of the person involved in a spouse's infidelity, would adultery be more likely? If you answered yes you basically agree with Davis's analysis.

A consequence of this formulation is that the only way to eliminate sexual jealousy is to eliminate sexual norms—and if Davis's initial assumption is correct, this cannot be done without producing much social instability. Functionalist explanations of this sort are still popular in sociology, but much less so than they once were. Thus, let us turn to other perspectives, beginning with conflict theory.

Conflict theory

Some conflict theorists, following Marx, lump cultural beliefs under the more general heading of "ideology," the system of thought that legitimates existing inequalities of wealth and power, or prevents the less powerful from seeing the true cause of this inequality. Conflict theorists also apply this same perspective to religion (also usually considered to be ideology). You will be considering the Marxist perspective on religion in Chapter 11.

A conflict approach has also been especially influential in the *sociology of knowledge*, a subfield of the sociology of culture that studies the influence of social factors on what constitutes knowledge in a society. For example, do you really think it is a coincidence, a conflict theorist might argue, that Darwin's theory of evolution first became popular in nineteenth-century England? Or are you willing to grant that Darwin's emphasis upon competition and survival of the fittest, as the keys to evolution, just might have been especially appealing in a society in which the rich favoured free economic competition and believed their high status to be mainly the result of their innate abilities?

The great value of the conflict perspective on culture is that it forces us to challenge a great many attitudes and beliefs that would otherwise be unexamined. Even if in the end we reject a particular conflict account, the exercise of considering it is very much in keeping with the purpose of education. With this in mind, you might try developing a conflict perspective on some of the many campaigns that are important in our society at the moment. Is there any basis for believing, for example, that the current cultural emphasis upon global ecology or upon household recycling works to divert our attention from prevailing injustices and from the groups responsible for them? Or what about those campaigns against cancer that adopt a purely medical model, seeing cancer mainly as a disease for which a medical cure must be found, rather than, say, mainly as a condition brought on by things put into our environment by industry? You might surprise yourself.

Cultural materialism

Cultural materialism is a third perspective used to study and explain culture. It de-emphasizes ideas and ideology as determinants of cultures, and instead *sees* cultures as adaptations to the needs forced upon social groups by their specific physical environments.

The essence of cultural materialism is best conveyed by examples, and the best examples of this approach are to be found in the applications developed by Harris (1985). One of his concerns was to explain the Hindu ban on the slaughter of cows. To many Western observers, this ban may seem utterly senseless, a classic example of how religion and the inertia of tradition can stand in the way of rational behaviour (religion and rationality will be discussed in Chapter 11, Religion). Nothing seems more tragic than for Hindu farmers in India to see their families starve rather than kill the sacred cows which wander the countryside. Nevertheless, Harris argued, if you think that the Hindu farmers are in a tragic situation right now, that is nothing compared with the misery and human devastation that would result if those farmers started to slaughter their cows.

How did Harris come to this very counter-intuitive position? He started by noting that there are two basic types of agricultural systems in the world today. One, the type used in Canada and most Western nations, is a highly mechanized system that relies on tractors for motive power. Such a system also relies heavily upon petrochemicals, both to fuel the tractors and to provide synthetic fertilizers. The second type is a non-mechanized system that relies on draft animals like oxen for motive power and uses dung for fertilizer. This is the system that characterizes modern India.

There are three reasons why India cannot convert to the more mechanized system of agriculture. First, India currently has insufficient capital either to purchase the required machinery or to establish a system for the distribution of petrochemical products. Second, the experiences in Western nations make it quite clear that one effect of agricultural mechanization is the displacement of people from the country to the city. India's urban areas are already overcrowded and simply cannot absorb a massive influx from the country. Third, although Westerners think that tractors are more efficient than oxen, Harris argued that this is not always true. In India, a tractor can plough a field about ten times faster than can a pair of oxen, but the initial cost of that tractor is something like twenty times the cost of the oxen. Given this fact, tractors are more cost-effective than oxen only in the case of large farms that require a lot of ploughing. In the case of small farms—and the vast majority of farms in India are small—oxen are more cost-effective than tractors. India, then, will probably continue to use the non-mechanical type of agriculture for some time to come.

Cultural materialism sees culture as an adaptation to the needs forced upon people by the nature of the physical environment in which they live.

At this point, Harris came up with an interesting statistic from Indian government reports: in an average year, the number of oxen available for use by Indian farmers is only about 66 percent of the number needed. This chronic shortage of oxen is one of the major reasons why thousands of Indian farms fail each year. If Western farmers want new tractors, they go to a dealer, but if Indian farmers want a new ox, they go to—a cow.

We begin to catch a glimmer of the reasoning behind Harris's position. Only by ensuring that most of its farms are productive can India feed itself. Only by maintaining a large population of cows can India's farmers be assured that sufficient oxen will be available to make the farms productive. Even with the current ban on the slaughter of cows, there are not enough oxen to go around. Think of how much greater the problem would be if a significant percentage of those cows were slaughtered.

But wait. Isn't there a flaw in the argument? If maintaining a large population of cows is so much in the farmers' self-interest, why do things have to be formalized under the guise of a religious ban? Wouldn't farmers just naturally refrain from slaughtering their cows? Harris's response to this criticism is simple. Rains in India are irregular and thus famine is recurrent. Indian farmers are like you or me; if they see their families starving, they will be strongly tempted to kill their cows to feed their families. Yet if they do kill those cows during famine, there will be an even greater shortage of oxen, and it will be even more difficult for agriculture to recover when the famine ends. In fact, killing the cows might easily mean that the famine would never end. The only solution is a total and absolute ban on the slaughter of cows. And only a religiously inspired ban has the remotest chance of overcoming the farmers' temptations to feed themselves and their families during times of famine.

Students who find this example of cultural materialism interesting should consult Harris (1985), in which he also provides explanations of why North Americans won't eat horse meat (though most of Europe does) but love milk (regarded as something like cow spit in traditional China), why Europeans don't eat insects but people living in the Amazon basin do, and why the Aztecs ate other human beings on a scale unheard of anywhere else in the world. Lunch anyone?

Feminism(s)

As you read in the last chapter and will read in Chapter 7, Gender Relations, feminism is a very diverse movement using a variety of theoretical approaches. Many of the contributions made by feminist investigators over the past three decades have been in the area of gender studies, and these will be discussed in Chapter 7. Another important feminist goal has been to uncover the androcentric biases mentioned earlier in this chapter. Beyond this, the most important feminist contributions to the study of culture have been concerned with (1) searching for the cause of female subordination throughout the world, and (2) importing into the study of culture a greater emphasis on women and the female experience.

With the rise of what was then called the Women's Liberation Movement in the 1960s feminists became concerned with finding "the" cause of female subordination. In contrast to the theories popular with non-academic publics (which usually emphasize male/female differences in physical strength), most of the feminist theories developed during this period trace female subordination to the fact that women conceive and give birth to children. In one particularly influential theory, for example, an anthropologist (Ortner, 1972) suggested that "female is to male as nature is to culture." What Ortner meant is that all societies make a distinction between things that "belong to nature" and things "that belong to culture," and that all societies invariably value the Culture category more highly than the Nature category. Since women were so closely tied to a biological process like giving birth, in all societies, Ortner argued, women would universally come to be associated with Nature—and this in turn ensured that men would come to be associated with the more highly valued Culture category. We shall return to nature/culture issues in the next chapter.

Unfortunately, as anthropologists went on to investigate gender relations, it became clear that there

was a diversity and subtlety to gender relations in different societies (and often in the same society across different historical periods) that seem unexplainable by any one variable. Ortner herself, for example, eventually repudiated her own theory since it became clear that there are many societies that do not associate women with Nature. Even in our own culture, there have been many periods in Western history when the "mother nature" metaphor so familiar to us today has been absent. Generally, as Di Leonardo (1991) pointed out, anthropological and sociological theories positing a single, universal cause for female subordination had been discredited by the late 1980s. Since then, feminist investigators have preferred to explain gender inequality in a particular society by careful consideration of the distinctive cluster of social and economic conditions prevailing in that society.

The second important contribution made by feminist investigators was to foster a greater emphasis on women and the female experience in studying culture. This has meant overcoming the view, latent in most traditional accounts, that what is important about a culture are the things that men do or care about. It has also meant interviewing both men and women in a particular society to find out how their experience of the same institution (say, the family or religion) differ. Finally, it has meant looking at things like sexual assault and gendered violence that were often overlooked in traditional accounts of culture.

This new emphasis on the female experience in the study of culture also affected the study of human prehistory. Traditional accounts of human prehistory, for example, had always argued that hunting (presumed to have been a male activity) and the technology surrounding hunting (arrowheads, spears, etc.) were the most important elements in human social evolution. A number of feminist scholars, by contrast, have argued that the gathering of food by females was far more important to the development of human social institutions than the hunting of animals by males. Not only did gathering provide most of the food in earliest human societies (just as it provides most of the food in modern hunting and gathering societies), but there are solid reasons for believing that systematic food-gathering would have been the source of complex patterns of group cooperation and communication.

Other feminist scholars (like Conkey, 1997) have challenged the presumption that there was a *gendered division of labour* (i.e., a pattern in which men do certain tasks and women do others) in our prehistoric past. There is nothing in the archaeological record, they point out, that suggests men were more likely to be hunters (and less likely to be gatherers) than women. What we have done, they argued, is simply to project the sort of division of labour that emerged in societies (like our own) onto the prehistoric past. Moreover, the traditional argument goes, if men and women have always engaged in different tasks, then assigning them different tasks in the present seems, well, "natural." The feminist argument, by contrast, is that once we recognize that there is no solid evidence for a gendered division of labour in our prehistoric past, then it becomes easier to imagine changing the gendered division of labour that exists in our own society.

From sociology to cultural studies

By the 1960s, the study of culture had slipped to the margins of sociology in North America. The reasons for this are still not entirely clear, though Smith (1998) has suggested that it was part of a general reaction against theoretical frameworks (like functionalism) and theoretical concepts (like culture) that emphasized social stability over social change. Over the past thirty years, however, the study of culture has once again become popular in sociology. One reason for this, Smith suggested, is that during the 1970s and 1980s sociologists in Canada and the United States came more and more to be influenced by those various European theorists who shared a common commitment to tracing previously unrecognized links between culture and other aspects of our social and mental experience.

One of the distinctive contributions made by these European theorists was that many things previously taken to be "natural" are in fact cultural inventions that arose at a particular point in historical time in response to particular societal conditions. For example, we now take it for granted that certain people are predisposed toward sexual activity with members of the same sex. We can debate whether this is the result of biology, the social environment, or some combination of the two, but that some people are homosexual seems obvious. Given this, it seems strange to realize—as Foucault (1978) pointed out—that in Western societies while people always knew about homosexual activity, the category "homosexual" was an invention of the nineteenth century. The *idea* that there is a category of persons who are generally predisposed (by their nature or their personality) to engage in

homosexual activity simply cannot be found in the writings of Western thinkers prior to this time.

Foucault's argument is that the cultural invention of the homosexual was an attempt at social control. In other words, by defining a deviant activity (in this case, homosexual behaviour) as resulting from a person's biology or personality, people engaging in such acts could now be defined as "sick" and so brought under the control of a powerful medical establishment. The invention of the "homosexual," in short, allowed the power of medical science to be co-opted to regulate what was then a culturally devalued activity.

Foucault's general argument here has been especially appealing to scholars interested in the interplay between gender, sex, and sexuality. Groneman (1995), for example, pointed out that it was only in the nineteenth century that medical doctors began to apply the term "nymphomaniac" to some of their female patients. Supposedly, this term referred to a medical condition that caused women to be characterized by excessive sexual desire. In principle, there was a corresponding term for males, satyriasis. But if you look at the indicators of nymphomania and satyriasis of the time, it is clear that the two terms were not symmetrical. In the case of women, things like adultery, wanting more sex than their spouses, excessive flirtation, and masturbation were often enough to merit a medical diagnosis of nymphomania. These same things were never enough to justify a diagnosis of satyriasis in men. Groneman, following Foucault, suggested that the category "nymphomaniac" was invented so that women who stepped outside the rigidly defined gender roles of the Victorian period (which characterized women as sexually passive) could be defined as "sick" and so treated (and brought into line) by a male-dominated medical establishment. The preferred method of treating nymphomania, incidentally, was surgical removal of the ovaries. To fully appreciate the horrific significance of this, imagine a society in which men who committed adultery, masturbated, or flirted excessively were routinely subjected to castration.

These two examples do not capture the diversity that exists in the new tradition of cultural studies that has taken root in North America and Europe. Interested students might want to consult the various essays in Smith (1998) and Long (1997) and learn, among other things, how the public discussion over AIDS has been shaped to reinforce prevailing notions of heterosexual monogamy; how popular child-rearing manuals are perfectly suited to the needs of a capitalistic society but work against the economic interests of women; and why the merger of animals and children in shows like *Sesame Street* is so appealing to us. Hint: in the Western tradition, undomesticated animals are often seen as a threat to human society but, even so, are rarely defined as inherently "bad."

Those working today in cultural studies have crossed disciplinary boundaries and borrowed freely from sociology, anthropology, literature and film studies, history, linguistics, philosophy, and psychoanalysis for their insights. A consequence of this interdisciplinary emphasis and the increasing popularity of cultural studies has been a destabilization of "sociology" as a distinct and separate category. Academic departments of sociology continue to exist, of course, as do specialized journals of sociology. Even so, sociology has quite literally vanished in some areas. Almost all large bookstores, for example, used to have a section entitled "sociology." Often that is no longer the case (you might want to check this out for yourself in your local area). So where do you find sociology books? Most often in a section called—what else?—"cultural studies." Even Durkheim's *Suicide*, long considered the prototypical study in sociology, is now often found in a "cultural studies" section. So what does the future hold? Are the subject headings posted in Chapters and other large bookstores quite literally the "writing on the wall" for sociology? Is "sociology" itself just a cultural construct that has served its historical purpose and is now in the process of being discarded?

Summary

Social life is patterned, not random, and much of this patterning can be attributed to the fact that every social group possesses a culture. A cultural element is something held in common by the members of a group, that affects their behaviour or the way they view the world, and is passed on to new members. A group's culture is simply the sum total of all the cultural elements associated with that group. There are many types of cultural elements, but the three most important ones for sociologists are values, norms, and roles.

Most students of culture are concerned with three observations: (1) that the content of culture varies greatly across the totality of the world's societies,

(2) that very few cultural elements are found in all the world's societies, and (3) that the elements of a given culture are often interrelated. However, much of what we see when studying cultures, whether our own or some other, is vulnerable to distortions produced by pre-existing biases. Ethnocentrism is always a danger, and Eurocentrism and androcentrism are especially common. The fact that different cultures can literally "see the same things in different ways" means that sociologist have a special responsibility to behave ethically when studying non-European cultures.

The most important theoretical perspectives used in the study of culture are: (1) functionalism, (2) conflict theory, (3) cultural materialism, and (4) feminism. Cultural studies is an interdisciplinary approach to the study of culture that is becoming increasingly popular among sociologists.

Questions for Review and Critical Thinking

1. Make a list of at least twenty norms and beliefs you hold and/or activities in which you engage. How would you defend them to an ethnocentric person from another culture? Could you explain smoking cigarettes, drinking alcohol, shaving, dieting, and watching summer reruns or baseball on television to such a person?

2. Choose some popular toys and for each identify the cultural beliefs and attitudes that it seems to reflect.

3. Read again the argument about Mother Teresa presented in the box "Rereading Mother Teresa: A Conflict Approach?" Then identify other individuals who are widely admired in this society, and develop and discuss conflict interpretations of why these individuals are so widely admired.

4. Make a list of some stereotypical differences between Canadians and Americans. Where did you acquire these stereotypes? From talking with Americans? From the media? How would you go about deciding if these stereotypes were based in anything "real"?

5. Edward Said and others have suggested that, while Eurocentric bias is less frequent today in scholarly analysis, it is still common in journalistic accounts. Can you find evidence of this claim in newspaper accounts of people living in non-Western cultures generally or in the Middle East specifically?

Key Terms

androcentrism, p. 50
cultural element, p. 38
cultural integration, p. 47
cultural materialism, p. 55
cultural universals, p. 46
culture, p. 38
ethnocentrism, p. 48
Eurocentrism, p. 48
folkways, p. 40
functionalism, p. 52
infantilization, p. 48
institution, p. 42
mores, p. 40
norms, p. 39
Orientalism, p. 49
popular culture, p. 42
role, p. 40
role conflict, p. 41
society, p. 40
subculture, p. 42
urban legends, p. 44
values, p. 38

Suggested Readings

Lipset, Seymour Martin
1996 *American Exceptionalism: A Double-Edged Sword.*
    New York: W.W. Norton.
Lipset systemically compares Canada with the U.S. along a number of different cultural dimensions and relates the differences he finds to the history of each country. His analysis should be read in conjunction with the critiques mentioned in the text.

Mead, Margaret
1935 *Sex and Temperament in Three Primitive Societies.*
    New York: Morrow.
This is one of the all-time classics in social science. By considering in depth three cultures radically different from our own, at least with regard to sex roles, Mead very forcibly establishes just how much the content of cultures can vary.

Ritzer, George
1996 *McDonaldization of Society.* Thousand Oaks, CA:
    Pine Forge Press.
Ritzer discusses how the principles of "rationalization," long associated with the fast-food industry, are increasingly structuring all aspects of our lives—and what can be done about it.

Ward, Martha C. and Monica Edelstein
2006 *A World Full of Women* (4th ed.). Boston: Pearson.
This book mixes feminist anthropology and feminist sociology to focus on activities involving women in a variety of societies, including our own, while simultaneously developing various critiques of the ways in which these activities have been viewed by traditional anthropologists and sociologists. It is written for the beginning student.

Websites

www.pre.ethics.gc.ca/english/index.cfm
Interagency Advisory Panel on Research Ethics
This provides a link to the Tri-Council Guidelines that provide the ethical standards that sociologists must meet in conducting research on human subjects generally and—especially—when conducting research on First Nations Communities.

www.snopes.com
Urban Legends Reference Pages
This is a commercial site (with ads) that lists and comments on a great many urban legends by category (e.g., most recent, most popular, college, cokelore, horrors, humour, etc.).

http://en.wikipedia.org
General reference
Wikipedia is the free online encyclopedia that provides mini-essays on a variety of topics, including many discussed in this chapter (folkways and mores, ethnocentrism, orientalism, functionalism in sociology, etc.)

Key Search Terms

Norms
Values
Culture
Subculture
Ethnocentrism

For more study tools to help you with your next exam, be sure to check out the Companion Website at **www.pearsoned.ca/hewitt**, as well as Chapter 3 in your Study Guide.

[4]

socialization

james côté

Introduction

For much of human history, it was believed that people's actions were determined by unseen but powerful forces. Often, these forces had spiritual or religious meanings. But in the early days of science, attention turned to genetic factors, with many people believing that human genetics determined much of our "nature." These beliefs were strong enough to stimulate the eugenics movement, which sought to perfect the human gene pool and thereby eliminate "lower" aspects of human behaviour like crime and poverty. This movement was rooted in Darwin's concept of *adaptation* and his theory of biological evolution into "higher" species. Eugenicists argued that if Darwin was right, we should be able to direct human evolution to "superior" levels (see Chapter 17, Social Change).

Out of this line of thinking grew the eugenics movement, stimulating efforts to develop techniques of genetic engineering involving the control of breeding within and between the "races." Not stopping there, many believed in the goal of race improvement through "selective breeding," with an implication that the "weak" should be left to die, or at least should not

be allowed to reproduce. These ideas affected immigration policies in the first part of the century and were key to the Nazi movement in Germany (see Broad and Wade, 1982).

To a large extent, it was the racism inherent in the eugenics movement that drew the attention of social scientists who had been studying "nurture"—or environmental—influences on human behaviour. The work of scholars like Ruth Benedict, Franz Boas, Margaret Mead, Ivan Pavlov, and John Watson suggested that it was unlikely that humans have genetic predispositions strong enough to fully determine their complex behaviour patterns, especially throughout their lives (see, for example, Mead, 1928). Instead, they argued that cultures can produce patterns of human behaviour that cannot be reduced to our genetic makeup (e.g., Benedict, 1934). This was especially evident in the wide range of cultural variation that early anthropologists found, as well as in the successes in human conditioning that early social scientists demonstrated.

The debate sparked by these two contrary positions—the **nature versus nurture** debate—was a lively one that can still be found in some form today. But, the fact that

Socialization begins at birth and continues throughout life.

humans are affected by experiences during their lifetime is no longer in dispute, and extreme pronouncements that poverty and crime are genetically based have long been discredited. As we now see, the key is to understand the changing nature of environmental influences and how these might interact with genetically based factors (Lerner, 2002). Still, questions remain concerning key issues such as: how much free will humans are capable of exercising; how much people—especially children—can resist attempts to influence them; and how much any one social institution can deliberately shape behaviours if there are many contradictory influences at work in people's lives. Thus, as we see, there are important questions to be answered regarding: (a) how much control parents can exercise over their children's development, (b) what schools can do to fully educate all of their students, and (c) the degree of self-direction we can expect of people growing up in societies with societal influences pulling them in different and contradictory directions. The study of socialization helps us to answer these types of questions.

Defining Socialization

There are several possible definitions of socialization. Most generally, **socialization** refers to the processes by which someone is taught to live among the other humans. These socialization processes are intended to ensure both the physical survival of individual members and the survival of the group or culture. This means that when someone is socialized, he or she has the motivation, skills, and knowledge necessary to live with others in group relationships. When any of these three factors (prosocial motivations, social skills, and cultural knowledge) is missing or deficient, a person can experience difficulties in getting along with others.

In order for cultures to perpetuate themselves, members need to be encouraged in some way to conform to their rules and values. As far as we know, this goes for all cultures and subcultures, including those found in extreme situations like prisons. When socialization processes are most effective, the enticements for conformity involve the *learning* of skills, roles, norms, and so forth. Sometimes, however, enticements for conformity involve *pressuring* people to obey in a variety of ways, from simple looks of disapproval by strangers to charging people with criminal offences.

In addition, some social scientists use socialization to refer to how people are *conditioned* so that inborn temperaments, potentials, and capacities are moulded to produce the desired traits that complement a given group or culture. This view of socialization takes a more complex form when people are viewed as having a number of preset stages through which they pass during their life course. In this more complex view, socialization contexts and processes differ at each stage of the life course, and the final outcome of socialization for a particular person is dependent on how well socialization contexts match the characteristics of that person "unfolding" at each stage. Some view these stages as largely cultural in origin, while others view them as "constitutional" in nature—part of an **epigenetic** makeup of the individual, in which the person is likened to a flower, with genetically preset stages of growth, the outcome of which depends on how well, or poorly, the environment nurtures it during each stage.

We see below how the various perspectives on socialization utilize one or more of these underlying assumptions.

Issues in the Study of Socialization

Implicit in the above discussion of socialization are several issues that represent disagreements about how to analyze specific circumstances. For example, one issue involves the extent to which in specific contexts, socialization is inherently benign or coercive, and for whom. This is an issue that often separates functionalists, who tend toward the "benign" approach, and conflict theorists, who often argue that socialization is "coercive." Do some, or even all, socialization processes help people "find themselves," or do they "force-fit" people, and make people only think they have been fulfilled? From a conflict perspective, much socialization simply involves getting people to want to do what they otherwise must do, without using excessive force. If this is true, and functionalists are mistakenly assuming that socialization is benign, then functionalists may simply be contributing to the

oppression of human beings by studying how to perfect coercive socialization processes. Such questions loom large today in attempts to understand what is happening in the various contexts in which young people now spend much of their time, especially high schools. Many people thrive in these environments, yet others react in a variety of negative ways, from social withdrawal to rampages of violence. Are those who do not thrive somehow personally deviant, or is the school to blame? Or both? In this case, we run the risk of "blaming the victim" if we focus only on individuals' reactions, because the deviant behaviour may simply be a result of socialization into a culture or subculture that we do not understand. Certainly, adults run the risk of doing this when dealing with those young people who have formed their own subcultures with different sets of rules. Deviance and rules are discussed in the next chapter.

A second issue concerns the extent to which people can resist attempts to socialize them. Regardless of whether the socialization attempts are benign or coercive, there are disagreements regarding how much free will people are capable of exercising in their dealings with the social structures that lie behind socialization efforts. This issue is more broadly known as the *structure–agency* debate.

On the one hand, the social structures responsible for socialization can be quite imperceptible, and even though no physical coercion is used in enforcing these structures, a high degree of conformity can result (e.g., conventions of personal appearance). Is our widespread conformity in dress simply a matter of people not having the willpower to resist social pressures? Or, is it a matter of people being unable to create their own truly unique behaviour patterns? Such questions have a relatively long history in sociology, and are related to an *oversocialized conception of humanity* held by previous generations of sociologists (Wrong, 1961), where people were viewed as not having the agency to resist, or deviate from, social pressures.

On the other hand, if people are capable of deciding things, even partly, on their own by exercising a free will, where does this agency come from? Is this an inherent mental capacity; is it something that we learn; or is it a combination of both? Is it a trait that varies among people, so that some people have more of it than others and are therefore more able to resist social pressures? Is it something that we use only when the opportunity arises? Or, is it exercised only when we are faced with a lack of guidance and structure from our culture, as under conditions of anomie in modern urban societies (see Chapter 17, Social Change)? The most recent thinking on this matter uses concepts such as "self-socialization" (Heinz, 2002), "intentional self-development" (Brandtstädter and Lerner, 1999), and "self-efficacy" (Bandura, 1989) to account for how people in complex societies can manage their life courses in spite of multiple, contradictory, and incomplete influences.

These questions have a long philosophical history, so we cannot hope to answer them in this chapter. But raising them helps us to better understand the tasks faced by those who attempt to grasp the nature of socialization and to apply socialization theory to real-life events. You may find yourself thinking of one or more of these questions as you read this chapter, as for example when it considers the effects of television and mass culture (see the box "Structure and Agency" on page 82).

Both genetic and environmental factors affect human personality and behaviour.

[Research Focus]

The Effects of Early Environmental Deprivation

Obviously, it is not possible to conduct experiments to deprive young children of human contact, but instances have occasionally been reported of child abandonment and serious neglect. In one case, a girl spent six years living in a dark room separated from the rest of her family (Davis, 1947). When discovered, she could only croak and in many ways behaved like a frightened animal. But with professional care, she quickly took on human characteristics and within a year, she could speak, write, and add. By the age of 8, she had caught up with her peers. More recently, a number of children who had been raised in poorly run Romanian orphanages in the 1980s were adopted by Canadian families as part of a humanitarian effort. Most of these children had been deprived of close bonds with caregivers in their first months and years of life. Follow-up studies found that those who had been adopted before six months of age suffered no lasting negative effects,

while those who were adopted later than six months of age showed lasting physiological impairment in their ability to handle stress (Chisholm, 1998).

While there are no well-documented cases of feral children—children raised by animals—a 9-year-old girl was found after having spent most of her waking hours in a chicken coop (*London Free Press*, 1 July 1980). She acted like a chicken; she could not talk, took small, quick steps, and flapped her arms like they were wings. She received professional help, but showed no real progress.

According the Bettelheim (1967), most reports of feral children are likely of autistic children who have been abandoned by their parents because they do not react to socialization processes like other children. Autism is not well understood, but the manifestations of this condition do give us some idea of what humans would be like without the capacity for, or receptivity to, socialization influences.

Given that human infants are so vulnerable and take such a long time to develop self-sufficiency, do you think it is plausible that infants could survive with only the help of animals?

[Research Focus]

Values As a Product of Experience

A large-scale ongoing longitudinal study of the life goals of hundreds of thousands of first-year college and university students in the United States (Astin et al., 1994) shows how populations can change their primary goals in life over rather short periods of time. Researchers found that while in the mid-1960s, only about 45 percent of college students rated "being very well off financially" as a very important objective, by the mid-1980s this figure reached about 75 percent. In contrast, in the mid-1960s "developing a meaningful philosophy of life" was endorsed by over 80 percent of incoming students. By the mid-1980s, however, this dropped to just over 30 percent. In other words, profit-seeking goals and meaning-seeking goals have traded

places among those undertaking a higher-education trajectory to adulthood. You can monitor the annual releases from this study by visiting the website of the Higher Education Research Institute at UCLA: http://www.gseis.ucla.edu/heri/news_freshman.html.

This dramatic cohort shift in values cannot be explained in terms of a changing genetic makeup over such a short period of time (nature). Instead, it appears that certain socialization influences (nurture) have changed, so that more university-attending people believe it more rewarding to be materialistic than philosophical or spiritual. This would suggest an examination of the socialization contexts to which these students were exposed before attending university.

After reading ahead in this chapter, come back to this example and determine which socialization perspective best explains these changes.

Perspectives on Socialization

The concept of socialization is fundamental to the social sciences, especially sociology and cultural anthropology. As we shall see, sociologists are interested in the content of what people learn, the contexts in which this learning takes place, and how the contents and contexts of socialization change over the life course (Hewitt, 1994: 3). In contrast, anthropologists study how these learning processes differ among cultures while still producing well-functioning humans. In this section, we briefly review how human socialization is viewed within both of these disciplines.

Sociological perspectives

Within sociology, we can find four distinct conceptions of socialization corresponding to the four classical theoretical perspectives: functionalism, conflict approaches, feminist approaches, and symbolic interactionism.

Functionalism

As mentioned above, functionalists tend to view socialization as a necessary and benign process inherent in all groups and societies. From this perspective, socialization performs several vital *functions* that maintain the structure of groups and societies, particularly from one generation to the next. Three major purposes to these processes are identified.

First, socialization plays a major role in the formation of the individual personality, while moulding people's attitudes and behaviours to conform to group values and needs. As a result, within groups people develop similar sets of outlooks and habits that make it easier for them to interact with each other. Second, socialization represents a set of processes and contexts responsible for cultural transmission. For example, within a particular group or culture, a common language is transmitted to all new members. Without socializing group members to speak a common language and to internalize a common set of symbols, cultures would be unable to support the cooperative activities necessary for an effective division of labour. Consequently, it would be difficult for members to share customs and traditions, or to agree upon a set of norms or laws. And, third, socialization performs the function of social integration. With their common personality characteristics and common language, people come to share common conceptions of their place in the world, as well as their places in their own cultures. These similarities help people to identify with one another, and to recognize their similar interests.

Of course, these functions of socialization are not necessarily perfectly or uniformly fulfilled among all members of a group. Within a culture, each person has a slightly different socialization history, even within the same family. Moreover, in the contemporary world, people from a variety of cultural backgrounds mix with one another, making socialization processes highly complex and often incomplete. For example, if you have travelled to a different culture, you might have encountered problems as simple as knowing how to eat a meal "properly" or how to express thanks for acts of kindness without offending someone.

Conflict approaches

Conflict theorists do not disagree with functionalists regarding the basic nature of socialization processes, but they tend to disagree about how benign some of these processes are, how neutral their outcomes can be, and even how necessary some socialization is. Instead, conflict theorists focus on the concept of **social reproduction**—namely, the ways in which societies reproduce themselves in terms of privilege and status. Conflict theorists argue that people do indeed learn about appropriate attitudes and behaviours, but these attitudes and behaviours vary by social class, gender, and race/ethnicity, so people within each of these social categories tend to learn things that perpetuate those categories. Thus,

The process by which language development occurs is central to socialization.

people with less privilege and status (e.g., the working class) tend to be taught to accept their position and not question who benefits from their uncritical acceptance of the class structure.

This reproduction can be compounded when the categories overlap—for example, when working-class males and females reproduce the socioeconomic outcomes of their parents, which are equal in terms of class, but not gender. Moreover, this uncritical acceptance of the class structure can come with a great price for the individuals concerned, as when schools treat those from less privileged backgrounds in an unsympathetic manner. Research has shown that public schools tend to be structured for students from middle-class backgrounds who have different language conventions than working-class students, and they tend to be taught by those from middle-class backgrounds. Accordingly, working-class students may be subtly, or even harshly, "cooled out"— namely, made to believe that they do not possess the intelligence or abilities to succeed academically. As a result, they may stop trying and eventually occupy social-class destinations similar to, or lower than, their parents'. In contrast, middle-class students are more likely to be "warmed up"—encouraged to excel. If so, they are likely to think more highly of themselves (and therefore have higher self-esteem), to try harder, and therefore to stand a better chance of occupying social-class destinations equal to or greater than that of their parents.

Feminist approaches

Feminist sociologists have many of the same concerns as conflict theorists with respect to the nature and outcome of socialization processes. They are particularly concerned with gender socialization, as specific sets of "processes through which individuals learn to become feminine and masculine according to expectations current in their society. In particular, individuals develop gender identity and learn to express gender norms. Especially important is the internalization of norms specifying gender inequality and gendered division of labour" (Mackie, 1991: 75). Most researchers believe that adolescence is a time of particular vulnerability to gender socialization processes, with femininity and masculinity being an intensified target, especially in peer groups— groups that share a common status or experience (Côté and Allahar, 2006; see also Chapter 7, Gender Relations).

Given these concerns, feminist sociologists (and also conflict theorists) are interested in first recognizing social inequalities and then modifying socialization processes to help address those inequalities (see the box "Youth, Social Control, and the Mass Media: A Conflict View").

[Social Trends]

Youth, Social Control, and the Mass Media: A Conflict View

Young people are enthusiastic consumers of the mass media, and over the years such enthusiasm has often been cause for concern. Today, for example, magazines directed at young women—"teenzines"—often send the message to girls that they should intensify their feminine characteristics with cosmetics and fashionable clothing. On the one hand, one could argue that these magazines are simply meeting a market need, insofar as young women want these things. Another, more critical perspective, however, is that such magazines are specifically engineered to create a consciousness among young women that only then becomes defined as a need.

An analysis of the content of the various mass media aimed at adolescents showed that all such media outlets share this vested interest. Some do so as agents for other economic interests (e.g., television programs, teenzines, and fashion magazines). Others, however, do it directly for themselves (e.g., the music industry, with television channels devoted entirely to this task). At the heart of much of this activity is the attempt to sell young people some element of an identity they have been taught to crave. With this accomplished, identities are sold back to them as products whose purpose is to provide a means of demonstrating their "individuality," however illusive or fleeting.

(continued)

As a result of decades of influence (and practice), the "leisure industries" that sell music, fashion, and cosmetics now have a largely uncritical army of consumers awaiting the next fads, which often seem more and more outlandish. In spite of their seemingly anti-establishment guise, these activities are tolerated by larger economic interests because the army of willing consumers is the same group that serves as a massive reserve of cheap labour, willing to work under poor conditions, for little pay and few benefits. In addition, distracting young people with these trivial identity-pursuits constitutes a form of social control because it helps prevent them from actively protesting their own disenfranchisement, lack of adult privileges, and the loss of a meaningful identity, denied them through a series of laws, customs, and institutional practices.

Instead of attempting to condition young people to spend money they do not have, the various media might have focused on helping them to develop their intellects and their sense of social responsibility.

Source: Adapted from James Côté and Anton Allahar, 1994. *Generation on Hold: Coming of Age in the Late Twentieth Century.* Toronto: Stoddart.

How do you feel about these influences? Many people believe that they are immune but see it in others. Is it really possible for anyone to entirely escape the effects of something that is so pervasive in their lives?

Symbolic interactionism

This approach to socialization takes the position that *interactions* among individuals are mediated by *symbols*, in the form of language and gestures, that form and shape the self—hence the term *symbolic interactionism*. Symbolic interactionists argue that individuals constantly monitor themselves and others in attempts to give meaning to events. In doing so, they observe the actions and reactions of other people toward them, and they then incorporate these responses into their self-structures. (For example, if individuals perceive that other people regard them as aggressive or smart or good-looking, they may come to define themselves as such.) They then take the meanings

about themselves and others they acquired from previous interactions and use them to give their current conduct meaning. In other words, for symbolic interactionists, people are meaning-seeking and self-referential, and through these activities they both create societies and socialize each other (Hewitt, 1994).

As mentioned in the introductory chapter, this theory has been a popular perspective in sociology for some time. Its basic ideas were developed by several philosophers and social scientists during the early years of the twentieth century, especially by Cooley (1902), who introduced the notion of the **looking-glass self** (the idea that personality is shaped as individuals see themselves mirrored in the reactions of others), Thomas (1923), who is noted for the idea of the *definition of the situation* (if a situation is defined as real, it is real in its consequences), and George Herbert Mead (1934), who developed a theory of how the self forms. G. H. Mead has been particularly influential, and is often considered synonymous with symbolic interactionism, so we will focus on his work.

At the centre of G. H. Mead's theory is the concept of **role-taking**. He asserted that effective communication between individuals requires that one "take the role of the other." He believed that people try to put themselves in others' shoes, imagining their thoughts and perceptions. As a result, humans are able to see themselves as others see them. Role-taking is possible because of the human ability to interact symbolically; the ability to take the role of the other is key to the development of the self.

G. H. Mead contended that the development of the self takes place in two stages. When children acquire a sufficient vocabulary to begin naming people and

Cooley argued that we come to see ourselves as others see us, much like the view in a mirror.

objects they observe, they begin to play-act roles. In this *play stage*, they pretend to be a mother, father, firefighter, or teacher. For the first time, they practise taking the roles of others whom they have observed, and are in a position to reflect upon themselves behaving in a variety of roles. For the first time, children can think of themselves as *objects* with specific qualities and capacities—they can now imagine how other people view them. Playing at roles in this way provides exercises in "being another to one's self" (G. H. Mead, 1934: 151). Thus, the basis of behaviour moves from mere imitation to more reflective self-direction.

In the *game stage*, children develop more unified conceptions of themselves as they learn to simultaneously take the role of multiple others. For example, in a game of baseball, a child might alternate roles between batter and pitcher, but also learns to appreciate the importance of all of the other players on the field. As this is experienced, the children imagine how those in the other roles think about their actions. As this is practised, the children learn to imagine themselves in terms of other children's perspectives toward them. By appreciating the interrelations of a set of roles rather than one isolated role, children develop a generalized conception of what is expected of them and how others will react to them. Thus, through informal and formal play, children learn how to conceive of a **generalized other** rather than simply of single, specific others. Eventually, children's perceptions of generalized others represent their ideas of what is expected in terms of social norms, and they provide a unified basis for self-reference. Hence, the self develops more fully and is capable of self-reference in terms of multiple viewpoints.

G. H. Mead also thought it useful to think of two complementary processes associated with the functioning self: the I and the me. The **I** represents the impulsive side of the self, which is spontaneous and creative. In contrast, the **me** is the more deliberate, reflective side of the self; it takes time to evaluate how others might react to the actions of the I. For example, the I might want to make a joke during a lively conversation, but the me might inhibit it by reflecting on how the joke might be received by others, mulling over whether the audience might think it off-colour or politically incorrect.

Finally, in addition to the generalized other, G. H. Mead also believed that people are influenced by **significant others**, persons who are well known to the person and whose attitudes and opinions affect their life. Significant others include family members and friends as

well as persons of high prestige, like teachers and celebrities. People are motivated to impress these others in certain ways, and engage in a number of techniques to manage how others perceive them. These techniques of *impression management* have been intensively studied by later symbolic interactionists like Goffman (1959).

Cultural anthropology

Cultural anthropologists help us better understand the relationships among socialization practices, cultural patterns, and personality characteristics. Their influence was greatest during the first half of the twentieth century, when anthropologists travelled to far-flung places on the globe, reporting on the tremendous variations in cultural arrangements. Common to all of these distant cultures are rites and rituals that provide concrete structure for the life course, while at the same time ensuring the continuity of the culture through the shaping of specific behaviours and personality characteristics compatible with the needs of the culture. Anthropologists found that the more individuals are integrated into a culture, both behaviourally and emotionally, the greater the chance of a culture perpetuating itself. In addition, cultures adopt childrearing practices that are consistent with their own institutional and behavioural patterns, but these childrearing practices can be very different from those found in other cultures. They can range from coddling children to being very harsh to them. It should be evident that cultural anthropologists share many assumptions with functionalists. In fact, as we saw in Chapter 3, Culture, a number of the early functionalists like Malinowski were anthropologists.

Because they sought out cultures that differ from Western ones, cultural anthropologists enjoyed a special place in the public's imagination. Through their efforts, Westerners have developed less ethnocentric and less racist attitudes and learned to accept the legitimacy of other cultural arrangements. Such tolerance, referred to as *cultural relativity*, involves "an awareness that different cultures have different ways of meeting life's demands. Different cultures have various guidelines regarding important decisions such as choosing a marriage partner, raising children, taking care of the infirm elderly, and so forth" (Brislin, 1993: 33). While this perspective involves a suspension of disparaging judgments, thereby opening one's mind and expanding one's awareness, it does have its limitations. It is difficult not to pass judgment on certain cultural practices, as in the obvious case of Nazi Germany, nor is it appropriate to suspend judgment when one sees obvious injustices (e.g., "bride burning," lynching, and the sexual exploitation of children). However, by appreciating that there is no one right way to socialize people, Westerners have come to appreciate how they can learn from other cultures in this regard.

Benedict (1938) did just this in a landmark essay on adolescence. She argued that most pre-industrial societies provide for a continuous passage from childhood to adulthood. By doing so, cultural continuity was safeguarded, and individual members of the society did not experience serious personal difficulties in making transitions through these social statuses. Western societies, however, are age-graded, largely segregating children, adolescents, and adults from each other. In pre-industrial societies it is thus easier for younger members to learn over a period of time the skills necessary for adult functioning, and experience the realities of life, like sex, work, and death. This occurs during the mid- to late-teens in most of these societies (Schlegel and Barry, 1991) so that by the time they reach their late teens or early twenties, most young people are prepared to assume mature roles and responsibilities.

Western societies have introduced three sets of discontinuities into the socialization process, according to Benedict. First, Western children are socialized into non-responsible roles, even though adulthood ostensibly requires a self-regulated responsibility. Second, children are socialized to be submissive, despite the expectation for adults to be dominant. And, third, children are shielded from sexuality (she first wrote about this in 1938), while Western adulthood requires a complex awareness of sexuality. Benedict's question was just when, where, and how are people to learn these three essential aspects of adulthood? Benedict did not believe Western societies have good mechanisms for transmitting these things, and leave adolescents largely on their own to learn them. Consequently, Western adolescence can be a difficult period of adjustment.

Margaret Mead, Benedict's colleague, took up this issue in a series of studies in the South Pacific. She was specifically interested in the belief that adolescence is inevitably a time of "storm and stress." As noted above, this idea was popular at the time among those who supported nature arguments about human behaviour.

Based on the work of Hall (1904), many people believed that adolescence was a period in which everyone inevitably went through a period of development that essentially reproduced human evolutionary history, in this case the long period in human history of "barbarism," preceding the "civilization" of the adult stage. Given the absoluteness of this claim (i.e., that everyone in every culture experiences adolescence as stressful), if one culture could be found where this was not the case (the *negative instance* method), then a cornerstone of the nature side of the nature–nurture debate would be upset.

Mead tackled this issue of the universality of adolescent storm and stress on the remote islands of Samoa. She reported her findings in a book that has been the best-selling book in the history of anthropology, *Coming of Age in Samoa* (1928). In it Mead compared three groups of females: those who had not yet experienced puberty, those who were experiencing it, and those who were past it. She reported that the experience of puberty made no significant differences in the character of these females. Mead attributed the lack of adolescent storm and stress in Samoa to its consistent and continuous socialization practices. In contrast, she argued, the difficulties affecting the adolescent of 1920s America were caused by conflicting standards of conduct and morality, and "the belief that every individual should make his or her own choices, coupled with a feeling that choice is an important matter." In contrast, she asserted that in 1920s Samoa (1928: 273):

> The gap between parents and children is narrow and painless, showing few of the unfortunate aspects usually present in a period of transition . . . essentially the children are still growing up in a homogeneous community with a uniform set of ideals and aspirations.

This evidence of cultural differences in the prevalence of adolescent difficulties led Mead to conclude that difficulties passing through adolescence cannot be considered a biological inevitability.

In spite of the fact that Mead's chief conclusion about the source of adolescent turmoil has been confirmed by subsequent research (Condon, 1987; Côté, 1992), the legacy of Hall's work lives on in the public mind—and in the mass media—to the extent that people still hold stereotypes about adolescent turmoil and "raging hormones."

Socialization Contexts and Agents

Now that we have examined the underlying assumptions regarding the nature of socialization, and the perspectives that various social scientists have taken toward it, we can move to a consideration of the question of how socialization takes place. Simply put, socialization takes place within a variety of social contexts, and within each context there are various socialization agents teaching and correcting others as to the "correct" way to act. We examine five contexts below, but do not focus on agents of socialization per se, such as teachers and parents. This is in part because agents are embedded in the contexts and in part because we are all socialization agents. That is, each of us participates in socialization processes in one way or another through our very participation in groups. In groups, we express our approval and disapproval, which shapes the subsequent conduct and thought of others, as symbolic interactionists argue. Thus, we are all informal socialization agents, and as such are also agents of social control in the sense that we enforce certain norms, beliefs, or practices.

The term *socialization context* refers to social settings that affect socialization processes, thereby influencing the individuals involved. In this sense, there is a concern with stable patterns of social interaction in groups through which common symbols are transmitted. Socialization contexts vary according to the characteristics of groups (e.g., size and boundaries), as well as the characteristics of group members (e.g., age, gender, race, and class). When undertaking this sort of analysis, the focus is on how socialization contexts (settings) set the stage for socialization processes and how individuals are affected by these contexts.

Most socialization takes place in subtle ways, so people often do not recognize efforts to shape them. In modern, industrialized societies many contexts are explicitly mandated to *change* people in ways that they may or may not want to be changed. In these contexts, specific socialization agents act within **role systems**, interrelated sets of social positions in power hierarchies based on a division of labour in which people share expectations about desired outcomes.

Sometimes these efforts are successful, especially when people want to be changed, as when they volunteer for military service. However, socialization efforts can be less than successful when people resist in various ways. When the socialization mandate is only partly realized as in the case of resistance, unintended consequences can result that set up a series of events that create new contexts or distort the originally intended consequence. At the same time, some people are too motivated to change, or are too susceptible to certain influences, so that socialization occurs when it was not intended. This problem may arise with the mass media, where the intention is to entertain, but some people (even a very small percentage) take it as a learning experience or internalize role models (see the box "Learning How to Be Violent").

One way to understand how problems can arise in socialization contexts is in terms of differences in **socialization ratios**, namely, the number of *socializers* (agents) to *socializees* (those being socialized). The lower the ratio (fewer agents), the less likely is the context to affect those being socialized. For example, if a professor (the agent) has a class of 400 students, chances are diminished that the professor will have an emotional or intellectual impact on any of those students. In contrast, a professor or teaching assistant with a class (or tutorial) of twenty students stands a much better chance of having an impact, other things being equal. What may not be equal is how willing or motivated the socializees are to being affected by the teacher or the material in the course. Students who are keen on the subject matter can be highly affected, even in a class of 400, but those who are not keen may not be affected even in the smaller class (Côté and Levine, 1997).

The socialization ratio is also related to how much potential power those being socialized have in a given context. The lower the ratio, the more they can exercise power just by their sheer numbers, effecting a form of reciprocal socialization (e.g., using collective class reactions like frowning and groaning to intimidate teachers they do not like or to get course requirements reduced). This is especially relevant when factors of motivation are taken into account. If individuals are not motivated to change, less change will take place. In fact, it is common for "subcultures" (cliques and gangs) to emerge in these contexts, which in turn have their own socialization potential. In these cases, socialization agents may have to be authoritarian to maintain their control of the context and their power in the socialization hierarchy, but this recourse to coercion can simply feed the "subculture of resistance." The most obvious example of this socialization problem is in prisons where a few guards must keep large numbers of unwilling inmates under control. However, the problem can also be found in high

[Debate]

Learning How to Be Violent

One of the last things people want to hear is that excessive television viewing can be harmful. This is probably because we all do so much of it yet feel that we have not been adversely affected. However, extensive research confirms that some people can be adversely affected, particularly in picking up aggressive behaviour habits during childhood that last into adulthood. This is the case because young children are more likely to imitate what they see on TV and take television characters as role models. For example, note how many play construction projects have been encouraged by Bob the Builder. Those attracted to more aggressive characters, and who are rewarded for their aggressive antics, are more likely to adopt them as part of their behavioural repertoire.

Bushman and Anderson (2001) noted that the scientific literature is conclusive on this issue, yet people's attitudes have not been influenced as is the case with other documented risks like second-hand smoke causing lung cancer and condoms preventing HIV infection. They found that, although many other risks have weaker statistical links than media violence and aggression, the news outlets have been downplaying this risk, even reassuring the public that there is nothing to be concerned about.

Why would news reports not accurately depict the scientific evidence about the impact of media violence on children? Has the scientific community failed to get its message out? Is there defensiveness on the part of the media? If so, to what can this defensiveness be attributed? Teen violence has increased in most industrialized countries, especially since the 1980s (Hoffman and Summers, 2001). Might we be inadvertently teaching some young people how and why to be violent when we are simply trying to entertain them?

schools, where a few teachers are supposed to be teaching (stimulating cognitive development in) large numbers of students. To the extent that mass education at the secondary level is resisted by a segment of the student body, the task confronting teachers becomes more difficult and the need for authoritarian measures increases. This only feeds the growth of "peer subcultures" in the schools that express their resistance in various ways, toward both the teachers (and what they represent) and the other peer subcultures that emerge. As universities continue to expand, similar problems are being encountered between professors and students.

Related problems with social contexts seem to be particularly common in societies that have dismantled many of their social control mechanisms, or have had them disrupted or weakened, as in modern, industrialized societies. For example, **inadequate socialization** can occur when people are not exposed to all experiences necessary to function in certain roles, as when educational systems fail to provide sufficient job training. **Defective socialization** happens when unintended outcomes or consequences arise. Some video games—

the point-and-shoot variety—actually provide training for murdering people (some of these games are used in weapons training by the military). Training young people to be violent murderers is not the intention behind these games (making money is), but it seems to have happened far too often. A number of the mass murderers in the recent American high-school rampages experienced this form of "gun training."

Finally, **disjunctive socialization** occurs in the ways described by Benedict earlier in the chapter. In fact, a lack of continuity of experience in moving between institutional settings is now common in modern societies, so much so that it is accepted as normal and of not much concern. For example, large numbers of people are regularly released from mental hospitals and prisons, with little support or means for re-entry into the community. When back in the community, they may find themselves stigmatized and shunned, and therefore with no useful social roles to play. For many in this situation, life back in the hospital or prison may be preferable because at least they have a means of subsistence there, as well as a sense of place and identity.

A positive consequence and the context of an action are both significant determinants of behaviour.

Of course, formal socialization agents are not unaware of these problems, but modern societies have increasingly opted to leave the solutions up to the individuals affected, rather than providing collective solutions, like providing the means for effective *resocialization*, the replacing of old behaviours and attitudes with new ones. However, individuals are often at a loss concerning what to do to fill the gaps within and among social contexts, and are left on their own to make their way into the social and economic institutions that establish security and fulfillment (e.g., securing a long-term profession or career). One individual response is **anticipatory socialization**, whereby people project themselves into the future in the hope of acquiring the characteristics appropriate to the institutional destination they hope to reach. This is a type of **self-socialization** in which people "construct their own life course by attempting to come to terms with opportunities and constraints . . . [by selecting] pathways, act and appraise the conse-

quences of their actions . . . in reference to social contexts" (Heinz, 2002: 58).

One way to understand why we live in a society with such complex socialization contexts is with a model developed by Margaret Mead (1970) in her book *Culture and Commitment: A Study of the Generation Gap*. In it Mead postulated a theory of intergenerational relations that reflects three stages of cultural change and associated patterns of commitment between children and parents: "*postfigurative*, in which children learn primarily from their forebears; *cofigurative*, in which both children and adults learn from their peers; and the *prefigurative*, in which adults learn also from their children" (1970: 1).

Mead's theory of changing intergenerational relations is straightforward, yet profound, because it encapsulates what appears to have happened in most world cultures in recent history. Indeed, Mead was fascinated with how preliterate societies had been affected by contact with technological societies.

Social Change and Childrearing

Mead's theory of changing intergenerational relations sheds light on a number of issues. For example, with Mead's theory we can make better sense of the recent laws in Canada affecting the right of parents to discipline their children. In a recent case, a mother and father (first-generation immigrants to Canada) found their 15-year-old son was out of control—stealing from them, skipping school, staying out past curfew, and getting violent (Corbella, 2000). After being physically disciplined for kicking in a door, stealing more money, and swearing at his parents when confronted, the son lodged a complaint with police and the father was charged with assault. The court ordered the parents to pay support for their son, who was placed in a foster home. Thousands of dollars in legal fees later, the father expressed confusion over the Canadian legal system: "In my culture, children do not speak to their parents the way my son speaks to us. They have more respect. I am doing what I believe to be right, what is done in the country I come from but the government and the courts are saying I am [a] criminal, [that] I am [a] bad parent."

The right of a parent to physically discipline a child generally would not likely be questioned in a postfigurative society, where discipline can be severe. In fact, as the above story illustrates, even today in many cultures around the world, *not disciplining* a child in a physical manner is seen as poor parenting. Indeed, throughout much of the history of Western societies, "sparing the rod" was viewed as "spoiling

the child." In an increasingly prefigurative society such as Canada's, we are witnessing a reversal of this, in which the act of physical discipline is viewed as negatively as not disciplining was in the past. Now, parents do not have as much traditional authority and there is less faith that they possess the wisdom to raise their children properly.

In prefigurative societies, the well-being of the current and future generations of children has been largely divorced from past practices. Consequently, there is now great confusion about how to raise children effectively. And, there is even more bewilderment about what the future holds for generations brought up with very little discipline, physical or otherwise. Mead would not be surprised, therefore, to hear that today these issues are of increasing concern. As Underwood (1999) wrote, "[S]omewhere along the line, things got little off track . . . . [Parents] began to let their youngsters call the shots. Children today are not only seen and heard, they expect to be obeyed: their war cry, 'You're not the boss of me!' is ringing out across the continent." In response to this increasing tyranny of childhood, bewildered and frustrated parents are looking for help in dealing with children, who they feel are behaving like spoiled brats who cannot control their impulses, take responsibility for their actions, or empathize properly with others. Bookstores are stocking titles like *Who's in Charge?* and *I'll Be the Parent, You Be the Kid* that offer advice to beleaguered parents.

In the past, strict disciplining practices were believed to build character; now they are viewed as abusive. Are the current attitudes toward even minor physical discipline merely an example of "present-ism" where people blindly believe that current practices are better than past ones, or are we really progressing? How can we be sure either way?

She noted how deep these effects ran, down to the day-to-day relations between children and adults, as both attempted to make sense out of their changing worlds.

In **postfigurative cultures**, the relations between parents and their offspring are governed by traditional norms beyond questioning by either parent or child. Child-disciplining practices are long-established and not

open to discussion. The postfigurative culture is stabilized by the co-residence of three generations (including grandparents) and the assignment of most social roles. Consequently, change is slow and intergenerational continuity great, even revered. These cultures often engage in ancestor worship and instill a sense of responsibility for many generations to come. Postfigurative cultures bear clear similarities with pre-industrial societies.

In **cofigurative cultures**, the intergenerational link-age becomes tenuous because of social change brought on by technological advancement, economic transformation, immigration, war, and so forth. One (or more) of these forces affect the culture, giving children a different set of experiences than their parents had, if only for a brief time. Consequently, to some extent, offspring look to non-traditional sources for components of their sense of meaning and identity, particularly from among their contemporaries. Thus, there is a fundamental change in the relations between parents and children, whereby the authority of the parent can be questioned, and the child can actually give direction to the parent in certain instances. As a result, the eventual adult roles of offspring are no longer as taken for granted by either parent or child, and young people seek new ways to establish a sense of identity. However, the schism between parent and child is limited because offspring are obliged to observe and respect significant elements of the traditional culture they share with their parents.

Finally, **prefigurative cultures** are characterized by rapid and massive social change. Because of the extent of social change, parents have little conception of what the future holds, so their past life-experiences are of little use to their offspring with respect to their present sense of meaning, ongoing identity formation, and future adult roles. As a result, parental guidance is not as well regarded by children. Moreover, parental belief systems (and a "traditional" culture, if applicable) may be dismissed as invalid by offspring (this is a common source of conflict in Canada between immigrant parents who want to maintain the values of their culture of origin and their first-generation Canadian-born offspring who are immersed in secular Canadian culture; Helm and Warren, 1998). In fact, Mead argued that in prefigurative cultures the young can actually teach their parents about the ongoing social changes, or achieve a higher social status, to the point where their parents can become subservient to them in various ways. Hence, the gap between parents and offspring that opened in the cofigurative culture is widened in the prefigurative one (see the box "Social Change and Childrearing").

We can see how socialization becomes more problematic as societies pass through these three stages, and we can see how it becomes more *reciprocal*, with offspring socializing their parents to increasing degrees (reciprocal socialization happens in all societies, but is minimized in postfigurative ones). As the collective supports of traditional society diminish, people are left more to their own devices to plan their lives, choose the beliefs upon which to base an identity, and regulate their behaviour. The resulting process is referred to as **individualization** (Furlong and Cartmel, 1997), which places demands on people to be self-socializing (Heinz, 2002) in making choices concerning their future life courses. There can be tremendous benefits associated with the individualization process, but there can also be significant liabilities that stem from the fact that people are under great pressure as they undertake identity formation in a contextually fragmented society. Pressures can be placed on them that they may not be equipped to handle (cf. Baumeister and Muraven, 1996). These pressures include the need to be reflexive about their behaviour and place in society, to plan for an indefinite future, to have information upon which to make life-altering choices, and to take responsibility for personal failings and limitations, even when they involve social-structural obstacles related to social class, race, gender, and age (cf. Furlong and Cartmel, 1997). It must be stressed, however, that individualization involves *freedoms from* normative constraints, not *freedoms to* pursue activities independent of systemic barriers like social class disadvantage and racial discrimination. Further, the freedom to individualize has emerged because of *a lack of structure*, whereas persisting social stratification along class and race lines presents *too much unwanted structure* for those placed at a disadvantage because of those structures.

With the above complexities concerning socialization contexts in mind, we can now explore how the life course is now quite different than in the past, presenting complex challenges for people in contemporary societies.

Social context and the life course

To illustrate some of the above principles, we shall now examine the changes in the socialization contexts governing the transition to adulthood in Canada, contrasting the present with changes over the past two centuries. Five contexts will be examined, each of which provides some of the **normative structure** for the transition to adulthood (normative structures provide direction for people regarding what to do, when to do it, why, where, and with whom). The contexts governing the transition to adulthood since about 1800 include the family, religion, education, the peer group, and mass (or popular) culture. Each of these contexts is an important determinant of a person's identity formation, and thus the course that their life will take throughout adulthood. Identity formation refers to the process by which a person develops a place in society, traditionally defined in terms of an adult identity based on commitments to various productive roles contributing to social integration. We see below how the relative importance of each context has shifted dramatically, affecting both the pace of identity formation and the types of identity people now form.

To provide a reference point at the middle of this historical illustration, about 100 years ago at the beginning of the twentieth century, what it meant to be a teenager was quite different than it is now. For one thing, the word "teenager" did not come into usage until the late 1930s, just as the word "tween" came into usage only in the late 1990s (both terms were coined by marketers to help them define market segments to target). Moreover, around 1900, only a small number of teens attended secondary schools, almost half were involved in agricultural or household labour, and the rest were employed in the industrial labour force, often making a living wage or close to it. While many lived with their families, there was paid work available for them (without the age prejudices we now witness) and, for those who lived with their parents, considerable financial contributions were made to the family. For working-class parents, their most prosperous years were often when their children worked and lived with them (Allahar and Côté, 1998).

Now, in the early twenty-first century, in most Western nations, the vast majority of teens attend secondary schools (see Table 4.1) and about two-thirds of secondary-school graduates go directly to postsecondary institutions (Montgomery and Côté, 2003). Only a minority (less than one-third) of those in the 18 to 24 age group is engaged in employment that is sufficiently well paid to afford them independence from their parents. But, those who co-reside with their parents rarely contribute much financially, and usually make only minor contributions to household labour (although young females do more housework than young males), leaving them free to pursue various leisure activities (White, 1994). In addition, their parents often subsidize them with free or cheap room and board, or allowances, and their mothers often provide "domestic" services for them. Referring to present Canadian youth, Almey and Normand (2002: 81) reported that those "aged 15 to 19 devote less time than older adults to productive activities, including paid and unpaid work as well as educational activities, while they have more free time and spend more time sleeping."

Table 4.1	Percentage of Young Men and Women Attending School Full-Time in Canada, 1921–2001			
	15- to 19-year-olds		20- to 24-year-olds	
	Men	Women	Men	Women
1921	23	27	3	2
1931	32	35	4	2
1941	34	37	5	3
1951	41	40	7	3
1961	62	56	12	5
1971	74	56	12	5
1981	66	66	21	16
1991	73	74	32	33
2001	72	75	37	43

Sources: Estimates for 1921–1981 from Normand, 1995; Estimates for 15- to 19-year-olds for 1991 and 2001 from Almey and Normand, 2002 (the 2001 estimate is based on figures for 1998–99); estimates for 20- to 24-year-olds for 1991 and 2001 from Statistics Canada, 2001 Census, Analysis Series, *Education in Canada: Raising the Standard*, Catalogue No. 96F0030XIE2001012.

Moreover, there was a recent decline in productive activities and an increase in leisure activities, with 15- to 24-year-olds spending less time on educational activities and more on leisure activities in 1998 than they did in 1986 (Fast, Frederick, Zukewich, and Franke, 2001). More specifically, students in this age range were spending one hour *less* per day on educational activities than they did in the mid-1980s, replacing it with leisure activities. Similarly, Arnett (1996: 162) argued that "adolescents in many American households are treated not like equal adults but like indulged guests." What is more, if they have a decent job, and do not pay room and board, some young people can have more discretionary income than their parents (Mogelonsky, 1996).

What happened over the last two centuries to transform young people from productive citizens on the cusp of adulthood to dependents on their families and educational systems, locked into a prolonged period of youth? And what justifications were used to exclude them from participating in their society and economy to their full productive capacities, blocking their entry into adulthood? Answers to these questions can be found in the shifting importance of institutional contexts in which socialization takes place.

Some 200 years ago, the family and religion were the contexts providing most of the normative structure in the transition to adulthood for the vast majority of the population. The family likely exerted the greatest influence for most people at the time, especially in frontier communities. Since then, however, the family has been in steady decline as a direct overriding influence (see Chapter 10, Families). Two centuries later, the family provides more of a "safety net" during the transition to adulthood, protecting the young from what can be an unwelcoming economy. At the same time, peer groups became more influential with the segregation of young people in schools. With the decline in traditional normative influences, young people have increasingly turned to—and been enticed by—popular culture activities to add purpose and structure to their lives. We will examine each of these changing influences in turn.

The changing role of the family

For many people, the family is no longer the dominant influence determining major life choices relevant to identity formation, future adulthood, or what to do along the way (e.g., what to do for a living, whom to marry, and how to find a secure place in society). Teens on average spend five minutes a day alone with their fathers and twenty minutes with their mothers (Bennett, 1994). Moreover, when they interact with their parents, they are not necessarily spending "quality time," because they usually meet in front of the television. This is hardly an ideal situation for adults of one generation to guide and relate to the next generation, especially in terms of communicating common cultural symbols. Television enters the picture even more, as we see below.

Despite the declining normative influence of the family in Canada and other developed countries, it is not true that young people and their parents experience an emotional distance, but, instead, that parents are not as directive as in the recent past. In fact, research evidence is accumulating that most parents do not attempt to exercise the types of guidance that were once considered the hallmark of adulthood and parenthood. Parental influence has been researched in terms of parenting styles, defined in terms of how much parents demand maturity and how responsive they are to their children's needs (Steinberg, 2001). Parents who are both demanding and responsive are referred to as "authoritative" and research shows that their children tend to

have good educational and behavioural outcomes. In contrast, adolescents with parents who are neither demanding nor responsive ("indifferent" parents) have poor educational and behavioural patterns, including greater tendencies toward delinquency, early sex, and drugs. Between these two extremes are "indulgent" parents, who demand little maturity of their children but are highly responsive to their needs, and "authoritarian" parents who demand high levels of maturity but are not very responsive. Adolescents with indulgent parents are more likely to be immature and irresponsible, while those with authoritarian ones are more likely to be conforming and passive (Steinberg, 2001). The accumulated findings of research on parenting styles suggest that more than half of contemporary parents are either indifferent or indulgent (together, referred to as permissive, preferring more of "friendship" relationship with their children), while only about one-third are authoritative in their relationships with their adolescent offspring.

This low level of what appears to be optimal parenting (authoritativeness) is likely unfortunate for contemporary young people who must make their way into a fragmented, confusing, and sometimes manipulative world. Moreover, the benefits of authoritativeness also seem to expand beyond the family— adolescents also benefit from having authoritative, versus authoritarian teachers, school principals, coaches, and bosses (Steinberg, 2001). On the other hand, it may be expecting too much of contemporary parents to function optimally in that same world, which also pulls them in many different directions (see the box "Authoritative Parenting: A Policy Panacea or Wishful Thinking?").

Declining religious observance

By the mid-1900s, religion had begun a sharp decline in influence as well (see Chapter 11, Religion). In Canada, only 12 percent of young people attended services regularly in the 1990s (Clark, 1998; cf. Bibby, 1993; Bibby and Posterski, 1992), down precipitously from mid-century. People are now more likely to "pick and choose" their religious beliefs independent of organized religions. This phenomenon is part of the individualization of the life course, identified above, where traditional collective socialization contexts are replaced by contexts in which self-socialization becomes important (Heinz, 2002). Its effect can be to create a "cafeteria-style" religiosity,

Authoritative Parenting: A Policy Panacea or Wishful Thinking?

Steinberg (2001) argued that authoritative parenting has benefits that cross the boundaries of ethnicity, socioeconomic status, and household composition and he called for policy-makers to undertake programs to improve how children and adolescents are raised. Although most of the research has been carried out on American samples, Steinberg concluded that regardless of racial or social background, or family composition, young people have more positive outcomes when exposed to authoritative parenting. Indeed, research carried out in other countries with a range of value systems (Canada, China, Pakistan, Hong Kong, Scotland, Australia, and Argentina), supports the cross-cultural validity of the beneficial impact of authoritative parenting, although it may take different forms in non-Western cultures (Arnett, 2000).

Mead's theory of culture and commitment helps us understand parenting styles in a cultural context. While we can likely find instances of each parenting style in Mead's three societies, each society would be more likely to give rise to one particular parenting style (making that style dominant in the culture). Accordingly, postfigurative societies should be more likely to require an authoritarian parenting style; cofigurative societies should facilitate the use of authoritative styles; prefigurative societies would be more likely to give rise to permissive styles. If the research on parenting styles is correct, from a health policy point of view, Canadian parents need to resist the deleterious aspects of prefigurative culture and teach their adolescent children how to do so as well.

It needs to be stressed, however, that like all theoretical models, the real-life situations parents face may be quite different from and more complex than what the parenting-styles model suggests. Day-to-day life involves give-and-take, especially in prefigurative societies, where there is more of a reciprocal relationship between the parent and the adolescent (Arnett, 2000). In contrast to young children, adolescents are more agentic in shaping the relationship with their parents, and more capable of intentional self-development (see Brandtstädter and Lerner, 1999). Taken together, the dispositions and capacities that adolescents bring into interactions with their parents can make authoritative parenting quite difficult. To cite an extreme example, trying to authoritatively reason with an adolescent who (temporarily or persistently) is stubborn, aggressive, or withdrawn may be fruitless simply because that adolescent may not be open to reasoning and discussion.

Accordingly, while it is tempting to use the parenting-style model as a basis for policy-making, in practice any policies would be difficult to implement. In addition to the problem of resistant adolescents, not all parents would be capable of adopting an authoritative style because of their own temperament (e.g., they may have authoritarian or permissive dispositions), because they cannot function at the relatively high level needed to act authoritatively, or they may simply be too busy trying to make a living. Some have suggested parenting courses, and even parenting licences, but such measures would be resisted by many parents and would be difficult to police.

Source: Adapted from *Parent–Adolescent Relationships and Identity Development: A Literature Review and Policy Statement*, by G. Adams, J. Côté, and S. Marshall. Report to Division of Childhood and Adolescence, Health Canada, Ottawa, Canada, September 16, 2001.

We require licences for driving cars and boats. Given the importance of effective parenting, does it make sense to have parents educated about childrearing practices and licensed before they can raise children, or is this too much of an infringement on personal rights?

where beliefs are based on what feels good at the moment and chosen from available options (Côté, 2000).

According to Statistics Canada, the percentage of Canadians reporting "no religion" on their census forms increased from less than 1 percent prior to 1971 to 16 percent in 2001. Almost 40 percent of those reporting no religion were 24 or younger, yet this age group represented only 33 percent of the total population (Statistics Canada, 2001 Census, Analysis Series, *Religion in Canada*, Catalogue No. 96F0030XIE2001015). We can expect this increase to continue as about one-quarter of children 14 and younger were listed on the 2001 Census forms (by their parents) as having no affiliation to an organized religion. With fewer and fewer children in each successive cohort being brought up in an organized religion, we can expect denominational religion to continue to decline as a normative influence in the transition to adulthood and therefore as a less important source of identity. At the same time, individualized religious and spiritual beliefs will likely become more common, as discussed in Chapter 11, Religion.

Educational influence: It expands and expands and expands and . . .

Educational systems are now pervasive socialization contexts influencing the first few decades of the life course for most people. Around 1850, private education began to emerge as an influence only for the children of affluent parents. Beginning in the early 1900s, its influence spread to the other segments of society, so that now it is one of the most important institutions providing structure to the transition to adulthood, as well as in childhood and adolescence. Currently, in most Western countries, the majority of teens are in school, and in some countries one-third of those in their early twenties are still in school (see Table 4.1). The role of student is now an important source of identity during the formative years of the transition to adulthood, while at the same time significantly delaying to adoption of adult roles. By the end of the twentieth century, public and private educational systems had become enterprises in their own right, occupying up to one-third of the population as teachers, administrators, or students, and holding a monopoly in the training of workers (Côté and Allahar, 1994).

As a result of this continual expansion, Canada now has one of the highest education participation rates in the world. As of 2000, 41 percent of Canadians between 25 and 64 had either a college diploma or a university degree, followed by the U.S. with 37 percent (Statistics Canada, 2001 Census, Analysis Series, *Education in Canada: Raising the Standard*, Catalogue No. 96F0030XIE2001012). However, in spite of Canada's successes in mass education, critics say that the current system of mass education at the primary and secondary levels too closely resembles the system developed to maximize industrial production. Critics also point to a "hidden curriculum" (Holt, 1964) of pedagogical practices and material that implicitly teaches certain beliefs and attitudes, such as a blind acceptance of the prevailing economic system or an obedience to authority (Bowles and Gintis, 1976). That curriculum can also communicate tacit expectations about social class origin, gender, and ethnicity that reduce the self-esteem and eventual educational attainment of working-class youth, young women, and youth from ethnic minorities (see Chapter 6, Social Inequality; Chapter 7, Gender Relations; and Chapter 8, Race and Ethnic Relations).

If schools were structured differently, and more relevant to the world young people are attempting to understand, we might not have a persistent dropout problem, and Canadian students would perform better in terms of international educational standards. Critics point out that people are not commodities that can be manufactured on assembly lines, but rather need individual care and attention. The large, factory-like schools that most young people attend can breed feelings of boredom, alienation, and resentment creating the conditions for clique formation and problems in identity formation that divert the person from more direct entry into the adult labour force. Smaller schools (with lower socialization ratios), critics argue, can avoid these problems, because teachers and students know each other better, and there are more chances per student for sports, music, and other extra-curricular activities. Even Al Gore, while vice-president of the United States, recognized this, when he said in a speech referring to violence in American high schools that we need to stop herding students "into overcrowded, factory-style schools [where] it becomes impossible to spot the early warning signs of violence, depression, or academic failure" (quoted in Christian, 1999: 19). In fact, students who attend smaller schools get better grades, attend more often, and participate in more extracurricular activities. They are also less likely to be part of a clique or gang, to fight or be attacked, and are more likely to discuss their problems with teachers (Christian, 1999).

Solutions to Canada's educational problems are continually being sought, but the momentum of expansion appears to have few limits. Canada currently has some one million university students (Statistics Canada, *The Daily*, October 11, 2005), with significant increases predicted by 2011 (Association of Universities and Colleges of Canada, 2002). Most people affected by this expansion have stopped complaining about the overcrowding in Canadian universities, and have just accepted the situation, but the nature of this socialization context has clearly changed as the socialization ratio has grown to the point where many students never get to know a professor.

The rise of peer groups

Peer groups have also changed over the last two centuries. In earlier times, especially in rural settings, peer groups had a minimal influence on the transition to adulthood: they were difficult to form, small, and on an *ad hoc* basis when formed. By the 1950s, peer groups were increasingly affected by the technologies of industrial society, especially the automobile, which gave young people greater opportunities to interact independently of their parents. At the same time, the burgeoning mass media transmitted youth-culture symbols to wide audiences, particularly through the then-popular transistor radio, giving young people in a country as diverse and expansive as Canada a common language with which to bind their peer groups together independent of their parents' cultures. This is not to say that young people and their parents have come to live in entirely separate worlds, but that the amount of common culture shared has diminished considerably, leaving young people open to other influences. Today, young people are now "hyperconnected" through cellphones, instant messaging, and e-mail in ways unimagined in the past, the positive and negative consequences of which are difficult to estimate.

One manifestation of this separation of generations is the spread of youth gangs, a problem that is growing in Canada (especially in cities like Toronto) in a way that imitates, but lags behind, the greater growth in the United States. Flannery et al. (2003) estimate that there are now some 30 000 youth gangs spread throughout 5000 American cities, and that these gangs are spreading to rural and suburban areas. According to Flannery et al., about one-half of suburbs now have gangs, as do

about one-third of small cities, and about one-quarter of rural communities. Youth gangs have historically been associated with extreme economic marginalization, but this marginalization appears to be increasingly normative as more young people join them to make statements of identity in the absence of roles leading to integration into adult society.

Those who are more cognitively developed, self-confident and autonomous, and with more mature forms of identity are able to participate in, and learn from, peer influences without any apparent difficulty (Conger and Galambos, 1997). However, a significant number of young people today show adverse effects from being too involved in youth-culture activities, as evidenced by the high casualty rate among this age group (e.g., suicides, youth-on-youth violence, car accidents; Arnett, 1996; Côté and Allahar, 2006). For a lively and controversial examination of the influence of the contemporary peer group, see Harris (1998), who argued that peers have a far greater influence on how children turn out than do parents.

Enter popular culture

Mass or popular culture, disseminated through the mass media, rose to ascendance along with, and through, peer groups. In the past, more members of society shared a popular culture, which represented their common roots (in contrast to an elite culture, in which only the rich could afford to participate). Popular-culture activities involving song and dance brought people of all ages together in community celebrations, binding communities through the sharing of common symbols (note the annual celebrations of "folklore" and other "ethnic" activities in many Canadian cities—these are leftovers from "traditional" culture). Over the twentieth century, however, driven primarily by the mass media, popular culture became increasingly segmented by age, with each successive cohort adopting its own forms of song and dance during its transition to adulthood (see Chapter 12, Media). This has introduced a symbolic wedge between successive generations of the twentieth century, reducing both the amount of time they spend with each other and the cultural symbols they share.

Since the mid-1900s, the transition to adulthood has been increasingly affected by mass cultures whose promoters seek out wide audiences, largely based on age. Mass culture is most easily delivered to the widest audience through a "dumbing down," whereby the lowest common denominator is targeted—namely, passive and uncritical consumers who prefer not to expend mental energy during their leisure time. We can predict, therefore, that it will be less effective in influencing those who are critical consumers of the media.

Television has been the main medium by which mass culture reaches its intended audiences, but it is quickly becoming eclipsed by the Internet, and the technologies associated with microcomputer chips. Strasburger and Donnerstein (1999: 129) argued that "an increasing number of studies document that a serious problem exists" with respect to "children, adolescents, and the media." Part of their concern is over the expansion of the media into video games and DVDs. When the time spent with these media is added to that of television, some teens spend as much as 55 hours per week in front of a TV or computer screen. One problem, they believe, is that these media exert a behavioural and subjective *displacement effect*. Behaviourally, the time spent watching television takes away from other activities, like physical exercise, reading, and face-to-face interaction with other people. Subjectively, the *content* (i.e., those ideas that occupy people's thoughts and to which they have ready mental access) of what is viewed can affect the consciousness of the viewer—and the younger the viewer, the greater the effect. The more one is exposed to certain ideas, or ways of thinking, the more likely these are to affect choices made and beliefs held, and therefore the identities formed.

It is now clear that all of the mass media have been exploited in one way or another as part of the attempt to make profits, and that attempts to sell people things and convince them of things have accelerated as technologies have become more sophisticated and miniaturized (e.g., witness what can now be done with a cellphone or iPod). And, again, it is not that people mindlessly buy into the mass-cultural messages that are bombarding them. People, including many young people, are able to resist these messages if they are so motivated. However, marketers have learned how to feed off this resistance, especially from young people, in the various youth-oriented industries that emerged in the latter half of the twentieth century. Now, many symbols of youth resistance to mainstream society and market forces are commodified and sold to younger cohorts so they too can feel "hip" or "cool" as an integral part of their sense of identity. Frank (1997a) documented these marketing tricks and showed ironically how marketers have used the concepts of "cool"

and "hip" to trick mass consumers into believing that they can show others how unique they are by wearing, using, driving, or consuming something that has been mass marketed (see the box "Structure and Agency: If Everybody Is Cool, Is Anyone Cool?"). This practice is now so widespread that the term "cool hunter" has entered our vocabulary (e.g., Klein, 2000).

Marketers have developed a variety of strategies to make people think that consuming their product is cool. The chief marketing strategy documented by Frank (1997b) is "liberation marketing": it presents ads critical of mindless, middle-class consumers, who are depicted as dumb suburbanites, trapped workers with sadistic bosses, or executive automatons in grey uniforms. Liberation ads tacitly admit that business now rules the world, but its own products or services can liberate consumers from this oppression, if only momentarily (e.g., the advertising of shampoos that give women orgasms in public, automobiles in which the driving experience is intoxicating, or soft drinks that enable impossible risk-taking adventures). Marketers have also nurtured new brand loyalties that provide models of existential rebellion, in which a product is used as an expression of resistance against, or escape from, the drudgeries of work and urban life. Companies have also worked to create brand identities, which help consumers assimilate a product into their own sense of identity (e.g., Apple computers attempt to appeal to those who have a humanistic vision of the future).

Marketing strategies now also involve multimedia penetrations of consumers' lives (products presented not only in explicit ads, but also in movies, music videos, television programs, the Internet, and magazine articles) and more direct peer-to-peer marketing, also called "viral marketing," in which (cool) people are hired to encourage friends or strangers (depending on the venue in which the marketing takes place) to try or buy a product (Schor, 2004; Quart, 2002). Youth-culture "spies" are even employed to report to marketing firms when corporations want intelligence reports about the latest trends (see the company website look.look.com for more on this tactic). A decade ago, Frank contended that the attempts to appropriate youth culture have been highly successful, noting that contemporary "youth culture is liberation marketing's native tongue" (1997b: 45), a trend that has clearly accelerated since.

One way to gauge how much effort has been put into influencing the mass consumption of the youth population is to consult the marketing literature, where we find that not only is there tremendous attention directed at understanding how young people think, but also great interest in influencing their thoughts. This stands to reason, given the vested interests of marketers. Because they make their wages by predicting and affecting future consumption patterns, they need to be able to chart out *current* consumption patterns. By the

[Social Trends]

Structure and Agency: If Everybody Is Cool, Is Anyone Cool?

Most young people today want to be hip or cool, or at least it seems that way. But what does it mean to be hip or cool? The term "hip" came into usage in the 1950s; born of urban-American black culture, "hip" made its way into mainstream English through the music and drug subcultures of that decade. For jazz musicians, it meant being tolerant. For heroin users, it implied a unique understanding of the world that accepted drug use. In general, for Beatniks, being hip meant a laid-back attitude. Whatever the take, the basic idea was to be nonconformist. Moreover, these meanings had relevance only in the context of anti-establishment subcultures, because they represented a rejection of mainstream society, which, by implication, cannot be hip.

In the 1960s, the desire to be hip spread, and a substantial proportion of a generation (hippies) adopted the knowledge and attitude representing hipness, which they referred to as being "cool." During this period, hippies could readily identify one another by means of their simple dress and hair styles, neither of which had a commercial basis. But cool still remained an intangible state of mind associated with a laid-back, non-materialistic view of the world.

Beatniks and hippies never really posed a threat to capitalist society, in spite of their rejection of it, but ironically it was capitalist society that learned to appropriate the disdain these groups held toward it. Playing on the young people's rebellious spirit and desire to be "in the know," marketers learned in the 1970s how to turn countercultural symbols into fashion trends. As Bellafonte, Gross, and Cray (1994) argued "[C]apitalism proved itself well-suited to absorb whatever was hip that might fascinate consumers, while discarding the uncomfortable parts. For every counterculture, there emerged the corresponding sales counterculture."

These marketing techniques have now been around for several decades now, and have convinced millions of people that they can buy hipness or coolness. But, as Bellafonte, Gross, and Cray (1994) noted, "[W]hen hipness is embraced from mainstream, much of the life gets squeezed from it. If the signs of hip—goatees, pierced nipples, and calf tattoos—are everywhere, what's so hip about them? If the attitudes of hip . . . are officially sponsored by the major media, what's so special?" In short, hip and cool cannot exist among the mainstream, yet literally billions of dollars and endless hours of leisure time are spent in pursuit of them by many mainstream youth.

This phenomenon is well illustrated in the three Woodstock music festivals held over the last thirty years. The first Woodstock in 1969 was largely a spontaneous event in which the organizers lost money, but made history and a cultural statement. The second Woodstock, held in 1994, is noted as being "history's largest convergence of the mass market," whose organizers test-marketed the line-up of bands, sold official refrigerator magnets and condoms, and were sponsored by several multinational corporations including Pepsi and Apple Computer. The organizers of this event made lots of money, but there was no cultural statement—only several hundred thousand people acting out what they had seen in film footage from the first Woodstock. Woodstock '99 likewise made lots of money, but will be remembered for the riots in which a dozen truck trailers—containing T-shirts and other official merchandise, as well as exorbitantly priced food and soft drinks ($4 for a Coke)—were set on fire. This may have been a "cultural statement" to the effect that some young people are tired of being exploited: however, it is hard to see how a rampage of violence is hip or cool, regardless of how one is dressed.

Has the agency originally represented by hipness and coolness been transformed into a new form of orchestrated conformity, or is it still possible to use attitude, behaviour, and appearance as anti-establishment statements?

mid-1990s, articles with the following titles appeared in *American Demographics: Consumer Trends for Business Leaders:* "Marketing to Generation X" (Ritchie, 1995); "Talking to Teens" (Zollo, 1995); "The Rocky Road to Adulthood" (Mogelonsky, 1996); "Getting Inside Kids' Heads" (McGee, 1997); and "College Come-ons" (Speer, 1998). Even more telling of the motivations of marketers are some of the captions for these articles, like "The teenage market is free-spending and loaded with untapped potential"; "Don't assume 18-to-24-year-olds are adults. The pre-adult life-stage is here to stay"; and "Today's college students have more money than their predecessors, and they don't mind parting with it. Product and service providers want a piece of the spending now, but the ultimate goal is to cultivate long-term customers." More recent articles targeting tweens and the so-called Generation Y or Millennial Generation carried titles like *Coming of Age in Consumerdom* (4 April 2004), *Getting Inside Gen Y* (Paul, 2001), and *Inside the Mind of Gen Y* (Nayyar, 2001).

Are mass marketers successful? Well, according to Palladino (1996), in 1990s America, teenagers constituted "a red-hot consumer market worth $89 billion," not counting the $200 billion their parents spend on them. This was a tenfold increase over the previous forty years, and the youth market continues to expand each year. Quart (2002) put the discretionary income of American teens at $155 billion in 2000 (not counting what they get from their parents). The most commonly cited estimate of total expenditures in the total youth market (teens and twenties) is about $300 billion (e.g., Rushkoff, 2001), a figure equivalent to the entire U.S. defence budget before the war in Iraq. (Because of the difference in population size, we can divide these figures by ten to get an estimate of the extent of these expenditures in Canada.) Inasmuch as mass culture is a potent socialization context to which people are now exposed during most of the formation of their adult identities, the expert advice is "buyer beware."

Summary

In this chapter, socialization was defined from a variety of perspectives, all of which involve teaching or inducing people to fit into, and cooperate with, human groups. From these definitions arose a number of issues associated with how much influence societies have in determining people's behaviour and how much personal control people can exert over their own behaviour in the face of cultural influences and societal pressures. In addition to cultural influences, scientists have also argued that evolutionary-based genetics plays a role in how people behave, both in terms of personality traits and in terms of how societies are structured. Referred to as the nature–nurture debate, positions have been adopted along the range, from total genetic influence to total cultural influence. Given the focus of this chapter, the impact of culture was emphasized with the acknowledgment that much remains to be learned about genetic influences and how they interact with cultural ones.

Within sociology, three perspectives have dominated the field. Functionalists emphasize the integrative function of socialization in maintaining existing social structures. Conflict theorists question how benign these socialization processes are, arguing that they often serve to perpetuate economic inequalities and social injustice. Symbolic interactionists, in contrast, focus on the micro level of analysis in terms of how individuals learn to interact with each other through negotiating and sharing symbols embodied in language and role-playing.

While sociologists tend to be interested in the contexts and content of socialization, cultural anthropologists study variations in socialization practices between cultures, and within cultures historically.

The substantive portion of this chapter focused on socialization contexts and agents, illustrating these in terms of how identity formation in the transition to adulthood has been transformed in Canadian society. Socialization contexts vary in the extent to which they can and do exert influence over people. In many contexts, people resist attempts to influence them, leading to unintended consequences and a variety of socialization problems. Socialization contexts also vary over the life course of the individual, and they have changed over the course of history. Using a 200-year time frame and five social contexts, it was argued that the family and religion have declined in the extent to which they socialize young people for adulthood and their place in the community, while education, peers, and mass culture have increased in influence. It appears that, increasingly, the socialization of new recruits to adulthood is in the hands of bureaucracies and businesses, rather than parents and other concerned adults.

Questions for Review and Critical Thinking

1. Can you cite examples from your own life experiences that would constitute defective socialization? Can you think of any examples in which you experienced anticipatory socialization?

2. Apply the structure–agency debate to your own day-to-day activities at university or college. Does your behaviour appear to be the result of agency or structure, or both? If both, in what ways is this demonstrated in your behaviour and how would you convince someone of your conclusions?

3. To what extent does your own upbringing reflect prefigurative influences? What is your relationship like with your parents? Are you close, but do you make up your own mind, feeling that you sometimes have to teach them things?

4. Think for a moment about children you have observed at home or a friend's house watching a violent cartoon. How did they spontaneously behave with each other following this exposure? Is there any evidence that at least some of their immediate behaviour was shaped by their television viewing?

5. Take time to reflect on your role as an informal agent of socialization. You are such an agent every time you correct someone about the "proper" way to dress or behave, or encourage them to buy a certain product like an iPod or cellphone. You also socialize other people every time you give them looks of approval and disapproval. Is there any way around this? Can people be neutral in their interactions with others, or will their acceptance of certain symbols always influence others' perception those symbols?

Key Terms

anticipatory socialization, p. 73
cofigurative culture, p. 74
defective socialization, p. 72
disjunctive socialization, p. 72
epigenetic, p. 63
generalized other, p. 69
I and me, p. 69
inadequate socialization, p. 72

individualization, p. 75
looking-glass self, p. 68
nature versus nurture, p. 61
normative structure, p. 75
postfigurative culture, p. 74
prefigurative culture, p. 75
role system, p. 71
role-taking, p. 68
self-socialization, p. 73
significant others, p. 70
social reproduction, p. 66
socialization, p. 62
socialization ratio, p. 72

Suggested Readings

Erikson, Erik H.
1968 *Identity: Youth and Crisis.* New York: Norton.
This is Erikson's seminal statement on human identity and how it has been made vulnerable by social change and the disruption of communities.

Gergen, Kenneth
1991 *The Saturated Self: Dilemmas of Identity in Contemporary Life.* New York: Basic.
Gergen argues that the self and identity are becoming "multiphrenic" and "relational" as a result of the changes in people's lives, brought on by the penetration of modern and "postmodern" technologies into their lives.

Heath, Joseph and Andrew Potter
2004 *The Rebel Sell: Why the Culture Can't Be Jammed.* Toronto: HarperCollins.
These Canadian professors take young counter-cultural rebels to task for actually contributing to the "conquest of cool" by providing marketers with ever-new symbols of youth dissent that they can use to define their products as cool. According to them, captialism feeds on change, not conformity, so youth culture has identified the wrong "enemy" in resisting symbols of conformity.

Schor, Julliet B.
2004 *Born To Buy: The Commercialized Child and the New Consumer Culture.* New York: Scribner.
This book provides extensive details into the inside world of predatorial marketing, which now begins with young children and tweens, and aims to produce life-long "branded" consumers.

Strasburger, Victor C. and Barbara J. Wilson
2002 *Children, Adolescents and the Media*. Thousand
Oaks, CA: Sage.
This up-to-date study examines the effect of various
forms of media upon the mental and physical well-
being of young people.

Websites

www.teenresearch.com/home.cfm
Teenage Research Unlimited
Visit a Canadian marketing firm where the strategies
to shape young people's consumption behaviour are
openly discussed.

www.adbusters.org/home/
Adbusters
At this Canadian site, online efforts to draw people's
attention to the attempts to shape their consumption
behaviour are reported.

www.unb.ca/crisp/index.php
Canadian Research Institute for Social Policy
See how a multidisciplinary research institute seeks to
improve social policy by helping Canadian communities provide better education and care for children.

Key Search Terms

Socialization
Roles
Individualization
Identity formation
Structure–agency
Nature–nurture
Education

For more study tools to help you with your next exam,
be sure to check out the Companion Website at
www.pearsoned.ca/hewitt, as well as Chapter 4 in your
Study Guide.

[5]

deviance

kevin d. haggerty

Pay attention to the public media and you will quickly notice a remarkable amount of deviance. Newspaper and magazine cover stories detail assorted forms of criminal victimization while police dramas are a staple of prime time network broadcasting. Daytime talk shows routinely recount the personal stories of certain classes of individual because the producers anticipate that they will appear bizarre to most viewers. One result of all of this exposure to crime and deviance is that the public often believes it is intimately familiar with crime trends and with the nature and dynamics of deviant behaviour. Many of those beliefs are, unfortunately, at odds with what sociologists and criminologists know about these topics.

This chapter introduces the social study of crime and deviance. At this juncture we will use the terms "crime" and "deviance" interchangeably but, as is outlined below, there are important differences between these concepts. At the conclusion of the chapter you will be able to differentiate between crime and deviance, be aware of some of the more important statistical trends pertaining to crime in Canada and be familiar with some of the strengths and weakness of different ways of studying crime. The second half of the chapter exposes

you to some of the more prominent social theories used to try to understand crime and deviance. By the end of the chapter you should be able to recognize these different theories and explain some of their limitations.

A useful way to commence this overview is to ask why criminology and deviance classes are consistently among the most popular university courses. Obviously there is a straightforward answer to this question, as some students take these courses just to get a credit or with an eye to a potential career in criminal justice. However, some students have more telling motivations for why they are drawn to the study of crime.

Some see studying deviance as a first step toward eliminating deviant behaviour. This can be an admirable ambition, as many forms of deviance cause considerable human suffering. However, as discussed later in this chapter, there is also the prospect that deviance and crime might never be eliminated because they serve necessary social functions.

Others want to help individuals who are suffering with problems associated with being treated as a criminal or deviant. Such ambitions to "reform" individuals become more complicated once we recognize how various efforts to "heal" deviants have themselves involved substantial abuses of power. In the name of rehabilitation people have been forced, often with the use of drugs, behaviour modification therapy, and corporal punishment, to adopt questionable standards of social propriety. The history of the official relationship to homosexuality, for example, consists of many attempts to "cure" such individuals of their deviant ways—often culminating in interventions that we now recognize as being misguided and profoundly cruel.

Some students claim that they are simply fascinated by the study of deviance. When pushed, however, many readily admit that what they are *really* fascinated by is a small subset of spectacular forms of deviance, such as serial killers or sex offenders. Students typically show less interest in the criminal acts of corporations or in more mundane forms of interpersonal deviance. This raises the question of whether the sociology of deviance involves a form of voyeurism, where the sufferings and peculiarities of certain classes of people are displayed for the guilty pleasure of academic audiences (Lyman, 1972).

These by no means exhaust the range of reasons why people study crime. They do, however, provide a sense of the diverse range of orientations found in this academic subspecialty, as well as some of the tensions inherent in each approach. As will become apparent, the study of crime and deviance is, in fact, *not* a single coherent field of study. Instead, it is a mixed endeavour that brings together assorted methodological, theoretical, and political orientations to the study of crime. This makes the field intellectually vibrant but it can also mean that newcomers must spend a considerable amount of time to firmly orient themselves to all of these different approaches. What follows is a preliminary effort to accentuate some issues that often arise in the study of crime and deviance.

The Relativism of Deviance

Can you identify a behaviour that is always deviant across different cultures and throughout history? Most students immediately say "murder," but murder is a legal classification, not a type of behaviour. When this is pointed out many then propose "killing." This, however is complicated by the fact that killing can assume a wide range of forms, including killing in warfare, self-defence, capital punishment, infanticide (the killing of children), killing to maintain family honour, killing to end a person's suffering (euthanasia), and so on.

Sometimes these are approved of, while in other contexts identical acts are severely punished.

Getting agreement on a behaviour that is and always has been deviant is a more difficult a task than it might first appear. Historians point out that many acts we now see as reprehensible were previously accepted. A prominent example is wife assault, which not very long ago was not only common, but also explicitly accepted within dominant male society. The reverse is also true; many acts that were once crimes are now common, such as drinking alcohol. Anthropologists who study other cultures further complicate this picture by accentuating how some acts that citizens of Western societies see as extremely reprehensible, such as infanticide, are often familiar and accepted behaviours in other cultures under certain circumstances (Shalinsky and Glascock, 1988). Even in North America behavioural standards can vary dramatically across different groups. Different social groups often embrace very unique rules about proper and improper behaviour, which can clash with dominant social standards. For example, there is an ancient tradition in warfare whereby soldiers collect human "trophies" from people they have killed in combat. In the words of a U.S. Marine who wore a string of human ears around his neck in Vietnam:

> We used to cut their ears off. We had a trophy. If a guy would have a necklace of ears, he was a good killer, a good trooper. It was encouraged to cut ears off, to cut the nose off, to gut the guy's penis off. A female, you cut her breasts off. It was encouraged to do these things. *The officers expected you to do it or something was wrong with you.* (Bourke, 1999: 42, emphasis added)

We have highlighted the last line of this disturbing statement because it neatly encapsulates the notion that standards of right and wrong, deviant and normal, depend on context. According to this soldier, his colleagues might have considered him deviant—might have suspected that something was a bit "wrong" with him—if he had refused to mutilate corpses.

In the face of these diverse reactions to deviance, academics who study crime and deviance tend to embrace a form of **relativism**. This is an orientation that recognizes that what counts as deviance varies across cultures and through history, and therefore does not judge whether such acts are right or wrong. Such relativism is typically a purely academic orientation—a way for sociologists to examine deviance in as disinterested a manner as possible. It does not translate into a form of "anything goes." In their day-to-day lives almost all academics are committed to a belief that some behaviours are simply wrong.

The Relationship between Crime and Deviance

Students interested in criminal behaviour often take courses in both criminology and the sociology of deviance. It quickly becomes apparent to them that there can be considerable overlap between these topics. This is not surprising. Many of the theories used to try to explain deviance can also apply to criminal behaviour, and vice versa. This is because there is a close, although not perfect, relationship between crime and deviance, which is represented in Figure 5.1. Note that of the two overlapping circles the one representing deviance is much larger than that for crime. That is because deviance is a much broader category, and refers to a pattern of norm violation. **Norms** are shared expectations of behaviour that prescribe what is culturally appropriate or desirable, and are a core concept in the sociology of deviance. For something to be **abnormal** means that it violates a norm, which implies a value judgment that the behaviour is wrong. As such, norms are akin to informal rules that are acquired through processes of socialization.

Crimes, in contrast, are behaviours that have been officially recognized by the state as serious forms of anti-social behaviour. Criminal justice officials can formally sanction individuals who engage in crimes, which is something they cannot do for non-criminal forms of deviance. A considerable volume of crimes are also forms of deviance, and this overlap is represented in the dark blue section of Figure 5.1. However, the relationship between crime and deviance is not necessarily straightforward. Not all deviant behaviours are criminal. There are many acts of which society might disapprove, but that are not seen as serious enough to justify being elevated to the status of crimes. Some homeowners, for example, display figurines on their lawns that many people perceive to be racist. Displaying these figurines is in extremely poor taste and offends the social norms of the dominant group, but that alone does not make this behaviour a crime. There are also several crimes on the books that many people do not see as violating social norms; these are represented in the white segment of Figure 5.1. Smoking marijuana, for example, is illegal, but large segments of Canadian society do not see this as deviant. The loose relationship between crime and deviance accentuates that there can be an

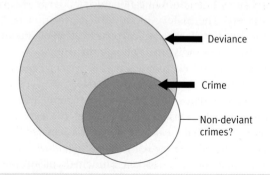

Figure 5.1 **Relationship between Crime and Deviance**

Note the loose relationship between "crime" and "deviance."

intense political dynamic to decisions about what types of behaviour become classified as crimes. Various groups have vested interests in defining the actions of other individuals as deviant, or in criminalizing particular behaviours. Currently, for example, the recording industry is engaged in a high-stakes political battle to convince the public that the free downloading of music is deviant, and is seeking to criminalize such behaviour. They are doing so notwithstanding the fact that free downloading is common among young Canadians and is not seen as deviant by most people.

Studying Crime and Deviance

Almost every social scientific discipline contributes to our understanding of deviance. The types of methodologies that have a bearing on this topic are consequently extremely diverse, and include such things as historical research, laboratory experiments, and legal analysis. Sociologists tend to employ the methods introduced in Chapter 2 of this volume. There are several unique methodological considerations to bear in mind when using sociological methods to study crime and deviance (see generally, Mosher, Miethe, and Phillips, 2002; Maguire, 2002).

Official data

Criminologists often analyze data produced by the Canadian Centre for Justice Statistics, which is the unit within Statistics Canada that collects and publishes national data on crime, courts, and corrections (Haggerty, 2001). Its most prominent data set is the Uniform Crime Reports (UCR), which produces standardized measures of officially recorded crimes in Canada. When journalists report on the crime rate they are typically referring to the numbers produced in the UCR. The Uniform Crime Reports have several advantages. The data are readily available and are produced using standardized definitions, which makes it straightforward to compare crime rates across the country. These data have also been collected since 1962, which allows for analysis of historical trends in crime patterns. The United States also has a form of UCR, which, although not identical to the Canadian system, nonetheless allows for useful cross-national comparisons.

Analysis of official crime data has produced important insights into the nature and dynamics of crime in Canada. The data reveal that crime, with some notable exceptions, is generally a male undertaking. Men, and young men in particular, are disproportionately involved in criminal behaviour. Indeed, in all societies young males are much more criminal than any other group. We also know that the vast majority of crime is not violent. Of all the crimes reported to the police in Canada in 2005 only 12 percent were violent. The remainder were property crimes (48 percent) and "other Criminal Code offences" (40 percent), which includes crimes such as mischief, disturbing the peace, and bail violation (Gannon, 2006) (see Figure 5.2). Looking exclusively at violent crimes (see Figure 5.3) reveals that the vast majority of violent

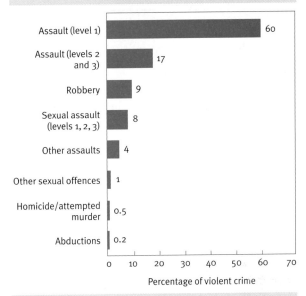

Figure 5.3	Breakdown of Violent Crime[1] Canada, 2005

Percentage of violent crime

Fully 60 percent of all violent crimes are "Level 1 Assaults," which are the least violent forms of assault.

Source: Adapted from Figure 3: "Majority of Violent Crimes are Level 1 Assaults, 2005," Statistics Canada publication "Juristat," *Crime Statistics in Canada, 2005*, Catalogue 85-002, Volume 26, Number 4, page 5, Released July 20, 2006.

[1] Percentages may not total 100 percent due to rounding.

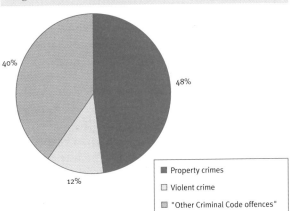

Figure 5.2	Distribution of Reported Crime

- 40%
- 48%
- 12%

■ Property crimes
□ Violent crime
▨ "Other Criminal Code offences"

Violent crime accounts for only 12 percent of all crime. Homicide accounts for only 0.05 percent of the violent crime in Canada.

Source: Maire Gannon, 2006. *Crime Statistics in Canada, 2005*. Ottawa: Statistics Canada.

crimes (60 percent) consist of "Level 1 Assaults," which are the least serious forms of assault, and can include shoving or verbal abuse. Homicide and attempted murder only account for 0.05 percent of all violent crimes in Canada.

One of the most notable developments in recent years has concerned the crime rate. From 1962 until 1991 the crime rate in Canada had steadily increased, reaching a peak rate of 10 342 crimes per 100 000 people in 1991 (see Figure 5.4). After 1991 the crime rate began a steady decline, and in 2005 the rate was 7761 crimes per 100 000. One reason why this decline is interesting is because it clashes with the assumption of most Canadians who typically believe that crime rates are high and climbing. Criminologists have hypothesized that many potential factors could account for this decline, including new policing practices, an aging population, new laws, different police reporting practices or new technologies.

Official crime statistics have several notable limitations. Most fundamentally, it is vital to always remember that rather than being a measure of crime, *crime statistics*

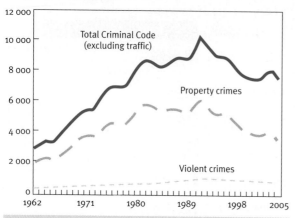

Figure 5.4 — Historical Crime Trends

Rate per 100 000 population

What do you think might account for the decline in the crime rate since 1990?

Source: Adapted from Figure 1: "Crime Rate Peaked in 1991," Statistics Canada publication "Juristat," *Crime Statistics in Canada, 2005*, Catalogue 85-002, Volume 26, Number 4, page 4, Released July 20, 2006.

are a measure of police activity. For a crime to be recorded on the official crime statistics a number of hurdles must be passed. At each hurdle there is an attrition process whereby crimes fall by the wayside, meaning that they never make it onto the official statistics. The first step in this process is that a person must recognize that he or she has been victimized, which is not as easy as one might think. A woman, for example, who thinks she has mislaid an electric drill that was really stolen from her garage, would obviously not call the police. The result would be that her victimization would never be recorded.

Even when people know they have been victimized, many never take the next step and contact the police. There are many reasons why people do not report crime to the police, including a belief that the police cannot do anything to rectify the situation, a distrust of the police in certain cultural communities, or a sense that calling the police might make things worse (as can be the case with reporting sexual assault). The cumulative effect of such non-reporting is that the police never learn about a considerable volume of crime. A recent Statistics Canada study found that only 34 percent of violent crimes are reported to the police. More disturbingly only 8 percent of sexual assaults are reported (Gannon and Mihorean, 2005). Such findings accentuate how the official crime statistics can severely underestimate the volume of certain types of crimes.

Even reporting a crime does not guarantee that it will be recorded on the official statistics. A police officer might decide that your problem is not a criminal matter and refer you to another social service organization (Meehan, 2000). Alternatively, an officer might conclude that there is no prospect of making an arrest and therefore not bother to do the paperwork necessary to ensure that the event is officially recorded. This process of filtering out crimes continues at every step of the criminal justice process. Criminologists typically characterize this as the **crime funnel**. At the top of the funnel are the very large number of cases that could potentially be recorded as crimes. At each step in the funnel more and more cases fall by the wayside. So, for most recorded crimes the police never make an arrest. For many arrests a charge is never laid. Even when the police lay a charge most of these cases never appear in court, but instead are resolved through a plea arrangement negotiated between the defence and the prosecution. Finally, most individuals convicted of a crime spend no time in prison, but instead receive some manner of alternative punishment such as probation or community service. Figure 5.5 provides a sense of how the crime funnel operates in relation to the crime of break-and-enter. A key thing to therefore keep in mind when working with official crime statistics is that they do not represent all of the crimes that occur in society. The unknown and unmeasured volume of crime is referred to by criminologists as the **dark figure of crime**.

Victimization and self-report studies

Victimization surveys and self-report studies are also used to study criminal behaviour. These are particularly helpful in shedding light on the dark figure of crime. **Victimization surveys**, such as Statistics Canada's General Social Survey, telephone Canadians to ask them whether and how they might have been victimized in the past twelve months. These studies provide a greater sense of the types of crimes that are not reported to the police. For example, victimization studies reveal how few sexually assaulted women report their victimization to the police. **Self-report studies** also ask individuals about their personal experience of crime, but in this case they ask people to identify the crimes that they have personally committed over the previous year. Again, an advantage of this approach is that it can measures crimes that never make their way onto the official statistics. One general insight derived from self-report studies is that crime is not a rare

Figure 5.5   Crime Funnel: Break-and-Enter Offences Processed
through the Canadian Criminal Justice System

ALL BREAK AND ENTER: Offences reported and not reported to the police

REPORTED: About 2 out of 3 break and enters are thought to the reported
to the police.

ACTUAL: The police assess slightly over 9 out of 10 offences
as actual.

CHARGED: For about every 8 offences that occur, 1 person is charged.

PROSECUTED: For about every 20 offences that occur,
1 person is prosecuted.

CONVICTED: For about every 23 offences that occur,
1 person is convicted.

SENTENCED: For about every 43 offences that
occur, 1 person is sentenced to
either a prison or penitentiary

The number of crimes gets smaller as cases proceed through the funnel.

Note: This diagram illustrates the processing of break-and-enter offences through various stages in the criminal justice system. Data are approximations.

Source: Solicitor General Canada, 1984. *Reported and Unreported Crimes*. Canadian Urban Victimization Survey, Bulletin No. 2; Solicitor General Canada, 1981: *Selected Trends in Canadian Criminal Justice*. Reproduced with the permission of the Minister of Public Works and Government Services Canada, 1999.

phenomenon undertaken by a few notorious individuals. Instead, crimes of various stripes are very common; in the words of criminologist Thomas Gabor (1994), "everybody does it." Not everyone commits heinous forms of violent crime, but many have engaged in more prosaic behaviours for which they could be prosecuted if they were caught, including tax evasion, impaired driving, overbilling, copyright infringement, theft (often from the workplace), illegal drug use, trading stocks on the basis of an insider "tip," simple assault (which can include shoving or verbally berating someone), and so on.

While victimization surveys and self-report studies provide an important alternative to official crime data, they are also not perfect. Like all survey research they only study a sample of the population, which means that a sufficient number of people must be contacted to ensure statistically significant findings. Some crimes are also not reported because individuals are unaware that they have been victimized. These problems are compounded by the fact that participants often forget prior victimization or cannot remember exactly when a crime occurred—one reason why they are asked only about

[Debate]

Race and Crime Statistics

One of the most contentious data-related issues in Canadian criminal justice concerns whether the police or Statistics Canada should collect information on the racial or ethnic status of offenders (Haggerty, 2001). Historically, Canadian crime statistics routinely included information on occupation, education, and religion, along with place of birth, and a crude measure of ethnicity. Criminologists used this information to discuss group differences in criminal behaviour. Ethnic differences in crime and delinquency were expected, and sociologists used the data to analyze forms of culture conflict that arose in the context of the widespread immigration that took place earlier last century—a form of conflict that some thought could account for certain types of criminal behaviour (Sellin, 1938).

Today, however, some groups fear that crime statistics based on race or ethnicity will be used to promote hatred and discrimination. Evidence for this can occasionally be seen in sensationalist stories about "Asian gangs," "Jamaican criminals," or the "Russian Mafia." Such stories typically ignore the fact that most members of any racial or ethnic group are not criminal. Consequently, there has been debate about whether such data should be collected or published. Below are some of the arguments against collecting this data.

1. Official crime rates are a function of police behaviour. Hence, differences in ethnic or racial crime rates might be a result of police paying over-attention to the behaviours of certain groups, more than such individuals being overly criminal.

2. Some ethnic differences in crime can be attributed to the crimes we choose to examine. For example, white-collar crimes are under-reported compared to arrests for street-level drug sales. Individuals from the predominately white Canadian establishment commit more of the former and recent immigrants more of the latter, thus creating a somewhat inaccurate picture of the relationship between ethnicity and crime. If ethnic or racial variations are reported, the specific crimes to which the generalizations do and do not apply need to be clearly stated.

3. It can be very difficult to achieve a rigorous and accurate definition of race and ethnicity (Roberts, 1994). Lack of agreement on the traits that distinguish ethnic groups lead to difficulties in unambiguously classifying many individuals into distinct ethnic and racial groups. Also, increasing intermarriage means that ever-fewer Canadians can claim that their ancestors came from only one group.

4. Finally, even if the crime rates for those individuals who can demonstrate only one racial or ethnic background were collected (which would leave out many Canadians), it would be important to examine the rates of these groups in their homelands, as immigrants to other lands besides Canada, and over time, to see if similar rates occurred. If they did not, then something besides ethnicity and race must account for their criminal behaviour.

Taken together, these measurement difficulties and the political controversy surrounding this issue have led Statistics Canada to not collect such data. This decision has also produced its own problems. For example, we know that some Canadian ethnic groups, most particular Aboriginal peoples, are overrepresented in terms of their arrest and incarceration rates. Without statistics identifying the ethic identity of offenders it is difficult or impossible to learn about the extent to which they are overrepresented, or to develop and evaluate programs that might help rectify this situation.

Do the potential problems associated with collecting race-related crime data outweigh the potential benefits of such data?

crimes committed in the past twelve months. Finally, one difficulty that is particularly acute when studying crime is that people will lie about their criminal behaviour. So, some respondents have been known to exaggerate their degree of criminal involvement. More commonly, even when reassured that research findings will be kept anonymous and confidential, individuals can be reluctant to admit to having committed serious crime.

Ethnography

A final methodology that has helped to develop an understanding of deviant groups is **ethnography**, also known as **participant observation**. It involves a researcher interviewing individuals or accompanying them on their day-to-day routines. This is quite different from the methods mentioned above in that it aims to learn about the world of deviance (and criminal justice) from the vantage point of the people who are personally involved in such activities. Through such efforts sociologists have learned important lessons about such things as the individual motivations for joining gangs, how illegal markets operate, and the real-world challenges of policing (Ericson, 1982; Ericson and Haggerty, 1997). One advantage of ethnographic research is that unlike statistical analysis, ethnographies provide a sense of the criminal as a human

being, someone who is often motivated by ambitions and desires that are familiar to everyone.

The limitations of ethnographic research include the fact that it tends to focus on individuals who are comparatively low on the social spectrum—street gangs, homeless people, and street-level drug dealers figure prominently in this literature. Ethnographic studies of elites are much rarer because of the additional difficulties in accessing such individuals or securing their permission. The fact that ethnographic research tends to focus on the actions of individuals can also mean that researchers downplay how individual behaviour can be shaped by larger structural factors. Finally, such studies can be incredibly difficult to conduct. While no social scientific methodology is easy, the personal commitments required to conduct extensive ethnographic research can be extremely daunting.

[Research Focus]

Dealing Crack

In 1994/1995 Bruce Jacobs (1999) conducted ethnographic research on street-level crack dealers in St. Louis, which has one of the largest illicit drug markets in the Midwestern United States. Crack is a hard crystal form of cocaine. When smoked in rock form it produces an intense euphoric high. Sold at a comparatively low cost (individual rocks can cost as little as $10) it is an attractive street drug for all but the most destitute. Crack is also extremely addictive.

Jacobs' research provides nice examples of the types of insights into an illegal occupation that can only be derived from extensive personal contact with people involved in such activities. He personally became acquainted with forty street-level dealers (thirty-four men and six women) who averaged 20 years of age. Extensive interviews were conducted with fourteen of these individuals. Predictably, he at first faced considerable suspicions from the dealers who feared that he was an undercover police officer. It was only after he himself was publicly harassed by the police that the dealers started to trust that he was not an informant.

To understand the dynamics of street-level crack dealing Jacobs looked at this practice as you might look

at any other job. This entailed considering why dealing crack might be an attractive occupation for some people, and also the unique challenges of earning a livelihood in this way.

He found that individuals sell crack largely because they have few other occupational alternatives. With an average educational level of Grade 10, most lack the credentials and social skills that would allow them to work in the traditional economy. Dealers also find the job flexibility attractive, as they are essentially individual entrepreneurs, working when they like, without the oversight of a boss. Living in a street culture where money is equated with status, the dealers also praise how dealing can allow them to make a lot of money quickly. Jacobs, however, found that the actual amounts they earn are often highly exaggerated and that dealers' lack of fiscal responsibility, combined with their continually buying flashy clothes, jewellery and so on, means that most will be penniless even after a long career of dealing.

The easiest part of their job involves getting the drugs. All participants know other dealers from personal

(continued)

or family connections. The drugs are purchased in rock form in small quantities, typically between ten to twenty-five packages. The dealers sell alone or in pairs, as group selling is discouraged because it is highly visible, which can draw the attention of the police.

Finding a clientele for their product is also fairly easy, as customers come to them. The fact that their customers are often poor addicts, and not uncommonly extremely edgy and irritable due to their being in the depths of a cocaine binge also gives the street trade some inherent tensions. A predatory dynamic characterizes the relationship between all groups involved in the actual selling of the drugs. Some dealers will occasionally sell fake product, and users often attempt petty forms of scams that involve underpaying for the drugs, seeking a discount, or requesting larger rocks. Consequently, when the exchange actually takes place, dealers are eager to be paid before they surrender the drugs, while the buyers often want to have the drugs in-hand before they give over their money, a situation that makes the typically quick exchange fraught with tension and danger. Users occasionally ask to purchase drugs on credit, which dealers sometimes do as a means to foster a kind of brand loyalty. This is not common, however, as, given the nature of their clientele, it is unlikely that dealers who sell on credit will ever be repaid.

The police represent an additional risk to dealers, and the prospect of being arrested shapes many attributes of how crack is sold. To avoid the prospect of more serious criminal charges if they are arrested, dealers typically keep only small amounts of crack physically on their body. They often store the plastic-wrapped crack in their mouths.

Should they come into contact with the police a dealer will swallow the drugs, and vomit it up later. When actively dealing they stash their extra supply of crack in nearby sites, including in dumpsters, pop cans, or buried under a distinctive-looking stick.

Dealers are also perpetually attuned to the fact that undercover police might pose as potential customers. This is not something that is necessarily easy for the police to accomplish. Crack addicts often have a ragged, dishevelled look, are extremely edgy, and have a runny nose, glossy eyes, and burns on their hands from using a crack pipe. One of dealers' most refined skills is their ability to scrutinize people for cues that they might be an undercover police officer. If they are still unsure about a customer a dealer might ask the individual to pass a "test," which could consist of naming other dealers he or she has bought from in the past or describing people he or she knows in the neighborhood. If suspicions are raised during such tests the dealers will not make the sale.

These are just some of the detailed insights that can come from in-depth ethnographic engagement with people involved in crime. Such research can be particularly helpful in challenging dominant assumptions about criminal behaviour. For example, Jacobs found that, contrary to many media accounts, the street-level drug trade is not operated by gangs. While all of the youths had some kind of gang affiliation, they were essentially entrepreneurs selling entirely independent of gang control. In addition, he also found that very few crack dealers actually used crack, something that contradicts the prevalent assumption that dealers are also addicts. Jacobs attributed this non-use to the fact that many of the dealers had seen the ravages of crack up close in their own community and family.

Can you think of any legal jobs that share some of the dynamics of the occupational dynamics of the illegal sale of drugs?

Deviance

We begin this section by discussing behaviours that people might see as strange or improper, but that are not crimes (see the grey area of Figure 5.1). In particular, we will briefly examine some of the social dynamics pertaining to: (a) manners and (b) human bodies. These examples have been chosen to accentuate the degree to which considerations of deviance and normality often unconsciously pervade our daily lives.

Manners

What would you do if your dinner companion consistently let food tumble out of her mouth? Or blew her nose into her hand? Or lit a cigarette—which she proceeded to butt out into her unfinished dessert? Most people would be shocked or disgusted. The offending party might be reprimanded or subjected to more subtle forms of ridicule or gossip.

This person is guilty of transgressing established **manners** or **etiquette**, which are the social rules that govern interpersonal relations. When most of us think about manners we envision highly refined situations where we must decide which fork to use from among the five options set out before us. Such scenarios, however, represent just a few of a core set of manners learned through a lengthy process of socialization. Rules for dining include protocols for seating and excusing oneself, how loud to chew, how large a spoonful to take, the types of foods that can and cannot be eaten with the hands, and how to dispose of food that is in your mouth that is disagreeable, or too hot. Manners are among the most elaborate and occasionally confusing set of social rules, which has also made them a longstanding source of social satire—for example, such as when George on the television show *Seinfeld* was severely reprimanded for "double dipping" his nacho chip. Manners are so ingrained that most of us are only reminded of their existence when they are broken, an event that can prompt surprisingly deep reactions in the offended party.

How we react to a breach of manners accentuates one of the important differences between crime and deviance. Criminal behaviours can be subject to a series of **formal social control mechanisms**. These are sanctions undertaken by the state and include such things as courts, prisons, and probation. In contrast, we respond to non-criminal deviant acts through a host of **informal social control mechanisms**. Such reactions typically come from individual citizens or community groups, and can include subjecting an individual to ridicule, shaming, gossip, and occasionally excluding them from the group. While such reactions might seem to be lesser forms of punishment, informal sanctions can be extremely effective. Indeed, criminologist John Braithwaite (1989) has advocated integrating the process of "shaming" more fully into the criminal justice system due to the ability of such reactions to change a person's behaviour.

Norbert Elias (1994) has done the most to advance the sociological study of manners. His historical research into changes in manners led him to propose that Western societies had undergone a long-term **civilizing process**. His choice of the term "civilizing" is

unfortunate, as most individuals interpret this to mean that things are improving. Elias, in contrast, does not believe that the civilizing process entails a value judgment about society becoming better. Instead, the civilizing process refers to a very long-term historical change to individual **sensibilities**, which are broad structures of feeling. Over the centuries these sensibilities have become much more refined such that modern individuals are now much more easily and deeply offended by a host of phenomena that people in earlier societies found unremarkable, including interpersonal violence, public sexuality, and human waste.

The driving force for this change in sensibilities was the historical rise of an elite society toward the end of the Middle Ages when people, for the first time, began to rely on complex chains of personal contacts to secure what they wanted. This ultimately reduced their need to rely on violence to achieve their goals. Manners emerged as a way for elites to distinguish and elevate themselves from more common sectors of society. As non-elites came to aspire to heightened social status they also embraced the manners of elite society, a process that accounts for the spread of manners into wider society.

Elias's work demonstrates that far from being idiosyncratic and comical phenomena, manners contribute to social processes that help to distinguish groups from one another and are also part of the broader dynamics of group power. Hence the rules that a person follows when eating, communicating, or greeting other people reveal a great deal about their identity and their position within society (Bourdieu, 1984). This is also true of how people choose to alter their bodies.

Deviance and the human body

"Bart, you got your ear pierced. How radical . . . in a conformist sort of way." (Lisa Simpson)

Contemporary society has a heightened fixation on the shape of the human body, which at times borders on an obsession. The body has become a project—something to be worked on, moulded, and transformed to meet specific criteria. Such efforts connect with questions of deviance in that many of these efforts are motivated by a desire to meet social norms about proper or perfect bodies. At the opposite extreme, a host of bodily transformations have emerged that challenge conventional norms about the look or shape of the human body.

Different cultures hold different standards of normal or beautiful bodies (Eco, 2002). The Paduang women of Myanmar, for example, secure social status by extending their necks to an often remarkable degree with the aid of metal rings. If a woman is unfaithful the rings are removed, a painful and potentially life-threatening procedure as the rings cause the neck muscles to atrophy, meaning that a woman could not hold up her unsupported head. In China the historical practice of the "Golden Lotus" involved binding a young girl's feet, which stunted their normal development. The aim was to ensure that her feet would never grow longer than three inches, a practice that was motivated by the male erotic fascination with women's feet (Levy, 1991). The result was that women's feet were so mangled that they often could not walk without aid. In Victorian times some of the European women who bound their bodies with corsets also, in the process, permanently relocated their internal organs and altered the shape of their spines and rib cages.

These examples suggest that women have traditionally felt the pressure of social norms that have necessitated that they transform their bodies in attempts to meet an often unattainable standard of beauty (Wolf, 1990). Such efforts continue today in Western society where young women are often afflicted with eating disorders such as anorexia and bulimia, occasionally risking death in a quest to attain a media-driven standard of thinness. The current media prominence of the "six pack"—highly defined male stomach muscles—suggests that such processes are also starting to inform how men shape their bodies.

Our bodies say a great deal about us, often revealing our group membership and our relationship to wider society. Bodies are also read for signs of a person's character. As Susan Bordo (1993) has pointed out, a woman's thin body is not just an aesthetic ideal, but also involves a moral evaluation of a woman's worth, as her body size reveals her ability to exercise restraint, self-control, and discipline.

Sociologist Erving Goffman (1963) introduced the concept of **stigma**, which he defined as a characteristic, behaviour, or attribute that is deeply discrediting. A stigmatized person can often be rebuked by others. The power of stigma derives from the fact that in our day-to-day encounters with others we typically interpret other people by reading a range of markers off of their bodies, including their body shape, skin colour,

physical fitness, and level of physical ability. Such quick readings are at the roots of stereotyping—making attributions about a person due to their perceived group membership. While such attributions are often inaccurate and unfair, they are also an inevitable part of interpersonal encounters. By reading assorted visual cues we try to determine, among other things, who might be bad, dangerous, mad, or weak. Such tainted attributes are all forms of stigma. Goffman suggested that there were three general categories of stigma: (1) *stigma of character* might involve interpreting someone as being dishonest, domineering, or having a weak will; (2) *tribal* stigma are related to a person's being a member of certain kinds of tainted groups, which might include particular nationalities, races, or religions; and finally (3) *stigma of the body* refers to culturally specific deviations from idealized body types. Although the specifics of what things will be stigmatized change over time, all forms of stigma can cause people to shun or avoid the stigmatized person, or not accord that person the respect that they would otherwise extend to them.

Fear of being stigmatized leads individuals to engage in assorted activities to try to counter or manage this identity. They might be extra cautious about their interpersonal demeanour, as when a person returns to work after having a mental illness and tries not to do anything that might make his co-workers think that he is having a relapse.

One of the more notable developments in this regard is cosmetic surgery. Originally cosmetic surgery involved efforts to repair extremely damaged bodies and return them to their normal functioning. In the sixteenth century this included attempts to restore noses lost to syphilis. It was in the twentieth century when cosmetic surgery truly came into its own, largely through efforts to reconstruct the mangled faces of soldiers returning from World War I. Over time, the surgical techniques designed to help people avoid the stigma of severe disfigurement have become more popular to the point that cosmetic surgery is now one of the fastest growing medical procedures in the world.

Table 5.1 presents a selection of cosmetic surgery procedures. When we connect these procedures with developments in physical education, pharmacology, nutrition, and also to the more mundane technologies of bodily transformation such as nutritional supplements, calorie counters, scales, and body fat indicators,

Table 5.1	Sample Cosmetic Surgery Procedures
Arm lift	Forehead lift
Breast augmentation	Foreskin reconstruction
Breast implant	Hair transplants
Breast implant removal	Liposuction
Breast tightening	Male breast reduction
Buttock lift	Neck lift
Calf (and other) implants	Nose job
Cheek implants	Penile enlargement
Chemical peel	Rib removal*
Chin augmentation	Scar revision
Collagen injections	Skin resurfacing
Ear pin-back	Thigh lift
Eyelid tightening	Transgender surgery
Face lift	Tummy tuck
Face transplants (entire face)	

* Women's lower ribs are removed to enhance hourglass figure.

Some forms of body modification explicitly challenge dominant norms.

we gain a sense of the considerable malleability of the contemporary body. These transformations are undertaken in light of considerations of what types of bodies are ideal, which are impossible to disentangle from considerations of what types of bodies are deviant or abnormal.

One problem with Goffman's work on stigma is that it presents an image of individuals living lives of almost quiet desperation, continually afraid that their particular form of deviance might be identified and stigmatized. Writing in the early 1960s, Goffman did not anticipate how assorted groups would come "out of the closet" to reclaim the value and worth of identities that were historically treated as stigmatized (Kitsuse, 1980). Notable among such groups are the gay rights movement, the black power movement, and the disability rights movement.

These efforts to affirm and revalue forms of difference have also had implications for the types of bodies on display in society. Rather than exclusively seek out bodily transformations that are in line with a societal consensus of what is acceptable or beautiful, different social groups now consciously use their bodies to challenge such norms. For some groups the body consciously became a billboard, a way of marking off your relationship to, or sometimes your exclusion from, dominant society. For example, the "Modern Primitives" movement (Wood, 1996) embraces various forms of scarification, extreme piercing, branding, extreme tattooing, and even amputations as ways to mark group identity and political commitment. If such manipulations had occurred several decades ago many of these individuals might have risked being committed to a psychiatric institution.

Theories of Crime

The following section turns our attention from deviance to crime. It outlines a number of theories that have been proposed to explain criminal behaviour. It should be noted that in presenting these theories we occasionally give the implication that one theory replaces its predecessor. This is misleading, as it is rarely the case that a particular theoretical approach is ever entirely abandoned. Some orientations lose favour, only to re-emerge in a slightly different guise. Hence while some of the specifics of the following

[Debate]

Designer Vaginas

Women from around the world flock to David Matlock's marble waiting room carrying purses stuffed with porn. The magazines are revealed only in the privacy of his office, where doctor and patient debate the finer points of each glossy photo.

The enterprising gynecologist sees countless images of naked women, but none are more popular than Playboy's fresh-faced playmates. They represent, he says with a knowing smile, the perceived ideal.

"Some women will say, 'Hey, you take this picture and hang it up in the operating room and refer back to it when you're sculpturing me,'" he said in an interview in his clinic overlooking hazy Los Angeles. "I say, 'Okay, all right, fine.'"

Dr. Matlock is a colourful pioneer in a controversial—and growing—frontier of plastic surgery: nipping and tucking vaginas. Patients from the United States and more than thirty other countries pay thousands of dollars for his "designer vagina," a purely aesthetic procedure that includes shortening or plumping up the labia, or vaginal lips. He attracts even more women for an operation he claims improves sex by tightening, or "rejuvenating," the vagina.

"There's a need for this," he said. "Women are driving this. I didn't create this market, the market was there."

While doctors have long known how to enhance women's genitals, demand for vaginal surgery has mushroomed in recent years because physicians—led by Dr. Matlock—market it as enhancing sexual satisfaction. Doctors working in the field, including those in Canada, report higher caseloads and longer waiting lists. And the American Society of Plastic Surgeons says the increase is so great that it expects to soon start tracking volumes.

The trend has even reached girls as young as 15. In the past eighteen months, the number of teens—and in one case an adolescent and her mother—who come to Dr. Matlock for designer vaginas has doubled. . . .

There is no textbook outlining the ways and means that doctors can beautify the vagina. So Dr. Matlock, as he likes to say, gets all of his ideas by listening to women. If they repeatedly make the same request, the man who has been called the Picasso of vaginas will attempt to turn wish into reality. He is currently developing what he calls a "lip tuck," a facelift of sorts that would shrink sagging skin around the vulva and create a more "youthful appearance."

He hones new techniques on animal parts—chicken thighs, turkey legs, and pigs' ears—until he is ready to work on women.

"It's basically all about art. I'm an artist."

Source: Jill Mahoney, *Globe and Mail*. 13 August 2005: A1. Reprinted with permission from *The Globe and Mail*.

Should Parliament ban vaginal cosmetic surgery as an unnecessary procedure that will further regulate women's bodies? What, if anything, makes vaginal cosmetic surgery different than any other type of cosmetic surgery?

---

approaches have been disavowed, the different logics of each approach can still be found in current research programs.

Prescientific theories

Religion

Historically, religious beliefs were used to understand crime and deviance (Pfohl, 1994). In Western societies this typically involved some appeal to notions of sin, with deviance being attributed to humanity's innate wickedness, a view derived from the biblical story of Adam and Eve. Alternatively, the Church explained the actions of peculiar individuals or extreme natural developments such as floods, diseases, and crop failures, through appeal to demonic possession—the suggestion that the devil had taken control of people so that he could have them do his bidding. The most notorious example of authorities acting in light of a fear of possession were the European witch burnings that occurred from the sixteenth through the eighteenth centuries (Currie, 1998). As records from this period are scarce and unreliable there is wide discrepancy in the estimates of the number of women killed, which range from approximately one million to seven million.

Religious explanations for deviance are outside of the predominantly secular framework of today's scientific establishment. Nonetheless, religion still plays an important role in the larger societal dynamics of deviance. A large number of Canadians proclaim some form of religions faith. The religious groups to which they belong are often active in the politics of deviance, advocating for their views on normal and deviant behaviour. The recent example of the multi-religious coalition that sought to stop the legalization of gay marriage is a prominent case in point. Some religious groups are themselves routinely characterized as deviant, including the assorted "cults" that embrace extreme religious beliefs or practices (Dawson, 2006). Moreover, Satan himself continues to make an appearance in this broader public culture of deviance. One recent example concerns the claims that children in American daycares were subjected to a widespread conspiracy of ritualistic satanic abuse. Although these claims were ultimately dismissed, the accusations and ensuing public investigation of this panic destroyed the lives of many daycare providers, some of whom, unable to cope with the strain of being officially investigated and the stigma of being accused of satanic abuse, killed themselves (de Young, 1998).

Classical criminology

Unlike satanic possession, the theory of classical criminology is so familiar and often common sense that students are sometimes surprised to see it listed as a theory. Classical criminology is the basis for all Western criminal justice systems. Like other theories it holds certain assumptions about society and humanity, and the questionable nature of these assumptions have produced lingering difficulties for the operation of the contemporary criminal justice system.

Classical criminology aims to deter crime through the rational and calibrated use of the state's formal system of punishment. Its origins can be traced to the work of Cesare Beccaria (1819), who in 1764 wrote his masterpiece *An Essay on Crimes and Punishments*. Part of the context for his work was the ongoing rational critique of the existing system of punishment, which was a characteristic theme of Enlightenment thinking. Prisons

were chastised for being both violent and ineffective. Truly horrible places, jails were little more than filthy dungeons where men and women, the sane and insane, paupers and criminals, were all housed together. Corporal punishment was routine, and in England there were over 350 individual crimes for which a person could be executed, including robbery, burglary, and, perhaps most bizarrely, "impersonating an Egyptian." The type and severity of punishment was entirely at the discretion of the judge, a situation that often lead to similar crimes receiving strikingly different punishments. Reformers sought to make the operation of criminal justice more humane by introducing rational and proportional principles.

The reformers were not scientists but philosophers and moralists. Therefore their approach was based on certain assumptions about human nature. In particular, they believed in the **hedonistic calculus**, the idea that people routinely behave in light of a rational consideration of the anticipated benefits and costs of their actions. Crime was therefore assumed to be the product of criminals anticipating its financial or other personal rewards, while not believing there was much risk in such behaviour. The purpose of the criminal justice system, the reformers argued, should be to establish a series of laws that clearly established the punishments that people would receive for engaging in criminal acts. Lists of crimes and their maximum punishments were publicized to provide the public a sense of the likely punishment for crimes. Such codes were also to guide judges about the appropriate range of sanctions for different crimes. The reformers believed that the level of punishment should be finely calibrated to match the seriousness of the crime, and that punishments should not be excessive. While it might seem logical that the prospect of extremely severe punishment might also deter criminals, the reformers opposed excessive punishment because they believed it could undermine the legitimacy of the criminal justice system and of the state itself.

For the principles of classical criminology to work effectively two additional factors must be in place:

1. Official punishments must be certain. The public must believe that if they commit a crime it will be almost inevitable that they will be caught and punished.

2. The punishments must occur as quickly as possible after a crime is committed—often referred to as the principle of "swiftness."

The limitations of classical criminology, and therefore with the operation of parts of the contemporary Canadian justice system, can partially be traced to these questionable assumptions. It appears that it is almost impossible for our criminal justice system to meet a standard of certainty. Criminals often commit many undetected crimes before they are ever caught (if they are even ever caught). The requirements of a large and bureaucratic criminal justice system can also undermine the aim of ensuring swift punishment. It can take months or years to resolve minor criminal cases through the courts, and major trials can drag on for over a decade. An additional difficulty with the classical approach is that the reformers' assumptions that individuals engage in some kind of a rational calculus before committing crimes is severely questionable. The factors that contribute to people committing a wide range of crimes are often not rational, but are much more spontaneous and emotional. Finally, classical criminology has been criticized for having an overly free vision of human nature that overlooks the other types of factors that might shape or limit a person's "choice" about whether to engage in crimes, including individual personality, biology, psychology, or a host of social structural variables, all of which have been emphasized in subsequent theories.

Environmental criminology

Environmental criminology shares with classical criminology the desire to reduce crime, but it does not rely on the formal system of law and punishment to produce that effect. Instead, environmental criminology uses principles of environmental design to make it more difficult or impossible for people to commit crimes (Felson, 2002). One of the more prominent versions of this approach is "Crime Prevention Through Environmental Design" (CPTED), although the name itself is a misnomer. CPTED is not just concerned with reducing crime, but with reducing or eliminating a wide range of different forms of deviance and disorder. The way that this is to be accomplished is by changing the local environment in which crime might occur.

Environmental criminology is also based on certain assumptions about criminals, in particular that they are largely lazy and as a result will tend to take advantage of only criminal opportunities that are readily available to them. Environmental criminologists seek to reduce such opportunities. They do this in at least three different ways:

1. *Target hardening*: This involves efforts to shape the physical environment such that the possibilities for deviance are severely reduced. Examples include the familiar use of more locks and higher fences. More innovative examples include using barriers to stop skateboarders from riding along the sides of benches. Occasionally these measures can be rather harsh, such as when a Los Angeles municipality installed an overhead sprinkler system to deter the homeless from sleeping in a park—anyone who stayed in the park received a nightly drenching (Davis, 1990: 233).

2. *Enhanced visibility*: Environmental criminologists also try to deter criminals by making potentially attractive criminal targets more visible. So, for example, they advocate cutting back the shrubbery on your property to remove a burglar's potential hiding spots. Entire suburban communities have been designed so that houses face one another, producing a form of natural surveillance where neighbour watches neighbour (Newman, 1973). In recent years such forms of "natural surveillance" have been greatly augmented with the use of new surveillance technologies, particularly closed-circuit television (CCTV) cameras, to deter crime (Haggerty and Ericson, 2006).

3. *More guardians*: Criminal behaviour is more likely to occur in unsupervised spaces. Hence environmental criminologists advocate increasing the number of people who monitor public or private locations. This can include more police officers or security guards, but also includes the use of assorted forms of "neighborhood watch" schemes where citizens keep an eye out for potential criminal activity (McConville and Shepherd, 1992). Other forms of effective supervision might include park wardens or lifeguards.

Part of the attraction of environmental criminology is that many of the procedures it advocates are both ingenious and involve a certain degree of common sense. One recent example comes from downtown Vancouver, a city that has an unfortunate history of considerable poverty, homelessness, and alcohol and drug addiction. Many of these poor and addicted people have effectively taken over Vancouver's few public washrooms, using them for shelter and as a place to inject or smoke drugs. Washrooms became filthy and most citizens refused to use them. Rather than try to use the legal system to

Cameras and other forms of monitoring have become very popular ways to try to address crime and deviant behaviour.

resolve these problems, local authorities contemplated installing new APTs, which come at no cost to tax payers because the APT is funded through advertising sales on other street furniture including bus shelters. JCDecaux makes no claim that their APT will deter or change anti-social behaviour. Hopefully, of course, homeless people will use the APT rather than the street, and APTs also serve the non-homeless population, including tourists and shoppers.

These APTs have a number of unique features designed to reduce the prospect of deviant behaviour. The toilet door, for example, will only remain locked for a maximum of twenty minutes, at which point it opens automatically. This feature was designed to stop homeless people or drug users from lingering. After each use the toilet bowl retracts into the wall where it is washed, sanitized, and dried. The sinks are "hands-free," which means that users do not have to touch unsanitary sink handles, and also reduces opportunities for

vandalism. Blue lights can be installed in the unit to discourage intravenous drug use—the blue lights make it harder for drug addicts to find their veins. The toilet floor is composed of corrugated metal which, after each use, rolls out a clean section of floor while the previously exposed flooring is rolled into a disinfecting system contained under the floor. Finally, each unit is equipped with an emergency 911 call button and with sensors that alert supervisors when vandalism is taking place or when someone is lurking in the unit, potentially waiting to assault the next user.

Notwithstanding the innovative nature of such design features, environmental criminology has been criticized for not addressing the structural causes of crime or deviance. The root causes that might cause people to commit crime, such as addiction, mental illness or poverty, remain unresolved in this framework. Consequently the various design features that this approach advocates might not actually reduce the total

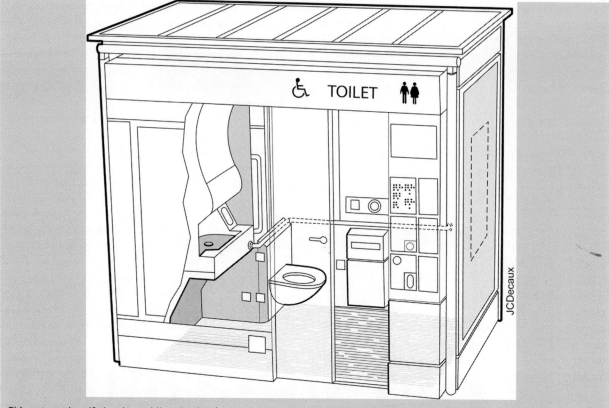

This automatic self-cleaning public toilet (APT) is an example of using design principles to alter human behaviour. The APT system has served 250 million people worldwide, including thousands in Vancouver, since it was invented by JCDecaux SA, the world leader in new street amenities. Among its many features, the door opens automatically after twenty minutes.

amount of crime, but instead simply move it around such that criminals move onto other targets that are less secure, a process known as **displacement**.

Biological and psychological theories

Biological theories *are* concerned with looking for the roots of deviant behaviour, which they believe lie in individuals. For example Dabbs (1990) concluded that testosterone level is related to violence and crime at a young age, trouble with parents and school, drug use, a greater number of sex partners, being absent without leave from the army, and being a fraternity "party animal." He also found that subjects from lower socio-economic backgrounds, on average, have higher levels of testosterone and a greater vulnerability to its effects than their better-off counterparts.

Researchers generally agree that biology plays a role in establishing some forms of mental illness. Schizophrenia, for example, is more genetic than social in origin, and biological factors are certainly important in the senile psychoses of the elderly. Other forms of mental illness, however, such as borderline personality disorder, are more likely caused by social factors such as physical abuse or the quality of parental care. In most cases, however, *both* social and biological factors are important. Beisner and Iacono (1990), for example, noted that a predisposition to schizophrenia is biological (and more common among males) but that environmental factors such as poverty and adverse working conditions play a role in triggering it. Part of the higher mental illness rates among the elderly is due to their loss of social status and their loneliness, not just biological aging.

Several selected psychological theories of deviance may also be briefly noted, as they also focus on individual causes. For example, criminal behaviour may be traced to individual personality, with the view that criminals crave excitement more than non-criminals (see Polakowski, 1994). Similarly, Freudians (recall Chapter 4, Socialization) may see some mental illness as the result of an inability of the ego, as mediator, to handle conflicts between the id, the superego, and the external world. This presentation of psychological theories is deliberately incomplete. It is intended merely to provide points of comparison for the sociological theories to come, which examine society's role in deviance.

Sociological criticisms of biological and psychological theories

Biological explanations of deviance are generally rejected by sociologists because they pay insufficient attention to the social factors that interact with their explanations. Thus it may not be the higher levels of testosterone (biological variable) in males that lead to crime, but the fact that they are more rewarded and encouraged by others (social variable) for their aggression and therefore learn to be more criminal. Also, because of their extroversion, they may be more noticed (social variable), thus inflating their deviance rates.

Another serious deficiency concerns the fluctuations in the amounts of deviance over time. Hartnagel's (2004) historical research demonstrates that conviction rates for indictable crimes were especially high from 1910 to 1920, a time of widespread immigration and mobility. These rates were at their lowest in the 1950s. Delinquency was also lower during the Depression, and higher during the World War II years (McCarthy and Hagan, 1987). Given that human biology is largely stable it is difficult to explain such dramatic shifts in criminal behaviour by appealing to purely biological causes.

In recent years developments in genetics have produced a great deal of optimism about the possibilities of explaining social behaviour in light of genetic causes. Occasionally one hears news of the discovery of a gene that causes crime. There are several problems with such claims. First, they present a single-cause model that is at odds with how genes operate. Genes work in combination with other genes; hence there is never a single gene for anything. Equally important, genetic factors do not operate on their own but are themselves shaped by environmental factors. For example, someone might have a genetic predisposition to being very tall, but if the person lives in an environment where nutritious food is scarce, he or she could be comparatively short (Lewontin, 1991).

Efforts to explain crime through genetics also ignores the fact that crime is a social category. Societies can and do change what is and is not a crime, which seems to undermine the notion that something as broad and diverse as crime can have a genetic cause. More sophisticated genetic approaches occasionally point out how genetic factors might contribute to some mediating factors, like the production of testosterone, which might then be correlated with increased aggression. However, this is a rather long and complicated causal chain. Aggression itself is not the cause of crime, as many crimes involve no aggression whatsoever. Moreover, even high levels of aggression do not necessarily translate into someone engaging in aggressive forms of criminality, as many people work out their aggression through socially approved outlets such as sports.

Psychological theories are also criticized by sociologists for the difficulty of measuring some of their concepts and for underestimating the influence of the social factors that precede psychological factors in deviance. Thus there is a difference in emphasis and focus between these two disciplines. Psychologists hold social variables such as race, sex, age, and social class constant, and then look for differences in psychological variables, while sociologists focus directly on those social variables. Sociologists thus take a step back in the causal chain; they want to know what social factors are related to psychological traits such as inadequate egos or extroversion.

Functionalism

One of the more curious propositions in the sociology of deviance is that deviance is normal. Here something is defined as normal if it is inevitable and if it serves positive social functions. Functionalist sociologists point out that deviance meets both of those criteria. Every known society has treated some behaviours as deviant. So long as these are not widespread and/or serious enough to undermine the basic fabric of society, deviance can be beneficial in several ways (Coser, 1964). First, deviants can become scapegoats, and in responding to the actions of scapegoats a society can unify itself. Deviants can also help unite conformists by serving as common enemies, especially when no external enemies exist. Deviants can also increase the conformists' cohesion, productivity, and well-being. As such, deviance helps to set the moral boundaries between groups, serving the social function of dividing "us" from "them."

Second, deviants can be used to mark the bottom layer of society and to clearly illustrate the meaning of abstract rules. Paying attention to deviants enables non-deviants to see exactly what is not allowed (proscribed) or what is demanded (prescribed). In fact, Erikson (1966) argued that if there were no deviants to serve as "inferior" comparisons, society would have to redefine some non-deviant behaviours as deviant in order to satisfy this need.

Third, deviance can call attention to flaws in the social system and serve as an early warning that something is wrong. Thus, like smoke detectors, deviance can help society avoid other potentially larger, more damaging problems.

Fourth, deviance can begin a process of social adaptation and progress to new and better norms and values. Many advocates of values now commonly accepted were once defined as deviant when they initially pressed for social change. Jesus and Gandhi were deviant in this sense. Nineteenth-century feminists who demanded equality for women were also labelled as deviant.

Fifth, minor forms of deviant behaviour can serve as societal safety valves. They permit individuals to let off steam, and in the process perhaps prevent more serious disruptions. For example, the minor deviance associated with fan celebrations after a home team world championship may actually prevent the greater deviance that could erupt without such an outlet.

Finally, deviance can serve as a source of employment. Thousands and perhaps millions of people now earn their livelihood in a way that is somehow connected to the existence of deviant individuals. This includes the people directly employed by the criminal justice system (Christie, 1993), but also a host of other occupations and industries including therapists, TV talk show hosts, pharmaceutical executives, and criminologists.

Strain

Acquiring wealth and material goods are widely shared ambitions. The education system, the mass media, parents, and peers may all encourage this pursuit. Not everyone, unfortunately, can have material success and there are not enough legitimate means available for everyone to own a Porsche, a mansion, and Tiffany diamonds. The discrepancy between the goals a society encourages and the legitimate means it provides to achieve those goals can lead to a state of normlessness, a large-scale breakdown of rules, called **anomie**. According

to Merton's (1968) functionalist model, the greater the discrepancy between means and goals, the greater the anomie, and the greater the amount of deviance that can be expected.

Most readers of this book are using the acceptable means of higher education to achieve material success, a legitimate goal. Merton called such behaviour *conformity*. Conformists accept the goals of society and possess the means to achieve them. Individuals without access to legitimate means have four additional options to achieve those goals, each of which Merton considered deviant in some way. First, they can lower their goals to the level of their means, and engage in **ritualism**. Ritualists are the honest, hard-working people who live in modest or rented homes, own older cars, and take few holidays. They are deviant to the extent that they have abandoned the fancy success goals, not that they have broken society's formal rules.

The second option for those who lack legitimate means is to keep the goals but to engage in what Merton called **innovation**. Innovators range from criminals to exam cheaters—individuals who use deviant means to achieve non-deviant ends. Rather than becoming bankers and lawyers, innovators become thieves and con artists in an effort to acquire material goods.

Retreatism, a third category in Merton's anomie model, involves rejecting both the means and the goals of society and, instead, withdrawing from society. Drug addicts, for example, represent a classic form of retreatism. Retreatists can also include members of religious groups who substitute different valued goals (e.g., salvation or contemplation) for the more common goal of worldly success. If such individuals become too controversial in their activities, as in the case of some religious sects (see Chapter 11, Religion), their behaviour may then be seen as **rebellion**, the fourth and final type of deviance in the model. Rebels are in essence active retreatists, loudly rejecting society's means and goals and advocating for a new social system. Merton's four types of deviance vary, but they all share an effort to look for the causes of deviance in the structure of society, not in individuals themselves.

In support of Merton's ideas, most research shows that official crime rates are higher among the disadvantaged. Those with less access to legitimate means, such as higher education and full employment engage in more serious and more violent crimes (Hartnagel, 2004). As before, these rates might be inflated by the biases of criminal justice officials, but the assaults and murders you read of in the paper are found more often among the underprivileged.

Merton's focus on the discrepancy between widely accepted goals and the supply of adequate legitimate means for their achievement set the stage for still other theories. For example, Cohen's (1955) theory of gang delinquency argues that many adolescents, especially lower-class boys, do not have the values and skills (means) necessary to succeed by the criteria (goals) demanded by the middle-class school system. Sensing failure and feeling disapproval from teachers and peers alike, the boys band together to seek a group solution to their problem. Rejecting the schools' middle-class standards, which they find almost impossible to achieve, they establish a **contraculture**, a way of life exactly opposite to the middle-class ideal, but one in which they can succeed. If middle-class values include politeness, promptness, and care of property, these boys will be rude, late, and destructive. Thus in a way they are similar to Merton's rebels. Cohen called this inversion of middle-class values **reaction formation**.

Problems with anomie theory

Merton's anomie theory generated much criticism. Some objected to his unproven assumption that everyone shares common success goals. Another criticism concerns the fact that anomie theory was developed in the United States and does not apply as well to other countries. Lipset's (1996) comparison of Canada and the United States would suggest that Canadians' greater respect for authority should result in less anomie here. Ironically, Canada has higher rates of property crime which, following Merton's argument, should not be the case given Canada's more generous social programs.

A larger criticism concerns Merton's apparent acceptance of official crime rates, data that may reflect lower-class crime better than middle- and upper-class crime. Anomie theory holds up less well when self-report studies show that many of the rich are innovators rather than conformists, such as the officials who accept bribes or kickbacks for work contracts or the corporate executives who fix prices (Glasbeek, 2002). Their deviance cannot be explained by a lack of means in any usual sense of the word. In their personal lives, more expensive cars and clothes; larger, more luxurious homes; and longer, more exotic holidays could be the lofty achievements that motivate the innovation of the rich. Only by arguing that these people lack legitimate means to allow them to achieve *extraordinary* goals would anomie theory work (see Snider, 1992).

Conflict-oriented theorists have noted that Merton simply takes it for granted that some people will lack the means. Anomie theory views crime as a dysfunction that greater opportunities can correct. But to many conflict critics, the inherent greed of the capitalist system is the cause of inadequate means. To these critics, only an extensive reconstruction of society, one that could remove inequality, will suffice. Welfare and unemployment insurance are insufficient (Schissel, 1992).

Cloward and Ohlin (1960) questioned Merton's assumption that everyone has access to deviant means, pointing out that individuals need access to *illegitimate* means to become innovators. Being a criminal is not necessarily easy. If most people wanted to become a computer hacker, for example, they would need to learn certain criminal skills, and then have access to opportunities to innovate. Such criminal opportunities are required for anyone who might want to engage in crimes.

Like many criminological theories (see the next section) Merton's theory can also be faulted for ignoring the situation of women. One might suspect that as women are more often denied means than men, they should be highly criminal. Yet women generally have low crime rates. Merton's failure to consider women is particularly unfortunate as his idea of crime being associated with illegitimate means might help explain some of the relationship between gender and crime. Part of the under-representation of women among criminals may be due to women being given fewer criminal opportunities (Reitsma-Street, 1999). Women may not be accepted by male criminals, they do not spend as much time in places where crimes occur, and they are less often in the positions of responsibility necessary to engage in white-collar crime.

Feminism

Feminists have presented some of the most powerful insights into the dynamics of deviance while drawing attention to many of the sexist assumptions that have pervaded the study of crime. Feminist perspectives on deviance arose in response to the imbalance inherent in a discipline written by, and generally about, men. They sought to supplement traditional male examinations of shoplifters, prostitutes, and strippers with a focus on sexual assault, spouse battering, and other forms of exploitation of women.

In both their research and politics feminists have challenged many myths about male and female criminality.

There are various forms of feminism, which can be differentiated according to politics, theory, and methodology. All share the common concern that rules are made by the powerful (men) to control the less powerful. This frequently leads to examinations of how gender-based forms of regulation limit women's opportunities. That said, feminists do not focus exclusively on women, but are concerned with gender dynamics more generally. For example, one of the important questions to have emerged recently concerns questioning the apparent *maleness* of crime. Such research examines how engaging in crime can help men form a distinctive masculine identity—and the implications of this process for both men and women (Newburn and Stanko, 1994). Feminists have also helped to broaden sociological analysis to examine how processes relating to deviance and normality operate across and between different sites of social exclusion and oppression including ethnicity, sexual orientation, and physical ability (Gelsthorpe and Morris, 1990).

Feminists have drawn particular attention to the operation of **gendered norms**, which refers to the processes whereby social rules and expectations operate differently between men and women, often producing a gendered-based double standard. For example, as noted previously, feminists have examined how norms regarding ideal physical appearance operate more coercively for women than men. Likewise, they have accentuated how efforts to control prostitution have almost always involved regulating women, and less often dealt with the male clients for commercial sex (Walkowitz, 1980). The realm of sexuality is rife with different gendered norms, as women have long been held to a different standard of sexual behaviour. For example, Nicole Hann Rafter's research on prisons in the United States from 1800 until 1935 (Rafter, 1990) found that in one New York prison for women at least half of the inmates were convicted of sexual misbehaviour.

Other institutions also play a role in regulating women. Gavigan (1987) has pointed out how the medical profession has often treated women's bodies as deviant. Likewise, psychiatrists have been criticized for their sexist views. Rohde-Dascher and Price (1992) have written about the patriarchal origins of psychoanalysis and its sexist view of women's roles. Psychiatrists disproportionately tend to treat women's problems as related to different forms of psychiatric illnesses, a process known as **pathologizing** (Menzies, Chun, and Webster, 1992). As Kaplan (1983) has noted, many of the traditional definitions of mental health were biased against women, with "normal" being equated with male behaviour.

Feminist criminologists are often asked to address the fact that women account for considerably less crime than men, typically only accounting for less than 20 percent of adult crime. This lesser involvement has meant that women's criminality has often been much less visible in criminology (Heidensohn, 1968). It has also meant that women who do come into contact with the criminal justice system typically have fewer possibilities for programming, training, and education, as the female population is often seen by officials to be too small to warrant such initiatives (Adelberg and Currie, 1987).

Historically the male-dominated approach to the discrepancy between male and female crime rates involved trying to explain why women commit so few crimes. This way of framing the issue is an example of using a male norm to evaluate female behaviour (Naffine, 1987). Feminists have sought to turn this question on its head, and asked what it is about men that accounts for their higher rates of crime. The few male authors who did examine female criminality typically revealed their sexist assumptions in the process. Writing in 1895, Caesare Lombroso and William Ferrero (Lombroso and Ferrero, 1895) argued that women's limited intelligence contributed to their criminality, and that female criminals were innately cunning and deceitful. The assumption that women were less intelligent than men even biased early IQ tests. Researchers conducting the first round of IQ tests found that women consistently had higher IQs than men. The (male) researchers responded by removing all of the questions on which women did better than men to ensure that the test results would meet their expectations about female intelligence (Hacking, 1995: 5).

This emphasis on intelligence was an early example of what became a widespread effort to locate female criminality in women's unique biology. Otto Pollack (1961), for example, proposed that the lower rate of female criminality could be attributed to both the chivalry of a predominantly male criminal justice system, but also to women's inherent cunning, which contributed to their being able to get men to do their criminal bidding. Pollack traced these deceptive skills to women's biology, specifically to the ability of women to fake orgasm, which he believed provided women with unique training and skills in deception, which they then used to commit crimes. While such obviously sexist theories have been abandoned, efforts continue to locate female criminality in female biology, including research on the role that premenstrual syndrome might play in female aggression. Feminists have been critical of such research for its various conceptual and mythological limitations (see Kendall, 1991).

In lieu of biological explanations, a number of researchers have sought to explain gender differences in crime by examining how sex roles are learned. One example is the **power-control theory** of Hagan and his colleagues (Hagan, Simpson, and Gillis, 1989). The crucial assumption in this approach is that mothers have a greater role in socializing children than do fathers, and that daughters are more controlled than sons. The result, claimed Hagan et al., is higher deviance rates among boys. This gender difference is least pronounced in homes where both mother and father have jobs. In these more egalitarian families, mothers have more power and they treat their daughters and sons more alike. The daughters, in turn, are more like the sons in their

deviance. Gender differences in deviance are greatest in patriarchal households, which are common when the father is controlled at work and the wife is either not employed outside the home or, if so, is also controlled. In such patriarchal families, mothers control their daughters more than their sons, leading the girls to be less inclined to take risks and to be less frequently deviant. Data for less serious forms of delinquency support this interpretation and may help to explain why wealthy adolescents engage in some forms of delinquency more than those less well off. They are less coerced, take more risks, and see themselves as above the rules and with freedom to deviate (Hagan and Kay, 1990).

Adler's (1975) research into female criminality also examined the operation of gender roles. She argued that women's lesser criminality could be attributed to their reduced position in society. Consequently, she proposed the **liberation hypothesis**, which holds that as women become more liberated and have greater job opportunities they will also engage in more crime, just like their male counterparts. And while there has been some evidence of a convergence between the crime rates for men and women, the gap has not been narrowed to the extent predicted by Adler's theory. More problematically, the types of women who are engaged in crime continue to be among the poorest and most disenfranchised segments of society, not those who are the most liberated. Finally, Adler is also guilty of taking male behaviour as the norm and setting out to explain why women are different (Naffine, 1997).

Feminists have also been central in efforts to understand the situation of crime victims, something that has contributed to the development of the field of *victimology*. Much of this work can be traced to early feminist concerns with the dynamics of rape (Brownmiller, 1976)—now legally referred to as "sexual assault" in Canada. Their interest in this topic has a dual focus. First, feminists have sought to develop greater knowledge about the general dynamics of male violence against women. From this has come an awareness that rape is consistently among women's greatest fears, and that it is comparatively common. Moreover, rape typically does not involve an assault by an unknown stranger, but is usually perpetrated by an acquaintance, friend, or family member, assaults that are referred to as "acquaintance rapes" and accunt for approximately 90 percent of all rapes.

The second major feminist agenda in relation to sexual assault has involved challenging and modifying many of the sexist assumptions that have been institutionalized in the Canadian legal system. This has included confronting the myths surrounding rape, which have included the view that rape is a sexual act, when in fact it is about violence; that women say "no" when they really mean "yes"; and that if a woman has had sex in the past she cannot be trusted when she says she did not consent to sex. Some of the notable feminist successes in this regard include the withdrawal of the legal "marital exemption," which made it impossible to convict a man for raping his wife; the removal of the requirement that a rape conviction could not occur without corroborating evidence—something that was based on the assumption that a woman could not be trusted. The recent introduction of "rape shield" laws also prohibits questioning a woman about her previous sexual history unless it is judged to have a direct bearing on the case.

[Research Focus]

Rape in Warfare

Only recently have criminologists examined the act of rape in the context of warfare. The large volume of rape committed during warfare suggests that this is a significant sociological oversight. Given that these offences often take place in a context when normal data-recording practices have collapsed, it is difficult to derive accurate numbers on the volume of rape in warfare. By any estimation it is massive. Some of the more prominent examples include the 20 000 to 50 000 women raped in Bosnia (mostly Muslims raped by Serbian forces) or the 200 000 to 400 000 women raped in Bangladesh by Pakistani soldiers in 1971 after a failed rebellion. Another prominent example involved the 1937 attack by the Japanese army on the city of Nanking, which was then the capital of China (Chang, 1997). The assault culminated in an orgy of mass murder and the systematic rape and murder of between 20 000 and 80 000 women over a six-week period. Such rapes were indiscriminate, and included assaults on prepubescent girls, grandmothers, and pregnant women. Many of these women were killed after they were raped as a way of keeping them silent.

Many reasons have been advanced to explain rape during warfare. Within the small-group context of the military, gang rape appears to promote group cohesion, and soldiers have participated in such acts to avoid becoming an outcast (recall the earlier example of soldiers who collect human trophies). Such assaults also occur in a context of normlessness where the normal rules of society have been abandoned and feelings of aggression have been cultivated. Early theories argued that rape could be attributed to the lack of normal sexual outlets that is characteristic of war. Such a position is flawed by virtue of the fact that it equates rape with sex, when rape is ultimately about violence. Goldstein (2001: 363) puts this matter succinctly: "Rape is a crime of domination and war has everything to do with domination."

Rape during warfare has served explicitly political purposes. Historically, mass rapes were an attempt to humiliate enemy males by despoiling their valued (female) property. The rape of approximately 100 000 German women by Russian solders in the Berlin area at the end of World War II appears to have entailed a form of revenge against the German people for the atrocities perpetrated by German troops in Russia. Rape also has been part of a conscious effort to destroy certain groups, as in Bosnia where rape was a part of a policy of ethnic cleansing, used to humiliate and terrorize a population and to drive them from their desirable territory.

While rape in wartime has long been illegal under international law, it has usually been treated as a crime against honour, not a crime of violence and has rarely been prosecuted. The war crimes tribunal for the former Yugoslavia was the first official agency to treat sexual assault as a "crime against humanity." Such small steps might mark a shift in the official response to wartime rape, something that was often ignored, or only seen to be a problem by military authorities to the extent that it might expose fighting troops to venereal disease.

There have been increasing pressures to punish individuals who commit rape in warfare by using criminal sanctions. What factors might inhibit the success of such efforts?

Differential association

The basic symbolic interactionist position explains deviance by examining how it is interpreted by individual deviants. Each act of deviance is seen as unique, and a subjective interpretation by the person who performs it will explain even its seemingly irrational aspects (Katz, 1988). One of the earliest symbolic interactionist theories of crime was advanced by Sutherland (1939), who argued that individuals learn crime the same way they learn conformity—in contact with others. He maintained that if behaviour—normal or deviant—is rewarded, it will be repeated. You read about this in Chapter 4, Socialization. The key to learning conformity as opposed to deviance is the group with which an individual interacts. If individuals interact more with others who socialize them to value deviance, either directly by rewarding it or indirectly by providing role models and perhaps vicarious reinforcement, they may develop an excess of pro-deviance definitions of the world and become deviant. If, on the other hand, they interact more with others who socialize them to value conformity, they should learn pro-social definitions of the world and become conformist. Thus the name of his theory is **differential association**: learning through association with groups having differing values.

Expanding on Sutherland's ideas, Sykes and Matza (1957) argued that most delinquents feel guilty and can engage in illegal behaviour only after rationalizing that guilt through **techniques of neutralization**. These techniques, which are learned and shared among delinquents, permit them to define their behaviour as acceptable, which allows them to stay basically committed to conventional society. They outlined five such techniques:

1. Denial of injury; for example, "No one gets hurt by shoplifting."

2. Denial of the victim; for example, "The victims deserved what they got."

3. Denial of personal responsibility; for example, "I was drunk when it happened."

4. Condemning the condemners; for example, "Everyone is doing it", or "Other people do worse things and get away with it."

5. Appeal to higher loyalties; for example, "I couldn't let my friends down; I had to help them."

Different individuals draw upon these techniques in different ways and at different times. The point is that individuals drift in and out of deviant activities, back and forth between conformity and deviance, in contrast to the views of functionalists and conflict theorists alike, who tend to draw a sharp distinction between deviants and conformists.

Evidence against this drift position comes from Sampson and Laub's (1990) findings that childhood delinquency is linked to adult crime, alcohol abuse, school failure, unemployment, divorce, economic dependency, and other deviance. No drift is apparent in that overall deviant pattern, and instead social deprivation may be a key contributing factor. It might therefore be that drift theory is less applicable to the socially disadvantaged. It appears that middle-class juvenile delinquency is more often transient, reducing or disappearing as a youth progresses into adulthood. Bias may also be a factor here. If caught (Hagan, 1992), middle-class delinquents are more likely to be given a second chance, thus allowing them to return to respectable society. Poorer delinquents are less frequently given those second chances. As a consequence, they cannot drift out of deviance as easily.

A more serious criticism of the whole differential association perspective is that it appears circular. What causes the culture that is passed on in intimate groups that then encourages or allows crime and deviance? Also, why do some learn to define deviance as acceptable, while others who live in similar circumstances do not? There are no definitive answers to these questions, but the next symbolic interactionist position attempts to provide at least a partial response.

Labelling

No matter what acts or conditions a society sees as deviant, not everyone who fits the definition will be discovered. This fact draws attention to an additional dynamic of deviance: once the definitions exist, the reaction of others (the audience) is crucial in deciding who is and who is not a deviant. Not only are the definitions of deviance social, their application to specific individuals is also social. Official counts (statistics) of deviance, such as crime and mental illness rates, are then also social products. These ideas are illustrated in Figure 5.6 and the discussion that follows.

In box (1) are *deviants*, so-called because they perform deviant acts or are perceived to be unusual in some way, and because their audiences respond to their deviance. In box (4) are *innocents*, who perform no deviant acts and

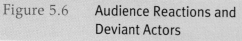

Figure 5.6   Audience Reactions and Deviant Actors

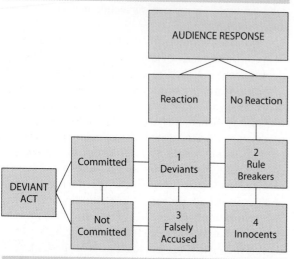

receive no audience reactions. The picture is more complicated in relation to boxes (2) and (3), rule breakers and the falsely accused, respectively. **Rule breakers** commit deviant acts, but for various reasons no one responds to their behaviour. Most individuals at one time or another are rule breakers, as we have all broken some rules for which we were not caught or for which we were excused for some reason. Such rule breakers can be compared to the *falsely* accused in box (3). Such individuals have not committed the deviant act for which they have been accused or even punished.

Conflict sociologists argue that there are at least as many rule breakers as deviants, with actual amounts (rule-breaking rates) of alcoholism, drug abuse, crime, and mental illness in Canada all much greater than shown in official data. The 32 466 Canadians in prison on any one day therefore represent the tip of the iceberg (Beattie, 2005). The same process is apparent in relationship to mental illness. Hagan (1991) estimated that as many as 25 percent of Canadians suffer psychological impairment. Only about half of that number sees a doctor for such problems in any one year.

A related point is that any change in the number of labellers, their deployment, and their resources can create corresponding increases or decreases in deviance,

without changes in the actual rule-breaking behaviour. So the introduction of more police can, for example, lead to an increase in the official crime rate because the police can now process more cases. In another context, provincial governments are quite aware that the greater the number of doctors licensed, the more illness that is treated.

Even with a constant number of labellers, any change in focus can affect deviance rates. For example, the recent decline in arrests for marijuana use is only partly attributed to fewer users; another factor relates to the courts and police turning attention from marijuana to harder drugs and from users to dealers. These examples show that deviance is a social activity involving more than the individual deviants. Reactors are a crucial part of the process, which is another reason why caution must always be exercised when interpreting official statistics of crime and deviance.

Finally, there are some fairly widely accepted rules for excusing deviance (Edgerton, 1985). Thus reactions to the same deviance do not fall equally on all groups of people. In a classic study William Chambliss (1973) examined the police relationships to two groups of youth—which he referred to as the "Saints" and the "Roughnecks." The Saints were upwardly mobile and came from respectable upper-class families, whereas the Roughnecks were poor and destined for working-class jobs. Chambliss monitored their criminal activity over an extended period of time and found that members of each group were engaged in approximately the same levels of deviant behaviour, including fighting, impaired driving, cheating in school, underage drinking, dangerous driving, and vandalism. However, none of the Saints had ever been arrested for their behaviour whereas the Roughnecks were constantly in trouble with the police. In fact, each member of the Roughnecks was arrested during the course of the research, several spent at least one night in jail, and two were sentenced to six months' incarceration in boys' schools. Such findings provide support for the suggestion that police biases about the types of people who commit crime can lead them to pay over-attention to such groups, which can, in turn, contribute to members of those groups being disproportionately charged with crimes.

This differential ability to respond to deviance is referred to as *discretion*, which provides officials with the *choice* to react or not. Discretion also gives rise to accusations of various forms of prejudice and discrimination. The racial profiling that lies behind the selective stopping

[Research Focus]

A Self-Fulfilling Prophecy

The general model of labelling theory is one of a *self-fulfilling prophecy*:

1. Deviance occurs; it is widespread and caused by diverse factors, by anomie, differential association, etc. This is called **primary deviance**.

2. An audience reacts, beginning the transformation of some of those involved from *rule breakers* into *deviants*.

3. Additional deviance occurs; again it has many sources.

4. This additional deviance is followed by stronger reactions from others, who begin to take steps to segregate the deviants from the conformists. On their part, the deviants seek out others, similarly labelled, who in turn welcome the new recruits as allies and provide them with additional opportunities for deviance.

5. Still more deviance may occur, and more reactions follow. Those labelled complain about being singled out and direct some hostility at the labellers.

6. These acts generally bring on even stronger audience reactions. In a process called *role engulfment,* "deviant" becomes the *master status* of those so labelled—that is, it is the dominant way in which they are identified. Their conformity is ignored or misinterpreted and their deviance magnified out of proportion. The audience expects deviant behaviour and tends to interpret otherwise normal behaviours as deviant.

7. The process continues as the labellers further isolate the deviants, who in turn spend more and more time with others similarly labelled. The deviants, starting perhaps with the weakest and most vulnerable among them, begin to define themselves as deviant.

Finally, secondary deviance occurs, caused not by the deviant self-concepts that arise from the isolation, segregation, alienation, and even self-hatred of those labelled deviant. Isolated acts of deviance can thus become regular and stabilized, changed into *deviant careers* because of the reactions of others.

The notion of a self-fulfilling prophecy has typically been applied to negative labels. Can you think instances where a comparable process might be at work with more positive labels?

---

of racial minority car drivers also results in an inflated number of charges for things like driving while intoxicated, drug possession, and violating past court orders.

In the area of mental illness, some conflict theorists argue that all people do things that could potentially be defined insane, but only some are labelled that way. Do you ever talk to yourself, feel claustrophobic in elevators or crowds, or believe in fantasies because they make you happy? Any one of these could be a sign of mental illness. Conflict theorists argue that a lack of power is often an important factor (although not the only one) in applying a mental illness label. Part of the higher official mental illness rates found among single or lower-class individuals may therefore be due to their relative lack of resources and greater vulnerability to being labelled (Scheff, 1984 [1966]). Similar behaviours engaged in by the rich and famous may be simply passed off as "eccentric" or treated in private facilities where they can avoid being officially labelled.

Social-control theory

The unique aspect of social-control theory is that rather than asking why people deviate, it asks why *don't* people deviate. To answer this question it focuses on families, schools, and other groups that serve as socialization agents, provide the bonds that discourage deviance, and include role models for conformist behaviour.

Hirschi (1969) popularized this position and maintained that meaningful attachment to family and friends pulls people away from deviance. This occurs as they consider the opinions of those significant others before acting. Besides attachment, other ties include involvement, or investment of time and energy in conventional activities, and beliefs in pro-social values. Like attachment, they lead to a commitment to and respect for the value of conformity, and thus less deviance. Correspondingly, such things as alienation from family, empty time and leisure, and pro-deviant sentiments weaken social control and permit deviance. Here we examine the effect on two specific ties only—family and school.

Families are a potentially important resource for both children and spouses. Regarding children, a meta-analysis—one that examines all previous research on a topic to reach a general conclusion—found that broken homes are related to delinquency, for both boys and girls. Broken homes play more of a factor in minor than in major forms of delinquency and, paralleling this, they are more strongly related to self-report than official data. For adults, the major familial social tie is marriage. Becoming unmarried has effects on drinking as does single status generally, especially among males. At the same time, marriage and job stability inhibit criminal behaviour (Sampson and Laub, 1990).

Turning to the school as a source of social ties, Hartnagel and Tanner (1986) found that school experience is an important factor in predicting delinquency. A weak attachment to high school, found more frequently among boys in lower-ability groups, is related to delinquency regardless of social class. Working part-time while in school may also be a factor. Tanner and Krahn (1991) argued that low attachment to school leads to the part-time work, which in turn leads to drinking and also to association with deviant peers who have sought a similar escape from school activities in their part-time work.

There are several criticisms of the social-control position. Some critics reject its assumption that all people would be deviant if they could. They do not believe that a release from social ties is all that stands between most people and robbing banks, or sexually assaulting or killing others. Rather than focusing on the absence of restraining factors as a cause of crime, these critics still want to look at *push* factors, at differences in individual motivation to commit crimes. They argue, for example, that anomie theory's concept of strain and the frustration of being encouraged to achieve what turn out to be unachievable goals must have some effect on individual decisions to commit crimes.

Critics also ask how control theory can account for the crimes and other deviance of the powerful, those who are closely attached to others, are deeply involved in conventional activities, and appear to be committed to conformity. Are these people tied perhaps to their corporations and not to society at large? For answers to these questions, we turn to structural theories that are more conflict oriented.

Conflict-structural explanations

Conflict theorists believe that society is held together by coercion not cooperation, and argue that definitions of deviance arise out of special interests. Those with power get to have their definitions of deviance prevail while those without power must get along as best they can. Feminism, noted above, can therefore be considered a variant of conflict theory.

Conflict theory has two main variants. According to the first, a more Weberian position sometimes called **pluralism**, various segments of society, such as the wealthy, the religious, or even bureaucrats in the criminal justice system, compete to have their definitions of deviance accepted. Becker (1973 [1963]) called these individuals **moral entrepreneurs**, people and groups who seek to influence the passing of rules and the setting of standards. Although these individuals often claim that they are working for the benefit of society, there are often more self-serving reasons for their behaviour. For example, labour groups supported early twentieth-century Canadian narcotics legislation. They saw in the anti-opium laws the potential for deporting Chinese immigrants, whom they saw as a threat to their own employment because of their willingness to accept lower wages (Solomon and Madison, 1986).

The second variant of the conflict position accepts Marxist principles and originates from what is sometimes called the *radical* or **critical school**. It sees an economic elite as the major force behind definitions of what is and what is not deviant (Comack, 1985). With either variant of the conflict position, whether it is a single economic elite or several competing groups that define deviance, the general conflict argument is that definitions of deviance often represent special interests. Conflict theorists do not deny the possibility of consensus, but they recognize that so long as social inequality exists, the powerful will use their position to ensure that their own interests are met. Relations of domination, then, ensure that those "on top" are in a position to define "the other" as deviant. Their investigations therefore tend to be directed toward the rules and standards themselves and the groups that profit (economically or otherwise), by providing definitions of deviance. Finally, conflict theorists do not see

Chuck Guité testified before the Gomery commission about widespread corruption at the highest Levels of the Canadian federal goverment in its awarding of federal sponsorship contracts leading up to the 1995 Quebec referendum.

deviance as functional. Deviance divides rather than unites, as it encourages people to be judgmental, sometimes distrustful of one another, even afraid of whole groups of people. In the process it deflects attention from the larger issues of inequality, racism, sexism, and the consequences of capitalist greed.

Less radical conflict theorists are aware of things like capitalist pollution and price-fixing, but also include crimes not specific to capitalists in their analyses, like the daily physical assaults to which the oppressed are so frequently vulnerable. These latter theorists also place somewhat less blame on the police and courts, and accept the possibility of reform. The two views do agree, however, that power is a crucial factor in any explanation of deviance. For radicals, it is economic power; for the less radical, other sources of power are important too.

More radical theorists focus more on problems created by capitalism, like unemployment and reduction in buying power for those with jobs, increasingly found in the developed world. Capitalists, they argue, use the law and prisons to remove the under-classes from a glutted labour market and to render them tame. The purpose of the law, according to Spitzer (1975), is to transform "social dynamite," like unemployed youth, into what he calls "social junk," a category in which he included the elderly and mentally ill, also potentially costly but less of a threat to the capitalist order. Some see the legal system as a tool to control the poor. Rather than legalize drugs, capitalists use the government to keep them illegal in order to reduce the potential of the "dangerous" classes for large-scale organized civil disturbance (Christie, 1993).

The other distinguishing mark of the radical position is its demand for a total restructuring of society, one that would eradicate inequality and replace current short-term and inadequate solutions to the problem of deviance by making more legitimate means available. Critical theorists think that researchers should be part of this transformation, to put their theories into action in what they call *praxis*, a term introduced in Chapter 2, Research Methods.

A few concluding comments are in order before we leave our discussion of theories. First, it should be apparent by now that there is no theory that is free from criticism. All theories are limited and it would be naïve to believe that we could develop a theory that was immune to criticism. It would also be naïve to think that the study of deviance could do without theory, as theories are essentially ways of looking at and thinking about the world. Without a theory of how the world operates there would be no reason to study crime and deviance. Moreover, researchers would be at a loss about how to proceed as it is theory that directs a researcher to examine particular social dynamics and processes.

Some of the theories outlined above have very different starting assumptions about the nature of society or humanity. Feminism, for example, which is often (wrongly) viewed by the uninitiated as a single approach, encompasses a variety of different theoretical orientations. Unfortunately, the different starting points for different theories can occasionally lead theorists to judge each other's positions too harshly. For example, radicals often portray functionalists as right-wingers and law-and-order advocates who blame the true victims of inequality and oppression (the criminals) and seek only minor adjustments to what are major structural faults. Functionalists see radicals as idealists who blame the rich for everything—as philosophers more than sociologists, holding theories that are contradicted by the data.

Michel Foucault

The nature of Michel Foucault's research makes his approach difficult to classify, which is compounded by the fact that his interests were in philosophy, not sociology or criminology. That said, sociologists and criminologists have been profoundly influenced by his work. The fact that his thinking touches on issues pertaining to deviance in the context of societies characterized by unequal power relations makes it reasonable to briefly introduce his work in the context of conflict theories.

One of Foucault's recurring themes involved large-scale historical changes in the dynamics of power in Western societies. His book *Discipline and Punish* (Foucault, 1977), for example, re-examined the historical transformations in punishment that occurred in Europe in the eighteenth century. Whereas many historians have interpreted the decline in corporal and capital punishment and the attendant rise in efforts to "reform" offenders as a story of humanitarian progress, Foucault saw these as more ambiguous and perhaps sinister developments.

Inside the penitentiaries of the eighteenth century there developed an optimistic program of "rehabilitation" that sought to reform offenders. Inmates were no longer to be beaten, tortured, and otherwise left to languish. Instead, new professions, such as criminology and psychiatry, took an active interest in learning as much as possible about inmates, all in hopes of transforming their behaviour. This entailed the development of a host of new practices, including segregating inmates in individual cells and the detailed documentation of their behaviour. This documentation typically occurred with the aid of elaborate charts and timetables that precisely ordered an inmate's entire day. Behavioural norms were explicitly outlined, and inmates were actively encouraged to meet these standards. To encourage their reform inmates were subjected to continuous evaluation through new testing procedures. Perhaps most notable among these practices was an emphasis on monitoring offenders, such that the prison authorities could keep a constant eye on how

inmates were behaving. It was hoped that by structuring this surveillance in such a way that the inmates would never know they were being scrutinized, they would embrace and internalize the norms established by prison authorities, and start to reform themselves.

Foucault saw these techniques as forming the basis for a new form of power, which he called "disciplinary power." Disciplinary power did not aim to punish an offender's body, but alter their character and their personality, all as a means of transforming their behaviour. What made these prison-based developments important was that they spread into wider society, and were instituted in various schools, reformatories, and hospitals. Such locations were the basis of a general increase in disciplinary power, a power that was more "soft" and subtle than the barbaric regime it replaced, but one that also represented a more effective and economical form of power that touched almost every member of society. In essence, Foucault's analysis of the prison took the humanitarian prison reform movement and suggested that it inaugurated a new more subtle and pervasive form of social power.

Foucault's influence on the social sciences has been profound. He reinvigorated the study of norms, drawing attention to the connection between norms and larger structures of power. His work also stimulated re-examinations of the contemporary criminal justice system. Such studies often outlined how ostensible "lesser" forms of punishment might actually involve an expansion of state power (Cohen, 1985). As one of the leading philosophers of the twentieth century, Foucault's work has also predictably been the subject of much criticism (see Hoy, 1986). Prominent among such criticisms is that his analysis might not apply to contemporary prisons where the aim of reforming inmates has been significantly reduced (see Garland, 2001). Also, Foucault's work can be very despairing as it appears to leave little room for the prospect of reform of resistance, as all reform initiatives appear to be inevitably incorporated into the general expansion of power.

Surveillance is a central component of disciplinary power. What are some of the major forms of contemporary anti-crime surveillance? What social issues does such surveillance raise?

The truth is less extreme. The two groups emphasize different aspects of deviance, but generally each is aware of its complexity. Some radicals, for example, have modified their views in a more pragmatic direction called *left realism* (Young and Matthews, 1992). Functionalists, for their part, are aware of the costs of inequality and of the relativity of law. They also know about the extent of white-collar crime and are fully aware that the crimes committed by the affluent are treated comparatively ligthly (see Snider, 1992).

Hence, while some theories are incompatible with one another, it is also the case that the differences between theories can amount to differences in emphasis. Researchers who examine the role that biological factors play in criminality will, for example, often acknowledge that social factors such as inequality and the reactions of official labellers also play a role in criminal behaviour. It is also the case that no single theory will work for all types of crime. Some approaches work better for violent crime, while others seem to offer better explanations for property crime. Nor will all theories work for all classes of criminal, as some might best explain adolescent delinquency while others might better explain white-collar crime. As feminists have pointed out, one of the longstanding problems with criminological analysis was that its theories were developed exclusively from studies of men or boys. The researchers then took the questionable step of generalizing such findings to the criminal behaviour of women, or, more routinely, ignored women entirely. It is also worth noting that many theories are concerned exclusively with criminal behaviour, and consequently offer very few insights into the dynamics of the larger mass of non-criminal forms of deviance.

Finally, not all theories have the same aims. Some, like classical criminology and environmental criminology, are explicitly interested in trying to stop crime. Other approaches are more scholarly, in that they seek to develop a deeper understating of the factors that might contribute to crime, but leave it to others to work out the social policy implications of their findings. Labelling theory turns the tables somewhat, in that it pays less attention to reducing crime, focusing instead on the implications of being labelled a criminal or deviant. Feminists take yet a different angle, concentrating on examining the dynamics of patriarchy while also developing initiatives to help alleviate the disadvantaged position of women and other disenfranchised groups. Conflict theorists are typically uninterested in reducing crime, but instead want to unmask the structural differences in power that shape which things are (and are not) treated as crimes.

Summary

This chapter has sought to accomplish something that at first seems paradoxical—it has tried to demonstrate that deviance, rather being rare and exceptional, is actually remarkably common. Issues pertaining to deviance and normality pervade our daily lives. It is only when informal social norms about something like manners are broken that we are reminded of the existence of those norms, and of the degree to which we might be offended when they are violated. We have also sought to foster an appreciation for the degree to which deviance varies across cultures, subcultures, and throughout history. Deviance, like beauty, is often in the eye of the beholder.

Society reacts to most forms of deviance in an informal fashion, through the interpersonal process of shaming or perhaps by ostracizing deviant individuals. This can involve a process of stigmatization, prompting certain classes of individual to embrace practices that will help them "pass" as normal. Cosmetic surgery is one example of such a process. Our discussion of bodily transformation also helped to accentuate some of the tensions inherent in social norms and efforts to "pass." Norms can be something that social groups aspire toward, but they can also occasionally be something that individuals explicitly seek to challenge. Since the 1970s one of the most important developments in the social dynamics of deviance has involved the emergence of groups who actively embrace previously tainted designations.

When dominant social groups deem that a particular deviant behaviour is sufficiently serious to justify formal state sanctioning these acts are elevated to the status of a crime. The line separating crimes and deviance can be complicated and is often highly politicized. On any given day a host of different moral entrepreneurs advocate for changes in how society responds to assorted forms of deviant (or potentially deviant) behaviours.

The study of deviance draws upon a wide range of research methodologies. In sociology this includes the analysis of official crime data, victimization studies, self-report studies, and ethnographies. Each approach draws upon a different form of data, and is consequently limited by the particular characteristics of how that data are produced. Criminologists are frequently concerned that certain forms of deviance or crime are excluded or under-represented by different data sources.

The data produced by these different methodologies only makes sense when looked at through the lenses provided by different theories. The theories advanced to understand the dynamics related to crime and deviance have been extremely diverse. The earliest theories explained deviance through appeal to a religious worldview, something that is not apparent in today's largely secular research environment. Nonetheless, many citizens continue to view issues of deviance in ways that are informed by religious principles.

The sheer variety of theories that have been advanced to try to explain deviance point out the complexity of trying to explain not only deviance, but any human behaviour. Different theories have different ambitions. Some, for example, seek to reduce crime, while others aim to unmask patriarchy, and still others hope to trace how contemporary definitions of crime serve established capitalist interests. Some propose that deviance is not necessarily an entirely bad thing, in that it can serve important social functions. As the study of crime and deviance advances, arguably the biggest challenge for the future will involve the question of how to balance and integrate the insights of these different perspectives.

Questions for Review and Critical Thinking

1. Have you engaged in any behaviours over the past year that could have resulted in your being criminally charged by the police if you had been caught? What might this suggest about our typical perceptions about criminals? What resources might you have been able to draw upon to avoid being labelled as a criminal?

2. What are the main ways in which feminism has challenged the traditional study of crime?

3. The public often expresses much less concern about white-collar economic crime than various forms of street crime, even though white-collar crime is more costly and often produces more social harms than street crime. What might account for this situation?

Key Terms

abnormal, p. 88
anomie, p. 104
civilizing process, p. 95
classical criminology, p. 99

contraculture, p. 105
crime, p. 88
crime funnel, p. 90
critical school, p. 113
dark figure of crime, p. 90
differential association, p. 109
displacement, p. 102
environmental criminology, p. 100
ethnography or participant observation, p. 93
formal social control mechanisms, p. 95
gendered norms, p. 106
hedonistic calculus, p. 99
informal social control mechanisms, p. 95
innovation, p. 104
liberation hypothesis, p. 107
manners or etiquette, p. 95
moral entrepreneurs, p. 112
norm, p. 88
pathologizing, p. 106
pluralism, p. 112
power-control theory, p. 107
primary deviance, p. 111
reaction formation, p. 105
rebellion, p. 104
ritualism, p. 104
relativism, p. 87
retreatism, p. 104
rule breakers, p. 110
self-fulfilling prophecy, p. 111
self-report studies, p. 90
sensibilities, p. 95
stigma, p. 96
techniques of neutralization, p. 109
victimization survey, p. 90

Suggested Readings

Gelsthorpe, Loraine and Allison Morris (eds.)
1990 *Feminist Perspectives in Criminology*. Milton Keynes: Open University Press.
This edited book is somewhat advanced, but the collected papers provide an excellent overview of feminist contributions to the discipline of criminology.

Mosher, Clayton J., Terance D. Miethe, and Dretha M. Phillips
2002 *The Mismeasure of Crime*. London: Sage.
This volume provides students with a detailed discussion of the advantages and disadvantages of different sociological methods for studying crime.

Reiman, J.

2007   *The Rich Get Richer and the Poor Get Prison: Ideology, Class, and Criminal Justice* (8th ed.). New York: Macmillan.

A very nice overview of critical approaches to the study of crime. The book is very popular and has gone through many different editions, which means that second-hand copies are often readily available.

Sumner, Colin

1994   *The Sociology of Deviance: An Obituary.* Buckingham: Open University Press.

Although this book is somewhat advanced, Sumner has produced an excellent overview of trends in the study of deviance that avoids the tendency of some "deviance" books to just talk about crime.

Websites

www.crimetheory.com/gallery.htm
Gallery of Criminologists and Their Influences
Links to discussions of many of the main criminological theorists.

www.sociology.org.uk/ddeviate.htm
Deviance and Social Control
Extensive and detailed overview of many of the key concepts in the sociology of deviance.

http://en.wikipedia.org/wiki/Deviant_behavior
Wikipedia: Deviant Behavior
Concise overview of some key concepts in the sociology of deviance.

Key Search Terms

Anomie
Deviance
Erving Goffman
Labelling
Beccaria
Moral entrepreneurs

For more study tools to help you with your next exam, be sure to check out the Companion Website at **www.pearsoned.ca/hewitt**, as well as Chapter 5 in your Study Guide.

part three

Social Differentiation

The previous chapters looked at culture and its acquisition, or lack of acquisition, by society's members. Research strategies to investigate these and other social phenomena were also examined. In this next section of the book, we focus on social differentiation. The sources of inequality and the fact that various groups are unequal in their power and privileges are the central concerns of Chapter 6, Social Inequality. The learning of male or female roles is a major focus of Chapter 7, Gender Relations. Various feminist perspectives are offered as the chapter discusses the differences between gender and sex, examines cultural definitions of "masculine" and "feminine," and describes the costs of being a female or male in contemporary Canada. Sexuality, poverty, and deviance are examined, in turn, as they relate to gender. Another major topic in this area, especially for Canadians, is the study of the various racial and ethnic groups in society. This topic is examined in Chapter 8, Race and Ethnic Relations. A topic of increasing importance in the twenty-first century will be Aging, the title of Chapter 9.

The analysis of social differentiation is central to all of sociology. First, as a dependent variable (recall Chapter 2, Research Methods), differentiation arises in part from, and then reinforces, various subcultures that are passed on to different groups and individuals in the socialization process. Individuals learn different roles, values, norms, and aspirations by virtue of their being born male or female, into different families, going to different schools, living in different geographical areas, and becoming members of different groups. When this differentiation becomes the basis of a ranking system and of inequality among the groups, it is relevant to the study of social stratification.

Second, social differentiation clearly can act as an independent variable, with important consequences for the lives of individuals in society. Membership in a gender group, in a minority or majority subculture, and the occupation of different social ranks can affect aspects of family life—for example, one's age at marriage and chance of divorce. It can affect religious practices, participation in social movements, and the size of one's family. These topics will receive greater attention in the next two sections of the book. For now, remember that social differentiation is a key factor explaining much of human behaviour. Keep this in mind as you read the rest of the book.

edward g. grabb

[6]

social inequality

Introduction

Modern societies are complex entities, filled with people working at various jobs, living in different circumstances, and engaging in a wide range of activities. Social scientists usually refer to this great diversity and complexity in social life as **social differentiation**. While societies vary in the degree to which social differentiation occurs, it seems that, in the course of human history, social differentiation has increased.

Logically, social differentiation involves only a distinction of duties and responsibilities in a social structure. An example would be the distinction between the various jobs performed in a factory or office. In virtually all but the simplest structures, however, this *division of labour* gives rise to a difference in the ranking and evaluation of the individual tasks and those who perform them. The process by which individuals, or categories of individuals, are ranked on the basis of socially differentiated characteristics leads to relatively enduring structures of **social inequality** among individuals and groups.

In this chapter, we examine basic concepts and definitions, and then consider classical theories of social inequality and some recent developments in the field. Subsequently, we look at the eight most important factors or patterns of social differentiation that give rise to the unequal distribution of privilege and prestige in Canadian society.

Concepts and Definitions

Power

Lenski (1966) asserted that the study of social inequality is concerned mainly with who gets what and why. In this view, social inequality is a *distributive process*, in which some people receive more of the valued things in life, especially wealth and prestige, than do others. In addition, social inequality is concerned with examining the *relations between* those groups who receive different amounts of wealth and prestige. Here, we argue that **power**, or the ability to command resources and thereby control social situations, is the basic concept to consider when attempting to explain both the distribution of these valued things and the relations between unequal groups in society. Hence, power is the essential determinant of social inequality.

Most sociologists are interested in studying structured or **institutionalized power**. Power is structured or institutionalized when it becomes a regular and recurring part of everyday existence, usually because it is established in formal laws or in accepted conventions and customs (Lenski, 1966; Grabb, 2002). We can identify three major forms of structured power in society: *economic power*, which stems mainly from control of material resources like property or wealth; *political power*, which arises largely from control over human resources or the activities of other people; and *ideological power*, which comes from control over the ideas, beliefs, knowledge, or information that guides social action (Giddens, 1981; Grabb, 2002, 2004a).

Status and stratum

How is power established or institutionalized in society? One approach to this question is to examine how power derives from the rights of individuals or groups occupying a certain position, or **status**, in the various spheres of social life. Social inequality represents institutionalized power differences in a set of these statuses. In earlier European societies, for example, the status of king had greater power than the status of duke, which in turn had greater power than the status of serf.

Sometimes those performing different functions and occupying different statuses are, nevertheless, of similar rank in terms of their command over resources. For example, carpenter, plumber, electrician, and auto mechanic are distinct occupational statuses, yet they are often considered of about equal rank in the system of inequality. This cluster of occupational statuses, which we might label "skilled labourers," is an example of a **stratum**, or status category. Those researchers who view social inequality as a series of ranked groupings of people, somewhat like geological strata or the layers of a wedding cake, are especially likely to use the term *stratification* to denote the system of social inequality.

Obviously, every individual can hold many statuses simultaneously. Consider a person who is female, 30 years old, married, a high-school graduate, and a real estate agent. These traits are, respectively, that individual's sex status, age status, marital status, educational status, and occupational status. The combination of all such statuses is a person's **status set**.

Status hierarchies and power dimensions

Those statuses that translate into significant power differences in society are the most crucial for the study of social inequality. We can isolate at least eight **status hierarchies** that seem most important in Canadian society: the three socioeconomic hierarchies of wealth (including income and property), occupation, and education; race or ethnicity; region or rural/urban location; gender; age; and political status.

These hierarchies represent eight power rankings that define most of the structure of inequality in Canada. As we shall see in Chapter 15, Social Movements, some of these rankings may also provide the basis for group conflict or integration in society and, hence, for collective action.

Social inequality in Canada can thus be seen as a multiple hierarchy phenomenon (Hurst, 1996; Curtis et al., 2004). **Status consistency** grows when individuals have consistently similar status levels within all or most of these hierarchies. Some individuals rank relatively high on all or most power rankings. An example might be a white, male, Ontario lawyer who earns over $200 000 per year, has a university education, and serves as a deputy minister in the federal government. A high degree of status consistency in a society tends to be indicative of a "closed" inequality system, one in which certain groups dominate and benefit most from the society.

The opposite of status consistency is **status inconsistency**, which occurs when an individual's ranking on one status hierarchy has little relationship to rankings on other hierarchies. An example might be a wealthy doctor living in a large Ontario city whose parents were poor immigrants when they came to Canada. A large degree of status inconsistency in a society may indicate a more "open" stratification structure in which traditionally disadvantaged groups, such as racial minorities or women, are able to achieve high status in other hierarchies—for example, in the educational or occupational hierarchies.

Ascribed and achieved status

The difference between open and closed systems of inequality relates to another pair of concepts: ascribed versus achieved status. An **ascribed status** is a feature assigned to an individual by circumstance rather than by accomplishment. These features tend to be characteristics an individual acquires at birth and cannot change. Race, ethnic origin, sex, and age are examples of ascribed statuses. **Achieved status** refers primarily to performance characteristics, traits attained by individual action. Perhaps the best examples in a society like ours are education and occupation. A society can be characterized as open if achieved statuses are more important than ascribed statuses in determining a person's rank in the overall system of inequality.

Some earlier social thinkers argued that the modern age is one in which achievement criteria have indeed become of increasing importance (Parsons, 1951; McClelland, 1961). While there may be some evidence for this argument, we shall see that achieved statuses and ascribed statuses tend to go hand in hand. In other words, while achieved statuses play a more important part in social inequality than was the case in centuries past, the opportunity to achieve, particularly in the education and occupation hierarchies, is strongly influenced by ascribed traits such as race, sex, or inherited

Race, ethnic origin, sex, and age are examples of ascribed statuses.

wealth. Hence, ascribed statuses have considerable influence, even in supposedly achievement-oriented societies such as Canada. A similar position is stated in Chapter 7, Gender Relations.

Social mobility

The question of an open system of inequality is also relevant to the concept of *social mobility*. If a society is open, there should be considerable opportunity for individuals to change their positions over time on the important status hierarchies. Consider occupational mobility, for example. This movement can involve changes in the occupation of the same individual during his or her life, or **intragenerational mobility**. Or it may entail differences between the occupational status of child and parent—that is, **intergenerational mobility**. While we usually discuss **vertical mobility**—movement up or down a status hierarchy—as most indicative of an open system, we can also examine **horizontal mobility**—movement between positions within the same rank or status category. An example would be a person who leaves a job as a government economist to teach economics in a university. Both jobs fall into approximately the same stratum in the occupational status hierarchy.

Class and social class

The final major concept to consider is class. This is probably the most frequently used term in the field of social inequality. However, because of the many different meanings attached to the concept, it is difficult to offer a single definition that is acceptable to everyone. In this chapter, we use class in a way more or less consistent with its use by the two principal classical theorists of inequality, Marx and Weber. For clarity, we can distinguish between the terms *class* and *social class*. Class refers only to one's position in the general economic hierarchy. As discussed later in the chapter, this corresponds to Weber's view of class as position in the economic "marketplace." It also parallels approximately Marx's concept of a "class in itself." In all cases, **class** refers to a category of individuals with similar economic power, as indicated by any of the following: property ownership, educational qualifications, labour power, or occupation (see Giddens, 1973).

For a **social class** to exist, however, more than just similar economic position or market capacity is required. The individuals involved must also have a common sense of identity, an awareness of their shared characteristics and interests, and a tendency to act together as a real group. As we shall see, this definition corresponds closely to Weber's view and approximates what Marx called a "class for itself." Whereas simple economic classes are often identifiable in societies, genuine social classes rarely exist. Marx expected that the class of wage labourers in the capitalist system eventually would become a social class in the complete sense: a class conscious, politically mobilized, revolutionary proletariat that would act as a group to produce fundamental change in the social structure. Our findings in Canada and other modern societies, however, suggest that this particular social class, this proletariat, has yet to take shape. Instead, the closest approximation to a real social class in modern times may be at the top of the system, among an upper set of controlling elites with the group consciousness and regular interaction necessary for a real group to exist (Porter, 1965; Clement, 1975; Francis, 1986; Carroll, 2004).

Now that we have considered the key concepts and definitions, we can examine more closely the theories that sociologists have offered to explain social inequality. We begin with the classical views of Marx and Weber, and then we compare these theories with a different school of thought, structural functionalism. Finally, we look at some recent attempts to combine the most important ideas from these earlier approaches into new explanations.

Major Theories of Social Inequality

Marx: Class, conflict, and the power of property

Historical roots

Marx's theory of classes and class conflict is the key starting point for understanding structured inequality in modern societies. Both supporters and opponents alike have devoted considerable effort to a critical evaluation of his ideas.

Marx was born in Germany in 1818 and died in England in 1883. His life spanned a period of great social change and political and economic turmoil in Europe. In the first half of his life, Marx witnessed and supported unsuccessful revolts in Germany and

France, events which he saw as attempts by the less privileged to achieve social justice and a more equitable share of the wealth in those societies. The latter part of Marx's life was spent in England, where industrial capitalism had developed most fully. The so-called "industrial revolution" taking place in Britain was transforming the social structure in a way that both fascinated and saddened Marx. Tremendous surplus wealth was generated by the efficient capitalist economic system, yet this wealth was largely given over to the owners of business while the great majority of working people lived in poverty.

It was out of this social and historical context that Marx's ideas emerged (and also the science of sociology itself, as mentioned in Chapter 1). The great gap between rich and poor in that period, and the fact that capitalism could produce such extraordinary wealth and yet leave so many people impoverished, were, for Marx, contradictions that required explanation. Marx tried to arrive at an explanation by analyzing societies from previous ages: ancient Greece, ancient Rome, and medieval Europe, in particular. He concluded that each major societal form is characterized by a clear split between "haves" and "have-nots": master and slave; feudal lord and serf; capitalist and worker. Moreover, each form of social organization is marked by struggle—either open conflict or underlying antagonism—between the two main groups.

The means of production and class structure

For Marx, what really underlies the division of societies into two opposing groups, apart from obvious differences in wealth and prestige, is the power that comes from the ownership or non-ownership of property. In particular, Marx focused on private ownership of productive property, or what he called the "means of production." Under capitalism, productive property includes resources necessary to produce the essentials of life (e.g., housing, tools, land) and the factories and machinery that transform raw materials into finished goods.

Marx argued that, historically, the dominant group in any society was the one that owned the means of production. It was because some people could own productive property that inequality among social groups and the formation of classes occurred. Private property meant that owners could determine the distribution of all wealth. Thus, under the capitalist system in Marx's time, the propertyless majority, who owned only their own labour power, had no choice but to rely on those who owned property to employ them as wage workers, often with only sufficient income to keep themselves and their families alive. Marx believed that a basic contradiction in this system would become more and more apparent to the people as capitalism developed and expanded.

The contradiction, in Marx's view, was that the mass of workers—the majority of the population—gained little benefit from the great wealth they themselves produced. Those who generated the riches of the society through their labour received only a small portion as a living wage, with the remainder going to the capitalist owning-class.

Marx claimed that under feudalism, the economic system that operated prior to capitalism, a similar contradiction had existed. The ruling class of feudal lords, who contributed little to the creation of wealth in their system but reaped most of its benefits, was opposed by the then new class of capitalists, who were a rising, dynamic force

seeking social change and a new economic system. Likewise, Marx expected that the working class, or **proletariat**, would become the rising new force under capitalism, one that would oppose the now obstructive and superfluous class of capitalists, the **bourgeoisie**. Just as the bourgeoisie had triumphed over and transformed feudalism, so too would the proletariat realize its potential, overthrow the bourgeoisie, and transform capitalism into socialism.

Revolt of the working class

The change from capitalism to socialism was, for Marx, the culmination of this historical process of class struggle. For socialism to triumph, however, the working class would have to become more than just a **class in itself**, a category of people sharing the same economic position as non-owners of productive property. In addition, an awareness of common position and a willingness to mobilize as a force for change

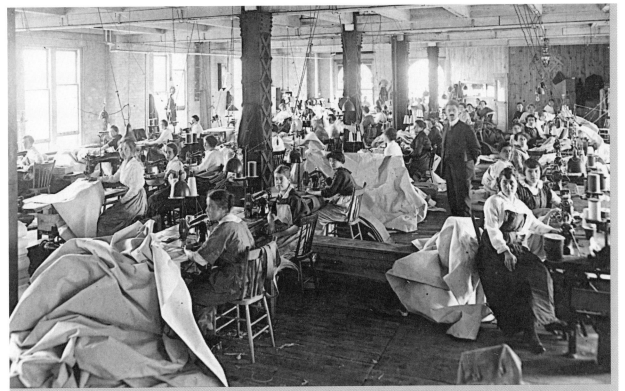

Marx argued that the propertyless majority, who owned only their labour power, had no choice but to rely on those who owned property to employ them as wage workers.

would be essential if the proletariat were to become a genuine **class for itself**, a group that would transform society. (social class)

To achieve the mobilization of the working class, several obstacles would have to be overcome. For example, apart from their economic power, the owners of property, in Marx's view, had great influence in various ideological structures: religious institutions, the communications media (see Chapter 12, Media), the educational systems, and so forth. The owning class could use each of these structures to manipulate or indoctrinate the workers and to justify its privileged position. Also, the owning class had effective control of the political structure, or state, and so could use legal, military, and police power to maintain its position if necessary.

Despite these obstacles, Marx believed that a successful revolution by the proletariat was possible, and that the circumstances necessary for this change would eventually occur. While Marx offered no precise predictions as to how the revolution would come about, he did expect a number of processes in the development of capitalism to spur the working class to action (Giddens, 1973). To begin with, capitalism encourages the rise of urban centres, since large numbers of propertyless rural inhabitants migrate to the cities in search of employment (see Chapter 16, Demography and Urbanization). This growing concentration of urban labourers is an initial step toward working-class awareness. A second important process in capitalism is the increasing expansion of production into large-scale factories employing many workers. This process also means a concentration of workers in close proximity to one another and a further basis for awareness of their common class position.

In addition, workers are made more aware of their common plight and their separation from the owning class by the workings of the capitalist economy. To Marx, capitalism is based on a rational and efficient, but relentless and self-interested, pursuit of profits by the owning class. The quest for increasing profits frequently has unfortunate consequences for the society as a whole. For example, in their desire for greater gain, owners often produce more goods than they can sell. This practice means a loss of money for the capitalist, whose most obvious recourse is to lay off workers to save money. But laying off workers means less money for the workers to purchase the capitalist's products. Hence, the

demand for these goods falls, and the capitalist loses even more money. In this downward-spiral fashion, economic crises tend to occur in the capitalist system, involving overproduction, high unemployment, and slow economic growth. After each crisis there is a period when the economy stabilizes, but always at the expense of the lower strata.

Several additional developments occur in the stabilization period to widen the gulf between the working and owning classes. First, the smaller capitalists, or *petty bourgeoisie*, who are the most vulnerable in bad economic times, either sell off their businesses or fail, and are taken over by larger capitalists. This leads to a growing concentration of ownership within a shrinking group of large-scale capitalists. This concentration, coupled with the gradual disappearance of the middle class of small owners, makes it more and more clear that workers and big capital are the only two classes of consequence in the system. Second, it is increasingly evident to the workers that they are the losers in economic crises, while most of the large-scale bourgeoisie prosper. As capitalism matures, *absolute* living standards for everyone, even the workers, are likely to rise because of the tremendous surplus wealth that is amassed. However, in Marx's view, the *relative* difference in economic well-being between owner and worker would widen. This widening gap and the realization by workers that they are the first to suffer in bad times stimulate class polarization still further.

One final factor that Marx believed would promote working-class consciousness and the polarization of the bourgeoisie and proletariat was the rise of the joint-stock company. In the earlier stages of capitalism, owners play an active role in the production process by managing operations and making administrative decisions. Under advanced capitalism, however, businesses are increasingly owned only on paper, with individuals buying shares in companies. Marx believed that, in such a system, it would become even more obvious to the workers that mere ownership is essentially superfluous to productive activity. That is, owners as shareholders control the means of production and accumulate rewards from it, but offer nothing constructive or valuable in return, not even managerial or administrative effort. Thus, the distinction between the productive proletariat and unnecessary capitalists would become increasingly clear.

Marx believed that all of these processes would produce an awareness among the workers of their exploitation and oppression by the bourgeoisie. The far greater numbers and, consequently, the potential power of the working class, coupled with consciousness of its class position and the desire to eliminate class inequalities, would set the stage for the workers to mobilize to overthrow the capitalist class. We should note that Marx did not see this revolution by the proletariat as automatic, in the sense that it would come about of its own accord. The basic conditions for the change were, to Marx, inherent in the capitalist mode of

[Debate]

Program for Revolution: Key Points in *The Communist Manifesto*

In 1848, Marx and Engels outlined the key changes that they believed were required in the transition from capitalism to socialism. The following passage is taken from their famous document, The Communist Manifesto.

. . . in the most advanced countries, the following will be pretty generally applicable.

1. Abolition of property in land and application of all rents of land to public purposes.

2. A heavy progressive or graduated income tax.

3. Abolition of all right of inheritance.

4. Confiscation of the property of all emigrants and rebels.

5. Centralization of credit in the hands of the state, by means of a national bank with state capital and an exclusive monopoly.

6. Centralization of the means of communication and transport in the hands of the state.

7. Extension of factories and instruments of production owned by the state; the bringing into cultivation of wastelands, and the improvement of the soil generally in accordance with a common plan.

8. Equal liability of all to labour. Establishment of industrial armies, especially for agriculture.

9. Combination of agriculture with manufacturing industries; gradual abolition of the distinction between town and country, by a more equable distribution of the population over the country.

10. Free education for all children in public schools. Abolition of children's factory labour in its present form. Combination of education with industrial production, etc., etc.

When, in the course of development, class distinctions have disappeared, and all production has been concentrated in the hands of a vast association of the whole nation, the public power will lose its political character. Political power, properly so called, is merely the organized power of one class for oppressing another. If the proletariat during its contest with the bourgeoisie is compelled, by the force of circumstances, to organize itself as a class, if, by means of a revolution, it makes itself the ruling class, and, as such, sweeps away by force the old conditions of production, then it will, along with these conditions, have swept away the conditions for the existence of class antagonisms and of classes generally, and will thereby have abolished its own supremacy as a class.

In place of the old bourgeois society, with its classes and class antagonisms, we shall have an association in which the free development of each is the condition for the free development of all.

Source: Karl Marx and Friedrich Engels, 1848. *The Communist Manifesto*. New York: Washington Square Press (1970, pp. 93–95).

A communist revolution in Canada is unlikely. Where else in the world might such a revolution occur today?

economic and social organization. However, the ultimate fate of the revolution depends on the actions of the proletariat to change society.

Classless society

What system would replace capitalism? Marx avoided specific predictions about this new system, but he suggested that two stages would follow the revolution. First, Marx foresaw a socialist phase, a "dictatorship of the proletariat," with the leaders of the revolution heading the political apparatus of the society, the state. The state would abolish private property, thus eliminating any distinction between owning and non-owning classes. The tremendous productive capacity of the old system would be retained, but the state would ensure that the wealth created by the economy was distributed equitably to the productive members of society, to the workers themselves.

In the second stage after the revolution, communism, the state as a political force would become unnecessary and would die away, although some individuals would still be required as administrators of the productive and other spheres of society. Communism would represent the first system without class distinctions, without a class structure, and without class conflict (Giddens, 1973).

Whether the classless society Marx envisioned will ever come to pass remains an open question. For many observers, the disappearance during the 1990s of communist regimes in the former Soviet Union and other countries raises doubts about Marx's projections, at least for the foreseeable future. It is also notable that, even in societies in which a socialist system has been implemented or still exists, inequality has not been eradicated. The need for a group of administrators to oversee the complex operations of any advanced society is probably one major reason why inequality has not yet been eliminated.

Weber's critique of Marx

One common criticism of Marx's theory of classes is that it paints too simple a picture of social inequality, especially in modern societies. Critics claim, first of all, that Marx overestimated the economic structure as the source of power in society. Second, many writers feel that Marx's splitting of society into two classes, the propertied and the propertyless, ignores the existence of other identifiable classes.

Multiple power sources

One of the first to raise such issues was another German thinker, Max Weber. Weber lived and wrote in a time after Marx's death and was able to observe certain developments in capitalism that Marx could not. Weber accepted Marx's emphasis on economic class and property ownership as fundamental to social inequality. However, Weber pointed out that economic class by itself was not the only source of power or criterion for ranking in the social structure. Weber noted that power or influence could also be gained from status honour, or prestige, deriving from membership in certain groups. Such *status groups*, which may include ethnic, religious, or other entities, involve exclusive membership; awareness of like tastes, lifestyles, and interests; and a tendency to act and interact as a unit. Similarly, Weber saw parties as an additional basis of power or command over resources in society. Party, in this sense, refers both to political parties and to other "special-interest" groups (e.g., trade unions, lobby groups) that can also operate in and influence political decisions. Weber was one of the first to view power in this multifaceted way. Each of the three factors—economic **class**, **status group**, and **party**—serves as a source of power and a basis for group formation in society (Giddens, 1973).

Weber conceded that these three aspects of inequality are frequently closely related, so that those who dominate the economic system tend also to have considerable status honour and political control. However, he disagreed with what he believed was Marx's contention, that all power derives ultimately from the control of the economy and the production process. Weber did not accept the view of some Marxists that the political, religious, educational, and other structures of society act only to serve the interests of the ruling economic class. To Weber, each of these structures possessed some power in its own right, some recognized sphere of influence and control. In this sense, Weber's view is one of the first *pluralist* conceptions of power in social theory. Power is pluralist here in the sense that it derives from more than a single source or structure.

The existence of "middle classes"

Weber's pluralist view of power is also revealed in his discussion of class structure. Weber argued that there were more than just two main economic classes, the bourgeoisie and proletariat. As discussed earlier, Marx also was aware of the existence of middle classes in capitalism, but he believed that these groups were transitional and would eventually become part of the two major classes. In his work, Weber included a range of middle classes, people who lack the privilege of large property ownership but who have more than just labour power to sell in the capitalist marketplace. These middle classes possess one or both of the following: (1) small amounts of productive property, such as shops, small businesses, or small farms; (2) valued skills, such as the special training or education of a physician, lawyer, or artisan.

Weber agreed with Marx that the small business segment of the middle classes was in decline. However, the other major segment, those with specialized skills or training, would not decrease but expand under capitalism. Many of these people would fill positions as technical and administrative workers in the huge, developing bureaucratic structures of modern society. According to Weber, the need for managers, accountants, bookkeepers, supervisors, engineers, architects, teachers, and so on in the business, government, and educational bureaucracies would ensure that the middle classes would not be a transitional group, but a growing force in modern society.

Classless society and bureaucracy

You will recall Marx's expectation that future societies would see the end of classes and inequality. If we employ Marx's criterion for defining classes—the ownership or non-ownership of property—it is possible to envision the disappearance of classes. We need only abolish private property, and the basis for class formation would not exist. This is the approach that was taken officially in socialist countries like China or the former Soviet Union. It appears, however, that the abolition of private property is insufficient to eliminate inequality between groups. Whether we call these unequal groups classes or strata, the fact of inequality persists, even with private property eliminated. In socialist societies, the bases for power differences and group formation have simply shifted from property ownership to other factors, particularly access to valued education or skills and to political power. Those who dominate these sources of power tend to dominate the society (Giddens, 1973, 1981; Parkin, 1979).

Weber's analysis of bureaucracy (see Chapter 14, Organizations and Work), provides some explanation for the persistence of structured inequality in both socialist and capitalist societies. In any social structure, people in decision-making positions must have the legitimate right or power to decide, if they are to ensure that their chosen course of action will be followed by others. By definition this means that hierarchies based on unequal power and control will arise. In the modern era, these power hierarchies have increasingly taken the form of bureaucracies. Bureaucracies are designed for the administration and performance of various important tasks—policy making, allocation of economic resources, health care, job placement, defence, and so forth. While socialism may attempt to remove material inequalities, it cannot eliminate the need for these administrative structures in making and implementing important decisions.

The problem of attaining individual equality and freedom in the face of bureaucratic dominance in societies of every type is probably the major dilemma facing Marxist and socialist theorists in the present day. In fact, Weber argued that bureaucracy would be even more common in socialist systems in which so many more aspects of life are regulated by government. Hence, power differences and inequality could be even greater in a socialist system than under capitalism. Certainly, the recent history of current and former communist countries points to this problem.

Weber clearly recognized the threat bureaucracy poses to equality and freedom, but believed the bureaucratic form was necessary for the efficient coordination and management of essential tasks in complex societies. Unlike another theorist, Michels (discussed in Chapter 14), Weber did not believe that an *iron law of oligarchy* operates in social structures, in which those in power inevitably abuse their position to gain special benefits for themselves. Nevertheless, Weber believed that the potential for such abuse of power is basic to modern social organizations, whether capitalist or socialist.

Structural functionalism: Consensus, individualism, and pluralism

While Marx stressed conflict, group (class) action, and the singular importance of economic power in understanding social inequality, the structural functionalist school of thought emphasizes consensus, individual action, and the pluralism of power in social structures (Davis and Moore, 1945; Parsons, 1953). Let us consider these three points.

Consensus or conflict

Marx believed t3hat conflict or struggle between groups is basic to the operation of all societies. In contrast, structural functionalist theorists, as mentioned in Chapter 1, concentrate on what they perceive as the harmony and agreement that mark social interaction. They argue that social groups could not survive as they do without considerable consensus on the norms and values that govern social life. Rather than viewing structured inequality as something imposed upon the people by those in power, structural functionalists argue that this inequality is based largely on an underlying awareness and agreement about the value put on various positions in the social structure. The value given to each position or status depends on two factors: its functional importance for society and the relative scarcity of people with the talent or training needed for the position. Some statuses, such as doctor, scientist, or judge, are said to be both more important and harder to fill than, for example, the positions of parking lot attendant or file clerk. Hence, the rewards attached to the more crucial positions and those requiring rare skills must be proportionately greater than the rewards attached to the less valuable statuses. Otherwise, the most qualified individuals would not aspire to the key positions or, if in them, would not perform their important duties properly. The rewards used to motivate individuals in this system are of three types: (1) "sustenance and comfort," which are most readily attainable from material and economic gains such as money or property; (2) "humour and diversion," which may come from material returns but also include such benefits as extra leisure time or a flexible and varied work schedule; and (3) "self-respect and ego expansion," which stem mainly from the prestige and honour given to those who occupy important positions.

Several assumptions underlie this functionalist argument, but a central one is that there is a high level of consensus among social actors: first, on the functional importance of each status—that is, on what the important jobs are; second, on what constitutes a "reward" in social life; and, third, on how rewards should be allotted to the various positions in the social structure. The further assumption that different rewards are essential to

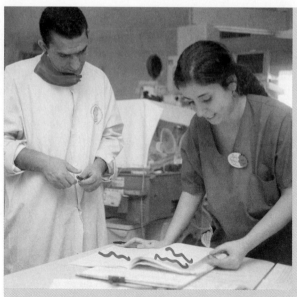

Some statuses are said to be more important and harder to fill than others.

motivate human beings leads to the conclusion that social inequality is inevitable and, in fact, performs a positive function for society by providing incentives for people to develop their talents to the full and to find their "proper" places in the system. Supposedly, those who are willing to work hard and apply themselves, and who can forego present rewards to achieve special skills and training, will achieve privileged positions and be rewarded with greater material benefits, prestige, and life satisfaction. It is assumed, once again, that there is general agreement on the importance of hard work, on the existence of opportunity for all, and on the rules that regulate the contest for success.

Individualism versus class action

The second aspect of structural functionalism that distinguishes it from Marxian theory is its general avoidance of the concept of class. Rather than proposing a class or group basis for understanding inequality in societies, structural functionalists focus mainly on individual action and individual status as the factors in social inequality. In modern societies, the most important status determining a person's position is occupational status. The functional importance of this status and not, for example, inherited wealth and privilege, generally indicates the rank of the individual.

Pluralism or property

While the structural functionalist analysis of social inequality differs considerably from the Weberian perspective, one view they share is that societies are pluralist or multifaceted. In the structural functionalist conception, social organization involves the coordination of interdependent subsystems, each with its own functions to perform if the overall system is to survive. The major subsystems, or *institutions*, of society include the economy, the polity (or political institutions), religion, education, and the agents of social control (police, military), among others. Each institution is said to operate in harmony with the others, to ensure social stability, maintenance of the system, and the general well-being of the population. The contrast between this formulation and Marx's focus on the overriding power of property ownership is apparent. For Marx, those who dominate the economy through ownership of the means of production ultimately hold sway in all other spheres and, moreover, can bring the power of the political and social control structures into play to protect their domination.

Combining the major theories to explain modern systems of inequality

We get very different views of social inequality depending on which theoretical perspective we consider. The differences exist primarily because each approach emphasizes different factors to explain structured inequality. It can be argued that no major theory by itself gives a complete picture, and that each applies better to some situations than to others. Consider the Marxian perspective. Marxism originated in nineteenth-century Europe and seems particularly suited to describe the group struggle and class divisions of that time and setting. Since then, however, Marxism has achieved its greatest following in the less industrialized countries of the world, and may not be as applicable to industrialized societies as it once was. In the less industrialized countries of Africa, Asia, and Latin America, for example, the continued sharp contrast between rich and poor has enabled class polarization and revolutionary potential to remain strong. In the industrialized capitalist countries of North America and Europe, however, absolute living standards have risen significantly, the middle strata have not disappeared, and opportunities

for mobility are still at least perceived to exist by many people. Hence, complete class polarization and outright revolution seem to be distant and unlikely developments in advanced capitalism at this time.

Nevertheless, many elements of Marxian theory are useful for understanding modern systems of inequality. The role of conflict and struggle in human affairs and the great power invested in those who own and control property are undeniably important facets of modern life that affect inequality.

The structural functionalist view of inequality originated in the United States where, historically, such ideas as equal opportunity, free competition, and individual achievement were cherished and accepted as realities by much of the population. It is unlikely, however, that anything resembling complete equality of opportunity has existed in any known society. Discrimination on the basis of race, gender, and family class background, for example, continues to play a significant role in defining inequality, even in supposedly egalitarian societies. However, certain aspects of the structural functionalist perspective do ring true. Some consensus, not just conflict, does operate in social systems; otherwise, social organization would not be possible. In addition, the expansion of the labour forces of most modern societies has provided opportunities for individual success on the basis of merit and training.

Some theorists have attempted to reconcile these disparate theoretical approaches by bringing together elements of each perspective that have the greatest merit. Dahrendorf (1959) and Lenski (1966), for example, attempted to show how both conflict and consensus operate in social systems. It is likely that a complete synthesis of theories is not possible. However, key features of the major theories can be combined to provide a more inclusive model for representing social inequality (Grabb, 2002). We suggest, first, that individual action, especially through educational and occupational attainment, does play a role in defining social inequality in countries like Canada. At the same time, group memberships play a major part in determining the structure of inequality. Most notable is membership in the upper class, and in that small set of elites that dominates the major institutions of society. Other group affiliations, such as race, ethnicity, and gender, also represent different bases of inequality, both inside and outside the elites, and are related to differences in command over scarce resources, including wealth, education, and prestige. The recognition of individual and group factors indicates that both the structural functionalist and Marxist approaches are relevant for understanding the overall pattern of social inequality.

Acknowledging that there are multiple bases for social inequality is consistent with both Weberian and structural functionalist theories. Each theory stresses the pluralist nature of power in systems of inequality. However, each ranking does not play an equally important role. Following Marx, we argue that control of property and wealth, particularly by large business enterprises, is the most important source of power in modern societies. We examine Canadian research on this point later in the chapter. At the same time, following Weber, we suggest that the other two socioeconomic status hierarchies, education and occupation, also are crucial in shaping the system of inequality.

Taken together, these three hierarchies have tended to promote the formation of a structure of three classes or strata in capitalist countries like Canada. This structure is made up of an upper class, which dominates large property ownership; a middle class, which, because of highly marketable skills, education, and training, holds the more powerful and rewarding jobs; and a working class, which has few skills other than labour power and so occupies the less powerful and less rewarding positions in the workforce. Of course, within these three broad groupings, many finer distinctions could be drawn. For example, sociologists sometimes speak of the "lower-middle class" or the "upper-working class" as subcategories in this three-class system. Some also include a fourth grouping, an "under class" of very poor and disadvantaged persons. This category includes people who may possess no property, education, or labour power and who may, for instance, be frequently unemployed because they cannot find work or are unable to work (Giddens, 1973; Grabb, 2002, 2004a).

In addition to the three socioeconomic hierarchies discussed above, five other hierarchies form Canada's overall system of social inequality. First, political power is crucial, especially when we consider that, officially at least, the ultimate power in society, even greater than that of the economic elite, is invested in the political leadership and the state. Generally, the interplay between those who control political power and those who dominate the economic sphere is the key process shaping the system of inequality in Canada and other modern societies. Second, differences in power and privilege between men and women are large in our society, so that gender has an important bearing on structured inequality. Recently, age has received increasing recognition as an important factor in social inequality. The remaining two rankings, based on ethnic and/or racial origin, and region or rural/urban location, are of particular importance in describing inequality in Canada, with its image as a "vertical mosaic" of diverse cultures and geographic areas (Porter, 1965). While other possible bases of social inequality could be considered, such as religion, for example, they will not be examined here because they are less salient in contemporary Canada than are the eight hierarchies suggested above. In the next section of this chapter, we take a detailed look at each of the eight rankings. We shall see that there are connections in many cases between the rank of individuals and groups in one hierarchy and their ranks in others. An understanding of these interrelationships among hierarchies should give the reader a relatively complete picture of the nature of social inequality in Canadian society.

Social Inequality in Canada

Socioeconomic hierarchies I: Wealth, income, and property

Wealth, including various forms of income and property, plays at least two major roles in social inequality. First, wealth is clearly a result or indicator of a person's position in the system of inequality. Wealth or income is the return people receive from their position in the economic structure. This return usually involves income from a job, but may include earnings from investments or property ownership. In all of these cases, wealth comes as a reward that can be high or low, depending on the market value of a person's job or property holdings. The distribution of wealth, then, is the most direct measure or indication of how groups or individuals rank in the overall structure of inequality. Nevertheless, wealth plays a second key part in social inequality, at least in capitalist societies like Canada, where private property and inheritance are protected by law. Wealth is itself a form of property that can be used through investment to acquire more wealth and property. In this sense, wealth is not only a consequence but also a cause or means by which a person's position in the system of inequality is maintained or changed.

Distribution of income and wealth

How are wealth and property distributed in Canada? Are these sources of power widely diffused throughout the population or are they concentrated in a small group of people? There is no doubt, first of all, that people in most industrialized societies have enjoyed an *absolute* increase in real wealth over the past 50 years or more. In Canada, between 1951 and 2001, the income of the average family more than doubled, even after the effects of inflation were taken into account. This increase was most pronounced prior to 1980, with some levelling off during most of the 1990s, followed by slight upturn again by the late 1990s (Urmetzer and Guppy, 2004: 76–77).

However, a key issue to consider is the distribution of this income. This question, in other words, is one of *relative* income, of how well certain strata have been doing compared to others. In one study of this topic, all families or individuals who earned money in a particular year were ranked by their total income for that year and then divided into *quintiles* (five strata of equal size). Results showed that the top quintile, the top 20 percent of the hierarchy, earned about 42.8 percent of all the before-tax income made in Canada in 1951, while the bottom quintile earned only 4.4 percent. By 1999, this unequal distribution of income had changed marginally, with the top quintile's share somewhat larger, at 45.3 percent, and the bottom quintile's portion at 4.3 percent (Urmetzer and Guppy, 2004: 78–79). The same study showed that, if the higher income taxes paid by the top quintile are taken into account, the amount of income inequality between the top and bottom decreases but only slightly. This study also found that income inequality would be far greater if it were not for the relatively higher amounts of "social transfers," such as employment insurance and welfare payments, that are given to poorer Canadians (see also O'Connor, 1999). Overall, then, the rich have generally remained rich and the poor remained poor during this period.

These figures for Canada, which correspond approximately to those reported in the United States and other developed countries, suggest that the unequal distribution of income has not changed much in recent decades. To establish a more complete picture of economic inequality in Canada, however, we must look beyond earned income alone. It is important to consider all the accumulated assets—stocks, real estate, durable goods, and the like—that together form the total wealth of an individual or group. Data from 1999 show that the top 10 percent of Canada's population held over half of all wealth, while the top 20 percent retained about 70 percent (J. Davies, 2004: 88). Thus, the distribution of wealth is even more unequal than the distribution of income.

Distribution of property

Besides income and wealth, the other major means for achieving economic power in a capitalist society is through ownership or control of property. Under the capitalist system, large property, especially in the form of giant corporations, is rarely owned outright by one person or even a few people. Instead, corporations are owned by shareholders, each "owning a piece of the rock." This is a popular image, suggesting a dispersion of economic power to the wider population. However, studies indicate that ownership tends to involve a relatively small number of shareholders in many cases. Moreover, even where ownership is dispersed, minority shareholdings rather than majority ownership are often all that is needed to achieve effective control of decision making in the corporations. Frequently, the shares in a company are spread across a large number of isolated individuals, most of whom do not attend shareholders' meetings, and some of whom may not have voting rights for electing company directors. In such instances, control of a small block of shares, perhaps only 10 or 20 percent, may be sufficient to determine how the company is run (Carroll, 2004; Grabb, 2004b). Therefore, ownership or control of property, and hence economic power, can be concentrated in a small group of people.

Perhaps even stronger evidence of the concentration of property ownership has been offered by various studies of corporate control in Canada. Carroll (2004: 201) has reported that, while there were about one million companies operating in Canada in 2001, the largest twenty-five enterprises alone accounted for more than 41 percent of all business assets (see also Grabb, 2004b: 22; Francis, 1986; O'Connor, 1999).

We can see, then, that Canada's system of inequality is marked by large differences in economic power, in the form of wealth and property holdings. A relatively small group of people at the top possesses much of the wealth. In addition, within this "upper class," an even smaller elite, including the owners and directors of dominant corporations, controls most of the society's economic resources.

[Social Trends]

Do the Rich Really Get Richer?

The gap between the incomes of Canada's top business executives and those of other workers has grown dramatically in recent years. A study by the consulting firm KPMG looked at the Chief Executive Officers, or CEOs, of 268 major companies listed on the Toronto Stock Exchange. The study showed that, from 1992 to 1995, annual incomes for CEOs rose by 32 percent, to an average of $776 000 per year. During the same period, the average income of Canadian workers increased by less than 3 percent. The survey also revealed that pay increases for executives were not related to how well their companies had performed. In fact, the CEOs of less profitable businesses actually received larger average raises than those running the more profitable companies. Such is an indication of how people with wealth and power in our society are able to protect and enhance their advantaged economic positions, sometimes regardless of their performance or contributions to the nation's economy.

Source: From a Southam News story by Bertrand Marotte, published in the *London Free Press*, September 25, 1996 (p. D5).

From a functionalist perspective, how can such differences be justified?

These findings are broadly consistent with a Marxist interpretation of social inequality. The continued unequal distribution of wealth, the relative decline in wealth and property holdings among the lower strata, and the concentration of economic power in a small elite all support such a view. However, these realities apparently have been insufficient to produce the class polarization and proletarian revolution Marx expected under advanced capitalism. While the explanation for this failure is complex, three possible reasons should be considered. First, the general population has done better economically, at least in absolute terms, than Marx anticipated. Such developments as worker unionization and the institution of government social programs—health insurance, old age pensions, and the like—have meant at least modest increases in living standards for most people.

Despite spending cuts by all levels of government that have weakened social programs in recent years, most workers may still feel their material position is adequate. Second, even those workers who are discontented may believe that they lack the power to change the situation. As a consequence, rather than becoming a unified force for revolution, much of the working class has remained passive, accepting their disadvantaged position in the system. Finally, despite the serious inequalities existing in Canada, there may be sufficient real or perceived upward mobility to maintain the belief among many workers that opportunities continue to be there for those who will take them. Such optimistic beliefs would tend to reduce class polarization.

We shall consider the question of mobility later in this chapter, but whatever the opportunity structure, economic inequalities in Canada in recent decades have apparently not been sufficient to promote a real move for change among the working and middle classes. In the next section, we examine occupation's role in the distribution of economic power, particularly for these two classes.

Socioeconomic hierarchies II: Occupation

Except for wealthy property holders, occupational status is the major source of economic power for most individuals. Because occupation correlates with other key variables—income, education, gender, ethnicity—it is sometimes viewed as the best single indicator of an individual's overall rank system of inequality. Therefore, we should examine trends in the occupational composition of the labour force. In this section, we consider some of the transformations in Canada's workforce and then look at changes in the distribution of income by occupational status over time. This will help us to assess how the market capacities of various occupations have changed in recent decades. Finally, we also look at research on occupational mobility in Canada. This allows us to evaluate the degree to which social inequality in our society is an open or closed system.

Occupational shifts

The first major trend to note is the great increase in the types of jobs that exist today compared with earlier times. Nuclear physicist, computer scientist, X-ray technician, and jet pilot are just a few of the jobs that have come into being in the relatively recent past. The growing variety of occupations is a prime example of the increasing social differentiation in modern societies, a process discussed earlier in this chapter.

In addition to the greater number of occupations, there has been a notable shift in the relative size of occupational categories over time. Occupations can be divided roughly into three groups: manual or blue-collar jobs, non-manual or white-collar jobs, and agricultural or farm occupations. Manual jobs normally entail physical labour or working with the hands, as the name implies.

In social research, these jobs are sometimes equated with the working class, and include such occupations as construction worker, factory labourer, miner, logger, and mechanic. Non-manual jobs typically involve working with symbols and ideas. Non-manual jobs are sometimes used as an indication of middle-class position by social scientists, and include such occupations as doctor, lawyer, teacher, nurse, business manager, salesperson, accountant, and clerk.

An examination of historical shifts in these three job categories is quite revealing (see Table 6.1). First, the proportion of agricultural occupations has declined greatly, from over 40 percent in 1901 to about 3 percent in 2001. Blue-collar occupations recently have declined somewhat, but still formed about 36 percent of the workforce in 2001. However, there have been shifts within the blue-collar group, including a move to more service work, such as food preparation, hairdressing, and housekeeping, plus a decline in unskilled labour and primary labour, such as fishing, logging, and mining. The white-collar sector has expanded the most, from 15 percent to almost 60 percent of the Canadian workforce by 2001. Much of the white-collar growth,

Table 6.1 Canadian Labour Force, Percentage Distribution by Major Occupational Groups, 1901–2001

	1901	1921	1941	1961	1981	1991	2001
All occupations	100	100	100	100	100	100	100
White-collar	15	25	25	39	53	57	59
Managerial	4	7	5	8	9	12	10
Professional/technical	5	5	7	10	16	18	24
Clerical	3	7	7	13	19	18	15
Sales	3	6	6	8	9	9	10
Blue-collar	45	42	49	49	43	38	36
Manuf./mech./construction	21	16	21	22			
Labourers	7	10	6	5	29[1]	23[1]	21[1]
Transport/communication	5	5	6	8			
Service	8	7	11	11	12	13	14
Fishing/logging/mining	4	4	5	3	2	2	1
Agriculture	40	33	26	10	4	3	3
Occupation not stated	—	—	—	3	1	4	2

[1] Because blue-collar categories differed after 1971 from previous years, these three occupational categories are combined for the years 1981 to 2001.

Sources: Kubat and Thornoton (1974: 153–55); Statistics Canada, *1981 Census of Canada*, Catalogue No. 92–917, Table 1; *1991 Census of Canada*, Catalogue No. 93–327, Table 1; *2001 Census of Canada*, February 11, 2003 Release, No. 97F0012XCB1017.

however, involves lower positions—sales clerks, typists, file clerks—which, in terms of income, power, and work activities, are similar to working-class occupations (see Rinehart, 2001; Lowe, 2004). Thus, part of the non-manual expansion may be indicative of a rising "new working class" of low-paid, semi-skilled, white-collar workers.

Occupation and income

As Table 6.2 reveals, blue-collar relative earning power has changed little since 1931, with incomes staying at about 10 to 15 percent below the national average. At the same time, white-collar incomes have declined from 2.09 times the national level in 1931 to 1.04 in 2001. On the surface, this relative income decline in the white-collar sector seems to support the new-working-class view. That is, with many white-collar incomes becoming more like blue-collar incomes, we might conclude that today's non-manual employees, in their market capacity and perhaps

other traits, are more like the working class than the middle class. However, several points should be noted here.

First, the white-collar income decline, as Table 6.2 indicates, appears to be most significant for clerical workers, who now earn incomes that are well below the Canadian average and that are also lower than those of blue-collar workers as a whole. Managerial and professional incomes, on the other hand, continue to be higher than those of blue-collar workers, although their incomes, too, have moved closer to the Canadian average over time.

A second important point about the general decline of white-collar incomes is that much of this trend is due to the flow of poorly paid women into many of these positions (see Krahn and Lowe, 2002; Lowe, 2004; Creese and Beagan, 2004, and see also Chapter 7, Gender Relations). White-collar males outside the clerical sector have maintained a significant edge over blue-collar workers. For example, in the full-time workforce in 2001, males in managerial jobs earned about 62 percent more

Table 6.2	Average Incomes of Major Occupational Groups (full-time employed), as a Percentage of the Average Income for all Occupations, 1931–2001						
	1931	1941	1951[1]	1961	1971[2]	1981	2001[3]
All occupations	100	100	100	100	100	100	100
White-collar	209	172	134	120	130	109	104
Managerial	314	253	169	184	204	179	127
Professional/technical	214	176	141	150	144	127	119
Clerical	125	112	102	92	89	72	74
Sales	140	122	107	106	108	90	90
Blue-collar	86	90	93	87	91	90	82
Manuf./mech./construction	101	102	106	99			
Labourers	53	61	73	60	97[4]	105	92
Transport/communication	115	104	100	94			
Service	97	85	84	76	80	60	66
Fishing/logging/mining	63	69	90	71	79	107	102
Agriculture	35	30	37	38	51	68	55

[1] Median income 1951.
[2] Figures after 1971 exclude those with no employment income and those whose occupations were not stated or included in the major categories.
[3] Figures for 2001 are based on average employment earnings for full-time, full-year workers ($43 298).
[4] Because blue-collar categories differ after 1971 from previous years, these three occupational categories are combined from 1971 on.

Sources: Derived from N.M. Meltz, 1965. *Changes in the Occupational Composition of the Canadian Labour Force: 1931–61.* Ottawa: Queen's Printer (pp. 64–65); Statistics Canada, *1971 Census of Canada*, Catalogue No. 94–765; *1981 Census of Canada*, Catalogue No. 92–930; *2001 Census of Canada*, Catalogue No. 97F0019XCB2001003.

[Debate]

Labour in the Working Class

In his book *The Tyranny of Work*, Rinehart (2001) assessed the nature of labour for the modern working class. He suggested that in more and more industries the jobs of blue-collar workers have gradually undergone a significant reduction in skill requirements in this century. Due to ever-improving technology, especially computers, and an

increasing division of labour, their work has become routine, easy to learn, unskilled, and repetitive. Even what was once skilled labour, such as machining, has been affected by these trends, thus blurring the previous, more clear-cut distinction between skilled and unskilled worker (Rinehart, 2001: Chapter 5).

Identify other potential consequences for society of deskilling.

than the Canadian average, while males in upper-tier professional areas, such as the medicine and health fields, for example, earned incomes more than 73 percent above the average (Statistics Canada, *2001 Census of Canada*, Catalogue No. 97F0019XCB2001003).

Finally, it should also be noted that these income figures give only a partial picture, since they do not include other economic advantages—job security, fringe benefits, and promotion opportunities—which have traditionally been more likely to benefit white-collar workers, especially those in the professional-technical and managerial categories (Lowe, 2004: 156–57).

Occupation and social mobility

The previous discussion of the occupational structure leads to another important issue: the process of social mobility in systems of inequality. Earlier, we described social mobility as any shift in status by an individual or group within a status hierarchy. Analyzing vertical intergenerational mobility is particularly helpful in assessing how open or closed a system of inequality is. If we can show that parents' statuses do not really affect their adult children's statuses in a particular system, this suggests a more open system. In an open system, individuals are neither helped nor hindered by the power of their parents, or by such ascribed characteristics as their family's race, ethnic origin, or class background. On the other hand, when children do gain or lose chances for success largely on the basis of their family backgrounds, we have a more closed system.

The most general approach to the study of social mobility is to take into account all of the eight major power dimensions considered in this chapter. Thus, social mobility may be defined as a change in the relative amount of all "power resources" held by a person or group. In most cases, however, social scientists have concentrated on the occupational status hierarchy when assessing social mobility. This is probably because, as was noted earlier in this chapter, occupation may be the best single indicator of overall class or stratum rank for most of the population.

One early study showed that occupational mobility patterns in Canada were similar to those of other industrialized nations. This analysis found a moderate relationship (a correlation of about .40) between fathers' and sons' occupational status (Goyder and Curtis, 1977: 304–8), suggesting that family class background, as measured by fathers' occupation, has a notable but not overwhelming impact on sons' adult occupational attainments. Goyder and Curtis also found that, if intergenerational mobility is traced over four generations, the association disappears. In other words, the effect of family class background on occupational attainments seems not to accumulate from great-grandfather through to great-grandson. Hence, the authors concluded that there is an "impermanence of family status over non-adjacent generations," suggesting that Canada is "an achievement society rather than an ascriptive one" (Goyder and Curtis, 1977: 316). More recent research on occupational mobility reveals other interesting patterns. One study found that the relationship

Occupation may be the best single indicator of overall class position for most of the population.

between father's occupational status and the occupational status of both sons and daughters declined significantly from 1973 to 1986, although it remained about the same between 1986 and 1994 (Wanner, 2004: 143). This implies that most people are less likely to inherit occupational privileges now than in the past, and suggests some increase in overall mobility, openness, and equality of opportunity in Canada's occupational structure since the 1970s. Of course, these findings do not mean that inheritance of occupational advantages has disappeared (Wanner, 2004: 144–45; see also Wanner and Hayes, 1996). Moreover, such research applies mainly to the broad range of individuals in the middle of the class structure, and not to the very poor and the very wealthy. For example, other evidence indicates considerable inheritance of privilege among wealthy families (Francis, 1986; J. Davies, 2004).

In summary, mobility does occur in our society, even though the overall opportunity structure is far from completely open. A major mechanism providing the chance for mobility across generations has been the education system. Especially for that large central group

from middle- and working-class backgrounds, the acquisition of skills and training through the schools is probably the best bet for individual advancement. In the next section we consider just how equally or unequally educational advantages are distributed in Canada.

Socioeconomic hierarchies III: Education

Education is included among the set of socioeconomic status hierarchies because it is closely linked to the acquisition of income, wealth, and occupational status. In Canada and other countries, the education system is the primary means by which most people achieve upward mobility and material success. Education plays a crucial role in sustaining the belief that our system of inequality is neither closed nor totally determined by ascribed status characteristics such as race, gender, or inherited wealth. If individual achievement in the education system consistently translates into higher incomes and better jobs, then the argument is more convincing that ours is an open, competitive, and fair society.

Recall that structural functionalism is most closely identified with the view that inequality is the result of a contest in which education and training are the key means to success. In Canada, there is some evidence to support such an assertion. Generally, higher education has a significant connection with higher income and occupational attainment. In 1996, for example, university graduates in Canada earned 61 percent more than high school graduates, a figure that was similar to that in other countries, including the United States, France, Germany, and Spain (Chauvel, 2003: 246). As for occupational differences, one study based on 1991 Census data found that more than 77 percent of Canadian university graduates and more than 90 percent of post-graduates held upper-level "discretionary" jobs in professional, technical, managerial, and administrative fields (Baer, 2004). In contrast, the same study found that about 75 percent of high school graduates and more than 80 percent of those with less than a high school diploma were engaged in "routine" jobs, involving less personal freedom and less stimulating work activities. Other research shows that, compared with non-graduates, graduates are less likely to be unemployed, less likely to remain unemployed if they do lose a job, and more likely to earn higher salaries when employed (Anisef and Axelrod, 1993; Guppy and Davies, 1998). Therefore, while higher education by itself is not sufficient for success and does not guarantee a better job to everyone, it is a necessary prerequisite in most cases.

An important question to ask when discussing education and social inequality is, who does and who does not acquire higher education, and why? For educational attainment to be an achieved status, there must be equal opportunity for everyone to acquire education, assuming they have the motivation and the ability to do so. Otherwise, education is like an ascribed characteristic, something that one possesses or lacks as a result of the inherited advantages or disadvantages of gender, race, or class background.

Early Canadian research showed that ascribed traits such as class background were significantly related to educational attainment. Porter (1965: 184) found that individuals whose families earned above-average incomes and whose fathers had high status occupations were greatly overrepresented in the university student population. More recent studies show increasing proportions of post-secondary students from lower socioeconomic backgrounds. These results suggest Canada's educational structure has become more "meritocratic," or more accessible to people on the basis of ability rather than class background, than in the past (e.g., Ali and Grabb, 1998; Fournier et al., 1999). However, these studies and others also show that students from the lower strata are still underrepresented compared to their proportion of the population (Nakhaie and Curtis, 1998; Guppy and Davies, 1998; Krahn, 2004).

Inequality of educational opportunity may not be the only reason why people from the lower strata are underrepresented in Canada's post-secondary institutions. Some studies indicate that other factors have an impact. Parents' and children's perceptions of the chances for education, their knowledge of educational programs, and their evaluation of the value of education in the job market all reduce the likelihood that lower-class children will go on in school. In addition, differences in parental encouragement of children's educational aspirations may make it more likely that middle- and upper-class children will continue in the education system (Guppy and Davies, 1998; S. Davies, 2004; Krahn, 2004).

Even if all of these factors are taken into account, it is likely that much of the difference in education in the population is due to inequality of access. Despite the availability of government assistance and student loans, post-secondary education is an expensive undertaking that low-income people often cannot afford. There is also reason to believe that continued government underfunding of higher education is beginning to restrict access to post-secondary education once again. All of these factors suggest unequal educational opportunity and threaten the major avenue of upward mobility for a large number of Canadians.

This completes our discussion of the major socio-economic status hierarchies. We have seen that wealth and property, occupational status, and education all play important parts in shaping the system of inequality or class structure. In the remaining sections of this chapter, we examine some of the interrelationships between these aspects of inequality and the five other key hierarchies.

Racial and ethnic inequality

Racial background and ethnic origin (discussed in Chapter 8, Race and Ethnic Relations) are important factors distinguishing people from one another in Canada.

It is also apparent that racial and ethnic diversity, or "multiculturalism," has important implications for the overall structure of inequality.

Various factors have made race and ethnicity important for the analysis of social inequality. First, different groups arrived in Canada at different times, so that some groups could make prior claims on power and property rights. Second, some cultures may put less stress than others on the importance of acquiring wealth and power; hence, differences in values may have contributed to racial or ethnic inequality. In addition, ethnic or racial background frequently has been used as a basis for favouritism or discrimination, making it difficult for some groups to enter the upper strata while allowing others ready access. These factors and others have produced in Canada what Porter (1965) called a "vertical mosaic," a social structure involving many diverse racial and ethnic groups, ranked along a hierarchy of power and privilege.

We begin our examination of the links between racial or ethnic background and social inequality by assessing the relationship between these factors and two socioeconomic status measures: income level and educational attainment. Then we look at the racial/ethnic composition of the economic elite. Finally, we focus on two groups that occupy unique positions in the system of social inequality: French Canadians and Native peoples.

Race, ethnicity, and socioeconomic status

Table 6.3 shows the rankings of 40 self-identified racial or ethnic categories in 2001, on two socioeconomic status indicators: average employment income as a percentage of the Canadian average, and the percentage of each ethnic group with a completed university education or more. One surprising result may be that those of British origin, while above the median rank on income, ranking seventh among the 40 groups, are only eighteenth on education. These figures suggest that, at least in the general population, the British no longer enjoy the dominant position they once did.

Some of the ethnic groups that rank above the British on one or both of the socioeconomic indicators are Europeans, including the Czech and Russian respondents, for example. However, people who identify themselves as Jewish rank the highest on both income and education. Also, at least on education, many "visible minorities," do well. These include Bangladeshis,

Koreans, Iranians, Pakistanis, Filipinos, Syrians, Japanese, Chinese, East Indians, Iraqis, and Lebanese, in particular. The situation of Jews and visible minorities is notable if we consider that all of these groups have been viewed historically as victims of significant discrimination and prejudice in Canada and elsewhere. Of course, their relatively high educational levels should not be seen as proof that discrimination or prejudice no longer exist in Canadian society (see Reitz and Breton, 1994; Allahar and Côté, 1998; Satzewich, 1998; Henry, 2004). This is suggested by the income rankings in Table 6.3, which show that, even though many visible minority groups have above-average levels of education, most earn below-average incomes. For example, while visible minorities make up nine of the top ten ethnic groups when ranked by education, only two of these groups—Japanese and Syrians—rank in the top ten on average income. Other research also shows that non-whites as a group still earn lower incomes than whites in Canada (Balakrishnan and Hou, 1996; Lian and Matthews, 1998; Pendakhur and Pendakhur, 2002). On balance, however, the research suggests that there are opportunities for socioeconomic success for many ethnic minorities in Canada today (see also Ali and Grabb, 1998).

Ethnic composition of the economic elite

Historically, the British dominated Canada's economy. Between 1885 and 1910, more than 90 percent of Canada's industrial leaders were of Anglo-Saxon background (Clement, 1975: 73). French Canadians made up 29 percent of the population but less than 7 percent of the elite, and other ethnic groups were virtually excluded.

By the 1950s, Porter found almost no change from these figures (Porter, 1965). Clement (1975: 234) revealed some erosion of British dominance by the early 1970s, with the Anglo-Canadian proportion of the economic elite dropping slightly (to 86 percent), the French rising somewhat (to 8 percent), and "other" groups, especially Jews, increasing moderately (to 5 percent). More recent research indicates some changes in the composition of the economic or business elite. The British still predominate, but now form less than two-thirds of the Canadian elite or upper class. The French make up another 18 percent, while other ethnic groups, including Jews, Germans, and Scandinavians in particular, account for the remainder (Carroll, 2004: 18–19; see also Ogmundson and McLaughlin, 1992). Even so, some

Table 6.3   Socioeconomic Ranking of 40 Selected Ethnic Groups[1] (Self-Identified), 2001

Average Income[2]	Education[3]
1. Jewish (170)	1. Jewish (39.4)
2. Japanese (130)	2. Bangladeshi (38.9)
3. Czech (118)	3. Korean (37.2)
4. Syrian (116)	4. Iranian (36.8)
5. Russian (115)	5. Pakistani (36.0)
6. Danish (115)	6. Filipino (30.5)
7. British (114)	7. Syrian (28.1)
8. Finnish (112)	8. Japanese (28.0)
9. Polish (112)	9. Chinese (27.1)
10. Italian (112)	10. East Indian (26.0)
11. Hungarian (111)	11. Russian (25.5)
12. Belgian (109)	12. Iraqi (24.0)
13. Norwegian (108)	13. Czech (22.1)
14. Ukrainian (108)	14. Lebanese (21.4)
15. Lebanese (108)	15. Spanish (19.8)
16. Dutch (107)	16. Polish (18.9)
17. German (107)	17. Belgian (18.8)
18. French (103)	18. British (17.6)
19. Pakistani (101)	19. Hungarian (17.4)
20. "Canadian" (100)	20. Finnish (17.3)
21. Iranian (100)	21. Danish (17.0)
22. Chinese (99)	22. Greek (16.7)
23. East Indian (99)	23. Ukrainian (16.3)
24. Greek (98)	24. Trinidadian/Tobagonian (16.1)
25. Trinidadian/Tobagonian (96)	25. Afghani (15.9)
26. Iraqi (96)	25. Norwegian (15.9)
27. Spanish (94)	27. German (15.2)
28. Portuguese (92)	28. French (14.9)
29. West Indian (92)	29. Italian (14.6)
30. Jamaican (90)	30. Dutch (14.0)
31. Aboriginal (87)	31. Vietnamese (13.0)
32. Black (87)	32. Haitian (12.4)
33. Korean (86)	33. "Canadian" (12.0)
34. Vietnamese (83)	34. West Indian (11.6)
35. Filipino (80)	35. Black (10.6)
36. Haitian (73)	36. Somali (10.4)
37. Bangladeshi (68)	37. Jamaican (10.0)
38. Salvadorean (66)	38. Portuguese (7.8)
39. Afghani (65)	39. Salvadorean (7.7)
40. Somali (64)	40. Aboriginal (6.4)

[1] Includes both single and multiple mentions of each group. Visible minorities and Aboriginal groups are in bold type. The British category includes English, Scottish, Irish, Welsh, and all other British.
[2] Average income refers to total annual employment income for full-time, full-year workers, aged 15 years and older. The Canadian average in 2000 was $41 226 and is set to 100 in the table.
[3] Ranked by the percentage of each group with a completed university degree or more in 2001. The Canadian average (for the adult population 25 or older) was 17.5 percent in 2001.

Source: Calculated from 2001 Census of Canada.

research suggests that the growth of non-British representation in Canada's economic elite is no greater than the growth of non-British representation in the population as a whole (Nakhaie, 1997).

Overall, then, people of Anglo-Saxon background continue to have an advantage at the elite level. However, as we have seen, outside this upper stratum, British origin has considerably less significance, with several other groups ranking higher in socioeconomic status. We turn now to a discussion of French Canadians and Native peoples, who historically, at least, have faced disadvantages in Canada's overall system of inequality.

French Canadians and social inequality

Until the last few decades, the French did not occupy a particularly privileged position in Canadian society. (This issue will be discussed more fully in the next chapter.) As of 2001, the French are still below the median on education but are above the median on income (see Table 6.3). The inequalities faced by the French in the past have been explained in different ways. Some have said that the French needed time to recover from the initial shock of the British economic and political takeover in the eighteenth century (Milner and Milner, 1973). Others saw the past avoidance by the French of "English-style" business and economic activity as a cause of their lower socioeconomic status (McRoberts, 1988: 178). Some have suggested that differences in values and upbringing put French Canadians at a disadvantage in the competition for material success, especially in business careers (Harvey, 1969; Richer and Laporte, 1971). Finally, ethnic prejudice and discrimination have been cited at times as an obstacle to French progress (Archibald, 1978).

Probably a combination of these factors contributed to the low position of French Canadians in the past. However, in the 1960s, during the "Quiet Revolution," there was a move in Quebec to catch up with English Canada. Since then, the French have come to dominate the Quebec government and civil service (McRoberts, 1988). The French now form an increasing portion of both the salaried middle class and the new business class in Quebec (Ogmundson and McLaughlin, 1992; Nakhaie, 1997; Carroll, 2004). Evidence also suggests that the economic advantages of the English over the French in Quebec have diminished

considerably. By 2000, the average employment income of French Canadians was about 3 percent above the overall Canadian average (see Table 6.3). Within Quebec, French-speaking Canadians not only earn above the Canadian average, but also earn slightly more than English-speaking Canadians (Canadian Press, 1994). Other recent evidence indicates that opportunities for occupational attainment, social mobility, and educational achievement have become increasingly similar for French and English (Guppy and Arai, 1993; Ali and Grabb, 1998). One analysis of income differences, using 1991 Census data, found that, as long as they have the same education level (and if the effects of other variables, like age and gender, are controlled), French Canadians "now earn significantly more than those of British ethnicity" (Lian and Matthews, 1998: 461–62).

These developments suggest that ethnic inequality involving French Canadians is changing, with the English becoming less powerful than before. Nevertheless, the English—both Canadian- and American-born—continue to hold somewhat greater economic power at the elite level in Quebec, through their positions in dominant corporations (McRoberts, 1988; Nakhaie, 1997; Carroll, 2004). For this reason and others, many French Canadians want greater economic control and political autonomy. Some favour the Parti Québécois program of sovereignty or outright independence for Quebec. Others support a new version of Canadian confederation, in which Quebec is formally acknowledged as a distinct society, and French rights and powers are given greater recognition than before. Quebec's 1995 referendum, in which almost half of the province's population voted for sovereignty, is one indication that French Canada's position in our society is still a serious issue. However, the election in 2003 of Jean Charest's pro-federalist government probably signals a period of improvement and optimism in Quebec–Canada relations at the present time (see Chapter 15, Social Movements).

Inequality and Native peoples

Native peoples also occupy an exceptional position in Canada's vertical mosaic. The erosion of their power, through the loss of land and natural resources, had a devastating initial impact on Native inhabitants (White et al., 2003; Menzies, 2004). The subsequent separation of many Natives from the rest of the population, due to voluntary avoidance, geographic isolation, and the government's policies of wardship for indigenous peoples, helped sustain and institutionalize their low status (Frideres, 1988; Wotherspoon and Satzewich, 1993). Such isolation may have helped to preserve Native identity, but probably at the expense of Native participation in the quest for jobs, education, and material affluence. Perhaps more than any other group, Native people face the dilemma of choosing between preserving their ethnic identities and succeeding in the larger society. Racial prejudice is also a factor, although in recent years this appears to have declined somewhat. While some people still hold negative stereotypes of Native groups, overall, the Canadian public has often been sympathetic toward, though also poorly informed about, Native peoples (Langford and Ponting, 1992: 141; Ponting, 1998).

Some recent developments suggest that the position of Canada's Native peoples may be improving. Funds derived from the settlement of Native land claims, as well as the increasing political awareness of Native leaders (see Chapter 15, Social Movements), may provide a means for Natives to achieve greater prosperity (Wotherspoon and Satzewich, 1993; White et al., 2003). The socioeconomic attainments of Natives have also risen in recent years, although serious inequalities remain (see Table 6.3). Natives increasingly hold white-collar jobs, though they are still underrepresented in such positions. Unemployment rates are still high and, even among employed Natives, incomes remain relatively low. In 1995, both individual income and family income levels were about 60 percent of the overall Canadian average (Maxim et al., 2001; Menzies, 2004: 297). Some educational improvements are evident: between 1969 and 1994, the number of Native people with at least some post-secondary education rose from under 1000 to almost 27 000 (Cairns, 2000: 185).

The prospects for Native peoples may still depend mainly on fuller acceptance of Native rights and the resolution of Native land claims. In the long run, the Native position may also hinge on how the dilemma of identity preservation versus participation in the larger socioeconomic structure is resolved.

Regional and rural/urban inequalities

Regional and rural/urban differences, perhaps as much as racial and ethnic diversity, give Canada its image as a mosaic of distinct parts. Canada's variability on these dimensions is apparent in the contrast between major urban centres like Toronto, Montreal, or Vancouver, and the less populous and more isolated areas of the Maritimes, the Prairies, and the North. Overall, geographic location has an important impact on social inequality among Canadians. In a sense, location is another source of power affecting the distribution of wealth and resources, because those who live in the urbanized, strategically located centres have considerably greater opportunity to achieve high positions in our society.

One theoretical approach that helps in thinking about such differences is the *metropolis–hinterland* perspective (Davis, 1971). In this view, Canada's social structure involves a complex network of regions and communities in which the rural and peripheral areas, or hinterlands, are ultimately connected by a series of intermediate links to a few major urban centres, or metropolises. The intermediate links in the system include local outposts, small towns, and middle-sized cities, all acting at different levels as depots between the outlying districts and the large population centres.

The metropolises are the focal points for industry, economic activity, politics, and education in the nation. Large-scale business enterprises, the major corporations, the seats of political power, and the largest universities are situated in the metropolitan centres. Economically, the hinterlands are sources of raw materials—primary resources like fish, wheat, petroleum, lumber, and ore—most of which are processed in the metropolises and then sold to hinterland inhabitants as finished goods. People constitute another resource that flows out of the hinterland and into the metropolis. More and more Canadians have left the hinterland areas for jobs in the big cities, taking with them their labour power, talents, and skills, and also their potential political affiliations and voting power (see also Chapter 16, Demography and Urbanization). All of this resource potential is lost by the hinterlands in favour of the large centres. Those who stay behind, near their family roots, historical heritage, and traditional communities, can be disadvantaged in regard to their relative power in the system of inequality. The local economy often has limited economic opportunities, so that job prospects are poorer and unemployment is higher. In addition, isolation from the central political power and from access to higher education helps to perpetuate and accentuate this disadvantage.

Metropolis–hinterland disparities are illustrated by differences in income by geographic location. Based on data provided by Beckstead and Brown (2005), we can calculate the per capita employment income of Canadians by province and community size (see Table 6.4). We can then express these figures, as a percentage of the per capita employment income of all Canadians in 2001, which was about $16 000 in 2001 and is assigned a score of 100. This procedure shows a number of interesting differences in income, by province and rural/urban category. First, in both Canada as a whole and in each separate province, income generally increases with an increase in community size. In other words, the most highly urbanized areas are the places in which average incomes are greatest, while rural districts show the lowest income levels. This result is consistent with the view that wealth is more highly concentrated in the metropolis. A second finding that conforms to the metropolis–hinterland argument concerns regional differences. The most economically developed and industrialized areas, particularly the urbanized areas of Ontario, British Columbia, and Alberta, appear to provide the highest standard of living. As of 2001, the four Atlantic provinces had the lowest incomes, especially in rural areas. To a lesser extent, the same pattern is observed for Saskatchewan, Manitoba, and Quebec. Some of the regional gaps in

employment income per capita are alleviated by social welfare programs that transfer funds from the wealthier to the poorer provinces and rural areas (Wien and Corrigall-Brown, 2004). Even so, we can see significant differences in economic well-being across the various provinces and rural-urban divisions (see also Serjak and Swan, 1993; Forcese, 1997: 58–81; Wien and Corrigall-Brown, 2004).

Other evidence related to business ownership and corporate concentration indicates that the metropolitan centres of Ontario form most of Canada's economic core. Toronto stands as the most influential financial and industrial centre in the nation, with Montreal a distant second and Calgary third. In and around these cities, most of Canada's major corporations are located and directed. Not only in terms of current residence, but also with respect to place of birth, urban southern Ontarians have for some time formed much of the economic elite (Carroll 2004: 92–96; see also Francis, 1986).

In general, then, economic power is heavily concentrated in the established urban locations of the nation. As noted earlier, these same locations are also the seats of political power and higher education. In combination, all these factors have promoted inequalities between regions in Canadian society.

Table 6.4   **Per Capita Employment Income by Province and Community Size, as a Percentage of the Canadian Average, 2001**

Region	Remote rural	Other rural	Urban under 100 000	Urban 100 000 to 499 999	Urban 500 000 or more	Total
All Canada	**63**	**76**	**88**	**99**	**116**	**100**
Newfoundland	34	43	80	89	—	63
PEI	47	59	82	—	—	74
Nova Scotia	41	65	73	89	—	78
New Brunswick	51	61	86	87	—	75
Quebec	56	70	81	83	102	90
Ontario	50	90	88	106	124	113
Manitoba	38	68	86	—	100	87
Saskatchewan	58	67	82	98	—	81
Alberta	63	91	110	—	123	113
British Columbia	66	82	87	99	116	100

The "Urban areas" header spans the "Urban under 100 000", "Urban 100 000 to 499 999", and "Urban 500 000 or more" columns.

Sources: Calculated from D. Beckstead and W. Mark Brown, 2005. *Provincial Income Disparities Through an Urban-Rural Lens: Evidence from the 2001 Census.* Statistics Canada Analytical Paper, Catalogue No. 11–624-MIE, No. 012, July. Table 3 and Figure 1, pp. 5–7.

Gender inequality in Canada

In recent decades, gender has become a central factor in the study of social inequality. The changing roles of women in modern society (see Chapter 7, Gender Relations) have done much to explain this focus on gender inequality. The major change in women's roles in the past century has been their movement into the paid labour force. As of 2000, women made up 46 percent of Canada's paid workforce, compared with only 13 percent in 1901 (Statistics Canada, *1961 Census of Canada* and *1971 Census of Canada, Historical Tables*; Creese and Beagan, 2004: 246). By 2000, 56 percent of women aged 15 or over worked outside the home (Creese and Beagan, 2004: 245). This great shift of women into the work world has provided a whole new pool of previously untapped talents and skills. However, the economic benefits gained by the average woman entering the workforce have often been limited. Female workers have consistently earned far less than male workers, even in advanced capitalist and socialist societies. In Canada, there has been a gradual improvement over the past few decades, but, by 2001, full-time working women still earned only about 71 percent of the male average (Statistics Canada, *2001 Census of Canada*, Catalogue No. 97F0019XCB2001003; see also Creese and Beagan, 2004).

Research also indicates that the lower socioeconomic rank of women cannot be explained by their lesser training and experience. Canadian studies have shown that, when the greater training and experience of male workers is taken into account, women still make only 80 to 90 percent of what men make (Calzavara, 1993: 315–16). Data for the 1990s suggest that, among those under the age of 25 who have university degrees, there is a much smaller difference in the average wages or incomes of males and females; however, a clear female disadvantage is still evident among the older and less-educated age cohorts (Beauchesne, 1994; see also Statistics Canada, 1998, *Earnings of Women and Men 1996*). These income differences have continued, even though, for some time now, women's average educational attainment has been catching up with, and in recent years surpassing, that of men (Guppy and Arai, 1993). It seems likely, then, that certain forms of gender discrimination, rather than differences in educational qualifications, are at the root of some of the income inequality between men and women.

In Canada, full-time working women in 1997 still earned just 73 percent of the male average.

Certain writers have suggested that female subordination in the system is so serious that the women's position is almost like that of a minority group, such as blacks or Native peoples. (We will discuss the feminization of poverty in Chapter 7, Gender Relations.) While there are problems with such a claim, some aspects of women's situation do parallel that of minority groups. First, sex, like ethnicity or race, is an ascribed trait that affects opportunities and life chances. Second, women share with racial and ethnic minorities a high degree of exclusion from the economic elite over the years (Francis, 1986; Carroll, 2004: 16–19). Such findings suggest that women continue to face disadvantages in our society.

Age and social inequality

The study of age and aging has been of increasing interest to sociologists in recent years (Novak, 1997; Connidis, 2001; see Chapter 9, Aging). Like sex or ethnicity, age is an ascribed attribute over which the individual has no control, but which has important implications for determining a person's rank in society.

Most research suggests that age has an up-and-down, or *curvilinear*, association with social inequality. In other words, as we move from the youngest to the oldest ends of the age spectrum, we generally find that people in the middle-age range enjoy the highest incomes and socioeconomic rank, with younger and older people ranking lower in most cases (Curtis et al., 2004: 307). For young people, this is often because their recent entry into the labour force means they begin at lower salaries or wage levels in their jobs. For elderly people, the lower economic standing is largely due to retirement from the labour force and having to live on reduced income from pensions and savings.

One obvious difference between young and old is that young people generally can hope to improve their position in society over time, as part of the normal process of joining the workforce and moving toward a future career. Most elderly people, however, must hope that their fixed incomes will not be eroded too severely over time by inflation and rising living costs.

This difference between young and old may explain why some researchers see the problems of the elderly as more serious, even though there is evidence that young people can also face an uncertain economic future (Côté and Allahar, 1994). In fact, not all elderly Canadians live in impoverished circumstances. Although more than 40 percent of families headed by persons over age 65 were living below the official low-income line in 1969, by 1999 this figure had dropped to about 17 percent (Guppy et al., 2004: 308). This trend indicates the success of government programs in alleviating the economic problems of Canada's elderly. Still, evidence shows that elderly women in Canada, especially those living alone, continue to endure economic difficulties (see also Chapter 7, Gender Relations). In 1999, 49 percent of all elderly females who lived alone were below the low-income line (Guppy et al., 2004: 308). This finding illustrates how two distinct inequality variables— gender and age—can combine to produce more complicated and more acute patterns of inequality. It also reveals the important impact of age on a person's life circumstances, even in an advanced and affluent society.

Political power and social inequality

The final component to consider in Canada's system of social inequality is the political power structure. We have saved this topic until the end because, in a sense, political power may be viewed as the ultimate manifestation of power and the ultimate determinant of structured inequality in society. In democratic countries, the political structure, or *state*, is the official representative of the power of all citizens. Thus, in theory at least, the political structure can act as the key mechanism for shaping all the major forms of inequality.

The concept of the state includes numerous substructures: the political leadership and elected representatives, the courts and judiciary, the civil service, the police, the military, and so forth (see Grabb, 2002). Virtually all societies are organized around the principle that the state is the means for creating and implementing laws, and thus the sanctions and rights that define power differences in society.

The state can establish and maintain political power differences, but the state can also affect the distribution of power in other realms. The creation of economic power advantages for the propertied over the propertyless, through the legally recognized institution of private property, is an illustration of how the political structure can be used to affect power differences outside the political sphere itself. Of course, political power also has the potential to remove or reduce power differences, through the creation of laws prohibiting race or sex discrimination in hiring practices, for example.

In these and other ways, position in the political hierarchy can be a source of power in itself and a potential means for establishing, enforcing, or altering power relations in other spheres. This is the basis for the argument that political power is a binding element, related to and interacting with all of the power sources that form the overall system. In addition, some observers see political power as the ultimate power source because, in a formal sense, those with power in other spheres must answer to those holding political power. Of course, other analysts have questioned whether the full authority of the state is really exercised when it confronts those in power in other areas, particularly the economic elite.

The state and the economic elite

We have noted that the state has the legally sanctioned power to control the actions of individuals and groups, even those who dominate the other institutions of society. In the economic sphere, for example, the government has acted against large corporations found guilty of price gouging, false advertising, environmental pollution, or making unsafe or defective products. Nevertheless, while we can think of specific instances in which political leaders have opposed the economic elite for the "common good" or the "public interest," it often seems that the state favours the economic elite and makes decisions on the basis of particular, rather than general, interests (see Clement, 1997).

It is from this point of view that Porter once criticized Canada's political leadership. He felt that Canada's major political parties engaged in "brokerage politics," making policy decisions based on what will get them reelected rather than what is best for the nation (Porter, 1965: 373–77). This may mean advocating policies favourable to the powerful and to special interests, in exchange for the campaign funds and voting power these groups can provide.

What is the significance of this alleged tendency for the political structure to favour the interests of the powerful, particularly the economic elite? Most social scientists reject the extreme view that the state is merely a tool in the hands of the economic elite, doing the bidding of big business at every turn. What seems to occur instead is that both state and economic leaders agree on the general goals and values that should prevail in society. Among these common goals are the need for political stability, economic development, and a continued promotion of capitalist expansion. State leaders accept the idea that the economic elite should make large profits. At the same time, however, the state must try to maintain social harmony and appear not to favour the economic elite too much, at the expense of other classes. Such action would undermine the state's basis for popular support, perhaps leading to severe disruptions in both political stability and economic development (Fox and Ornstein, 1993; O'Connor, 1999).

Composition of the state elite

Our previous discussion suggests that state leaders and the economic elite have much in common, at least in regard to goals, interests, and values. Another way of assessing the links between elites is to examine the social origins of state leaders. We might expect a considerable overrepresentation of individuals from upper-class backgrounds in the Canadian state elite. Porter's early analysis in the 1950s and Olsen's subsequent study in the 1970s did find that the upper class was overrepresented compared to its proportion of the general population (Porter, 1965; Olsen, 1980). However, the level of upper-class representation declined during the period between the two studies. Furthermore, the

Hilary Weston, former Lieutenant-Governor of Ontario, is the wife of Galen Weston, head of George Weston Ltd. Individuals who are nearer the top of the various power rankings are also likely to exercise above-average political power.

majority (almost three-quarters) of the state elite in the 1970s was from middle-class origins. While the working-class representation was low in both cases, these findings indicate that the state leadership is clearly open to those with non-elite origins. More recent evidence shows that, while numerous political leaders in Canada have served as directors of large businesses (and vice versa) over the years, these linkages are not nearly large enough to produce corporate domination of the government (Fox and Ornstein, 1993; see also Carroll, 2004). This suggests that the political leadership is not directly dominated by those controlling wealth and property in Canada. Instead, the state and big business are two separate but compatible forces in our society.

Political power and the individual

To this point, we have discussed political power mainly at the elite level. However, in liberal democracies, even

How Does Your Rank Affect You?

The importance of social inequality in sociology is apparent from the wide use of social inequality variables as explanatory factors in social research. Each of the eight power hierarchies discussed represents a distinct variety of structured inequality that can have consequences for many social phenomena. The literature that has developed around the effects of social inequality is massive. Here, we briefly examine some of the work that has been done, to illustrate the effects of social inequality on the lives of Canadians. We focus specifically on differences across socioeconomic groupings in life chances, lifestyles, values, and beliefs.

Life chances

Probably the most crucial consequence of social inequality concerns the life chances of people from different socioeconomic backgrounds. Generally, the term *life chances* refers to the ability to lead a healthy, happy, and prosperous existence. Studies show consistently that life chances decline as one moves down the socioeconomic ladder. As will be discussed in Chapter 16, Demography and Urbanization, lower-status individuals have shorter life expectancies and they are more susceptible to a broad spectrum of physical and mental health problems (National Council of Welfare, 1993; Health Canada, 1999a). The poorer strata also are more likely to suffer malnutrition, are less likely to use medical facilities and services, and experience poorer and more hazardous working conditions (Forcese, 1997). All of these elements, coupled with lower economic resources and fewer educational opportunities, lessen the quality of life in the lower strata and make the chances for a satisfying and rewarding existence less likely than they are for the higher strata.

Lifestyles

Social inequality also has a bearing on lifestyle. Differing economic resources, education levels, and life experiences lead to variations in a host of phenomena: consumption habits, manner of dress, speech patterns, and leisure activities, to name just a few. Generally, life in the lower strata is more restrictive than in the upper strata: less leisure time, less freedom of action, less flexibility in daily routine, and less variety in experiences and interests. The limited activities and experiences of working-class people are revealed in a number of ways. People from the lower strata are less likely to belong to clubs and organizations, do less reading, and participate less in community life than do other people (Kohn et al., 1990; Curtis et al., 2004). Instead, home life tends to receive greater emphasis. Nevertheless, even home activities often are disrupted by the need for working-class parents to work overtime or take part-time jobs to supplement incomes (Rinehart, 2001: 122, 164–65; Lowe, 2004: 154–56).

Values and beliefs

Another important consequence of social inequality is the tendency for different values and beliefs to be generated within social strata. Some studies suggest that greater economic deprivation and occupational instability in the working class lead its members to place a high value on material success, good pay, and financial security (Form, 1985).

Other research indicates that differences in the nature of the jobs done by people from different classes can lead to important differences in values and beliefs. For example, studies in several countries suggest that, because members of the working class have little personal freedom at work or control over their job environment, they place a lower value on individual independence or "self-direction" than do people in middle-class occupations. Some research shows that working-class parents are, in turn, more likely than middle-class parents to teach their children such values as obedience and conformity, rather than self-direction or independence (Kohn et al., 1990; see also Baer et al., 1996).

In what ways have your life chances, lifestyle, or values and beliefs been affected by your social class?

those dominated by elites, some power exists in the hands of the people. Voting, joining political parties and other voluntary associations, and, of course, running for election are some of the ways in which the individual can exercise political power. But what groups are most likely to use these means of political expression? In particular, which social strata are most likely to participate in the political structure?

Given the general pattern of social inequality suggested in this chapter, it may be no surprise that individuals who are nearer the top of the various power rankings are also likely to exercise above-average political power. Research shows that Canadians from higher socioeconomic backgrounds are more likely to vote, join political organizations, take an interest in politics, run for public office, and be elected to positions in government (Curtis et al., 2004).

In all these ways, the political power structure is closely bound up with the more general configuration of social inequality in Canada. At the elite level, and for the whole range of individual Canadians, political power is associated with the other sources of power that determine the distribution of wealth, prestige, and other resources in this country. Those who tend to dominate the other status hierarchies—especially the economically privileged, but also men, central Canadians, and those of British background—tend as well to hold sway in the political sphere (Ogmundson and McLaughlin, 1992; Nakhaie, 1997; Carroll, 2004). Although there are exceptions, the consistency in this pattern is a clear feature of social inequality in Canadian society.

Summary

This chapter has introduced you to the topic of social inequality in Canadian society. We looked at basic concepts and definitions and discussed the major theories advanced to explain the process of social inequality in modern societies. We proposed eight principal components to consider when examining Canada's system of inequality: wealth (including income and property), occupation, education, race or ethnicity, region or rural/urban location, gender, age, and political status. Each of these is the basis for a status hierarchy and corresponding power ranking, reflecting the distribution of resources and privileges in the population.

Our analysis indicates some fairly close linkages among the eight status hierarchies, with high status on one hierarchy often associated with high status on the others. Certain rankings seem to have a relatively greater influence. In particular, power deriving from wealth and property tends to have the greatest impact on the overall system of social inequality. The group that dominates in this hierarchy, the economic elite, is the single most powerful entity in the structure. Along with the political leadership, or state elite, they make most of the major decisions affecting the operation of the country, the distribution of wealth and resources, and the extent of inequality experienced by other Canadians.

And what can we say about the future of social inequality in Canada? Is it possible to predict whether the current patterns will continue as they are, or change in dramatic ways as we enter the new millennium? Different researchers are bound to offer different answers to such questions. However, the evidence we have reviewed in this chapter indicates that social inequality will remain a significant problem in our society for many years to come. Of course, there is reason to be optimistic that there will be some decline in the amount of inequality on certain dimensions. For example, the gradual increases in women's occupation, income, and especially education levels that we have seen in recent decades seem likely to be sustained in the future. At the same time, though, the evidence offers little basis for expecting much improvement in other areas. This is illustrated by the absence of any real change in the unequal distribution of income and wealth to the rich and the poor in Canada over the last half-century or more, and by the increasing concentration of ownership among large-scale business enterprises in this same period. Together, these patterns suggest that Canada, like other capitalist societies, will continue to be a country in which major inequalities exist between the powerful and the powerless, or the haves and the have-nots. These are much the same inequalities that sociologists have been studying since the time of Marx and Weber, and they seem destined to be subjects of concern to us for the foreseeable future.

Questions for Review and Critical Thinking

1. Structural functionalists argue that social inequality, or what they usually refer to as social "stratification," is necessary to motivate the best or most qualified individuals to seek the most important positions in society. What does this view imply about the motivations or

abilities of those individuals and groups that do not attain high positions? How would they respond to this argument?

2. Some have said that Marx's theory of classes and revolution is not relevant to modern societies such as Canada. Can you think of some ways in which this statement is true and some in which it is false? How might recent events in the former Soviet Union, China, and elsewhere influence your response?

3. You have learned in this chapter that the structure of inequality in Canada has remained fairly constant over the years, with both rich and poor maintaining their relative proportions within the total population. What main proposals or programs do you believe could be instituted to eliminate or decrease persistent inequality in Canada?

4. Sociologists have always debated the precise meaning of the concept of social class. Less often do they consider what people in general think about social class. What important characteristics and behaviours, in your opinion, distinguish social classes? Is there one key criterion or are there many? In a mini-research project, ask a sample of your friends or fellow students what social class means to them. See if there are any differences of opinion among them. For example, do men and women give different responses? Older and younger people? Poorer and richer people?

5. How hard is it to "get ahead" in Canadian society? What are some of the principal barriers to social mobility in Canada? How might these be removed?

Key Terms

achieved status, p. 121
ascribed status, p. 120
bourgeoisie, p. 123
class, p. 121
class for itself, p. 124
class in itself, p. 123
class, status group, party, p. 126
horizontal mobility, p. 121
institutionalized power, p. 120
intergenerational mobility, p. 121
intragenerational mobility, p. 121

power, p. 119
proletariat, p. 123
social class, p. 121
social differentiation, p. 119
social inequality, p. 119
status, p. 120
status consistency, p. 120
status hierarchy, p. 120
status inconsistency, p. 120
status set, p. 120
stratum, p. 120
vertical mobility, p. 121

Suggested Readings

Allahar, Anton, and James Côté
1998 *Richer and Poorer: The Structure of Inequality in Canada.* Toronto: James Lorimer.
The authors use a framework that centres on the role of dominant ideology to examine social inequality in Canada, with a special focus on class, gender, age, and race/ethnicity.

Carroll, William
2004 *Corporate Power in a Globalizing World. A Study in Elite Organization.* Don Mills, ON: Oxford University Press.
This analysis is the most recent and detailed study on the nature of corporate power in Canada. The book also has the added dimension of assessing the role of Canada's corporate elite and economic structure within the larger global capitalist system.

Curtis, James, Edward Grabb, and Neil Guppy (eds.)
2004 *Social Inequality in Canada: Patterns, Problems, and Policies* (4th ed.). Toronto: Pearson Education Canada.
This book, a collection of articles dealing with all the major social hierarchies in Canada, also considers some of the important consequences of social inequality for people, as well as policies that could be implemented to alleviate problems of inequality.

Grabb, Edward G.
2002 *Theories of Social Inequality: Classical and Contemporary Perspectives* (4th ed.). Toronto: Thomson Nelson.
This book reviews and evaluates the major perspectives on social inequality that have emerged from classical and contemporary social theory.

Krahn, Harvey, and Graham Lowe
2002 *Work, Industry, and Canadian Society* (4th ed.).
Toronto: Thomson Nelson.
This book reviews a range of sociological issues pertaining to the study of work and industry in Canada, including labour force trends, women's employment, the organization of work, and questions of power and control at work.

Websites

www.hewett.norfolk.sch.uk/curric/soc/marx/
marx1.htm
The Karl Marx Page
Read more about the man and his work at this site.

www.ccsd.ca/
The Canadian Council on Social Development
This site provides a wealth of statistical and other data on income inequality, poverty, and welfare in Canada.

Key Search Terms

Inequality
Social Class
Social Mobility
Status

For more study tools to help you with your next exam, be sure to check out the Companion Website at **www.pearsoned.ca/hewitt**, as well as Chapter 6 in your Study Guide.

[7]

gender relations

james j. teevan

Introduction[1]

Some of the gender chapters in other introductory sociology texts are dated, or have errors in data interpretation, and some are more ideological (saying what "should be") than sociological (what is). This Gender Relations chapter is critical and, written by the same person who wrote Chapter 2, Research Methods, it reminds students to examine the adequacy of current research on gender.

This chapter starts with a controversial issue: sex (gender) differences. Imagine that you have just read of two spousal homicides. In one, the victim's body had one fatal knife wound to the chest. In the other, the victim was struck by multiple bullets, children were also killed, and the killer committed suicide. Can you guess which scenario was a husband killing his wife and which was a wife killing her husband? Without ever taking a criminology course most people get the right answer (the husband repeatedly shot his wife). In the end, he committed suicide and the woman with the knife lived to investigate the potential of a battered wife syndrome defence.

Now put on your methodological cap. The data are clear (e.g., weapon, number of bodies), so measurement of this gender difference is adequate. Next, recall the discussion about sampling. There are very few spouse murderers, or murderers of any kind, in Canada. Therefore, we must not generalize from this example to all spouse killers much less to the millions of Canadians innocent of this crime by saying, for example, "men are brutal." There are always exceptions: some men spare their children and some women do not. What other factors—*control* variables—are relevant? For example, is the gender gap less obvious when alcohol is involved in a spousal murder? Further, what is it specifically about being male that leads to the excess—could it be that high levels of testosterone lead to impulsiveness and then to brutality? Could chronic unemployment be a source? These are examples of the kinds of questions one should ask when examining gender differences.

A second example illustrates a greater difficulty in determining gender differences. A recent report said that females outnumber males by almost 3 to 1 among

[1]In this chapter, *CST* will be used in parentheses (along with a year and volume number) as an abbreviation for *Canadian Social Trends*, a quarterly Statistics Canada publication containing articles on a variety of social topics.

15- to 19-year-olds hospitalized for attempted suicide. Is this another example of how it is harder to be a woman in Canada? Recall from Chapter 1 that Durkheim, in the earliest of sociological research, noted a higher suicide rate for males than for females. So what is going on, have things changed? No. This trend still holds true in Canada today where, among 15- to 19-year-olds, three males kill themselves for every female who does so (*CST*, 2002: 66). So, part of the reason that there are more females in hospital is because the males are in the morgue. As an aside, who is more likely to take poison and who shoots himself in these suicidal acts? The answer lies in the pronoun.

This chapter begins with a discussion of gender differences in the context of the nurture and nature positions introduced in Chapter 4, Socialization. What can nature and what can nurture tell us about gender differences regarding longevity, fatal car accidents, concern for the environment, etc.? The chapter then moves to a vigorously debated subtopic: numeracy and literacy differences between boys and girls, with an evaluation of recent research framing that discussion.

A second major section of the chapter looks at the explanations offered for the differential treatment of men and women and at gender socialization, the process in which one learns how to be male or female and how much of each. Finally, as it would be impossible in an introductory book to cover all of the research in the burgeoning study of gender, a third section examines three important areas in gender research: body image, work and pay issues, and abuse. The chapter concludes with a discussion of the future of gender differences.

Biological and Social Determinism

In Chapter 4, Socialization, we saw that human behaviour is influenced by both culture (nurture) and biology (nature). For example, childrearing books will tell you that while a small number of children are fearful of the unfamiliar from birth (nature), parents can reduce that fear in almost half of the cases (nurture). Let us now examine gender differences in this light, keeping in mind the political implications—nurture implies a possibility of change, nature is more fixed—and how the weight assigned to one factor or the other varies with the specific behaviour being explained.

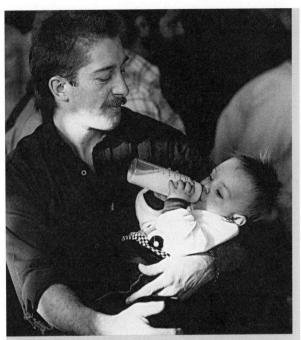

Biological determinism applied to gender relations is seen increasingly as myth.

A greater support among women than men for protecting the environment (Dietz, Kalof, and Stern, 2002) is an intriguing difference, but probably not a genetic one. That men are more likely to vote for conservative political candidates and that they are more sarcastic are also probably due to social factors. What about gender differences in health and longevity? Here, both biology and social factors are at work: genes and lifestyle. At the end of the last century, women could expect to live 81.4 years and men 75.9 years (see Chapter 16, Demography and Urbanization). Is this biology? Maybe not, as when deaths from preventable causes like unsafe sex, poor driving, smoking, and excessive drinking are factored out, the gap reverses and men have a slight advantage (*London Free Press*, 30/9/2003, p. C8). Thus, social variables also affect the gender gap. Changes over time in the size of that longevity gap (while gene pools remained relatively constant over that time) and different-sized gaps in different ethnic groups in the same society also suggest social influences. But it is not an either/or nature/nurture situation. More male than female infants die immediately after birth and castration increases male life expectancy. These facts may need biological, not social, explanations.

Moreover, that five-and-a-half-year gap does not mean that all women outlive all men. Many men outlive a wife or sister and some live to be 100. In fact, the normal range of age at death for both men and women is much greater than the gap separating the two. In the field of statistics the first is called *within* variation (comparing males to males or females to females), the second *between* variation (comparing males to females) (see Figure 7.1). Let's say the great majority of men who live to adulthood die between ages 55 and 95; women, 60 and 100—each a range of about forty years, still with many women dying at younger ages than

men (2001 Census). To use gender as a substitute for longevity, as traditional pension plans did (i.e., male = fewer pensionable years and female = more pensionable years), would oversimplify the data.

Numeracy and literacy differences

The debate surrounding differences in mathematical ability is quite intense, for while something like degree of environmental concern generally has little immediate personal consequence for individuals, gender differences in mathematics skills may lead to discouraging

Figure 7.1   "Within" and "Between" Variations for Age at Death

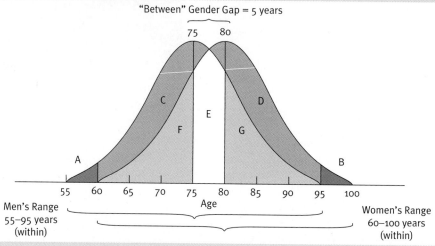

Because, on average, men die earlier and women later, pension plans used to pay the men more per month (for fewer months), and paid women less (for more months). While that system should equalize total *lifetime* payments for all men and women as *groups*, the figure above shows how it creates inequities for *individual* male and female pensioners, both to those women who die at a young age and to the men who do not.

Area A: all of these men die at younger ages than women.

Area B: all of these women die at older ages than men.

> No bias; paying these men more monthly for a shorter period and these women less per month for a longer period matches their mortality.

Area C: the greater number of men than women who die at ages 60–75.

Area D: the greater number of women than men alive at ages 80–95.

> Along with above, the basis of the "pay men more, pay women less" policy; bias begins but excused, with cases not fitting the general model seen as "exceptions."

Area E: women dying a bit younger than female average; men dying a little later than male average.

> Some bias but less than below since rates are close to expected.

Area F: women dying at younger age than male average.

Area G: men dying at older age than female average.

> Great bias; these men should be paid less and these women more if longevity is the only factor behind pension differences.

Remembering Research Methods When Studying Gender Differences

After hearing about a scoutmaster abusing his scouts some people will say that homosexuals are pedophiles and should not be allowed to lead youth organizations. But probably about 90 percent of pedophiles are actually heterosexual and only 10 percent homosexual. What is going on here? Recalling Chapter 2, Research Methods, how many variables do you see in this example? Sexuality is one: either homosexual or heterosexual. Pedophilia, however, is not a variable but a *constant* (discussed in Chapter 2, Research Methods). Instances where pedophilia do not occur are not counted.

We also introduced independent and dependent variables in that chapter, and pointed out that, in analysis, the independent variable should add to 100 percent. Does being a pedophile determine sexual orientation? No. In the general argument, sexual orientation is the "cause" or independent variable and pedophilia the dependent variable. But here pedophilia is the variable adding to 100 percent.

To evaluate a "sexuality leads to pedophilia argument," a comparison between the incidence of pedophilia among homosexuals and heterosexuals is needed. Such a comparison will show that *heterosexuals* are the majority of pedophiles. But this should not be overplayed. In fact, heterosexuals are the majority of astronauts, left-handed people, comic book readers, and poor drivers, not because of their sexuality but *because there are so many more of them than homosexuals.* Comparing the percents will show which group actually has the higher rate.

An exception

Now consider the statement that 95 percent of pedophiles are men. While gender is a variable (women are the other 5 percent of pedophiles), pedophilia is again a constant. Having said that, the 95 percent of pedophiles are men figure actually might have some use. If you were in charge of an over-stretched police force and heard rumours of a pedophile ring in town, how many officers would you deploy to put women under surveillance? Even amidst charges of *gender profiling*, you would concentrate on males. Also note that there are fewer men than women in Canada, so the explanation used in the previous example does not work here. Indeed more men than women are pedophiles despite the fact that there are fewer men than women. So sometimes the figures are useful. Just be especially careful when you do not have a variable, and when you do, make sure that it is the independent variable, not the dependent, that adds to 100 percent.

Are there similar issues that should be considered in concluding that the majority of abortions are performed on married women rather than on single women?

the over 60 percent of women in today's paid labour force from entering certain occupations.

Gender imbalances in postsecondary education are well documented. Female students are overrepresented in the humanities and social sciences while male students are the majority in mathematics, technology, and sciences (see Table 7.1 on page 163). An Israeli study (Ayalon, 2003) found high school to be one source of the differences: girls do not take as many advanced math courses as boys do. Even when they do, a U.S. study (Leahey and Guo, 2001) found a faster rate of acceleration for high school boys, despite relative gender equality in elementary school. By grade 12, a slight gender difference is apparent, especially in geometry, which requires spatial reasoning. Canadian data also show that girls use computers less at school than do boys (*CST*, 2003: 69).

One would then expect to find women underrepresented among applicants to mathematics-related fields of study at university, and they are. Actually, strong mathematics skills in high school are related to applications to the *non-math*-related, but high-demand and selective, fields of study at university, thus expanding its effects (Ayalon, 2003). That influence of mathematics skills continues thus into the workforce. Mitra (2002) found that, although women earn significantly less money than men, possession of mathematics skills leads to significant wage premiums across all groups of workers, and that women with superior mathematics abilities enjoy wage premiums equal to *or greater than* those of men. The gender wage gap is not significant among professionals with above-average mathematics skills.

Are such findings a result of society valuing mathematical ability, a skill possessed more often by males, over literacy, at which females excel? Indeed there is growing concern today about growing gender differences in literacy, with boys lagging further behind girls in literacy than girls lag behind boys in math. Some think that the greater physical activity among boys (biological factor?) discourages parents from reading to them as often as they do to girls (a social factor). But improving that situation is very difficult. Thus most research tends to look at problems that are easier to solve—at the high school curriculum, segregated classes, and teaching styles, among other things—to see if the gap can be reduced. But that, too, can be difficult. For example, Duffy, Warren, and Walsh (2001) found that female mathematics teachers, potential role models for girls, tend to interact somewhat more with their male than their female students, a discrepancy *not* caused by the boys verbally initiating the contact. On the other hand, an interesting experiment found that girls told that they may not do well on a math test actually do less well, while boys given the same message do *better*, perhaps in an "I'll show you" fashion. Positive expectations thus may be even more important for girls than for boys (Brown and Josephs, 1999).

While such studies point to social explanations for at least part of the gender difference in mathematics, nature and biological sources exist and more are still being uncovered. Just as men and women have different body mass, strength, and a preponderance of certain hormones, there are differences in their brain structures, too. A problem occurs when these biological explanations exaggerate what we called *between* variation and ignore the greater *within* variation, a situation compounded when lower expectations in mathematics for women lead to their lessened abilities in a self-fulfilling prophecy. Let us say it again: All boys do not do better at math than all girls, at any age. Data like those presented in Figure 7.1 can reveal just how much overlap there is and then the nurture position will argue that any gap can be lessened.

This discussion touches only the tip of this crucial topic. Rosenfeld (2002), a feminist scholar, said that all research on gender differences should be context-specific, encourage cross-cultural extensions, look for similarities as well as differences, examine variation within as well as between groups, and go beyond gender as a category per se to see it as one of many bases of inequality. And finally, when researchers repeatedly find little or no inequality, they should accept this, she said. Continuing to argue as some do that despite finding no inequality it still *must* exist, begins to turn research into ideology.

Sex and Gender: Some Definitions

For sociologists, sex and gender are not the same. A person's **sex** is a *biological* trait characterized by the XX chromosomes and estrogen for a female and the XY chromosomes and testosterone for a male. Males are typically larger, more muscular, have more hair, and have deeper voices. The reproductive organs are different, though complementary. **Gender** is a *social* construct based, in part, on definitions of masculinity and femininity and consisting largely of the norms and expectations that encourage people to behave in a "sex-appropriate" manner. Learning masculine and feminine gender roles occurs early in the socialization process and the specific content of that learning varies across cultures and over time (cf. Bonvillain, 2001). Recall the three societies described in Chapter 3, Culture, especially the Arapesh, in which both men and women were nurturing and cooperative (things traditionally thought of as more feminine) and the Mundugamor, where both men and women were hostile and uncaring. While one's sex is rarely changed (see the box "Difficulties in Classification"), one's gender can be changed though often with difficulty. Gender can be likened to *achieved* statuses (described in Chapter 6, Social Inequality) to highlight this greater flexibility. So were the differences at the beginning of the chapter sex or gender differences? Testosterone's relation to longevity suggests a strong sexual underpinning; concern for the environment is probably gender related; the real battle is over math ability—how much of it is sex (biology, and therefore very hard to change) and how much is gender (social, and perhaps easier to change)? The choice of terminology may reflect the bias of the researcher.

Gender roles are socially created and then learned; people are not born with them.

Gender identity is the perception, developed probably by age three, of oneself as male or female. It is not to be confused with sexual orientation, and is not necessarily consistent with a person's sex (cf. Kroger, 2000). **Gendered order** is a macro-level concept and refers not to individuals but to social structure. It includes gendered norms, gendered roles, and a gendered ideology, which together make social life gendered, directing how males and females *should* act. Its biggest influence is to create a **gendered division of labour** in which males and females, in both the unpaid and paid labour arenas, tend to act "gender-appropriately." Men take on more demanding jobs and less housework, and women, the opposite. The terms introduced in this section will help investigate gender theory, the next section.

Major Theoretical Perspectives on Gender

The four theoretical perspectives introduced in Chapter 1 can be applied to the topic of gender relations. We begin with an examination of structural functionalism, then symbolic interactionism, next a conflict-oriented (Marxist) approach, and conclude with feminist views.

Structural functionalism

Functionalist arguments about gender appear less frequently in sociology today than in the past. The main functionalist position, as you have seen, is that social practices, such as a gendered division of labour, persist because they benefit society in some way. Gender, then, is just another of the social conventions, such as family and law, that maintain order and promote social stability. More specifically, given a society's need to reproduce for it to survive, and given women's greater vulnerability and reduced mobility in the later stages of pregnancy and postpartum breastfeeding, they need protection and care at this time. One can debate how long the vulnerability really lasts, whether breastfeeding is necessary for all mothers or even necessary at all, and if non-pregnant women could perform the protective role instead of men. But let us assume that the general functional argument has some validity. The greater problem arises when that temporary vulnerability expands to include broader

Difficulties in Classification

Sociologist Aaron Devor, Dean of Graduate Studies at the University of Victoria, is wearing a charcoal grey suit, grey shirt, and black and white tie for an interview published in *Maclean's* (26 May 2003). He was once Holly Devor, a masculine, pants-wearing, female sociologist who studied "gender blenders"—women who, because of their physical appearance, are regularly mistaken for men. The name change to Aaron was merely another step in a long process traceable back to his childhood.

He misses the greater ease women have in exposing their feelings to others. On the other hand, he appreciates the greater freedom of movement men have; men can walk down a dark street relatively unafraid of a sexual assault (Devor, 1989).

Using our terms, Professor Devor's gender is masculine. His sex was not revealed in the article and may still be female. His example brings up some of the difficulties in gender identity, and specifically of the **transgendered**, those who include aspects of both genders. *Transvestite*,

for example, is a common term for a cross-dresser and is applied more often to males than females. Recall from Chapter 3, Culture, that Zuni society allowed men known as *berdaches* to dress and work as women (Lorber, 1994). In Canada, the practice is more often intermittent, with the person dressing sometimes as a man and at other times a woman, but still it means that there is not a match between sex and gender.

There are also *transsexuals* who anatomically are one sex, but feel like and want to be treated as a member of the other sex. So inconsistent are their gender identity and their sex that some may seek medical procedures to change their sex, removing the sexual parts of their anatomy. Hormonal therapy aids in the transformation and in some instances an artificial vagina or a penis can be created. This is an example of the social construction not only of gender but also of sex. The fact that more men than women undergo the operation may be related to the especially strong intolerance of effeminate males by other males.

How would adding sexuality distinctions (preferring same sex: homosexuality; either sex: bisexuality; and different sex: heterosexuality) complicate these distinctions? For example, how are female heterosexual transvestites different from male heterosexual transvestites?

Is homosexuality more common among the male or the female transgendered?

gender stereotypes. For example, a mother's initial primary responsibility for infant care can lead to pressures that she take permanent responsibility for all childcare and housework, then to avoiding occupations that require time away from the home, and finally to the father's becoming the permanent "breadwinner."

Occupying such a status, then, implies other functional imperatives for men. Breadwinners have access to the **public realm** of paid labour and perform the *instrumental tasks* needed for survival. In a competitive workplace, they must be strong, even aggressive, and smart. Rationality is preferred over emotionality. On the other hand, in the traditional functional argument, women are relegated to the **private realm** of the home, providing unpaid domestic labour and responsible for *expressive tasks* like nurturing and providing emotional support. The private sphere is valued less than the

public one, and its inhabitants are generally dependent on inhabitants of the public realm. When both husband and wife work in the paid labour market, his job is the more important one; they move if his job requires it and it is usually her responsibility to miss work to care for sick children. In this public/private division of labour, partners are seen as complementing each other, making social order possible.

By now, you are probably ready to debate such functionalist thought. Just look at its assumptions: that a family needs both a mother and a father (Statistics Canada, *Annual Demographic Statistics*, Catalogue No. 91-213, estimated that 15.8 percent of families with children had a lone parent in 2000); that heterosexual unions are the only type of union possible; and it overlooks the fact that many parents, especially women, work a *double shift* as paid employees and unpaid homemakers. You also know by now that gender differences are relative, not absolute. Each binary duality, for example, public/private, should be thought of as a continuum: most men do some housework and some women none; most women earn some money and some men none, even though neither realm is equally shared. Next we examine a less dated and more relevant perspective (cf. Rosaldo, 2002).

The symbolic interactionist perspective

Symbolic interactionists, you will recall, see the world as socially constructed and changeable. Unlike functionalists, they do not see the gendered division of labour as a natural outcome of the need to reproduce, and are especially critical of any extensions of this position that generalize to a female dependency and a male dominance. Definitions of masculinity and femininity, gender roles, and gender norms are all *negotiable*. Even gender identity is not fixed and immutable as can be seen in the cases of transsexuals and other exceptions to a male/female duality (see the box "Difficulties in Classification").

Norms surrounding definitions of masculinity and femininity, defining behaviours as more appropriate to one sex or the other, are still very powerful in our society. While men may be more sensitive and openly affectionate than they were in previous generations, limits still remain. Hints of homosexuality are avoided; men can hug, but in ways that minimize any genital contact and they generally cannot kiss other men. Women can be executives, but calling attention to the lesser competence of male colleagues too often or too publicly can bring informal sanctions.

The main contribution of symbolic interactionist thought in the current context is in the area of socialization. Brown and Gilligan (1992) argued that children *learn* gendered behaviour through a variety of processes, such as imitating others (especially significant others) and receiving rewards and punishments (including shame and name-calling) for behaviour defined as gender-appropriate or -inappropriate. They saw gender more as a product of social and cultural, rather than biological, influences. Parents and siblings and then peers, schools, religions, the mass media, and the workplace all play roles in continuing the gendered order. Verbal cues are also

I Hope It's a Boy

In Canada each year, a slightly greater number of males than females are born. You might wonder if the gap is because expectant parents, especially fathers, want a son. In fact, women anticipating a pregnancy also prefer sons, changing to a daughter preference only after conception (Marleau and Saucier, 2002).

Much of the discrepancy is because, from a *functionalist* standpoint, more males at birth are needed, for from day one, males have a higher mortality rate than females. By young adulthood and reproduction time, the numbers are about equal (see Chapter 16, Demography and Urbanization), a functional balance not achievable if the numbers had been equal at birth.

Although exact figures are in dispute, in some countries like China, Vietnam, India, and Bangladesh, fewer female than male babies are born (Arnold, Kishor, and Roy, 2002). Here it is not biology at work, but selective abortion. The difference is found especially in cultures where a groom takes his dowry-bearing bride from her family to live with his, with the expectation that she will care for his parents in their old age. As long as some other families produce daugh-ters, a preference for a son is thus functional, as long as you recall the question of Chapter 1: "Functional for whom?"

Does already having one or more children of one sex make selective abortion to ensure a child of a different sex more acceptable than if the abortion is performed on a first pregnancy?

thought to play a role (see the box "Language and Cultural Values").

Most behaviour is affected by what is defined as gender-appropriate, from the clothes worn, to more serious matters like the amount of food eaten, to life-altering issues of safety, choice of occupation, and parental responsibilities. The norms are sometimes loudly proclaimed (boys do not wear bows in their hair) and sometimes less so (in disagreements in a math competition, a girl should defer to her boy partner's answer). A dress, shiny shoes, and long hair may not fully dictate behaviour, but they certainly convey a different message than pants, sneakers, and short hair. The toys and clothes in stores (Raag and Rackliffe, 1998) give off subtle and not-so-subtle messages about gender expectations. Any doubts will be cleared up when peer group terms like "gay," "fag," "sissy," "tomboy," and "dyke" are publicly and loudly expressed.

Finally we should mention again that gender is really a continuum rather than a duality, from very masculine, through *androgyny* (blending both masculine and feminine), to very feminine. Stereotypes can be changed, but it is a slow process, and pioneers face a hard battle in any society not yet ready for such change.

A Marxist conflict perspective

Marxists put primary emphasis on economic forces. They view the economy as the driving force in society, influencing such things as religion (see Chapter 11, Religion), the law (see Chapter 5, Deviance), and communications (see Chapter 12, Media). This position implies that concentrating on ethnic, racial, and gender inequalities instead of social class inequities can lead to divisions and infighting within those groups (e.g., men against women, French Canada versus English Canada) that will

[Social Trends]

Language and Cultural Values

Compared to French, the English language is relatively gender-neutral. French has *la chasteté,* for chastity and *la comerre,* for gossip (both feminine words), but a hammer is *le marteau* and a chisel *le ciseau* (both masculine words). Before we go too far, we should note that the French words for ambition, adventure, and chemistry are also feminine.

The question here is the extent to which language communicates cultural values that in turn may affect behaviour. More broadly, what is the role of language in the ideology of gender inequality? When we say "man and wife," rather than the parallel "husband and wife" or a parallel but reversed "wife and husband," does this encourage differential treatment of men and women? Did widespread use of terms like fireman, businessman, and chairman make girls think they could not play such roles?

The use of gender-neutral terms in English is now widely accepted and today there are many more women firefighters, businesspeople, and chairpersons (or the less

hierarchical term *facilitators*). How much of this can be attributed to efforts to eradicate linguistic sexism? This topic has not been fully studied, probably because it cannot be: an experiment on vocational choices, in which half of the children are exposed to sexist terminology (fireman, chairman, etc.) and half are not would be highly unethical.

There is an alternative, however, to that unethical experiment. Quebec has a gendered language while Ontario does not; the traditional Québécois equivalent of Ontario's gender neutral "doctor" is *le medecin.* Showing that fewer Quebec than Ontario women are becoming doctors could be evidence of the adverse effects of linguistic sexism. The data, however, show that Quebec actually has proportionally *more* women in medical school than other provinces. While this does not disconfirm the effects of linguistic sexism, it does encourage looking for other factors. For example, perhaps lobbying, legislation, government pressure, and a growing number of female doctor role models encourage women to study medicine.

What effects could be expected from dressing infants in gender-neutral colours, thus avoiding the traditional practice of pastels for a girl and dark colours for a boy?

Young children are encouraged to behave in ways considered sex-appropriate.

delay the ultimate revolution of the workers against the ruling class. Some Marxists even suggest that capitalists deliberately fuel such disputes for this purpose.

With this economic focus, it is not surprising that gender inequality was not an issue for Marx. Indeed, today he would be called sexist as most of his writings were about male workers. Women were seen as mothers and housewives, a view shared by functionalists, the intellectual opponents of Marxists. Marx's co-author Engels (1884) did pay more attention to women, likening their position in the family to that of the oppressed working class in the larger society. Neither men nor women possessed the means of production and each was in fact like property: workers of the capitalists, wives of their husbands. In the end, early feminists also found Engels lacking; male dominance has to be more than just a parallel to the divide between capitalists and proletariat.

Some modern socialists have responded by trying to unite Marx and later feminist thought. First they link the subordination of women to the Industrial Revolution and thus capitalism. Factories took workers away from their homes, resulting in a need for someone to stay at home and care for children, resulting in a gender inequality greater than had existed in the farm economy that preceded industrialism. This "cult of domesticity" reinforced the earlier biologically constructed beliefs about pregnancy and childbearing, strengthening the position that men and women have different innate interests and capabilities. The culture of the Victorian age then solidified—perhaps even worsened—the division.

Feminist perspectives

There is no single feminist perspective; heterosexual and homosexual feminists often disagree, as may those who are members of visible minority groups and those who are not. They do, however, generally concur that the main force behind women's oppression, in Canada and elsewhere, is **patriarchy**, a system in which the traits associated with men are valued more than those associated with women. This gives men *unearned* privilege relative to women (Calasanti, 1996). Although there is some agreement about the role of patriarchy in oppression, different views become apparent when it comes to dealing with it.

Liberal feminism argues that gender inequality can be remedied by giving women greater opportunity. Legislation for pay equity and employment equity policies, free universal day care, and ending the sexism in our high schools and universities that restricts women's choice or occupation, are some of its focuses. The basic assumption of liberal feminism is an essential equality between males and females, one often suppressed, but achievable. Moreover, according to liberal feminists gender inequality is the main problem in today's society, bigger than the inequalities of race, age, region, and social class. It is this second assumption that is most offensive to the next feminist position. Also see the box "Working Toward Change" at the end of the chapter, which includes a discussion of employment equity.

Socialist feminism agrees that patriarchy must be eradicated, but methodologically speaking, seeks a longer causal chain. Capitalism is the real issue they say. Just as it leads to factories for husbands, it is a cause of patriarchy and the relegation of wives to isolated homes and domestic labour that is always undervalued. An end to capitalism will lead to the end of patriarchy (cf. Kourany, Sterba, and Tong, 1999). This view also questions claims from senior women corporate executives that sexism limits their careers. Theoretically, the relentless greed of capitalists should outweigh such limits with promotions awarded to anyone who can bring in the most money.

From a male viewpoint, one can see another link between capitalism and patriarchy. Men must subordinate themselves, sometimes in ways they would prefer not to, to their employers and one way to maintain their dignity is to control others, starting with a wife and children. This idea was extended by Johnson (1997), who argued that patriarchy is sustained by men's fear of other men, with fear of their male capitalist bosses a major component. Only increasing workers' sense of control at work can reduce this fear, thus lessening men's needs to control their families.

Radical feminism has one goal, the abolition of male supremacy, and two connected focuses: biological reproduction and paid labour. It says that as long as women have full responsibility for children in the home, they cannot be equal in the workplace. Some radical feminists thus argue for alternative reproduction strategies, like *in vitro* fertilization, to permanently eliminate men's domination of women's bodies. They suggest that employers will always get around the employment equity programs of liberal feminists. And few today, except for a few diehard Marxists, really expect an end to capitalism. Control over one's body is thus the key to ending women's oppression and it must not involve pills or patches with side effects, inserts that can damage one's internal organs, or awkward devices that lessen a woman's sexual pleasure.

Three Areas of Difference

As mentioned in the introduction, it would be difficult to examine all of the recent research on gender. This next section covers only three areas in gender research: body image, work and pay issues, and abuse. These topics should suffice as they encompass a varied and contentious territory.

Body image

Obesity among children aged 7 to 18 has tripled in the recent past, and that generation is the first in modern history to potentially have a shorter life span than its parents' generation (*London Free Press*, 2 Nov. 2003: 15).

Weight is the largest factor—more important than all others combined—in satisfaction with one's appearance (Garner, 1997). Dieting is epidemic, with new fads appearing yearly, and although health is sometimes the reason, an improved appearance is virtually always a goal. But the focus of this chapter is on gender differences in such behaviour.

Let us begin with a look at adolescent girls and young women. Many females in North America are victims of what Hesse-Bieber called the *cult of thinness* (1996: 11), the never-ending fight to be (unnaturally) slim. Some girls even smoke to suppress appetite, and girls now outnumber boys among adolescent users of tobacco. Manufacturers may even target girls by calling some cigarettes "slim." The full price for this practice will be realized as the female death rates from lung cancer catch up with those of men. The desire to be slim also may have more immediate and sometimes deadly consequences. *Anorexia*, a voluntary starvation, is a serious illness that begins at earlier ages and, when combined with emetics to induce vomiting, can be fatal. *Bulimia*, a pattern of (binge) overeating and then purging through the use of laxatives and emetics, is less often fatal but still damaging; bulimics often lose teeth (stomach acids eat away the enamel) and suffer serious vitamin and mineral deficiencies.

Such eating disorders affect thousands of young Canadian women, but extreme cases are the minority. More girls binge-eat without the vomiting and others limit themselves to dieting and obsessive exercise. Measurement of the problem is fairly good although there may be problems in diagnosis and some under-reporting does occur. (Boys, whom some estimate at 10 percent of those with eating disorders, more often fail to report it, not wanting to admit having what is perceived as a "girls' disease" [Drummond, 2002].) Girls who are prone to obesity and those who are subject to repeated negative comments concerning their shape, weight, and eating habits are especially vulnerable to eating disorders, again demonstrating a combination of biological and social factors. A 2003 report from Statistics Canada (Health Reports Supplement: *How Healthy Are Canadians?* Catalogue No. 82-003-SIE) added that a girl's poor self-concept can lead to depression and then obesity. For a boy, the poor self-concept leads to physical inactivity and then obesity. This difference reminds us of the need to compare girls' eating and body-image problems with those of boys.

Boys suffer eating disorders much less frequently (Boles and Johnson, 2001) and are usually trying to *gain* weight. This occurs despite the fact that they are slightly more likely to be obese than girls, 19 percent versus 17 percent (*CST*, 2003: 68) and much less likely to be underweight, 5 percent versus 13 percent (*CST* 2002: 67). This gap widens among 15- to 19-year-olds. Most men would like a trim muscular body, to be "buff," but this desire generally does not lead to the excesses that women use to conform to society's beauty norms. Adolescent male steroid use is increasing (Labre, 2002) despite the publicity surrounding its dangers, but obsessive jogging and visits to the gym are the more common male approach. Still, the Web contains offers of "pec" implants and tummy liposuction, and such operations occur with growing frequency among men.

The average size of the erect male penis is 15 centimetres, both for those men who, in an unaroused state, appear smaller ("grow-ers") and those who look bigger ("show-ers"). The fact that some men feel inadequate in this area may be related to a lack of knowledge of this

Ideas of beauty and attractiveness are culturally produced, especially by the mass media and fashion industry.

fact, but for others it may be what they see in the locker and shower rooms of their high school physical education classes (cf. Drummond, 2003). The "larger" boys, some because of an earlier puberty, may be more willing to use the traditionally open and shared showers, the "smaller" boys less so, thus increasing observer estimates of what average penis size is. Other factors include sexual myths, competitive spirit, and the numerous ads on the Web, but whatever the cause, most men would like a larger penis. Some men shave their pubic area to make their penis *appear* larger. Others have an operation that cuts the skin that holds the penis in, allowing it to fall out more and *appear* larger, even despite a small chance of post-operation impotence.

For women, hips and breasts are common sources of dissatisfaction, the latter more frequently a focus of self-improvement techniques. Magazines tell them that men like women with moderate-sized breasts. To achieve this, some young girls will stuff their bras or do special exercises; later they will buy enhancing bras and a few even get surgical implants. Still others will seek uplift and breast-reduction surgery to reduce sagging, or modifications to specific breast parts. A small percentage of these women will lose breast sensitivity as a result.

The media and the fashion industry get a large share of the blame for the widespread body image dissatisfaction of both men and women. Their actual responsibility can never be directly proved, as a true experiment is ethically unacceptable, and gathering a real control group, one unexposed to such influences, would be impossible. Natural field studies are probably the closest we can get to an experiment. Kilbourne, a media critic, for example, claimed that dieting among girls in Fiji increased greatly after television was introduced, an especially interesting finding since the prior norm was for fuller-bodied women. Botta (2003) also documented how girls' fashion magazines and sports magazines for those boys who buy into them, are a source for body image dissatisfaction. With computer enhancement of images common in these magazines, an even more impossible-to-achieve goal is created. Recall the discussion in Chapter 3, Culture, on the impossibility of achieving the body measurements of toys like Barbie or GI Joe, each an expression of a cultural norm of physical attractiveness.

Such blaming of the media takes away some of the *agency* of these women and men. Are they not able to define what they see on the television or magazines as fantasy, as they do in other instances like space travel movies, and to counter peer pressure? Indeed advocates for equality in the workplace are especially careful not to depict women as so vulnerable to suggestion and incapable of independent thought. Or, as Marx would have suggested, are they just additional victims of capitalist exploitation, a class *in* themselves but not *for* themselves?

Whoever is to blame, not meeting these impossible-to-achieve norms leads not only to punishing diets and excessive exercise, but also to lower self-esteem problems and even suicide. Those who fail in their attempts to alter their bodies suffer blame and guilt, perceiving that they did not buy the right stuff or try hard enough. Even those who fight back against unrealistic body appearance norms may never totally erase doubts about their decision.

Objectification is a deeper problem, and involves viewing a person as an object, usually a sexual object. Advertisements routinely encourage the practice, more often with female than male models, as when on television women's bodies are used to sell a product such as beer. Revealing clothes are substituted for an illustration of the merits of the product. In the area of seductive poses, the gender gap grows. For an exercise, take a sample of ads and compare the number of men versus the number of women with their or someone else's finger in their mouths, or their legs suggestively positioned. A glance at department store ads gives the impression that women must be buying a new bra at least once a week, so prevalent are the depictions. But demonstrating, not just asserting, that such objectification leads to seeing women as things and then to greater violence against them is still an unfinished task.

The loudest criticisms arise when objectification occurs in the workplace, interfering with women's achievements there. In this instance, it is perhaps more clear to say that a role conflict occurs, as when someone busy at work gets an important but not emergency personal phone call, and must choose which role takes precedence. Here, the situation is even more difficult because, for most women, the sexual role is not one they want to occupy at work but it arises too often.

Certainly the preference in ads is for attractive, thin, young women with beautiful hair and ample breasts. But what kind of men does advertising favour? The men who appear in male cologne ads, for example, are often almost nude, and almost always young, slim, and handsome. Men's hair and fashion magazines also rarely feature average looking, hairy, heavy, or short men, or men with bald spots. This may be a factor in the increase in male hair implants (a solution not popular among the many older women with thinning hair issues) and why some men shave their chests. And while it is true that roles for aging female actors dry up more quickly than for aging male actors, and an older male more often than an older female is shown being romantically linked with someone younger, it is the younger men and women who sell the most tickets. As the pioneering feminist Germaine Greer (1992) noted, it is not only women who become invisible in their fifties; men become invisible too. A content analysis of several soap operas would allow you to evaluate her assertion.

To conclude, while the gap is narrowing, more importance is placed on women's appearance than on men's. Women are still the great majority of those having facelifts or undergoing other plastic surgery (Hesse-Bieber, 1996), despite the small, but growing number of men who are seeking tummy tucks and other surgical interventions (Labre, 2002). Most women and men, however, will not go that far.

The gendered wage gap

This section considers the different worlds of work experienced by men and women. Education (normally a prerequisite of occupational choice), gender-related differences in attitudes about paid labour and childcare responsibility, and pay are the specific topics examined.

The great increase of women in the paid workforce over the last 50 years is widely known. In 2002, 59.9 percent of adult women were in the labour force (versus 73.3 percent of adult men). Adding part-time workers to the mix gives women a slight advantage in those working (*CST*, 2003: 69). These differences can be related to women more frequently taking temporary leaves to care for small children and the older generation of women who gave up paid work upon marriage. The discrepancies might have been even higher except that the unemployment rate for males aged 15 to 24 (15.3 percent) is higher than the female rate (11.6 percent), reflecting 2001 data that 17 percent of men versus 13 percent of women do not finish high school (Statistics Canada, Cansim II, Table 282-2002). Further, men are generally found in most occupations, but female ghettoes of teachers and nurses have not disappeared entirely (see Lust and Minot, 2003, on the hidden advantages of men in "female" professions). Table 7.1 shows the percentage of women majoring in education, fine arts, humanities, and nursing in 1998.

As seen in Table 7.1, women are now less likely to major in these four areas; from comprising 69.9 percent of your grandmothers' majors to 38.3 percent of your sisters'. The figures for males also decreased (44.5 percent to 30.6 percent) indicating contributing factors besides gender. Nursing shows the greatest convergence, with more male and fewer female nursing students. Still, women are almost half of physiotherapists, librarians, and primary school educators today. And recall from the last chapter that the broader picture shows many more women entering the growing but poorly paid clerical and retail sales occupations.

A broader examination of postsecondary education shows another imbalance. Women now receive 58 percent and men 42 percent of all university degrees (Statistics

Table 7.1	Percentage of Postsecondary Degrees Granted to Women by Subject and Age Group			
	Age Group			
Field	**20–34**	**35–44**	**45–64**	**65+**
Education	17.9	19.6	32.6	37.0
Fine Arts	3.6	3.5	3.3	3.9
Humanities	12.6	11.7	14.0	16.6
Nursing	4.2	5.9	8.8	12.4
Total (for all four subject areas)	38.3	40.7	58.7	69.9

Source: Adapted from Statistics Canada, 2001 Census, *Education in Canada: Major Fields of Study*, Catalogue No. 97F0018X1E.

Canada, CANSIM, Table 0058-0602), a reversal of the past suggesting future gender differences in the workforce. Women are more often enrolled in social science and commerce, and when in science, they are likely to choose biology. The gender gap is greater in math, engineering, and the physical sciences. The data in Table 7.2 show a growing percentage of women in each science major over time. The exception to this growth is computer science, where women have remained at about 22 percent of the total. Notice that as you move left from the 65+ age group column to the 20-to-34 age group, the numbers generally get bigger, showing more women entering these fields over time. Column 1 is then lower as it is the total of the other columns and includes those 65+ who were most under-represented. Studies that look only at the total could note that women are only 13.2 percent of engineering degree holders. If one looks at the age breakdown, the same data show that women have gone from 3.6 percent to 19.7 percent, a 400+ percent increase; or you could say the percentage of men has gone down somewhat. All figures are correct; they just do not convey the same story.

Both the greater tendency for women to avoid certain types of paid work and to feel a greater responsibility for the unpaid work of the home are part of what was earlier called a *gendered division of labour*. The unpaid work includes *wifework*, meeting a husband's sexual, physical, and emotional needs; *motherwork*, fulfilling the emotional and physical needs of children; and *housework*, care of the home, including cleaning, shopping, cooking, and laundry (Rosenberg, 1990). Today, more of that work is shared

Table 7.2	Percentage of Degrees Granted to Women in Various Science Subjects by Age Group				
	Age Group				
Major	**1** **All**	**2** **20–34**	**3** **35–44**	**4** **45–64**	**5** **65+**
Biology	35.3	38.1	35.2	29.8	29.8
Chemistry	25.8	31.4	28.8	20.9	18.1
Physics	14.9	20.0	14.8	13.1	11.3
Mathematics	27.2	32.0	28.8	24.0	22.3
Computer Science	22.0	21.9	22.5	20.9	24.2
Engineering	13.2	19.7	14.6	7.2	3.6

Source: Adapted from Statistics Canada, 2001 Census, *Education in Canada: Major Fields of Study*, Catalogue No. 97F0018X1IE.

(see the box "When Equal Is Not Equal"); more women (and fewer men) are taking jobs requiring long hours, extended absences from home, and giving precedence to the breadwinner over the parent role. But a gendered division of labour at home still persists. The existence of children in the family widens the gap, with the wife taking on even more unpaid duties (McQuillan and Belle, 2004); she is usually the one who stays home to care for a sick child and who spends more time with an infant than does her partner (*CST*, 2000: 57). It is perhaps for this reason that terms like *husbandwork* and *fatherwork* have not yet become popularized.

The unequal division of labour reinforces the tendency for women to take the "second" job in the family, the one that, although necessary, must be flexible enough to accommodate the unexpected. Often this is not a sexist response directly, but an economic decision based on the larger income. In marriages between doctors and nurses,

[Debate]

When Equal Is Not Equal

I went to the library to read articles about the household division of labour but I could have just asked my wife. We each have our designated chores. She would have told me that I "do" the lawn. This is true and is harder than first appears. I have to consider weather: rain means a delay, evening mosquitoes may mean West Nile, and noon is bad for my fair skin and bald spot. I also have to make sure I have enough gasoline. It takes an hour each week, unless the grass grows really fast. Inside I vacuum and have to decide in which room to start and when to do it. I also have to do the laundry. Sometimes I have too few darks and too many lights for two balanced loads so I save the darks for another week. Lastly, I have to pay the monthly bills and get gas for the car.

My wife makes the meals. She, too, has much to consider beyond the chore itself: Are the ingredients

Source: A conversation with Bonnie Teevan.

still fresh? Will everyone like it? Can it all be prepared at the last minute? Can I substitute an ingredient if I run out of something? Should I make a lot or just enough for tonight? What if one part of the meal unexpectedly takes more time to cook? Will the rest dry out, taste good cold? Did I make the tasty substitutions for the choosy eater? Overall is the meal economical, nourishing, and not fattening? Whew, those are a lot of questions, but she is done . . . until tomorrow. Indeed, women are more often responsible for the routine, tiring, and recurring household tasks—those that can never ever be crossed off a "to do" list (*CST*, 2003: 70). Of course, in an emergency and with all the potential for attention and thanks, I will step in and "help" in these routine chores.

How can the emotional burden and the feelings of ultimate responsibility for things like sick children and balanced meals be better shared? How can the more responsible person learn to overlook an untidy house or an over-reliance on fast food?

Most working women encounter a second or even third shift when they get home from work. According to researchers, employed women still do most of the daily household chores and most of the childcare.

the nurse, male or female, yields. Renk et al. (2003) found that only given equal earning status does the sex of the parent predict the level of parental responsibility for child-related activities. So in a two-dentist family, the mother is more responsible. Moreover, home-oriented or (traditionally) more feminine fathers are happier than career-oriented (masculine) mothers in taking on these responsibilities, challenging the tendency to view men's and women's work and home orientation as distinct and non-overlapping (Charles and James, 2003).

This economic decision has long-term economic consequences. Intermittent work histories, marked by part-time employment for mothers, often mean that women never catch up. Women who postpone child-bearing until their careers are established earn 6 percent more than women who have children earlier (*CST*, 2003: 68). Keith et al. (2002) found that scholarly publishing differences between male and female academics in a university setting occur within the first six years after the doctorate, a time when many women are new mothers. Will this affect pay? Definitely, so let us look a bit more at that literature.

Historically, even when men and women did the same job, men were generally paid more. One (functional) rationale was that most of the men were family men, supporting not only themselves but also a wife and children. Indeed, women often were forced to leave their paid jobs upon marriage, certainly upon pregnancy. As a

result, most working women were single, thus "needing" less. While those practices and thoughts are generally diminished today, there is still a well-publicized gender wage gap. According to Statistics Canada (2001, *Occupation and Gender*, Catalogue No.13-217, *Labour Force*), women earn 73 cents for every dollar men earn. The figure is somewhat misleading, however, and the inclusion of additional variables in the analysis reduces the gap. For example, among single women the figure is 93 cents (versus 69 cents for married women). Does this mean that single women experience less discrimination at work than do married women? Another set of income data may help to answer that question. Most lawyers are self-employed; female lawyers earn 68 percent of what male lawyers do. Part of this gap may be due to more clients preferring men to women or women charging less. We do not have data to examine these possibilities. At least part of the gap is due to factors already mentioned: choosing certain specialties (family law pays less than corporate) and refusing to work a 60-hour week (Robson and Wallace, 2001). We do know that female doctors are more likely to work part time than male doctors. Additionally, even in marriages where house-work is shared, women are more likely to take on traditionally feminine (never-ending and immediate) tasks while men take on traditionally masculine (intermittent and postponable) tasks. Also, if the wage gaps are closing it may partly be due to a lowering of men's salaries (Lowe, 2004).

Another variable in pay differences is starting salary, generally a good predictor of later salary. Heckert et al. (2002) found, consistent with past research, that women expect lower entry salaries than men. A recent Canadian study (Desmarais and Curtis, 2001) found, however, that differences in expected salary have diminished to the point that today more women than men *over*estimate their worth on the job market. Still, if you add any lower expectations to women's greater propensity to enter lower wage occupations and the greater importance women attach to work that can accommodate a family, the gap can be hard to close fully.

Although other factors are at work, bias is still important. Drolet (2002) found that Canadian women's average hourly wage rate is 82 to 89.5 percent that of men after controlling for a variety of productivity-related characteristics. More specifically, gender differences in actual work experience explain 12 percent of the gap, differences in major field of study justify 5 percent, and differences in job responsibility account for about 6 percent; in sum about one-quarter (23 percent) of the total gap. This leaves 77 percent of the gap, or *eight cents to fourteen cents on the dollar*, to be explained by other factors, including discrimination and some of the factors, like the unequal household division of labour, mentioned above.

Before deciding that a gap of eleven cents (on average) is relatively small (albeit unfair), it should be added that small and large are often value-laden terms. Researchers should limit themselves to describing the difference and noting whether it is growing or shrinking in any consistent way and be careful to avoid such subjective terms. For example, the average number of days lost to sickness for female workers was 8.6 versus 6.4 for males in 2002, a gap of 2.2 days (Statistics Canada, CANSIM, Table 279-0029). Is that large or small? In a related sense, researchers can present this data as a gap of 2.2 sick days or they can say that women take almost one-third more sick days than do men. Each statement is correct but one seems more value-laden.

In this instance it is eleven cents over a lifetime and that adds up. There is much poverty among older women, especially among widows who must survive on the reduced pensions that follow a spouse's death. This happens to widowers too but they are fewer in number and tend to possess the better pension of the two. Moreover, pensions are for workers in the paid workforce and employers are reluctant to give parents (more likely mothers) pension credits for the time they stayed at home to raise children (Canada Pension does give some credit). Adding this discrepancy to the eleven-cent gap results in an even greater gender imbalance in poverty among the elderly. (Also see Tessler, Rosenheck, and Gamache [2001] for gender differences in reasons for homelessness.)

Experiencing violence

Finally, let us examine gender differences in experiencing violence, beginning with *spousal abuse*, an early attempt at gender-neutral language. Traditional research focused on female victims, and we have discussed the problems of not having a variable. Later research, therefore, also looked at men and found wives abusing husbands and abuse in homosexual partnerships; some even found that abuse is an equal-opportunity problem. For example, in a study of university faculty (DeSouza and Fansler, 2003), over one-half of *both* the male and the female professors experience sexual harassment from a

student at least once. In heterosexual dating relationships, Katz, Kuffel, and Coblentz (2002) found little "severe" violence, that university men and women students are victimized at similar rates, and that, if anything, the women are more violent.

How can these findings be explained? One issue is measurement. These and similar studies tend to ask questions about simple incidence, "Have you ever?" or "How often have you experienced?" In this type of question, a yes equals a yes, and a slap equals a slap. But, there is generally so much more to the story: who started it? How hard was the slap? What were the long-term repercussions: fear, sleeplessness, lost self-esteem? Is a woman who slaps a screaming, menacing, and perhaps drunk man—but one who has not raised his hand to her—the more violent of the two? Answers to these questions are needed to clarify the data, and the traditional follow-up question (whether medical treatment was needed) to measure seriousness is only a beginning. For a closer look at the methodological issues surrounding this topic, see Kimmel (2002).

In the workplace, an area where the data are in less dispute, women are much more likely to experience problems of sexism, from sexist jokes (cf. Ryan and Kanjorski, 1998) to threats that a refusal of sexual favours will jeopardize promotions and even continuation of employment. Here the issue of prevalence again is important. How many men must be involved in this type of sexism before a workplace is labelled as having a *chilly climate* for women? Is it all, most, a few, one? There is great disagreement on the figure required, but whatever the number, only part of the difference between rates of harassment by men and by women can be traced to the greater power that men enjoy in the workplace. We know this because female bosses with similar powers are less likely to sexually harass subordinates than are their male counterparts, and this holds up even after taking into account the fact that men may be less likely to define the behaviour as a problem. A second reason is that even some of the less-powerful, rank-and-file male workers poison the work atmosphere for their female colleagues. Legislation, resulting in money lost in sexual harassment lawsuits, will help change this situation, but such harassment continues for now.

Before claiming sexism, however, there must be a variable. This can reveal that some bosses are not sexist but power players, bullying both men and women subordinates. Similarly, comments such as "You have to be less emotional in your decisions" can be just a heads up, and

"You look great today" can mean "Keep up the new standard, you have been looking unprofessional." Sexism is the appropriate label only if men's experiences are different or when the average observer would feel that the experience is really not innocent. Finally, in a confrontation at work, is calling a woman a "b——" different from calling a man a "p——"? Are either or both of the terms sexist? Such labels are hurtful and inappropriate, but are they sexist? If the "p" word is used for an especially abusive male boss but "b— buster" and not the "b" word is used for a female boss, the choice is probably sexist. Confusion arises if any of these tactics are used more often on physically weaker or more vulnerable people; more women than men, more at extreme ages than those of average age, more new employees than veterans. Are these instances of sexism or ageism, for example, or targeted strategies where the attack is directed where the expected resistance is lowest?

What about pornography in the workplace—for example, depictions of nudity and sexual activity in either hard copy or virtual form? Feminists have led relatively successful campaigns to remove pornography from the workplace, but many want to go further, outlawing pornography anywhere, seeing it as one of the worst remnants of patriarchy. The Canadian Charter of Rights and Freedoms, however, includes a guarantee of freedom of expression, and so a compromise has been worked out. The courts have ruled that the combining of sexual activity and *violence*, even simulated, is pornographic by its very nature, demeaning and degrading and thus illegal, just as is child pornography, the simple possession of which is a criminal act. For depictions of adults in non-violent sexual situations, however, objectors must now demonstrate its harm.

Proving that non-violent, adult pornography is harmful is a large task that is still largely undemonstrated. Showing that most men charged with sexual assault once viewed violent pornography is not proof, for here we again have only one variable, and what is called the "after this, therefore because of this" fallacy. The questions in this case are: What else was the offender doing prior to the assault? How many men have viewed violent pornography and not committed a sexual assault? Further, a third factor, such as being sexually abused as a child, may lead both to a choice to watch violent pornography and to commit a sexual assault. We called this *spuriousness* in Chapter 2, Research Methods, meaning that the link is artificial and that eliminating pornography will not reduce sexual assault as childhood sexual abuse is the cause. Also, an examination of women's use of pornography, thus using a variable and not a constant (only men), may shed light on this issue as may homosexual pornography. For example, in lesbian pornography (deemed "erotica" by one lesbian bookstore importing it), women, not men, are doing the degrading. It is less clear in such instances that patriarchy is at fault, just as something besides patriarchy is needed to explain gay erotica, even its sado-masochistic variant. Any linking of pornography to sexual assault in these instances also needs closer scrutiny.

Finally we turn our attention to crime victimization. Homicides are committed against men twice as often as against women (Statistics Canada, CANSIM, Table 253-0003) and visible minorities are also over-represented. Whether homosexuals are also over-represented is harder to determine, as data on sexuality is often not collected. Still, the existence of a "homosexual panic defence" for a man who kills another man he thinks has propositioned him suggests the possibility. Sexual assault data suffer from under-reporting, but victimization data show a 9:1 female to male victim ratio, with males less likely than females to call the police, especially if the incident jeopardizes their masculine self-identity (Pino and Meier, 1999). Data on other assaults, especially those occurring at home, are also harder to read as so many are unreported. How much of this imbalance represents patriarchy and how much is due to factors such as proximity, alcohol, and unequal size, must be examined, especially when the violence is in lesbian or gay households. In a particularly interesting study, biology gets part of the blame for lesbian domestic violence. High-testosterone lesbian partners are more violent than low-testosterone partners but alcohol use by low-testosterone partners narrows the gap (Baker and Dabbs, 2002).

Convergence?

The gender gap is closing with respect to things like pay, job tenure, and household responsibilities. This is called *convergence*. The question of whether women and men will ever be totally equal should be carefully deconstructed, so let us examine convergence more closely. The first thing to note is that, in some areas, removing gender imbalances may not be a high priority. Most ballet dancers and synchronized swimmers are female; race-car drivers and skydivers are more likely male as are most of the people who go "polar" swimming on

Boxing Day. How many women really want to take advantage of the hard-fought court battle ruling that Ontario women may, like men, appear topless in public? And certainly women do not want to live shorter lives, spend more time in prison, or suffer liver cirrhosis in greater numbers to support gender equality. On the other hand, more female members of Parliament could be a goal. Indeed some politicians argued in the 2006 election that more women would make Parliament more civil. Of course this would be true only if all women running and no men seeking office are civil.

A second issue relates to how the gender gap is closed, as this can occur in several ways. The model most often implied is that of women catching up to men. Sweeney (2002), for example, noted this kind of convergence in how women and men approach marriage. No longer do young couples accept the traditional family division of labour of a woman's trading sex, childcare, and housework for economic security. The convergence was driven primarily by changing patterns of marriage among women who now see marriage as including both career and home and secondarily by men accepting a share of household responsibilities. On the other hand, men can also catch up with women—for example, the increasing numbers of men who wear makeup, undergo cosmetic surgery, or become male strippers. Maybe men can also learn to be more concerned about the environment.

Convergence can also occur with men decreasing and women increasing. Bergdahl and Norris (2002) found this to be the case in fatal car accidents. The number of women drivers killed has gone up, not because they are copying males and taking more risks, but because more women are driving and for greater distances, exposing them to the fatal accidents that plague even the most careful of drivers. In addition, the male fatality rate has been going down due to greater care and less risk-taking. A similar pattern occurs in the area of delinquency, where the rates for girls are increasing while the rates for boys may be decreasing (Fedders, 2001). Boys are more frequently crime victims and they are less attached to school than girls, but being a crime victim is more strongly related to girls' than to boys' violent delinquency, just as their low school attachment is more strongly related to property crime than it is for boys (Fitzgerald, 2003).

Decreasing rates for both men and women, with men's rates decreasing more quickly, would also close the gap, a pattern one might find in the case of Canadian manufacturing. As jobs are lost to countries with lower labour costs, the numbers of both male and female factory workers will decrease, but especially so for men who traditionally outnumbered women in that sector. This closing of the gap is not welcomed.

Additionally, the gap could be closed by the male rate going down while the women's rate remains constant. Closing the gap thus can be achieved in multiple ways, each with different implications for those involved. But before convergence, the first question is always whether parity is a worthwhile goal.

But change has begun. Primarily through the efforts of the women's movement, social organizations at all levels are more aware of gender issues, at least nominally. Consciousness of the dangers of sexism is gradually filtering through. Most women will work for pay for a good part of their lives and less often in gender

Working toward Change

While we await the control over reproduction that would free women to pursue careers as easily as men (as suggested by radical feminists) let us go back to the tools of the liberal feminists. We begin by looking at seniors discounts, something seemingly unrelated. On public transit, at the movies, and at special sales older people pay less for things than younger people. Some say it is a way of thanking seniors for the years they have served society. A more common justification is that seniors live on reduced incomes following retirement. Age is used as a proxy for need, and is easily demonstrable by showing a driver's licence or other identification. Poverty or financial need is a much more sensitive issue and less easy to demonstrate. Can you imagine showing your tax return to the bus driver? So we use age as a proxy for poverty, fully aware that many seniors are very wealthy and many young people very poor.

A similar difficulty occurs in employment equity programs that try to help those groups whose history was marked by consistent workplace discrimination. Historical group oppression scores are open to interpretation and dispute, so Canada uses gender, visible minority status, physical disability, and membership in First Nations as proxies instead.

Let us consider gender. Employment equity means that, in some instances, an employer must demonstrate why a male applicant would be better than a female before hiring him; his being equal would not suffice as an explanation. In other instances no demonstration is needed; statistical data showing that women are not making inroads quickly enough into a certain arena suffice to demonstrate discrimination. In these instances, the quality of individual male applicants is irrelevant; the competition is for females only. Practically, this could mean that the granddaughter of one of Canada's 100 wealthiest families would be preferred over a man who came to Canada from Poland or Russia, having recently learned English and finished his education, and who is ineligible for inclusion in any of the four employment equity-designated groups. So gender is used as a proxy for discrimination, just as it once was used for mathematics ability and ability to nurture, but in this instance, strong justifications—not protests—follow. A more targeted process, giving advantage to most women and to some men, could be more easily defended, if harder to design.

In addition, not all women have benefited equally from the employment equity legislation. Often it is upper-middle-class women who become doctors and lawyers, joining their upper-middle-class brothers and boyfriends in their pursuit of higher education. Upward mobility channels for working-class males and females shrink in the process. The working class is split along gender lines and loses sight of its real problems. Marx would love this picture: Using the rhetoric of feminism, just like they used the ideology of religion, the rich win again. As the number

of two-income professional couples grows, so does class polarity and the gap between rich and poor. The rich balance their work and family responsibilities with nannies and housekeepers who are overwhelmingly female and from lower economic groups.

Notice the emphasis in much of the discussion of gender inequality on the lack of women professors, doctors, lawyers, and engineers (see Table 7.3 for the actual improvements). A *glass ceiling*, invisible but limiting, thwarts women who aspire to be upper managers and industry executives. Older Hollywood actresses can no longer demand $10 million for a film. Less often do we hear about the long hours nannies (often immigrants) work, their general lack of paid maternity leave, or the low wages of the service industry. Two million Canadians make less than $10 an hour; most lack sick leave, disability insurance, and pension plans. Two-thirds of this group are women (*The Globe and Mail*, 14 Nov. 2003: C1) who have yet to feel any significant trickle-down effect from the changes described in this chapter.

Table 7.3 Percentage of Degrees Granted to Women in Various Professional Subjects by Age

Profession	20–34	35–44	45–64	65+
Actuary	31.4	27.9	13.9	4.0
Architect	32.8	26.8	14.7	9.6
Dentist	33.9	27.2	15.6	10.6
Lawyer	33.9	29.9	19.3	9.7
Medical Doctor	34.8	30.5	21.8	15.6
Optometrist	36.5	34.0	19.1	10.9
Pharmacist	38.0	36.9	33.2	21.5
Veterinarian	39.0	33.5	16.1	4.0

Source: Adapted from Statistics Canada, 2001 Census, *Education in Canada: Major Fields of Study*, Catalogue No. 97F0018X1E.

The above discussion implies that feminist efforts should focus more on the poor women in Canada. The October 18, 2003, edition of *The Globe and Mail*, however, had an article describing how poverty in parts of the old Soviet Union has led to wholesale kidnapping of girls and women to become prostitutes in the West. Should Canadian feminists give that an even higher priority?

ghettos. The wage gap is closing. But feminism, and gender consciousness in general, has been disproportionately a white, middle-class, urban social movement. It is for these groups that things have improved the most. The voices of visible minority and poor women, however, grow ever louder. They are changing the face of feminism, forcing it to further modify its historical tendency to relegate their issues to a secondary status. Men are still excluded but maybe women in a future "Take Back the Night" march will invite gay friends, male senior citizens, or bullied male adolescents to protest the after-dark violence they fear.

Sociology is an evolving social entity too. It has made that transition with much current research now including race, class, and gender. For a recent example, see *Understanding Social Inequality: Intersections of Class, Age, Gender, Race, and Ethnicity in Canada*, Oxford University Press, 2004, by Julie McMullin.

Summary

The chapter began with some examples of gender differences and looked briefly at methodological issues in research in that area. The idea that *within* variation is greater than *between* variation was introduced to temper any tendencies to dichotomize the sexes. The roles of nature and nurture in the development of such differences were also examined, using the example of mathematical ability.

The next section provided some important definitions including the difference between the terms *sex* and *gender*. Transvestites and transsexuals were discussed to further illustrate the distinction. Also included was a presentation of the theoretical positions used throughout this book. Functionalism was briefly discussed and criticized while symbolic interactionism was given more weight, particularly with the creation of definitions of masculinity and femininity. Marxist and feminist positions on the causes of the gendered division of labour (that women do more unpaid work than men and are not equal partners in the world of work) were also presented. For cause, Marxists see capitalism, moderate feminists a correctable lack of opportunity, and more radical feminists the need for women fully to control reproduction.

Next we examined three areas of gender differences: norms surrounding body appearance, the workplace (including pay), and violence. Although gender norms affect both men and women, women are usually affected to a greater degree. There is bias in the workplace but some issues of advancement arise from factors outside of work, especially in the homes of dual-career families. The chilly climate does exist, but it may have more to do with things other than sexism, and better analyses, including two variables, are needed before drawing conclusions.

A final section looked at convergence, and whether the sexes will ever be truly equal. On some things, like the care of children, it may never happen; on others, like pay, there is more optimism. But a decision on whether equity in a specific area is desired must first be made.

Questions for Review and Critical Thinking

1. Some say that research on breast cancer is greatly underfunded. On the other hand, manufacturers of ASA (best-known by the brand name Aspirin) remind women that they are eight times more likely to die of heart disease than they are of breast cancer. Further, the National Cancer Institute of Canada's *Canadian Cancer Statistics 2001* (Steering Committee on Cancer Statistics, 2001: Table 12), shows that men have an 11.2 percent chance of getting prostate cancer in a lifetime and a 3.6 percent chance of dying from it versus a 10.6 percent incidence and 3.9 percent chance for death from breast cancer, yet there is still no national blue ribbon campaign for men. What do you take from this situation?

2. Do you see evidence among those you know of movement to an androgynous fashion sense in which male and female lines are blurred, with more makeup and cosmetic surgery for men and less emphasis on large breasts for women, more tattooing, even women body builders? What are the implications for such changes?

3. Assuming some convergence in the criminality of men and women, for which crimes do you predict the gender gap will be reduced the least, with women not really catching up to men? Which crimes will show the greatest convergence?

Key Terms

gender, p. 154
gender identity, p. 155
gendered division of labour, p. 155

gendered order, p. 155
liberal feminism, p. 160
objectification, p. 162
patriarchy, p. 160
private realm, p. 156
public realm, p. 156
radical feminism, p. 160
sex, p. 154
socialist feminism, p. 160
transgendered, p. 156

Suggested Readings

Blum, Deborah
1997 *Sex on the Brain: The Biological Differences between Men and Women.* New York: Viking.
This book reviews the scientific literature on biological differences between males and females.

Hussey, Mark
2003 *Masculinities: Interdisciplinary Readings.* Upper Saddle River, NJ: Prentice Hall.
This is a collection of articles by over twenty authors on such topics as "act like a man," "the medical construction of gender," and "a father's story."

Renzetti, Claire, Jeffrey Edelson, and Raquel Bergen (eds.)
2001 *The Sourcebook on Violence against Women.* Thousand Oaks, CA: Sage.
This comprehensive book includes explanations and a discussion of methodological issues in research on the topic.

Websites

www.genderwatchers.org
Gender Watch
A collection of references to recent articles on gender, available in most academic libraries to supplement the more scholarly databases also found there.

Key Search Terms

Gender
Sex
Patriarchy
Feminism

For more study tools to help you with your next exam, be sure to check out the Companion Website, at **www.pearsoned.ca/hewitt**, as well as Chapter 7 in your Study Guide.

[8]

race and ethnic relations

carol agòcs

Introduction

Throughout human history the land now called Canada has been a place of great diversity. Before the first Europeans (the Norse) arrived in Canada about 1000 CE, the land had been populated for thousands of years by many peoples—the First Nations—who differed greatly from each other in language, culture, and systems of government (Dickason, 2002: x). At the time of Confederation, Canada's total population was approximately 60 percent of British origin, 31 percent of French origin, and 8 percent of other ethnic origins. By that time the Aboriginal population had been decimated by diseases and warfare introduced by the European settlers. By the early 1980s the Aboriginal population had reached the same size it is estimated to have been before European settlement (Royal Commission on Aboriginal Peoples, 1996: 2). Today the proportion of Canada's population that is Aboriginal is second only to that of New Zealand. Furthermore, Canada is recognized as a multicultural, multiracial, and multi-ethnic country where, according to Statistics Canada, people claim membership in more than two hundred different ethnic groups. Canada has a larger percentage of immigrants in its population than any other country

except Australia, and immigrants comprise a larger proportion of Canada's total population now than at any time in the past seventy years.

Census definitions of ethnic origin and Aboriginal identification have changed over time. Recently, the census has collected data on multiple as well as single ethnic origins and on visible minority status of Canadians, making it problematic to compare data from various census years. The 2001 Census found that 39 percent claimed Canadian origin, 20 percent reported some English origin, 14 percent Scottish origin, 13 percent Irish origin, 16 percent some French ancestry, and about 4 percent Aboriginal origins. The other most frequently mentioned ethnic origins in 2001, in order of relative size, included German, Italian, Chinese, and Ukrainian. The 2001 Census found that visible minorities comprise more than 13 percent of the Canadian population, including in order of size, Chinese, South Asian, Black, Filipino, Arab/West Asian, Latin American, Southeast Asian, Korean, and Japanese. About one-third of the visible minority population was born in Canada, and the rest are immigrants (Statistics Canada, 2003c, pp. 5, 10, 11, 14, 45, 46).

Canadians often describe their society as an "ethnic mosaic," a varied composition of many peoples whose distinctive cultures give colour and texture to the whole. The image of the mosaic symbolizes the reality of the ethnic and racial diversity that is characteristic of Canada. Canadian society is a social system of coexisting ethnic groups and peoples. To some degree each maintains its own distinctive communities, social networks, culture and social organizations, such as clubs and religious institutions, while at the same time, each participates in Canada's common cultural, economic, and political institutions. However, ethnic populations in Canada, as in most pluralistic societies, are hierarchically ranked. Some groups, such as the English, have historically dominated positions of economic, political, and social power while others, such as Aboriginal peoples, have been, and remain, relatively powerless within Canadian society. In referring to Canadian society as a vertical mosaic, Porter (1965) called attention to the fact that ethnicity is a major source of social, economic, and political inequality, cleavage, and conflict. More recent research has documented the growing importance of racial diversity as a basis of inequality in this country. (You will recall that we discussed such inequality in Chapter 6, Social Inequality, and we will do so again in Chapter 15, Social Movements.) At the same time, diversity is a hallmark of Canadian society and is among its greatest strengths, resources, and sources of national pride. Nurturing and benefiting from diversity, while addressing the growing problem of racial inequality, is a fundamental challenge for Canada.

We begin this chapter on race and ethnic relations in Canada with a discussion of the processes involved in the formation and development of immigrant communities. Once we have an understanding of local ethnic communities as social entities, we shall consider the meanings of the concepts of ethnic group, race, and minority group, and some of the manifestations of ethnic and racial discrimination and inequality. We shall then discuss the historical processes of colonialism, conquest, and migration, forces that laid the foundation for Canada's vertical mosaic. Finally, we shall examine influential interpretations of the past, present, and future of ethnic and race relations—assimilationism, pluralism, and views influenced by post-colonial and postmodern theoretical approaches. We shall consider some of the implications of each of these perspectives for social policy affecting Aboriginal peoples, French Canadians, and Canada's diverse immigrant and racial minority populations. Our concluding theme will be the continued importance of racial and ethnic pluralism, inequality, and conflict in the modern world, and in Canada in particular, and the opportunities and challenges these social realities pose for this generation.

Local Ethnic Communities: Formation and Development

One day in 2005, a young man stepped off a plane in Toronto after a long and tiring flight from Beijing. He had torn up his roots for the dream of an opportunity for higher education, a job in a high-tech field, a good standard of living for his family, and an education for his children—things less attainable at home. He was welcomed by a friend and former classmate from his hometown in China, with whom he would stay until he could afford his own place. Before long he was introduced to his friend's family and circle of friends over dinner in Toronto's Chinese community, and began to learn from their experiences of gaining access to educational and employment opportunities in the new city. His hope was to eventually afford to have his girlfriend and his brother join him in Toronto.

The experience of this man is far from unique; Table 8.1 illustrates the importance of immigrants, as well as visible minorities and Aboriginal people, to the populations of Canada's largest cities. For many immigrants, settling in a new country means separation from loved ones and leaving behind familiar ways of life and the support systems available in the home country. Immigration also places the individual in an immensely difficult position of becoming part of a confusing, and often unwelcoming, world of strangers. In today's global village, however, it is possible for immigrants who have access to technologies of communication and transportation to maintain connections with the home country.

Studies of the immigration experience suggest that migration is frequently a social act, with primary social relationships a strong influence on the decision to migrate and the subsequent process of settlement. (We shall discuss the reasons for migration more fully in Chapter 16, Demography and Urbanization.) The migrant's destination is often a place where relatives, friends, or others from the same town have already settled. Chain migration is a sequential movement of persons from a common place of origin to a common destination, with the assistance of relatives or compatriots

Table 8.1   Immigrants, Visible Minorities, and Persons of Aboriginal Identity: Percentage of Census Metropolitan Areas: 2001*

	Aboriginal Identity	Immigrants	Members of Visible Minorities
Toronto	0.4	43.7	36.8
Vancouver	1.9	37.5	36.9
Hamilton	1.1	23.6	9.8
Kitchener	—	22.1	10.7
Windsor	—	22.3	12.9
Calgary	2.3	20.9	17.5
Victoria	2.8	18.8	8.9
London	1.3	18.8	9.0
Edmonton	4.4	17.8	14.6
St. Catharines-Niagara	—	17.8	4.5
Montreal	0.3	18.4	13.6
Winnipeg	8.4	16.5	12.5
Oshawa	—	15.7	7.0
Ottawa-Gatineau	1.3	17.6	14.1
Kingston	—	12.4	4.7
Thunder Bay	6.8	11.1	2.2
Regina	8.3	7.4	5.2
Saskatoon	9.1	7.6	5.6
Sudbury	4.8	7.0	2.0
Halifax	—	6.9	7.0
Saint John	—	3.8	2.6
Sherbrooke	—	4.6	2.6
St. John's	—	2.9	1.4
Quebec	—	2.9	1.6
Trois-Rivières	—	1.5	0.9
Saguenay	—	0.9	0.6

* Percentage is shown where the population of Aboriginal ancestry numbered 5000 or more.

Source: Statistics Canada, 2001 Census, Analysis Series, *Canada's Ethnocultural Portrait: The Changing Mosaic*, Catalogue No. 96F0030XIE2001008; 2001 Census, Analysis Series, *Aboriginal Peoples of Canada: A Demographic Portrait*, Catalogue No. 96F0030XIE2001007.

already settled in the new location (Campani, 1992). Assistance may take the form of information helpful in weighing the decision to migrate, money for transportation, a place to stay upon arrival, information about how to function in Canadian society, job offers, or legal sponsorship. Through chain migration, separated family members and friends may be reunited and a supportive community formed to help immigrants cope with the difficulties of confronting a new and strange culture.

Whole families, even entire villages, have been transplanted from Lebanon, Italy, Portugal, Greece, and many other parts of the world to urban neighbourhoods in Canada. Business relationships formed in other locations, such as Hong Kong, are often extended to include Canada (see Campani, 1992; Hamilton, 1999). Thus chain migration is an adaptation and extension of kinship and friendship ties and reciprocal commitments. Over a period of time, an ethnic community takes shape around a widening network of such exchanges. Statistics Canada's *Longitudinal Survey of Immigrants in Canada* found that 59 percent of recent immigrants chose to live in a particular city because of the presence there of a spouse or partner, family member, or friends, while 14 percent chose their destination based on job prospects (Heisz, 2005: 13).

An ethnic community forms around a social network shaped by chain migration.

Most ethnic communities develop *institutions*—organized, patterned ways of behaving and carrying on social interaction to accomplish specific goals and meet the collective needs of the group. These institutions include religious organizations, separate schools, businesses, social agencies, political or advocacy groups, and cultural and social organizations. Rosenberg and Jedwab (1992) suggested that ethnic groups develop such organizations as a means of coping with community needs that are not otherwise met by mainstream institutions of Canadian society. In a study of the Italian, Jewish, and Greek communities of Montreal, they found that each group developed and used ethnic organizations in different ways, depending on how the group was treated by the surrounding Quebec society.

The degree to which an ethnic population develops a strong sense of solidarity and ethnic identity and self-sufficient ethnic institutions, referred to as **institutional completeness**, depends upon many factors (Breton, 1964). These may include the group's cultural values and social patterns, the treatment it receives from the society around

it, the size of the city and of the ethnic population, its prosperity, and its access to employment opportunities. If an ethnic community builds a secure niche within a local economic structure, it may grow in size and affluence, be able to support ethnic organizations, and develop common economic and political interests as well. For example, in postwar Toronto, Italian immigrants established themselves in the construction industry as labourers and craftspeople, and increasingly, as contractors and developers (Reitz, 1990). As a consequence of such occupational specialization, ethnic community members may come to share values that go beyond language, culture, and social ties, to encompass well-defined economic and political interests.

Occupational specialization is often rooted in the desires of immigrants who come to Canada seeking opportunities to farm, own a business, or practise a trade or profession—goals that may be difficult to achieve in their homelands. Canada has encouraged the immigration of experienced and trained farmers, entrepreneurs, and professionals. Recently, Canadian immigration policy has recruited highly educated professionals such as medical doctors and nurses, scientists, and immigrants with technical education. It is clear, however, that these highly trained immigrants are often unable to find employment commensurate with their qualifications, and are forced to accept jobs in which their knowledge and skills are wasted.

This waste of talent is often a result of discrimination, limited opportunities, or a combination of these factors. For example, Giles (2002: ch. 4) found that most Portuguese women who immigrated to Canada a generation ago entered low-paying unskilled jobs because of a lack of educational opportunity in their home country as well as minimal access to English-language and job skills training provided by the Canadian government to male immigrants as "heads of households." Self-employment, such as operating a small business within an ethnic or immigrant neighbourhood, may reflect a lack of employment opportunities in Canadian society outside that community (Li, 2000).

Canada's current immigration legislation recognizes several objectives including family reunification, economic benefits for both newcomers and Canadian society, and the provision of "safe haven" to refugees fleeing persecution. In 2001, about 27 percent of immigrants admitted were family class, about 11 percent were refugees, and 61 percent were economic immigrants whom immigration authorities viewed as contributors to Canada's employment and investment priorities (Li, 2003: 25). Canada's economy and quality of life depend upon immigrants' contributions as workers, business people, taxpayers, and consumers, because natural increase is not adequate to maintain our population. Therefore, Canada's success in attracting, integrating,

and using the talents of immigrants is essential to our collective future.

We have begun our discussion of Canadian race and ethnic relations by trying to understand something of the origin, development, institutional framework, and economic base of the local community that originates as a consequence of migration, the critical contributions of immigrants to Canadian society, and some of the obstacles they face. It is now necessary to examine the meaning of the terms *ethnicity, race,* and *minority-group status.*

Ethnic Group, Race, and Minority Group: Some Definitions

The ethnic group

An **ethnic group** is a highly variable and complex social entity that has assumed various and changing forms in different societies and historical eras. The Turks of Germany, the Scots of Cape Breton, the Italians of Australia, and the Kurds of Iraq all may be seen as examples of *ethnic groups*. These populations exist within pluralistic societies in which peoples of various cultural, religious, or ethnic backgrounds live side by side, however uneasily, within a single social, economic, and political system. While scholars disagree on its definition, the influential theoretical perspectives of Weber (1946) and Barth (1969) suggest that ethnicity has four major dimensions, listed in Chart 8.1, with their manifestations at the individual and group levels.

Chart 8.1 Some Defining Characteristics of the Ethnic Group

	Dimensions of ethnicity			
	An ascribed status	*A form of social organization*	*A subculture*	*A focus of identity*
Individual ethnic group members	inherit ethnic group membership	are involved in interaction and a shared institutional framework	tend to share some fundamental values	feel a sense of belonging with other members
The ethnic group as a whole	is self-perpetuating	has boundaries	transmits a culture rooted in historical experience	is recognized as a collectivity by others in the society

Ethnicity as an ascribed status

To say that membership in a social group is ascribed means that it is usually conferred at birth, inherited from parents and other ancestors. Ethnicity, like race, gender, and age, is rarely something that individuals aspire to, strive for, choose, or achieve in life. And like other gifts or accidents of birth, ethnicity is relatively enduring, rather than something that can be set aside or changed, as an occupation can be. It is one of those givens of social existence that become deeply embedded within individual identity. Of course, individuals vary in the degree to which they consider ethnicity central to their identity.

As an ascribed status, ethnicity is also self-perpetuating, an important characteristic differentiating ethnic groups from other kinds of social groups such as voluntary associations. The ethnic group, then, includes ancestors long dead, as well as those who are the present-day carriers of the group's culture, and probably at least some of their children as well. Because the ethnicity of parents and ancestors is visited upon their children and grandchildren, the ethnic group itself continues to exist from generation to generation, at least as a potential that may be realized under certain conditions.

Ethnicity as a form of social organization

From the perspective of its individual members, the ethnic group may be viewed as a set of social relationships originating within a family, and radiating outward to include primary ties with kin, friends, neighbours, fellow worshippers, and others with whom interaction is frequent. If informal interaction and communication patterns tend to be particularly intense among persons of the same ethnicity, then these relationships may be said to form an *ethnic network*. Members of a network frequently share values and a way of life, and individuals may identify their personal fates with these people. For some, being part of an ethnic group may meet needs for social relatedness and belonging.

As one element of a **pluralistic society**, then, the ethnic community is a product of social interaction rather than formal organization. The ethnic community has no rules of membership, no coordinating agency, no official leadership. Yet it does have norms that regulate membership, an internal social hierarchy, a shared history and culture, and formal organizations that promote group solidarity and meet collective needs. An important feature of the ethnic group as a form of social organization is that it also has boundaries that include some individuals but exclude others. If a social group is to have an identity, it must have boundaries that are set and maintained by patterns of interaction. Some kinds of social interactions may be confined largely within the group while others are not. In part, ethnic group boundaries may be culturally defined; for example, an Irish Protestant who marries a Jew may be included within the boundaries of the Jewish community by converting to its religion or joining in its social gatherings. Sometimes geographic concentration and isolation from other groups contribute to the maintenance of ethnic boundaries, as among Old Order Mennonites, who often minimize social contact with the surrounding population. Segregation of a group may be imposed by the institutions of Canadian society. The isolation imposed upon some First Nations as a result of the reserve system has helped to maintain boundaries between them and other Canadians, and has contributed to their lack of access to opportunities and the standard of living generally available to Canadians.

However, the survival of an ethnic group or nation usually does not depend on physical isolation. In many plural societies, ethnic groups meet in the marketplace, at work, or in school. Indeed contacts that do not threaten group boundaries may be easily permitted. It is ethnic *endogamy*—marriage within an ethnic group—that is perhaps the critical factor in the maintenance of ethnic group boundaries. Isajiw (1990: 77–81) found that Toronto ethnic groups differ in their emphasis on marriage within the group. Endogamy remained an important value into the third generation for those of Jewish origin, while for Ukrainians, Germans, and Italians, it decreased in importance with each generation in Canada. Thus the Jewish community retains ethnic identity, solidarity, and community involvement within the context of a highly urbanized and cosmopolitan lifestyle (Isajiw, 1990; Breton, 1990). The prevalence of marriage across ethnic and racial boundaries is increasing, and nearly 40 percent of Canadians today report mixed ancestry (Statistics Canada, 2001 Census, Analysis Series, *Canada's Ethnocultural Portrait: The Changing Mosaic,"* Catalogue No. 96F0030XIE2001008, p. 15).

The ethnic group as a subculture

An ethnic group as a social organization, with boundaries maintained by social norms governing interaction, has an existence of its own, independent of its individual members. It persists from generation to generation; it has a history. The sharing of experience over time gives specific cultural meanings to the social relationships that ethnic group members have with one another. These historical experiences are unique to each group, and are an important dimension of the ethnic identity that is passed down to succeeding generations during socialization. They shape understandings of what it means to belong to the ethnic group.

Generally speaking, the sharing of cultural traits such as food preferences or distinctive styles of musical expression need not be a defining characteristic of an ethnic group. Italians may remain Italians even if they do not read Italian newspapers or eat pasta. And Poles who do these things will not be defined as Italians. The maintenance of language has been considered a fundamental aspect of collective existence for some groups, such as French Canadians and Ukrainians, but has not been as strongly emphasized by others, such as German, Italian, or Jewish Canadians (Isajiw, 1990: 51). Among some Aboriginal peoples, there is currently a strong interest in teaching their original language to the young as a part of cultural survival and spiritual renewal (Lawrence, 1999: 1). Language may be a focus of nationhood and governmental institutions as well as cultural life, as is the case for French in Quebec and Inuktitut in Nunavut.

Primarily as a result of immigration, the mother tongue of a growing number of Canadians is a language other than English or French. The Census of Canada defines "mother tongue" as the first language a person learns at home in childhood and still understands. In 2001, about 18 percent of Canadians reported a mother tongue other than the two official languages. The most frequently reported languages (in order) are Chinese, Italian, German, Punjabi, Spanish, Portuguese, Polish, Aboriginal languages, Ukrainian, Arabic, and Tagalog (Statistics Canada, "Population by mother tongue, provinces and territories, 2001 Census," www40.statcan.ca/l01/cst01/demo11a.htm).

Ethnicity as a focus of identity

Socialization, discussed in Chapter 4, is the critical factor in the acquisition of ethnic identity, which is integral to a person's self-concept. If both parents are members of the same ethnic group, or if the family participates actively in the life of a community, children may form a strong identification with that group.

To the extent that individuals become firmly linked with the historical experience, values, way of life, and social patterns and relationships that are at the core of group life, personal identity and collective identity become intertwined.

However, the process of acquiring ethnic identity is usually not simple in contemporary pluralistic societies. As children grow up, they typically confront many influences that go beyond the home and primary social network to include educational, communications, governmental, and other institutions of the larger society, as well as popular culture and a variety of informal social contacts. In such encounters, children may also learn that social mobility or acceptance by the larger society may involve pressures to compromise their ethnic identity. An extreme example is the treatment of Aboriginal children in Canadian residential schools, where they were forced to live apart from their families and communities. Many children were punished for speaking their own languages or maintaining their communities' beliefs and values, and many were victims of abuse (Fournier and Crey, 1997; Miller, 1996). The consequences of the residential school system included severe damage both to individuals and their communities.

Because of such oppressive experiences—and because it may be painful to be singled out for being "different"—children and youth may experience considerable conflict between their two worlds: the ethnic community where they make their home, and the larger society with its dominant social, cultural, economic, and political systems.

Children of immigrants sometimes live on the margin between two worlds, bearing two competing identities that are equally important.

Racialization

Inherited physical traits, such as skin colour and hair texture, in themselves have no necessary consequences for behaviour. Yet such identifying features often become *socially defined* as very significant. Individuals who have a particular characteristic, such as dark skin, or a common religious practice or language, may be seen by others as members of a single **social category**, defined as a collection of individuals who share traits that are regarded as socially meaningful.

The social meaning attached to racial or ethnic categories often includes the assignment of a rank within the hierarchy of society. This position is not necessarily subordinate; ethnicity is not always stigmatizing, nor always associated with oppression. It is quite possible for an ethnic group to occupy an elite or privileged status, as English Canadians did prior to the Quiet Revolution in the economic life of Quebec. More frequently, racial or ethnic labels become criteria for assigning individuals or groups to subordinate positions within a social hierarchy.

Members of a social category may not have anything in common beyond their shared identifying features. However, if as a consequence of their treatment and position in society they become involved in social interaction with one another, and come to share values and a sense of identity and common interests, they may actually *become* a social group. This process of *ethnogenesis* occurred among the First Nations of North America, who lived as separate and frequently warring peoples until Europeans forced a common label and identity as Indians or Natives on them. These labels exist along with their identities as distinct nations.

A prime example of an arbitrary social category is race, popularly thought of as a category based on inherited physical characteristics such as skin colour and facial features. But **race** is a social construction, not a social or biological fact (see the box, "Race: An Arbitrary Social Category"). Indeed, scientific evidence has proved that genetically separate races of human beings never existed. A recent comprehensive review of evidence from genetic research (Templeton, 1999: 632) concluded that human "races" are not "pure" and that "human evolution has been and is characterized by many locally differentiated populations coexisting at any given time, but with sufficient genetic contact to make all of humanity a single lineage sharing a common

evolutionary fate." From a scientific perspective there is no such entity as a race; yet there is clear evidence of the sociological reality of **racialization**—assigning people to socially constructed racial categories and behaving toward them as though these categories were real. **Racist ideologies** regard racial or ethnic categories as natural genetic groupings, and attribute behavioural and psychological characteristics to the genetic nature of these groupings. In racist thinking, biological traits are used to label some human beings—invariably those belonging to categories other than the one doing the labelling—as inherently inferior, and therefore proper objects of exploitation and domination. The so-called "races" thus can best be understood as social constructs defined by dominant groups in a society (Li, 1988: 23) in order to justify the exploitation and oppression of minority groups. Racist ideologies have been used to rationalize and legitimate countless forms of racist behaviour, including the oppression of Aboriginal peoples, the Nazi extermination of Jews and Gypsies, and laws restricting the immigration of southern European and Asian peoples to Canada and the United States.

Social scientists, like others who influence public opinion, have contributed to racist thinking (Gould, 1981). However, largely through the efforts of later generations of social and biological scientists and of political, human rights, ethnic and community leaders and organizations, racist ideas have been challenged and have weakened their hold on popular thinking in Canada. Still, racist conceptions continue to be held by many, and racist assumptions are regularly reflected in everyday life. In Canada today, Aboriginal people, immigrants, and racialized minorities are especially disadvantaged by racist thinking and negative stereotypes (see Ponting, 1998; Henry and Tator, 2002; James, 1998).

Minority groups and patterns of subordination

A **minority group** is a social category that occupies a subordinate rank in a social hierarchy; such a group is accorded unequal treatment and excluded from full participation in the life of society. The term *minority* refers not to the size of the group—a minority may outnumber dominant groups, as in South Africa under apartheid—but to its position in a context of power relationships. In post-Confederation Canada, Japanese, Chinese, First Nations, Inuit, and Blacks have suffered restrictions on their freedom of access to employment, housing,

Race: An Arbitrary Social Category

The term race refers not to "real" social groupings whose membership can be specified objectively or empirically, but to arbitrary categories that reflect a social process of labelling and classification that has been called "racialization." The concept of race has changed through time, and has taken on various social meanings with profoundly negative effects upon groups of people. So while race is a product of human decisions without scientific basis, the reality of "race" as a social concept and construction cannot be denied. Nor can we deny the fact that the concept of race has been used as the basis for social stratification, oppression, and the denial of the humanity of the majority of the world's people.

In today's pluralistic society, a variety of terms are used to refer to the concepts of race, colour, or minority status based upon physical characteristics. It is probably true that all of these terms create discomfort and misunderstanding, especially when used primarily by dominant white majorities to refer to people whom they consider to be "other" or different. For example, in government policy and data reported by Statistics Canada, the term *visible minorities* is widely used to refer to people who look different from the white majority because of the colour of their skin, and who often are disadvantaged in the workplace and other settings as a consequence. A great variety of peoples are lumped into the category of visible minorities, including Chinese, South Asians, Blacks, Arab/West Asians, Filipinos,

Southeast Asians, Latin Americans, Japanese, Koreans, and Pacific Islanders (www.statcan.ca/english/Pgdlo/People/Population/def/defdemo40h.htm). Clearly, the term *visible minority* does not refer to a social group. Other terms including *people of colour* and *racial minorities* are also used to refer to this category. The term *racialized minorities* is often preferred because it connotes the social construction of race as a category, and makes reference to the fact that it is the dominant society that creates and employs racial categories and labels.

It should be noted that Aboriginal peoples in Canada do not see themselves as a "visible minority" or an ethnic group within the multicultural population of Canada, but as Canada's First Nations—sovereign peoples whose relationship to the government and people of Canada has yet to be defined.

Deconstructing the various terms that refer to race and to Aboriginal ancestry, and subjecting them to historical and critical analysis, is an important project for interdisciplinary research. Any terminology imposed upon minorities by dominant majorities, rather than developed and proposed by these groups to refer to themselves, will be problematic and implicated in the structure of racism in society. Later in this chapter the discussion of postmodern approaches to the study of race and ethnic relations considers the construction of whiteness as a racial identity.

Identify another example of social groups in Canada that have been thus "racialized." Can this process be "undone" or reversed?

education, and citizenship (Boyko, 1998). The right to vote has at some time been denied to each of these groups.

In the modern world, extreme forms of social control have been used to subordinate minorities identified on the basis of race or ethnicity. Such measures include *expulsion*, the forcible removal of a minority from its homeland—a fate suffered by Canada's First Nations during the settlement of the country, and by West Coast Japanese

Canadians during World War II. Soon after Canada declared war on Japan, all persons of Japanese origin living within 100 miles of British Columbia's coastline, the majority of them Canadian citizens, were forcibly evacuated from their homes. They were stripped of their property and placed in "relocation centres" in Alberta, Ontario, and other provinces, where they lived in camps and worked as farm labourers. After the war, many were not able to return to their West Coast communities, but remained dispersed in other areas (Sunahara, 1981).

The modern world has also seen instances of *annihilation* or *genocide*—the intentional massacre of peoples. The most frequent scenario for genocide occurs when the state, acting for or with a dominant ethnic group, seeks to eliminate a target ethnic group through the use of large-scale violence (Oberschall, 2000). The destruction of certain Aboriginal groups as a result of the European conquest of the Americas, of European Jews and Gypsies by the Nazis, of Armenians in Turkey, and of Muslims in Bosnia-Herzegovina, are but a few items in a catalogue of horrors (Chalk and Jonassohn, 1990). The "ethnic cleansing" operations in Serbia and Rwanda are more recent examples.

Dominant groups frequently control and restrict the economic, social, and political participation of minorities by means of **discrimination**, the practice of denying to members of certain social categories opportunities that are generally available within the society. Discrimination may in some instances occur by legal means (*de jure*). For example, until 1960 an article of the Indian Act withheld the vote from Native peoples in all provinces except Newfoundland. More common in Canada today is *de facto* discrimination that occurs as a matter of common practice, often in violation of the law. Examples would include a landlord who, in contravention of provincial human rights statutes, finds an excuse for refusing to rent an apartment to someone of another race, or an employer who will not hire minorities.

There is considerable evidence in the sociological research literature of discrimination on the basis of race and gender in contemporary Canadian society. For example, a 1995–96 survey of 1081 graduates of York University tracked experiences with the job market a few months after graduation. Looking just at graduates who had found or were looking for full-time jobs, the researchers found that parents' income and ethno-racial origin made a large difference. While 58 percent of graduates of European origin had found full-time employment, only 40 percent of Black, 54 percent of South Asian, and 35 percent of Chinese origin were employed full time. The impact of class and ethno-racial origin strongly influenced success in getting full-time work, even when skills, area and type of degree, grade point average, and other factors were taken into account (Grayson, 1997). See the box "Land of Opportunity for Whom?" for another example.

[Social Trends]

Land of Opportunity for Whom?

A telephone poll of 1575 adults in the Greater Toronto Area conducted by Goldfarb Consultants for the *Toronto Star* found that members of racialized minority groups were much more likely than other Toronto residents to personally experience discrimination. The *Star* reported that 62 percent of Blacks, 37 percent of Chinese, 40 percent of Filipinos, and 37 percent of Hispanics say they have experienced discrimination, compared with 29 percent of the non-minority Torontonians surveyed.

Discrimination was found to affect the search for a job, wage levels, and access to raises and promotions. Respondents from the black, West Asian/Arab, and South Asian groups were most likely to state that finding a job is their most serious problem; these communities also reported the lowest household income, and the least satisfaction with life in Toronto. In contrast, 80 percent of Italian and Portuguese respondents indicated that they feel they have fair and equitable pay, access to jobs, promotions, and raises. While 86 percent of the general population felt that their community is treated fairly by the media, only 32 percent of blacks and 49 percent of South Asians believed that their communities get fair treatment in the media. (Results from the total sample are considered accurate within 2 percentage points, 19 times out of 20; the margin of error is higher for individual minority groups).

Source: Adapted from "Opportunity knocks ... but not for all." *Toronto Star,* 2 May 1999.

Have you ever experienced discrimination, or do you know of others who have? Why does discrimination persist in Canadian society?

The example of inequality in the job market suggests that discrimination is not simply a matter of individuals acting out their racist attitudes. Sociological theorists and researchers have given extensive attention to the ways in which racism and discrimination become institutionalized or embedded in the structures of society. By participating in the social, political, and economic institutions of our society, we enact racism and engage in discrimination in our daily lives.

Systemic or **institutionalized discrimination** occurs as a by-product of the ordinary functioning of our social institutions, rather than as a consequence of isolated actions by prejudiced individuals, or a deliberate policy or motive to discriminate. Systemic discrimination consists of institutional practices that perpetuate majority-group privilege and create disadvantage for minorities simply by conducting "business as usual." The practices of employers, governments, the justice system, schools, universities, churches, the media, or any other institution or organizational setting may perpetuate systemic discrimination. For example, by only hiring job applicants who have Canadian educational credentials and work experience, an employer may give advantages to applicants born in Canada and exclude immigrants whose knowledge, skills, and experience acquired in another country have prepared them to do the job.

Systemic discrimination in the workplace may also take the form of exclusion of minority women and men from informal communication and social networks, or biased decision making about promotions, job assignment, or pay (Agòcs, 2002: ch.1). Hence systemic discrimination is perpetuated in social relations and also in cultural practices, which are often mutually reinforcing. In Canadian society, whiteness and European cultural origins are considered normative and dominant, while people of colour, or whose cultural roots are Aboriginal or non-European, are generally viewed as "different" or "other." Systemic discrimination is difficult to identify, challenge, and change because it is embedded in customary practices that serve the interests of those who have the power to make and enforce the rules that shape organizational behaviour. We have already mentioned many examples of this, including the attempt by government and the churches to force Aboriginal children to forsake their own cultures and learn the "Canadian" culture.

Social scientists often examine intergroup differences in wages, when types of work and worker characteristics are similar, as a means of testing for the possible presence of systemic discrimination in employment. In an analysis of 1991 census data, Li (1998) found that native-born and foreign-born white Canadians have an earnings advantage, while native-born and foreign-born visible minorities and Aboriginal peoples have an earnings disadvantage when years of education, age, nativity, full-time vs. part-time employment, gender, industry, occupation, and number of weeks worked are statistically controlled. (For recent research presenting similar findings see Kunz et al., 2002; Pendakur and Pendakur, 2002). The most severe pay disadvantage was suffered by foreign-born visible minorities, despite their higher than average level of education (Li, 1998: 123) (see also Chapter 6, Social Inequality). Women who are members of minority groups are doubly disadvantaged in employment because of gender *and* minority-group discrimination (Das Gupta, 1996; Neallani, 1992).

Discrimination is reinforced in some societies by the practice of segregation on the basis of minority status. **Segregation** is a form of social control whereby physical distance is maintained to ensure social distance from groups with whom contact is not wanted. Segregation involves the exclusion of ethnic, racial, or other minorities from the facilities, residential space, or institutions used by dominant groups. For most of the twentieth century in South Africa, under an elaborate system of legislated racial segregation known as *apartheid*, or "apartness," every individual was classified by race. Interracial sex and marriage were banned and racially separate public facilities, educational systems, residential space, and work arrangements were enforced. After a struggle that lasted for generations and cost the deaths, imprisonment, and torture of thousands, the key segregation laws were repealed in 1991.

In Canadian cities, while housing discrimination is illegal and there is no legal basis for ethnic and racial groups to live separately, some researchers have found indications of residential separation or concentrations of minority groups. In an analysis of census tract data coving the past twenty years, Hou and Picot (2003) found that Chinese, Black, and South Asian residential enclaves have become more numerous in Toronto and Vancouver, and that about half of recent Chinese immigrants live in Chinese neighbourhoods in Toronto and Vancouver. Despite this pattern, it is clear that most new immigrants to Canada do not live in residential enclaves of people from the same ethnic background. Today, ethnic and immigrant populations and communities in Canada tend to be geographically dispersed rather than

Throughout history, extreme forms of social control have been used to subordinate minority groups. When Canada declared war on Japan during World War II, Japanese Canadians—most of them Canadian citizens—were stripped of their belongings and property, and forced into "relocation centres" in several provinces, where they worked as labourers.

concentrated in neighbourhoods. Black residential concentration in Canada is lower than that of other visible minority groups, and black-owned businesses rely less on the patronage of their own group than is the case for other groups (Hou and Picot, 2003: 3; Teixeira, 2000). Nevertheless, Kazemipur and Halli (2000) suggested that some Canadian cities are manifesting a "new poverty" marked by ghettos where impoverished Aboriginal and visible minority immigrant populations are concentrated, although this pattern is far less prevalent in Canada than in the United States.

Research suggests that discrimination, poverty, and people's desire to live near others of the same background may all be explanations for ethnic and racial residential separation. Sociologists who study black–white residential separation in the United States generally view this as part of an oppressive pattern of systemic racism that limits opportunity for blacks. However, some Canadian sociologists are inclined to see residential separation as a choice that can benefit immigrants and their children by providing opportunities for employment, social support, and cultural maintenance within the neighbourhood setting. Whether residential concentrations are detrimental or beneficial may depend on whether they are symptoms of poverty and housing discrimination or whether they reflect peoples' choices and a healthy pattern of cultural pluralism. When poverty and ethnic or racial residential concentration are found together, it is important to examine whether the concentration is a result or a cause of the poverty.

Explaining discrimination

In their attempt to explain discrimination in modern societies, social scientists have studied various kinds of influences. Before the 1960s, there was much interest in the role of ideas and beliefs in motivating discriminatory acts against minority group members. Of special importance was the concept of **prejudice**, an attitude

[Applied Sociology]

"Get Lost, Jap. We beat you!"

In his autobiography, renowned Canadian environmentalist, scientist, and broadcaster David Suzuki reflects on his boyhood experience in a war-time internment camp in British Columbia.

He tells how Japan's 1941 "sneak attack" against the U.S. Navy at Pearl Harbor, and the war that followed, threw his family and some 20 000 other Japanese Canadians and Japanese nationals into a turbulent sequence of events that deprived them of all rights of citizenship. Suzuki writes that pre-war Canada was a racist society. He describes how First Nations peoples in Prince Rupert in northern B.C. lived under conditions not unlike apartheid in South Africa—they were not allowed to stay in most hotels, were refused restaurant service, and required to sit in certain designated sections of theatres.

Modern Canada boasts high ideals of democracy with all the rights that are guaranteed by the Charter of Rights and Freedoms. Suzuki reminds us that many of these rights are recent, have been hard-won, and some have yet to become part of the accepted rights of all citizens. In 1942, the Canadian government invoked the War Measures Act and in effect declared that race alone was a sufficient threat to Canadian security to justify revoking rights of citizenship for Canadians of Japanese descent. He writes that to the white community, Japanese Canadians looked different—looked just like the enemy—and so were treated like the enemy.

Under the War Measures Act, bank accounts were frozen, personal property was confiscated, possessions were looted, and within the first few months all Japanese Canadians were removed from coastal British Columbia and sent to other provinces or relocated to hastily constructed internment camps located in the interior of British Columbia. Suzuki describes how his father volunteered to go to a road camp where Japanese Canadians were helping to build the Trans-Canada Highway. He writes that his father hoped that by volunteering, he would demonstrate his good intentions and trustworthiness as a citizen and thus ensure his family would be allowed to remain in Vancouver. Shortly after his father left for the work camp,

Suzuki, his mother, and two his two sisters were moved to an internment camp located in interior British Columbia. Along with hundreds of other Japanese Canadians, a long train ride brought them to their new home—Slocan City, an abandoned mining town north of Nelson. The Suzuki family's new home was a single room in a rotting building with glassless windows. Suzuki describes how the tiny room reeked from past generations of occupants, and they would wake each morning covered in bedbug bites. He reiterates that, for Japanese, cleanliness is like a religion, and can only imagine the revulsion his mother must have felt.

Suzuki relates that his parents were second-generation Canadians. They were bilingual, but spoke English at home. This was problematic for the young Suzuki—almost all the other children in the camps were fluently bilingual but he didn't speak Japanese and often could not understand what they were saying. Because of this linguistic deficiency, he was picked on, taunted, and isolated from the other Japanese children. He writes that it took a long time for him to overcome distrust and resentment of Japanese Canadians because of the way he was treated in the camp.

Suzuki writes that in his teenage years, his identity was based on the belief that in the eyes of white Canadians, he was Japanese first and Canadian second. He describes a street scene in 1945 Kaslo, B.C., where people were celebrating and setting off firecrackers. When he edged closer to the crowd, a big boy kicked his behind and shouted, "Get lost, Jap. We beat you!" This experience, along with the years of camp life only showed the young Suzuki that he was not a Canadian. This sense of alienation has remained a fundamental part of Suzuki's identity, despite the acquired veneer of adult maturity. He writes that, as an adult, his drive to do well was motivated by the desire to demonstrate to fellow Canadians that he and his family did not deserve to be treated as they were during the war years. Further, Suzuki wonders that if this psychic burden he carries as a result of a few years during the war is this profound, what then of the untold consequences for First Nations people who have experienced similar treatment since first contact.

Source: Adapted from *David Suzuki: The Autobiography.* Greystone Books, 2006, from *The Globe and Mail*, April 8, 2006: F1 and F6.

Extreme forms of discrimination and injustice were practised by the Canadian government and society against Canadians of Japanese ethnic origin forty years ago. What is the significance of these events for Canadians today?

that prejudges individuals because of characteristics assumed to be shared by all members of their group. Those assumptions may be based on **stereotypes**— mental images that exaggerate what are usually perceived to be undesirable traits of typical members of a group, and applied to all of its members.

A prejudice is not a product of experience, and may persist despite contrary evidence, particularly when prejudice serves to rationalize a position of privilege. One reason prejudice is often so deeply entrenched is that it is a part of culture that is learned early, and that it is a product of negative emotions as well as mental images (see Sniderman et al., 1993). The teachings of parents, teachers and other experts, the stories, the television shows and media that children and adults are exposed to all contain assumptions and evaluations concerning social groups and their attributes and social ranks. Indeed, the mass media in Canada continue to be criticized for ignoring ethnic and racialized minorities and for presenting them in ways that are stereotyped, inaccurate, and insulting. Henry and Tator (2002) pointed out that for many white Canadians, who have limited first-hand experiences with those who are "different" from them, the media are the primary source of information about immigrants, Aboriginal people, and racialized groups. The media play a significant role in the reproduction of racism to the extent that they selectively present these groups as people with problems, or as threatening to Canadian society. These practices partly reflect the fact that media decision makers and influential journalists include few members of racialized minorities (see the box "Do the Media View Racial Minorities Through a 'Prism of Whiteness'?").

[Debate]

Do the Media View Racial Minorities through a "Prism of Whiteness"?

Few would dispute the prominence of the media in guiding, shaping, and transforming the way we look at the world ... how we understand it ... and the manner by which we experience and relate to it .... A media-dominated society such as ours elevates the electronic and print media into an important source of information on how to shape an operational image of the world .... Those in control of media information define the beliefs, values, and myths by which we live and organize our lives. They impose a cultural context for framing our experiences of social reality, in the process sending out a clear message about who is normal and what is desirable and important in society ....

Media values are designed around those priorities that can capture as large an audience as possible for maximizing advertising revenues .... Media messages come across as safe, simple, and predictable in order to appeal to the lowest common denominator in society. Information about the world, if it attracts a broad audience, is included. Otherwise it is excluded, especially if any potential exists to offend significant markets. Especially in advertising, the media acknowledge the necessity to cater to dominant attitudes and prejudice. The logic of these circumstances dictates media mistreatment of racial (and other) minorities as the norm rather than the exception ....

The media in Canada relay information about who racial minorities are, what they want and why, how they propose to achieve their goals, and with what consequence for Canadian society. How responsibly have the media acted in this respect? ...

Certain patterns can be extrapolated from media (mis)treatment of racial minorities. Minorities are defined and categorized (a) as invisible, (b) in terms of race-role stereotyping, (c) as a social problem, and (d) as amusement ....

(a) Minorities as invisible
Racial minorities are reduced to invisible status through under-representation in programming, staffing, and

(continued)

decision making. Minorities are deemed unworthy of coverage unless caught up in situations of conflict or crisis . . . . This marginalization continues into advertising, where they are excluded because of minimal purchasing power or low socioeconomic status and prestige . . . . Media "whitewashing" (especially in advertising) contributes to the invisibility of minorities in society. Racial minorities are restricted in [a] way that "denies their existence, devalues their contribution to society, and trivializes their aspirations to participate, as fully fledged members" . . . .

(b) Minorities as stereotypes

Minorities have long complained of stereotyping by the mass media. Notwithstanding some improvements in this area, the report card on mass media stereotyping shows only negligible improvement. Race-role images continue to be reinforced, perpetuated, and even legitimized through media dissemination and selective coverage. When appearing in advertising, racial minorities are often cast in slots that reflect a "natural" propensity for the product in question. Who better to sell foreign airlines, quality chambermaid service in hotels, or high-cut gym shoes? . . .

(c) Minorities as social problem

Racial minorities are frequently singled out by the media as a "social problem." They are described in the context of "having problems" that require solutions requiring an inordinate amount of political attention and consuming a disproportionate slice of national resources . . . . In addition, the media are likely to define minorities in terms of "creating problems" by making demands unacceptable to the social, political, or moral order of society.

For example, Aboriginal peoples in Canada are portrayed time and again as "troublesome constituents" whose demands for self-determination and self-government are anathema to Canada's liberal-democratic tradition. This "us versus them" mentality fostered by the media is conducive to the scapegoating of racial minorities, who are blamed for an assortment of social ills or economic misfortunes . . . .

(d) Minorities as amusement

Racial minorities are often portrayed as irrelevant to society at large. This decorative effect is achieved by casting minorities in the role of entertainment by which to amuse or divert the audience. On-air television programming creates a situation where racial minorities find themselves ghettoized into roles as sitcom comedians. The restrictive effects of such an orientation serve to trivialize minority aspirations, as well as to diminish their importance as serious contributors to Canadian society . . . .

Racial minorities are victimized by media treatment that confirms and endorses audience prejudice . . . . Compounding the difficulties is the absence of racial minorities in creative positions, such as those of director, producer, editor, or screenwriter. Fewer still are positioned in the upper levels of management where key decision making occurs. The experiences and realities of racial minorities are distorted by the media, largely because of the inability of largely white, middle-class media personnel to perceive and understand the world from a different point of view.

Source: Augie Fleras and Jean Leonard Elliott (1992). *Multiculturalism in Canada: The Challenge of Diversity*, 1st edition, Scarborough, ON: Nelson Canada (pp. 234–43). Reprinted by permission of Nelson, a division of Thompson Learning: www.thompsonrights.com.

For each of the categories, give examples of how minorities have been portrayed by the media. Is there evidence that things are changing?

The connection between prejudiced attitudes and discriminatory behaviour has been the subject of a great deal of research, which suggests that the relationship between attitudes and behaviour is extremely complex. A prejudiced person does not always act in a discriminatory way, and there is little evidence that discriminatory behaviour by individuals is caused by prejudiced attitudes. A 1999 survey of anglophone and francophone Canadian university students found that feelings of personal and cultural security were related to positive attitudes toward immigration and ethnic diversity (Bourhis and Montreuil, 2003: 40).

Survey evidence has shown that, with the passing generations, majority attitudes toward minority racial and ethnic groups have become more tolerant and accepting. A 1990 survey by Decima found that 90 percent of Canadians and 86 percent of Americans agreed, "all races are created equal" (Reitz and Breton, 1994: 67–68).

Yet Aboriginal people and immigrants who are visible minorities in Canada continue to suffer from disproportionate rates of poverty, unemployment, menial occupational status, and poor living conditions as mentioned above (Small, 1998; Kazemipur and Halli, 2000). Clearly, improvement in the attitudes publicly expressed by members of the dominant group is not in itself a solution to the problems of inequality and discrimination. Indeed, the racialization process, and the ongoing generation and reproduction of new negative assumptions and stereotypes about minorities, can be viewed as part of the larger structure of social relations that developed through Canada's history of race and ethnic relations, and which perpetuates today's vertical mosaic.

The Development of Race and Ethnic Relations in Canadian Society: An Overview

Intergroup relationships in Canada in this century have been shaped by the historical processes of colonialism, conquest, and migration, processes that continue to have influence generations after these events originated. Colonized groups such as the First Nations of North America became part of a plural society involuntarily, by coercion, and remain economically and politically marginal to that society. The military conquest of Canada's French by the British shaped subsequent relationships between the two majority groups. Migrating groups, such as the many peoples of Asian, South or Central American, or European origin who now populate Canada, entered the society voluntarily, although economic need or political repression may have driven them from their homelands. The communities and institutions they have established in Canada are not transplants, but new social forms created in response to the challenges that they face here. We shall discuss each of these historical processes in turn.

Colonialism and the First Nations

The struggles and accommodations that have characterized contacts between Aboriginal peoples—the First Nations, Métis, and Inuit—and the rest of Canadian society reflect a system of intergroup relations that grew out of **colonialism**. In colonial situations, whether in the Americas, Africa, or elsewhere, a settler culture and society have invaded and dominated an indigenous population, controlling and exploiting the land, resources, and institutions of that population, and over time undermining and sometimes even destroying its culture and way of life.

During the earliest period in the colonization of Canada, both the French and English used trading relationships with First Nations for economic gain and to enlist them as allies against their enemies. But as political and economic realities changed, and these alliances and trade relationships became less useful and profitable, the British increasingly made war upon First Nations and sought treaties to remove them from much of their traditional land, which was to be occupied by settlers. Some of these encroachments were met with armed resistance, as in the 1869 and 1885 rebellions of Indians and Métis under the leadership of Louis Riel in the Red River and Saskatchewan River regions. The first rebellion ended with limited gains for the Natives, but the second ended in complete defeat and the hanging of Riel. Wars, forced resettlement, and disease brought an absolute decline in the size of Canada's First Nations population, from an estimated 200 000 to 500 000 at the beginning of European settlement to not many more than 100 000 by 1871 (Royal Commission on Aboriginal Peoples, 1996: 2).

The practice of negotiating treaties with individual bands, begun by the British Crown and continuing after Confederation (1867), resulted in the forced surrender by some First Nations of their interests in their ancestral lands, sometimes in exchange for the right to live on reserves as wards of the state, segregated from the rest of Canadian society. Under the terms of the Indian Act (first passed in 1876 and subsequently revised), *registered* or *status Indians* are entitled to live on reserve lands and to receive certain government programs and services, such as education and health care. However, some First Nations have opted out of certain sections of the Indian Act and some are self-governing, never having signed treaties.

Since Confederation, the affairs of status Indians have been managed by various branches and departments of the federal government, which has administered the reserves, band funds, property, education, welfare, and the fulfillment of treaty obligations. As the reserve system and residential schools became entrenched, many First Nations communities manifested the demoralization that has affected powerless colonized peoples in many parts of the world. Indian residents of reserves had few ways to influence the paternalistic colonial government bureaucracies. Yet resistance to the system of colonialism, both individual and collective, has persisted (see Chapter 15, Social Movements). *Non-status Indians* are those who do not meet the criteria of status Indians under the Indian Act, and are thus exempt from the Act's provisions. So too are the Métis, a people descended from marriages between Indian women and early settlers, traders, and trappers, mainly of French and British stock. Although these groups suffered many of the same injustices and deprivations endured by status Indians, they do not have the same entitlements.

Canada's 45 000 Inuit are also exempt from the provisions of the Indian Act, and no historic treaties were ever made between the Inuit and the Government of Canada. (See the film *Atanarjurat: The Fast Runner* for a realistic portrayal of traditional Inuit life.) Sustained contact between Inuit and other Canadians began with the construction of large military installations in the North during World War II. Since that time, change in the Inuit way of life has been rapid and dramatic, involving impoverishment, social disorganization, and disruption of traditional ways of life, as is usual when a settler society invades and dominates an indigenous population. Government policy, including the forced removal of communities, as well as economic change have led to the concentration of many Inuit in urban centres, where educational and social service facilities and housing are located. The rapid importation of southern workers, institutions, consumer goods, and social patterns has further transformed traditional Inuit culture, economy, and family life, and created marginality among the young.

As a result of a comprehensive land claim settlement in 1993 between the federal government and the Inuit people, Canada's third territory, Nunavut, was created in the central and eastern Arctic in 1999. Nunavut, which means "our land" in Inuktitut, constitutes more than a fifth of Canada's land mass.

In the post-World War II years, the size of the Aboriginal population increased substantially, and in 2001, over 1.3 million people reported having some Aboriginal ancestry (Statistics Canada, 2001 Census, Analysis Series, *Aboriginal Peoples of Canada: A Demographic Profile*, Catalogue No. 96F0030XIE2001007).

Many Aboriginal women were finally recognized and given band membership rights when a 1985 amendment to the Indian Act ended its discriminatory exclusion of First Nations women who had married non-Natives, and their children. The Aboriginal population is also more likely now than in the past to identify themselves as Aboriginal in the census. Moreover, the rate of population increase among Aboriginal people exceeds that of the rest of Canada, resulting in a population that is younger than the Canadian average. Thus Aboriginal people will form an increasing proportion of Canada's total population over time.

Today, approximately half of registered or status Indians live on the more than 2000 reserves in Canada; some of these are in cities. Living conditions vary considerably from one reserve to another, but generally speaking the reserve population is impoverished and lacks opportunity for higher education and employment. The average income on reserves is less than half the Canadian average (Northern Affairs Canada, *Information*, November 1997: 1). Life expectancy for Aboriginals is below the Canadian average, and infant mortality is above the national average. Many reserve communities face severe environmental hazards resulting from industrial and resource development, which has polluted waterways and disrupted the fish and game stocks upon which many communities have depended for a livelihood.

About half of Aboriginal people live in urban centres, including large cities such as Vancouver, Calgary, Edmonton, Regina, Saskatoon, Winnipeg, and Toronto, as well as smaller centres such as Thunder Bay and Prince George (Graham and Peters, 2002). Most off-reserve Aboriginal people suffer economic and social disadvantage, and the unemployment rate for Aboriginal people living off-reserve is roughly double the rate for the Canadian population. The earnings of Aboriginal people who work full time, full year are on average about 10 percent less than those of non-Aboriginal people, and Aboriginal people are more likely to live in poverty than visible minorities and recent immigrants in most cities (Maxim et al., 2001: 468; Lee, 2000). However, many urban Aboriginal people have university degrees and middle-class incomes, so it is important not to make assumptions. There is considerable mobility among Aboriginal people between urban areas and reserves or rural areas, and between cities (Graham and Peters, 2002). To many, rural reserve communities are more attractive residential

The need to implement an alternative to the reserve system and the movement toward self-government by Aboriginal peoples present a major policy dilemma for Canada's pluralistic society.

locations than cities, especially if economic opportunity exists there.

For First Nations people in Canadian society, whether living on or off reserves, the past generation has been a time of collective commitment and action directed toward change and renewal, and ultimately self-government and self-determination. Aboriginal associations, community organizations, and individuals are engaged in struggles to reclaim and strengthen their political and economic institutions, cultures, languages, religions, lands, communities, and families, which have been profoundly damaged by the impact of colonialism and its legacy of discrimination and racism. Lengthy land claims negotiations and struggles over fishing and hunting rights have preoccupied many communities and led to some success. These collective and individual efforts have brought a strengthening of many First Nations communities as well as a flourishing of entrepreneurship and of cultural and artistic productivity. Involvement in higher education and in the professions has also increased greatly. The achievements, contributions, and capacities of Aboriginal people provide

strong evidence that the conventional stereotypes, a legacy of colonialism, are false and must be challenged.

French and British Canadians: Two majorities, two solitudes

Conquest is another historical process that brings pluralist societies into being. In Canada, the British conquest of New France was followed by events that established the foundations of French–British dualism. The dominant metaphors in Canadian scholarship as well as in law and popular tradition have long described Canada as a bicultural country composed of "two societies," "two majorities," "two charter groups"—and, some have added, "two solitudes."

The French–British relationship has distant historical roots that should be familiar to all Canadians. The primary economic value of New France was its resource of furs, and Britain and France fought to control the fur trade the colonists had begun with Native peoples living in New France.

Not only commercial rivalry, but also differences of religion, economic life, and culture figured in the British–French conflict.

The Treaty of Paris (1763) transferred virtually all Canadian lands under French control to the British, whose empire now stretched from the Atlantic to the Mississippi. Britain then faced the problem of governing some 65 000 French-speaking Roman Catholics, who possessed a distinct way of life, history, language, and set of institutions. The British chose to deal with this challenge by establishing a policy of cultural and political pluralism that recognized the "French fact," legally acknowledging the special status of the French in Lower Canada in the Quebec Act of 1774.

With Confederation in 1867, the foundation of contemporary language rights was established in the British North America Act, which guaranteed the right to use either English or French in the Canadian and Quebec governments and courts.

The Manitoba Act, passed three years later in the aftermath of the Métis rebellion, confirmed the official equality of French and English in the public life of Manitoba. However, this important legal guarantee of French language rights outside Quebec did not survive the rapid influx of English-speaking settlers. By 1890 the French were reduced to a small proportion of Manitoba's population, and the provincial legislature, reflecting the assimilationist and anti-Catholic mood of the time, abolished separate schools and adopted the English Language Act, making English the sole language of public affairs in the province. This act was not disallowed by the federal government nor tested in court until 1979, when the Supreme Court ruled that all legislative acts of the province must be rewritten in both languages.

Outside Quebec there has generally been little recognition by the other provinces of the "French fact." New Brunswick, with less than 3 percent of Canada's population, is the only officially bilingual province. Federally, the Royal Commission on Bilingualism and Biculturalism (1967) was established in response to Quebec's Quiet Revolution of the 1960s (see also Chapter 15, Social Movements), which brought rapid modernization to the economic, political, and cultural institutions of the province and stirred nationalistic and separatist currents. Following the Commission the federal government enacted the Official Languages Act (1969), which extended the use of French within the federal civil service and sought to make public services

available in French wherever concentrations of Francophones reside.

The legal foundation of Canadian bilingualism and biculturalism is one essential ingredient of modern French–English relationships. Another is the territorial concentration of about 77 percent of Canada's single-origin French ethnic population in the province of Quebec, whose population was 41 percent of French ethnic origin in 1996, according to the census. Québécois influence over the province's territory and its major educational, religious, judicial, and governmental institutions has been a crucial resource in the struggle of French Canadians to maintain their language and culture and to develop as a nation.

Sociologists who have studied Quebec society over the years have used the concepts of "race", "ethnic group", "society," and "nation" at various times to refer to both the uniqueness and the marginalization of francophone Quebec society within Canada. Over the past half century, sociological analysis has evolved beyond a preoccupation with French Canadians as an ethnic minority within Canada, and Quebec as a society going through a modernization process. Contemporary Quebec sociologists generally view Quebec society as a nation, and Quebec nationalism as a movement with social, cultural, and political dimensions (Fournier, 2001).

The Québécois struggle for national self-determination, whether within the Canadian federation or as a sovereign state, is both a sociological and a political development that must be seen in the context of dramatic political events. For example, the proclamation of the War Measures Act by the Government of Canada in reaction to the October Crisis of 1970, in which the Front de Libération du Québec kidnapped two public officials and murdered one of them, brought the suspension of civil liberties, the arrest of hundreds, and tanks in the streets. This defining event fuelled sovereigntist sentiment (you will remember that this Act was also used to remove the Japanese Canadians from their West Coast homes during World War II). With the 1976 victory of the Parti Québécois in the Quebec provincial election the nationalist movement became a legitimate and enduring political force. The first important initiative by the new government, the 1977 language legislation known as the Charter of the French Language, or Bill 101, specified that the language of Quebec's French majority would be the official language of Quebec, and the legal language of work, business, education, and all public functions within the province.

Quebec scholars such as Guindon (1988) have pointed out that French Canadians historically responded collectively to their marginal position in Canadian political, cultural, and economic life as ethnic groups generally do, by creating a complex system of parallel institutions and social networks. French Catholic schools, parishes, credit unions, labour organizations, communications media, voluntary associations, and a wide range of other institutions, some with government support, met the collective needs of French Canadians. British Canadians in Quebec also developed a fairly high degree of institutional completeness, and traditionally dominated the economic sector. As a result, in past generations British–French contacts in Quebec were largely confined to the public sphere, to formal bureaucratic settings such as the factory. But even within the factory, the presence of occupational stratification often meant that French assembly-line workers worked and ate lunch side-by-side with other French workers, and were linked weakly to English-speaking white-collar workers and management by bilingual supervisors.

However, the Quiet Revolution, language legislation, and the development of national consciousness and political power have increased francophone socioeconomic mobility and cultural vibrancy. After Bill 101, the use of French rapidly increased in the workplace and in public life generally. Most francophones are now able to work in their own language in Quebec, and the proportion of anglophones who are bilingual has increased greatly, according to census information.

One element of this change in Quebec was the outmigration of many anglophones, especially unilingual people uncertain about their future in an increasingly French Quebec. Their departure in turn heightened a trend toward polarization in Canada. Official bilingualism and legal guarantees have not altered English cultural and economic dominance and the erosion of the French language and culture outside Quebec. This erosion has complex sources, including: English-speaking immigrants vastly outnumbering French-speaking immigrants, the adoption of the English language both by the French outside Quebec and by other ethnic groups, and the decline in Quebec's birth rate.

The vision of a bilingual and multicultural Canada is not easy to reconcile with that of a sovereign Quebec as the homeland of French culture in North America. Constitutional and political developments have not brought together the two solitudes. In recent years, public opinion in Quebec appears to have cooled somewhat toward sovereignty, but the relationship between the two majority groups in Canadian society remains troubled as the Québécois nation continues to evolve, despite resistance from the rest of Canada. The influence of a global economy and international popular culture, particularly among young Quebecers, has presented new and creative possibilities for the future of French language and culture within a multicultural Canada.

A fundamental development in Quebec society in recent years has been the increased ethnic and racial diversity of the population as a result of immigration. In Quebec today, the central sociological issue is no longer seen as the relationship between the French and English collectivities in Canada, but the relationship between the francophone majority and the "other ethnic groups" in Quebec. "Francophones, once viewed as a dominated group inside Canada, are now defined as a dominant group inside Quebec" (Fournier, 2001: 345).

The "other ethnic groups": The shaping of the Canadian mosaic

It is inaccurate to think of Canadian society as nothing but a struggle between two founding nations, complex as the implications of such an image may be. Along with the Aboriginal presence, a history of massive immigration has created a much more complex pluralism in Canada, one marked by a high degree of ethnic and class diversity.

In the first decade of the twentieth century, the economy and society of Canada were still largely agrarian, and government policy was oriented toward agricultural development. Government sponsorship of recruitment and transportation for immigrant peasants and farmers from Europe and the United States, and the availability of free land that had been stolen from the First Nations, combined to rapidly increase the immigration of settlers from Britain and the United States. They were joined by Ukrainians, Poles, Hungarians, Russians, and many others from Central and Eastern Europe. We have already mentioned some of the consequences of this influx for the Aboriginal and French populations of western Canada.

The era of the farmer-immigrant was a relatively brief one in Canada's history, for the predominant pattern of immigrant settlement has long been urban. As early as 1921, the first year for which data are available, 56 percent of Canada's foreign-born were living in urban areas, compared with only 48 percent of the Canadian-born. The transformation of Canada from an agrarian to an urban-industrial society was already well under way at that time, and opportunities for industrial employment in the growing cities attracted both farm-reared Canadians and immigrants.

Heavy immigration following World War II also contributed to urban-ethnic diversity, since the vast majority of newcomers settled in the seven largest metropolitan areas of Canada. Job opportunities are most plentiful in the largest cities and the effects of chain migration are also seen in the congregation of immigrants there. By 2001, nearly three-quarters of all immigrants to Canada were living in Toronto, Montreal, and Vancouver compared with about one-third of the total Canadian-born population, according to the census (Statistics Canada, 2001 Census, Analysis Series, *Canada's Ethnocultural Portrait: The Changing Mosaic*, Catalogue No. 96F0030XIE2001008, p. 7). Look again at Table 8.1, which shows immigrants as a percentage of selected city populations as of 2001.

Before 1970, immigrants originating in Europe made up 70 percent of newcomers to Canada. In the 1990s, immigrants from Asia contributed 58 percent of total immigration while Europeans made up 20 percent (Statistics Canada, 2001 Census, Analysis Series, *Canada's Ethnocultural Portrait: The Changing Mosaic*, Catalogue No. 96F0030XIE2001008, pp. 6, 39).

In addition, since the end of World War II, hundreds of thousands of people have come to Canada as refugees, displaced by wars and political oppression in their homelands (see Figure 8.1). The numbers seeking asylum from violence and oppression grew throughout the 1990s and, as a signatory of the United Nations Geneva Convention, Canada has a duty to accept refugees (for details on recent immigration and refugees to Canada see Citizenship and Immigration Canada, http://cicnet.ci.gc.ca/english/).

Before 1967 discriminatory immigration policies severely restricted the settlement of Chinese, South Asian, black, Japanese, and other racialized minorities in Canada. With the refocusing of immigration policy in the 1970s to emphasize occupational skills, educational qualifications, demands of the economy, family reunification, and refugee criteria instead of national origin, the immigrant population has become increasingly heterogeneous and representative of Asia, Africa, and Latin America. The administration of policies regarding admission of immigrants and refugees, however, continues to

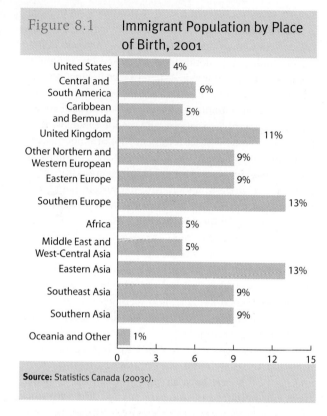

Figure 8.1 Immigrant Population by Place of Birth, 2001

Source: Statistics Canada (2003c).

adversely affect racialized minorities. Domestic and farm workers from the Caribbean and Mexico, who are admitted to Canada on a temporary basis to work in private households or on farms at low wages, are especially disadvantaged and deprived of the rights taken for granted by Canadians (Avery, 1995; Henry et al., 1995: 75–78; Sharma, 2001). There is evidence that Muslims in Canada experienced an upsurge of hate crimes and negative media coverage following September 11, 2001, as well as ethnic profiling by police and intelligence officials, and survey responses reported experiences of discrimination (Helly, 2004).

Researchers have found that urban immigrants generally experience higher rates of poverty than non-immigrants (Lee, 2000) and that the economic disadvantage of recent immigrants as compared with non-immigrants has increased since 1980 regardless of age group, language group, and educational level (Picot and Hou, 2003). Still, immigrants are less likely than the Canadian-born to make use of social assistance or unemployment insurance, although the taxes they pay support these services (Picot and Hou, 2003: 5; Papillion, 2002: 10).

The average educational level of immigrants has been rising in line with an immigration policy that gives preference to those with a postsecondary education. However immigrants do not receive the same economic returns for their investment in education that the Canadian-born do. This may reflect, in part, a lack of recognition by employers of credentials and work experience acquired by immigrants in their home countries (Papillion, 2002: 11). Whether or not they are immigrants, blacks are much more likely to be unemployed and to live in poverty than whites, even when education, age, and full-time versus part-time job status are taken into account (Kazemipur and Halli, 2003). Pendakur and Pendakur (2002) found that the pay gap between whites and Canadian-born visible minorities and Aboriginals increased during the 1990s. Focus group research has also documented systemic employment discrimination against racialized men and women in the culture, social relations, and decision-making practices of workplaces (Agòcs and Jain, 1999; Kunz, Milan, and Schetagne, 2002).

Reitz (1998) has found evidence that there is less inequality between recent immigrants and non-immigrants in Canada than in the United States, perhaps reflecting a better support system for immigrants here. However, the substantial and growing level of poverty and earnings inequality affecting racialized minorities and immigrants in Canada signals a need to do much more to ensure social inclusion and the sustainability of our multiracial and ethnically diverse urban communities.

Perspectives on Canadian Race and Ethnic Relations

We now turn our attention to three influential perspectives on intergroup relations within pluralistic societies such as Canada—assimilationism, pluralism, and postmodern approaches. Each functions in two ways at the same time, first as a description of social reality, and second, as a goal or vision for social policy.

Assimilationism

The interpretation of ethnic group relations that dominated North American thought for at least the first half of the twentieth century was **assimilationism**—the view that ethnic diversity gradually and inevitably will decline as ethnic group members are integrated or absorbed into the general population of the society. Assimilation involves becoming more and more like the dominant group, so that in time Polish Canadians, for example, would be indistinguishable from the British or French Canadians with whom they live. As a group they are unique only while they are relatively recent arrivals. In time they will improve their social and economic position and disappear into the great melting pot, in which various ethnic groups and cultures blend into a single culture and society.

The melting-pot image has been a prominent feature of national identity in the United States, but assimilationism as a description and social ideal has also had its adherents in Canada (see, for example, Porter, 1980). Assimilationist assumptions were reflected in official policy toward immigrants and ethnic groups before World War II. The preference for British immigrants and the existence of severe restrictions on the immigration of racially and culturally different peoples have already been mentioned. These restrictions were based, in part, on the assumption that those peoples who are most

Assimilation is the process of becoming part of the larger surrounding society and culture by becoming more and more like the dominant group.

similar to the dominant Canadian population—the British—would most readily adapt to life in Canada, cause fewest problems for the dominant group, and ultimately assimilate.

The sociological theory of assimilationism is rooted to a large degree in the work of Robert Park (1950; 1952), one of North America's first and most important sociologists, and leader of the Chicago school of urban sociology between 1915 and 1940. As we saw in Chapter 1, What Is Sociology?, Park's theories became influential in Canada through the work of Charles Dawson, a scholar and teacher in the field of Canadian ethnic group relations, who was Park's student at the University of Chicago and later founder of the first Canadian department of sociology at McGill University.

Park viewed the modern world as a melting pot, a total system characterized by large-scale geographic and social mobility that tended to break down the isolation of local cultures, causing cultural and social patterns in the global society to become uniform and homogeneous. Park considered the breakdown of small-scale, local societies and cultures, with their ascribed class and status distinctions, to be a positive development. He felt it would help to liberate individuals by making status dependent upon achieved rather than ascribed criteria.

Park developed the notion of a **race relations cycle** to describe four successive stages in the relationships between dominant and minority groups in any society. These stages are contact, competition, accommodation, and assimilation. Through exploration, migration, or conquest, groups come into *contact*, beginning a process of communication that breaks down the isolation of each. If these groups begin to draw from a common pool of limited resources, *competition* ensues between them. The competitive stage may eventually be resolved through the *accommodation* of the weaker group, which adopts the language and culture of the more powerful. In time, if the distinctive external signs that differentiated one group from another are erased, *assimilation* is complete. The peoples intermingle and the offspring of intergroup unions belong fully to neither group. Ultimately, the ethnic group member becomes "a mere individual, indistinguishable in the cosmopolitan mass of the population . . . " (Park, 1950: 208–9).

There would, however, be instances of intergroup contact in which the race relations cycle would not run full course, for Park believed that distinctions among peoples may be maintained when ethnic or racial characteristics are highly visible. He considered physical traits such as colour to be the chief obstacles to the universal assimilation he envisioned, for these external marks cannot be changed, and constitute lightning rods for animosities and prejudice. Their presence perpetuates an endless vicious circle of majority prejudice, and minority withdrawal and defensiveness.

Other sociologists, after Park, contributed substantially to assimilationist theory, among them Gordon (1964), who noted that the concept of assimilation must be broken down to reflect the many-sided nature of individual and group life. It is especially important to distinguish between cultural assimilation, or **acculturation**, and **structural assimilation**. Gordon argued that individuals may acculturate quite readily—that is, they may learn the language, values, and customs of the dominant group and make them their own. But this does not mean that they will be assimilated into the social structure—that is, accepted into intimate or primary social relationships with the dominant group. The majority group may still hold back from entering into friendship, marriage, or neighbour relationships with the minority. Thus, even though a group may acculturate, it may never succeed in assimilating into the social structure of the larger society.

Assimilationist thinkers generally hold liberal, individualistic values, and assume that it is only through individual achievement that upward mobility in the social hierarchy can occur. They further assume, as in Park's thought, that maintaining one's ethnic culture and language hinders upward mobility because it reduces acceptance of the ethnic group member by the majority group. Thus, ethnic group members must accept a trade-off: giving up their ethnicity in return for social acceptance, improved status, and a good standard of living.

As a social goal and guide to policy, assimilationism has been subjected to damaging criticism. For example, it follows from the assimilationist perspective that public institutions must apply the same rules to everyone, "regardless of race, religion, or national origin." Groups, then, are officially ignored, and only the claims of individuals are recognized by assimilationist theorists. It is assumed that, in order to be equal, people must all be alike, and that equality means treating everyone alike, regardless of their differences.

It had become apparent by the 1960s that the condition of blacks and Aboriginal peoples as groups was not improving through the process of social mobility whereby individuals play by the universalistic rules of the game. The goal of bringing these groups into the mainstream of American and Canadian societies has seemed farther and farther away as census data chart the continuing gap between the incomes and unemployment rates of blacks and Natives, on the one hand, and the rest of the population on the other. Many observers in academic and public life concluded that assimilation is not happening because of the barriers that stem from longstanding patterns of discrimination and disadvantage. The historical legacy of slavery, colonialism, discrimination, and cultural destruction has shaped the structure of race relations and weighs heavily upon present generations. The application of universalistic rules and standards is resulting in what we earlier called systemic or institutionalized discrimination. Inequality is built into the occupational structure and many minority group members are not even getting to the starting gate in the race for advancement. The rules of the game are not fair to all, since they were established by the majority and serve to maintain their positions of privilege. It follows that the rules must be changed in order to remove those barriers that have excluded minorities from access to jobs, promotions, and career advancement.

The critique of assimilationism generated new policy approaches in Canada and the United States. **Employment equity** is a broad strategy for change in the policies, practices, and culture of the Canadian workplace (Agòcs, 2002). Its objectives are to increase the representation of disadvantaged groups at all levels of the occupational structure, to remove barriers to their career advancement, and to create a workplace culture free of discrimination. In Canada at the present time, the designated employment equity groups are Aboriginal peoples, visible minorities, women, and people with disabilities. Under the 1986 federal Employment Equity Act (as revised in 1995), employers in the federal jurisdiction and the federal public service are required to implement employment equity programs and to report annually on their results. The Federal Contractors Program requires employers who sell goods and services to the federal government to implement employment equity requirements as well.

Research on affirmative action in the United States and employment equity in Canada has shown that legislated requirements and enforcement can make a difference. When employers are required to set goals and timetables for improved representation, to remove practices that stand in the way of achieving these goals, and when these requirements are enforced, representation improves and there is less inequality in pay (Agòcs, 2002: ch. 1). However, federal employment equity requirements and enforcement have been weak, and their impact on the representation of visible minorities and Aboriginal people in employment has been small (e.g., Leck and Saunders, 1996; Jain et al., 1997). Furthermore, progress in eliminating systemic discrimination requires the enactment of strong employment equity legislation at the provincial level, since most workplaces fall within the provincial jurisdiction. The potential of employment equity to break the cycle of systemic discrimination that impedes the integration of minorities in the workplace is yet to be fully realized.

Pluralism and multiculturalism

The worldwide rise of modern nationalistic movements has shaken loose historic accommodations between ethnic and racial groups, not only in Canada and the United States, but also in many parts of Africa, Europe, Asia, and the territory of the former Soviet Union. Ethnic and racial diversity, as well as inequality and conflict, are very much a part of our contemporary society, and "assimilation" seems as far away as ever. Quebecois, First Nations, Jews, Chinese, Muslims, Sikhs, and many other groups in Canada still ask: Can't we all enjoy equal opportunities as members of one society while maintaining our differences, our identities, and our communities? Can we not coexist as equals within a single society, even though we do not all look the same or share the same values and culture?

Pluralism is the view that ethnic diversity (and conflict) remains a central feature of contemporary societies and that ethnicity continues to be an important aspect of individual identity and group behaviour. In the post-World War II era the image of the ethnic mosaic, an intricate tapestry of many hues woven from the strands of many ethnic and regional subcultures, has become integral to Canadian national identity and is said to distinguish Canadian from American values and culture. It is generally understood today that "Canadian culture" is not a homogeneous whole and that diversity is one of its hallmarks.

Since Canada is a pluralistic society, both assimilation and ethnic and racial differentiation are going on at the same time. While in some respects Canada's ethnic groups become more alike as time passes, in many ways their influence brings an increasing diversity to the

A Reverse Brain Drain?

We read in the paper about the brain drain to the U.S. or other countries where taxes are supposedly lower. Canada actually gains in this exchange as ever-greater numbers of educated people from other, especially developing, countries come here to work. Indeed, the federal government makes education and skills its paramount criteria for immigrants (this does not apply to family class or refugee immigrants).

The educational credentials that immigrants received in their home countries, however, are not always recognized by accreditation bodies and regulatory agencies in Canada as equivalent to Canadian degrees. Hence immigrants may not be permitted to practise their professions or trades in this country. Added to this barrier are the effects of discrimination, an uncertain economy, and in some cases lack of facility in English or French.

As a result, we see many foreign-trained doctors and other professionals working as taxi drivers or cleaners; university graduates become sales clerks in stores and take on other jobs in which they are under-employed. Immigrants are also more likely than the Canadian-born to be unemployed; as the last hired, they may be the first fired in economic downturns. The situation of racialized immigrants is particularly difficult, as is suggested by data that reveal that visible minority immigrants earn less than White immigrants—most likely because of discrimination.

Source: Adapted from Mark McKinnon, "Give us your highly educated." *The Globe and Mail,* 24 May 1999, p. B1.

Would internships for such professionals, followed by a requirement to work in an under-serviced area, solve the problem?

Pluralism is the view that ethnic diversity remains a central feature of modern urban society and that ethnicity is an important aspect of individual identity and group behaviour.

cultural, social, and political life shared by all Canadians. For example, immigrants, by becoming citizens and voting, may show signs of assimilation. Yet in local elections they may support candidates who represent their own ethnic group's interests, thus bringing diversity to the political spectrum.

In fact, many pluralists contend that ethnic group members make progress and improve their positions in the social hierarchy not by individual achievement and dissociation from their roots, as assimilationists would argue, but by group efforts, using ethnic solidarity as a resource. It is collective action that benefits the group, and thereby its individual members. When members of an ethnic community vote in a bloc, they force the political system to recognize and respond to their concerns. When relatives pool their resources to start a business, they not only provide jobs for their kin, but also contribute to the economic life of their community. When members of the community patronize ethnic businesses, they strengthen the community's overall business climate. In these examples it is the collective action of the community, rather than the efforts of isolated individuals to achieve upward mobility, that brings progress to members of the group. Still, we should add that many studies (e.g., Breton et al., 1990) have provided evidence that ethnic and Aboriginal communities, as well as individuals, adopt a variety of different approaches as they integrate into Canadian society and improve their socioeconomic position, while retaining varying degrees of ethnic identity and community solidarity.

The increasing heterogeneity of Canada's population, the growing numerical strength and voting power of ethnic groups, and the acceptance of a collectivist strategy have coincided with a shift from the official image of Canada as a bicultural country toward a recognition of it as multicultural. In 1971, Prime Minister Trudeau, with the support of all political parties, announced a policy of "multiculturalism within a bilingual framework," under which federal recognition and support would be extended to the various ethnic groups that constitute the Canadian mosaic (Government of Canada, 1971). The Multiculturalism Act of 1988 affirms the government's commitment to the preservation and appreciation of cultural diversity, and to the promotion of the full and equal participation of individuals and communities in all aspects of Canadian society (Fleras and Elliott, 1992). However, critics have noted a lack of results and questioned the government's real commitment to these principles. For example, it has been argued that the official policy of tolerance, exemplified in multiculturalism, provides a cloak of legitimacy for the federal government's pursuit of immigration policies that exploit temporary workers while benefiting employers seeking a cheap labour supply (Sharma, 2001).

The institutions of Canadian society have begun to grapple with the fact that ethnic and racial diversity and inequality are not just individual traits, but fundamental characteristics of the social system as a whole. Canadians now face the challenge and opportunity of learning to live in harmony and mutual respect, and making the value of equality a reality, in a society in which ethnic and racial diversity will continue to grow.

Post-colonial and postmodern perspectives

In recent years, theory and research on race and ethnic relations have increasingly understood ethnic and racial inequality and conflict as products of social structures and systems of social relations. In this analysis, discrimination is not simply a matter of individuals motivated by prejudiced attitudes hurting other individuals, although this certainly occurs. Instead, discrimination is built into the institutional and cultural life of society and, thus, a structure of inequality on the basis of race and gender is continuously reproduced.

As mentioned in our earlier discussion of systemic or institutionalized discrimination, the everyday functioning of institutional settings such as the workplace, the media, the government office, and even the family may perpetuate racist and sexist thinking and behaviour. In this way, the legacy of the past, which includes colonialism and conquest as well as immigration, interacts with emerging forms of inequality associated with the rise of a global economy and labour market to shape today's Canadian vertical mosaic. Prominent features of the contemporary structure of inequality include the persisting poverty and absence of opportunity characteristic in many First Nations communities. Other examples include the powerlessness of refugee families whose fate depends on the decision of a government official (see the box "Who Will Take Care of Our Children?"). There are many other examples of how our social institutions and the assumptions embedded in our culture create a structure of inequality.

From this perspective, racism is not only an ideology, it is integral to the structure and culture of a society. All members of that society, at least to some degree, participate in racist social arrangements and practices that privilege some and disadvantage others. Hence when we look at the photographs of Boards of Directors and senior executives in corporate annual reports, or see government ministers and parliamentarians on the evening news, the faces we see are predominantly white and male. But when we leave our office buildings at the end of our workday, the faces of the cleaning staff whose night of work is just beginning are often brown and female.

It is these institutionalized social arrangements that shape the opportunities and choices of the individuals who make up our society: they create the stage on which life stories are played out. Yet each individual is fundamentally unique and no assumptions can be made about what a person will achieve or contribute based on ancestry or gender. According to Giddens (1984), each of us has *agency*: although our choices are constrained by the rules of social institutions and by the resources to which we have access our lives are not predetermined by social structures. Hence we can be inspired by the achievements of individuals who have struggled against racism and sexism to survive, contribute to their families and communities, and attain success in the public sphere.

Who Will Take Care of Our Children?

Milton Daschevi installs drywall and lays bricks in . . . [Toronto's] booming home-construction trade. The father of two is a union member. He works long hours. He pays income tax. On Tuesday he, his wife, and their two children are supposed to be deported. . . .

[Daschevi is an example of] the many underground workers in Greater Toronto whose labour helps keep the city humming, but have no legal immigrant status. "Between 35 000 and 45 000 housing units are annually built in the GTA," says . . . a spokesperson for the Central Ontario Regional Council of Carpenters, Drywall and Allied Workers. "If you were to take out the estimated number of potentially undocumented workers in the construction market, I think it would be difficult to meet that demand. Hard labour jobs are hard to fill . . . Canadians are more interested in going into the high-tech, white-collared jobs."

The phenomenon is not just confined to the construction trades. Non-documented workers are in every aspect of our society. . . . If we deport all of them tomorrow, who will clean the homes? Who will take care of our children? Who will clean our office buildings?

[The union spokesperson pointed out that] "they're illegal and they're trying to get status . . . They don't want to be living like a criminal part of society. There should be a way to help these people." . . .

There are widely varying estimates about the number of undocumented workers in Canada. Some peg the

number at a low of 20 000. Others think it is as high as 200 000—maybe even higher. Citizenship and Immigration Canada's official position is that it doesn't know for sure and won't hazard a guess. . . . "It's like asking a police officer how many people speed," [said a spokesperson for Citizenship and Immigration]. . . .

Daschevi and his wife Jane came to Canada from Brazil 3½ years ago on a visitor's visa, along with their son Adelino, then 7, and their one-year-old daughter Julia. "My life is here now," says Daschevi, 43, as his wife interprets. "I just want to have a chance to build a future for my children in Canada." The family contacted immigration officials after they had been here for a year. . . .

Lawyer Avvy Go speaks for a group called Status, a coalition of community and social service agencies that advocates for people living here without legal immigrant status. She says she doesn't want to see these people used as disposable workers, who can be discarded when they are no longer needed. She argues it is time to examine how the evolution of Canada's immigration policy, which now emphasizes recruiting only the best and brightest, means that the kind of people who typically migrated here for generations no longer qualify to come legally. "For a lot of people, the only way to come is by so called illegal means," says Go. "We're defining skills by way of postsecondary education . . . but we still need people to build our houses."

. . . Status wants Ottawa to give everyone working underground the opportunity to "regularize their status."

Source: Excerpted from Maureen Murray, "Who Will Take Care of Our Children?" *Toronto Star*, August 10, 2003, pp. A1, A10. Reprinted with permission of Torstar Syndication Services.

When people work in Canada illegally they may be hurting those unwilling to jump the queue, especially if the government, believing that more workers are not needed, reduces its immigration quotas. How can we resolve that dilemma?

Post-colonial and postmodern theoretical approaches in sociology are extremely varied but share a limited number of themes in the pursuit to understand racism (see Delgado and Stefancic, 2000; Memmi, 2000). One such theme is the study of the way historical experience, be it that of the colonizer or the colonized, marks human and institutional behaviour in the present (e.g., Foucault, 1991). Another theme is how the centrality of power relations and the human struggle against domination contributes to sociological understanding. A third theme is the variety of human experience as well as the postmodern reality of constant change, so central in the lives of immigrants. A fourth theme is the need to understand how ideas are constructed and controlled, and by whom. For example, Mackey (1999) is concerned with how the ideology of multiculturalism and images of Aboriginal people, French people, and immigrants are used as part of the construction of Canadian nationality.

The **postmodern perspective** is skeptical, critical, and self-aware, seeking to "deconstruct" or demystify the claims of those with power and authority, including those of earlier generations of sociologists. Many postmodern theorists appear to be more preoccupied with understanding what lies behind dominant assumptions and social conventions than with developing theories to explain and predict behaviour, solving social problems, influencing social policy, or prompting social change. There is generally an assumption that "universal truth is impossible, and relativism is our fate" (Butler, 2002: 16).

Contemporary sociologists are also concerned with the study of anti-racism, the ways and means of working toward a non-racist society in which diversity and equality can coexist. Such a transformation requires both individual and institutional change, processes that necessarily begin with learning and deliberating about the causes and consequences of racism (Johnson, Rush, and Feagin, 2000). The opportunity to begin that learning is here.

Summary

Canada is a pluralistic society, a social system composed of ethnic groups that coexist in both peace and conflict within a common cultural, economic, and political framework, while maintaining cultures and social institutions that are to some extent distinctive. Canada has been called a vertical mosaic in recognition of the fact that racialized and ethnic groups occupy differing ranks within its stratification system: some groups enjoy relative privilege, while others lack access to power and opportunity in Canadian society.

A major form of ethnic group life in Canada, the local immigrant community, often develops through a process of chain migration, the sequential movement of people from a common place of origin to a common destination, with the assistance of relatives or compatriots who settled there earlier. In the ethnic community, newcomers find a familiar social network and an array of institutions to meet their needs. As the community grows, it establishes a place for itself within the local economic structure. Economic interests combine with cultural and social patterns to shape the community's distinctive adaptation to the new environment.

As a concept, ethnicity has several dimensions. Ethnicity is an ascribed status, a potential conferred upon individuals at birth, which becomes a part of personal identity during socialization within an ethnic community. The ethnic group is self-perpetuating and has boundaries set and maintained by patterns of interaction rather than by formal structures, cultural traits, or isolation. The ethnic group is also a subculture, the product of shared historical experiences that shape present understandings about values important to the group.

While members of a social group share values, interests, and patterns of interaction, a social category such as a race is socially constructed, referring to a collection of individuals who share certain physical features that are charged with social meaning. Racist ideologies rationalize the exploitation of certain categories of human beings on the basis of inherited characteristics. Minority groups are categories of people that are oppressed and relegated to subordinate ranks in the social hierarchy, regardless of their numbers. Various forms of social control, including annihilation, expulsion, discrimination, and segregation, have perpetuated the oppression and subordination of minority groups in modern societies.

The historical processes of colonialism, conquest, and migration have shaped Canadian race and ethnic relations. Colonized groups such as Aboriginal peoples become part of a plural society involuntarily. They often suffer longstanding and severe discrimination and disadvantage and remain economically and politically marginal to that society. The Indian Act and the reserve system have been the cornerstones of Canada's Aboriginal policy. Today, Canada's Aboriginal population is highly diverse, as it was historically, and is increasingly represented among urban residents and the middle class. First Nations continue to resist the oppressive legacy of colonialism and to struggle for self-government and self-determination.

The conquest of the French by the British shaped the subsequent relationship between Canada's two "founding peoples." Legal guarantees at the federal level provide for the perpetuation of the language, religion, and culture of French Canadians, and the concentration of the French within Quebec provides a powerful territorial and institutional base in the struggle of the Quebecois to perpetuate their culture and national identity. But, for a variety of reasons, the French language and culture have eroded in the rest of

Canada, where English cultural dominance has accompanied the economic dominance of what was once British North America.

Immigrant groups enter a society voluntarily, although they may have been driven from their home lands by economic want or political oppression. Historically, the British and Americans were Canada's dominant immigrant groups, but in the post–World War II era, immigrant origins have diversified, with increasing representation of peoples from Africa, Asia, and Latin America. Canadian policy is "multiculturalism within a bilingual framework," and the diversity that immigration brings is officially celebrated. Yet there is evidence that recent immigrants, especially those who are members of racialized minorities, are more likely than the rest of the Canadian population to suffer unemployment, poverty, and pay inequality. Researchers have documented the presence of racial discrimination, inequality, and disadvantage as issues that challenge Canadians today.

Interpretations of ethnic and race relations encompass two tasks: describing and making sense of social reality, and proposing social goals or visions of what Canadian society should be like. Assimilationism is the view that diversity declines as ethnic-group members achieve economic prosperity and are absorbed into the general population and culture of the society. This view of society as a melting pot has proven to be an inaccurate description of social reality and a doubtful guide to social policy. Pluralism, the perspective that recognizes the central place of ethnic diversity and conflict in modern societies, has long typified Canadian thought on ethnic and race relations, and is expressed in the policy of multiculturalism. Postmodern approaches provide insight into the structures of power relations and the ideological constructions that institutionalize racism. Inequality remains a central feature of most pluralistic societies today, including Canada, and racism and ethnic conflict continue to pose dilemmas for Canada and the modern world.

Questions for Review and Critical Thinking

1. Compare and contrast the experiences of post–World War II immigrants and refugees from Europe with those of immigrants and refugees arriving in Canada today. What policies are needed to ensure the successful settlement of today's immigrants and refugees?

2. Describe the historical development of a local ethnic community with which you are familiar. Examine the degree to which ethnicity continues to influence the attitudes and behaviours of members of this group. Compare your results with those who have studied other groups.

3. Examine the migration, marriage, and occupational patterns in your family by charting your genealogy and then listing the occupations, geographic movements, and marriages of as many family members as possible. Summarize any patterns you observe, applying concepts used in this chapter such as chain migration, occupational specialization, ethnic network, discrimination, ethnic stratification, occupational mobility, and ethnic endogamy.

4. What is racism? Give examples of the various forms it may take. Who suffers and who benefits from racism, and how? Why does racism persist in the modern world?

Key Terms

acculturation, p. 194
assimilationism, p. 193
chain migration, p. 173
colonialism, p. 187
discrimination, p. 181
employment equity, p. 195
ethnic group, p. 176
institutional completeness, p. 175
minority group, p. 179
pluralism, p. 195
pluralistic society, p. 177
postmodern perspective, p. 199
prejudice, p. 183
race, p. 179
race relations cycle, p. 194
racialization, p. 179
racist ideology, p. 179
segregation, p. 182
social category, p. 179
stereotypes, p. 185
structural assimilation, p. 194
systemic or institutionalized discrimination, p. 182
vertical mosaic, p. 173

Suggested Readings

Driedger, Leo and Shiva Halli (eds.)
2000 *Race and Racism: Canada's Challenge.* Toronto: University of Toronto Press.

Fournier, Marcel, Michael Rosenberg, and Deena White
1997 *Quebec Society: Critical Issues.* Scarborough: Prentice-Hall Canada.

Helms-Hayes, Rick and James Curtis (eds.)
1998 *The Vertical Mosaic Revisited.* Toronto: University of Toronto Press.
Leading Canadian sociologists provide a readable overview of the state of Canadian society and scholarship on ethnic and race relations since the publication of John Porter's classic, *The Vertical Mosaic* (1965).

Henry, Frances and Carol Tator
1995 *The Colour of Democracy: Racism in Canadian Society.* Toronto: Harcourt Brace.
The authors, social scientists and long-time activists for racial equality, examine the dynamics and impacts of racism in Canadian society today.

Long, David Alan and Olive P. Dickason (eds.)
1996 *Visions of the Heart: Canadian Aboriginal Issues.* Toronto: Harcourt Brace.
Eminent First Nations scholars analyze a variety of current social and legal issues.

Alfred, Taiaiake
1999 *Peace, Power, Righteousness: An Indigenous Manifesto.* Don Mills: Oxford University Press.
Taiaiake Alfred, raised in Mohawk territory, is Director of the Indigenous Governance Program at the University of Victoria and an authority on Native nationalism and traditional governance.

Websites

www.canada.metropolis.net
The Metropolis Project
This website provides research and information resources on migration, immigration, refugees, and ethnicity in Canada and other countries.

www.uottawa.ca/hrrec
Human Rights Research and Education Centre
This site, based at the University of Ottawa, provides information and links to many sources on human rights and equality issues in a wide variety of fields, in Canada and internationally.

www.crr.ca
Canadian Race Relations Foundation
This foundation's website provides information on examples of current research and community action on issues of racism in Canada.

Key Search Terms

Race
Racism
Ethnicity
Prejudice
Discrimination
Minority group
Assimilation

For more study tools to help you with your next exam, be sure to check out the Companion Website at **www.pearsoned.ca/hewitt**, as well as Chapter 8 in your Study Guide.

[9]

aging

ingrid arnet connidis and andrea e. willson

Introduction

Population aging occurs when a society is experiencing a growth in the proportion of its people who are older, typically 65 and over. Due to a drop in the birth rate over several decades, and less so to better health, Canada's population has been aging steadily. As this century begins, 12 percent of Canadians are in this category, a figure that will peak at 23 percent in 2041, when the last of the baby boomers have reached 65 years of age (see Chapter 16, Demography and Urbanization). Canadians aged 85 years and over are the fastest-growing portion of our population. The average life expectancy of women born in 2003 is just over 82 years, and of men 77. This is good news, as it means more of us can look forward to an unprecedented long life. And yet, as we shall see, population aging is often treated as bad news, as a serious problem to be solved rather than as an advance to be celebrated.

As the population ages, interest in examining aging issues has increased. Two specialties, *geriatrics* and *gerontology*, focus on aging. **Geriatrics** involves studying the physiological aspects of aging and the unique health concerns of older persons. **Gerontology** takes an interdisciplinary approach to studying aging that involves the physical, psychological, and social processes related

to growing older and being an older person. While a multidisciplinary approach has the benefit of different vantage points (e.g., the physical, psychological, and social aspects of aging), this chapter focuses on the *sociological* study of aging, which means an emphasis on the social aspects of aging.

The objective of this chapter is to present a balanced portrayal of old age, aging, and health, by demonstrating that for most older persons, later life, like the rest of the life course, has both ups and downs, and that most older persons are able to enjoy the former and weather the latter quite effectively. At the same time, the aging of the population and the cumulative effects of inequalities over a lifetime mean that there are very important social policy issues related to aging. The fact that older people tend to be resilient should not be the basis for downplaying their very real needs.

Aging: A Personal Matter

Personalizing aging

Take a moment to reflect on your own life and the key people in it. Is anyone in your family aged 65 or more, the age typically used to delineate the old from the middle-aged? While it is an arbitrary cut-off, 65 is a *social marker* of later life, the conventional retirement age and age of entitlement to economic benefits in most Western countries. Perhaps you are thinking of a grandparent or parent. How often do you see this person? Do you enjoy each other's company? What is this person's marital status? How many children does this person have? Siblings? Are there ways in which you help this person? Does she help you in any way? What was this person's life like when he was your age? Do you know his or her work history? Is this person retired? Happily? How would you describe this person's health? Does this person receive any social services or government benefits? How would this person compare this stage of life with earlier stages?

You might find yourself wanting to ask this person these questions directly; you will have an interesting conversation if you do. One thing that may strike you is how connected old age is to the rest of life. Experience of later life is fundamentally shaped by the decisions made and the lives led as younger persons. Now, as you read about various theories, issues, and experiences of aging in the sections ahead, think about the older person you know. Consider how your background (gender, class, ethnicity/race, the nature of your ties to your parents, siblings, or other family members), the decisions you make (e.g., which university to attend, where to live, which job to take, whether to marry and/or have children), and other experiences (not always fully in your control) are likely to shape your own old age.

Stereotypes of old age

"Life is trouble. Only death is not." This quotation from *Zorba the Greek* (Kazantzakis, 1952) is a good starting point for thinking about aging. Too often, aging is equated with trouble, leading us to feel that there is not much to look forward to in older age. And yet, how many of us would choose an early death over a long life? Indeed, older people have uniformly high scores in studies of happiness and life satisfaction, and studies of the stress created by various life events show us quite vividly that life at all ages includes "trouble." One traditional scale of stressful life events ranks the top ten stressful events, starting with the tenth, as: retirement, marital reconciliation, being fired from work, marriage, personal injury or illness, death of a close family member, a jail term, marital separation, divorce, and—the number one stressful life event—death of a spouse (Holmes and Rahe, 1967). While some of these events

are more likely in older age (losing a spouse and retirement), others are more likely at younger ages (being fired, marriage, marital separation, and divorce). The others are not age specific. Yet, the changes associated with younger years tend to be treated as challenges to be met, those of older age more often as insurmountable setbacks. At all ages we confront change, and change, whether negative or positive, tends to be stressful.

The negative view of aging is also reflected in stereotypes of the old as sick, isolated, ignored, and lonely. There have been attempts to counter such a disheartening view by creating equally atypical positive stereotypes that focus on the 80-year-old marathon runner, or the woman who just completed her medical degree at age 75, or the wealthy, globe-trotting, retired couple. These can hide some of the real benefits of older age by essentially linking happiness with traditionally youthful activity. Positive stereotypes also deny some of the harsher realities of aging, like illness, loss of a spouse, and financial worries, impeding the development of creative and effective coping strategies by individuals and by society. The challenge is to portray realistic pictures of later life that capture important variations among older Canadians.

The Study of Aging

In many instances, the study of aging picks up where some of the other substantive areas of sociology leave off. For example, family issues (see Chapter 10, Families) such as marriage in later life, intergenerational ties between older parents and adult children, the sibling ties of adults, and involvement with family of single and childless persons tend to receive limited attention in courses and books on the family. But, they are central considerations when studying aging. Exploring such issues forces a move from regarding the family as a fixed structure in a particular location (the household) to viewing family ties as negotiated relationships in an extended family network. In the sociology of health, the focus on the medical model and responses to acute illness has been balanced by concerns about the unique circumstances of older persons. The study of retirement extends our understanding of work and its longer-term consequences. Similarly, the study of stratification (recall Chapter 6, Social Inequality) is enhanced by incorporating age as another system of inequality and by examining the accumulated effects of other sources of inequality, including gender, in old age.

Sociologists adopt a variety of approaches in their study of aging. For example, aging may be looked at as a *process* or as the study of *older persons*. Related to this distinction are three separate points of emphasis in sociological research on aging. First, an interest in older persons as a group is often accompanied by an interest in comparing older people with other age groups. Second, when looked at as a process, researchers are interested in examining the changes that are a result of aging, what some have termed **age effects** and others **maturation**. Third, confounding such examinations is the need to determine whether any observed changes are a direct function of aging or of *period effects*. **Period effects** refer to outcomes that result from having been a certain age at a certain point in time (for example, a teenager during wartime) and capture the impact of an historical time or period. The study of age differences can be accomplished using *cross-sectional* data, but the study of age change requires longitudinal data (see Chapter 2, Research Methods). To determine period effects, longitudinal data for several age cohorts are necessary in order to determine whether different cohorts experience similar (supporting age as the reason for the outcome) or different (supporting the influence of historical context) changes over time.

One can also examine aging at an individual or at a social structural level. *Micro-level* analysis of individual aging asks such questions as: What is it like to be an older person in Canada? How does one plan for and adjust to retirement, and how does one cope with increasing health problems? What is family life like in older age? A *macro-level* approach asks questions about things like the impact of population aging on society, how social structure shapes the experience of aging through such organizing features of social life as gender, the role of society in providing support for older persons, and social policy questions concerning the distribution of benefits (e.g., pensions) based on age. Ideally, theoretical perspectives that combine both micro and macro levels of analysis or incorporate bridging concepts that facilitate their connection will result (Marshall, 1995a).

Theoretical approaches

Current theoretical work on the social aspects of aging tends to emphasize the diversity of the aged population (some are rich, some poor, some healthy, some not), a critical view of social processes themselves, and the link between the individual and society (the macro-micro link). It generally adopts an *interpretive* view of aging, one that sees social structure as *socially constructed* and, therefore, subject to change, and emphasizes *individual agency* (ability to act on one's own behalf) in the negotiation of social life. This symbolic interactionist approach differs from the *normative* approach, which tends to portray social structure in quite static terms and individuals as fairly passive followers of society's norms and rules as Durkheim might have argued. We will consider these issues as we briefly review key theories on aging.

Changes in fashion in sociology are reflected in shifts in theoretical approaches to studying aging over the years (for reviews of aging theory see Bengtson, Burgess, and Parrott, 1997; Marshall, 1996; McPherson, 2004). Here we highlight some of the dominant social perspectives of the past sixty years.

The functionalist paradigm of sociology, more dominant in the 1950s and 1960s, was represented in the aging field by disengagement theory (Cumming and Henry, 1961). Proponents of **disengagement theory** argued that the withdrawal of older persons from active social life (particularly the labour force) is functional for both the individual and the larger society. Disengaging permits older individuals to preserve their limited resources and energy and allows for their smoother exit from society, reducing the awkward interruption created by death. **Activity theory** countered disengagement theory by taking the view that the best prescription for a successful old age is to remain active and to take on new activities in later life to supplant those that have been left behind (Havighurst, 1943). Both perspectives received heavy criticism over the years, especially disengagement theory for effectively putting older people on the shelf for the benefit of society's smooth functioning. However, much of the logic of each perspective is still evident today in arguments about intergenerational equity, avenues for successful aging, as well as ongoing social policy such as mandatory retirement.

Despite taking apparently opposite approaches in their view of what is good for older persons, disengagement and activity theories share the fundamental weakness of treating older persons as a *homogeneous* group. Yet, of all age groups, the old are likely to be the most *heterogeneous*, given the time that they have had to accumulate both a broader range of experience and the effects of intra-cohort differences based on such factors as gender, class, ethnicity, and race (Dannefer, 1987).

The **age-stratification perspective**, still currently used, incorporates several strands of theoretical thinking about aging. As originally formulated (Riley, Johnson, and Foner, 1972), this macro-level approach focused primarily on a *stratified age structure* that favours young and middle-aged adults, and the *age cohort* (individuals in the same age group). Each age cohort must make its way through a system of expectations and rewards that are based on age. Hence, society is described as **age-graded**. The approach made explicit the significance of age as a basis for social differentiation, and highlighted the variability of experience among age cohorts, moving away from a focus on individual adjustment. At the same time, however, the age-stratification model failed to address diversity *within* age cohorts, and treated individuals as passive followers of age-graded expectations. Recent extensions of the age-stratification perspective have included the functionalist concept of *structural lag*, referring to society's failure to respond fast enough to the aging of the population and to changes in the life

course of individuals, such as a lengthy period of retirement (Riley, Kahn, and Foner, 1994; Riley and Riley, 1994). This extension provides a link between micro and macro levels of analysis.

A more recent and more conflict-oriented perspective is **exchange theory** (Dowd, 1975), which focuses on the relatively weak bargaining position of older persons in their exchanges with younger ones. This inequity violates basic assumptions of exchange, particularly the expectation of reciprocity—the idea that partners in an exchange expect to give and receive in roughly equal measure. Exchange theory introduced the possibility of differential resources among the old, but the focus was on their generally weaker power position vis-à-vis the young. More recent formulations have taken a longer view of exchange by considering reciprocity over a life course rather than in relation to immediate exchanges only.

[Research Focus]

Family Ties and Qualitative Data

The personal accounts of family relationships obtained in qualitative research help bring key themes alive. Some examples from studies of older persons conducted by Connidis (1989–1999) follow.

Intergenerational ties tend to be stronger along the matrilineal (mother) line, and singlehood may be due to strong commitment to the family of origin. A woman talks about her ties to her grandparents, aunts, and uncles: "Mother was from a large family. Dad was from a large family, but he was the youngest of nine and, therefore, his family had all gone. I used to see his sisters once in a while when they came home, but we weren't as close to our father's family as we were to our mother's. My grandfather and grandmother [mother's parents] used to come to the house and we used to fight about who was going to sleep with Grandma. We just adored her. She was just a darling . . . . Aunt Kate had never been married and she thought one daughter should stay home and look after the father and mother the way they used to. [A fellow]

wanted to marry her, but she said no, that she felt that all her sisters were married and it was her responsibility to look after her mother and father."

The ongoing responsibility to older parents often continues into retirement. At the same time, retirement can bring opportunities for renewed contact with siblings. A retired woman observes: "Of course, my husband told me I was always retired; I had never worked since I had the children. I did have a business, but I didn't have to work at it full-time, so it didn't take a lot of time from me. [Retirement] means that Eleanor [sister] and I can spend more time together and we do elder hostelling— we did an elder hostel together before she was ill and we will be doing more, I think, when we get Mother kind of settled.

At the present time, that situation is really taking a lot of our time, Eleanor's and mine. I guess we hope that retirement will continue and that it will be a time of doing things together."

Do you expect to spend more time with your family or your partner's family once you are settled in a long-term relationship? Why?

Building in part on Marxist, conflict, and critical foundations, the **political economy of aging perspective** (Myles, 1984) takes a macro-level view of how political and economic processes create a social structure that tends to place constraints on the lives of older persons. In general, older persons are seen to lose power to varying degrees, depending upon class, gender, race, and ethnicity, in a society that seeks to maximize economic returns while attempting to honour democratic ideals. One outcome has been to institutionalize retirement as a method of ensuring productivity at the lowest cost, while offering a "citizen's wage" in the form of pension benefits. This perspective provides a critical view of social structure in its interpretive treatment of social structure as a creation of political and economic interests and of the old as a diverse group. A weakness, however, is its tendency to see older individuals as passive rather than active agents.

The currently popular **life course perspective** encourages us to connect the lives of older persons to their earlier lives and seeks to make explicit the link between the individual and society. It is perhaps best thought of as a framework with several linking concepts rather than a theory in its own right (Marshall, 1995b; 1996). The life course involves a series of age-related transitions that occur along a trajectory across the age structure. This approach emphasizes aging as a process, highlighting the connection of older persons to their own life histories, the history of their times, and to younger generations, while connecting their biographies to social structure. Major advantages of this approach include a focus on connections between past and present as well as between generations, an interpretive emphasis on possible disjunction between individual lives and the age structure, the perception that individuals can regain control when circumstances change, and the incorporation of institutions such as the family that link the individual and society (Elder, 1991). A drawback of the framework is its tendency to treat social structure as a given.

Feminist theories on aging often describe aging as a women's issue, largely because there are more older women than older men. They can examine men, as when the greater isolation of men after retirement is seen as a gendered issue, but most theorists emphasize the lifelong gendered nature of social life and how it fundamentally shapes women's experience in old age. They focus, for example, on the effects of a lifetime of unpaid labour, erratic labour-force participation, and family obligations in older age. Applications of feminist theory to aging tend to examine both the macro (e.g., the social construction of gender and gender as a dimension of inequality in old age) and micro (e.g., women's experiences as caregivers) levels (see Chapter 7, Gender Relations).

Major themes of **critical theory** are woven through several of the perspectives reviewed here, particularly the political economy and feminist approaches. Reflecting a strong interpretive tradition, critical theory focuses on power, social action, culture, and the economy (Bengtson et al., 1997). As related to aging, this includes examining the social construction of old age and dependency and of old-age policy. Applications of critical theory also focus on the need to incorporate *praxis* or practical change that benefits older persons when theorizing about aging. Critical theory's characterization of social structure as constraining, and the individual as acting with agency, provides a linking mechanism between macro and micro levels of analysis (see Marshall, 1996).

Finally, the *symbolic interactionist* perspective, more recently referred to as the **social constructionist perspective**, is also influential in theoretical approaches to aging. This micro-level approach emphasizes the subjective experience of older persons and their ability to negotiate with others. As powerful as the effects of gender, class, ethnicity, race, and age are in organizing our society, they do not guarantee identical outcomes for everyone in shared circumstances. Instead, older individuals negotiate their situations as best they can to meet their preferences, some more effectively than others. Thus, how life is lived in old age can be viewed as the outcome of the lifetime interplay between social structure and individual action.

A profile of older Canadians

While one can draw general conclusions about the aging of Canada's population, it is important to note substantial variations across the country. First, there are provincial differences in the size of the population aged 65 and over, ranging in 2005 from a low of 10 percent in Alberta to a high of almost 15 percent in Saskatchewan. These variations are projected to shift over the next twenty years, with estimates for 2011 of a low of 14 percent in Alberta to a high of nearly 19 percent in Newfoundland, Nova Scotia, and New Brunswick. As analyses by census tract show, population aging is greatest in communities characterized by stagnant economies, fewer financial resources, aging in place (local residents stay and grow older), and net migration effects resulting from the exodus of younger residents (McGuinness, Moore, and Rosenberg, 1997). On the other hand, the average age of the Aboriginal population is much younger than for the total Canadian population, reflecting lower life expectancy, higher rates of some diseases (e.g., heart disease), and poorer services (Wister and Moore, 1998).

The longer lives of women mean that, with each successive age group, the ratio of women to men increases. Sixty-one percent of Canadians aged 75 to 84 years are women, and this increases to 70 percent among those aged 85 and over. Gender differences are also evident in living arrangements (see box below). Finally, income levels of the older population reveal important differences (Statistics Canada, 2006). The personal income of women is far lower than is men's, which means that loss of a spouse leaves women in a far worse financial position than is true of men who lose a wife. Never-married women are an exception; single older women have higher incomes than single older men. For widowed women, access to survivor benefits often means an actual increase in *personal* income (but not in household income) reflecting the gendered nature of labour-force participation among the current elderly, and the greater financial repercussions of marital status to women than to men.

The balance of the chapter focuses on three key topics about later life: family ties, health, and work and retirement. As you read each section, consider its connection to the other main topics. You will see that they are highly interconnected, which suggests their mutual importance to social policy, the final topic addressed in this chapter.

Family Ties and Social Support in Later Life

Who is your family? Make a quick list. Now, think about an older person in your family. Who is his or her family? Make a list beside yours. For years a portrait of the family as a husband and wife with two children has been promoted as the "typical" Canadian family (see Chapter 10, Families). How does this compare with your family and those of your older family members? With changes in family life over the past few decades the nuclear family has been eroded for all age groups, as growing numbers of families have different compositions (single-parent families; shared-custody families; gay or lesbian parents; childless couples; single adults; as well as two parents and their [combined] children). For older persons, the nuclear family in one household has never been an accurate portrayal of family life. We will discuss three key familial relationships of older

[Social Trends]

Where Do Older Canadians Live?

Gender differences among older Canadians are evident in their living arrangements. While 76 percent of men aged 75 to 84 live with a spouse, only 42 percent of women in this age group do so, reflecting primarily their higher rates of widowhood. Looked at from another way, 47 percent of women aged 75 to 84 live alone, while only 19 percent of men do so. Living alone is generally a preferred option among those who do not have a spouse because it allows for independence. Living alone also reflects the improved financial circumstances of today's elderly compared with previous generations. When it comes to institutional

living, Canada's rates are fairly high. For the same age group, 6 percent of men and almost 10 percent of women are in this situation. This compares with 6 percent of men and 16 percent of women who are living with family other than a spouse. While we tend to think that older persons would prefer living with children over living in a facility for seniors, research suggests that many older people would prefer not to, fearing loss of independence and burdening their children (Connidis, 1983). Living alone often means less healthy eating patterns as people do not take the trouble to cook for just one.

Source: Statistics Canada, *2001 Census*.

Would separate apartments with a shared cooking area solve this problem? Can you identify any downsides to this solution?

Intimate ties among family members often span generations.

Table 9.1	Percentage Distribution of Marital Status by Age and Gender, Canada, 2001			
Age	Married	Widowed	Separated/ Divorced	Single
WOMEN				
65–74	55	29	10	6
75–84	33	56	5	6
85+	11	78	2	9
MEN				
65–74	76	8	10	7
75–84	70	18	6	6
85+	53	37	4	6

Source: Adapted from Statistics Canada, *2001 Census*.

persons: intimate ties (mostly marriage at present); intergenerational ties (parent–child and grandparent–grandchild ties); and sibling ties.

Intimate ties

A spouse is the most likely source of support for married persons and most persons 65 and over are married. Indeed, despite increases in divorce over time, the likelihood of being married is greater among today's older population than it was for the entire twentieth century, primarily because the likelihood of spousal death has declined. This trend is more marked among women and is due to the greater life expectancy of both men and women and the narrowing of the gap in life expectancy between them (Connidis, 1997; 1999a).

But there are very important differences based on age and gender in the availability of a spouse (see Table 9.1). As age increases, the likelihood of being married decreases, and the probability of being widowed increases. This probability is greater for women than men because of their greater longevity and tendency to marry men who are slightly older. Still, marriage remains the modal experience for all men, even the oldest (85 and

over) and for women 65 to 74. For women over 75, the most common experience is to be widowed.

Note also that only a small percentage of older persons is divorced, although about 10 percent of those included under "married" in Table 9.1 were previously divorced (Gee, 1995). Nonetheless, trends indicate that growing proportions of Canadians will enter old age divorced, though not to the extent that media coverage of divorce would lead us to expect. As well, while remarriage means a partner in older age for some, it does not necessarily erase the consequences of divorce for relationships with children and grandchildren, as will be discussed later.

Marriage in the later years

One consequence of living longer is that our relationships with family members are also lasting longer, especially for those who stay married to a first spouse. A long-held view was that happiness in marriage follows a curvilinear pattern, with marital satisfaction greatest in the early and later years. However, more recent research indicates that the apparent curvilinear trend in marriages is a function of relying upon *retrospective* data (information obtained by asking older persons to reflect on their satisfaction with marriage over time). When couples are asked about the current state of their marriage at different points over the course of their relationship, instead of following a curvilinear pattern, marital satisfaction decreases over time, especially among women (Vaillant and Vaillant, 1993). This conclusion is supported by other studies of marital satisfaction that compare different cohorts and find marital satisfaction to decrease for each successive cohort (Glenn, 1998). And rather than the middle years being the low point, they can be happy for those living in an empty nest, free to enjoy adult activities and one another. For those who were unhappy and did not realize it or stayed together for the children, however, the departure of children can serve as a reason for divorce.

Retirement also reshapes the marital tie. To date, we know more about the impact of male retirement on traditional marriage than about the effect of either male or female retirement on the marriage of dual-job couples. We do know that the retirement decision of women is affected by their marital status. Married women are likely to retire early in order to retire at the same time as their usually older husbands. This, of course, reduces the economic benefits that women receive in retirement by shortening what was already a shorter career with fewer benefits than typically experienced by men.

On balance, marriage following retirement tends to be positive but, among the current elderly, does require a transition as the previously employed husband finds a niche in his new social world and his wife finds room for her partner in her long-term household patterns. For those in reasonable health and with adequate incomes, retirement can be a time of particular contentment. Conversely, the minority for whom work served as a primary source of identity and a diversion from intimacy may discover a hollow relationship in retirement.

The impact of caring

If one is married, a spouse is the most likely source of help, support, and caring. Women are more likely than men to find themselves caring for an ill spouse because they are more likely to outlive their partner. Thus, data on who cares for whom can give the misleading impression that women are neglected by their husbands when, in fact, a key reason that women rely more heavily on other sources of support is that they no longer have a spouse. However, while both men and women come to the aid of their partners, the kind of aid they give and the consequences of giving it differ.

The long-term illness of one partner in a marriage can have multiple consequences. First, of course, is the sorrow of serious illness. A mutual sense of loss and the need for support by one partner can actually enhance the *interdependence* of the marital tie, bringing rewards to both partners, in the form of a renewed sense of emotional closeness. At the same time, both providing and requiring care can be stressful. Men are more likely than women to employ a management style of care, making sure that care and support are delivered, but not necessarily personally. Women, on the other hand, tend to provide more extensive care, including the personal hands-on care that men are more likely to delegate to others (Stobert and Cranswick, 2004). This reflects the gendered nature of family life in which women typically feel more obliged than do men to provide all forms of support to family members. This difference may be the key reason that women experience more stress than do men when caring for a partner. More generally, the well-being of women is tied more closely to the well-being of those to whom they are close than is true of men.

As well as the immediate demands of providing care, the emotional challenge of facing the physical and/or mental decline of a long-term partner is stressful. For those caring for a partner suffering from dementia, there is the particularly difficult situation of simultaneously caring for and mourning the loss of a partner as the spouse becomes a different person from the one known over the years.

Widowhood and divorce

Losing a partner has both subjective and objective consequences (Martin Matthews, 1991). On the subjective level are the feelings that accompany loss and the change of one's identity to an individual rather than a member of a couple. On the objective level are changes in such tangibles as finances and the social and practical skills of the partner. The period of bereavement that follows the death of a spouse is a process of about four years during which a new identity as a widowed person evolves. If widowed when older rather than younger, the adjustment is easier. Because women are more likely to be widowed, they are also more likely to have a network of widowed friends and family, particularly sisters, who can share their experiences and provide companionship. Widowed men, on the other hand, have fewer male counterparts but have a larger pool of available women for potential companionship or remarriage. For both men and women, however, remarriage rates have been falling (Milan, 2000).

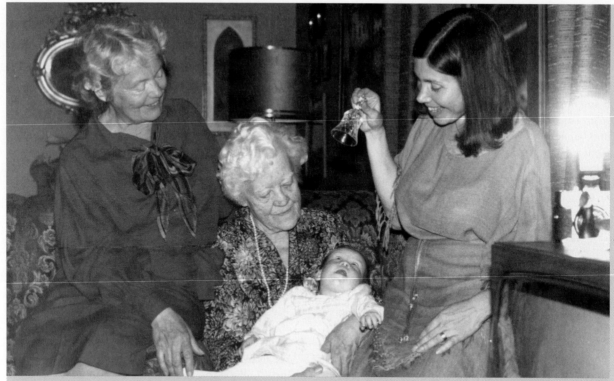

Intergenerational ties have been the focus of much research on aging.

The gendered nature of social and family life (see also Chapter 10, Families) is reflected in the fact that widowed women are far more likely to be financially deprived than either their married counterparts or widowed men. They are also more likely to have an active network of family and friends, having nurtured these ties over a lifetime. Widowed men, who often relied on a spouse's networking skills in the gendered division of labour, suffer greater isolation than widowed women. While widowhood is ranked as the most stressful of life transitions, most older persons make a successful personal adjustment to this change in status. This resilience can be tested especially for women left financially strapped in old age as a consequence of a lifetime of inequality.

As mentioned, while the proportion of older divorced persons is increasing, the numbers are still quite small (see Table 9.1). As with widowhood, there are feelings of loss and loneliness following divorce. Similar gender differences also apply, with older divorced men a particularly isolated group, in part because of the traditional awarding of child custody to mothers. At the same time, divorced women typically suffer greater financial hardship than other women and than divorced men, and do not have the same benefit entitlements in older age as do widowed women. The challenge of remaining married in the current context of longer lives and higher expectations is noted by Gillis (1996: 151):

> [W]hen lifetimes are as much as one-third longer than they used to be, it becomes very difficult to sustain romance for the duration of a marriage . . . [a] situation made even worse by the fact that . . . [t]he perfect couple now must be everything to one another—good providers, super sexual partners, best friends, stimulating companions—roles that earlier generations turned to others to fulfill.

The single (never-married)

Those who never marry tend to be childless and thus excluded from spousal and parent–child ties. Yet, single persons may play very active family roles and, ironically, it was often their obligation to family of origin that precluded marriage, for older women especially (O'Brien, 1991). Then as now, daughters were more likely than sons to meet the obligation of caring for older parents, a responsibility that often overrode forming their own unions. Women from past generations who wanted a career often had to choose between work and marriage rather than combine the two.

More is known about single women than men, but both require further study. Single women have been described as "la crème de la crème" because they tend to have higher levels of education and occupational prestige than their married counterparts. Single men, on the other hand, tend to compare less favourably to their married counterparts. Despite the far more positive image of being a "bachelor" than being a "spinster," it is single men, not women, who appear to be isolated in older age. In general, single older persons have adapted to being single over a lifetime, with friends, siblings, and parents serving as important sources of companionship and support. Nonetheless, when compared with married persons and with parents, today's older single persons are less likely to have extensive support available to them when needed.

Other intimate ties

Little is known about the intimate relationships of long- or short-term cohabiting couples, of gay and lesbian couples, or of those in less committed relationships in older age (what would traditionally be termed "dating"). Concerning gay and lesbian ties, the historical failure of Canadian legislation to formally and fully support gay and lesbian relationships (Carter, 1998) limited the extent to which such ties are public, as they could not be made "official." The likelihood of keeping same-sex bonds hidden is higher in the older population, who grew up in a time when the stigma of homosexuality was far greater than it is today. Much research is needed on the nature of such unions and, more generally, the lives of gay and lesbian individuals in old age. Some suggest that dealing with the challenge of being gay or lesbian in a heterosexist society actually leaves older gays and lesbians better equipped to deal with the challenges of aging (Friend, 1991). On June 28, 2005, same-sex marriage was approved by Canada's House of Commons, which may eventually create a better environment for gays and lesbians of all ages to negotiate family ties.

Intergenerational ties

Much of the research on intergenerational ties is motivated by concerns about who looks after older persons (a concern shared by researchers who identify more personally with adult children than with older parents). Two approaches to studying intergenerational relationships have dominated North American research. The *solidarity perspective* (Roberts, Richards, and Bengtson, 1991) focuses upon the strength of family ties between generations. The approach is criticized for its conservative bias: its tendency to emphasize consensus and its underplaying of the conflict and contradiction in familial ties (Luescher and Pillemer, 1998). In response, a substantial body of research on adult child–older parent relationships takes a *social problems approach*. It documents the shortcomings of older persons' social networks, the burdens of providing care, the conflicts that may ensue between older parents and their children and, more generally, the negative impact of the ups and downs of old age on the parent–child relationship. This perspective tends to heighten the negative stereotype of old age in its overemphasis of problems between the generations.

A recent and third approach to intergenerational ties sees them as *ambivalent*; family members are torn between feelings of love and obligation, competing interests for their time, and a social world that places contradictory demands on them, through, for example, the competing expectations of individualism and filial obligation or the competing demands of work and family (Luescher and Pillemer, 1998; Connidis and McMullin, 2002a, 2002b). Addressing how such fundamental ambivalence is resolved involves a conception of familial ties that emphasizes interaction, negotiation between family members, the possibility of both solidarity and conflict in familial bonds, even the creation of *legitimate excuses* for avoiding obligations toward family members (Finch, 1989).

Relations between older parents and their adult children

Lower fertility rates lead many to conclude that a crisis in informal support is near, due to the growing numbers of childless older persons and growing numbers of adult children without siblings with whom to share the responsibilities of supporting their parent(s) (see Chapter 16, Demography and Urbanization). Yet, an examination of family size since 1961 shows that the shift in fertility is due primarily to a decline in the number of women who are having five or more children (Connidis, 2002). As of 1991, the proportion of ever-married women aged 45 and over who had no or only one child was actually lower than for preceding cohorts, while the proportions having two or three children were up. Thus the issue may have been overblown. Indeed in 1996, among women of all marital statuses aged 75 to 84, only 12 percent had no children, 11 percent one, 23 percent two, while 54 percent had three or more children. Thus, as before, most older persons have living children. The question then becomes, what kind of relationship do they have with them?

Older parents tend to have active ties with their children, and daughters and sons serve as important support persons when needed. At the same time, parents are also significant support providers to their adult children, a fact that is often downplayed in debates on intergenerational equity that focus on government transfers to seniors (Stone, Rosenthal, and Connidis, 1998). A realistic portrayal of parental ties with adult children should emphasize exchange and reciprocity over the life course. Exchanges of material goods favour adult children (that is, older parents give more to their grown children than they receive from them). Older parents often provide housing to their adult children (the refilling of the empty nest following job loss, marital separation, or unemployment of the adult child as well as long-term support for children with various disabilities or chronic conditions), and offer various forms of instrumental assistance including caring for grandchildren. More generally, adult children can benefit from the experiences of their older parents, learning from them as they go through life transitions such as marriage, the arrival of children, or widowhood (Connidis, 1989a). As well, problems like alcoholism and marital separation experienced by adult children have an ongoing impact on the lives of their parents (Pillemer and Suitor, 1991).

Nonetheless, as older parents age, their children are crucial sources of support, particularly among women who are more likely to be on their own and to have cultivated strong ties with their children over the years. The gendered nature of family life is again reflected in the greater likelihood that daughters rather than sons will provide assistance to their parent(s), including daughters who are in the labour force. Among employed adults, unmarried women give more hours of help and

are more likely to be primary caregivers than any other gender and marital status combination (Connidis, Rosenthal, and McMullin, 1996).

When daughters are unavailable (there are none, they live far away, or they have other demands that take precedence), sons do step in. Daughters and sons tend, however, to take a different approach to negotiating care. Daughters are more oriented to consulting siblings about how to meet the needs of their parents, while sons are more likely to deal directly with their parent (usually mother) in determining how much and what type of support is needed. While daughters provide more hands-on care than do sons, the approach of sons may actually benefit older parents because it fosters independence (Matthews and Heidorn, 1998). A key difference between daughters and sons, paralleling differences between husbands and wives, is that sons are more likely to use a management style of care, ensuring that help is provided, though not necessarily by them. A similar difference is emerging among women, with those in the labour force more likely to use this management style than homemakers, who provide more of the help personally.

Labour-force participation has not meant an abdication of parental support but rather a shift in how it is provided. This shift poses a serious policy challenge. Needed services must be in place for orchestration by adult children, particularly daughters who, thus far, are combining the responsibility of labour-force participation with care of older parents and, for some, children as well (Martin Matthews and Campbell, 1995; Martin Matthews and Rosenthal, 1993). A key issue is the responsibility that employers should assume to accommodate the situation of the worker responsible for a frail parent.

Rising rates of divorce in both generations also have long-term consequences for the parent–child relationship. The divorce of parents, whether it occurs when children are young or adult, has negative effects on relationship quality and the amount of contact and support exchanged once parents are older, especially between fathers and their children (Cooney and Uhlenberg, 1992; Kaufman and Uhlenberg, 1998). In turn, the divorce of children may limit their ability to assist their parents at the same time as it increases the need for and provision of support from older parents. Maternal grandmothers, in particular, are often central players in the care received by their grandchildren following their daughter's separation or divorce (Milan and Hamm, 2003).

Childless older persons

Childlessness tends to be treated as an issue of childbearing years, not of older age, except for the concern that those without children are lacking a primary source of informal support and will thus require more state-funded formal assistance in old age. Research tends to show little difference between older childless persons and parents in subjective well-being, life satisfaction, loneliness, social participation, or social support (Connidis, 1992, 1994; Connidis and McMullin, 1996; McMullin and Marshall, 1996). This indicates the successful negotiation of childlessness over the life course by most older people.

When asked to discuss childlessness, older persons report both advantages and disadvantages (Connidis and McMullin, 1999). The main advantages are fewer worries and problems, financial benefits, greater freedom, and career flexibility. The major drawbacks are being alone and loneliness, the missed experience of parenting, and a prediction of lack of support and care when older. There is no question that childlessness does have repercussions for support. For example, institutionalization in old age is more likely among the non-married, the childless, and women, who more often than men lose a partner. Yet, childless people who report loneliness and lack of support as a shortcoming of not having children are no more likely to actually be lonely and lack support than those who do not. Thus, the view that children fend off loneliness and guarantee support may be more a cultural bias about the potential support of children than actual experience.

Siblings

There are few studies on adult sibling ties. About 80 percent of persons aged 65 and over have at least one living sibling and this will continue to be true in the foreseeable future. For most of us who have siblings, our brothers and/or sisters will be our longest-lasting family tie when we reach old age. Unlike a spouse or children, siblings have known us since early childhood and served as our training ground for negotiating peer relationships. Unlike parents and children, siblings are horizontal rather than vertical ties, making them more egalitarian. Sibling relationships tend also to be more voluntary and less obligatory than is true of ties between parents and children or between spouses.

Siblings tend to have quite close ties in older age despite a somewhat fallow period during earlier adulthood, when careers are being launched and commitments to others made. Among persons aged 55 and over, 70 percent say that they are somewhat, very, or extremely close to at least one of their siblings (Connidis, 1994), and among those 65 and over, nearly 80 percent describe at least one sibling as a close friend (Connidis, 1989b). Siblings connect us with our past and are ideal companions for reminiscence, a favoured pastime in old age. Emotional closeness to siblings increases with age among those aged 55 or more and is greater among women than men (Connidis and Campbell, 1995). These emotional connections are evident in the fact that siblings often serve as confidants in later life, especially for women, and are a particularly significant part of older single women's confidant networks (Connidis and Davies, 1990, 1992; Campbell, Connidis, and Davies, 1999). Emotional closeness also increases personal and telephone contact with siblings, again especially for women (Connidis and Campbell, 1995).

How do key life transitions affect the sibling tie? Qualitative research shows that marriage has varied effects ranging from making sibling ties closer to inhibiting closeness and contact, usually depending upon how a sibling views his or her in-law. However, when siblings have children, divorce, or are widowed, changes in the sibling tie are positive, leading to greater emotional closeness, more contact, and greater support from siblings (Connidis, 1992).

Another important transition in sibling ties is often triggered by their parents' need for support. The poor health or death of a family member tends to bring siblings emotionally closer to one another. Interesting dynamics in sibling ties are evident when examining how siblings negotiate who will support parents (Matthews, 2002; Coward and Dwyer, 1990). For both men and women, having sisters increases the likelihood that help to parents will be shared with others (Connidis, Rosenthal, and McMullin, 1996). Families of two sisters share the care of parents most equitably; in families with more sisters, two of them will provide most of the help, with periodic assistance from the others. When there are brothers and sisters, sisters provide most of the care, with occasional or no help from brothers. Men in families of brothers only tend to work out supportive arrangements directly with parents, rather than with one another. Finally, siblings who are emotionally closer tend to share parental care more equitably and to be more accepting of inequities when they exist.

What about support among siblings in older age? While most older persons do not report actually receiving help from their siblings, the majority perceive siblings as potential support providers, should the need arise (Connidis, 1994). Marital and parental statuses make a difference; siblings are more important as providers of support to the widowed, single, and childless (Campbell, Connidis, and Davies, 1999). At the same time, single, widowed, and divorced siblings are also more likely to be willing to *offer* support to their siblings, if needed. In sum, sibling relationships remain important across the life course, both in their own right and in terms of support received by older parents from their children.

Aging and Health

The health of the older population has improved steadily over this century, as reflected in longer life expectancy as well as subjective indicators that show that the majority of older persons consider themselves to be in good to excellent health (McPherson, 2004). While women continue to outlive men, the gap is narrowing, and lifestyle changes among women (more smoking, alcohol consumption, and driving in particular) are already taking their toll in elevated rates of lung and heart disease and deaths among women. Despite the fact that women live longer than men, women have higher rates of morbidity (illness) than men, controlling for age (Denton, Prus, and Walters, 2004). Social concerns regarding aging and health include the provision of health care, alternatives to institution-based care, and the disruption of social roles due to poor health. Balanced against these are individual-level concerns about maintaining good health, burdening others, losing personal autonomy, the economic costs of lengthy health care, chronic illness, and the illness of close family members.

Aging versus illness

There is no question that aging brings a physiological decline. The five senses (sight, hearing, touch, taste, and smell) become less acute and strength and endurance wane as muscles lose their mass, and lung capacity decreases. These represent normal aging processes and must not be mistaken for illness. For example, hearing loss can lead to confusion, correctable by a hearing device. If misperceived as the first signs of dementia, however, the response could be quite different.

The decline in the senses alters the symptoms of illness as well. Because they are less likely to feel pain or to experience a rise in temperature, a similar illness does not trigger the same response in older persons, making it harder to diagnose. For this reason, any decline in health or capacity should not be assumed to be a function of age until other possible explanations have been eliminated. Otherwise, there is a risk of misdiagnosing or mistreating illness in older people, based on our assumptions about old age and on transferring our understanding of symptoms based on younger persons to older ones. According to the *Canadian Family Physician* (May 1999), depression is often not diagnosed among the elderly, in part because their symptoms are taken as part of being an older person. Consequently, necessary medication and therapy are often not forthcoming.

Another important consideration is whether limitations incurred with age are a function of disuse. Research shows that half of what used to be viewed as normal decline of physical abilities with age is actually a result of not using muscle and bone tissue, leading to their degeneration and loss of function (Health Canada, 1995). Physical activity among seniors enhances psychological well-being, heart function, and bone strength; reduces the pain and stiffness of arthritis, the risk of colon cancer and high blood pressure; and helps maintain a healthy weight.

With age, the number of chronic ailments increases, and older people often experience more than one condition simultaneously. The most common chronic illnesses are arthritis, hypertension, heart-related illness, respiratory problems, and diabetes (McPherson, 1998). The accumulated risk of life-threatening diseases also takes its toll. As well, as the recent outbreaks of SARS and West Nile Virus in the early 2000s have reminded us, older persons are particularly vulnerable to such health threats. These are not matters to be taken lightly and there is no point in pretending that older persons are just as healthy as any other age group (Matthews, 1993). A key sociological question is the extent to which such physical decline and health problems shape interaction with significant others, and how this, in turn, affects the costs of a health-care system for an older population.

Delivering health care

The support provided to older people can be either informal or formal. Informal support refers to the help that they get from people they know, usually family members, and formal support is care provided by professionals and services, often government funded. In reality, informal support typically continues in conjunction with formal support as when grandchildren visit their grandmother in a nursing home or serve as her advocates. Thus, the transition from informal to formal care is best viewed as one of relative balance rather than as a case of formal versus informal support. A continuum of care is then more clearly seen as moving from needing less to more care, not moving from informal to formal support. Of course, as the need for care increases, so too does the need for additional formal as well as informal support. While the willingness of families to support their older members has not waned, the ability to do so has been altered by several realities, particularly labour-force participation among women, traditionally the providers of such help (Connidis, 2001).

Perhaps no issue raises more concern about an aging population than the potential escalation of health costs. While younger people who arrive in hospital tend to require short-term treatment for an acute illness, older persons suffer more chronic diseases that require a focus on care rather than cure. Consequently, there has been an ongoing concern that our health-care system should move away from the traditional medical-model focus on cure, and toward a care-centred approach. This requires the training of more specialists in geriatric medicine, nursing, and other allied professions; a greater focus on community-based care; a greater emphasis on health promotion; and more support for improved long-term care in institutional settings. Unfortunately, recent initiatives have more often involved "off-loading" of health-care responsibilities from government-supported health care to private support from family members, often in the guise of moving from institutional to community-based care. As well, there is ongoing debate between the federal and provincial governments about the need for larger transfer payments to meet rising health-care costs, which largely fall within the jurisdiction of the provinces.

Debates rage over whether having more old people will mean a crisis in health-care financing. Some difference of opinion rests on employing different time frames about when and for how long health-care costs will escalate. The generally improved health of younger generations is a basis for arguing that the onset of their increased need for health care will occur at older ages, shortening the period during which they will place a greater strain on health-care budgets (Evans, McGrail, Morgan, Barer, and Hertzman, 2001). Failure to separate

age-based reasons for increases in health-care costs from others also contributes to a view of aging as a crisis. Key contributors to rising health-care costs are expensive drug treatments and diagnostic testing, not the aging of the population. Because the elderly are not alone in contributing to this expense, blaming the aging population for an expensive health-care system is misplaced. Recent research also indicates that those aged 65 and over contribute disproportionately to health-care costs in the last year of life because their mortality rates are higher, not because costs per older person for such care are higher (Demers, 1998).

Another basis for the contrasting views about whether an aging population will bring about a health-care crisis is whether projections focus on traditional approaches to health care or on new options. Providing formal support in the home has become increasingly popular in political rhetoric and has been shown to be both cost-effective and preferred by older persons (Chappell and Penning, 2001). Yet, despite strong endorsement from the Romanow report (2002), home care continues to be an under-supported option for meeting the needs of older Canadians. For those whose need for care exceeds what can reasonably be brought to the home, options for long-term housing and/or residential care that is less expensive than acute-care beds in hospital—beds that are in short supply—remain elusive. Yet, the particularly fast increase in the size of Canada's oldest age groups will make residential care as well as home care a necessity for growing numbers.

Good public policy requires health promotion initiatives rather than responding to illness only (Marshall, 1994). For an aging population, this includes augmenting community-based support, recognizing that most assistance to older persons is self-provided or provided by family, friends, and neighbours. Thus, all age groups have a shared interest in strategies that improve the health of older Canadians. Introducing and enhancing new forms of support to the formal support system are likely to mean additional expenditures in the short run. However, in the long run, a multi-pronged approach to health care that involves coordinating self-care, informal support, home-based formal care, residential options, and the more traditional interventions of acute, hospital-based care is likely to improve both the well-being of older Canadians and the bottom line. Anticipating the future with information rather than rhetoric will mean that changed circumstances are anticipated rather than surprising. Viewing population aging as a health-care

Government Income for Older Canadians

There are several sources of state-supported income for older Canadians. These include:

- *The Canada/Quebec Pension Plan (CPP).* Based on contributions made from earnings in the labour force. Eligibility is 60 to 64 for early retirement, 65 for normal, and up to age 70 for late retirement. Recent changes allow one parent (mother or father) to claim a Child Rearing Drop-out Provision for children born after December 31, 1958, if the parent dropped out of the labour force to be the child(ren)'s primary caregiver up to the age of 7. If qualified, the claimant receives a credit toward CPP benefits.

- *Old Age Security Pension (OAS).* General eligibility for a full pension is having lived in Canada for a total of 40 years after the age of 18.

Source: Human Resources Development Canada.

- *Guaranteed Income Supplement (GIS).* An income-tested supplement for Old Age Security Pensioners with limited incomes. (Some studies use qualifying for GIS as an indicator of poverty.)

- *Spouse's Allowance/Widowed Spouse's Allowance.* Low-income-based benefits available to the 60- to 64-year-old spouse of an Old Age Security Pensioner or to widowed persons aged 60 to 64. (The Widowed Spouse's Allowance has sparked some controversy on the grounds that divorced and single women do not have access to similar benefits despite the fact that divorced women are at least as financially insecure as are widowed women.)

Some economists have suggested that the working poor should not put money into their own Registered Retirement Savings Plans (RRSPs) as this will later count against them by reducing amounts they would receive from OAS and GIS (as above). Does this advice raise any ethical questions?

---

crisis is a perfect example of turning something very positive—the unprecedented opportunity to live a long and mostly healthy life—into a problem rather than a welcome challenge.

Retirement

Retirement can be examined at both the individual (micro) and societal (macro) levels. Issues at the individual level include personal planning for retirement, the decision to retire, and adjustment to retirement. At the societal level, topics include social policy and legislation regarding retirement and security, the impact of social and economic trends on retirement (e.g., labour-force participation rates, aging of the population, levels of employment), and the impact of retirement on society (e.g., costs of publicly funded pensions; the balance of public- and private-sector responsibility for providing retirement benefits). Examining retirement at both levels of analysis requires considering the impact of factors

such as the organization of work and family, gender, health, income, and the economy.

At the macro level, a major concern in Canada is how to meet the costs of a growing number of retirees. What is the appropriate balance between public (social) and personal (individual) responsibility for the welfare of Canadians in old age? It is generally agreed that the two basic objectives of our retirement income system—"ensuring both an adequate basic income for all seniors (the anti-poverty objective) and an adequate standard of living in retirement when Canadians [leave] the labour force (the earnings-replacement objective)"—have not been met (Battle, 1997: 521). The outcome of considerable debate on revising income policy for seniors and retirees has been a moderate tinkering with the existing system. Consequently, the retirement income system continues to be unbalanced because only relatively well-off labour-force participants have adequate pensions and registered retirement savings plans. Meanwhile, "the majority of Canadians depend upon the public parts of the pension system for most or all of their retirement income. Yet public pension programs were not designed to achieve on their own the earnings-replacement objective" (Battle, 1997: 525). Recent changes to the retirement income programs mean, on balance, that workers under 65 years of age as of December 31, 1997, will see increased contributions but decreased benefits down the road.

Over the years there has been considerable debate about mandatory retirement. This debate reflects the ongoing tension between *individual justice* (emphasized by proponents of flexible retirement) and *comparative justice*, or group rights (emphasized by proponents of mandatory retirement). In support of *mandatory retirement* is the argument embedded in disengagement theory that a uniform age of retirement ensures the smooth exit of older persons from the labour market, freeing a predictable number of positions for younger persons to fill. Another advantage of mandatory retirement, some argue, is that it avoids the need to assess job performance and to have to inform workers that they are no longer capable of performing their job and, therefore, they must retire. Instead, all workers can retire with the belief that they have retired only by virtue of being a given age, not because they are no longer competent. Those who favour *flexible* retirement hold the view that all adults should have the right to employment and that, particularly in the absence of adequate financial support in old age, the state should not have the right to deny access to income. Mandatory retirement violates principles of individual justice by forcing everyone to retire regardless of ability and desire to continue working.

Canadian law generally supports age-based mandatory retirement, usually at the age of 65. For occupations where age can be related to job performance—for example, an airline pilot—a younger age can be set. While reaction time and acquiring new skills tend to take longer as we age, most older workers are good workers whose job performance has benefited from experience (National Advisory Council on Aging, 1992). There have been some successful appeals of mandatory retirement (e.g., professors at the University of Manitoba) but these are exceptions, and appealing on the basis of the Charter of Rights' protections against discrimination based on age has often been unsuccessful. Currently, there is no mandatory retirement age in Alberta, Manitoba, Ontario, Quebec, Prince Edward Island, New Brunswick, Nunavut, Northwest Territories, and Yukon. In Newfoundland and Labrador, retirement can be

mandated when there is a retirement or pension plan, and in Nova Scotia, Saskatchewan, and British Columbia, employers can require retirement at age 65.

While the typical mandatory age of retirement and the age of entitlement to full government pension benefits is 65, the average age at retirement has been lower than this for some time—62 for men and just under 61 for women in 1996 (Norris, 1999). Initially, this trend reflected an increase in voluntary early retirement, as growing numbers of workers chose to leave the labour force before the mandatory age of retirement (primarily men because they were more likely to be lifetime earners and, therefore, to have pension benefits that made retirement possible). More recently, early retirement was actively encouraged through incentive programs designed to free jobs for younger persons in a labour market that is glutted with baby boomers. However, such incentives have declined and pressure to raise the age of retirement and of pension entitlement (to ensure that there are enough labour-force participants) has grown as baby boomers approach retirement.

Accruing deficits and a weak economy tend to encourage cost-saving efforts such as downsizing, prompting employers to force exit through layoffs, creating growing numbers of involuntary retirees. Forced early retirement has substantial consequences for retirees and their families. The shift in identity from being retired to unemployable, the negative consequences for retirement income, and the negative effect on health of forced early exit detract from the retirement years for both the retiree and his or her family (Marshall, 1995a, 1995b; Guillemard, 1996).

The experience of retirement is intricately tied to the experience of work, including salary and benefits, length of employment, full- versus part-time employment, and the nature of employment (e.g., self-employed versus employee; white- versus blue-collar). Prior to any of these issues is whether one spent all or much of a lifetime in paid versus unpaid labour. Historically, the majority of Canadian men have been labour-force participants until full retirement at age 65 or older. However, trends over the past few decades indicate that men are leaving the labour force earlier, some by choice and some following a failure to find new employment after a layoff. For example, among men aged 55 to 64, 80 percent were in the labour force in 1971 compared with 64 percent in 2002. Among those aged 65 to 69, 37 percent were still working in 1971 versus 16 percent in 1991. In 2002, just over 10 percent of all men aged 65 and over were in the labour force.

The proportion of people who are 65 years and older, currently about 13 percent, is more than double that of fifty years ago.

Among women, trends have generally been in the opposite direction, except among those aged 65 and over where the numbers have always been low (12 percent in 1971 versus 10 percent in 1991 for women 65 to 69 years old). By 2002 just under 4 percent of all women aged 65 and over were in the labour force. The dramatic increase in women's labour-force participation over this century is evident among those aged 45 to 54, of whom 41 percent were in the labour force in 1971 compared with 78 percent in 2002. Corresponding figures for women aged 55 to 64 in 1971 are 33 percent versus 44 percent in 2002. Labour-force histories vary among women according to age, with today's older women much more likely than younger women to have interrupted their employment for lengthy periods to stay at home with their children.

Among those engaged in paid labour, there are substantial differences in the pension support available through work. Compared to men, women of all ages are more likely to interrupt their paid work to care for family,

to be employed part-time rather than full-time, and to be in jobs with poorer pension benefits (Street and Connidis, 2001). Thus, one must delve deeply into labour-force participation data to get an accurate picture of the respective positions of men and women at work and, consequently, in retirement. A critical question for all new employees should concern their pension package. Over a lifetime, a pension can mean much more in real dollars and in old-age security than a higher salary.

The nature of work for most Canadians makes retirement attractive. Most retirees enjoy retirement, appreciating the time available to engage in chosen activities, to spend time with children and grandchildren, and to travel. Of course, these pursuits require reasonable health and financial security. Retirement is more difficult for those who have fewer financial resources, who did not develop interests and/or friendships outside of work, who relied heavily on a job for a sense of self-worth, and who are in poorer health (McDonald and Wanner, 1990; McPherson, 1998). The gendered nature of social life makes these factors apply differently to men and women. Today's older men tended to invest quite heavily in their jobs, while today's older women invested more heavily in their families. Thus, the retirement experience at present tends to be gendered as well; men are more likely to face the challenge of finding alternatives to work as a source of activity, identity, and social contacts. Women, on the other hand, have developed ties with family and friends outside the work domain, but are more likely to face the serious challenges of inadequate financial resources in retirement. The cumulative effects of the gendered division of labour are thus felt in retirement. To the extent that the experiences of men and women as labour-force participants and family members become more parallel, these differences in retirement may diminish, to the benefit of both men and women.

Shifts in the economy can have a particularly dramatic impact on the financial welfare of retirees, because the vast majority of them are on fixed incomes. Thus, if inflation is high and interest rates low, the net effect is to reduce the incomes of many older persons. When inflation is low and interest rates high, incomes stretch further. The economy also shapes views and policies about appropriate retirement ages (high unemployment generates pressure for a lower retirement age, low unemployment for a higher retirement age) and pension benefits (the current pressure to lower benefits is based on assumptions of a slow economy and a large number of future retirees).

Pension Benefits and Same-Sex Couples

The Supreme Court of Canada decision allowing partners of same-sex unions to entitlements following separation, paralleling those of married and common-law heterosexual couples, has caused quite a stir, from dismay among those promoting traditional family structures to pleasure among those who believe the ruling is long overdue. This represents an example of relying on litigation as a way of obtaining rights for gay and lesbian partners in the absence of legislative change by politicians (Carter, 1998). The failure of politicians to make legislative changes to grant gay and lesbian partners access to spousal pension benefits has also led to litigation, which, so far, has been unsuccessful. A major obstacle is the federal Income Tax Act, which does not allow extension of pension plans to same-sex couples. But anticipating that successful litigation to provide pension benefits to same-sex couples was inevitable, on May 25, 1999, the government passed a bill allowing the retroactive claim of a $30-billion surplus in the public service pension plan, to be used in a variety of ways by the government. The opposition parties voted against it as an inappropriate money grab. However, the bill was also fraught with controversy within the Liberal Party because some of the money would be spent on same-sex benefits, and six backbenchers refused to support the bill. Ironically, so did Svend Robinson, then one of Canada's two openly gay members of Parliament. Opposing the bill on the grounds that appropriating the surplus amounted to theft, Robinson was quoted as saying, "I would do anything to vote for equal pensions for gay and lesbian people. It hurts terribly to vote against that part of the bill but . . . I'll swallow my pain and I'll vote against the bill and I'll fight for equal pensions another day" (*London Free Press*, May 26, 1999, p. A7). Four years later, Robinson was addressing the anticipated acceptance of same-sex marriage by the federal government. In response to queries about whether he and his partner, Max, will marry, Robinson replied: "I'm still unsure if Max and I will marry anytime soon. After nine years in a committed, loving relationship, how would the state's imprimatur change anything? What has changed, fundamentally, is the fact that we now have the choice. Not a choice for some kind of 'separate but equal' registry, but marriage. We are no longer second-class citizens in our own country . . . ." (*The Globe and Mail*, June 24, 2003).

Should everyone, even single people, be allowed to share benefits with someone? A brother and sister, an aunt and nephew, two friends? If not, why not?

Social Policy and Future Directions

Reflect on the material that you have just read and see if you can think of some policy implications. How does one turn information into the basis for sound policy? This is the challenge before policy makers and researchers when they are asked to link research findings with policy recommendations. Research findings do not in themselves offer clear directives for policy. Instead, biases about the kind of society we want influence our view of what constitutes good policy decisions. In comparisons with the United States, Canada has been described as a country that favours a more collective (rather than individual) solution to problems, as is evident in universal social programs such as health care (Clark, 1993). However, this orientation has been eroded over the past few years as some programs are no longer universal (e.g., child allowance, referred to as the "baby bonus") and others place much heavier emphasis on individual responsibility (e.g., independent contributions to a registered retirement savings plan; earlier discharge from hospitals to informal care at home).

The position one takes on the balance between individual versus social responsibility will determine the extent of support for government-based programs to deal with an aging population. Years ago, Mills (1959) made this distinction by talking about *private troubles* versus *public issues*. Treating social issues as private troubles means that the ultimate responsibility for dealing with them rests with the individual and his or her significant others. Conversely, a public-issues approach looks for collective solutions to the challenges that citizens face. A particular issue may have elements of both. For example, in the case of widowhood, bereavement is very much a private trouble, and there are limits to what any social policy can do to alleviate this fact. The greatest strength is likely to be drawn from oneself and close family and friends. Yet, some of the consequences of widowhood are socially constructed and require social solutions. A clear case in point is the financial setback suffered by many women when a husband dies, a consequence of a social world built upon a gendered division of labour in which women depend upon their partners for financial security. This outcome can be dealt with as a public issue on several possible fronts such as better survivor benefits for widows, payment for their domestic labour so that women can secure their own financial future, and income entitlements in older age not based only on work history or marital status.

Taking a broad view is essential to forming good social policy and in this instance older persons should not be considered the only beneficiaries of age-based policies. For example, we have seen the very important role played by adult children in providing support to their older parents. However, the high labour-force participation rates of both men and women make this care a greater challenge than it once was. Public policies and initiatives in the private sector that support employee efforts to care for older family members are needed to enhance the probability and quality of care provided by children. Life for both generations is improved as older persons receive support from loved ones, and children are relieved of the stress that can come with providing such support. At the moment, the general absence of such policies in the workplace means that employees are paying a substantial price to aid their parents. This is particularly true of women, who are likely to use holiday time to provide care, to miss employment opportunities, and to forfeit promotions as strategies for balancing care and work (Martin Matthews and Rosenthal, 1993). The irony is that these short-term costs persist in the long term, as these women enter their own old age less financially secure than they would have been otherwise and, in turn, unduly reliant on others and the government for support. Thus, supporting younger persons benefits older

ones, while providing support directly to older persons alleviates pressures on younger family members.

The heavy reliance of the government on the family (which translates predominantly into a reliance on women) to take care of its older members has been an ongoing concern in several Western nations (Myles, 1991; Walker, 1991). The current government focus on deficit reduction and cost savings escalates this concern. Cutbacks in service provision are placing greater demands on the family at precisely the same time the combination of labour-force participation and changes in the family (e.g., rising divorce rates, more lone-parent families, and high unemployment rates) makes it more difficult for family members to increase their level of support.

Another compelling reason for assuming public responsibility for the older population is our requirement that most older persons must retire (the self-employed are an exception here). Having withdrawn their access to financial livelihood in order to provide jobs for younger persons, there is surely an unspoken agreement to offer economic and social support to ensure a secure old age. Yet, as we saw in our discussion of retirement, it is the rare Canadian who can expect to sustain the same standard of living in retirement as he or she enjoyed while working.

Historically, there has been disproportionate attention paid to the help given to older persons. While this has been corrected somewhat in the literature on informal support, the current debate about intergenerational equity has involved a renewed focus on the receipt of support by older persons, this time in the form of government transfers. Discussions of intergenerational equity focus on the equitability of funds expended by government on different age groups in the population (e.g., build a new school or a home for the elderly). Those who engage in generational accounting argue that the old are receiving more than their share at the expense of the young and that measures should be taken to make public transfers more equitable, in part to avoid inter-generational conflict (Corak, 1998). Critics of this position argue that such accounting procedures focus too narrowly on government transfer payments and on one point in time. They argue that a lifelong perspective that considers personal contributions and includes informal transfers is needed (McDaniel, 1997; Stone, Rosenthal, and Connidis, 1998). Moreover, studies of public opinion indicate that Canadians are willing to spend more in tax dollars to support their older citizens (Northcott, 1994).

Looking ahead

As baby boomers age, so too will Canada's population, peaking in 2041. The population will then become younger as the mortality of baby boomers grows. Before that happens we will probably see older workers being encouraged to remain in the labour force, not bought out as today to provide opportunities for younger (and cheaper) workers. Because so many baby boomers will want to retire at the same time, strains on pension plans will reinforce this trend. Generally, the older population will be healthier, wealthier, and, if not wiser, more educated, as successive cohorts reach old age. Yet, concerns remain regarding the financial situation of retirees, particularly women who, despite increasing years spent in paid work, will continue to have poorer pension benefits and a longer period of time in old age than men.

Changes in labour-force participation among women, declines in labour-force participation for older men, and increases in divorce rates for all age cohorts, will mean shifts in the family ties of older persons. Divorce among both the older generation and their children have the long-term effect of diminishing the amount of informal support and emotional closeness between parents and children, especially between fathers and their offspring (Connidis, 2002). Such general trends will affect the lives of older Canadians. Two outcomes may be the increased importance of siblings and of building relationships with other family and non-family members.

As Canadians continue to live longer and healthier lives, we can also complement our attention to the genuine needs of some older people by considering the contribution that Canadians can continue to make in their older age. Our current customs are predicated on a time when the age of 65 represented a long life. Today, Canadians who live to 65 can expect to live another eighteen years. Nine of these years are typically disability free, followed by three years of slight, three years of moderate, and three years of serious disability (National Advisory Council on Aging, 1999). This has been the basis for distinguishing between the third and fourth ages, the third age characterized by retirement, independence, and good health, and the fourth representing a period of growing vulnerability. The challenge before us is to formulate research projects and social policy that address methods of enhancing opportunities for those in the third age to capitalize, personally and socially, on their improved circumstances while meeting the needs of growing dependency during the fourth age.

An anticipated period of retirement, the ongoing availability of family to most older persons, and the general improvement in health combine to enrich the experience of old age for Canadians. This includes more active participation in physical activities, travel (including visits to family), and other leisure pursuits at an unprecedented rate. Yet, while the general picture is rosy, a substantial minority of older persons faces serious restrictions in their lives. Many of these constraints can be alleviated by better social policy designed to meet more effectively the needs of particular pockets of older persons including: women, those without family ties, the poor, immigrants, and the physically and intellectually challenged. Aiding these older persons requires redressing current inequities among the old and longstanding inequities among all Canadians based on age, gender, class, race, ethnicity, and sexual orientation.

The challenge to researchers is not only to provide useful information. Indeed, we have accumulated a wealth of facts regarding aging and old age. Researchers can make important contributions in two additional ways. First, reflective and analytical syntheses of existing information can help clarify what we know and what we need to know. Second, delving beyond the facts by examining the processes that create them and by applying and developing theory can turn information into understanding.

Remember the older person you pictured at the beginning of the chapter? Do you see that person's life any differently now? What does your own old age look like? The actions you take now will shape your future as an older person. This chapter has introduced you to a very rich area of sociology. The more that you understand about aging issues, the better prepared you will be for your own aging and old age, for appreciating the situation of older persons close to you, and for contributing wisely to the ongoing debate about how to respond to an aging population.

Summary

Canada's population is aging, due mostly to the decline in birth rates of the past few decades. In 2001, almost 13 percent of Canadians were 65 years or older. A realistic picture of old age leads us to reject the negative stereotype of this stage as a time of loss, as well as the stereotype that tends to equate successful aging with youthfulness. Sociologists seek to understand aging at both the societal and individual levels, examining the balance between social structural forces and the experiences of older persons themselves. Theories on aging have progressed over the past twenty years, and the best of them emphasize heterogeneity among older persons, the role of power and conflicting interests in shaping aging across the life course, and the ability of older individuals to exercise agency over their lives.

Women generally outlive men, creating one basis for the quite different life experiences of older men and women. Older women are more likely to experience old age on their own, while older men are most likely to be married. The greater financial resources of men than women in later life reflect a lifetime of difference due to socially constructed opportunities based on gender. The majority of older men and women have children and siblings, relationships that loom larger in the lives of women, in part because they are less likely to have a spouse in old age. Rising rates of divorce will change the experience of being unattached in older age, given that divorce has different implications for family ties than does widowhood.

The private domain of the family is under strong pressure to provide support for all members in need, including those older persons who require care. A key policy issue is the extent to which Canadians judge it appropriate for the fate of older persons to rest heavily in the hands of family members who generally care for one another, but who find themselves overextended with competing commitments to work as well as family. While older Canadians are enjoying better health than ever, the oldest-old, the fastest-growing age group in our population, experience high levels of chronic illness.

Questions for Review and Critical Thinking

1. Gender is a critical organizing feature of social life. Discuss three ways in which the accumulated effects of gender are apparent in older age by comparing the experiences of older women and men.

2. How do the experiences of your grandparents fit in with what you have read? Are they typical or different? Why?

3. Widowhood is an age-related transition that has elements of both a private and public nature. What other age-related transitions involve both personal and social responsibility?

4. This chapter covered three main topics related to aging: family ties, health, and retirement. Discuss five ways in which these topics are interrelated.

Key Terms

activity theory, p. 204
age effects, p. 204
age-graded, p. 205
age-stratification perspective, p. 204
critical theory, p. 206
disengagement theory, p. 204
exchange theory, p. 205
geriatrics, p. 202
gerontology, p. 202
life course perspective, p. 206
maturation (see *age effects*)
period effects, p. 204
political economy of aging perspective, p. 206
social constructionist perspective, p. 206

Suggested Readings

Chappell, Neena, Ellen Gee, Lynn McDonald, and Michael Stones
2003 *Aging in Contemporary Canada.* Toronto: Pearson Education Canada.
The authors provide a current and interdisciplinary overview of aging in Canada.

Cheal, David (ed.)
2002 *Aging and Demographic Change in Canadian Context.* Toronto: University of Toronto Press.
In this edited volume, one of a series, the authors explore policy issues surrounding aging from their differing perspectives.

Connidis, Ingrid Arnet
2001 *Family Ties and Aging.* Thousand Oaks, CA: Sage.
An in-depth exploration of family ties across the life course, this book examines sibling relationships and the roles of childless, single, gay, and lesbian adults in a family.

Gee, Ellen M. and Gloria M. Gutman (eds.)
2002 *The Overselling of Population Aging: Apocalyptic Demography, Intergenerational Challenges, and Social Policy.* Don Mills: Oxford University Press.
This volume takes a critical approach to aging and concludes with a warning not to exaggerate the effects of aging on Canadian society.

Websites

www.cagacg.ca
Canadian Association on Gerontology
Canada's national association is multidisciplinary and
includes a Social Sciences Division.

www.geron.org
Gerontological Society of America
The national association of the United States has a
Behavioral and Social Sciences Division.

www.naca.ca
**National Advisory Council on Aging, Ottawa (Health
Canada)**
This site has much useful information on aging in
Canada.

Key Search Terms

Aging
Gerontology
Life course
Health
Geriatrics

For more study tools to help you with your next
exam, be sure to check out the Companion Website at
www.pearsoned.ca/hewitt, as well as Chapter 9 in your
Study Guide.

part four

Social Institutions

Social institutions are structures organized around the performance of a society's central activities. They include the beliefs, values, and norms concerning the manner in which a society's needs should be met and the groups that serve these needs. Important activities such as marriage, reproduction, and the raising of children, for example, are generally conducted within families and another institution, schools. The acquisition of a particular sense of the meaning of life can take place within religious institutions. The media can have a powerful influence over our day-to-day lives and our perceptions of the world. Finally, the institution of education teaches social roles and skills. This next section examines these social institutions.

We introduced social differentiation by saying it is both a cause and an effect of social phenomena. The same can be said about social institutions. As causes, institutions influence culture, norms, values, and roles. Certain institutions, especially families, religion, the media, and schools, socialize individuals to acquire culture. Religious institutions define what is deviant and the media may strengthen reactions to that deviance. The same two

institutions may provide a platform for the birth and development of social movements.

In turn, institutions are affected by social differentiation. For example, race and ethnicity affect the type of family life individuals experience and their religious practices. Finally, institutions affect one another, as when the media affect family and religion affects political life. Thus, there is extensive interdependence among the various institutions, and important links among institutions, culture, and socialization. All contribute to the structure of social life, which impinges on individuals and affects their behaviour.

Because institutions serve social needs they are often portrayed as structures built upon consensus. But there is also conflict between and within each of these institutions, as when religion clashes with the media over proper entertainment standards, or when family needs and the world of work collide. As before, when you read a functionalist, conflict, symbolic interactionist, feminist, or other explanation in the following chapters, ask yourself what a sociologist with a differing perspective might say.

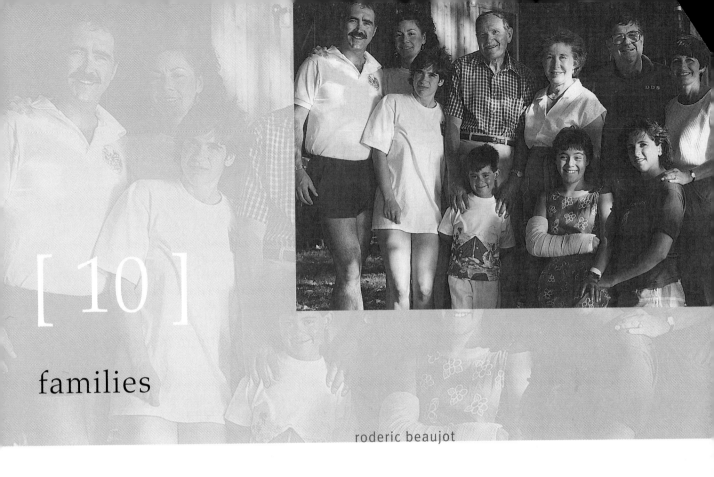

[10]

families

roderic beaujot

Introduction

The study of families is an important part of the study of society. The chapter on culture introduced examples from the sociology of families: definitions of "mother," an explanation of sexual jealousy, and the existence of incest taboos in almost all societies. The chapter on socialization pointed out that much of socialization takes place in families. And in the last chapter you saw the importance of family ties in later life.

Two further points underscore the place of families in social research. First, families are the social arena in which most people spend most of their lives. Thus, if we want to find out how people live and how their lives are organized, it is important to know something about what happens in their families. Second, as one of the institutions of society, families affect and are affected by other social institutions. For example, the desire to combine work and child-raising has been partly responsible for the increase in part-time work and other forms of non-standard work in a 24-hour economy. That is, family change has brought change in the organization of the economy. At the same time, the move toward a service economy (e.g., lawn care, fast food), has allowed families to spend a higher proportion of their total time in the labour market.

While the study of families is important for understanding society, at least two factors make this study difficult. First, we are too frequently willing to make generalizations about families based on our own limited experiences, making it difficult to take a broader look at family behaviour. The second difficulty is that family behaviour is generally considered private. Consequently, researchers are often barred from studying families in their natural settings. Even when they do observe families, much normal behaviour may be hidden from them or altered, as they attempt, either consciously or unconsciously, to present themselves in a favourable light.

We shall begin this chapter with definitions of marriage and related family terms and then highlight some of the differences and uniformities in family patterns across societies. This will remind us of the necessity for viewing families against the background of the larger society. Family change will be described and then interpreted through theoretical perspectives that consider both the evolving role of families in society and the changing importance of families in individuals' lives. We then consider family questions over the life course, including socialization for marriage, childbearing and childrearing, and marital dissolution. The final section considers the general question of change and continuity in family patterns in the recent past and immediate future.

Definitions of Marriage and Family

Marriage can be defined as a commitment and an ongoing exchange. A commitment involves a more or less explicit contract that spells out the rights and obligations between partners and can be defined at either the personal or social level. At the personal level, it means that marriage is undertaken with considerable seriousness. At the social level, it means that certain customs and laws govern entering or leaving a marriage.

Ongoing exchanges involve a continuing interdependence between partners. Expressive exchanges—the emotional dimension of marriage—include love, sexual gratification, companionship, and empathy. Instrumental exchanges—the task-oriented dimension—include earning a living, spending money, and maintaining a household. In virtually all marriages, expressive and instrumental exchanges take place, but in some the economic dimension may be more important, while in others the expressive level may be foremost.

Marriages do not just happen; they have to be maintained as ongoing exchanges. In the process, one partner may provide more of some things (e.g., earning), while the other provides more of other things (e.g., caring). Such sharing will continue if the pair sees some equity in the exchanges, so that each finds marriage to be rewarding. The exchange can be based on complementary roles or on shared roles as when both are involved in earning a living and caring for family members. We shall return to a discussion of alternative models for the sharing of paid and unpaid work.

A family can be defined as two or more people who are related by blood, adoption, or some other form of extended commitment (e.g., individuals who care for each other), and who reside together. There are two crucial aspects to this definition: the persons must be related in some way and they must customarily maintain a common residence. Relationships include heterosexual couples without children, same-sex families, couples with children, and lone-parent families, among others. If the individuals involved are not related, they may form a household but not a family.

If individuals are related but do not live together, they are kin and not a family as defined here. Kin often live in close proximity and are socially and economically integrated with other kin, but they are not considered a family unless they share a dwelling. The one exception would be a couple that lives apart for job reasons for much of the year yet still define themselves as a family unit.

Variability in Family Patterns

As indicated in Chart 10.1, there are considerable differences across societies in marriage and family structure. To demonstrate this variability, we shall consider three aspects of families: number of partners in the marriage, sex codes, and emphasis on a nuclear family versus a kinship network.

Number of partners in the marriage

There are four possible compositions of the marriage group: **monogamy**, **polygyny**, **polyandry**, and **group marriage**. (For definitions of these terms, see Chart 10.1.) One classic survey of 565 societies shows, however, that historically monogamy is the most prevalent marital form and the majority of marriages in almost all societies (Murdock, 1957). At the same time, 75 percent of the world's societies (but not 75 percent of the world's population) appear to accept polygyny. Polygyny is an option in many Muslim countries. In West Africa, half of women aged 35–44 are in polygynous unions (Tabutin and Schoumaker, 2004). When polygyny is common, it is usually the older, more established men who marry young women. While most women are married in such a situation, many men are unable to marry, at least until they are older.

Polyandry is even more rare and typically involves brothers who share a wife. Polyandry prevents the land the brothers will inherit from their father from being subdivided into parcels too small for subsistence and enables the inheritance to stay within the male line.

Group marriage is similarly rare. Although no longer the case, it was for a time practised among the Nayar in Southern India. At or before puberty, each girl was given a "ritual husband," but the couple's obligations to each other were mostly of a ceremonial nature, partly because the Nayar men acted as mercenary warriors for neighbouring kingdoms and were often absent. After marriage, women could receive any of the men of the neighbourhood group as sexual partners. At the birth of a child, one or more of them had to acknowledge paternity and pay for the delivery of the child. If no man came

Chart 10.1   Family Terms

Family and kin

Nuclear family	A "traditional" family consisting of at most two generations, including a couple and their unmarried children
Lone-parent family	One parent and one or more children
Common-law union	A nuclear family consisting of partners who are not formally married, with or without children
Reconstituted family	A nuclear family with children from a prior union of one of the spouses
Blended family	A nuclear family that includes children from more than one marriage or union
Extended family	A family that includes more than spouses and unmarried children (e.g., grandparents, married children, other relatives) living in the same residence
Consanguine family	A family organization in which the primary emphasis is on the biological relatedness (e.g., parents and children or brothers and sisters) rather than on the spousal relationship
Kin	People related by blood, adoption or marriage

Number of partners

Monogamy	Marriage involving only two partners
Polygamy	Marriage involving more than two partners
Polygyny	One man married to two or more women; husband-sharing
Polyandry	One woman married to two or more men; wife-sharing
Group marriage	Marriage involving multiple partners not specified above

Sex of partners

Heterosexual	Male and female partner
Same sex	Two men or two women

Choice of partners

Exogamy	Partner must be chosen from outside a defined group
Endogamy	Partners must be members of the same group

Descent

Patrilineal	Descent traced through male line; children not related to mother's relatives
Matrilineal	Descent traced through female line; children not related to father's relatives
Bilateral	Descent that follows both lines; children related to both parents' relatives

Residence

Patrilocal	Couple takes up residence with the husband's parents
Matrilocal	Couple takes up residence with wife's parents
Neolocal	Couple resides alone

Authority and dominance

Patriarchal	Males are the formal head and ruling power
Matriarchal	Females are the formal head and ruling power
Egalitarian	Equal dominance of partners

forward, it was assumed that the father was either of a lower caste or a Christian, and the woman was put to death (Gough, 1959).

Sex codes

The regulation of sexual behaviour outside of marriage also varies. In a sample of 158 societies, Murdock (1960: 265) found that premarital intercourse was permitted in 41 percent of societies, conditionally approved of in 27 percent, mildly disapproved of in 4 percent, and forbidden in 28 percent. Thus, the majority of societies at least tolerated premarital intercourse. An example of a particularly relaxed attitude is that of Trobriand Islanders, the users of magic discussed in Chapter 3, Culture, among whom premarital coitus was taken for granted (Malinowski, 1929). In this group, sex was seen as a natural expression of personality, and children began their sexual activities at an early age with a number of partners. After puberty, each person tended to form a more permanent relationship with one person and, if the association continued, the couple was expected to marry.

In general, extramarital coitus is more stringently prohibited than is premarital coitus. However, this too varies, since it was freely allowed in 3 percent of societies, conditionally permitted in 13 percent, and socially disapproved of but not strictly forbidden in 3 percent (Murdock, 1960: 265). Even where it is forbidden, many people consider adultery to be acceptable as long as its existence remains a secret.

Consanguine versus nuclear bonds

All societies recognize both consanguine and nuclear family bonds but vary considerably in the importance accorded to each. In tribal societies the consanguine family is generally paramount, and kinship may predominate in all spheres of life: groups based on kin ties are economic units for production and consumption, political units with regard to power, and religious units with an emphasis on ancestral worship. The Yoruba of Nigeria provide a good example of the importance of consanguine bonds in a tribal society. Communal residence and occupational cooperation would be endangered if Yoruba men listened to their wives rather than to their brothers and fathers:

> In fact ... relationships between spouses, even
> in monogamous marriages, are not very strong
> in traditional Yoruba society and parents do not

exclusively focus their attention on their biological children. Even in 1973 only one-third of Yoruba spouses slept in the same room or even ate together (admittedly indexes of affection regarded as less significant by Yorubas than by outsiders), and fewer still identified the person to whom they felt closest as their spouse, while children were commonly brought up by a number of kinsmen. (Caldwell, 1976: 340)

Networks of relatives are important in this type of society. They provide economic security, attend family ceremonies, and are valued political allies. Both marriage and reproduction are at a premium in such tribal societies. Marriage increases the number of alliances with other kin groups and since the marriages are for the benefit of the kin rather than for the couple, they are usually arranged by parents. Children expand the number of links and are expected to provide services to their parents starting from a very young age and throughout the lives of their parents.

In a nuclear family, the kin network is considerably less important. The emphasis is on the spousal bond,

In the nuclear family, the kin network exists but is less important than the bond between spouses.

and thus it is important that spouses choose each other rather than accept a parentally arranged marriage. Couples are less concerned with ancestors and kin than they are with their own children. In fact, they are likely to have only a small number of children and to "spoil" their children, giving them more than they can ever expect in return so that each of them can have the best possible chance in life.

We could go on stressing the variability in family patterns, so visible that the 2001 census release on families used the subtitle "Diversification Continues." This was the first census that specifically identified same-sex couples, which represented 0.5 percent of all couples (Statistics Canada, 2002a). See the box "Pushing the Boundaries of Tolerance: Gay and Lesbian Relationships in Canada."

We have focused on three elements of diversity: number of spouses, sex codes, and consanguine versus nuclear bonds. It is important as well to note the elements of uniformity in this diversity: (1) although polygyny is accepted in many societies, most marriages are in fact monogamous; (2) although there are different orientations toward premarital and extramarital sex, reproduction and sex are generally controlled for the benefit of families; and (3) although some societies emphasize consanguinity and others a nuclear family, both always are in existence. A number of other uniformities in family patterns also exist, as we discuss below.

Uniformity and Family Patterns

Importance of marriage

Most societies place a high premium on marriage, at least for reproduction and socialization of the young, and the majority of adults are expected to fulfill these roles. Most adults are motivated to live in an enduring relationship. Cultural norms support the premium on marriage including the expectation that the parents of a newborn be in a state of union, the discouraging of activities that impinge on marriage, particularly adultery and homosexuality, and the dim view taken of marital dissolution. In *Embattled Paradise*, Skolnick (1991: 220) concluded that there is more tolerance for variation, but lifelong heterosexual marriage with children remains the preferred cultural norm in North America.

Incest taboo

The incest taboo, prohibiting sex and marriage for close biological relatives, is another almost uniform feature across societies (see also Chapter 3, Culture). The taboo reinforces the family in two ways. First, restricting legitimate sexual activity to spouses prevents sexual rivalry from breaking up the family. Second, the requirement to marry outside of the nuclear family enlarges the kinship network through alliances with other families. Mead reported the following imaginary dialogue from an Arapesh informant whose friend wanted to marry his own sister:

> What? Do you not want brothers-in-law? If you marry another man's sister and another man marries your sister, you have two brothers-in-law. If you marry your own sister, you have none. With whom will you visit? With whom will you talk? With whom will you hunt? (Mead, 1971: 52)

Importance of inheritance

Another virtual uniformity is the importance of inheritance; families can be joined across generations by the passing on of property. The inheritance that links generations produces social relationships that will continue into the future. On the other hand, intergenerational transfers in families perpetuate inequality. Children of the wealthy can consolidate their positions while those of the poor cannot get the leg up they desire. As well, historically at least, inheritances were for sons not daughters, thus entrenching gender inequality. And while daughters today do better than before, the social class issue remains. Quite simply, we have not erased the differential transfer of wealth from parents to children between families of different classes (Wanner, 1999).

In concluding this section on uniformities in family patterns, it is important to note the exceptions to these uniformities. For example, the early Israeli kibbutz placed a lower premium on marriage. The family was seen as endangering communal solidarity, and given little importance; the marriage ceremony was reduced to the simplest ritual, and children did not eat or sleep with their parents. Second, no society requires that all adults be married all the time. Also, the incest taboo is almost universal (there are exceptions) and the taboo

[Social Trends]

Pushing the Boundaries of Tolerance: Gay and Lesbian Relationships in Canada

In 1969, Prime Minister Pierre Elliott Trudeau said that the government had no place in the nation's bedrooms. Until that time consensual homosexual activity in the privacy of one's home was a criminal offence. By 2003, the province of Ontario had legalized gay marriage. While visitors, fearing SARS, avoided Toronto, gays and lesbians went there to marry. The same police precinct that had raided gay baths in Toronto twenty years earlier recruited at the annual Pride Parade. Leaders of every political party except the Canadian Alliance gave support to such marriages, some going so far as to say that their first responsibility was to their society not to their religion, earning open opposition from some religious leaders. Today all of Canada has been joined by Spain and other countries in accepting those unions.

This sounds like a success story for tolerance. Still Victor Dwyer, in an essay in *Maclean's*, pondered about some loss of the fun of homosexuality, replaced by

houses and mortgages in the suburbs, long-term relationships, regular visits to mothers-in-law, and friendly interactions with neighbours. Sounds too much like straight society, he said. We could add that while homophobia is not stamped out, as evidenced by continuing hate crimes, day-to-day intolerance occurs less frequently and the future may be even brighter, as younger Canadians are more accepting of homosexuality than their parents and grandparents. There is further legal recognition through survivor benefits from pension plans, expanded insurance coverage, and greater adoption possibilities.

Will there be convergence? It is unlikely. Dwyer claims that gays dance better and are still much more likely to be excited about their purchase of Depression glass than straights. And as for his life becoming boring, he says he will take that any day, compared with previous levels of intolerance.

Source: Adapted from Victor Dwyer, 2003. "Not so Queer as Folk." *Maclean's*, June 23, pp. 42–44.

What types of people or groups tend to resist these changes? Why?

does not necessarily prevent incestuous behaviour. Moreover, while inheritance along family lines is the general rule, this practice can be interrupted in times of revolutionary change.

Family Change

Historical transformations in families can be described in terms of two transitions (Lesthaeghe, 1995). The first transition (1870 to 1950) brought about smaller families and involved a change in the economic costs and benefits of children, along with a new cultural environment that made it more appropriate to control family size. In effect, this transition changed family dynamics surrounding fertility (see Chapter 16, Demography and

Urbanization) from an emphasis on child quantity to a focus on child quality.

In discussing the second transition in Western countries (1960 to the present), Lesthaeghe (1995) proposed that it is useful to consider three sub-stages. The first, from about 1960 to 1970, involved the end of the baby boom, the end of the trend to younger age at marriage, and the beginning of the rise in divorces. The second, from 1970 to 1985, involved the growth of common-law unions and, eventually, of children in cohabiting unions. The third stage, since 1985, brought a levelling of divorce levels, an increase in post-marital cohabitation (consequently a decline in remarriage), a plateau in fertility, and higher proportions of births after age 30.

Table 10.1 presents some Canadian statistics that capture these trends. The average births per woman had reached a peak of 3.9 in 1957 before declining to 2.1 in 1971 and 1.5 in 2003. The median age at first marriage declined over this century to reach a low of just over 21 years for brides and 23 years for grooms in the early 1970s, then increased to ages 27 and 29 for women and men respectively in 2002. The law permitting divorces on grounds other than adultery dates only from 1968. For every 100 000 married women, there were under 200 divorces in each year over the period 1951–1966 compared to 990 in 1976 and 1080 in 2003.

The 1981 Census indicated that 6.4 percent of couples were living common-law and this increased to 16.4 percent by 2001. The proportion of births occurring to women who are not married, most of whom are cohabiting, increased from 9 percent in 1971 to 36 percent in 2003. The proportion of births to women aged 30 and over increased from 19.6 percent in 1976 to 47.9 percent in 2003.

These changes in births, marriage, cohabitation, and divorce brought fewer children, but also a higher proportion of children who are not living with both biological parents. In particular, lone-parent families as a proportion of all families with children increased from 11.4 percent in 1961 to 24.7 percent in 2001.

The data also confirm the uniqueness of the 1950s, a "golden age of the family," a period when life was family centred. Not only was this the peak of the baby boom, but it was also a period of the marriage "rush," as marriage occurred at young ages, and almost everyone married. Many families, especially those in the suburbs corresponded to the ideal of domesticity (Skolnick, 1996: 134–41).

Subsequent research made it clear that not all was ideal in this golden age. Since the task of maintaining the home had been assigned to women, men became less competent at the social skills needed to nourish and maintain relationships (Goldscheider and Waite, 1991: 19). There was also violence and abuse but given a general denial that such things could ever occur in families, little recourse for the victims of violence. Isolated housewives in particular experienced what has been called the

Table 10.1 Summary Statistics on Family Change, Canada, 1941–2003

	1941	1951	1961	1971	1976	1981	1986	1991	1996	2003
Total fertility rate (average births per woman)	2.8	3.5	3.8	2.1	1.8	1.7	1.6	1.7	1.6	1.5
Median age at first marriage										
Brides	23.0	22.0	21.1	21.3	21.6	22.5	23.9	25.1	26.3	27.0
Grooms	26.3	24.8	24.0	23.5	23.7	24.6	25.8	27.0	28.3	29.3
Divorces per 100 000 married couples	—	180	180	600	990	1180	1302	1235	1222	1080
Common-law couples as a percent of all couples	—	—	—	—	—	6.4	8.2	11.2	13.7	16.4
Births to non-married women as a percent of all births	4.0	3.8	4.5	9.0	10.9	14.2	18.8	28.6	36.3	36.2
Births to women aged 30+ as a percent of all births	35.6	36.2	34.1	21.6	19.6	23.6	29.2	36.0	43.7	47.9
Lone-parent families as a percent of all families with children	9.8	9.8	11.4	13.2	14.0	16.6	18.8	20.0	22.3	24.7

Notes: For 1941–71 births to non-married women are designated as illegitimate births. Data for 2001 are shown as 2003 for common-law couples and for lone-parent families. Data for 2002 are shown as 2003 for median age at first marriage.

Source: Beaujot (2000); Beaujot, Ravanera, and Burch (2006).

"problem with no name." There was a lack of autonomy to pursue routes other than the accepted path. Childless couples were considered selfish; single persons were seen as deviants; working mothers were considered to be harming their children; and single women who became pregnant were required either to marry or to give up the child to preserve the integrity of the family. In Canada, sentiment was strong to move women out of the labour force once their contribution to the war effort was complete. The following magazine quotation is an example of the subtle pressures put on women to return to a more traditional family form:

> What will they [women workers] demand of [post-war] society? Perhaps—and we can only hope—they'll be tired of it all [working outside the home] and yearn in the old womanly way for a home and a baby and a big brave man. (*Maclean's*, 15 June, 1942; as quoted in Boutilier, 1977: 23)

The restriction on alternative lifestyles did mean that there were few lone-parent families, and consequently the difficulties associated with this kind of arrangement were limited. In hindsight, we can nonetheless observe that pent-up problems were preparing the way for the second transition, which started in the 1960s.

Theoretical Perspectives on Family Change

The phenomenon of family change has been addressed through two broadly competing explanations at the macro level, as a societal institution, and at the micro level, as the social arena in which people spend most of their lives. The macro or structural perspective considers the relationship of family to other parts of society, and tends to see a reduction in the instrumental functions of families. The micro or cultural perspective looks within families, and observes in particular the greater importance of the expressive dimension. Both perspectives effectively argue that the family is weaker, either because it plays fewer roles in society, or because families easily fall short of satisfying high expectations for personal fulfillment.

Macro or structural explanations

Structural functionalism, defined in earlier chapters, maintains that changes in any one part of society affect other parts, and that each part of society serves some

function for the whole. From this perspective family and kin groups had a larger number of functions in pre-industrial societies (Goode, 1977) where besides being the chief units of reproduction and socialization of the young, families were also the units of economic production, and sometimes of political action and religious observance. For the most part, living space, workplace, and childrearing space were the same. Individuals depended on their families for protection and to cope with problems of age, sickness, and incapacity. In particular, the overlap between family and economy meant that economic activities occurred in family relationships.

Industrialization and modernization (see Chapter 17, Social Change) brought *structural differentiation* and, increasingly, separate structures in society came to serve specific functions. The family lost many of its roles in economic production, education, social security, and care of the aged to non-family institutions such as factories, schools, medical and public health organizations, the police, and even commercialized leisure.

Consequently, in a functionalist view, long-term changes in the family are related to societal changes, especially changes in economic structures. Families have become less central to the organization of society, a reduced role that allows for more flexibility in family arrangements. For instance, the growth of wage labour for the young undermined parental authority and removed barriers to early marriage. More broadly, families have become weaker institutions, in the sense of having less cohesion, fewer functions, less power over other institutions, less influence on behaviour and opinion, and consequently less importance (Popenoe, 1998). This can be called *de-institutionalization* in the sense that there are fewer constraints on family behaviour. For instance, families have less control over the sexual behaviour of adolescents and are less involved in socializing their children. In terms of the more recent transformations, the functionalist explanation pays attention to the shift to a service economy, which increased the demand for women's involvement in paid work (Chafetz and Hagan, 1996). Until the 1960s, the division of labour encouraged a reciprocal state of dependency between the sexes. Economic and policy structures favoured a breadwinner model, with wives dependent on their husbands' incomes, and husbands dependent on wives for the care of home and children. The early 1960s' expansion in the labour market for women involved mostly jobs that might be seen as extensions of

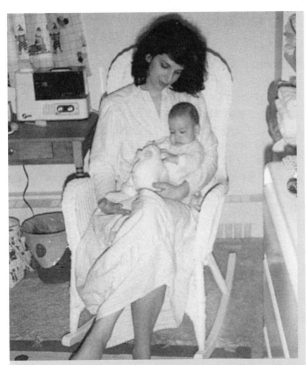

Childrearing restricts labour-force activities and disrupts earning continuity.

women's unpaid work, particularly in clerical work, teaching, nursing, and other services. This put pressure on women to postpone marriage as they extended their period of education and invested in their work lives. For both young women and young men, marriage became less important as a means of structuring their relationships and understandings, and consequently cohabitation became an alternative. Women's greater self-sufficiency broke the dependency associated with the breadwinner model. Women became less dependent on marriage, making divorce and cohabitation more feasible alternatives for both sexes.

Micro or cultural explanations

Other explanations of family change have looked *within* families, proposing that expressive activities have become increasingly important (e.g., Shorter, 1977). In non-industrial societies individuals obtained much of their emotional gratification through religion and community. To use Durkheim's terms, these societies were held together by *mechanical solidarity*, a sense of belonging

and immediate identity with the surrounding community (see Chapter 17, Social Change). In the industrial world, societies are held together more by *organic solidarity*, a division of labour whereby individuals are dependent on each other's specialized abilities. But such societies are also competitive and impersonal, providing individuals with less psychological support and security, and less of a sense of identity. In the transition from a non-industrial to an industrial society, families became considerably more important as sources of emotional gratification, affective involvement, and a sense of personal identity for individuals. Families are centres of nurturing and affection; individuals seek emotional support from them as a retreat from the achievement-oriented struggles of the outside world, placing heavy demands on family relationships. If they do not fulfill expectations, if their emotional well-being is not satisfied, people will abandon their family ties.

Roussel (1989) suggested that the 1970s and 1980s involved a cultural change wherein people became less interested in living up to external norms and more interested in living up to personal standards. Marriage changed from an institution to a *projet de couple* with fewer social constraints. Legislative changes making divorces easier and equating cohabitation with marriage also signified a greater acceptability of alternate sexual and marital arrangements. Instead of the norm that marriages should stay intact regardless of the costs, the prevalent view came to be that "a good divorce is better than a bad marriage" (Lesthaeghe and Surkyn, 1998).

This is not to imply that family behaviour was, in the past, constrained by strict norms, while people are now free to do as they please. Cultural norms continue to operate; all societies will constrain individual behaviour in such crucial areas as sex, family, and procreation. The greater acceptability of individualism and self-fulfillment has relaxed, but not removed, the normative context of these behaviours.

Others, who have written about the long-term changes in the family, speak of a movement from institution to companionship (Burgess et al., 1963), with children being transformed from duty-bound workers to emotionally precious objects (Coltrane, 1998). These perspectives imply a loosening up of relationships and a greater priority on emotional gratification. To use Durkheim's terms, the family has changed from a unit of survival, where relationships are based on a "division of labour," to a unit of "mechanical solidarity" based on a sense of common identity. Obviously, sentiment is a weaker basis for relationships than is instrumentality, and the need for continuous gratification puts heavy, and sometimes contradictory, demands on relationships. Spouses are expected to give each other the autonomy necessary to develop their potential, but at the same time to "be there for each other." Likewise, each is to develop his or her potential, yet remain the person that one once married.

Other authors have used similar frameworks. For Kettle (1980), the parents of the baby boom were a "dutiful generation" committed to sacrificing themselves for groups beyond themselves, while their children are now a "me generation" with high expectations of success and personal gratification. This is sometimes called "affective individualism." Based on Giddens, Hall (1996) used the concepts of "pure relationships" and "reproductive individualism," which refer to relationships based on personal choice rather than normative considerations, and reproduction that is oriented to self-fulfillment. Others have called this a companionship model of marriage, based on few children, attributing high value to the quality of spousal relationships, and involving instability due both to the complexities of the collaborative endeavour and to the greater ability of partners to seek alternatives (Goldscheider and Waite, 1991; Oppenheimer, 1994).

In summary, the last century and a half has seen many of the functions previously performed by families transferred to the larger society, and, at the individual level, a change from meeting instrumental needs to meeting expressive needs. Families became more important as a source of emotional gratification for individuals. Today people still say that they need each other, but now it is for the emotional gratification that marriage and family can provide. As a result, families are quicker to break apart when individual members do not find a particular arrangement to be gratifying.

Anticipating Marriage and Mate Selection

Having examined variability and uniformity in family patterns, and family change, let us now look more closely at family questions over the life course. This section starts with an overview of the average life course, then considers questions of socialization for marriage, dating, premarital sex, home leaving, cohabitation, love, and mate selection.

Family behaviour over the life course

Over the cohorts of persons born from 1915 to 1945, there was a general downward trend in the age at home leaving, first marriage, first birth, last birth, and home leaving of the children (Ravanera and Rajulton, 1996). Conversely, subsequent cohorts have experienced an upward trend with later ages at home leaving, first union, and first childbirth. Not only has there been a delay in the life course events of younger generations, but the transitions themselves are more fluid or less defined, and less standardized, with more variability from case to case (Beaujot, 2004).

There have also been changes in the extent to which some *typical* patterns have been followed (Ravanera et al., 1995. For instance, the pattern of leaving home, getting married, then having a first child reached a peak in the 1931–40 cohort at 65.6 percent of men and 65.8 percent of women. In the 1961–70 cohort, only 26.3 percent of men and 23.2 percent of women followed this pattern. These authors concluded that the younger cohorts have not yet established a path or sequence that can be called typical.

Important changes have therefore occurred in the typical marital life cycle from pre-modern to modern times. The years of childbearing have been reduced, and a new and often happy stage of the empty nest has emerged, between the moving out of the last child and the death of one of the spouses. The increased life expectancy and the decreased family size of today's societies also present a very different context for family life. In earlier times family life patterns were subject to sudden changes, since death so often interfered in the family life cycle. Orphanhood, once a common experience, is now rare. The increased rate of survival of parents means that the nuclear family can now be much more self-sufficient. Under high mortality conditions, it was very risky to depend on the nuclear family alone.

In the mid-nineteenth century, only 6 percent of couples would have celebrated their fiftieth wedding anniversary, compared with 39 percent under 1981 mortality conditions. Couples now live a longer life together, changing the meaning of "till death do us part." When romantic love was introduced into Western civilization as the basis for marriage, the promise to "love each other for life" had a vastly different time horizon. When young lovers make a similar promise today, they probably do not realize that it likely will be for almost fifty years. Even when divorces are entered

Couples now live a longer life together: the average duration of marriages that do not end in divorce is close to fifty years.

into the calculation, the average duration of marriage is thirty years (Nault and Bélanger, 1996: 36, 42). The instability caused by death has been replaced by the personal instability of the marital relationship itself.

Socialization for marriage

To be properly socialized for any role, one needs the motivation to practise the appropriate behaviour, the ability to perform the requirements of the role, and the knowledge of what is expected. With regard to marriage, the overwhelming majority of people are *motivated* to be married or to live in an enduring relationship. In terms of practice and *abilities*, dating provides various relevant experiences. However, unmarried individuals may have difficulty learning about what is actually *expected* of marriage partners, insofar as other people's marriages are generally private. In addition, most people anticipating marriage are very confident, believing that their good intentions will be sufficient to ensure a successful union. As a consequence, they do not seek out information.

The problem of lack of knowledge is further complicated by the fact that, traditionally in our society, boys and girls tend to be socialized differently. Mostly through their peer groups, adolescent girls become adept at interpersonal communication and in the language and actions of romantic love. The male subculture, however, is more sexual and achievement-oriented. As Skolnick (1996: 216) further observed, the order of

priorities is reversed between the sexes: "If boys like sex more than they like girls, girls like boys much more than they like sex."

Also, by the late teens and early twenties, marriage may represent a more important life goal for women than for men, for whom marriage becomes an important life goal at a later stage. Courtship partly involves each gender training the other to be more responsive to what each wants and expects. Boys train girls to see sex as part of a relationship, while girls train boys to see love and commitment as part of a relationship.

Dating and premarital intercourse

Waller (1937) described dating on a U.S. campus during the Depression in a way that may sound slightly exaggerated, but which remains relevant today. He felt that dating was a more or less explicit (often conflict-filled) bargaining relationship, in which each person tried to get the best possible deal. Dating, like marriage, can thus be seen as involving exchanges. In a sense, people who are dating can bargain even harder than those who are married, since they are not formally committed to each other. For instance, if the dating partners are not equal in their desirability as dates, then the one with the higher "rating" has more power in the bargaining and can exploit the other party. Another feature of the dating process, according to Waller, is the "principle of least interest." This means that the less involved person has more power because he or she has less to lose if the relationship ends. The unethical will remain uncommitted but pretend to be committed in order to get the partner committed.

Sex before marriage, as a specific aspect of dating, has also received considerable attention from sociologists of the family. Hobart (1993) studied premarital sexuality of students in ten postsecondary institutions in 1988. He inquired both about attitudes (what do you think is right for males and for females?) and about behaviour (what have you done?). Table 10.2 presents some of the results. It is useful to consider the extent to which these findings support "old moralities" or "new moralities" of **premarital sexual standards**. There are two old moralities: the **abstinence standard**, which forbids premarital sex, and the **double standard**, which grants men premarital sexual licence but expects premarital virginity of women. The data show that only about 10 percent of the students favoured the abstinence standard and that the double standard is also not very prevalent.

Table 10.2	Attitudes toward Sexual Intercourse and Incidence of Various Sexual Experiences, by Sex of Respondent, 1988, in Percentages		
		Males %	Females %
Abstinence standard		10	9
Love standard		48	68
Fun standard		42	23
Has never petted		7	8
Has experienced intercourse		74	78
Engaged to all intercourse partners		1	2
In love with all intercourse partners		26	23
Number of Respondents		940	946

Source: Adapted from Charles W. Hobart. (1993). "Sexual behaviour." In G.N. Ramu, *Marriage and Family in Canada Today* (2nd ed.), pp. 60, 62. Scarborough, ON: Prentice Hall.

The two new moralities of sexual behaviour received greater approval among Hobart's respondents. The **love standard** regards sex as a physical expression of love and sees premarital sex as acceptable when love or strong affection is present. The **fun standard** views sex as primarily a giving and receiving of sexual pleasure; intercourse is acceptable as long as the partners are willing. The love standard receives the greatest support, with slightly more than half of students considering premarital intercourse acceptable for partners in love. About a third of students subscribe to the fun standard of sexual behaviour.

There are a few notable attitude differences between males and females in the study, with females more likely to support the love standard and males the fun standard. For instance, 42 percent of men compared with 23 percent of women subscribed to the fun standard. At the same time, little difference between males and females is in evidence when actual behaviour is concerned.

Hobart showed that, between the sexes, the percentage experiencing premarital intercourse per se has, over the years, roughly equalized. Other studies indicate that 25 percent of youth in Grade 9 have had sexual intercourse, and the figure reaches 50 percent somewhere between Grades 11 and 12 (Wadhera and Millar, 1997: 15). Based on the 1994–95 National Population Health Survey, 44 percent of persons aged 15 to 19 had at least one sex partner in the previous year (Galambos and Tilton-Weaver, 1998). Of those who were sexually active, about a third had two or more partners.

The long-term increase in permissiveness can be related to general changes in gender roles (see Chapter 7, Gender Relations). Premarital sex codes are more permissive when women have greater equality and are subject to less occupational differentiation. As women become less dependent on marriage for their major source of status, it is less necessary for them to keep sex out of the dating relationship in order to exchange it for the marriage contract. Sex and marriage, then, have become less closely linked for both men and women. Reliable birth-control methods have greatly enhanced this separation, and it would appear that the fear of disease, including AIDS, has not encouraged a return to more conservative standards.

Home leaving

After having declined decade by decade, the average age at home leaving started to rise in the late 1970s, producing what some have called a "cluttered nest" (Ravanera et al., 1995; Boyd and Norris, 1998). In addition, some children have returned home after having left for a period of time, a pattern very rare in the past. For instance, at age 20 to 29, 41.1 percent were living with their parents in 2001 compared to 27.5 percent in 1981 (Statistics Canada, 2002a: 27).

There are clearly *economic* factors at stake, such as the difficulty of "Generation X" or the "Generation on Hold" to establish itself in the labour market (Côté and Allahar, 1994; see also Chapter 4, Socialization). Not only are younger generations staying longer in school, but young people trying to get established through a first job are also more likely today to return home (Wister et al., 1997). Lapierre-Adamcyk et al. (1995) found that economic factors play a larger role for men's than for women's leaving home.

However, there are also *cultural* factors operating. Children are less likely to be living at home when the parents are more religious, remarried, or from certain ethnic groups (Wister et al., 1997). According to Boyd and Norris (1998) average age at home leaving is latest in intact families. If parents have separated, children are most likely to live with their mother, except if she has established a new relationship. In effect, children tend to prefer living with a father who is not in a relationship over a mother who is in a new relationship (Boyd and Norris, 1998).

Cohabitation

While some common-law unions have always existed, especially in the case of persons not allowed to marry, the modern phenomenon of cohabitation started with university students, especially in Scandinavia and North America, in the 1960s. The behaviour then spread to professional classes in the 1970s and subsequently to much of the population. Initially, cohabitation often was a short pre-honeymoon period. Later it became a longer period and the normal form of entry into unions for persons who are single, but especially for the previously married. Among Canadian women aged 60 to 69 in 2001, only 2 percent of first unions had been cohabitations, but 63 percent of first unions were cohabitations for women aged 20 to 29 (Statistics Canada, 2002b: 4). At the 2001 Census, 16.4 percent of all couples were cohabiting, compared to 6.4 percent in 1981 (Statistics Canada, 2002a: 25).

To some extent, less formal relationships are simply a substitute for marriage, but in other respects, cohabitation is not the same as a formal marriage. Comparing various characteristics of cohabiting people with those who are single and those who are married, Rindfuss and VandenHeuvel (1990) found that the cohabiting were more similar to the single than to the married. People living together often do not consider themselves married; their cohabitation can be seen as an *alternative to being single.* However, increasing numbers consider cohabitation as an *alternative to marriage.* Le Bourdais and Lapierre-Adamcyk (2004) propose that, at least in Quebec, cohabitation may well be on the way to losing its marginal status, becoming more like marriage, with a similar long-term commitment, only less formal. Indeed, by 1996, 47 percent of common-law unions involved children, sometimes from a previous relationship. In 2001, half of step-families were cohabiting rather than married.

Kiernan (2001) proposes that cohabitation undergoes various stages in societies. At first, cohabitation is a prelude to marriage, and then it is seen as a probationary period where the strength of the relationship may be tested prior to committing to marriage. In this second stage, cohabitation is a form of conjugal life, largely without children. In the third stage, cohabitation is socially acceptable and becoming a parent is no longer restricted to marriage. In the fourth stage, cohabitation is a substitute or alternative to marriage, including being a lasting arrangement in which to raise children. Le Bourdais and Lapierre-Adamcyk (2004) propose that Quebec is somewhere between the third and fourth stages in this development, while the rest of Canada is between the second and third stages. For instance, nearly 60 percent of births occurring in 2000 in Quebec were to unmarried mothers, and 75 percent of step-families are cohabiting. The change brought by the Quiet Revolution in Quebec would be part of the reason for the less rigid attitudes on family and gender. On gender questions, these authors propose that the feminist movement is stronger and more deeply rooted in Quebec.

There are also fewer differences in Quebec with regard to the likelihood of separation, across types of unions. Considering only unions with children, in Quebec, the likelihood of separation is about the same for direct marriages as it is for marriages that follow cohabitation, while it is twice as high for cohabitations that are not followed by marriage (Le Bourdais and Lapierre-Adamcyk, 2004: 937). In the rest of Canada, for these unions with children, compared to direct marriages, the likelihood of separation is 66 percent higher in marriages following cohabitation, and it is five times as high in cohabitations that are not followed by marriage.

Researchers such as Leridon and Villeneuve-Gokalp (1994) see the spread of cohabitation as the most radical change to families in the past twenty-five years. Cohabitation is displacing marriage as a form of first union, and its duration is increasing. It signals flexibility in unions, transforming premarital, marital, and post-marital relationships, and with significant consequences for children.

Homogamy in mate selection

In conversations about mate selection, two contradictory principles often emerge: "opposites attract" and "like marries like." Clearly, most people choose someone of the other sex, but beyond that, the idea that opposites attract receives little research support. There is more support for **homogamy**, the idea that people marry others like themselves.

Among marriages occurring in 2000, more than half in each of the following groups married others of the same religion: Jewish, Mennonite, Pentecostal, Jehovah's Witness, Catholic, Eastern Orthodox, other Christian, and non-Christian groups. Even those whose religion was "unknown or not stated" are more likely to marry someone in the same category (Statistics Canada, 2003a: 20–21). Homogamy is also significant by education and social class (Kalmijn, 1991).

The general conclusion, then, is that most people are likely to marry someone who is pretty much like themselves in most social and economic characteristics, and who has similar things to exchange in the marriage bargain. This departs considerably from the romantic notion that love and marriage are individualistic and determined by chance. Note also that this is an average tendency; obviously, some marriages involve partners who are very different from each other.

The timing and propensity to marry

One example of dissimilarity between married partners—i.e., **heterogamy**—occurs with respect to age. On average, women marry at a younger age than men. In some societies, the ideal age gap is a five- to ten-year difference. In Canada, the difference in the median age at first marriage is two years, a decline from about three years in the 1960s, and four in the early part of the century. Among the currently married population, the 1990 General Social Survey found that 41 percent of couples are within two years of age. In 51 percent of cases the man is two or more years older, and in 38 percent three or more years older (McDaniel, 1994: 21). In contrast, only 6 percent of women are two or more years older than their husbands.

Although a two-year gap is small, it is important. A younger person is likely to be less experienced at taking responsibility and playing leadership roles and to have achieved less in economic or career terms, a condition known as the **mating gradient**. In the average marriage, then, the husband will earn more money, partly because he is older and more established and his job may be given priority (for example, the family is more likely to move for the sake of his job than for hers), and the wife is more likely than he to withdraw from the labour force for the sake of the children. What this means, of course, is that the slight disadvantage with which the wife started, because she is younger, can become entrenched over the course of the marriage.

Until the beginning of the twentieth century, marriage patterns involved relatively late age at marriages and significant proportions that did not marry (Gee, 1986). Over the first six or seven decades of the century, except for a slight reversal in the 1930s, marriages occurred earlier in people's lives, and higher proportions were married.

Then in the late 1960s and early 1970s these trends reversed, with marriages occurring later in life, and a lower frequency of marriage. In the early 1970s, for example, over 90 percent of adults could be expected to marry at some point in their lives, compared to under 75 percent in the early 1990s (Nault and Bélanger, 1996). The changes in entry into first marriage are partly a function of more cohabitation. However, especially under age 35, the combined proportion married or cohabiting has declined appreciably between the 1981 and 2001 censuses (Beaujot, 2000; Statistics Canada, 2002a). As achieved characteristics, particularly education and occupation, play an increasing role in the lives of women, the timing of the transition to marital relationships is delayed while stable work careers are being established. Women's greater economic independence also allows them to search longer for the right person (Oppenheimer, 1994). For both sexes, marriage has become less central to the transition to adulthood and to the set of roles that define adult status.

Goldscheider and Waite (1991) found that *employment* today is a prerequisite for marriage especially for men, but also for women. Many people probably consider that two jobs are needed to marry. The time needed to establish these two jobs may well be an important part of the delay of marriage. Analyzing the propensity to marry among American cohorts marrying in the 1970s and 1980s, Sweeney (1997) also found that economic prospects are positively related to marriage and that men and women now resemble one another in terms of the relationship between economic prospects and marriage. In general, later marriage is associated with higher socioeconomic status (Ravanera et al., 1998a; 1998b).

Marital and Family Interactions

Having considered socialization for marriage, premarital interaction, mate selection, and timing of marriage, we can now move into the study of some specific aspects of marital and family interactions, some of which were introduced in Chapter 9, Aging. We will consider models of the division of work, lone-parent families, childbearing, and children.

Models of the division of paid and unpaid work

Durkheim argued for a division of labour based on complementary roles for husbands and wives. He did not envisage a collaborative model of shared roles where partners collaborate at both earning a living and caring for the family. Becker (1981) proposed that such sharing is inefficient because different forms of capital are needed for market and household production. Cultural factors may then support that traditional division of labour. For instance, Brines (1994) spoke of a "gender display perspective" that prompts men to avoid housework as a means to establish their masculinity, especially men who lack other avenues for recognition—for example, because they are experiencing difficulties in the labour market. But while a division of labour between paid and unpaid work may be an efficient strategy, it is also a high-risk strategy when marriages become unstable (Oppenheimer, 1997). There is a risk for the partner who has specialized in unpaid caring when the one who has specialized in the market is unable or unwilling to provide for children and a former spouse.

Given the importance of both paid and unpaid work, it is useful to consider how couples divide their time into these categories. At the level of couples, this allows for the three-by-three cross-classification shown in Table 10.3. Compared to one's spouse, one could be doing more, less, or the same amount of each of paid and unpaid work.

[Social Trends]

One Is the Loneliest Number . . .

In 1971, 15 percent of women at ages 25 to 34 were neither married nor cohabiting, compared to 35 percent in 2001. Men not in a union at these ages increased from 21 to 45 percent. That is, even when cohabitation is included, living in relationships is down compared to levels experienced over the last fifty years (Beaujot, 1995: 40).

A larger proportion of people are now living alone. For the whole population aged 15 and over, 12 percent were living alone in 1996. By age group, the figures are 10 percent or lower until age 55, but they reach 34 percent at ages 85 and over (Statistics Canada, 2002a: 26). Between 1981 and 2001, living in union decreased for all age groups (Beaujot and Kerr, 2004: 220). Living alone is particularly predominant among older widows (recall the last chapter), including 35 percent of women over 65 in 2001 (Statistics Canada, 2002a: 26).

At younger ages, while there is a delay in leaving home, significant numbers are in relationships. In the 2001 General Social Survey, persons who were neither married nor cohabiting were asked "Are you in an intimate relationship with someone who lives in a separate household?" At ages 20 to 29, 56 percent of persons were in these relationships, which the authors defined as "couples living apart" (Milan and Peters, 2003).

What differences would there be in the lives of older versus younger couples living apart?

Table 10.3	Relative Contributions to Paid Work and Unpaid Work (Domestic Activity) in Husband–Wife Households, Canada, 1998 (Percentage of Sample)		
	Compared to husband, wife does		
	More paid work	Same paid work	Less paid work
More Domestic Activity	5.7	17.2	48.5
Same Domestic Activity	1.9	5.7	5.5
Less Domestic Activity	5.3	4.5	5.5

Notes: The sample size is 3794 married and cohabiting couples. This table excludes persons with missing data on weekly estimates of time use for respondent or spouse and couples where one or both are aged 65 or over.

Source: Statistics Canada. *1998 General Social Survey on Time Use.*

The dominant category, amounting to 48.5 percent, is the traditional **complementary-roles model** where the husband spends more time at paid work and the wife at unpaid work. The complementary-gender-reversed comprised 5.5 percent of the sample. The second largest category is the women's **double burden** where typically the wife is doing the same amount of paid work but more unpaid work. This corresponds to 23 percent of the sample. The men's double burdens amounted to 10 percent of the sample. The remaining 13.2 percent of the sample can be called a **collaborative** or **role-sharing model**.

Comparisons between 1992 and 1998 time-use surveys show only slight change, but this tends to be in the direction of somewhat greater symmetry, with slight reduction in complementary-traditional, a greater proportion of men with a double burden, and a slight increase in shared roles (Beaujot and Liu, 2005). We can also see that the symmetrical family, in which both partners contribute more or less equally to economic and domestic activities, is more an ideal than an actual arrangement. Despite the fact that the dual-earner model has become the norm, close to half of families could be described as "neo-traditional" because the major responsibility for paid and unpaid work remains divided along traditional gender lines.

It is important to note as well that, although the shared-roles arrangement occurs in only a minority of families, equality of partnership rights is enshrined in law. For example, in Ontario, the Family Law Act says, "it is necessary to recognize the equal position of spouses as individuals within marriage and to recognize

marriage as a form of partnership" (Ontario Family Law Act 1990). The act goes on to indicate that, as a default condition, family assets are to be divided in equal shares upon a marital dissolution. Generally speaking, these conditions also hold for persons who have cohabited for three years, or for those who are cohabiting and have a child.

Lone-parent families

Just as marriages can take a number of alternative forms, so too can families. The largest increases in the 1980s and 1990s have, in fact, involved lone-parent families. Among families with children, 24.7 percent were lone-parent in 2001 (Table 10.1). In 1951 most one-parent families were led by a widowed parent. In contrast, by 1996 the separated or divorced constituted 58 percent of the total, with another 20 percent involving a never-married parent (Milan, 2000: 9). The proportion of male-headed families among the lone-parent families has been stable, amounting to 16.9 percent in 1996. Over the life course, the experience of lone parenthood is in fact quite common, representing a lifetime probability of 34 percent for women and 23 percent for men (Péron et al., 1999: 124, 181). Almost all lone parents (92 percent) leave this state within 20 years, with about a quarter of cases involving the departure of the children and three-quarters the formation of new unions, thus involving step-parenting.

Compared with currently married women of the same age, female lone parents are more likely to have

Among families with children, 25 percent were lone-parent families, and over 80 percent of those were led by a female parent.

lived in common-law relationships, to have had their children earlier, and to have less education (Ravanera et al., 1995). In effect, they must raise children while facing a double disadvantage of lack of support from a

spouse and fewer job skills. McQuillan (1992) found that between 1971 and 1986, as participation of married women in the labour force increased, the income gap between lone-parent and two-parent families grew. (See the box "What Are the Challenges and Rewards of Lone-Parenting?")

Childbearing and Children

Childbearing is a part of marital interaction that deserves special attention, especially given the considerable changes since World War II in the ease with which couples can control their reproduction. In fact, few aspects of family behaviour have changed so fundamentally as the extent and effectiveness of control over marital fertility.

Just as marriage can be regarded as involving ongoing instrumental and expressive exchanges, so too children can be examined in terms of both economic (instrumental) and non-economic (expressive) components. At the economic level, children are very costly, since they are largely dependent on their parents and do not contribute to family income. Gauthier (1991) calculated the direct costs to age 18 of a first child, excluding childcare, at $190 000 for a higher income family and $78 000 for a lower income family (in 2001 dollars). The average costs for three children would be $285 000. This figure rises to $575 000 if one includes childcare and indirect costs associated with lower labour-force participation.

[Research Focus]

What Are the Challenges and Rewards of Lone-Parenting?

In 2001, the average income of two-parent families with children under 18 in Canada was $6962, compared with $26 008 for one-parent families. In the excerpt that follows, Cherlin noted the problems associated with the lower standard of living of lone-parent families, as well as some of the non-economic rewards of parenting alone.

Saddled with sole or primary responsibility for supporting themselves and their children, lone mothers frequently have too little time and too few resources to manage effectively. There are three common sources of strain. One is responsibility overload: lone parents must

make all the decisions and provide all the needs for their families, a responsibility that at times can be overwhelming. Another is task overload: many lone parents simply have too much to do, with working, housekeeping, and parenting; consequently, there is no slack time to meet unexpected demands. A third is emotional overload: lone parents are always on call to give emotional support to their children, whether or not their own emotional resources are temporarily depleted. Moreover, divorced and separated women who are raising children often find that their economic position has deteriorated. Many of those

(continued)

who were not employed in the years preceding their separation have difficulty re-entering the job market. As a result of their limited earning power and of the low level of child support, lone mothers and their children often experience a decline in their standard of living after a separation.

[Yet] to be sure, life in a lone-parent family also has its rewards, foremost the relief from marital conflict. In addition, lone parents may gain increased self-esteem from their ability to manage the demands of work life and family life by themselves. They may enjoy their independence and their close relationships to their children. Some writers argue that women are particularly likely to develop an increased sense of self-worth from the independence and greater control over the life they achieve after divorce. . . .

Goldscheider and Waite (1991) observed that many bad marriages are also marked by poor parenting, and consequently that divorce can be a benefit to children. However, they also note that many other parents with marital problems can parent effectively. Overall, they conclude, children are less likely than parents to benefit from divorce and remarriage.

Source: Reprinted by permission of the publisher from *Marriage, Divorce, Remarriage: Revised and Enlarged Edition,* by Andrew J. Cherin, pp. 73–74, Cambridge, Mass.: Harvard University Press, Copyright 1981, 1992 by the President and Fellows of Harvard College.

Under what conditions might children experience more of the rewards or fewer of the costs of a divorce?

The non-economic costs and values of children are more difficult to determine. Children are costly in the sense that parents have less time and energy for themselves. Children are sometimes emotional and psychological burdens; parents worry about them and have to put up with various inconveniences, ranging from a messy place at the table to a dented car fender. On the positive side, children offer certain advantages: people's status as adults can be more firmly established when they are parents; having children can provide a sense of achievement, of power and influence, of continuity beyond death; children provide immediate pleasure in the form of fun, excitement, and laughter in the home.

However, the value and cost of children do not cover the whole dynamics of childbearing. People are not completely free in the decision to have children. There are often normative influences, stronger in some groups than in others, that encourage couples to have children. The traditionally higher fertility in Quebec that lasted until the 1960s was partly the result of considerable pressure on parents in French Canadian communities to have large families to preserve "the French fact" in Canada. This changed in the 1960s as the influence of the Roman Catholic Church weakened and parents became more concerned with the cost of children. French Canadians are now more likely to have fewer children in order to take advantage of the new opportunities for social mobility that have opened up for them since the Quiet Revolution of the 1960s (see Chapter 15, Social Movements).

Although the level of fertility in Canada has gone down (see Chapter 16, Demography and Urbanization), most couples want to have children. According to the 2001 General Social Survey, only 7 percent of persons aged 20 to 34 intend to not have children. At age 30 to 34, 74 percent of women have children, and another 20 percent intend to have children; for men at this age, the figures are 57 percent with children and another 34 percent intending to have children (Kemeny and Stobert, 2003: 8).

Family change and children

Given delays in marriage and childbearing, the family units into which children are born have changed. In the early 1960s, 25 percent of births were *first births*, compared with 44 percent in the early 1980s (Marcil-Gratton, 1988). Consequently, greater proportions of children have "inexperienced" parents. With fewer brothers and sisters, they also have *fewer older siblings*. For instance, half of the generation born in the early 1960s had two older brothers or sisters, compared with one-fifth of those born twenty years later. One in five had a brother or sister ten or more years older, compared with one in twenty for the later generation. Fewer births, and their concentration over a shorter time in the lives of adults, mean more potential parental resources per child, but also that children have less opportunity to interact with and learn from siblings.

Among children born in the early 1960s, 8 percent were either born to a *lone parent* or experienced the separation of their parents by age 6, compared with 22 percent for those born in the mid-1980s (Table 10.4). By age 16, more than a quarter (27 percent) of the 1971–73 birth cohort had experienced similar conditions.

The experience of lone parenthood is occurring earlier and earlier in the lives of children and now applies to more than one-fifth of children by age 6 (Marcil-Gratton, 1998). Of children who were born in a two-parent family, 20.5 percent experienced lone parenthood by age 10, and 60 percent of these had also experienced a *step-family* as a second major family change, all by age 10.

There are also very strong differences in the experience of lone parenthood depending on whether or not the parents had ever cohabited. The family lives of children have also been affected by the changing propensities for cohabitation and separation. In the early 1960s, 95 percent of children were born in marriages, compared with 64 percent in the year 2003 (see Table 10.1). What has changed is not the births to single mothers, but *births to cohabiting couples*. For instance, by age 6 in the 1987–88 cohort, among children born to two-parent families, 8 percent had experienced a parental separation if the parents had never cohabited, but 25 percent if they had (Table 10.4). The proportion experiencing the separation of parents by age 6 reaches 43 percent if the parents cohabited and never married (Marcil-Gratton 1998: 18). Consequently, the family life of children born to parents having ever cohabited involves more change and it is particularly unstable (Marcil-Gratton, 1998).

Many children therefore live through a *diversity of family trajectories*. Cohabitation, births outside of marriage, increased divorce, and family reconstitution either through cohabitation or marriage: all these trends represent reduced family stability for children. Within 15 years of seeing their parents separate, 85 percent experience the arrival of at least one new parent, and 45 percent the arrival of two new parents. About half of these step-families become blended families with the birth of a child in the new relationship (Juby et al., 2001). And while family reconstitution often provides children with multiple parents, it does not lessen the instability. For instance, step-fathers often invest more in non-biological children who are present than in their biological children who are absent (Marsiglio, 1998). But if they are no longer living with the child's mother (Kaplan et al., 1998), step-fathers largely remove themselves from the lives of step-children.

There are clearly strong variations in the economic well-being of children by family type. Comparing children in the top and bottom income quintiles (Figure 10.1) we see that among children under 18 in the top quintile, 93.9 percent are in families with married parents, 4.8 percent with cohabiting parents, and 1.3 percent with a lone parent. In contrast, children in the bottom quintile include 44.1 percent with married parents, 7.8 percent

Table 10.4	Cumulative Percentage of Canadian Children Experiencing Family Disruption, by Cohort		
	Age		
	6	16	20
Percentage born to a lone parent or experiencing separation of parents			
1961–63 birth cohort	7.8	19.8	24.2
1971–73 birth cohort	13.0	27.3	–
1981–83 birth cohort	18.1	–	–
1987–88 birth cohort	22.6	–	–
Of children born to two-parent family, percentage experiencing separation of parents			
Parents never cohabited			
1971–73 cohort	6.0	19.5	–
1981–83 cohort	8.0	–	–
1987–88 cohort	8.1	–	–
Parents ever cohabitated			
1971–73 cohort	18.0	53.2	–
1981–83 cohort	23.1	–	–
1987–88 cohort	24.6	–	–

Source: Beaujot (2000). Reprinted with permission of Broadview Press.

with cohabiting parents, and 48.1 percent with a lone parent. Other data confirm the increasing proportions of poor children from lone parent families; those living with one parent comprised 21 percent of poor children in 1971 but 46 percent in 2001.

In summary, some of the family changes have benefited children. Smaller family sizes, later ages at parenthood, and greater proportions of two-income families mean that parents are more likely to have the necessary resources to care for children. However, the greater propensity of parents to separate has had a negative consequence. Coleman (1988) analyzed the situation of children in terms of financial, human, and social capital. Children in lone-parent families are more likely to have relative deficiencies on all three levels. The financial capital is easiest to document, as indicated above. The reduced human capital involves fewer adults and consequently a

reduced ability to learn from the experience of parents. Social capital refers to relationships to other family members beyond the household and to other members of the community. Here again, one parent is likely to provide fewer such relationships for children.

Marital Dissolution

We turn our attention in this section to marital dissolution. We have proposed that a marriage involves ongoing instrumental and expressive exchanges and that it involves a form of commitment. How can we use this recognition of exchange and commitment to help us understand divorce trends?

The most observable ways in which families have changed are in terms of entry into unions and exit from

Figure 10.1 Distribution of Children under Age 18 Whose Families Are in the 1st and 5th Income Quintiles, by Family Environment, 1990

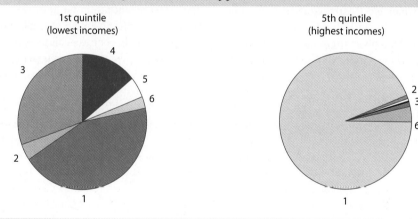

	1st quintile (lowest incomes)		5th quintile (highest incomes)	
1. Married couples	44.1%	(8.1%)	93.9%	(18.2%)
2. Lone fathers	4.1%	(0.8%)	0.7%	(0.1%)
3. Lone mothers (separated, divorced, or widowed)	30.0%	(5.5%)	0.6%	(0.1%)
4. Never-married lone mothers	14.0%	(2.6%)	–	(0.0%)
5. Common-law couples, both spouses never married	5.0%	(0.9%)	1.1%	(0.2%)
6. Common-law couples, at least one spouse ever married	2.8%	(0.5%)	3.7%	(0.7%)
	100%		100%	

–nil or zero
[1]In brackets is the percentage each group represents of all children under age 18.

Source: Péron et al. (1999); Statistics Canada, *Report on the Demographic Situation in Canada, 1997*, Catalogue No. 91-209.

Figure 10.2   Cumulative Incidence of Separations by Length of Union, per 1000 Unions of Each Type, Canada, 1995

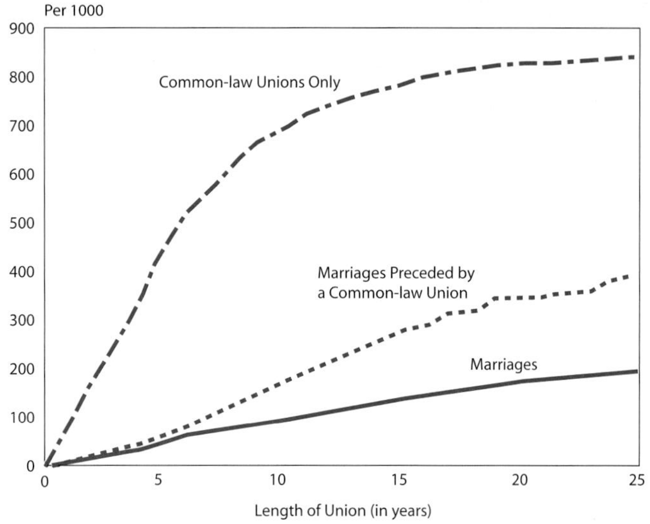

Per 1000

Common-law Unions Only

Marriages Preceded by a Common-law Union

Marriages

Length of Union (in years)

Source: Bélanger and Dumas (1998: 41); Statistics Canada, *General Social Survey*, Catalogue No. 11-612.

marriages, both of which imply greater flexibility in relationships. Separation and divorce have certainly increased since the 1960s, but it is also important to appreciate that the most common situation is for people to be married only once. For instance, at ages 30 to 54 in 1990, some 10 percent are never married, another 10 percent are formerly married, 67 percent are married or cohabiting with no previous marriage, and 12 percent are married or cohabiting after a previous marriage (Beaujot, 1995: 42). In terms of family units, the 1995 General Social Survey found that 70 percent of families with children include both biological parents, while 22 percent involve only one parent and 8 percent are step-families with one biological parent and a step-parent.

Nonetheless, it is estimated that at least one-third of marriages taking place in the last two decades will end in divorce within 25 years (Péron et al., 1999). For instance, the divorce rates by duration of marriage imply that at the rates for the year 2000, 35.5 percent of marriages will end in divorce within 25 years (Belanger, 2003: 30).

Separations vary considerably according to the type of union (Figure 10.2). After 25 years, 20 percent of marriages not preceded by cohabitation have separated. This compares to 40 percent of marriages preceded by cohabitation, and close to 85 percent of cohabitations that did not involve marriages. Even after five years, there are significant differences, with half of unions

having dissolved if they involved cohabitations not converted into a marriage, compared to only 5 percent dissolution for unions that started as a marriage not preceded by cohabitation.

In their analysis of the *transition to divorce*, Goldscheider and Waite (1991: 104–6) found that the risk of divorce in the U.S. is greater when one's parents have separated, or when parents have higher education. However, higher education for husbands reduces this risk, as does higher husband's earnings. Canadian data show similar patterns (Balakrishnan et al., 1993). Higher men's incomes reduce divorce. A lower income means that the instrumental exchanges in the marriage are less rewarding, making the prospect of divorce less negative for working-class individuals.

Divorce propensities are particularly high for those who married at a young age and who had premarital births. Furthermore, those marrying young are more likely to be downwardly mobile, especially if the wife is pregnant at the time of marriage, because this detracts from the possibility of pursuing further education. Divorce is also higher for couples raising step-children, for those who have a larger age difference at marriage, and for persons whose parents had separated (Hall and Zhao, 1995). Divorce levels are also higher at lower levels of socioeconomic status.

Love has become more important as the focus of marriage in the twenty-first century, while economic considerations have lessened.

Decrease in instrumental functions

It should be quite evident by now that there has been a decrease in the instrumental functions fulfilled by families. Thus, families have less to hold them together. This is particularly true in the economic domain, where families now involve considerably less economic interdependence. For the wife, it is much easier to get out of an unhappy marriage if she is employed than if she is in a complementary-roles marriage. Women with higher incomes have higher divorce prospects.

Considering instrumental functions helps us to understand several other things about the incidence of divorce. Divorces are less likely to occur when there are young, dependent children because the family is more economically interdependent at that time. Indeed, both childless couples and those in the empty nest stage have higher risks of divorce (Rowe, 1989).

Importance of the expressive dimension

We have argued that marriage now is seen much more as an arrangement for the mutual gratification of participants. Spouses now expect more from families in terms of intimacy and interpersonal affect. In addition, individual well-being and self-fulfillment are seen as important values. Families are expected to serve individual needs, rather than individuals serving family needs. Therefore, divorce may be more prevalent today because it represents a natural solution to marriages that do not serve the mutual gratification of the persons involved. For instance, 88 to 95 percent of respondents to the 1995 General Social Survey consider that divorce is justified if there is "lack of love and respect from the partner," "unfaithful behaviour," or "abusive behaviour" (Frederick and Hamel, 1998: 8). Still, Ambert and Baker (1988) found that significant numbers of people regret their decision to divorce. In a third of separations, the partners have no serious grounds for divorce. While some divorces are due to "taking a risk" with an affair, others happen because of circumstances that have little to do with marriage, such as problems at work, mid-life crises, or unresolved and long-standing emotional problems.

As noted earlier, one of the most consistent findings in divorce research is the higher probability of divorce for those getting married at an early age. The same applies to the risk of dissolution of common-law unions, especially if there was a conception before the union (Turcotte and Bélanger, 1998: 19–20). Regarding the expressive dimension, one can hypothesize that as these young married persons mature, they no longer receive the expected gratification and find their spouse a poor choice. It may even be that, for persons marrying at younger ages, emotional gratification is particularly important. Early marriage may have been a way of escaping an unrewarding situation in their original families. If the expressive dimension is especially important to them, they will be more likely to separate if this dimension is not working.

The higher incidence of divorce for second marriages can be seen in this light as well. The lowest dissolution rate is for marriages involving two previously single people, while those involving a divorced woman and a single man or two divorced persons have the highest dissolution rates (Dumas, 1990: 28). Persons who have already divorced are more likely to see marriage in terms of mutual gratification and to leave a marriage that is not rewarding. But it is clear that the rejection of one marriage is not to be confused with the rejection of marriage per se. Persons getting divorced are generally not doing so because they do not want to be married; instead, they do so because they find the exchanges with a particular partner to be unrewarding.

Redefinition of the marital commitment

Obviously, divorce would be less common if everyone frowned on it and if the legal restrictions were formidable. But there has been a significant change in the attitudes toward divorce in Western societies. Its social stigma has lessened considerably and people now accept that divorce occurs frequently among the "normal" population. There has also been considerable change in the definition of acceptable grounds for dissolving marital commitments. Until 1968, adultery was the only grounds for divorce in Canada. The 1968 Divorce Act extended the grounds for divorce to include both fault-related grounds and marriage-breakdown grounds. Fault-related grounds include adultery and other sexual behaviours, prolonged alcohol or drug addiction, and physical and mental cruelty. To obtain a divorce on these grounds, there must be an injured party who brings the other spouse to trial, which then finds him or her guilty. As of 1986, divorce under marriage-breakdown grounds can occur for any reason so long as the spouses have lived apart for one year.

Table 10.1 indicates quite clearly the jump in divorce levels with the advent of the 1968 Act. Part of this jump includes the backlog of separations that occurred before 1968. Even taking this into account, there still has been a great increase in divorce since 1968. Life-table techniques that extrapolate on the basis of the data from a given year suggest that there was a stabilization of divorce levels in the 1990s with some 35 percent of marriages ending in divorce within 25 years (Bélanger, 2003: 30). Compared to other countries, Canadian divorce rates are higher than in Japan, France, or Germany, roughly the same as those of Sweden and the United Kingdom, and considerably lower than in the United States.

Anticipating Future Change and Continuity

There has been considerable change in family patterns over the last few decades. Families may not play the same roles, or as many roles as in the past, and they are not as permanent, but they remain crucial to the lives of most people. For the majority of people, there is considerable continuity in family patterns. There is no evidence that marriage, or at least the desirability of durable relationships, will go out of style. The level of divorce has gone up significantly, but it is best viewed as a form of family reorganization. Although the proportion of adults living alone has increased, this applies mostly to those not yet in a relationship, or older people who have been widowed. Although separation and divorce are a much more common family experience, estimates are that close to seven out of ten will experience a lifelong relationship. Childbearing has also gone down, but only a small minority do not intend to have children.

Perhaps the largest change relates to the liberation of gender roles. While, on average, husbands continue to earn more of the family income, there has been a considerable move to more equality in terms of labour-force participation, some equalization in the propensity to work full-time, and increasing numbers of couples in which the wife earns more than the husband. Perhaps the greatest difficulty is the resistance to a more equal sharing of the unpaid family work. Nonetheless, there are also examples of change in this caring dimension, in terms of both attitudes and behaviour (Beaujot, 2000).

The study of examples that depart from the typical patterns helps us to understand that there are possibilities for change in these gendered processes associated with caring activities. Coltrane (1996) predicted an increase in future sharing of unpaid work because sharing is more likely to occur in the following conditions: wives who are employed more hours and more attached to their jobs, women earning more of the total household income and especially co-providers, wives negotiating for change and relinquishing control over managing the home and children, more ideological support for gender equality, husbands employed fewer hours, fathers who are involved in the care of infants, and smaller family sizes. In addition, women who delay parenting and who are remarried are more likely to be able to negotiate a more equitable arrangement.

This unlinking of gender and caring may well be crucial to changing gender relations in the broader society. In particular, this change in the broader society is enhanced by an evolution to collaborative marriages in which spouses are co-providers and co-parents, and where the default condition would be the sharing of responsibility for children in the case of separations. Just as the largest change in the past thirty years has involved women's earning activities, perhaps the next thirty years will see changes in men's caring activities.

[Debate]

The Family in Crisis?

In a book entitled *The Canadian Family in Crisis*, John F. Conway depicted the family as undergoing a major transition, from the traditional patriarchal family (dominant since industrialization) to an egalitarian family, and argued that, while this transition is underway, the family is in a state of serious crisis. This crisis partly involves the family's ability to do what it is supposed to do—support children, women, and men—and is caused by various contradictions between the move toward gender equality and the assumptions of the traditional patriarchal family based on complementary husband and wife roles.

According to Conway, we see many of the consequences of this crisis in the lives of children who are without adequate childcare and subject to the insecurity of family dissolution and absent fathers. We see the vulnerability of children in the numbers who are abused, living in poverty, or even committing suicide. In effect, the family is not providing the support that children need.

Other consequences of the crisis are felt by women who are caught in various contradictions. In particular, they are expected to be involved in the labour force, yet the work world is not ready to accept them on an equal footing with men. At home, some are abused but more are fatigued as they perform a double duty, because husbands are not taking on an equal share of housework and childcare. Many women decide to move out of a marriage in order to resolve some of the conflict, but that brings the additional problems of lone parenthood, especially poverty.

Conway proposed that men also suffer the consequences of the crisis in the family. They have a sense of unease—that is, they are not sure what is expected of them. They too are suffering from the contradictions between the traditional and the egalitarian assumptions. In some ways, they are also subject to a double burden in terms of work and family life, expected to give a hundred percent to career achievements yet also expected to do more at home. In addition, many men are separated from their children and miss the basic human interactions with children that they consider to be an important part of family life.

While Conway saw the family in crisis, he also was optimistic, seeing the void created by the death of the traditional family being filled by an egalitarian family. While the whole book is about family difficulties, he ended with the concept of a "joyous funeral" for the family's previous form. At the same time, much social change is needed to bring about this egalitarian family. In particular, for women there is the need for equality in the work world—that is, pay equity and employment equity. For children, there is the need for support mechanisms, in particular daycare, while parents are at work. For both mothers and fathers, there is the need for various changes, such as parental leave and flexible work-time, to enable a better accommodation between roles inside and outside the family.

Source: Adapted from R. Beaujot, 1995. "Review of John F. Conway, The Canadian Family in Crisis," *Journal of Comparative Family Studies*, 26(2): 284–86. Reprinted with permission.

Is the family in a state of crisis? Will an egalitarian family resolve the conflicts between the world of work and the private world? Will an egalitarian family be more stable? Are young adults ready for egalitarian families?

Summary

A family is two or more people related by an enduring commitment, blood, or adoption, and who reside together. Marriage involves a commitment and ongoing expressive and instrumental exchanges between partners. A look at various cultures shows uniformity in family patterns in some aspects, such as the incest taboo, but variability in others, such as monogamy and polygyny. Thus, there is much variety and complexity to family behaviour, and it is necessary to view family questions against the background of the larger society.

In the theory section, we attempted to understand some of the historical changes in families through both macro and micro considerations. The macro perspective highlights the structural differentiation through which families no longer perform some of the functions they previously provided for the larger society. On the other hand, a look inside families at the micro level shows that families now play a more important role in the emotional gratification of their individual members.

In the section on anticipating marriage and mate selection, we first noted that socialization provides little systematic knowledge regarding expectations from marriage. Also, boys tend to be socialized more toward the sexual, and girls more toward the emotional, aspect of heterosexual relationships. Dating was described as an exchange or bargaining situation in which the person with the most to offer has the most power. Within this dating "environment," moreover, there are several normative standards in existence. As we saw, the abstinence standard has decreased, while the love standard, or permissiveness with affection, is the most representative of postsecondary-school students. Homogamy is important to mate selection, with similar people getting married to each other more often than those who are different in social, economic, and physical characteristics. In addition, the woman in a marriage is often younger than the man. This age gap tends to entrench traditional gender differences.

In terms of marital interactions, the empty-nest stage is an important and relatively new stage in the life course. Another new stage is a premarital one involving young people living together before marriage. Considering models of the division of paid and unpaid work, about half of couples are in complementary-roles arrangements, with about a third in double burden, and one in eight a collaborative or role-sharing model.

Regarding childbearing, it was shown that children are expensive and that people are having fewer of them. There has been a weakening of the norm that childbearing is an essential part of marriage. Nonetheless, most couples have children and want to perform well in the difficult job of childrearing.

The rising level of marital dissolution was related to the decrease in instrumental functions played by the family, the increase in the importance of the expressive dimension in marriage, and the changing definition of the commitment.

Finally, while there is a larger variety of family forms today, including especially common-law unions and lone-parent families, there is also much continuity in the family patterns, with high priority for living in enduring relationships and having children. Just as the biggest change in the past thirty years has been associated with women's earning activities, there is some basis to anticipate that the future will show important changes in men's caring activities.

Questions for Review and Critical Thinking

1. There are a number of alternatives to the traditional husband/wife/two-children family (e.g., homosexual union, reconstituted family, patrilocality, and polygyny). Choose several alternatives and describe the strengths and weaknesses of each with respect to both instrumental and expressive functions.

2. Talk to your friends and try to determine how much expectations about mate selection and marriage vary by gender.

3. Is it cohabitation, per se, or is it the factors that encourage one to choose cohabitation over marriage, that lead to divorce?

4. What must occur before men and women will equally share caring activities in families?

Key Terms

abstinence standard, **p. 235**
collaborative or role-sharing model, **p. 240**
complementary-roles model, **p. 240**
double burden, **p. 240**
double standard, **p. 235**
expressive exchanges, **p. 226**
family, **p. 226**
fun standard, **p. 236**
heterogamy, **p. 238**
homogamy, **p. 238**
instrumental exchanges, **p. 226**
love standard, **p. 236**
marriage, **p. 226**
mating gradient, **p. 238**
premarital sexual standards, **p. 235**

Note: Other important terms are defined in Chart 10.1, **p. 227.**

Suggested Readings

Ambert, Anne-Marie

1992   *The Effect of Children on Parents.* New York: Haworth. Ambert considers the two-way relationships between parents and children, as well as the relevance of the broader social context. Children clearly have considerable effects on parents, and these are often not properly recognized.

Beaujot, Roderic

2004. *Delayed Life Transitions: Trends and Implications.* Contemporary Family Trends Paper on The Modern Life Course. Ottawa: Vanier Institute of the Family. **www.ivfamille.ca/library/cft/delayed_life.html**

The trends in delayed early life transitions, including home leaving, starting relationships and childbearing are put in the context of other changes affecting a lengthening of adolescents. Implications are discussed on questions relating to fertility, the life course, and retirement.

Beaujot, Roderic

2000   *Earning and Caring in Canadian Families.* Peterborough: Broadview.

This focus on the earning and caring activities of families provides a synthesis of research on family change, anticipating that more and more couples will adopt family models of co-providing and co-parenting.

Coltrane, Scott

1998   *Gender and Families.* Thousand Oaks, CA: Pine Forge Press.

Taking a social constructionist approach, and with much richness of historical detail, the author considers how family and gender are forged together.

Conway, John F.

2001   *The Canadian Family in Crisis.* Toronto: James Lorimer.

This book considers how family change affects the lives of children, women, and men. Relevant public policy considerations are offered for improving people's lives in a variety of family forms.

Goldscheider, Frances K. and Linda J. Waite

1991   *New Families, No Families?* Berkeley, CA: University of California Press.

The authors consider that unless families evolve toward new models of more egalitarian relations, many people will abandon them.

Péron, Yves, Hélène Desrosiers, Heather Juby, Evelyne Lapierre-Adamcyk, Céline Le Bourdais, Nicole Marcil-Gratton, and Jael Mongeau

1999   *Canadian Families at the Approach of the Year 2000.* Ottawa: Statistics Canada Catalogue No. 96-321, no. 4.

Using an abundance of data and analysis, this census monograph considers the changing family relations of women, men, and children.

Websites

www.yahoo.com/Society_and_Culture/Families
Yahoo! Society and Culture: Families
The perfect resource for doing research on family issues, this site provides links to dozens of sites worldwide dealing with topics from fatherhood to dating and marriage, to parenting generally.

www.cprn.org
Canadian Policy Research Network
The Family Network of the Canadian Policy Research Network is dedicated to advancing public debate on a full range of policy issues that relate to Canadian families.

www.vifamily.ca
The Vanier Institute of the Family
Since 1965 The Vanier Institute of the Family has done research on Canadian families and advocated on their behalf. This website is designed to enhance the understanding of issues and trends critical to Canadian families.

Key Search Terms

Family
Marriage
Children
Same-sex marriage
Divorce

For more study tools to help you with your next exam, be sure to check out the Companion Website at **www.pearsoned.ca/hewitt**, as well as Chapter 10 in your Study Guide.

[11]

religion

michael p. carroll and lorne l. dawson

Introduction

Throughout the first half of the twentieth century, Canada appeared to be a very religious nation. Most Canadians attended church services with some regularity, and almost everyone was baptized and got married in a church. A great many Canadians contributed money to religious charities, volunteered their time and labour to a wide variety of religious organizations, and participated in an array of social activities centred on their church. Religious leaders carried real influence in the affairs of their communities. In these respects, there were few differences between Canadians and Americans, and between Canadians and much of the rest of the Western world.

As North American families achieved new levels of affluence after World War II, they moved to the suburbs and built new churches at an unprecedented rate. Look around you, at your own community, and you will see the result: churches, and their associated auditoriums, schools, and community centres. Reflecting our heritage and the dominant patterns of immigration to that point, Canada was a Christian nation, and it thought of itself as such. In the first decades after the founding of

this country in 1867, during the Victorian era, it is no exaggeration to say that Christianity exercised a profound influence "on both the character of the nation and the Canadian character" (O'Toole, 2000: 67). There was a remarkable uniformity to the religious life of Canadians, since all but a tiny minority of people belonged either to the Catholic Church, the United Church of Canada, the Anglican Church, or the Presbyterian Church. These churches worked to bolster the middle-class values, norms, and goals favoured by the majority of Canadians. They helped to extend God's blessing to the status quo and to exhort Canadians to strive harder to achieve greater prosperity and social respectability. They also helped to temper the disruptive effects of industrialization and urbanization (see Chapter 15, Social Movements, and Chapter 16, Demography and Urbanization), and played an important role in creating the culture of concern for the social welfare of all that distinguishes Canadian public life from the politics of free-enterprise individualism in the United States.

The only significant religious division in the nation was between Catholics and Protestants, and in some parts of the country the traditional animosities between these groups were perpetuated. But the differences did not run deep. Canadians had learned long ago to accommodate these religious distinctions and to fashion a public world that did not significantly discriminate between Protestants and Catholics. Like most North Americans, we prided ourselves on leaving behind the serious conflicts over religion that plagued the "old world." In the "new world," many of our ancestors fervently believed, there was the opportunity to lay the foundation for a truly Christian society.

Some things have changed over the past half-century. In the late 1940s and early 1950s about 60 percent of Canadians attended church weekly. For Catholics the figure was as high as 83 percent. By the mid-1990s only 20 percent of Protestants and about 30 percent of Catholics attended church. Across North America, levels of religious participation began to plummet in the 1960s as many baby boomers rebelled against "the establishment," and about half of this huge demographic group chose to follow the ethic of the counter-culture, to "turn on, tune in, and drop out." In the 1980s many did return to the churches as they married and started to raise families. In fact, recent surveys provide some evidence suggesting that attendance levels may be rebounding a bit, especially in the case of conservative Protestant groups (Bibby, 2002; Table 11.1). Still, there is no denying that attendance levels in general are nowhere near what they were in the recent past.

There is also evidence suggesting that over the last fifty years Canada has become an increasingly secular society. The influence of religious symbols, ideas, and organizations on both the daily life and public affairs of this nation has waned dramatically. A Gallup poll done in 1955, the heyday of religious growth, found that 68 percent of Canadians felt that "religion as a whole is becoming a greater influence in Canadian life." By 1995,

Table 11.1 Weekly Religious Service Attendance in Canada, 1957–2000 (Percentage of Total Population)

	1957	1975	1990	2000
Total	53	31	24	21
Protestant	38	27	22	25
Conservative	51	41	49	58
Mainline	35	23	14	15
Catholic	83	45	33	26
Outside Quebec	75	48	37	32
Quebec	88	42	28	20

Sources: Bibby (2002: 73); Gallup poll, March 1957; 1975, 1990, 2000: Project Canada survey.

only 17 percent of Canadians would say the same thing (Bibby, 1995).

And yet appearances can be deceiving. Canadians continue to hold tenaciously to their traditional religious affiliations and, when questioned continue to display a relatively strong interest in religious and spiritual issues. For example, although proportionally fewer Canadians attend church on a regular basis, the vast majority of Canadians (83 percent) still identify with some particular religion (see the final column in Table 11.2). It is also the case that most Canadians report that they engage in private religious activities (like prayer, meditation, reading sacred texts, etc.) at least once a month (Clark and Schellenberg, 2006). As well, the number of Canadians who claim to believe in God, or to have personally experienced God in their lives, is

Table 11.2 Religious Identification of Canadians, 1871–2001 (Percentage of Total Population)

	1871	1901	1931	1961	1991	2001
Catholic	42	42	41	47	46	43
Eastern Orthodox	<1	<1	1	1	1	1
Protestant	56	56	54	49	36	29
Jewish	<1	<1	1	1	1	1
Other faiths	2	2	2	1	3	9
No religion	<1	<1	<1	<1	12	16

Source: Bibby (2002: 85); Statistics Canada, 2001 Census data, www.statcan.ca

Table 11.3   Religious Beliefs of Canadians (Percentage Responding "Definitely believe in" or "Think so")

	1975	1980	1985	1990	1995	2000
Does God exist?	89	85	84	82	80	81
Is there life after death?	73	69	65	68	71	68
Have you experienced God's presence?	48	43	44	43	41	47

Source: Adapted from Bibby (1995: 131–32; 2002: 119, 140, 147).

now as great as at any time in our past (Table 11.3). And although we live in a supposedly secular society, we tend increasingly to believe in such things as "near-death experiences," contact with spiritual beings (e.g., angels), and reincarnation (Bibby, 2002).

Are Canadians becoming less religious? Is religion destined to disappear from the modern world, and the Canadian experience typical? Is the continued interest in the supernatural and the spiritual merely a cultural rem-nant of a bygone era? Or are we in the midst of a significant shift in the nature of North American religiosity?

Throughout this century, most sociologists antici-pated that religion would decline into insignificance as societies modernized. But the United States, that most modern of all nations, has remained a surprisingly contrary case. This stark fact, along with the other counter-indicators detected in Canada and elsewhere are leading a growing number of sociologists to believe

[Social Trends]

Inventing the Religious Past We Need in the Present: The Goddess Meets da Vinci

During the 1970s and 1980s, as the feminist movement was gaining strength in North America, a number of books and documentary films (at least three of which were made by the National Film Board of Canada) advanced a startling thesis about religion: up until about 5000 years ago—well before the rise of known historical religions like the religions of Greece and Rome, Judaism, Christianity, and Islam—the dominant form of religion in most communities throughout the world, including Europe, was a Goddess religion. The "Goddess" involved might have had different names in different places, but in all places She was intimately associated with the Earth and the women who served Her possessed spiritual authority. In addition, the traditions that formed around the Goddess promoted a number of other things, among them the equality of females and males, and an emphasis on living in harmony with nature and with other human communities. It was a time of peace and well-being.

According to the view of prehistory advanced in these books and films, the idyllic world of the Goddess came to a crashing halt with the rise of patriarchal and warlike cultures whose male-centered religions came to supplant the religion of the Goddess.

Although the Goddess hypothesis still has some supporters, it is not nearly as popular now, in large part because archaeologists—many of whom are deeply com-mitted to feminism (Eller, 2000)—have pointed out the lack of any real archaeological evidence to support it. Basically, what seems to have happened is that proponents of the Goddess hypothesis took a number of gender beliefs that were popular in the 1970s and 1980s (women and men are fundamentally different; women are more "connected" to nature; men are innately aggressive; etc.) and projected these beliefs onto an invented past. Why? ... because it served a social function in the present. Solutions to global warming, environmental degradation, and the threat of

(continued)

nuclear war were available in the return to a time when the Goddess ruled, when "womanly virtues" were predominant, and when societies lived in tune with nature.

Although support for the Goddess hypothesis has faded, the pattern encountered in this case—inventing a religious past in order to change the present—is still with us. Consider, for example, the immense popularity of the novel *The Da Vinci Code* (Brown, 2003.)

The premise of *The Da Vinci Code* is simple: Jesus and Mary Magdalene were a married couple and of equal importance in the early Church. By extension, Christianity was originally characterized by gender equality. Unfortunately, during the fourth century, the male leaders of the Church effected their own patriarchal revolution and suppressed all knowledge of Mary Magdalene's role in the early Church and exaggerated Jesus' role by making him divine. Knowledge of that historical truth survived, however, and came to be encoded into certain objects (after all, doesn't Leonardo da Vinci's *Last Supper* show, clearly and unambiguously, Jesus and a *woman* presiding over, well, the Last Supper?).

Although *The Da Vinci Code* is identified as a novel, it is nevertheless an interesting mixture of scholarship and invention. For example, its suggestion that a belief in the divinity of Jesus was not at all central to the earliest Christian traditions, but only became increasingly popular among Christians over time, is one routinely encountered in the scholarly literature on early Christianity. On the other hand, most of the statements relating to Mary Magdalene and her role in the early Church, though they are statements made in other popular books (and often presented as fact), are generally seen by knowledgeable scholars as unsupported. Even so, a great many people seem willing to entertain the possibility that the book's story line is roughly accurate. So, how do we explain the book's popularity? One possibility is that *The Da Vinci Code* was popular because like the Goddess hypothesis it presents a story that uses the past to legitimate a current concern.

Thus, it is common in both the Catholic and Protestant tradition to legitimate a particular belief or practice by suggesting that this is what "Jesus intended." The Catholic Church, for instance, legitimates its insistence that only males can be priests by pointing to Biblical stories that say that Jesus chose only males to be his Apostles and thus suggests that these stories are evidence that Jesus intended priests to be male. In the context of this sort of reasoning what better way to legitimate the belief, held by many modern Christians, that women should share in the leadership of Christian communities (and in the Catholic case specially, that women should be allowed to be priests) than by promoting the belief that Jesus himself shared his leadership with a woman?

Can you think of any other stories about "religion in the past" that are likely popular not because they rest on any solid evidence but rather because these stories can be used to legitimate beliefs about "the ways things should change" in today's society?

that religion will continue to be an important element of our societies for the foreseeable future. Complete secularization now seems unlikely. Industrialization, urbanization, the growth of science, education, and the state, have all effected a permanent change in the forms and functions of religion as a social institution. But it seems that religiosity and modernity can coexist. How this is the case and for how long is another matter, as are the consequences of these changes for other aspects of the social order. In much of the rest of the world religion not only continues to be a primary marker of social identity, but its salience has increased in the face of threats to cultural autonomy posed by the processes of globalization. Islamic, Hindu, and Buddhist nationalist movements now dominate the political life of countries like Iran, Pakistan, and Myanmar. Christians and Muslims waged war in Bosnia-Herzegovina and in Kosovo in the 1980s and 1990s, Buddhists and Tamil Hindus have been at war since the 1980s in Sri Lanka, and violent clashes between Christians and Muslims are now common in India and the Philippines. In China the ruling Communist Party has struggled to suppress such increasingly popular expressions of mass cultural and social discontent as the Falun Gong, a new religious movement, and the so-called "underground" Christian churches. Tens of millions of Chinese are turning their backs on decades of official atheism.

Studying Religious Life Sociologically

In light of the central role of religion in shaping social relations throughout history, sociologists have long been concerned with questions about the role of religion. The founding figures of sociology—Marx, Durkheim, and Weber—all paid extensive and careful attention to religion, and their insights continue to inform contemporary sociological discussions of religion. Living in the late nineteenth and early twentieth centuries, they were able to see first-hand how changes in religion were part of a larger and disruptive social transformation from a premodern to a modern social order. Today, sociologists are equally intent on understanding the transition from a modern to a postmodern society. Are these social changes, and

our responses to them, being reflected once again in the changing nature of the religious life of Canadians? To even begin to answer this question, we must first pause to consider a few special features of the academic study of religion.

The challenges of research on religion

In trying to understand religion from a social-scientific perspective, scholars have struggled with a number of methodological and conceptual issues: Can social science study the religious experience? How can it define religion? How can it measure *religiosity*, the act of being religious? How is the experience of religion today different, if it is different, from the experience of religion in times past? Each of these questions is the

Throughout the world, religion continues to be a primary marker of social identity. Even in countries where the government has actively suppressed religion and religious practices because they are perceived as being disruptive to social order, expressions of religion continue to be active and, if necessary, move underground. In China, for example, followers of the Falun Gong movement continue to practise despite having come under attack by government officials.

subject of long, complex, and still largely unresolved debates. But for our purposes, it is sufficient to specify a few key points.

Studying the religious experience

Many of the greatest scholars of religion have long argued that religious experience, in its essence, is unique. It cannot be explained in terms of anything else, and most certainly not the kinds of things that social scientists can measure, compare, and criticize. The "religious" is, as Otto (1917) said, "wholly other." In the face of the fervent claims made for the core experience of religion, most sociologists of religion have adopted a position of methodological "detachment." They do not seek to determine the truth or falsity of religious assertions about the **supernatural**, or that which lies beyond day-to-day experience. The task of sociology is to detect and gauge the nature and significance of the human consequences of such claims and experiences. For the purposes of sociological analysis, it can remain an open question whether the gods or God exist; that is a matter for the philosophers and theologians to debate. Sociologists will confine their attention to those aspects of people's religious life that can be observed and measured in some way.

Defining religion

The great diversity of things that people have held to be holy or sacred through the centuries and across the world poses a fundamental problem for sociologists of religion. What is it that they are studying? No consensus on a definition has ever been reached due, in part, to a split between substantive and functional definitions.

Substantive definitions of religion emphasize what religion "is," by focusing on some crucial and presumably universal feature of religious activity. A classic illustration of this substantive approach is provided by Tylor (1903), the eminent British anthropologist, who suggested that *religion* be defined as "belief in Spiritual Beings." He is the same man who provided an early definition of *culture* in Chapter 3, Culture. On first glance, this simple definition seems plausible enough. But in fact most scholars have found it to be too exclusive. In the first place, many argue that belief is only one aspect of religion, and in many religions, both old and new, belief is secondary to various forms of action and

practice. Contemporary Wiccans and Neo-Pagans, for example, practise similar forms of magic and ritual, yet their beliefs are tremendously diverse. Participation in rituals takes precedence over beliefs. Indeed a stress on *beliefs* in studying religion, though common in sociology, may reflect an ethnocentric bias and, in particular, a bias that derives from the European Protestant tradition (given that that tradition sees the Biblical text as central to religion). Secondly, many Wiccans and Neo-Pagans, like many Buddhists, simply reject the reality of supernatural beings. Are these groups to be excluded from the study of religion? Finally, like most substantive definitions of religion, Tylor's definition suffers from an additional problem. It relies on a term that is itself in need of further definition. What, we should ask, constitutes a "spiritual being"?

Functionalist definitions of religion focus on what religion "does," and tend to suffer from the reverse limitation: they can be too broad and inclusive. The American sociologist of religion Yinger (1970) framed a well-known functionalist definition of religion: "Religion [is] a system of beliefs and practices by means of which a group struggles with [the] ultimate problems of human life." Certainly this approach could encompass both the Wiccans and the Buddhists, along with most other conventional religions. But these terms of reference make it difficult to differentiate between religion and various other "functional equivalents" to religion in society. Some people may throw themselves quite whole-heartedly into the service of some cause, like the fight for political freedom or an attempt to save the environment. They may derive much of their understanding of the world, and a sense of ultimate meaning and worth, from engaging in these activities. But is this the same as being religious?

In most cases, sociologists of religion work with a rather commonsensical definition of their subject matter, and, when pressed, defend it as best suited to their present research interests. They work at all times, however, with an appreciation of the intrinsic limitations of any one definition of religion. This said, as a working definition we shall simply suggest that a **religion** is a system of beliefs and practices about transcendent things, their nature, and their consequences for humanity. The transcendent refers here to some level, type, or dimension of reality that is thought to be intrinsically different from, and in some sense higher than, or beyond, our ordinary experience of the world.

Measuring religiosity

Given the difficulties sociologists have in coping with the core experience of much of religious life, and in defining religion, it should come as no surprise that measuring how religious people are, their *religiosity*, is problematic as well. Survey researchers regularly ask people about their religious affiliations, levels of attendance, belief in God, and so on. But as almost everyone recognizes, if only from personal experience, the answers to these questions can be poor indicators of how truly religious people are. Some people attend religious services with great regularity, but do not seem to put their religion into practice in their daily lives. Others strike us as being really very pious or spiritual, though they rarely attend any organized religious services. Religiosity is a complex blend of states of mind, attitudes, and behaviours, and people can be religious in several ways. An adequate measure of religiosity should access information about all the aspects and ways of being religious. With this in mind, Glock and Stark (1965) recommended inquiring into at least eight dimensions of religious life to assess: (1) the *experiential*, whether people think they have had contact with the supernatural; (2) the *ritualistic*, their level of participation in public rites; (3) the *devotional*, their level of participation in activities like praying or saying grace before meals; (4) *belief*, the degree

to which they agree with the doctrines of their faith; (5) *knowledge*, their degree of recognition and understanding of the beliefs of their religion; (6) the *consequential*, the effects of their religion on their everyday life; (7) the *communal*, the extent to which they associate with others members of the same religion; and lastly, (8) the *particularistic*, the degree to which they think their religion is the one and only true path to salvation.

This multidimensional approach stimulated a great deal of research. One finding, now widely appreciated, is that a person may score high on any one or a cluster of these dimensions and thus appear very religious, while scoring low on other dimensions, in seeming contradiction of that religiosity. Much can be learned then about both the style and the degree of the religiosity of individuals, groups, and whole societies, by devising survey and interview questions that measure these dimensions. The design of these research instruments can be quite complicated, however, and poses additional problems. Glock and Stark tended to use conventional criteria to measure each dimension in their work on American piety with at least two undesirable consequences. First, unconventional religious practices, like the belief in astrology, were simply excluded from their study. Second, a bias toward a more conservative style of Christianity was implicitly built into their measures. At every point, then, the sociology of religion is dogged by conceptual difficulties posed by the sheer diversity of ways in which people can be religious.

Moreover, no matter how one chooses to measure religiosity, every approach is plagued by the problems of self-reporting. Hadaway, Long-Marler, and Chaves (1993; 1998), and others, have found serious discrepancies between the levels of church attendance Americans commonly report to pollsters and the actual number of people counted in the pews of a sample of Protestant and Catholic churches. In general, people are inclined to provide researchers with answers that exaggerate their religiosity because it is still thought of as socially desirable to be at least somewhat religious, especially in the United States.

The Insights and Issues of Classical Theory

The founding figures of sociology studied religion because they were interested in understanding the changes occurring in their own European society as it

Mystics reject the world perceived with the senses as illusory, and seek a passive endurance of earthly trials and tribulations through a learned detachment.

[Social Trends]

The Golden Age That Wasn't

It is common, in thinking about religion in the world today, to make some implicit assumptions about religion in the past. The problem is that quite often these assumptions are wrong. For instance, a great many people believe that religion is far less important to ordinary people today than it was centuries ago. But does the historical evidence support this? Not at all—at least, not at all if we are talking about European societies. There are many historical studies (reviewed in Greeley, 1995) suggesting just the reverse: religion was hardly important at all. In most European communities, for instance, people rarely if ever attended church services (and they certainly did not attend on a weekly basis) and, as any number of local bishops loudly complained, most villagers were completely ignorant of core Christian beliefs. Nor did the Church play a role in activities that we today take for granted. Consider marriage. The aristocracy aside, the vast majority of people living in European communities did not get married in a church or even with a priest in

attendance. They simply set up what today would be a common-law arrangement. Such marriages were considered perfectly lawful both by Church and civil authorities and remained the norm in European societies well into the 1600s. On the other hand, from the 1600s forward the Church increasingly played a role in life events like marriage. Over time, in other words, and partly due to the Protestant Reformation, the Catholic Church and new Protestant churches gradually began to play a greater, not a lesser, role in the daily lives of ordinary people.

What all this means is that in thinking about religion we must avoid thinking of it as something that has declined in a simple linear fashion over time. Quite the contrary, the historical evidence suggests that the popularity of religion has waxed and waned over time and not always in the same way in all locations. One of the goals of the sociologist, then, in studying religion, is to identify the changing social conditions that fuel the rise and fall (and rise and fall again) of particular religions in particular locations.

What social factors do you think are driving the resurgence in conservative religious belief?

was jolted from traditional order into the modern world. Marx, Durkheim, and Weber had diverse responses to these changes and they focused on different aspects of the role that religious beliefs and practices played in promoting or resisting the social changes associated with modernity. But they all recognized the importance of the sociology of religion to the discipline of sociology as a whole.

Marx: Religion and ideology

Marx (1818–1883) believed that, in every age, religion served to justify the rule of one class over another. That hierarchy was seen either as divinely ordained or as part of the natural order of things. Fundamentally, Marx proposed—quite scandalously—that humanity had not been created in the image of God, as the Bible said. On the contrary, the gods or God had been created in the image of humanity. The beliefs and teachings of religion, he

stated, are comforting illusions, designed to compensate people for the sacrifices and misery of their present lives with promises of rewards for good behaviour in another life. Today he is still famous for his colourful phrase characterizing religion as "the opium of the people" (Marx, 1972 [1844]: 38). The quest for religious virtue subdues the mind and distorts thinking, he argued, just like a powerful narcotic, distracting people from developing a critical appreciation of the real source of their deprivation: their economic and political exploitation at the hands of a dominant class. In their visions of heaven they thus acknowledge the inadequacies of this world, but misidentify the reasons for their disappointment.

For Marx, Christianity was a clear example of how religion served the interests of the ruling class to the detriment of the working class. After all, in most Christian traditions, what is the one thing that should be of utmost importance to all true Christians? Obviously: to do what needs to be done in order to get to heaven and spend eternity with God. In other words, Marx argued, the Christian message suggests that what happens in *this* world—including the fact that one is poor, oppressed, etc.—is far less important than what happens in a supposed *next* world and so it discourages people from thinking about their lot in this world. For Marx, Christianity also promoted the interests of the ruling classes to the extent that particular Christian denominations stress blind obedience to authority or beliefs that certain forms of inequality (the inequality of males and females, for example) are established by God.

But Christianity is not the only religion to which a Marxist analysis can be applied. Central to most Hindu traditions, for instance, is a belief in continuous reincarnation. People are born, live a life, die, and then are re-born to live another life—and the process continues again. In any particular life, what determines your social position within Hindu society? Well, basically, it's how well one fulfilled the ritual obligations (which are very specifically defined) associated with the social position occupied in a previous life. What that means, in effect, is that if a Hindu is poor in this life it is because of what was done in the preceding life. Not blamed are the dominant elites in society whose decisions affect the distribution of wealth.

Durkheim: Religion and social solidarity

Durkheim, while no more religious than Marx, saw a greater purpose for religion in society. Seeking to help create a stable modern state in France during the social and political disruptions of the late nineteenth and early twentieth centuries, Durkheim was keenly interested in understanding the processes that held societies together, that kept them unified and strong in the face of adversity and change. Throughout his life, this central concern led him to the study of religion.

In the past, he believed, religious beliefs and practices had protected the moral integrity of social relations. They worked to hold individualistic impulses at bay, while cultivating an altruistic desire to serve the needs of the group even above those of the individual. Unlike Marx, then, Durkheim had no interest in dismissing religion as an unnecessary illusion. On the contrary, he was worried about what might happen to the social solidarity of society should religion wane in the modern world. But like Marx, Durkheim sought a natural and not a supernatural explanation for the persistence of religious convictions. He did not doubt the reality and the power of religious experience and instead argued that the origins of religion are to be found in the experience of *society* itself.

Durkheim devised a theory of religion based on the study of what was then thought to be one of the simplest of religions, that of an Australian Aboriginal group, the Arunta. The information available to Durkheim was seriously flawed and much of what he said about the Arunta is now considered to be mistaken. But this deficiency has done little to diminish the lasting impact of his perceptive insights into the more general nature and functioning of religion. With his study of Aboriginal religion in mind, Durkheim defined religion as "a unified system of beliefs and practices relative to sacred things . . . which unite into one single moral community . . . all those who adhere to them" (1965). This definition combines both substantive and functional elements. Concern with the sacred is the substantive element that differentiates religion from other activities, while functionally, religion is to be identified with the social processes that create a sense of community. In a rather circular manner, these elements are both assumed and supposedly demonstrated by Durkheim's theory of religion.

Durkheim began his analysis of religion with a fundamental observation or assumption that then posed a problem that he, in turn, addressed with another observation or assumption. The most distinctive trait of traditional religious life, Durkheim stipulated, is the division of all things into two opposed categories: the *sacred* and the *profane*. The **sacred**, Durkheim said, is that which is set apart and treated with special awe and respect. What is sacred in any society is highly variable, and, as Durkheim acknowledged, almost every kind of thing has been sacred for someone at some time, from particular trees and rocks, to blessed spaces within magnificent temples, particular writings, or the stars in the heavens. The sacred, whatever it may be, is thought to possess a tremendous and unique power that requires people to take special care in its presence. The sacred provides a kind of fixed point in reality, around which the ordinary or everyday—the **profane**—circulates. Religious systems place people in controlled contact with the sacred in order to call upon its power to protect them from the challenges of profane life. But, Durkheim asked, "What has been able to lead men to see in the world two heterogeneous and incompatible worlds, though nothing in sensible experience seems able to suggest the idea of so radical a duality?" (1965). The answer, he proposed, is to be found in another elemental fact of religious life. Religion, unlike the mere practice of magic or superstition, is always a *group* activity. It is a social phenomenon and, like the religion of the Arunta, deeply concerned with the regulation of the internal and external relations of the group. In traditional societies, religious rites are almost always associated with special times of collective festivity. In the repetitive performance of these group rituals, the Arunta and others, Durkheim thought, encounter the true experiential basis for their belief in the reality and power of the sacred.

Durkheim observed two features of being in the presence of things deemed sacred. First, devotees are moved by feelings of heightened strength. Second, believers feel that this strength comes from sharing in a power that is both outside of themselves and greater than themselves, and capable of acting upon them with or without their consent. There is a real basis for both beliefs, Durkheim reasoned, but it is not the one that religious people interpret it to be. By participating in the concerted action of a group, in the performance of a religious cult of worship and sacrifice, individuals are bringing themselves into intimate contact with two powerful aspects of social life itself: what Durkheim called the *collective conscience* and *collective effervescence*. The carefully orchestrated and solemn acts of ritual have a disciplining effect on participants, directing their attention to the ideals and sentiments they share with their group. They are lifted, for a time, out of the limited horizon of their own personal preoccupations, and exposed through highly condensed symbols, gestures, and stories to an intuitive grasp of the collective wisdom of their society—to the **collective conscience**. This moving reaffirmation of their heritage and their secure place in a larger cultural whole is, Durkheim argued, both invigorating and reassuring and all the more so because the sheer numbers of people involved and their physical closeness have their own psychological effect upon them. Caught up in the emotional and almost contagious energy of a crowd, people will often experience levels of enthusiasm, ecstasy, pride, and fear quite out of keeping with their solitary experience. This sense of **collective effervescence** can inspire, for a time at least, a sense of quite superhuman strength in each individual, like soldiers entering battle or participants in large political rallies or sporting events. More on this topic will come in Chapter 15, Social Movements.

The social experience itself, then, contains the properties of religious experience, as understood by Durkheim. Through the practice of the religion, the members of a group are bonded together, and the uplifting effect of this bond serves to perpetuate their feelings of empowerment, and hence, in endless circular fashion, their continued belief in the things deemed sacred and their social solidarity.

Weber: Protestantism and the rise of capitalism

Weber provided us with one of the most profound and comprehensive sociologies of religion. His works reflect an encyclopaedic knowledge of religious traditions worldwide and the historical circumstances of their development. Yet in some respects Weber's abiding interest in religion was merely a by-product of his initial

Durkheim believed that the power the sacred seems to have over the minds of individuals is really the power the group has over the minds of individuals.

and chief concern: the origins and nature of modernity. In examining such institutional manifestations of modernity as capitalism, bureaucratic administration, and the creation of autonomous legal systems (see Chapter 14, Organizations and Work), Weber believed he could detect a common and essential feature of modernity: an *ascetic* ethic of vocation. Unlike their medieval counterparts, the people involved in the creation and operation of the early systems of modern commerce, government, and law performed their tasks with an unprecedented diligence and lack of concern for their immediate material benefit. The first capitalists, Weber argued for instance, differed from traditional merchants because they would forgo spending the profits earned on new luxuries in favour of reinvesting the profits in their businesses. By adopting this more **ascetic** approach, and denying themselves the pleasures of the material world, they prospered as their investments earned them greater profits and they accumulated capital. This approach to their work, their **vocation**, Weber concluded, fuelled the spirit of capitalism that emerged from Western Europe to transform the world.

But how, Weber asked, did this rather unnatural ascetic ethic of vocation arise? Noting the disproportionate number of Protestants over Catholics involved in business and related professions in his own times, Weber argued that the ascetic impulse underlying capitalism might be the unique legacy of the Protestant Reformation. He developed this idea in his famous book *The Protestant Ethic and the Spirit of Capitalism* (1958 [1904]), where he traced the spirit of capitalism to the psychological effects of two doctrines introduced by the Protestant reformers who broke with Catholicism in the sixteenth century: Martin Luther's concept of the *calling* and John Calvin's *doctrine of predestination*.

Like the medieval Church, Luther believed that all people have a divinely ordained **calling** (i.e., an occupation to which God has assigned them). Some people are called by God to be peasants, others to be lawyers, etc.— and some are called to be capitalists. But whereas the medieval Church had suggested that some callings (like being a monk) were more valuable in God's eyes than others, Luther argued that all callings were equal in importance. For Weber, this meant that Luther's doctrine contributed to the rise of capitalism because it gave labour, even in the pursuit of profit, a moral legitimacy that it did not previously possess.

But for Weber what really gave rise to values and behaviours that defined the spirit of modern capitalism was the **doctrine of predestination** developed by John Calvin, another Reformation leader. Stressing the omnipotence and the omniscience of God, Calvin argued that the ultimate status of believers, whether they are saved or damned, is something God has predetermined. Individuals can do nothing to either know or change their predestined status without calling into question God's supremacy. It is not appropriate for lowly and largely sinful humans to question the ways of God. Thus the Catholic belief in the power of good deeds, confession, or the sacraments, was illusory.

Faced with such a severe view of our fate, Weber speculated that many ordinary Protestants were driven to find solace in some covert sign of their salvation. For these truly religious people, the uncertainty of their destiny would be an agony. Protestant pastors were advised to tell their parishioners to work hard at their lay callings, have faith in their fate, and avoid the doubts about salvation that are the temptation of the devil. Idle hands, they were repeatedly told, are the devil's helpmates. So with time, and through sheer hard labour, success in one's worldly calling became an unofficial sign that one was saved. But this success could stand as a sign of God's favour only if one did not indulge in the obvious displays of wealth that signified one had succumbed to the contaminating pleasures of the flesh. Thus to secure individual peace of mind and social prestige in their communities, the early Protestants were induced to lead relatively humble and industrious lives, faithfully reinvesting their profits in their businesses. In this ironic way, then, out of deep religious devotion and need, the motivation was provided for the endless cycle of accumulation and reinvestment so pivotal to the rise of capitalism. With time and mounting material success, this new spirit of capitalism would itself succeed the Protestant ethic (the ethical orientation toward work as a divine calling) as the motivational wellspring of modern society.

Understanding the forms of religious life

Much of the work done in the sociology of religion, particularly since World War II, has been dedicated to the empirical study of specific aspects of religious life. Thousands of studies have tried to determine how religious beliefs and practices influence or are influenced by such other features of our social existence as racial prejudice, mental health, sexual attitudes, and political

Legitimating Religion in Contemporary Society

The traditional legitimating task of religion is being disrupted by two new realities of religious life: *privatization* and *pluralism*. In the past, people almost automatically practised the faith of their families, and in largely the same way as their parents and grandparents. Over the course of the twentieth century, however, religious beliefs and practices became a private matter—a matter of individual choice. But as religion becomes increasingly private, it cannot be called upon to support a truly common and transcendent universe of meaning and order. Likewise, in the face of the growing plurality of religions available in most Western societies, it is becoming more difficult to convince oneself and others of the absolute truth of one's faith, that one's religion is something more than a mere preference. In these societies there is a revival of various Neo-Pagan practices from medieval times; the East and West are being integrated with ever-greater presence of Hindu, Buddhist, and other traditions in North America and Europe; and all the established religions are being confronted with new competition from innovative faiths, ranging from Mormonism to Scientology and Eckankar. In these circumstances, when most public institutions and day-to-day social contacts may no longer reinforce one's beliefs, religion loses its taken-for-granted quality. Instead, for both the exponents and potential followers of many religions, religion becomes more like a product to be sold, using the latest marketing techniques, to an increasingly wary public of religious consumers. Can such commodified religions perform the primary function of religion effectively? Alternatively, will other religions elect to retreat from the conditions of the modern world in order to still perform this function effectively, if at the cost of cutting themselves off from the source of new members and hence any real chance of growing and influencing contemporary society?

Does the satisfaction of religious needs require a belief that the chosen path to salvation is the only one and true way?

preferences. In other words, researchers have been exploring ways in which religion operates as either an *independent* or the *dependent* variable in the shaping of our societies (see Chapter 2, Research Methods). Likewise, a strong need persists to simply acquire reliable information about the size, nature, and functioning of an enormous variety of religious groups, ranging from such mainstream organizations as the Catholic Church or the Lutherans through more recent and rapidly growing groups like the Mormons (Church of Jesus Christ of Latter-day Saints) and the Pentecostals. In the last few decades, for example, a lot of research has been undertaken into the nature of new religious movements (or cults) like the Unification Church (i.e., the Moonies), Krishna Consciousness, Scientology, or Wicca (i.e., contemporary witchcraft). The seemingly sudden conversion of many well-educated, middle-class, young people to these alternative religions, beginning in the 1960s, stirred up a great deal of controversy (see Dawson, 1998). So did the shocking mass suicides and murders perpetrated by members of the Branch Davidians (1993), the Solar Temple (1994, and again in 1995 and 1997), Aum Shinrikyo (1995), Heaven's Gate (1997), and The Movement for the Restoration of the Ten Commandments (2000). Using questionnaires, interviews, and participant observation, sociologists have striven to analyze, classify, and explain the current various forms of religious life.

In classifying religious groups, sociologists have traditionally taken their lead from an initial distinction drawn by Weber (1958 [1904]) between *church* and *sect*, and further developed by Troeltsch (1931). The church/sect typology, which is based largely on a Christian organizational model, has been modified in myriad ways, creating a confusing array of types and subtypes of religious organizations. Here we need only consider a few of the most basic and popular schemes.

According to Troeltsch, **churches** are organizations into which people are born and baptized as infants. Membership is involuntary. **Sects** are voluntary organizations to which people usually convert, frequently as the result of very emotional experiences. All kinds of people can and do belong to churches; they are inclusive and their membership is heterogeneous. Sects tend to be much more homogeneous in their membership, drawing disproportionately from the underprivileged elements of society. This situation often reflects the fact that sects are created by schisms within a church that is aligned with the dominant social structure. The beliefs and practices of sects, then, tend to be more radical and ethically stern than those of churches, and constitute an act of protest against the values of the rest of society. Sects tend to be exclusive: individuals must meet and maintain certain clear requirements to belong. Sectarians perceive themselves as an elect, and those who contravene the group's precepts are subject to expulsion much more readily than in churches. The leadership of churches is usually hired or appointed on the basis of special educational qualifications. It operates within a hierarchical and impersonal administrative structure. Sectarian leadership tends to be charismatic, and, in line with this feature, sects tend to have smaller, more democratic, and personal organizational structures. In theology and liturgy, churches are inclined to be dogmatic and ritualistic. Sects reflect a more inspirational, volatile, and even anti-ritualistic orientation.

This fundamental distinction has been expanded to encompass a wider array of additional types of religious groups. In one well-known formulation Yinger (1970) proposed a six-fold typology, based on two criteria: how inclusive or exclusive a group is and its attention to the integration of its members into the dominant society. In order of decreasing inclusiveness and decreasing attention to integration, Yinger distinguished between the **universal church** (e.g., the Catholic Church); the **ecclesia**—that is, the established national church (e.g., the Church of England or the Sunni Islamic faith of Saudi Arabia); the **denomination** (e.g., Presbyterians or Baptists); the *established sect* (e.g., Jehovah's Witnesses or Christian Science);

[Applied Sociology]

Why Do Cult Suicides Happen?

Thirty-nine members of Heaven's Gate killed themselves in Rancho Santa Fe, California. Why? Five members of the Solar Temple committed suicide in Saint-Casimir, Quebec. Why? We cannot really say with precision, but we can say more than is commonly supposed.

Each of these tragedies stems from the interplay of a rather complex set of external and internal factors. The external factors—such as the nature and levels of hostility, stigmatization, and persecution experienced by a group— vary widely and make comparisons difficult. But analysts have linked at least three internal features of new religious movements to the outbreak of violence: apocalyptic belief systems, heavy investments in charismatic leadership, and processes of social encapsulation. These are among the prime conditions necessary for the eruption of major incidents of cult-related violence, though they may not be sufficient to predict this violence.

In each of the recent cases, *apocalyptic* beliefs— prophecies about the ultimate end of human history— played a crucial role, structuring and motivating the acts of those who died. The Book of Revelation presents a terrifying narrative of the world's destruction, laced with obscure symbolism and exotic imagery. Since the early Christians, in every generation there have been those who eagerly awaited the end and the return of Christ. In their eyes the events they experience conform to those prophesied and they have prepared to face the tribulations foretold and to meet their Maker. This was the case with the Branch Davidians in Waco. For the Solar Temple and Heaven's Gate members, another element was added to the mix: an eclectic blend of occult and New Age beliefs drawn from the lore, for example, of the medieval Knights Templar, alternative forms of medicine, and a belief in the reality of UFOs and alien interventions in human history.

(continued)

A number of behavioural consequences commonly follow from these apocalyptic beliefs. First, anticipation of the apocalypse tends to lead to a questioning of conventional norms and rules, even the law itself. What good are the codes of an inadequate humanity in the face of the ultimate acts of divine justice and retribution? The righteous will not require the force of law to live in peace and joy, and the evil are destined to perish. Second, serious anticipation entails preparing to deal with violent times and the persecution of the righteous. Weapons must be secured and defences prepared (building shelters, storing supplies, generally training to be self-sufficient). These preparations set the stage for actual violence, as people look for evidence to confirm their fears and legitimize their plans.

This leads to a third behavioural consequence: the emotionally volatile conception of one's fate bolsters the common tendency to "demonize" perceived enemies. Opponents are portrayed as being capable of the most heinous acts, and thus they can be resisted with extreme force. Fourth, a life lived in serious expectation of the end tends to instil a level of enthusiasm that alters judgment.

Yet tens of millions of North Americans hold apocalyptic beliefs today, and they are not violent. It is the association of this world view with a messianic charismatic leader—a man or woman who identifies the signs of the apocalypse with the events of his or her own life—that makes the difference. The authority of such leaders is founded in a deeply personal relationship of extraordinary faith and trust. But this kind of authority is intrinsically precarious. Even the success of their own group poses a threat, for it diminishes the amount of personal contact and dependency crucial to the maintenance of the leader's personal charisma.

To counteract this loss of authority, charismatic leaders often revert to strategies that reinforce the destabilizing effects of an apocalyptic world view. By instituting

sudden shifts in doctrines and policies, for example, they seek to reassert their superiority, forcing some of the old guard to the margins while elevating new people to power. Similarly, these leaders will initiate a progressive escalation of the demands on members for service and sacrifice to the group, as a test of their loyalty and commitment. Close relationships among followers are disrupted to prevent alternative sources of power from arising. The demonization of "outsiders" is extended, crises are invented, and dissidents are expelled to galvanize the solidarity of the group and its focus on the leader.

This struggle to overcome the precariousness of charismatic authority leads to a progressive intensifying of the leader's power, along with the increased homogenization, dependency, and social and physical isolation of the followers, setting the conditions for some of these leaders to indulge the darker desires of their subconscious.

In such a cycle, the new religions that are subject to these tendencies will become ever more extreme in their beliefs and practices and suspicious of others, while the surrounding society will become ever more repelled by or hostile to these groups. Socially and physically, new barriers to meaningful contact and feedback will be erected. A process of social encapsulation will set in. For example, the Solar Temple worked very hard to increase the symbolic distance between its spiritual elite and the uninitiated.

As the gulf between the group and the rest of society widens, it is increasingly difficult for the members to gauge whether their behaviour is becoming bizarre and maladaptive. In the absence of alternative views, and in the face of a perceived threat of dissolution or final promise of rapture, the ultimate solution may be invoked: the "transit" to another world of the Solar Temple and Heaven's Gate. In most cases, this will not happen; but with greater public awareness and appropriate vigilance, it need never happen.

Source: Lorne Dawson (2000). Originally published in *The Globe and Mail*, 31 March 1997. Reprinted with permission of the author.

What other factors might play a role in precipitating these tragic events?

the *sect* (e.g., Pentecostal churches or the Worldwide Church of God); and the **cult**, a closed religious system in which the members often live, work, and worship in close proximity (e.g., the Unification Church or Scientology). These categories have been

subdivided further by other sociologists (see Dawson, 1998).

In each case, it must be recognized that religious groups may be transformed. As Niebuhr observed in *The Social Sources of Denominationalism* (1929), as sects develop they tend to become more like churches. New generations are born to the faith and socialized into the set ways of the community, and the original sense of protest against the norms of the dominant society fades from memory. Likewise, if a cult manages to grow, it may take on the features and increased stability of a sect. In either case, the movement toward establishment may spawn new acts of religious dissent, and hence new sects or cults.

In the end, the strengths and weaknesses of the various typologies are open for debate. So is the classification of specific groups. Are the Mormons, for example, a cult, sect, established sect, denomination, or even church? The answer will depend on whom you ask, what period of history you have in mind, and in what part of the world. In the context of southern Ontario, the Mormons may be viewed as a sect, but a denomination or even an ecclesia in the state of Utah. Despite some differences of opinion, however, sociologists still use the basic church/sect/cult typology in their analyses and discussions.

Within an established church, religious experience is highly ritualized.

Contemporary Conceptions of Religion: Secularization

Building on the insights of Durkheim and Weber, sociologists like Wilson (1982) and Luckmann (1967) argued that the process of rationalization works against the interests and power of traditional religions in society, by reducing the scope of the functions of religion. Where once almost all aspects of social life fell under the influence, if not direct rule, of religion, what has happened over the last several centuries is that ever-larger segments of daily life have been segregated from religious authority and relegated to other institutions. Authority has been transferred, in other words, from religion to economic, political, medical, educational, recreational, and even family institutions. This process, what sociologists call *institutional differentiation*, not only stripped religious institutions of their manifest power in social affairs, but also subverted the many latent or unintended functions that religions long performed. In this most fundamental way, contemporary society has been secularized, and few sociologists would disagree.

Yet, as indicated earlier, there is significant disagreement about whether these and other developments are destined to bring an end to religion altogether, as anticipated by Marx. Contemporary opinions have been influenced heavily by a recent and seminal theory of religion that epitomizes the subtle but important differences in the way **secularization**, the process by which sectors of society are removed from the domination of religious institutions and symbols, can be interpreted. This new theory of religion is called the theory of religious economies, and it has been advanced most forcefully by Stark, an American sociologist, and a variety of associates (Finke and Stark, 1992; Stark 1996; Stark and Finke, 2000).

The theory of religious economies

Central to the theory of religious economies is the view that one should think of religions, or more specifically, of particular religious organizations, as business firms. This means thinking of religious organizations as having a product they want to sell to the public and as a way of attracting members and other resources. The only difference is that the products marketed by religious organizations, unlike most (other) business firms, have something to do with the supernatural.

For Stark and his associates, the most important product that religious firms market are *compensators*. A compensator is a strategy for obtaining a reward at a later date, and Stark suggested that the compensator that sells best always has two attributes. First, the reward involved will be of immense value, and second, it will be difficult for people to evaluate if the specified strategy will indeed lead to the promised reward. For example, suppose I said "Join my church and follow its rules and God will make you a millionaire." Certainly, there is a strategy here (follow the rules of my church) that supposedly leads to a desired reward (becoming a millionaire). The problem, however, is that the strategy is too easy to evaluate; after all, most people joining a church will clearly not become millionaires and thus eventually leave. But suppose I say "Join my church and follow the rules and you will spend eternity in Heaven with God." In this case the reward is immense but it is virtually impossible to disprove that the strategy will work. *Voila*: the perfect compensator (which is why, so the argument goes, it a compensator that so many different religions market to the public).

One of the most interesting features of the theory of religious economies is what it says about competition. Stark and his associates argued that if we think of religious groups as firms having a product to sell, then success (how many people you get to buy your particular product, or more simply, how many people join your group) is affected by the same things that affect sales in the business world. For example, what happens when one particular religion is in a monopoly situation (i.e., more or less is the only game in town)? Well, the argument goes, in this situation priests or ministers—like any sales staff—will have little incentive to market their product aggressively. The result: few people will buy that product (which means few people will attend church services). For Stark this argument explained, say, why Catholics are more likely to attend church services in places like the United States, where Catholics are in a minority, than in areas of the world (like Latin America) where Catholics are a majority.

Religion and identity: Ireland and Quebec

The matter of competition aside, something else that can affect the rise or fall of a religious tradition is the degree to which it becomes central to a national or ethnic identity. Take, for example, the Irish. By the late 1800s, Irish Catholics were among the most devout Catholics in the Catholic world. Yet, earlier in that same century, things had been quite different. Indeed, in terms of measures like knowledge of core Catholic doctrines and weekly attendance at church services, Irish Catholics in Ireland were really quite lax. What changed? Although there were a number of contributing factors, most historians (see the review in Carroll, 1999) suggest that the critical element was (1) rising support for Irish nationalism and Irish independence and (2) the idea, promoted by Irish nationalist leaders, that "being Catholic" was a central element in an Irish identity.

Prior to the nineteenth century, in other words, you could be strongly committed to Irish nationalism and be Protestant; indeed, many of the most important Irish political leaders promoting Irish nationalism in the eighteenth century *were* Protestant. But as "being Catholic" became increasingly central to an Irish national identity, the rising support for Irish nationalism brought along with it a greater commitment to Catholicism. Phrased differently, as "being Catholic" and "being committed to Irish nationalism" became increasingly intertwined over the course of the nineteenth century, "being a *good* Catholic" became a way of identifying with the nationalist cause in Ireland.

Quebec is another case where "identity" issues help to explain religious behaviour, although the pattern here is almost exactly the reverse of the Irish one. In the early part of the twentieth century, Quebec was a devoutly Catholic society. By the 1990s, all that had changed. Thus, for example, during the 1940s a solid majority of the French Catholic population attended Mass on a weekly basis; by the 1990s, only a minority of Quebec Catholics attended weekly Mass and they were less likely to attend weekly Mass than Catholics elsewhere in Canada (Finke and Stark, 2003). Here again: what changed? Finke and Stark (2003) argued that the critical event was the Quiet Revolution in the 1960s (described in Chapter 8, Race and Ethnic Relations).

Prior to the Quiet Revolution, the Catholic Church was for all practical purposes the only organization in Quebec that had the power and the will to promote and protect the interests of the French population in that Province, with the result that Catholic Quebeckers felt a strong tie to the Church. But with the Quiet Revolution, francophone Quebeckers increasingly took control of a range of important economic and political institutions in the province. Because it was now possible, Finke and Stark argued, to promote the interests of French

The Rise of Religious Fundamentalism: Myths and Realities

Although everyone agrees that religious fundamentalism is on the rise throughout the world, it is surprisingly difficult to come up with a definition of "fundamentalism" that fits all cases. At least in the Protestant case, however, fundamentalism typically implies a belief in Biblical inerrancy, that the Bible is to be taken literally in every instance. And although there is a tendency thus to think of Christian fundamentalism as "old time religion," this is historically incorrect. During the nineteenth century, the predominant form of Protestantism in both Canada and the United States, especially outside the Anglican/ Episcopalian tradition, was evangelical Protestantism (Choquette, 2004). And although the terms fundamentalist and evangelical are now often confused, evangelical Protestants—at least in the nineteenth century—were Protestants who emphasized the importance of a "conversion" experience to salvation and who were committed to the view that Christian principles should be used to transform society as a whole for the better. It only was in the early part of the twentieth century that religious fundamentalism, in the sense of Biblical inerrancy, became increasingly popular among Protestants and came to be fused with the evangelical tradition. A thriving tradition of Protestant fundamentalism, in other words, is much a product of the twentieth century.

It is common in the popular press to depict Protestant fundamentalists as people who represent a threat to social progress because of their views on such things as gender inequality and family values. And yet, if we move beyond the popular stereotypes and look instead to sociological studies, the truth proves more complex. For example, while contemporary evangelical/fundamentalist Protestants, both male and females, are more likely than other Protestants and Catholics to say that a husband should provide the spiritual leadership in a family (Gallagher, 2003), they are just as likely as other Protestants and Catholics to say that marriage "should be an equal partnership." Moreover, as a purely practical matter, wives in evangelical/fundamentalist families are just as likely to

be working outside the home as wives in other Protestant families (Gallagher, 2003). In some cases, even when strong differences exist between evangelical/ fundamentalist Protestants and other Christians, it is hard to decide who is more "progressive." For example, evangelical/fundamentalist fathers are far more involved in the day-to-day care and parenting of children than fathers in other Protestant families (Gallagher, 2003). Isn't this something that, say, most modern feminists would in fact see as progressive?

As mentioned above, defining what "fundamentalism" means in all cases is difficult. In the case of Islam, for example, fundamentalism seems to mean—at least in the Western press—a desire to reverse the process of secularization—that is, a desire to eliminate the institutional separation between religion and politics. Here again, there is a general tendency, at least among non-Muslim publics, to see this as a step backwards in time, and here again sociological research suggests that the truth is more complicated.

In Ontario, a 2004 government task force recommended that family arbitrators—in adjudicating things like divorce, child custody, and inheritance—should be allowed to make decisions using the principles of Shariah law, a set of traditional principles that govern the Islamic way of life (CBC, 2005). The general principle here was not at all new. During the 1990s, in an effort to relieve a clogged court system, the Ontario government permitted faith-based (religious) arbitration *if* both parties (i.e., husband and wife) wanted to do this and *if* such arbitration conformed to the Canadian Charter of Rights and Freedoms. Furthermore, this system of religious arbitration did in fact come to be used by many Christian and Jewish families (CBC, 2005). Nevertheless, there was strong opposition from a number of groups who did not want faith-based arbitration to be extended to the use of Shariah law. A common concern was that Shariah law would disadvantage women who might be coerced into taking part in the process. In 2006 the government of Ontario made it clear that Shariah law would not be used in Ontario (the government of Quebec had made

(continued)

a similar decision for Quebec in 2005) and Ontario also promised legislation to outlaw all faith-based arbitration.

Implicit in much of the discussion of Shariah law in the press is the suggestion that support for Shariah law represents a type of religious fundamentalism that is regressive—that is, it seeks to return society to a past characterized by social injustices of various sorts. Is this popular stereotype true? There is not a lot of research on this issue, but at least one recent sociological study suggests that—here again—the truth is more complicated than the stereotype. Davis and Robinson (2006) used survey data from seven predominantly Muslim nations (Algeria, Bangladesh, Egypt, Indonesia, Jordan, Pakistan, and Saudi Arabia) to assess the relationship between "support for Shariah law" (that is, support for the suggestion that Shariah law be made the law of the state) and

other attitudes. On the one hand, the respondents who supported Shariah law were more likely to endorse the view that things like divorce, homosexuality, and abortion are never justified. On the other hand, and perhaps surprisingly, support for Shariah law was also correlated with support for a number of economic reforms that might be viewed as progressive. For example, respondents who supported Shariah law were far more likely, as compared to respondents who did not support it, to say that governments had a responsibility to provide for the poor and to say that income inequality in society should be reduced.

In the end, remember, sociology's goal is not to decide if something like religious fundamentalism is "good" or "bad" but only to provide insight and evidence that establish the relationship—in all its complexity—between religious fundamentalism and other aspects of social life.

Does the use of Shariah law conflict with or complement presumed Canadian values with respect to the separation of Church and State?

Quebeckers without reliance on the Church, there was far less incentive for French Quebeckers to remain attached to the Church.

Thinking further about religion in Canada

Canada clearly presents a hybrid case, which simultaneously demonstrates the utility and the limitations of the theory of religious economies. In England, for example, the Anglican Church, also known as the Church of England, has long been the established church. Non-Anglicans were a disadvantaged minority in most sectors of British society until well into this century. In Germany, the Lutheran church is supported by tax dollars, and only fifteen other religions are legally recognized as religions (though hundreds of others exist). In both nations, despite state support for the churches, regular religious practice has fallen to about 10 percent. In the United States, as indicated, under conditions of religious free enterprise, the level of regular practice has stayed at about 40 percent for decades. In Canada, where no formal establishment of religion has existed since the mid-nineteenth century, levels of regular practice have declined to about 20 to 30 percent. But Canada's colonial history has produced what the British

sociologist Martin (2000) called *shadow establishments*. In English Canada, the extended political ties with Britain made the Anglican and Presbyterian churches predominant among the social, political, and economic elites of Canada. In Quebec, the Catholic Church virtually ruled supreme, in defence of French Canadian culture, from the time of the English conquest to the 1960s. Things changed dramatically in Quebec following the Quiet Revolution of the 1960s (also see Chapter 15, Social Movements). With the rise of a secular form of Quebec nationalism, the state expanded its responsibilities, displacing the church from the important social functions (e.g., healthcare and education) that it performed long after other churches had abandoned them in the rest of Canada and elsewhere. With this belated change, the European model of secularization has been repeated in Quebec. The end of the virtual monopoly of the Catholic Church did not open up the religious economy of the province to new religious competition and growth. Rather, in the space of three decades (1960–1990) the people of Quebec went from being one of the most religious populations in the world, by conventional measures like church attendance, to being one of the least religious populations. English Canada, where the presence of the shadow establishments was balanced by a greater measure of denominationalism, was less religious to begin with and has been secularized at a slower pace and to a lesser extent. But it, too, now seems to be emulating the European, more than the American, path of religious development. At this point, however, it is too difficult to clearly specify what might really be accounting for the differences between Quebec and the rest of Canada, and Canada and the United States. The theory of religious economies is suggestive, but the situation is more complex (see also Chapter 3, Culture).

Exploring the differences in religiosity between the United States and Canada, for example, the Canadian sociologist Reimer (1995) found evidence to support the supposition, long held by others (e.g., Wilson, 1966; Luckmann, 1967), that Americans are not nearly as religious as they appear. A generalized commitment to basic religious ideas and at least modest church attendance seem to be synonymous with the American way of life. It is a part of the American culture and not necessarily an indication of greater or more sincere religious conviction. Fewer Canadians attend church, but Reimer (1990: 7) found that these Canadians display higher levels of orthodoxy in their beliefs and practices than their American counterparts. What is more, the differences between the levels of orthodoxy recorded for Americans who do and do not attend church are much lower than for Canadians. In other words, church attendance seems

Canadians continue to maintain, at least officially, a religious identification with the faith of their parents.

to be less relevant to the determination of the moderate orthodoxy, displayed by most Americans, than it is to the determination of the relatively higher religiosity of Canadians. Fewer Canadians may be religious, but they are more truly religious. The religiosity of Americans, on the other hand, tends to be, as the American pollster Gallup stated, "broad, but not deep." It seems that the higher levels of church attendance in the United States may be a product of the cultural values to which all Americans are socialized, and not some true difference in the religiosity of the peoples of Europe, Canada, and the United States. In other words, the differences in the levels of secularization between these three areas of the world may be more the result of cultural differences than differences in the structure of their religious economies.

Thinking about these and other kinds of cultural and historical complications, another Canadian sociologist of religion, Beyer (1997; 2000), called into question the quest for some "master trend" in the development of religion in modern times. The theory of religious economies should be superseded, he argued, by a recognition that several different, regionally specific, developmental patterns may occur, and that there is a third option: **invisible religion**. This is a term Luckmann (1967) introduced to describe the kind of pervasive, non-institutionalized, and highly individualistic religiosity or spirituality practised by so many modern people. For example, reading the empirical evidence of alternative patterns of secularization, with these three forms of religiosity in mind, Beyer suggested that at least three different developmental patterns are emerging for religion in the modern world. In Europe, where churches have historically been at the centre of religious life, religious change has not produced a switch to denominations. Rather, religious change has been expressed through the enhanced presence of invisible religion that complements the continued presence of churches (Davie, 2000). Contrastingly, in the United States, denominations persist as the dominant form of religious life, but again with a growing co-presence of invisible religion. In Canada, as indicated, the European accommodation to modernity has been replicated in Quebec, while the rest of Canada has displayed a mixed version of the European and American realities. Most Canadians inhabit a religious environment of denominations and invisible religion, but the dominance of denominationalism is less than in the United States. In each case, Beyer observed, two things stand out: the co-existence of different religious forms and the strong presence of invisible religion. These observations are congruent with the religious trends that other sociologists, with an eye to the future of religion, have been noting.

Religious Change in the Twenty-First Century

In thinking about religious change, it is important not to lose sight of what is *not* changing. In terms of "market share," for example, Catholics now account for the same proportion (about 42 to 43 percent) of the Canadian population as they did 130 years ago (see Table 11.2). Moreover, as mentioned earlier, the proportion of Canadians who believe in God and in an afterlife has remained unchanged (Table 11.3). Still, religious changes are occurring and sociologists have documented and studied many of these changes. One such change and one that has been especially well documented and studied, is the increasing popularity of fundamentalist Christianity.

In the United States the fundamentalist-led Southern Baptist Convention is now one of the largest Protestant denominations, and across the nation the more conservative forms of Christianity have been growing at the expense of the more liberal and long-dominant denominations like the Congregationalists, Methodists, and Episcopalians. In times of uncertainty and moral flux, many people seem to want religions with clear and certain conceptions of what is good and bad and how to behave in the face of the growing temptations of contemporary life. They also want a context of strong and uncluttered worship and preaching in their churches, where religion is deeply felt and experienced, and seek the greater sense of community often found in such churches. As frequently noted by commentators, there is a marked element of resistance to modernity in these communities. There is a strong desire to place things firmly within a sacred context, once again, to balance a scientific education with renewed Bible studies—for example, modern medical practice with belief in the power of prayer. These new evangelicals and fundamentalists are, on the whole, members of a rising and prosperous middle class. While most of the research on the evangelical/fundamentalist resurgence has focused on the United States, Reimer (2003) has compared evangelical/fundamentalist congregations in the United States and Canada. In general, he found that

evangelical/fundamentalist Protestants in both countries share the same beliefs and can reasonably be characterized as a cohesive subculture that in each case is different in significant ways from the dominant culture in each country.

Another change that has caught the attention of sociologists is the emergence of new religious movements. In particular, sociologists have paid attention over the last several decades to aspects of religious revivalism (i.e., sects) on the one hand, and religious innovation (i.e., cults) on the other. In the United States in particular, but elsewhere in the Western world as well, the single greatest area of religious growth has been among groups like the Mormons, Seventh-day Adventists, and the Pentecostal and Charismatic movements. Likewise, there has been an explosion of new kinds of religion, ranging from Asian-based meditational traditions through to New Age trance-channelling groups, in Western Europe and North America. It is difficult to gauge the number of people involved in the latter types of groups, unlike the millions of people known to have been swept up in the surge of Pentecostal and Charismatic activity worldwide. Estimates of the numbers with some involvement in cults range from as low as 1 percent to as high as 10 percent of the population. It is the sheer existence, however, of thousands of truly new and unusual religions, no matter how small most of these groups may be, that points to a shift in the religious sensibilities of Western societies. The cultural significance of these groups, as the harbingers of true religious and cultural pluralism, clearly exceeds their present demographic impact.

In studying both kinds of groups, many sociologists are detecting a structural similarity in the kind of religiosity favoured, one that seems to transcend the differences in the specific beliefs and practices of the groups. Moreover, the similarities noted seem to be in line with broader shifts appearing in the religious consciousness of most Americans and Canadians.

There are roughly six interrelated features of this new religious consciousness:

1. There is an emphasis on individualism. Not only is religion increasingly thought to be a matter of personal choice, but the focus of concern is on what involvement can do for the individual. The social or group implications or benefits are quite secondary. Correspondingly, the primary motivation for participation lies with the development of personal

identity, and the sacred is identified with a reality interior to the self, not exterior.

2. There is an emphasis on religious experience. The demand for a moving religious experience has been democratized. It is no longer thought to be the preserve of the religiously virtuous. Rather, people wish to be moved intellectually and emotionally by their dealings with the sacred. Mere belief and passive faith are no longer enough.

3. There is a more pragmatic approach to questions of religious authority and practice. Both aspects of religious life are linked now more than ever to the actual provision of worthwhile religious experiences for individuals. Religious leaders must display their skills with some regularity. They cannot rest on their credentials.

4. There is a greater tolerance for other religious systems, rooted in a greater acceptance of the relativism of all religious perspectives. In fact this tolerance often crosses over into a pragmatic **syncretism**, in which beliefs and practices from different traditions are integrated into new systems.

5. There is a greater emphasis on a holistic approach to life. The traditional dualisms (either/or) of Western culture are either rejected or reduced in scope and significance. This applies to the dualisms of God and humanity, the transcendent and the immanent, the spiritual and the material, humanity and nature, the mind and the body, male and female, good and evil, and science and religion.

6. There is a greater suspicion of institutionalization and a preference for more organizational openness. Networks of small, grassroots communities are favoured, to protect the focus on the individual and the here and now, over the formation of bureaucracies justified by claims of efficiency.

None of these features of the new emerging religious consciousness is particularly new in itself. All have precedents in the religious history of the West, and the turn to individualism, experience, and pragmatism is rather characteristic of American culture. It is the convergence and strength of these trends that has attracted attention. Will these trends persist and produce a lasting transformation in the form and style of religion practised by Canadians? Will the individualistic invisible religion of so many Canadians take on more visible forms and displace the denomination and the church?

Predicting the future is a foolish endeavour, especially with so subtle and volatile a subject as religion. But these trends mirror developments in many other aspects of Canadian lives (e.g., how we work, play, educate ourselves, and engage in politics), and this continuity suggests the trends will last and be consequential.

Summary

We began this chapter by talking about how the conventional religious life of Canadians is changing. Canada was once quite a religious country, but it has been secularizing at a quite rapid pace since the 1960s. This is especially and most surprisingly the case in the province of Quebec. On the one hand, this decline in the fortunes of mainstream religion has brought Canada in line with more long-term developments in Western Europe, though we are still more religious than the Europeans. On the other hand, it is putting us increasingly at odds with our close neighbours, the Americans, who continue to be quite religious. Whether this pattern of development will continue, and why, are open questions and the subject of much research. In all three regions, Europe, Canada, and the United States, however, surveys also reveal that most people identify with some particular religion, and continue to believe in God and other supernatural phenomena.

Marx, Durkheim, and Weber all recognized long ago that changes in the fate of religion were indicative of other sweeping social transformations. Thus each sought to understand something of the fundamental nature and functioning of religion. The social-scientific study of religion, however, entails grappling with a number of methodological and theoretical problems: How can we study a phenomenon whose ultimate nature is thought to elude empirical assessment? How can we define religion? How can we measure the religiosity of people? In thinking about religion in the present are we making assumptions about religion in the past that are not historically accurate?

In line with his critique of capitalism, Marx captured the primary role of religious beliefs and institutions in the legitimation of the status quo. He portrayed religions as human creations serving the vested interests of ruling classes by deceiving the masses about the true source of their deprivation, and persuading them to accept their fate as divinely imposed. He felt that Christianity, with its emphasis on otherworldly salvation, provided a particularly clear example of a religion that diverts people from their this-worldly oppression. More comprehensively, Durkheim captured how religion plays a crucial role in the creation and maintenance of social solidarity through the detailed study of the religious life of Australian Aboriginals. Individuals and groups are strengthened in their capacity to persevere in the face of the trials and tribulations of life by participating in the religious rituals through which society worships itself in symbolic guise. Alternatively, Weber captured the ways in which religion acts, often unintentionally, as a powerful agent of social change. Seeking the origins of the spirit of capitalism, Weber argued that the Protestant Reformation represented the culmination of a religiously inspired process of rationalization that gave rise to the first true capitalists. In particular he pointed to the combined psychological impact of the doctrines of the calling and predestination in rendering worldly success a sign of salvation.

As the functions of religion are diverse, so are its forms. Sociologists have tried to capture some of this diversity with the development of the church/sect typology. Framed in different ways by different theorists, this typology identifies how religious groups vary in terms of their degree of formality, institutionalization, and integration with the dominant society, with churches being the most formal, institutionalized, and integrated groups, and cults the least.

The contemporary debate about the forms and functions of religion is still framed very much by the theory of religious economies, which posits an ongoing need in every society for the kinds of general compensators based on supernatural assumptions that religion uniquely offers. We are not witnessing the end of religion, the argument goes, just the slow demise of the form in which religion has been delivered for the last few centuries. In general, religions actually succeed better in an environment of religious competition. Taking a supply-side view of religious growth, the theory of religious economies argues that it is monopoly and not pluralism that undermines faith. Theorists working in this tradition also recognize that religion can prosper when a particular religious tradition becomes central to a social identity.

Although it is easy to overlook what has remained unchanged, there is no denying that the past century has seen a number of important changes in religion. Sociologists have been concerned, in particular, with the rise of religious fundamentalism (and what this does and doe not mean), and with the emergence of new forms of spirituality and new religions.

Questions for Review and Critical Thinking

1. Have you noticed any signs of continued or renewed interest in religious and spiritual concerns among your friends, or in your community?

2. When you have participated in a religious service, baptism, marriage, or funeral, did you experience some of the elements of the collective conscience and collective effervescence discussed by Durkheim? If so, describe the feelings you experienced.

3. Design a small empirical study to test some aspects of the theory of religious economies.

4. If you yourself do not think of yourself as a religious fundamentalist, what beliefs do you hold about religious fundamentalists? Where do these beliefs come from? How would you go about designing a study to determine how "fundamentalists" differ from "non-fundamentalists" in any particular faith tradition?

Key Terms

ascetic, p. 261
calling, p. 261
church, p. 262
collective conscience, p. 260
collective effervescence, p. 260
cult, p. 264
denomination, p. 263
doctrine of predestination, p. 261
ecclesia, p. 263
functionalist definitions of religion, p. 256
invisible religion, p. 269
profane, p. 259
religion, p. 256
sacred, p. 259
sect, p. 262
secularization, p. 265
substantive definitions of religion, p. 256
supernatural, p. 256
syncretism, p. 271
universal church, p. 263
vocation, p. 261

Suggested Readings

Dawson, Lorne L.

1998 *Comprehending Cults: The Sociology of New Religious Movements.* Toronto and New York: Oxford University Press.

This small book provides a comprehensive overview of post-1970 new religions. The discussion is organized in terms of six questions: What are cults? Why did they emerge? Who joins them and why? Are converts brainwashed? Why do some cults become violent? What is the cultural significance of the cults?

Bibby, Reginald

2002 *Restless Gods: The Renaissance of Religion in Canada.* Toronto: Stoddart Publishing.

Bibby's book remains one of the best sources for survey data relating to a wide range of religious beliefs and practices in Canada.

Stark, Rodney and Roger Finke

2000 *Acts of Faith: Explaining the Human Side of Religion.* Berkeley, CA: University of California Press.

This compilation of previously published papers offers the latest statement of the principles and an empirical application of the authors' influential and controversial theory of religion based on rational choice theory and supply-side economic modelling.

Weber, Max

1958 [1904] *The Protestant Ethic and the Spirit of Capitalism.* New York: Scribners.

One of the most accessible classical studies of religion, this seminal book seeks to demonstrate how religious ideas can have profound and often unanticipated consequences for social life. Weber presents the controversial thesis that Protestantism was central to the rise of the capitalist economic ethos that dominates life throughout much of the contemporary world.

Websites

www.adherents.com

Religion Statistics

Ever wanted to know how many Hindus live in Canada? What percentage of the world is Catholic? This is the site for you. Search world religions by name and location and find statistical information on all types of faith groups from around the world.

www.ccc-cce.ca

The Canadian Council of Churches

This site contains information on an organization representing Canada's main Christian faiths. Links to its various working groups, such as the Commission on Justice and Peace, and various ecumenical organizations, are provided.

www.religioustolerance.org

Ontario Consultants on Religious Tolerance

This private website has won international acclaim for its promotion of religious understanding. It provides profiles of many religious groups and balanced discussions of many controversial religious topics (e.g., brainwashing accusations against cults, assisted suicide, evolutionary theory and creationist science).

Key Search Terms

Sacred
Profane
Church
Sect
Cult
Denomination

For more study tools to help you with your next exam, be sure to check out the Companion Website at **www.pearsoned.ca/hewitt**, as well as Chapter 11 in your Study Guide.

[12]

media

nick dyer-witheford

Introduction

No topic is more up-to-date and fashionable than the role of media in society. But to get a perspective on the issue, and on the very meaning of the word "media," let's step back in time for a moment. The term *media* comes from the Latin *medium*, meaning "in the middle." In seventeenth- and eighteenth-century English, "medium" could mean a connection between two things, or a way of conveying something from one place to another (Williams, 1983: 203). People spoke of newspapers as a "medium" for communicating ideas to the public. This then became shortened to "media," the plural of the word. The press, and later radio and television, were often referred to as "mass media," suggesting communication addressed to a large, anonymous, and in many ways unknown audience. Today, when we talk of media, we generally include print publications—newspapers, books, and magazines; telecommunications—such as the fax machine and telephone; broadcast technologies, like radio and television; cable television; domestic electronic devices like video games and CD players; and an array of new digital means of communication, including computer networks such as the Internet.

Over a relatively short time successive waves of media innovations have altered everyday life (see Chart 12.1). A few generations ago, most people had very little information about the events occurring any distance from where they lived. Most people lived and died within thirty kilometres of where they were born. The maximum speed of communication was usually that of a person on horse (on land) or sailing ship (by sea). When such news did arrive, it was with an enormous time lag. In 1814 the British fought a deadly battle with the Americans at New Orleans,

Chart 12.1	A Timeline of Media Technologies
1837	Telegraph
1876	Telephone
1895	Radio
1920s	Television
1966	Satellite Communication
1970s	Internet
1989	World Wide Web
1990s	Wireless Net
2000s	Mobile Computing

taking thousands of casualties, simply because news of a peace treaty had not completed the weeks-long journey across the Atlantic. Today, media technologies have accomplished what Marx (1973: 525) called the "annihilation of space by time," as the near-instantaneous transmission of messages around the globe makes physical distance less and less of a barrier to communication.

Media have reshaped not only our sense of space, but also our use of time. Anyone who has visited a historical site from the nineteenth century will have noticed how little packaged entertainment the inhabitants had. No Game Cubes or PlayStations for them! Without televisions, MP3 players, or video games, they depended on reading aloud, or they made up games, or gave their own live performances of music and song. As you will see in Table 12.1, our leisure time today is much more heavily devoted to technologically based amusement. Just watching television is a major occupation of most people in North America, and indeed around the planet. In this sense, our lives have become increasingly *mediated*—more reliant on a technically sophisticated, socially organized communication apparatus that conveys, filters, and constructs our experience. Some theorists try to catch this aspect of our society by saying that we now inhabit a "mediascape" (Appadurai, 1990), or "datasphere" (Rushkoff, 1994), that is as much a part of our environment as the landscape or biosphere.

In this chapter, we review some of the approaches sociologists and other communication scholars take to understanding the media. We review theoretical models of the information society, analyses of social power and communication, discussions of media audiences, debates about representations of gender and of violence in the media, the role of media in globalization, and the importance of the Internet. We conclude with some predictions for the future.

Perspectives on Media Transformation
Technological change and the information society

Some theorists believe that media are so important today that they have created a new sort of society, often referred to as an "information society" (Wilhelm, 2006), or "the network society" (Castells, 2001). Sociologist Daniel Bell originated this idea in *The Coming of Post-Industrial Society* (1973), where he argued that North America was witnessing the appearance of a new type of society, to be fully visible sometime around the year 2000. He called this society "post-industrial" to distinguish it from the "industrial society" that had characterized the last 200 to 300 years and the "preindustrial" or agricultural society of the preceding centuries (see Chapter 17, Social Change).

The main force driving the shift to the "post-industrial" society was the advance in scientific knowledge, systematically organized to create new wealth-producing technologies. This was associated also with other changes: a shift from a manufacturing to a service economy; a move from manual jobs to more technical work; increasing capacities to forecast the trends of social change; and a new "intellectual technology" of computerized systems. The birth pangs of this new society would inevitably involve dislocation, anxiety, and resistance to change. But the post-industrial era society could, Bell argued, be a time of extraordinary promise—one that would finally escape from the poverty and class division of the old "industrial" society.

Bell emphasized the role of the media in making the new system. He wrote of an "information explosion" arising from scientific advances and a:

> Growing demand for news, entertainment, and instrumental knowledge, all in the context of rapidly increasing population, more literate and more educated, living in a vastly enlarged world that is

Table 12.1	Percentage of Canadian Households with Selected Media Access, 2004
Technology	**% of Households**
Television	99
Radio	99
Telephone	96
Cellphone	60
VCR	90
CD Player	80
Cable TV	66
Computer	69
Internet	60

Source: Statistics Canada, *Selected Dwelling Characteristics and Household Equipment*, www40.statcan.ca/l01/cst01/famil09b.htm (accessed 19 April, 2006).

[Social Trends]

Mobile Networks: The Next Media Revolution?

The latest wave of new media is mobile, networked communications devices. Cellphones have been around for a while: there are probably a billion subscribers worldwide, and revenues from them will soon exceed those from fixed-line phones. The laptop computer was a step toward always-available e-mail but mobile communication devices like portable phones and hand-held computers now have digital text and graphics capacity. These devices enable you to check your e-mail at a moment's notice, send text messages, use location-finding devices, send pictures through tiny digital cameras, and even conduct colour videoconferences.

For once, North America is not at the very front of this new wave of networked communication. Adoption rates have been higher in parts of Europe—especially Finland—and in Japan and some other parts of Asia. There, "hand-helds" are an integral part of youth culture. In the United Kingdom, for example, nearly 80 percent of 18- to 24-year-olds use short-text messaging.

There is no shortage of sociological prediction about the consequences of this media innovation. There are already several studies of new on-the-move networked sociability—for example, the use of mobile communications to get instant dates or by fans tracking celebrity movements. Some claim that easy, always-on communication will promote democracy, through the creation of "smart mobs" (Rheingold, 2002)—ad hoc mobilizations of well-informed, well-connected citizens. We have already seen examples of this in the practice of "peer to peer" journalism, using mobile phones to upload digital video reports directly to the Web. Protestors from the Philippines to Seattle have used mobile communications to coordinate and publicize their activities.

Some hope that wireless phone and mobile Internet will be a "bypass technology," allowing people in the developing world to connect to the global communication networks without incurring the considerable costs of wired infrastructure. In Bangladesh, for example, development agencies and progressive banks provide loans for peasant communities to purchase cellphones so farmers can check market prices for crops. China has more cellphone subscribers than any country except the United States, and the average subscriber chats three times longer than the average American. Other predictions are negative—the lack of privacy, people always on call for work, endless spamming and commercial solicitation, and increased accidents from multi-tasking inattention (already a consideration with using a cellphone while driving).

For better or worse (from the technologically determinist perspective) mobile communications, the latest stage in the information revolution, will likely bring big changes. Political economists who keep an eye on institutional power already are concerned about the power mobile communications give individual citizens relative to say, the Pentagon, or a multinational corporation.

Sources: Balnaves et al. (2000). *The Penguin Atlas of Media and Information: Key Issues and Global Trends.* New York: Penguin; Howard Rheingold (2002). *Smart Mobs: The Next Social Revolution.* Boulder, CO: Perseus Books.

One effect of the revolution in mobile communications is a generation of men who communicate more than their fathers' and grandfathers' generations. Is this a sign of the convergence of male and female roles as some researchers claim?

now tied together, almost in real time, by cable, telephone and international satellite . . . and that has at its disposal large data banks of computerized information (1980: 526).

In fact, Bell's notion of "post-industrial society" was soon renamed the **information society**. Whatever the name, the basic idea is that information technologies—machines that transfer, process, store, and disseminate data—are moving us to a new stage of civilization. The most important of these technologies are computers and telecommunications, though some theorists also include biotechnologies that manipulate genetic code. These machines play a role in the "information revolution" equivalent to the steam engine and railway in the nineteenth-century "industrial revolution." Underlying many such prophecies is the idea that the real force propelling social change is the introduction of new tools and machines, including new media. Economic, cultural, and political transformations are seen as following behind. This concept is known as **technological determinism** (see the box "Mobile Networks: The Next Media Revolution?").

In general, the arrival of the information society is seen as a good thing. Thinkers who celebrate it are not unaware of possible problems. Technological unemployment, intrusive surveillance, and electronic crime are all acknowledged as real perils. But they are represented as problems of adjustment, temporary setbacks, or avoidable hazards on what remains an ascending path, the next stage in the march of progress. The promises

include great increases in prosperity, a decrease in manual labour in favour of more creative and interesting jobs, a broader dissemination of knowledge, and, consequently, the potential for a more democratic and participatory society. At the extreme, some of these thinkers see the information revolution marking not only a new phase in human civilization, but also a new stage in the development of life itself, with forms of artificial intelligence as silicon-based successors to humanity (Kurzweil, 2005).

A great deal of this optimism is focused around new media technologies—for example, computer networks, fax, cellphone, and satellite television. These are seen as increasing people's choice of information sources and channels of communication. Because some of these technologies (such as the Internet) bring with them the capacity for a two-way, rather than one-way,

[Research Focus]

Seeing Is Believing

In Chapter 1, you briefly encountered the ideas of McLuhan, arguably Canada's most famous social theorist. According to him, the media extend our senses—specifically, the capacities to see and hear. The significance of any new medium relates to how it alters the balance or "ratio" between the different senses. Drawing on the work of earlier theorists, McLuhan proposed three great stages in the development of media. The first was the oral, spoken culture of traditional societies, which relied on hearing; the second, the era of the written word, which relied on sight; and third, the current era of the electronic media, which uses both sight and hearing.

In McLuhan's view, each shift in the means of communication alters attitudes, institutions, patterns of behaviour, and modes of thinking. Oral societies were relatively harmonious; language did not dominate but took its place alongside other means of expression such as touching, music, and dance. On the other hand, a reliance on speech does imply small-scale, spatially close communities marked by face-to-face interpersonal exchanges.

All this changed with the advent of writing and, in particular, with the printing press. Once something is written, it can be separated from its original context, split-off from the originator in a way the spoken word cannot be. Also, writing, unlike speaking, can be denied to many, as when schools were closed to women in Afghanistan. Print can subordinate the richness of actual experience and the senses to the intellectual capacities encouraged by reading. Print became linked to rationality, linear thinking, and a split between head and heart.

With the advent of electronic media, however, the situation changed again. Television, because it involves sight and sound, reintegrates the balance between the senses. The effect, McLuhan argued, is to "re-tribalize" humankind, restoring the emotional excitement and intimacy that had once existed in small-scale pre-print societies on a planetary scale, creating the "global village" (1964: 87). McLuhan (unlike some of his disciples) was not a naive optimist. Still, some have argued that his thoughts amount to a theory of salvation through better media.

Some people are more visual, some more oral, and some more kinetic (touchers). How does this relate to what McLuhan said about the various media?

communication, they enable citizens to be transmitters as well as receivers of information—active producers, not just passive consumers. The result, information-society theorists claim, is personally empowering and politically democratizing. With the common nervous system and senses of the world population now in the care of satellites, and with machines approximating the condition of mind and the minds of humans connecting across time and space, the future can and should be more a matter of choice than destiny.

The political economy of media: Power and wealth

A contrasting perspective is provided by the **political economy of media**. Instead of focusing just on technological changes, this approach situates the media in relation to issues of power and wealth. Sociologists who study the political economy of media look at the social institutions that govern the production, distribution, and consumption of information. They are interested in who controls access to the means of communication, and how that control is used to solidify or subvert social power (McChesney, 2004). This view sometimes yields a much more critical perspective than the rather rose-tinted view that comes from just looking at improvements in media technologies.

You may immediately think of government's control of media—and with good reason. In most social systems, the elites or classes that exercise state power regard control over channels of communication as crucial to maintaining their position (Innis, 1950). Conversely, groups challenging the established regime have consistently seen access to the media as critical to mobilizing support for their cause. Media have therefore been centrally involved in conflicts over state power. Struggles for freedom of assembly, freedom of speech, and freedom of the press have marked our society. Today, the existence of what is sometimes called a "public sphere," where opinion and discussion can circulate without government interference, is regarded as a central element in liberal democracy (Habermas, 1989).

The media systems of liberal democracies are often sharply contrasted with the state-controlled media of totalitarian or authoritarian regimes. Hitler's dramatic use of radio in the 1930s alerted many people to the capacity of broadcast mass media to shape opinion in the service of a political agenda. This example, and that of the Soviet Union under Stalin, have given us the image, unforgettably captured in George Orwell's *1984*, of the state that uses the media both to transmit propaganda to its citizens and to gather information about them through ceaseless surveillance. One of the great hopes associated with the idea of an information revolution is that easy-to-use, speedy, decentralized means of communication will be **technologies of freedom** that empower citizens and make despotic top-down state control of media more difficult to maintain (Pool, 1983). The fall of state socialism seems to provide some support for this idea. Secretly printed or photocopied *samizadat* books and pamphlets, illegal radio stations, underground music, and computer networks all played an important part in undermining authoritarian regimes of the Soviet Union and Eastern Europe. In China, student revolt in Tiananmen Square received global publicity from satellite television. But this did not stop the government from crushing the revolt; in fact, it used the television footage to identify and pick up political suspects.

But a number of political economists of media, some influenced by Marx, challenge the idea that communication systems in liberal democracies are in fact "free." Under capitalism, the means of production—the technologies and raw resources required to make socially useful things—are privately owned, and organized to make a profit. This is also the case with the means of communication. Television, newspapers, film, radio, books, magazines, video, and other media, by and large, constitute a vast commercially operated

The sector comprising media, telecommunications, and computer industries is the largest and fastest-growing component of the global market.

culture industry, a vital part of the capitalist economy. If one counts media, telecommunications, and computer industries as a single sector, it is today the largest and fastest-growing component of the global market.

In many fields of media, there is a high *concentration of ownership*, as the largest companies control a high proportion of the market. In North America, and indeed globally, film production is dominated by the major Hollywood studios (Paramount, Twentieth-Century Fox, Warner, Universal, Disney, Columbia); the recorded music business by "the big six" (Warner Music, Sony Music, PolyGram, BMG, EMI, MCA); and computer operating systems by a single giant—Microsoft, despite legal challenges. In a Canadian context, we can think of the leading role of Rogers and Shaw in cable television, and of the Asper newspaper chains. A famous series of studies by Ben Bagdikian (2004) has documented the intensification of this trend. In the U.S., there are some 37 000 media companies—perhaps more, depending on how one counts. But most are small, local, and subsidiary to or dependent on larger companies. In each field—film, television, and newspapers—there are a handful of "dominant corporations" that among them control more than 50 percent of the market. When Bagdikian first researched the field in 1983, he found fifty dominant communications corporations; twenty years later, in 2003, he claimed the number had fallen to five. The issue becomes complicated because there are both different ways of evaluating the degree of concentration of ownership, and different assessments of the degree to which this squashes diversity of expression (Demers, 2002). But there is undoubtedly a trend toward the formation of gigantic media conglomerates. Moreover, although in the past such companies usually specialized in one type of media, today the most powerful combine interests in many different areas to form vast media conglomerates (see the box "Freedom of the Press: Reality or Myth?").

Why should we be concerned about commercial media, concentration of ownership, and conglomeration? As Liebling, a famous American journalist, once remarked, "Freedom of the press is guaranteed only to those who own one." Many media analysts argue that commercial ownership introduces serious distortions into communication systems (McChesney, Newman, and Scott, 2005). The owners of the communications companies are members of a class of people—capitalist owners—who have a very particular interest in seeing society run in a way that allows them to continue reaping

profits and wielding power. They will use their control over the means of communication to direct the flow of news and entertainment to support the social order. They will screen out reports sympathetic to alternative regimes, or about activities that threaten their interest, such as trade unions, poor people's movements, or environmental organizations. For example, outrages committed by regimes or movements hostile to U.S.-style capitalism are extensively reported and criticized, but similar or greater atrocities committed by regimes sympathetic to U.S. state and business interests are massively neglected (Chomsky, 2002).

According to this line of analysis, commercial media will favour entertainment that keep people in a buying mood and distract them from social criticism. Although nominally competing with one another, such media empires in reality act in collusion to maintain the dominance of a world view of consumerism. The perspective of critical political economy suggests that the multiplicity of media outlets and channels celebrated by information revolution theorists is deceptive—because all transmit a common "corporate-speak" that hides issues of labour exploitation, social injustice, and ecological destruction in favour of an air-brushed depiction of happy consumerism.

This is a depressing prospect. But one countervailing trend that may partially offset the power of media conglomerates is the explosion of "do-it-yourself media." Underground or alternative media—from "zines" to community radio—have always been part of the communication scene. But the digital revolution has massively increased the scope of such citizen self-expression. Today, many people, all around the world, can put up a Web page, send an e-mail, or write a "blog" (weblog). Such efforts are not an automatic solution to corporate control. It is one thing to launch a blog, another to get anyone to read it: without massive advertising budgets and established media presence, many (perhaps most) "DIY" media are fated to marginalization or oblivion. Nonetheless, many see in the tendency toward grassroots reporting and guerrilla news an important challenge to corporate media (Gilmor, 2004).

Media audiences: From couch potato to co-creator?

Up to this point, we have talked about media as both a technology and as an instrument of state and market power. But neither of these perspectives deals with media audiences. For a long time, the assumption of much mass-media theory was that the audience was indeed just a mass—inert and manipulated. It assumed a linear, cause-and-effect connection between media messages and people's behaviour. Thus it was supposed that television images of violence instil in people a predisposition to act violently. If radio stations broadcast messages favouring a particular political party, this makes people vote for that party, and so on. Such a view

drew support from a bizarre episode in the early history of radio. In 1938, CBS broadcast, during prime time, a dramatized version of H.G. Wells's science-fiction story about a Martian invasion of earth, *War of the Worlds*. Thousands of Americans panicked, fleeing their homes and phoning emergency services, convinced they were hearing reports of a real event. This seemed to demonstrate a very direct connection between media content and audience behaviour.

[Debate]

Freedom of the Press: Reality or Myth?

A large corporation that controls a number of subsidiary companies, often called a conglomerate, is organized through two kinds of integration. *Horizontal integration* refers to a corporation that controls several different enterprises in the same business, all producing the same thing. Media examples would be a newspaper chain, like Sun Media, or the group of cable companies owned by Rogers. *Vertical integration* exists where a corporation owns different stages or steps in a related economic process, so that companies under the same owner supply and consume each other's products. For example, a studio that makes movies and owns a chain of cinemas to exhibit these films, the video-rental stores that sell these films, and a cable network that shows them on television, would be vertically integrated.

Political economists of media distinguish between *general conglomerate* and *communications conglomerates*. A general conglomerate has interests in communications that are matched by or exceeded by its involvement in other industries. For example, General Electric, which owns NBC-TV, is heavily involved in nuclear power and weapons production—controversial areas in which impartial news coverage might be considered important. A **communications conglomerate** operates mainly within the media sector and often aims to control as many different media as possible: news, magazines, radio, television, books, motion pictures, cable systems, satellite channels, recordings, videocassettes/DVDs, and chains of movie theatres. In addition, these giant companies, although nominally competing with each other, often actually collude

through joint ventures and strategic alliances or by sharing members on their boards of directors.

Some of these companies are very big indeed, and are called *transnational* communications conglomerates. They are usually based in one country, typically the United States, Japan, or Western European nations, but operate in many others. Time Warner is such a conglomerate. It is the largest magazine publisher in the U.S., one of the largest book dealers in the world, runs the second-largest cable television operation, owns one of the six Hollywood studios—and these are only a fraction of its total holdings. Time Warner could publish a novel, review it in its magazines, make it into a movie, and eventually show it on its cable television station. They call this potential "synergy"; others might call it control of information.

The power possessed by these companies is of obvious concern. With the total value of Time Warner exceeding the combined gross domestic product of Jordan, Bolivia, Nicaragua, Albania, Laos, Liberia, and Mali (and this was before it merged with AOL and then EMI), conglomerates like these raise concerns about the displacement of economic power beyond the control of national governments.

Anxieties about corporate control often focus on the power wielded by the individuals who own these giant conglomerates. The quintessential modern media mogul Rupert Murdoch owns over 130 daily newspapers, including the *Times* of London and the *New York Post*, the U.S. Fox television network and 22 television stations covering 40 percent of the U.S. population, Twentieth-Century Fox

(*continued*)

film studios, the book publisher HarperCollins, and major satellite broadcasting operations in Europe, Asia, China, and Latin America (again, that's only for starters). Murdoch was an ardent supporter of Margaret Thatcher, whose electoral success many political analysts partially attribute to the support of his British newspaper empire,

Sources: Bagdikian (2005); McChesney (2004).

and was accused of exercising similar clout in national elections in Australia, and in city politics in New York. But although their personal power is a real issue, concentrating on individual owners may actually obscure the larger problem posed by the overall system of concentrated commercial media ownership.

How can a democracy—like Canada or Finland, for example—protect itself from conglomerates?

This is sometimes called the **hypodermic model**, because it sees media as "injecting" audiences with messages that make them act in a certain way (Lasswell, 1927). The association with drugs is not accidental. In this perspective, media tend to be regarded as dangerous and addictive, the audience as passive zombies or glassy-eyed dupes. Such a view is shared by both conservatives, who hold the media responsible for the breakdown of family and religious values, and left and liberal critics, who see media as instruments of capitalist indoctrination.

Although this view is intuitively appealing, it has some serious problems. For example, it has been notoriously difficult to isolate the supposed effects of media from a host of other social influences, such as social class or gender roles, which are always simultaneously working on people. Moreover, in practice most studies have shown a variety of responses to specific messages, rather than uniform "mass" effects. It is also worth noting that few media researchers believe that media have taken over *their* minds; television zombies or "vidiots" are always other people!

These difficulties led some social scientists to ask not "what do the media do to people?" but "what do people do with the media? For example, researchers of the **cultural studies school** began to investigate popular culture as an arena where contending cultural codes and agendas are in conflict. Mass media are not only sites where powerful institutions, such as corporations or the state, try to instil identities and values—those of "consumer" or "citizen," for example. They are also a zone where these values and identities can be opposed and subverted. This process involves not only how programs are produced, or "encoded," but also how they are received or "decoded" (Hall, 1980).

An early focus of cultural studies theorists was television news. They showed news broadcasts to groups of people from different socioeconomic groupings— managers, management trainees, shop stewards, trade-union members, and students from various institutions— and analyzed their responses (Morely, 1980). Suppose a newscaster begins a broadcast with a statement like, "In a turn of events that significantly worsens Canada's economic crisis, Wall Street traders sold Canadian dollars." People watching the news might accept the "dominant" interpretation, in effect saying, "Wow, there is an economic crisis; something has to be done right away." Others might come up with a "negotiated" reading, accepting the broad picture laid out by the newscast, but with some qualification or modification: "Seems the economy is in bad shape—but we mustn't lose sight of even more important environmental problems."

Or, a viewer might make an "oppositional" reading, which rejects the dominant message completely. For example, a person might watch the news and comment, "What economic crisis? This is just the corporate agenda for cutting our social programs and wages and increasing their profits." The researchers concluded that the "meaning" of the news depends on the audience member's class and ethnic position and not simply on how it is produced. It also depends on how it is received.

Today a whole school of media analysis rejects the idea of audiences as "couch potatoes" and depicts them as creative co-participants in the construction of meaning (Fiske, 1994). This does not mean that a program is just an inkblot from which an audience can make anything. It has a definite structure that favours a "preferred reading." But, equally, viewers are not blank slates waiting to be inscribed with whatever message is transmitted. Rather, they are active agents of interpretation and criticism. This concept has now been applied to many different kinds of programs—not just news, but also more entertaining media products.

There have, for example, been several studies of the audience activity generated by *Star Trek* (Jenkins, 1994). In addition to their famous conventions, the program's fans, known as "Trekkies," generate a stream of newsletters, books, and discussion groups. These, in effect, constantly add to, reinterpret, and rewrite the "official" *Star Trek* story. Audiences thus start to "poach" on producers' control over their characters, by investing them with an alternative life—perhaps one that more closely reflects some of the issues audiences find important. Much of this activity has been taken by women and often elaborates on the role of female characters, or adds dimensions of personal relationships that are missing in the television drama—for example, speculating on a homoerotic relationship between Captain Kirk and Mr. Spock. This can be seen as an attempt to transform the series from the somewhat traditional masculine-dominated, science-fiction genre in which it was originally cast. Interestingly enough, with the introduction of a female captain, these negotiated readings actually seem to have succeeded in altering the predominant version of *Star Trek* culture.

[Research Focus]

Filtering the Media

A controversial analysis of how the corporate media shape world views was presented by the celebrated linguist Noam Chomsky and his co-author, political economist Edward Herman. They noted that while we fear thought control—a world in which powerful institutions shape perception of reality, an accusation made about totalitarian societies—it also happens here. U.S. media, although apparently free, control people's thoughts, including those of a growing numbers of Canadians, by the operation of five "filters":

1. the size, concentrated ownership, owner wealth, and profit orientation of the dominant mass media firms;

2. the reliance of media on advertising as their primary income source;

3. the dependency of the media on information provided by business, government, and "experts" funded and approved by these sources;

4. "flak"—that is, the ability of corporations and governments to discipline media by threatening expensive lawsuits in response to critical coverage;

5. "mobilization against threats"—then communism, today terrorism—to serve as a national secular religion and ideological control mechanism.

Sources: Chomsky (2002); Chomsky and Herman (1988).

Chomsky and Hermann tested their thesis by comparing U.S. media coverage of human rights atrocities around the globe in areas from Indonesia, to El Salvador and Guatemala, to Lebanon. They found that outrages committed by regimes or movements hostile to U.S.-style capitalism are extensively reported and criticized, but similar or greater atrocities committed by regimes sympathetic to U.S. state and business interests are greatly neglected. They concluded that the U.S. media act on a "propaganda model"—one that is actually as, or even more, effective in controlling public opinion than media in overtly authoritarian societies.

Of course many people strongly disagree with Chomsky and Herman. Some critics dismiss them as "conspiracy theorists"; others claim that their work focuses on a handful of special cases, or underestimates the independence of editors and reporters. Others say that while their theories have some truth with respect to the traditional mass media such as television or newspapers, the growth of alternative media, such as the Internet, is enough to counterbalance the corporate influence. Nonetheless, their work is a serious challenge to complacency about the fairness and freedom of our own media system.

You can see a good presentation of Chomsky and Herman's views in the film *Manufacturing Consent*, which is an interesting demonstration of the way independent media can be used to contest mainstream views.

To what extent do state-owned media, like the CBC, ensure media independence?

By showing that people can respond to and reinterpret media in different ways, such **active audience theory** has made a crucial addition to media theory. And it has shown that this activity can be a significant element in struggles over cultural authority. But it is also important to acknowledge the limitations of this perspective. In focusing on the micro choices we make in interpreting media, it is easy to lose sight of the macro structures that shape their overall agenda. Concentrating too much on alternative readings of a single episode of, say, *The Sopranos* or *Desperate Housewives* can actually make us lose sight of the way all these readings are situated in a framework dictated by television networks' need to attract advertising audiences. A balanced media analysis needs both to acknowledge the power of the meanings inscribed by media producers, *and* to recognize how these meanings can be challenged and changed by viewers and readers in the act of reception.

Arguments about active or passive audiences are intensified by the trend toward so-called "reality" television. Shows like *Survivor* and *The Apprentice* feature "ordinary" people in supposedly "real"—though carefully engineered—situations. One point of view suggests that this type of programming boosts the "couch potato" aspect of television watching, making viewers into voyeurs not just of celebrity performance, but also of everyday life. People may even begin to consider life as one continuous spectacle put on for viewing pleasure, with little requirement for participation or serious social involvement.

The contrary argument is that there is something empowering about "reality TV." It affirms that ordinary people—even you and me—are interesting enough to merit camera attention and asserts that our normal activities of self-presentation, such as trying to get a date or negotiate an agreement, can sometimes be performances, worthy of any television star. A cynic, of course, would suggest that the networks are just happy that the production costs of "reality TV" are a fraction of those for other prime-time shows.

Gender and the Media

Much of the most interesting recent work on media has focused around issues of gender. If our identities as male or female, heterosexual or homosexual, are not entirely biologically given but to some degree socially constructed, images and messages distributed through the media play a crucial role in this process. Television, film, video, and music help define what we consider attractive or sexy, "truly" masculine or feminine looks and behaviour, or the "typical" conduct or appearance of gays and lesbians.

Feminist sociologists have argued that men have generally commanded access to the most powerful means of communication of the age. For example, think of the monopoly of predominantly male clerics over reading and writing in the medieval period, or of the predominance of men as both players and producers of video and computer games today. Despite the prominence of female stars and performers in the contemporary media, a number of studies suggest that, behind the scenes, men continue to occupy a majority of the crucial positions in media ownership, management, and production. Later in the chapter, you will read about Rupert Murdoch and his immense influence in Great Britain; in Canada we have Paul Desmarais, and now, the sons of Izzy Asper.

Given this, it is perhaps hardly surprising that media are full of stereotypical images and messages that support masculine control over women. Television still reinforces gender norms when it includes soft nurturing sounds for girls but louder explosive sounds for boys. Feminists have long accused Hollywood of making films that are constructed for the pleasure of the "male gaze," which makes women objects of voyeuristic spectacle. If all channels of communication disseminate such images, the information revolution is obviously of little good to women. At the same time, however, media are a crucial arena in which sexist images and messages can be changed (Byerly and Ross, 2006).

Some of the earliest debates in this field focused on "soap operas"—television dramas that deal with everyday events of family, domesticity, and romance. These have long been regarded as typically "female" programs, in contrast to "masculine" news, sports, or action movies. Indeed, the "soaps" were so called because such shows were at first sponsored on radio by Procter and Gamble, a producer of domestic cleaners and detergents, to attract the female viewers to whom their products could be advertised.

This was part of a larger pattern. When media-based advertising got into full swing in the early twentieth century, women were very rapidly targeted as a key audience. In the gendered division of labour associated with industrial production, men went to work and women stayed at home to labour in the house (recall Chapter 7,

Gender Relations). Women did most of the shopping. They were also responsible for organizing and operating the new domestic appliances, from gas stoves to washing machines and vacuum cleaners, which were changing the household from a site of subsistence activities to a centre of consumption. Advertising was mobilized to win popular acceptance for these innovations, targeting women in campaigns that drew on traditional images of beauty, domesticity, and incompetence, but tied them in a quite new way to the acquisition of goods. "Soaps" were

among the programs designed to support these campaigns. They were structured to fit the rhythm of a housewife's work, scheduled to punctuate the day with a break, but designed to allow distracted viewing.

For a long time, soap operas were regarded as the epitome of trivial mass media, and dismissed by male critics as mindless entertainment. Insofar as they were discussed, they were often criticized for indoctrinating women into conventional domestic roles—as "good" wives and mothers. Then researchers who studied

---

[Social Trends]

I Can't Believe It . . . Not Another Ad!

Advertising is such a fundamental part of our media system that we usually take it completely for granted. But advertising is big business. Newspapers get 75 percent of their revenue from ads, general-circulation magazines 50 percent, commercial broadcast television almost 100 percent, and cable television around 20 percent. Even film media, which we do not think of as advertising-based, are involved in practices like product placement (e.g., featuring actors drinking an identifiable soft drink). World Wide Web sites are full of advertising streamers and sidebars inviting a click. In constant dollars, global expenditures have risen by 30 percent in the last decade and are forecast to increase at greater rates than general economic growth for some time to come. This activity is led by a handful of advertising agencies based in New York, London, Paris, and Tokyo. One firm, Saatchi and Saatchi of London, with offices in eighty countries, buys 20 percent of all commercial time in world television.

There is, of course, enormous debate as to whether media advertising is positive or negative. Supporters say it provides the funding that assures the media's independence from government and provides free television programs for large numbers of people. Advertising plays a valuable role in informing the public about the availability, merits, and competing prices of goods. They also add that many ads are creative and entertaining.

Critics say that advertisers sometimes specify what content may or may not accompany an ad. More generally, dependence on advertising revenues orients media to "lifestyle" issues that encourage people to spend on fashion, holidays, homes, and toys, and away from hard news or controversial topics that might break the "buying mood." Advertising revenues encourage media to pay less attention to the views and interests of those who do not have buying power. On top of this, critics accuse advertising of making people acquisitive and fostering "false needs." They say advertisements encourage unrealistic and unattainable expectations about lifestyle and body image, promote some very dangerous practices, like smoking, and, by constantly exhorting us to consume, contribute to the assault on the environment.

Try the following experiment. Try to remember all of the ads you saw or heard yesterday—in newspapers, on radio and television, on billboards and signs, and on the Internet—from the time you got up to the time you went to sleep. Then imagine that all had been exhorting you, not to buy things, but to recycle used products, reduce world poverty, or follow a particular religious faith. Think about what it would do to your mind to be surrounded by a media system that depended on those kinds of message. Now you will probably understand what Williams (1980) was getting at when he called advertising "the propaganda of capitalism."

Sources: Leiss, Kline, and Jhally (1986); Williams (1980).

Does the existence of free public service ads weaken left-wing criticisms of the media?

actual soap-opera audiences challenged this idea (Hobson, 2003). They found that viewers, far from being passive sponges that absorb what is presented to them, interpret and discuss what they watch, and sharply distinguish fantasy from reality. There is enormous variety in the characters viewers like and identify with. Women viewing soaps do not show much sign of easy indoctrination in domestic virtue. Many identify not with the conventionally "good" heroines, but with the female villains who disrupt and destroy the stability of the nuclear family. They are sometimes quite open about how this expressed their hostility about domestic subordination. The plot lines of these shows became topics for conversation among soap-opera watchers, a forum for working out or discussing views about fidelity, monogamy, marriage, abortion, and homosexuality. Rather than being just vehicles for patriarchal ideology, soaps are a rich symbolic resource out of which women construct scripts for everyday life and affirm important aspects of it that men in general overlook or disparage.

A different but related approach to the gendering of mass media looked at the control of both technology and time in domestic settings. A study of working-class families in England examined the effects of gender in terms of styles of television viewing. Men, who often control the remote, practise uninterrupted, silent viewing. For women, watching television is usually done while performing at least one domestic task or social activity. Solo viewing is a "guilty pleasure" only to be indulged when the rest of the family is not there. Men plan their viewing more systematically than women, but talk less about television with friends. These different viewing styles, the researchers argued, reflect the cultural and economic shaping of female and male roles by which the home is defined for men primarily as a site of leisure, while for women, it is primarily a sphere of work, whether or not they also work outside the home. Television viewing is therefore something men are better placed to do wholeheartedly, and which women seem only to be able to do distractedly because of their sense of domestic responsibility. Significantly, some of these patterns—such as control of the remote—change when women are wage earners and men are unemployed.

Of course, the gendered division of labour on which soap-opera culture was founded has slowly been eroding. This process has been both reflected and reinforced by changing media images of women. In the 1960s and 1970s, women became increasingly rebellious against

stereotypes. Feminist analysis accused advertisers of portraying women only in sexualized, decorative, and subordinate roles, as physically passive, emotionally dependent, and intellectually incompetent (Friedan, 1963). Reactions against such derogatory and demeaning images included defacing advertisements, product boycotts, picketing, legal cases, and attempts by women inside of the media industries to alter advertising practices. There were also other forces in play. As more and more women entered the paid workforce, and gained independent control of their income, advertisers and media producers had an incentive to appeal to potential female buyers on a new basis. Similarly, alterations in the acceptability of homosexuality in media have come at least in part from corporate recognition that the gay and lesbian community is a demographically attractive consumer group (Gauntlett, 2002). Better media treatment of women and sexual minorities arose because, while "sex sells," it is just as important that "money talks."

Whatever the reason, the last three decades have seen significant alteration in representation of both women and men in television advertising, and the programs it supports. There are still plenty of smiling housewives and seductive sex mannequins. But a growing proportion of consumer goods' advertising stresses women's expanding opportunities for achieving success and equality. Television is full of new images: professional or career women, self-confident and secure, beautiful, independent, and successful—liberated, yet feminine and romantic.

Analysts are divided as to the significance of this shift. Many see it as emancipating, a real improvement on the female stereotypes of the 1950s, with their compulsory domesticity and normalized subservience to men. Others, however, believe that "superwoman ads" simply create a yet more demanding ideal image of femininity, in which women must be professionally successful, caring mothers, and stunningly good-looking—all at the same time. Researchers such as Kilbourne (1999) argued that the new advertising regimes focused on supposedly positive images of confident female sexuality have in fact had a deeply destructive effect on women's well-being. She argued that such advertisements encourage girls and young women to see themselves (and be seen) as sex objects at ever-earlier ages, and, by promoting totally unattainable body images, help cause serious health disorders such as depression and anorexia. In her view, television today is, if anything, less female-friendly than it was thirty years ago.

At the same time, men are increasingly targeted for fashion, cosmetic, and exercise regimes (Gauntlett, 2002). To some extent, advertisers' representation of domestic work has also changed; it is not unusual today to see images featuring fathers taking care of children. The predominantly heterosexist codes of advertising have also changed a bit. Homosexuality was long taboo to the advertising agencies. Outside of publications or programs specifically aimed at the gay or lesbian communities, overtly homosexual representation is still largely excluded. Some analysts, however, argue that certain media—for example, men's fashion magazines—now practise "gay window advertising" (Clark, 1995: 490). This doesn't make explicit reference to homosexual desire (male or female) but offers opportunities for readers to perceive it if they want to, thus creating a space for formerly inadmissible sexual preferences. Both within individual ads and across the entire span of advertising a more complex cultural construction of gender identities is gradually emerging.

The gender codes of prime-time television programming have also shifted. It is now common in soap operas and situation comedies to see champions of "macho"

The role of television in the socialization process is the subject of ongoing debate.

sexist values held up as figures of fun or criticism. Programs such as *Roseanne*, still widely seen in reruns, played an important role in giving a public discussion to hidden crimes such as domestic violence and childhood sexual molestation. The on-screen "coming out" of the central character of the comedy *Ellen*, several years before audiences became aware of talk-show host Rosie O'Donnell's sexuality, was widely regarded as a landmark in making lesbianism more publicly acceptable in North America. Even the now-in-syndication television show *Baywatch*, notorious for its displays of bikinis on its female lifeguards, chiselled chests for its males, and perfect idealized heterosexuality, was caught up in such change when the decision of its world-famous star, Pamela Anderson, to remove her breast implants provided a catalyst for discussion about cosmetic norms of female beauty. More recently, *Sex and the City* has given an eloquent television voice to single women's perspectives on sexuality, relationships, and social codes, with debates raging over whether its female protagonists are third-wave feminists who won't conform to a preconceived image of emancipation or merely recapitualating the traditional search for Mr. Right (Akass and McCab, 2004), while many saw *Buffy the Vampire Slayer* as a humorous but groundbreaking assertion of teenage female empowerment. These examples show how media constitute a public forum for negotiation and discussion of gender codes that are in a state of flux (Gauntlett, 2002; Cortes, 2000; Byerly and Ross, 2006).

Violence in the Media

An issue of fierce public controversy is that of violence in the media. Many popular books, comics, films and television programs, and, most recently, video games, involve the depiction of death and injury. Thrillers, detective shows, westerns, war films, horror shows, and even many cartoons all, in different ways, hinge on violent encounters. What the relationship is, if any, between this simulated mayhem and the actual incidence of murder, assault, and other violent crimes is hotly debated (see Chapter 4, Socialization). One writer observed that the topic of television violence alone "may qualify for some sort of world record" in the number of research studies devoted to it (Cashmore, 1994: 59).

Those who believe media violence promotes real-life violence base their argument on the intuitively appealing idea that people learn from media. Repeated exposure to media representations of violent acts provides models for behaviour that may later, under the right circumstances, be acted out for real. This is especially the case when the violent acts are glorified or glamorized, or when those perpetrating them do not suffer any negative consequences—as with shows or games that celebrate killers who get away scot-free. Proponents of this view say that the types of violence represented are becoming more graphic and extreme—consider the decapitations and disembowelling common in many recent films and games. Not surprisingly, such views focus on the effects of media violence on children and adolescents, who are believed to be particularly vulnerable.

However, there is a counter-case. Though the idea that we learn by media example is an attractive one, there is a contrary and equally intuitive theory about the psychological effects of violent spectacles. This says that vicariously experiencing aggression provides a *substitute* for actually expressing it, and acts as a sort of "safety valve." This is the **surrogate theory**. So, if you have had an unpleasant confrontation with the boss, going home to play a gory video game such as *Soldier of Fortune* may work off the frustration and help you calm down, rather than inspire you to check into work next day with a semi-automatic weapon. Further, it is often argued, the idea that media violence is some recent and awful invention is nonsense. Our myths and stories have always found fascination in the violent and gruesome; a glance at traditional children's fairy stories will reveal enough cut-off fingers, beheadings, and general cruelty to keep even Freddy Krueger happy. These stories have played an important and useful part in coming to terms with the "dark side" of our psyches. If we are searching for the causes of violent crime, the skeptics say, there are much more important places to look than media: poverty, drugs, family disintegration, the availability of guns, and so on.

But the critics of media violence come right back with rebuttals. Media industries themselves seem to subscribe to the idea that they are modelling actual behaviour. On what is advertising (on which television relies for its revenues) based, other than learning by watching? Moreover, to suggest that video games and films are no more dangerous than traditional stories, ignores their new level of technological realism and immediacy. In an influential book, Grossman (1995), a psychologist and military officer, pointed out that exposure to elaborate simulations of violence is precisely the way armies increase the deadliness of their soldiers. He suggested that the proliferation of violent video games and films amounts to a sort of informal training to kill, administered to a youthful population.

Faced with this array of arguments, all plausible, yet totally contradictory, what is a media analyst to do? The answer may seem obvious: set up an experiment to test the competing hypotheses. The media violence debate is, however, a startling demonstration of just how difficult it is to convincingly test sociological theories. Many researchers have tried to demonstrate the effects of media violence on experimental subjects. An early, famous experiment was conducted in the 1960s in which two groups of children were shown different pieces of film in which a human interacted with an inflatable, three-foot doll—known as the "Bobo doll." In one film, an adult beats Bobo with a mallet; in the other, Bobo is treated gently. After watching the film, children were left alone with a similar doll. The group who had seen the gentle film treated Bobo nicely, while those who had viewed the violent film gave him a distinctly rough time. Bandura, Ross, and Ross (1963) claimed the children's behaviour had been learned through simple observation and mimicry.

Subsequently there have been many similar but more sophisticated tests. The majority, though by no means all, conclude that exposure to media violence leads to effects such as **desensitization**—making the subject less sensitive to real violence (Drabman and Thomas, 1974) or to **disinhibition**—inclining the subject to shed barriers toward physical expression of aggressive feelings (Berkowitz, 1975). There are, however, some that support the alternative "surrogate" theory of dissipated or reduced aggression. All, however, found a range of variation in responses to violent programs. And they also found many cultural and context-bound variations—for example, with very different results from tests carried out in the U.S., Israel, and Finland. To make things even more difficult, two researchers discovered intensification in aggression among children following extended viewing not only of violent cartoons, but also of *Sesame Street*. This suggests it is not the content, but the pace of a show, or perhaps even the very nature of television as a medium, that is aggressively stimulating. Lots of fast, colourful action, rather than images of fighting and injury, may be the crucial factor (Cashmore, 1994: 66).

The problem with all these experiments is that leaping from findings in a highly controlled laboratory to conclusions about real-life behaviour is risky. There are a host of other influences at work on people shaping

Video Games: Masters of the New Media

New technologies are constantly spurring the creation of new media industries. One of the most dramatic recent examples is video and computer gaming. Three decades have seen their transformation from a whimsical invention of bored Pentagon researchers into the most rapidly expanding sector of the entertainment industry. The U.S. video-game business is now as large as the Hollywood box office. Globally, the value of the industry is estimated at between $20 and $30 billion.

The first digital game, *Spacewar*, was created on the mainframe computers of defence-related researchers at U.S. universities. In 1972 Bushnell commercialized this innovation, launching Atari, the company that made the first home console system, an 8-bit mini-computer connected to a television screen. With games such as *Pong* and *Asteroid*, Atari introduced video gaming to millions of households, and spawned scores of imitative companies. In 1984, however, the U.S. industry experienced an over-production crisis, destroying consumer interest with a glut of inferior games. Thousands of unsold cartridges were bulldozed into landfill sites in Nevada, and the U.S. industry was all but extinguished.

Its revival was the achievement of a Japanese playing card and electronic novelty company, Nintendo. In the 1970s Nintendo licensed video-game technology from U.S. producers, then developed its own consoles, and finally took control of the Japanese industry. In the mid-1980s, it invaded the North American market. Nintendo fostered video-game culture not just with cheaper and better game-playing machines, but also with lavish promotional ventures, magazines, phone lines, and Disney-style licensing deals. By the early 1990s, its signature character, the Italian-American plumber Mario, had higher name recognition among U.S. children than Mickey Mouse.

Then, in a classic instance of the technological leapfrogging that drives the industry, a challenger, Sega, introduced a newer, faster, 16-bit console. It supported this with an aggressively "cool" campaign of television advertising, aimed at older boys—a demographic targeting

underlined by Sega's violent games, such as the notorious heart-ripping version of *Mortal Kombat*, which Nintendo, with its carefully chosen family image, had avoided. Although Nintendo dominated North America and Japan, Sega found a toehold in the growing European market, and support from a variety of independent software developers who resented Nintendo's strict licensing agreements. Throughout the early 1990s, the Sega–Nintendo game wars drove the business to new technological improvements, ever more extravagant promotional techniques, and a steadily increasing share of leisure expenditures. Eventually, Sega made some bad business gambles, suffered financial disaster, and pulled out of the console wars, its place rapidly taken by two competing industry giants, Sony and Microsoft. Today there is a three-way fight for corporate dominance in the console gaming field, among Sony with its *PlayStation 3*, Microsoft with its *Xbox*, and Nintendo with its *Wii*. And not just video games are booming. Computer games, pioneered by titles such as *Myst* and *Doom*, have become ever more impressive, with contemporary games such as *Grand Theft Auto, The Sims*, or *Medieval: Total War* representing massive leaps in the quality of graphics, performance speed, and artificial intelligence. Indeed, many people argue that it is hard-core gamers' demand for top-quality machines capable of playing such sophisticated software that now drives the consumer computer market.

Digital play is now central to North American popular culture. Lara Croft, the shapely digital heroine of the hit game *Tomb Raider*, experienced via the forty million PlayStation consoles sold worldwide, became among the hottest of current media celebrities. All the major Hollywood film studios have investments in or alliances with digital gaming enterprises. Indeed, many successful video games today come from movie blockbusters—*The Matrix, Star Wars, Harry Potter, James Bond, Lord of the Rings, Spiderman, The Hulk*—and sometimes the revenues from the game versions match or exceed the take from cinema seats. This may be only a beginning. Online gaming, played by connection to the Internet, has become increasingly important. Virtual communities formed

(continued)

around games such as *World of Warcraft, Battlefield,* and *Second Life* are eagerly scanned by business analysis as potentially profitable areas of experimentation with e-commerce. Many believe that digital gaming will play a major role in the commercial development of computer-mediated communication, and tout it as a "killer application" in the wave of interactive entertainment that will transform leisure time across the planet. At the same time, many aspects of video games—their frequent violence, supposedly addictive qualities, and tendency to attract boys and men rather than women and girls—crystallize some people's worst fears about a digital world, even while others find it a fascinating and enjoyable new realm of cultural experimentation.

How can the digital game culture be changed to appeal more to women and girls?

---

attitudes toward violence—including family, school, gender, and class. It is very difficult indeed to control for these variables, to isolate the effects of, say, television. Even if we discover that people who watch a lot of violent television behave more aggressively than those who do not, what we have demonstrated is a correlation, not a causal relation (see Chapter 2, Research Methods). We have shown that the two things are associated with each other, not that one leads to another. Watching violent media and behaving violently could both be the products of a third factor. Perhaps, for example, lonely, alienated, depressed people like watching violent television and are also more likely to be violent because they are lonely, alienated, and depressed.

In this quagmire, there is one research program that stands out by virtue of its clear design and long-term investigation. It is the study of the so-called **cultivation effect** conducted by Gerbner at the Annenberg School of Communication in Philadelphia over the last thirty years. First, Gerbner and his associates conducted a systematic analysis of the "message system" of television. They focused not on individual programs, but rather on the overall content of television, doing round-the-clock viewing. Using detailed coding systems, they charted the content of what they saw to find out what the world depicted on television was like. They found it had a lot more men than women, more young people than old, more professionals and law enforcement officers than manual workers. It was also a very violent world. In the 1980s, for example, Gerbner and his crew found that "crime in prime time is at least ten times as rampant as in the real world. An average of five to six acts of overt physical violence per hour involves over half of all major characters. Yet pain, suffering, and medical help rarely follow this mayhem" (Gerbner, Gross, Morgan, and Signorelli, 1987: 445).

The researchers then took a sample of viewers and asked them questions about their perceptions of the world, to find out how closely they reflect the potential lessons of television. How far are the apparent facts of television accepted as truth? Dividing viewers into heavy, average, and light viewers, they found that on many issues the assumptions, beliefs, and values of heavy viewers are quite consistent and differ systematically from those of light viewers in the same demographic group. They termed this tendency for heavy viewers to adopt a similar or homogenous world view "mainstreaming" (Gerbner, Gross, Morgan, and Signorelli, 1987: 441). In particular, heavy viewers tend to believe that the real world is a far more "scary" place than light viewers do. Those who watch more television express greater interpersonal mistrust, perceive the world as "mean," and endorse statements that reflect fear and vulnerability. Gerbner concluded that television systematically "cultivates" certain perceptions of the real world—hence the term "cultivation effect." He did not assert that the heavy television viewers' apprehensive view of reality necessarily translates into violent behaviour. But he did suggest that as people see a violent world portrayed on television, they may become fearful, demand protection, and welcome the use of force by police and other authorities. They may re-create the world as television depicts it. We should note that this part of his analysis is speculative. Moreover, some of the statistical techniques used by Gerbner have been seriously challenged. Nonetheless, his research remains one of the most sustained systematic attempts to demonstrate how media violence affects perceptions of the world.

None of this, however, establishes an indisputable causal connection between media and real-life violence. Opponents of censorship or regulation argue that critics of media violence have not met the burden of proof. They say that any evidence of the negative effects of media violence is too slender to warrant the abridgement of valued social rights such as freedom of expression. Further, no sensible researcher in the field would pretend that media are the sole—or even primary—cause of real-life violence. If media studies are to inform policy makers on the issue, the question has to be what action is appropriate in an uncertain, complex, and tangled situation. A strict innocent-until-proven-guilty approach will not favour intensified regulation, since there will always be room for reasonable doubt about media culpability. On the other hand, in some other fields—such as ecology—policy makers have started considering the "precautionary principle," which says that in situations where toxic effects are possible, though not proven, it is better to hold back. This sort of perspective might provide a different approach to regulating media representations of violence. In any case, those who demand unequivocal answers on this question will be waiting for a long time (for more on this issue, return to Chapter 4, Socialization).

One World: Media and Globalization

In the introductory chapter you briefly encountered the ideas of McLuhan, arguably Canada's best-known social theorist. One of McLuhan's most powerful predictions was that advances in communication technology would create a "global village" (1964: 87), a planetary community united by electronic media. In some ways, this promise appears to be fulfilled. New media enable images and messages to be transmitted around the world at a speed and over distances unimaginable a century ago. We are accustomed to seeing live news broadcasts of horrifying or inspiring events from points as distant as Baghdad, Kandahar, and Beijing. Events like World Cup soccer finals, watched by billions on television sets, do seem like mediated global community experiences. Recently, these developments have been cited as evidence of a globalizing process in which media play a crucial role in integrating the planet economically, politically, and culturally.

However, global integration is not the same as global equality (see Chapter 17, Social Change). Just as there are vast differences in the material resources available to different sections of the global population, so there are massive disparities in the distribution of media resources. Media resources are massively concentrated in the developed world (see Table 12.2). There are more phone lines in Manhattan or Tokyo than in the whole of sub-Saharan Africa. As Hamelink (1990) put it, the planetary information society is characterized by an **information imbalance** that gives some people much better capacities to produce, record, process, and distribute information than others.

Some analysts see the ever-expanding reach of global media as a weapon of **cultural imperialism**.

Table 12.2   Pervasiveness of Global Media, 2003

Region	Youth literacy (% of population)	Telephone lines (per 1000)	Cell subscribers (per 1000)	Internet users (per 1000)
Least developed countries	57%	8	16	4
Arab states	68%	94	118	49
East Asia (includes China)	95%	172	212	80
South Asia (includes India)	62%	47	24	18
Latin America/Caribbean	93%	165	239	n/a
Central & Eastern Europe	99%	232	287	n/a
High Income OECD (North America & Western Europe)	99%	567	705	480
WORLD	n/a	184	226	120

Source: Adapted from *United Nations Human Development Report 2005*. http://hdr.undp.org/reports/global/2005/pdf/HDR05_HDI.pdf.

European nations once directly occupied colonial territories in Africa, Asia, and Latin America. But today, it is argued, the "developed" nations—most notably the United States—exercise a more insidious but equally effective long-distance, neo-colonial control through economic and cultural means. A major aspect of this neo-colonial regime is that developing nations are swamped by Western cultural imports: films, television programs, music, newspapers, and magazines. Indigenous ways of life are overwhelmed by an electronically transmitted global culture whose content is, in fact, determined at the centre of the world system, and whose advertisements and entertainment are geared to promote dependence on Western consumer goods and political systems.

Recently, however, the cultural imperialism concept has been critically re-examined (Tomlinson, 1991). The idea of Western media indoctrinating people in the developing world depends on a very passive view of media reception, of precisely the sort rejected by "active audience" theory. In a famous study, Liebes and Katz (1993) looked at viewers' responses to the U.S. soap opera *Dallas*, a program often seen as typifying North American greed, materialism, and sexual promiscuity. They examined the reactions of a variety of ethnic groups in Israel—Arabs, newly arrived Russian Jews, Moroccan Jews, and long-time Israeli citizens—and also conducted a comparison study in Japan. They found a wide diversity of interpretations and reactions. Some viewers "read" the show in a way to make its events consistent with norms of their own culture—for example, reinterpreting personal relations to make them fit their own codes of sexual propriety. Others recognize the difference between the values of *Dallas* and that of their own cultures, but see the program as a critique, rather than a celebration, of consumerist values, exposing the superficiality and misery of its characters' lives. This finding seems to contradict the idea that Western media impose uniform values on international audiences.

It has also been suggested that the concept of U.S. cultural imperialism has been overtaken by the increasingly diversified international patterns of media ownership. The rise of "Bollywood," the Indian film industry; Middle Eastern satellite television, such as Al Jazeera; and Japanese video-game companies suggests that what is happening is more complex than cultural imperialism. Rather than a one-way stream of media messages from the West to the rest, what is occurring is a two-way process of **hybridization** (Martin-

Barbero, 1993; Morely and Robins, 1995). If reliance on standardized Hollywood products is one key strategy by which media corporations establish a world presence, another is the selling of exotic cultural items to cosmopolitan North American consumers. At the same time, people all over the planet are adapting, improvising, and changing media products, appropriating them to create novel and unexpected forms. An example would be the emergence of various sorts of "world music"—reggae, ska, bhangra, ethno-pop—that can variously be described as "Western pop-stars appropriating non-Western sounds, as developing-world musicians using Western rock and pop, or as the Western consumption of non-Western folk music" (Wallis and Malm, 1984: 15).

All this has led some proponents of the cultural imperialism thesis to revise their arguments. In the "not yet the post-imperial era" Schiller (1991) agreed that while American cultural imperialism is not dead, it no longer adequately describes the global cultural condition. It has given way to a new form of transnational corporate cultural domination. The problem with this new order is not that it imposes one national culture on the planet but that it absorbs a variety of regional, national, and ethnic idioms into a single, placeless consumerism, in which anything can find a place—at a price. What this global commercial order squeezes out is any form of cultural production that is not for sale. Whereas previously art was created in diverse contexts, to express religious devotion, political protest, or communal togetherness, in the world market it has one overriding role: to be a profitable commodity.

This process does not unfold without conflict. Barber (1995) suggested that global media are caught up in a cultural contest he terms "Jihad versus McWorld." "McWorld" is the placeless, global consumer capitalism we have just described. "Jihad" refers to movements asserting traditional religious, ethnic, or nationalist identity. (It is important to note that Barber is not just talking about Islam. His concept of "Jihad" could also include Christian or Hindu fundamentalism, or Serbian or Québecois nationalism.) The faith- or place-based movements of Jihad fiercely resist the dominance of the secular, commercial McWorld. Clearly, the giant infotainment corporations are among the most potent forces of McWorld. But, ironically, nationalist and religious forces also use new media, as when videocassettes spread the message of the Islamic revolution in Iran, or evangelical radio and television create fundamentalist Christian communities in North America. In Barber's view, the new planetary mediascape thus promises to be swept over by contradictory currents of both global and local identity.

A striking example of this complexity was provided by the television coverage of the war in Iraq during 2003. Major U.S. television networks such as CNN, ABC, and Fox used new communications technology to provide extraordinary up-to-the-minute war reporting from journalists "embedded" with frontline U.S. troops. Much of this coverage, transmitted around the world, was framed in a patriotic discourse that probably confirmed or amplified many Americans' beliefs that the invasion of Iraq was necessary and justified.

On the other hand, the Arab-speaking world got much of its news about the war from the Al-Jazeera satellite television station broadcasting out of Qatar. It used the same global communication technologies as the U.S. stations, and largely modelled its journalistic practices and reporting style on those of CNN. But the content of its broadcasts gave a very different picture of the war, because Al-Jazeera addressed issues of concern to Arab audiences. For example, it gave much greater attention to issues of civilian casualties, to the similarities of the U.S. attack to former colonial invasions, and to the relation of the Iraq war to the conflict between Israel and Palestine. The emergence of Al-Jazeera suggests that while the power and reach of Western media systems remains strong, it may face mounting challenges as countries outside North America and Europe gain access to powerful communication technologies.

Cyberspace: Virtual Community, Virtual Commerce, Virtual Protest

Of all recent developments in media, none has provoked more interest than the emergence of computer networks—in particular, the global network of networks, the Internet. The connection of computers and telecommunication allows messages to be sent with unprecedented speed and scope. Although in reality these messages exist only in electronic impulses stored in computer memories and whizzing through fibre-optic cables and satellite links, we often speak as if they existed in some distinct, new dimension. We talk of **cyberspace**—a term invented by Gibson, the Canadian science-fiction author (1984: 51).

The first steps in the construction of cyberspace were taken in the late 1960s by the U.S. Defense Department in its attempt to build a communications system that could survive nuclear war. Later, it used the same technologies to connect university research centres working on military research. In an unforeseen development, the faculty, students, and systems managers extended the network beyond its original scope, connecting more and more sites into the main backbone, and using it not only for research, but to exchange e-mail, chat in electronic discussion groups, play games, and generally explore the new technology. Eventually, in the 1980s, the military withdrew and set up its own, separate system, leaving what had become the Internet to be managed by a decentralized collection of civilian users (Cassidy, 2002).

The result was a system that in many ways seems to realize the most radical dreams of democratic communication. Unlike one-way, centralized broadcast systems, with all programs sent from a radio or television station, the Internet is a decentralized system, with many participants, all capable of transmitting as well as receiving, allowing not just one-to-one but one-to-many communications. Although initially the Internet was a text-based system, depending on the onscreen display of words typed on a keyboard, by the 1990s the development of the World Wide Web brought both image and audio capacity. In North America and Europe, universities and other big institutions that pay a flat rate for their Internet connection are offering relatively large numbers of people access for little or no cost. The more affluent sectors of society can connect from home.

On this basis, Internet use exploded in a way totally unforeseen by its early pioneers. In 1970 there had been fewer than a hundred people using the Internet. By the early 1980s, there were only a few thousand. It is extremely difficult to find an accurate census of today's Internet population. Not only may several people be using a single computer connection or e-mail account, many of the firms and organizations making estimates have a vested interest in optimistic calculations. However, it is probably fair to say that that as of 2004 there were about one billion Internet users worldwide, roughly 15 percent of the global population.

This activity in cyberspace has attracted considerable attention from professional and amateur sociologists. One of the most influential theories is Rheingold's (1993) idea of **virtual community**. The roots of his thinking go back to the German sociologist Tönnies who argued that modern society was characterized by a loss of "we feeling" that exists in traditional communities and being replaced by an impersonal, faceless association typical of industrial, urban life. (We shall return to this topic in Chapter 17, Social Change.) According to Rheingold, people search virtual interactions for a way of reversing this tendency to isolation. They migrate into cyberspace for the "togetherness" lacking in a society fragmented into malls, freeways, and corporate workplaces. They are searching not just for information, but also for relationship.

Rheingold and other cyberspace enthusiasts suggested that virtual communities have advantages over those based on physical presence. People can connect on the basis of mutual interests, rather than accidents of geographic proximity. Because they cannot see one another, they do not form prejudices about others on the basis of race, gender, age, national origin, and physical appearance. The anonymity of online relationships gives the opportunity to experiment with a more flexible and fluid sense of self, exploring roles and personae that they might not feel free to express "in real life" (Turkle, 1995; Bruckman, 1996). Impressed by the capacity of computer networking to overleap censorship and political restriction, Rheingold and others hope for the growth of an "electronic civil society" reviving direct participation in political life and overcoming the remoteness many people feel from electoral democracy.

Others are more skeptical (Mosco, 2005). They point out that the loss of physical presence in cyberspace makes it easy to misinterpret communication, opens enormous possibilities for deception, and removes many of the commitments and constraints that compel people to act more or less responsibly in face-to-face situations. This leads to the frequent eruptions in online discussion groups called *flame wars* in which people go on long and vicious harangues against people who have offended them. It can also lead to more bizarre problems. A study by Dibbell (1996) documented a "rape in cyberspace" when a member in a role-playing cyber community used his superior programming powers to inflict sexually humiliating behaviour on other participants' virtual personae. This violation of "netiquette" caused the victims serious

Internet use has exploded—in 2004 there were probably more than one billion Internet users worldwide.

psychological distress. It also raised a host of problems about how to expel the offender from the virtual community he had abused, and prevent his return under another virtual identity.

Critics of the virtual-community concept say that the more time people spend as "mouse potatoes," in front of computer screens, the more face-to-face community will deteriorate. In this view, rather than providing a replacement for the crumbling public realm, virtual communities actually contribute to its decline. Although cyber-communication may reinforce social relationships among like-minded individuals, those groups will have a decreasing need or opportunity to interact with other members of the larger society. One U.S. study seems to support these concerns (Kraut and Lundmark, 1998). The researchers found 160 people in Pittsburgh who had never been online before, put computers in their homes, tracked their Internet use, and then used psychological questionnaires to measure alterations in their emotional well-being. They discovered a statistically significant connection between hours online and intensified feelings of loneliness and depression. The researchers suggested that, in spending time on the Net, people were trading the "strong" social bonds of face-to-face friendships and relationships for the "weak" ties of the disembodied online realm. It is also the case that the lonely and depressed may be more attracted to the Net.

Although the debate over these issues will continue for some time, the focus of activity in cyberspace is rapidly shifting from "virtual community" to **virtual commerce**. The corporate sector did not pioneer the exploration of computer-mediated communication, but the unexpected growth of the Internet roused intense commercial interest. In the 1990s business caught on to the profitable possibilities of computer networks not only as a new space for advertising but to connect customers with suppliers, monitor employees, eliminate jobs, cut travel costs, gather competitive data, and launch new goods and services. Telephone, cable, video, and software companies rushed in with supposedly "killer" applications—video-on-demand, tele-gambling, pay-per-use computer games, and infomercials (Gates, 1995). The experiments of companies such as the online bookseller Amazon.com, and the even more successful online pornography business, stirred interest in all kinds of "e-commerce."

Some of these "dot.com" ventures paid off—at least in the short term. But it soon became apparent that

many of the Net-based business ventures were more hype than substance. Consumers were much slower to adopt Internet services, and much more resistant to Internet advertising, than had been imagined. In 2000, the stock market value of many Net businesses collapsed when people realized that skyrocketing stock values were not being matched by real profits. The "Internet bubble" burst, destroying the value of companies such America Online, Nortel, and WorldCom. It was the biggest stock market crash in history, inflicting as much financial damage as if all the houses in North America had been wiped out by a gigantic tornado (Cassidy, 2002). But although the dot.com bust slowed the commercialization of the Net, it certainly hasn't stopped it. The companies that survived have consolidated in a new cycle of Internet business—in which search engines such as Google have been particularly important—and go on to make buying, selling, and advertising increasingly common in the virtual world (Abramson, 2005).

It is, however, important to note that, despite the intensifying corporate dominance of the Internet, it continues to provide expression for a diversity of interests. Some of these are opposed to the corporate agenda. In 1994 peasant farmers in a remote province of Mexico launched a revolt against conditions of poverty and social injustice that they believed were being worsened by international free-trade agreements. This movement—the Zapatistas—succeeded in attracting worldwide attention to their cause by distributing their communiqués on the Internet (Cleaver, 1994). In 2000 the major protests against the World Trade Organization in Seattle were also the occasion for the founding of a major cyber-activist network of "Independent Media Centres"—and this type of practice continues to spread across the planet. More sinisterly, terrorist organizations such as Al Quaeda are known to make extensive use of digital networks.

Certainly, it is now apparent that cyberspace, far from providing easy solutions to social dilemmas, is as complex as any terrestrial society. In its early days, the Internet was often referred to as an "electronic frontier." Today, there is an ongoing debate about the appropriate reach for "law and order" on this frontier. The issues provoking this debate include "hacking"—virtual trespass and theft; destructive computer "viruses"; online "hate speech" and pornography; and digital invasions of privacy by individuals, corporations, or government. These issues are made more difficult by the transnational nature of the Internet, which makes it extremely difficult to police. One possibility is that the Internet will persist as an area of relatively unregulated communication activity, with both the freedoms and problems this implies. Another is that the need to cope with such issues will be among the forces propelling our civilization toward more global institutions.

It is, however, important to realize that, on a world scale, relatively few people are in cyberspace. Although some 15 percent of the global population—approximately one billion out of six billion—may be connected, by far the majority of these are in the developed world (see Table 12.3). While some 60 percent of Canadian households are online, in many countries in sub-Saharan Africa less than 1 percent are connected. Across the planet, access is strongly associated with differences in income, gender, and ethnicity. Users are more likely to be male and tend to be drawn from the most affluent sections of society (Wilhelm, 2006). Although access rates are growing and the gender imbalance is diminishing, there is a significant digital divide that excludes major sections of the population because of cost, education, and time barriers. On a global scale, these obstacles are vast.

Predictions for the Future

Over the last two decades, predictions about the "information highway," "500-channel universe," or "wired world" have become commonplace. These prophecies

have often been optimistic in estimating the speed of such developments, because they tend to disregard the size and risk of investments required to construct new media systems, and the real barriers—in terms of expense, education, and habit—to their widespread public acceptance.

Because of futurists' failures to take these factors into account, it is sometimes tempting to dismiss their promises as just so much "hype." This would be a mistake. The commercial and cost-saving opportunities presented by new means of communication are so attractive to corporations and government that we can expect to see continuing innovation and applications in media technologies, and huge pressures and incentives to weave these inventions into the fabric of everyday life—at least in the affluent, "developed" world.

Rapid expansion of "e-commerce"; the fusion of phone, television, and computer into multipurpose domestic communication devices—such as "Web TV" (combining both many digitalized channels and the capacity to "surf" the Internet); the proliferation of hand-held and personalized computing devices, linked by wireless technologies; the emergence of new forms of simulation-based entertainment (of which today's video games are only a pale shadow); and the elaboration of "virtual universities" and "tele-health" systems, orienting both education and medical consultation around computer-mediated communications—all these are very much in the cards now being played by corporate and state planners. If the game goes as they hope, then our lives will be dramatically changed, not necessarily

Table 12.3   Global Online Population, 2006

World regions	Population (2006 est.)	% of world population	Internet users	% of population online	% of world users
Africa	915 210 928	14.1%	23 649 000	2.6%	2.3%
Asia	3 667 774 066	56.4%	364 270 713	9.9%	35.6%
Europe	807 289 020	12.4%	291 600 898	36.1%	28.5%
Middle East	190 084 161	2.9%	18 203 500	9.6%	1.8%
North America	331 473 276	5.1%	227 303 680	68.6%	22.2%
Latin America/Caribbean	553 908 632	8.5%	79 962 809	14.4%	7.8%
Oceania/Australia	33 956 977	0.5%	17 827 707	52.6%	1.7%
WORLD TOTAL	6 499 697 060	100%	1 022 863 307	15.7%	100%

Source: Internet World Stats. "World Internet Users and Population Statistics." www.internetworldstats.com/stats.htm (accessed 6 May, 2006).

transformed overnight, but nevertheless altered irrevocably and deeply by a series of incremental shifts in our habitual, daily ways of communicating. For example, it is quite possible that, within a decade, texts such as this will have a diminishing role in an education system increasingly oriented around various forms of online delivery.

However, we should never assume that this multiplication of media channels and information technologies amounts in any simple way to social "progress." One of the most extreme and attractive promises of the prophets of "information revolution" is that new media will create some sort of group-mind or world-brain. In this story, the enhanced capability of the planet's six billion or so inhabitants to easily and speedily circulate information and ideas will significantly improve its collective capacity to solve some of the formidable problems facing it, such as the preservation of the biosphere, the avoidance of nuclear/chemical/biological war, the elimination of poverty and disease, and the direction of the genetic future.

There seem at least two formidable barriers to the fulfillment of this dream. The first is the extraordinarily uneven social distribution of the new media. Even within advanced capitalist societies, the "digital divide" among "haves" and "have-nots" is significant; on a planetary scale, it is a gaping chasm. Without a systematic redress of these inequalities, connection to the information revolution will become a sign of global privilege, and access to communicational wealth will be seen as a source of intensified division, rather than enlarged community. The second obstacle involves the nature of the content filtered through the new media channels. Insofar as the emerging global media system is being formed primarily by commercial interests, it contains strong tendencies to select in favour of content that encourages, or at least does not challenge, the daily habits on which consumer capitalism depends. Advertisements, infotainment, and politically innocuous content will predominate, while issues such as our ecological crisis and global inequality, though not completely excluded, will be marginalized and drowned out by the exhortations to buy and have fun. In this case, advanced communications systems may make us more oblivious to, not more aware of, the future dangers confronting humankind. Only if alert planetary citizens contest these tendencies to inequality and indoctrination will our new global media system contribute to the creation of a true collective intelligence.

Summary

We began this chapter by looking at the vision of an information revolution, and its promise of a world transformed by better communications technology. To many, computer networks seem like the fulfillment of this vision. The Internet and the information highway represent the latest stage of a process that, over a couple of centuries, has taken us from a predominantly oral culture, through the spread of print literacy, and into an era of electronic and digital culture. In many respects these rapid changes have meant huge increases in knowledge, creativity, and enjoyment for millions of people—a point we hope this chapter has sufficiently acknowledged.

At the same time, however, we want to sound a note of caution about the unqualified optimism often expressed about the information revolution. It is important to look not just at technological changes, but also at the political economy of media. Control over the means of communication has always involved massive vested interests and intense social conflict. In liberal democracies, our political traditions make us at least somewhat alert to issues of governmental censorship and state direction of media systems. But it is perhaps harder for us to grasp the blind spots and blockages that arise from a market-driven media system, dominated by multinational conglomerates operating on a purely commercial basis. It is in this area that some of the most important critical media studies are now being done.

In studying issues of ownership and control, it is important not to lapse into simplistic notions about media audiences. We saw how straightforward models of media effects, which portray people as passive victims of indoctrination, have been challenged by theories that ascribe a much more active role to audiences in interpreting and criticizing what they read, hear, and see. The cultural studies school of media theory suggests that dominant values encoded in media products can be opposed or subverted by such audience decoding. This is a valuable corrective to notions of monolithic mind-control by media owners. In emphasizing the creativity of audiences, cultural studies theorists sometimes bend the stick too far the other way. But it is clear that media meanings must now be understood as arising not just in production, but also in reception.

We went on to see how these issues played out in some concrete cases. Studies of gender in media have shown that the major means of communication—

historically controlled mainly by men—have played an important role in maintaining patriarchal authority. But they also show how media can become a site of struggle. Women have reappropriated and reinterpreted texts and programs that might seem just to confirm their subordinate roles and domestic identities. Through campaigns of media activism, and because of increasing independent economic power, women and also sexual minorities have, over the last few decades, significantly altered the stereotypes transmitted by the mainstream media—even if this process sometimes seems painfully long.

The issues of onscreen and in-print violence show how difficult it can be to conclusively determine the social effects of media. Both critics of media violence and their opponents have strong intuitive arguments as to why representations of violence may or may not lead to real-life aggression. Although the huge volume of research on the topic probably suggests *some* linkage, decades of sociological and psychological work have failed to give a definitive answer to the question, largely because of the difficulty of separating the effects of media from all the other potential factors causing real-life violence. This is a case that indicates how far public policy decisions about media need to take into account the many unknowns in the media environment.

Next, we placed media in a global context. Here, the paradoxes of the information revolution are clearly revealed. In complex ways, new communications technologies *are* making something of a global village, creating exciting transnational cultural cross-fertilizations and dramatic accelerations in the circulation of knowledge. But there are also staggering inequities in the distribution of information resources. Nowhere is this clearer than in the case of that ultimate information-age media, computer networks. Here we have to simultaneously hold in mind two apparently contradictory tendencies. On the one hand, the Internet is, in speed and ease of communication, a truly global media. On the other, its use is still limited to a privileged minority of the planet's population. We should remember that there are still large numbers of people who do not read or write. It is estimated that some 880 million adults (the majority of them women) in developing countries have never been taught these skills. Even in the industrial world, there may be as many as 200 million people who do not possess adequate literacy skills. Arguably the most basic social need in the field of media is not for computer literacy, but for the skills of reading and writing. None of this is to say that media technologies are insignificant in making cultural change; instead, it is to insist that other social institutions are important too.

Our civilization has the technological power to create universal communication. But a market economy rations and stratifies access to media according to purchasing power in a way that sharply divides the global population. This tension between the technological potential for truly global communication and the limitations our economic system places on such networks may eventually prove to be the central issue of the information age.

Questions for Review and Critical Thinking

1. Which model of audience behaviour better fits your experience as a media watcher and listener—the "active audience" concept or the "hypodermic model"?

2. Take your favourite television shows. To what degree do they reinforce or challenge gender stereotypes? Can you think of a way to test this formally?

3. Do the media you encounter in daily life adequately inform you about the issues of global poverty and inequality? What factors shape their coverage of such matters?

4. Have you discovered "virtual community" on the Internet? Is it possible to have a real relationship in cyberspace?

Key Terms

active audience theory, p. 283
communications conglomerate, p. 280
cultivation effect, p. 289
cultural imperialism, p. 290
cultural studies school, p. 281
culture industry, p. 279
cyberspace, p. 292
desensitization, p. 287
disinhibition, p. 287
hybridization, p. 291
hypodermic model, p. 281
information imbalance, p. 290
information society, p. 276
political economy of media, p. 278

Suggested Readings

Balnaves, Mark, James Donald, and Stephanie Hemelryk

2001 *The Penguin Atlas of Media and Information: Key Issues and Global Trends.* Harmondsworth: Penguin.

This compendium of information about global media has flashy graphics and maps.

Abramson, Bruce

2001 *Digital Phoenix: Why the Information Economy Collapsed and How It Will Rise Again.* Cambridge: MA: MIT Press.

This book provides a knowledgeable overview of the ups and downs of the Internet economy.

Castells, Manuel

2005 *The Internet Galaxy: Reflections on the Internet, Business and Society.* Oxford: Oxford University Press.

This text is a concise summary of the findings of one of the leading sociologists of "network society."

Kline, Stephen, Nick Dyer-Witheford, and Greig de Peuter

2003 *Digital Play: The Interaction of Technology, Culture and Marketing.* Montreal: McGill-Queens University Press.

In addition to giving a detailed account of the video- and computer-game industry, this book develops a theoretical model to analyze the introduction of new media in society.

Rheingold, Howard

2002 *Smart Mobs: The Next Social Revolution.* Cambridge, MA: Perseus.

This book provides a fascinating, though highly speculative, discussion of the possible social consequences of mobile communications networks.

Byerly, Carolyn and Karen Ross (eds.)

2006 *Women And Media: A Critical Introduction.* Oxford: Blackwell.

A collection that gives a good overview of recent research on female media presence

Websites

www.mediawatch.com
MediaWatch

This site provides a view of Canadian media through a female lens. The site also allows visitors to make their views on the media known, by facilitating direct contact with media corporations, retailers, and advertisers.

www.cnn.com
CNN

This site is an example of the public face of a major media transnational corporation.

www.indymedia.org/en/index.shtml
Independent Media Center

In contrast to CNN, this is the site of the major "indy" media network, founded following the famous street protests against the World Trade Organization.

Key Search Terms

Culture industry
Information technology
Media
Advertising
Cyberspace

For more study tools to help you with your next exam, be sure to check out the Companion Website at **www.pearsoned.ca/hewitt**, as well as Chapter 12 in your Study Guide.

wolfgang lehmann

[13]

education

Introduction

Participation in some form of education is one of the defining social experiences shared by most individuals in Western industrialized societies. This may explain the consistent popularity of education as a topic in all forms of popular entertainment. The hugely successful Harry Potter book and movie series follows its heroes as they progress through an educational institution (albeit one rather different from the schools to be discussed in the remainder of this chapter). From the earnestness of *Blackboard Jungle* in the 1950s, to the countercultural resistance of *If* in the 1960s, to the inspired silliness of *Old School* and *Napoleon Dynamite* fifty years later, movies with educational themes seem to define the mood of their times. Some of the most popular television programs either take place in and around schools (one of the most successful Canadia TV programs, the *Degrassi* series and its spin-offs, are good examples), or have frequent education-themed episodes, as in *The Simpsons*.

Education has also been, either directly or indirectly, a focus of sociological research since the inception of the discipline. This should come as no surprise, as, during our most formative years growing up, we spend the majority of our time in schools. Maybe because we do spend so much time in educational institutions, we rarely consider how schooling and education not only affect individual experiences and outcomes, but also have societal implications. In this chapter, we will take a closer look at how different individuals experience education, but also at the role education plays in creating stability in a society, and how it is implicated in either minimizing or reproducing existing social inequalities.

Functions of Education

Socialization

Schools are key institutions fulfilling social needs and making contributions to social order. In school, we learn about norms and values of the society in which we live and in which we eventually have to assume responsible roles as adults. Schools accomplish this not only by what they teach explicitly—that is, by what is in the **formal curriculum**, but also through a **hidden curriculum**. Through the formal curriculum, we learn to write, read, perform mathematical calculations, and solve problems. We also learn about the culture in which we live, its rules, laws, politics, and history. Through the hidden curriculum, we learn the type of informal knowledge that is considered important for the smooth functioning of everyday life. For instance, in school we learn to work and cooperate with others (schoolmates) and we learn to submit to formal authority (teachers, principals). More importantly, we learn to behave in certain ways. We learn to come to school on time, do our homework, and not speak out of order. We become accustomed to certain ways in which our day is being organized, sometimes subconsciously, and to specific ways to process knowledge. After all, we rarely question that schools break down knowledge into definable subject areas (English, Math, History) and that we learn these subjects in specified time blocks over a clearly defined school day, and in a hierarchically structured and authoritarian classroom. All of this, of course, is not unlike what we will experience once we enter employment, become spouses and parents, and take on roles within our respective communities.

This view of education as fulfilling specific needs within society is part of a sociological traditional called functionalism. Talcott Parsons (1902–1979), whose work dominated sociological theory in North America throughout the 1950s and most of the 1960s, interpreted social institutions (like the education system) as responsible for inculcating common social values. This means that the task of schools is more complex than simply transmitting knowledge and values. What is more important is that this knowledge and these values are internalized as part of an individual's personality (Parsons, 1959). A properly schooled person intuitively knows, understands, and can act upon social expectations, rules, and norms. According to Parsons, a key function of education is to redirect young people from the emotional and person-centred demands of home and family life toward the more formalized, competitive, and achievement-oriented demands of adult life. This process has to take place gradually, which explains why there is less emphasis on testing or specific subjects in our early years of elementary schooling. We tend to have one teacher, work in one classroom, and are basically socialized into learning about learning, getting along with others, and

respecting authority and structure. Writing in the late 1950s, Parsons also argued that it makes sense for the elementary teacher to be a female, as she mirrors the nurturing role of the mother at home.

As you move through the grades, the emphasis shifts to competitiveness, performance, testing, and a division of subjects. This is accomplished by increased streaming and tracking of students into different programs, levels, and courses. Testing, grading, streaming, and credentialling sort individuals into different positions in the social and occupational hierarchy. In other words, these processes help determine who will eventually become the doctors, lawyers, teachers, managers, factory workers, carpenters, hairdressers, and garbage collectors. Furthermore, individuals are socialized to accept and understand their future positions in the social hierarchy, through a different emphasis on knowledge and social interactions in their respective streams and the courses they take. From a functionalist perspective, passing through the school system not only prepares individuals for different roles in the workplace and the nature of social life more generally, it also creates conditions by which this *role differentiation* is accepted as being based on fair and *meritocratic* principles. The latter is particularly important for the maintenance of social stability. The way functionalists see it, we do not inherit the different roles we assume as adults, but we achieve them through open and fair competition in schools.

Employment

Preparing individuals for employment and developing a skilled and productive labour force are also key functions of education. Increasingly, it is believed that the economic prosperity of nations and successful careers and life courses for individuals are related to high levels of formal education. This belief is tied up with debates regarding what we call the post-industrial or knowledge economy. Obviously, most economies throughout history were knowledge economies in some sense: during the feudal period, for example, peasants had to have knowledge about farming practices and blacksmiths about blacksmithing practices. Yet, there are reasonably convincing arguments that we now live in a world in which economic success is mostly determined by education and knowledge.

It has been argued that, under recent conditions of globalization, the economies of industrialized nations can no longer be based on the production of mass consumer products. Labour costs in newly industrializing nations like Vietnam or China are substantially lower than in countries like Canada or the United States and most firms have been relocating factory production to these low-cost countries. This has created concerns over questionable labour practices in these countries. Most prominently, the issue of sweatshop and child labour has been associated with such well-known brands as Nike and Gap and with such celebrities as the former morning TV show host Kathie-Lee Gifford and the clothing line bearing her name. At home, this means that industrial employment is being replaced with various forms of service employment and that national economic success depends on the ability to innovate and to provide value-added products and services (e.g., Reich, 1992). These value-added services and products are to be provided by engineers, managers, brokers, lawyers, communication experts, consultants, programmers, and researchers. These arguments have obvious implications for education: all of these forms of employment can be categorized as professional-type employment requiring a substantial amount of postsecondary and most likely postgraduate education. Another catch-phrase associated with this new knowledge economy is **lifelong learning**. The skills in demand in a knowledge economy constantly shift and evolve and it therefore becomes necessary to engage in constant learning and upgrading of skills and knowledge.

Economic success in advanced, industrialized countries is said to be mostly determined by high levels of education and knowledge.

Table 13.1 Unemployment Rate in Canada by Educational Attainment, 1992, 1995, 2000

	All Levels of Education	Less than High School	High School	College or Trade	University
1992	11.2	16.9	10.9	9.5	5.7
1995	9.4	15.0	9.6	8.0	5.2
2000	6.8	12.4	7.0	5.2	4.0

Source: Adapted from Canadian Education Statistics Council (2003: 393).

Statistical data support this argument. Seventy-five percent of Canada's workforce is now employed in the service industry (Statistics Canada, 2005b). Educational attainment is positively related to labour market outcomes such as salary and job security. Average salaries increase and chances of being unemployed decrease with higher levels of educational attainment (see Table 13.1 and Table 13.2).

Both of these relationships are at the core of **human capital** theories, which—put simply—propose that there is a direct relationship between educational attainment and labour market outcomes: as you get more education, you will gain access to better jobs and a higher income. Not surprisingly, most government policies aimed at reducing unemployment focus on human capital deficiencies. In recent years, governments have looked for more direct relationships between businesses and schools, through internships, co-op placements, and youth apprenticeship programs. Often these programs are aimed at filling growing shortages of young, qualified workers in specific occupations and trades, and at offering an educational alternative to students who have little interest in traditional, academically focused education. Although students enrolled in these programs generally speak very positively about their experience and agree

that this has renewed their interest in finishing high school, critics are concerned that these programs are too narrowly focused and that they tend to operate without proper learning plans and guidelines (Lehmann and Taylor, 2003). More importantly, it has been argued that students in these programs are not given the opportunity to reflect on their experiences in the workplace, which seriously limits their ability to critically reflect on employment practices and their roles in the workplace (Lehmann, 2005b). Unlike the functionalist assumptions underlying human capital theory, these critiques are based on conflict perspectives of education. The main goal of conflict sociologists is to understand how education, either intentionally or unintentionally, is implicated in the reproduction of social inequalities.

Education and Social Inequality

Functionalist theories of education, like human capital theory, do not contest the fact that inequality exists in society. Functionalist sociologists argue that inequality is both a necessary condition of modern society and that it is based on meritocratic principles. **Meritocracy** is the

Table 13.2 Average Wages in Canada by Educational Attainment, 2000

All Levels of Education	Less than High School	High School	Trades Diploma or Certificate	College Diploma or Certificate	University
$32 183	$21 713	$25 807	$33 868	$33 531	$48 183

Source: Adapted from Statistics Canada (2003d), 2001 Census.

[Research Focus]

Underemployment

Many observers are critical about the focus on education and the improvement of human capital, as this relationship is perceived as too narrowly defining the role of education. Others, like Canadian sociologist David Livingstone, challenge the very assumption that such a clear-cut relationship exists. Livingstone provides evidence that credential inflation has actually led to a mismatch between educational credentials and labour market outcomes. Using a measure of the skill content of jobs and the formal education of job incumbents, Livingstone found that in 1996, 57 percent of employees in Ontario worked in jobs in which they did not get to use the full extent of the skills, knowledge, and abilities they acquired through formal education. Livingstone called this mismatch **underemployment** (Livingstone, 2004). This figure actually represents an increase of 13 percent of

underemployment since 1980. Using a questionnaire that directly asked workers about the match between the job demands and their education, Livingstone further found that in 1996 in Ontario, 41 percent of workers agreed that they have skills from education, training, and experience they would like to use at work, but don't get a chance to use, and 33 percent agreed with the statement that given their level of schooling, they should be entitled to a better job than what they have. This can be explained through the concept of **credential inflation** (Collins, 1979), which generally means that credential requirements for entry into many occupations and professions have increased, even though the job demands have not (or at least not to the same magnitude). But the findings also raise some doubts about the validity of claims that we have truly entered a knowledge economy.

Do you think Canadians are entitled to jobs that reflect their level of education?

principle that persons are selected for social positions based on merit, or achievement in accordance with universal standards and criteria, such as talent, motivation, tenacity, and hard work (Wotherspoon, 2004). Those working within conflict and critical sociological traditions challenge these assumptions. Rather than living in a society in which achievement is based on merit, conflict theorists argue that we see inequalities that are clearly based on ascribed characteristics such as gender, race, ethnicity, or social class. In particular, schools are considered to be institutions that perpetuate these inequalities, rather than removing them. Schools are said to keep dominant groups in power, while creating an illusion of opportunity, objectivity, neutrality, and fairness.

Gender

In recent decades, feminist challenges to education systems have been central to critical discourses on education and have been crucial in updating curricula in

Canadian provinces. There are fairly diverse strands of feminist analysis of education (e.g., Forman et al., 1990; Gaskell et al., 1989; Gaskell and McLaren, 1991). Feminists have studied the early struggles of women to be educated and to be allowed access to universities and continue to be concerned about the unequal gender distribution of teachers and administrators in the education system. In terms of how we experience and what we learn at school, feminist scholarship has looked at gendered interactions in the classroom, as well as gender-stereotyping in curriculum. For instance, researchers have found that boys tend to dominate classroom interactions and that their more aggressive behaviour is likely to be rewarded by teachers. This generally reflects how we have been socialized to expect most boys to be competitive and girls to be less so, even nurturing. This gender-stereotyping has also long been present in how men and women are portrayed in textbooks and other school materials. In large part due to the efforts of feminist scholars and activists, we have seen rather significant efforts to show men and women in non-gender-traditional roles in school materials. Nevertheless, many of these improvements are hotly contested by more conservative critics of education, while feminists argue that women's experiences are still often disregarded in curriculum. If you think back to your high school history curriculum, for instance, you probably learned a lot about the role of men in war and politics, but less about the reality of social life and the role of women in different historical periods.

The most recent data about gender and educational inequality as a dimension of social inequality is that women have not only closed the gap in educational attainment, but have actually surpassed men in recent years. Of all undergraduate degrees awarded in 2001 in Canada, 60 percent went to women. The only areas of study in which fewer women than men graduated were engineering, mathematics, and computing. Although there are still more men than women graduating with doctorate degrees, women received 52 percent of all Master's degrees in 2001. Similarly, women compose the majority of graduates from most professional post-degree programs, with, for example, 60 percent of law degree recipients and 55 percent of medical degree recipients being women. Only engineering and business programs are still dominated by men (Canadian Association of University Teachers, 2004). This is a long way from 1872, when Mount Allison University in Sackville, New Brunswick, was the first Canadian university to admit a woman and most of the first women students were relegated to especially created "female" subject areas (e.g., home economics).

Although the status change of women in the education system is a real success story, the situation in the labour market is still a bit different. Women are still more ikely to be found in gender-typical occupations. Those who have broken into traditionally male careers (like law or medicine) tend to practise in less prestigious sub-disciplines (e.g., family medicine rather than surgery or real estate law rather than corporate law or litigation) and generally earn lower incomes (Krahn, Lowe, and Hughes, 2007: 192). Despite high levels of educational attainment, most women also still encounter very serious barriers in their attempts to climb corporate ladders. Held back by what has become known as the *glass ceiling*—referring to the fact that women can see the top, but not reach it—less than 20 percent of top executives in

North America are women. Despite the success of women in graduate studies, older faculty in most Canadian university departments are still mostly men; among younger faculty there is much more equality.

Ethnicity

Similar concerns to those of feminists are raised by theorists and researchers who engage in *anti-racism education* (e.g., Dei, 1996). Topics of interest include the lack of minority teachers; the white, Caucasian focus of curriculum; and undercurrents of racism that might run through school practices and knowledge.

Canada defines itself as a multicultural society and in recent decades, provinces have made efforts to integrate multicultural perspective into school curriculum. Canadian census data indeed show that members of numerous ethnic minority groups have above-average educational attainment. For instance in 2001, 23.7 percent of white Canadians between the ages of 25 and 34 held a university degree, compared to 41 percent of Canadians of Asian descent. In contrast, Aboriginal Canadians have by far the lowest average level of educational attainment of any ethnic group in Canada (Davies and Guppy, 2006: 118). Using older, 1991 Census data, Guppy and Davies (2006) have shown that substantially more Canadians of Chinese and Filipino origin have university degrees than the average of all Canadians combined. The only group that has a higher percentage of members with a university degree are Jewish Canadians. Furthermore, the average new immigrant arrives in Canada with higher levels of educational attainment than the average Canadian-born person.

John Ogbu, a U.S. educational sociologist, applied three distinct categories to analyze how minorities relate to the education system that may be able to help us understand the differences in educational attainment for different ethnic groups identified by Guppy and Davies (Ogbu, 1992). According to Ogbu *autonomous minorities* are minorities in a numerical sense (e.g., members of a religious group like Jews, Mormons, or Mennonites). Ogbu considered these groups as largely integrated into the culture of mainstream society and saw their relationship to the education system as no different. *Voluntary minorities* are immigrants who have moved to the host country voluntarily. For many immigrants, the purpose of immigration is to improve their and their children's overall opportunities and education becomes a central institution to achieve this. *Involuntary minorities* are those whose minority status within the mainstream is not voluntary. African Americans were brought to the U.S. as slaves. Aboriginals in Canada became minorities through subordination. The specific needs of involuntary minorities are often defined in opposition to the mainstream. Involuntary minorities are the least likely to see their cultural values reflected in the education system and curriculum and therefore find less motivation to do well. In addition, overt discrimination makes them the least likely group to see their human capital translate into labour market success. The most successful students from involuntary minorities, according to Ogbu, are those who end up "emulating" or at least accommodating the mainstream culture while at school. Some accomplish this by maintaining a different cultural identity outside school. At the other end of the spectrum are those involuntary minority students who increasingly identify themselves in opposition to the mainstream. This opposition is often accompanied by peer group norms and activities, which, at worst, might be expressed through membership in gangs. Members of involuntary minorities are thus faced with the dilemma of choosing between a denial of ethnic identity, or a denial of mainstream values and norms. In contrast, members from voluntary minorities, at least according to Ogbu, have far fewer problems in consolidating ethnic identities with the mainstream norms and values of

their new home society and often actually experience immense family pressures to succeed in education.

Although attempts have been made to expand curriculum to reflect a commitment to multiculturalism, it has also been argued that some minority groups, like Aboriginals in Canada, would best be served in schools over which they have more control and which more directly reflect the culture of the group (see the box "Ethnocentric Schools").

Both feminist and anti-racist theories of education are closely connected to **critical pedagogy** (Freire, 1970; McLaren, 2002). Critical pedagogy looks at ways in which education can become more empowering and be a catalyst for social change. Proponents of critical pedagogy argue that education should enable both students and teachers to understand their respective roles in the educational process and in the social structure. Such a form of education would help students and teachers deconstruct different aspects of schooling (e.g., classroom interactions or curriculum) and challenge taken-for-granted assumptions about social life. This, in turn, would lead to a deeper and more critical understanding of social relations. Ultimately, the goal of a critical pedagogy is to empower all those involved in the educational process to become more active and critical about their life, to understand the social context in which they live, and to envision and work toward positive change.

[Social Trends]

Ethnocentric Schools

Control over education can be a hotly contested issue. Various First Nations in Canada have long sought greater control over schools on reserves. The key argument put forward is that young Aboriginals are losing touch with their roots and that many problems plaguing Aboriginal communities can be traced to the decline in their culture. The experiences of First Nations members with the education system have been particularly painful. The Canadian government operated so-called "residential schools" from the 1870s until the mid-1970s. The intention of residential schools was to forcefully integrate Aboriginal children into the white, Christian, and anglophone mainstream. This was accom-

plished by removing Aboriginal children from their families and communities and putting them into boarding schools, often run by various churches. During the school year, the children were not allowed to speak their native languages, play their games and sing their songs, or communicate with their families. It was, however, not only the cultural repression, but also the tales of mental and physical abuse of Aboriginal children in residential schools that make this a particularly shameful part of Canada's history. In 2006, the Government of Canada approved the Indian Residential Schools Settlement Agreement, which is intended to compensate residential school students for the

(continued)

abuse they suffered at these schools, and to provide measures to support healing and commemorative activities. Residential school experiences have also been used as an argument for the need to allow First Nations greater control over the education of their members.

Although the educational experiences of African Canadians are not as harrowing as those of many Aboriginal children, leaders in the African Canadian community have looked at the potential of Afro-centric schools to improve educational experiences in their communities. Nelson Whynder Elementary School in North Preston, Nova Scotia, is the only publicly funded Afro-centric school in Canada. Although following the provincial curriculum like any other public school in Nova Scotia, students at Nelson Whynder learn with an emphasis on African culture and what are considered uniquely African forms of learning (e.g., learning more visually and preferring hands-on participation).

As with schools under the control of First Nations, ethnocentric schools like Nelson Whynder hope to accomplish a number of goals. Foremost is a respect of differences in interests and learning styles, which can more directly address inequities in learning outcomes (e.g., by offering more focused instruction). These schools provide leadership opportunities that might not be accessible to minority students in regular schools. They create safer and more comfortable environments (e.g., from harassment and racism). Finally, they can teach and instill pride and better understanding of the accomplishments of ethnic minority members and thus increase self-confidence in ethnic minority students.

Ethnocentric schools have, however, been criticized—even by members from within ethnic minority communities—for posing a number of serious problems. Potentially, the racial segregation that results from ethnocentric schooling might actually perpetuate and even increase racial stereotypes. Segregation, according to critics, does nothing to address inequalities within the public system, which is where we should focus our efforts. Furthermore, once students return from a segregated school environment to an inclusive one, the transition might be more difficult.

How would you evaluate the arguments for and against ethnocentric schools? Could we make the same arguments for school segregation based on other social factors, such as gender and social class?

Social Class

Although postmodern sociologists have argued that traditional structural factors such as social class have lost their significance in shaping individual lives, empirical studies persistently show that social class continues to be the most important predictor of educational and occupational attainment (e.g., Andres et al., 1999; Davies, 2004). Parents' level of education as one specific measure of social class has been shown to be particularly strongly related to their children's occupational aspirations, expectations, and achievement. Young people with university-educated parents are more likely to be enrolled in academic high school programs and eventually attend university, while those young people not participating in any form of postsecondary education tend to come from families in which neither parent has attended university (Andres and Krahn, 1999).

In a longitudinal study of transitions from school to work, Harvey Krahn at the University of Alberta has followed a cohort of high school graduates into their adult years (Krahn, 2004). In 1985, Grade 12 Edmonton high school seniors were first interviewed about their high school experience, educational and occupational plans, and their social background. Krahn found that students with at least one university-educated parent were more likely to be enrolled in an academic program and had overall higher educational and occupational aspirations than their peers without university-educated parents. When Krahn revisited the study participants fourteen years later in 1999, these initial expectations had been largely realized. Individuals with university-educated parents were substantially more likely to have completed a university degree, while individuals with non-university-educated parents were more likely to have been enrolled in apprenticeships, technical school, or college programs. Krahn's 1999 data also showed that individuals with university-educated parents were more likely to have moved into professional and managerial careers. Similarly, a group of researchers from York University followed a cohort of individuals who graduated from high school in 1973 over a period of more than

20 years (Anisef et al., 2000). Much like Krahn, Anisef et al. found that the social-class background of students in 1973 very strongly influenced their educational and occupational patterns after high school. Although their study showed some amounts of upward social mobility over time, those from privileged-class backgrounds in 1973 had substantially solidified their privileged position through high levels of educational and occupational attainment.

While these empirical facts are indisputable, it is more difficult to explain why social class continues to affect us in this way. Are these persistent class differences the outcome of individual choices or are they in some way determined by social and institutional structures (like the education system)?

Resistance theory

In 1977, Paul Willis, a British sociologist, addressed this issue in his book *Learning to Labour*, probably one of the most cited and influential books in the sociology of education. Willis spent considerable amounts of time observing a group of working-class students in their final years of middle school in an industrial town in England. This group of boys, which he called the "lads," would skip school, not do their homework, take pride in performing badly, fight, threaten teachers, and engage in other deviant behaviour inside and outside of school (e.g., drinking and coming to school drunk). In his lengthy conversations with the lads, Willis also found that they rejected the theoretical-academic aspect of schooling. Instead, they were looking forward to getting out of school as soon as possible and starting in manual, working-class types of factory or construction jobs, just like their fathers. Willis concluded that these lads were not the passive "victims" of abstract institutional or social processes, but actively rejected the middle-class values of school, while embracing the working-class values of manual labour. Through their own actions, existing inequalities were being reproduced (i.e., the working-class lads ended up in working-class jobs). His work has become known as **resistance theory** (Willis, 1977). Although almost thirty years later Willis' work is still acknowledged as groundbreaking, it has also received its fair share of criticism. Willis has been criticized for describing the behaviour of a relatively small group of working-class boys as emblematic of all working-class youths and ignoring what Brown (1987) has called "ordinary" working-class students and their everyday struggle to do well in school and to perceive schools as a way to achieve solid careers and social mobility. Feminists in particular have accused Willis of overlooking the struggle of girls and for romanticizing male, aggressive behaviour that may also be described as sexist, racist, and bullying (see McFadden, 1995).

Rational choice theory

Another individualistic, yet completely opposite explanation can be found in what is known as **rational choice theory**, which proposes that individuals make decisions based on how they can maximize the return on their investments in their education. From a rational choice perspective, individuals from lower-class families are less likely to invest in higher levels of education because they have limited financial resources and are more concerned with failing to succeed at, for instance, university. If a young student from a lower-income family fails, the return on the initial investment would be very low. Yet, their likelihood of success is smaller than for the middle and upper middle classes. Hence, their rational choices would suggest that they invest in other forms of education, such as college, technical schools, and apprenticeship, or don't invest in advance education at all (Goldthorpe, 1996). In other words, the empirical fact that fewer individuals from working-class families attend university is explained by their own, rational choices. Our own individual experiences as well as research with high school and university students suggest, however, that few would make educational decisions based on such rational choice considerations (Brown, 1987; Lehmann, 2005a). Instead, decisions to attend higher education are framed around educational and vocational interests and aspirations. Some have argued that these interests and aspirations are steered, fostered, and thwarted by schools and teachers through streaming and tracking and the corresponding different educational experiences.

Correspondence theory

Many critical studies in educational sociology are based on Marxist thought. They interpret schools and the education system as integrated into the capitalist system of production. As such, schools assume the role of legitimizing class differences and of socializing individuals to accept their future exploited status in society. The 1970s was a particularly productive decade for conflict and neo-Marxist scholarship in the sociology of education. Most famously, in 1976 Samuel Bowles and Herbert Gintis published their influential book *Schooling in Capitalist America* in which they laid out a concept called **correspondence theory**. In this book, they argued that the rise of mass secondary education corresponds to industrialization and the need for a disciplined workforce. Similarly, the transition from a manufacturing to a white-collar, service economy and the rise of professional occupations is related to the expansion of postsecondary education. In terms of what students learn at school, they argued that educational processes and individual experiences in education correspond to future roles in workplaces. These differences in education are accomplished by streaming and tracking students in ways that largely reflect the social class backgrounds of students and provide students with a different curriculum focus and educational experience in the different streams. Lower-class students learn basic skills, with a focus on strict rule following, discipline, punctuality, cleanliness, and manual skills. In contrast, upper-class kids learn problem solving, critical thinking, and leadership skills (Bowles and Gintis, 1976).

Other researchers have found empirical support for Bowles and Gintis' theoretical assumptions. Jean Anyon (1980) an American educational sociologist, studied five schools in different socioeconomic areas and with a different student population. She found that in schools in working-class communities and with a working-class student population, students encountered very mechanical and rote forms of learning (e.g., a focus on memorizing facts) with a very strict emphasis on rule following in all subjects. Students were offered few decision-making options in class. Teachers were in complete control and rarely explained the reasons behind classroom activities. In contrast, students attending schools in upper- and upper-middle class communities were given more decision-making power in class through active discussions and negotiation and the educational emphasis was less on memorization, but on creative and critical expression. Much like Bowles and Gintis, Anyon concluded that students learn to develop different attitudes about how work is being done, which in turn prepares them for the different roles they will eventually assume in the workplace. We will return to the issue of streaming and tracking later in this chapter.

Habitus and cultural reproduction

The work and ideas of the French sociologist Pierre Bourdieu (1930–2002) are increasingly applied in the sociology of education in attempts to bridge the divide between structural (e.g., correspondence theory) and individual (e.g., resistance theory) accounts of educational processes. Bourdieu tried to understand how an individual's social background and upbringing shapes how he or she comes to see the world and his or her experiences in it. Two concepts are particularly important when applying Bourdieu's ideas to the sociology of education: cultural capital and habitus (Bourdieu, 1990; Bourdieu and Wacquant, 1992).

Cultural capital, like economic capital (money) or human capital (education, skills), describes a form of capital we can use to negotiate our lives. Cultural capital means the knowledge and skills we have in understanding and manipulating the dominant culture of the society in which we live. In modern Western societies, the dominant culture is seen as that of the upper middle class. Schools in particular are institutions that are characterized by middle- and upper-class values. Theoretical/academic knowledge has priority over manual/applied knowledge. School curriculum reflects middle- and upper-class values as we study Shakespeare, languages, music, and art. Teachers are mostly from middle-class backgrounds and have been socialized during their own education in ways that make them more likely to relate well to their middle-class students.

Children from middle- and upper-class families, surrounded by books at home and with access to cultural resources (e.g., museum visits or vacations to foreign countries), have a better chance of doing well at school, as they have already been socialized at home to read, think critically, express themselves, and appreciate art, music, and literature. In contrast, students who grew up in working-class environments in which working with their hands is more important, are less likely to see their own experiences and culture reflected at school, which in turn disadvantages them from the outset.

A related concept is that of **habitus**, which suggests that in many ways, we are products of our social environments. For example, if you grow up in a family in which everybody has worked in construction or other manual types of employment, it is much more difficult to see yourself as a doctor or lawyer in the future (and vice versa). Put simply, habitus means that through our upbringing and social environment (including our cultural capital), we come to see the world and our place in it in a certain way, which in turn creates dispositions to act, interpret experiences, and think in a certain way.

Through the cultural capital processes outlined above, education ultimately reinforces expectations already present in your habitus. While school may come relatively easily and naturally to many middle-class students, it is often experienced as a struggle for working-class children and youth. Bourdieu describes the ways in which working-class students' life experience find little resonance in the school curriculum as **symbolic violence**, which ultimately leads working-class students to engage in forms of self-selection and self-censorship (e.g., by dropping out of school or deciding not to continue to postsecondary education). It is important to note that Bourdieu saw these processes of social reproduction as affected by both institutional structures (e.g., curriculum) and individual dispositions.

Lehmann (2005a) has used Bourdieu's concepts to show how social class background affects high school students' educational choices and aspirations. Talking to senior high school students enrolled in either academic or vocational programs, he found that students largely discuss their educational and occupational aspirations as extensions of what their parents do or have done. Most of the working-class students in the vocational stream speak about their love for "real" work and working with their hands, and agree that academic/theoretical learning is simply not for them. Many of them see their occupational aspirations as based on the fact that this is what their families have done all their lives and that it comes naturally to them. Similarly, those who have grown up in homes in which parents have high levels of formal education and work in professional employment (e.g., teachers and lawyers) never consider anything but university. Lehmann interprets these findings as expressions of habitus. In terms of cultural capital, the students in the different streams express distinctly different attitudes toward schooling and what they learn at school. While most students in the academic streams claim to see the value of learning for the sake of learning and talk about very positive relationships with their teachers, working-class students in the vocational streams reject the academic/theoretical aspect of schooling and have either adversarial or nearly non-existing relationships with their teachers. For them, learning needs to be immediately applicable and have relevance for their chosen career paths. The few working-class students who plan on going to university after high school see their prospects as fraught with risk and uncertainty, mostly because of the lack of role models in their immediate families. In contrast, middle-class students talk about university with excited anticipation (Lehmann, 2004).

This example illustrates how we need to understand the reproduction of social inequality through education as a complex interplay between institutional forces and individual dispositions and actions.

Labelling, Tracking, and Streaming

Education in Canada is under the control of the different provinces and territories. Although this suggests a diversity of education systems across the country, formal structures of education are remarkably similar. All provinces and territories provide free, public elementary and secondary education, offered in a comprehensive school setting. Yet experiences in schools can be completely different from student to student. As Bourdieu has shown, both the institutional structures of education systems and how we individually relate to them affect how we experience schooling. In an ethnographic study of a kindergarten class, Harry Gracey found that the foundations for educational socialization and success are laid very early on in our educational life (Gracey, 2004). Gracey argued that kindergarten socializes young children into the expectations of grade school through carefully created physical set-ups that mimic adult worlds, or at least grade school classrooms. The social structures of the kindergarten he observed were organized around rituals and routines, such as designated play time, clean-up time, study time, and rest time. This structure is completely controlled by the teacher and creative expression and spontaneity are systematically eliminated in favour of unquestioned obedience to authority and role learning of imposed, prepared, and controlled material (Gracey 2004: 147). Depending on how well they relate to these structures, kindergarten students quickly become labelled as good, adequate, or bad students. Other sociologists have used similar ethnographic methods to study students in elementary and secondary schools and have found that these labels tend to be perpetuated throughout a young person's education.

Dropping Out of University

In 2005 the Educational Policy Institute published a report entitled *A Little Knowledge is a Dangerous Thing* (Usher, 2005). Using Canadian survey data on financial barriers to university access (Ipsos-Reid, 2004), the report argues that Canadians in general, and low-income Canadians in particular, overestimate the cost of university tuition while at the same time underestimating the income-generating potential of a university degree (Usher, 2005: 3). The report concludes that these mis-estimates of the costs and benefits lead lower-income Canadians to reject university as a viable option. But getting to university is not the only problem for young people from working-class backgrounds. In a series entitled *Class Matters*, the *New York Times* recently published a feature article on the college dropout boom. In it, college dropouts are described as the largest and fastest-growing group of young adults in the United States. The article continues to state that almost one in three Americans in their mid-twenties is a college dropout and that most of them come from poor and working-class families (Leonhardt, 2005).

Why is it that working-class university students become more likely to drop out of university? Comparing different university dropouts, Lehmann (2005c) found that university students with a working-class background leave university without graduating for very different reasons than those from middle- and upper-class backgrounds. The latter are more likely to be forced to leave university because of academic achievement problems, while working-class students leave early on despite relatively high marks. These students describe their reasons for leaving university as not *feeling* university, not fitting in, and not being able to relate to other students and the institutional culture of university. Many also insist that they discover their true vocational interests during their time at university and consequently enter colleges, technical schools, and apprenticeships.

What theoretical perspectives might help us explain the working-class students' reasons for dropping out?
What do you think universities could do to improve the experiences of working-class students? Or do you think university simply is not for everybody?
Why did you decide to come to university?

Labelling

Students are labelled by teachers based on a number of characteristics. For instance, attractiveness and neatness in dress are often equated with upper- or middle-class status, which is in turn equated with being studious, disciplined, and smart. Unattractiveness and being poorly dressed may immediately create the label of poverty and academic incapability. Rist (1977) began his ethnographic observation on student labelling in a U.S. inner-city kindergarten. He found that after only eight days of kindergarten, the kindergarten teacher made permanent seating assignments based on what she assumed were variations in academic ability. Rist soon realized that these seating arrangements also reflect students' socioeconomic characteristics: the poorest children from families on welfare sat together, the slightly more affluent working-class children sat together, and the middle-class kids sat together. The teacher ended up treating the children quite differently in terms of her teaching approach, the time she spent with them, the praise given, and the amount of autonomy allowed. Rist followed the same classroom and children into Grades 1 and 2 and found that by Grade 2, these labels had not only been perpetuated, but substantially solidified. In other words, these labels, which are initially based on very subjective assumptions, become objectified, stick with the kids, and in many ways affect their learning and their status as students. The *self-fulfilling prophecies* these labels create take on a particular relevance when we look at how they affect students' later placement in streams and tracks and how these placements affect long-term academic and occupational achievement.

Streaming

Streaming is often a taken-for-granted school practice. Although we might take exception to specific placements of individual students, we rarely pause to reflect on the assumptions on which streaming and tracking rest. Proponents of streaming and tracking argue that students learn better when they are grouped with other students who are considered like them academically. This "likeness" is to be determined by fair and objective assessments of a student's academic ability. Once they have been grouped by ability, students are said to learn at the same rate, have similar knowledge, and support each other in their future learning. Bright students would be held back if they were together with slower learners, while slower learners would be overwhelmed if they were together with bright students and fast learners. Ultimately, grouped students can develop better and more positive attitudes about themselves (particularly the slower learners), and teachers can more effectively target their instructional methods and materials. As should be clear from what you have read so far, these assumptions reflect the functionalist tradition of sociological reasoning.

In a review of research on streaming and tracking conducted over the past half century, Jeannie Oakes (2005) found little evidence that these assumptions stand up to scrutiny. Her review indicates convincingly that the assumption that students learn better in homogeneous groups is not correct. There is no evidence that, on average, bright students are held back and slower learners are falling further behind in mixed groups. Furthermore, research shows that rather than creating a more positive self-image, students placed in lower streams actually develop lower levels of self-esteem. Within the school, tracking and streaming is a fairly public process. Students do know who is placed in which stream. Teachers and peers develop more negative attitudes toward those placed in lower tracks, which in turn affects the students' self-esteem negatively. It has also been shown that those placed in higher streams may develop inflated self-concepts as the result of their placement. We already know from labelling theory, that these

placements can have long-term effects on students' educational experiences and their future educational and occupational aspirations. Once placed in lower streams, students tend to become less involved in extracurricular activities, exhibit more deviant behaviour (like being disruptive in class), and are more likely to drop out of school altogether.

Finally, Oakes's research challenges the fairness and objectivity of the assessment mechanisms used to determine track placements. To a large degree, track placement is based on standardized tests. Despite various claims that standardized tests are fair measures of student ability, they have been shown to have a number of serious shortcomings. Some tests are poorly designed, and minimal test differences can potentially lead to different track placements. Also, the practice of using a normal curve distribution to determine test results means that many placements are not necessarily a true reflection of actual aptitude. Experts on testing (e.g., psychologists and psychometric experts) have further argued that standardized tests do not measure any "fixed" ability, but can only tell us about the differences in what people do or know at the point the test is taken. Clearly, this is an important concern when we consider the long-term implications of track placements (Gillborn and Youdell, 2001). The most consistent criticism of standardized tests is that such tests are culturally biased, as they test white, middle-class knowledge and reward what is considered inherently a white, middle-class way of learning, retaining, and recalling information. Besides test results, track placement is also influenced by recommendations of teachers and counsellors. As our earlier discussion of labelling theory has shown, there is a good chance that at least some of these recommendations are based on ascribed characteristics. Finally, tracking decisions can also be affected by parental decisions. Parents from middle- and upper-class families tend to be more involved with their children's educational decisions and are more likely to push for and insist on their children being placed in higher level tracks.

Most research on streaming and tracking shows social class and race difference in stream placements, with white, middle-class students the majority of students in higher-level streams. To the extend that IQ is relatively equally distributed across class, gender, and ethnicity, then this outcome of streaming suggests that some of it is not based on a fair and meritocratic process.

Tests form an important basis on which streaming decisions are made, even though tests and their results are often criticized for being culturally biased and an unreliable measure of long-term ability.

leading to track placements are compounded by the different educational experiences in respective streams. Oakes found that students in higher-level tracks are exposed to material of academic and challenging content, allowed to work independently, and encouraged to engage in critical thinking, problem solving, self-direction, and creativity. In the lower tracks, material content remains very basic and unchallenging and the focus is on conformity, rule following, getting along with others, discipline, punctuality, cleanliness, and the development of rudimentary study habits. This is problematic in at least two ways. First, the lack of challenge in the lower stream will increase the students' cultural capital deficits. Recall our earlier discussion of Bourdieu, who argued that cultural capital is an essential element to successfully navigate through the education system. Second, students from lower tracks see their chances for further, postsecondary education reduced and may also be perceived as lacking essential employability skills. Employers increasingly argue that success in a modern workplace requires such skills as problem solving, critical thinking, communication, teamwork, and relatively high levels of literacy and numeracy, all of which are characteristic of education at the upper streams, and much less at the lower streams. This last point also reflects our earlier discussion of Bowles and Gintis' (1976) correspondence principle, as students in different streams are prepared for vastly different roles in their later working lives.

In her own study of twenty-five schools (both junior high and high) in different neighbourhoods in different U.S. cities, Oakes (2005) found that the inequalities

[Applied Sociology]

Streaming in Germany

Although streaming and tracking does take place in Canadian high schools, most students still attend comprehensive high schools. In Germany, streaming happens at a far more institutional level. In most parts of Germany, students are streamed after Grade 4 (when the student is approximately 10 years old). Based on tests, teacher recommendations, and parent's wishes, a student enters one of three different types of secondary school in Grade 5. The *Hauptschule* (secondary modern school) is the lowest level of secondary schooling, and covers Grades 5 to 9. Here students learn basic skills and are prepared to take up apprenticeship training in construction or similar trades once they graduate from Grade 9 (age 14 or 15). The *Realschule* (middle school) covers Grades 5 to 10 and its curriculum is more advanced than that of the *Hauptschule*. Traditionally, students are prepared in this school stream to take up training and eventually employment in administrative and technical

(continued)

occupations upon graduation from this stream (age 15 or 16). Only *Gymnasium* (grammar school), the highest school stream, provides students with the diploma to enter university. *Gymnasium* covers Grades 5 to 13 and resembles the academic stream in Canadian schools. In the past, fewer than 10 percent of all students would graduate from the *Gymnasium* and subsequently enter university. The majority of students graduated from the lowest stream (*Hauptschule*). This very strict form of streaming laid the foundation for a workforce in Germany that was highly skilled in industrial production. Starting in the 1970s, educational reforms led to a significant shift in enrolment patterns. Although the three-stream education system stayed intact, there are now essentially equal levels of enrolment in all three school types. The lowest school type (*Hauptschule*) has witnessed the greatest problems as a result of these changing educational decisions. While it was the main type of secondary school until the 1970s, it has now become a "remainder" school for the most disadvantaged children. The focus of these schools has shifted away from learning to disciplining and controlling students.

While many educators in Germany continue to defend this formal streaming process as one that targets education to different student needs, international test results suggest otherwise. Germany's 15-year-olds performed substantially below average in various tests (e.g., reading comprehension) administered by the Program for International Student Assessment (PISA). PISA is an internationally standardized assessment tool designed to measure the reading, math, and scientific literacy of 15-year-olds. PISA also collects data on the socioeconomic background of the students taking the tests. When breaking down the test results by socioeconomic status (SES), researchers have found that there is a far greater discrepancy between the test results of high and low SES students in Germany than in Canada. This means that students from less affluent families in Germany perform far worse on the test (compared to their peers from more affluent families) than do students from poor families in Canada (see Table 13.3).

Table 13.3	Mean Scores in the PISA Combined Reading Literacy Scale by Family Socioeconomic Status, Canada and Selected Countries

Country	Average Score Lowest SES	Average Score Highest SES	Difference between Highest and Lowest SES
Canada	503	568	65
United States	466	554	89
Sweden	484	557	72
France	468	552	84
Germany	424	540	116

Source: Adapted from Table C6.11: "Mean Scores and Standard Errors in the PISA Combined Reading Literacy Scale by Quarter of Family Socio-Economic Status, Canada, Provinces and Selected Countries, 2000", Statistics Canada publication *Education Indicators in Canada: Report of the Pan-Canadian Education Indicators Program, 2005*, Catalogue 81 582, Chapter C, page 335, Released April 12, 2006.

How can we relate the findings from Germany to Jeannie Oakes's concerns about streaming and tracking? Some people argue that without streaming and tracking, we would all become mediocre, as schools would end up teaching to the lowest common denominator. Do you think that is true?

Experiencing Schools

Student roles

Schools have the responsibility to impart to students cognitive skills (what we learn through the formal curriculum) and social norms and values (much of which we learn through the hidden curriculum). We all remember, however, from our own time spent in elementary and high school that schooling meant far more than simply learning. Students establish their own cultural norms and coping mechanisms, which are often quite different from what educators have in mind.

Student coping mechanisms encompass a substantial range, from conforming, working hard, being studious, and taking on extracurricular and leadership roles, to being the class clown, cheating, withdrawal, and other forms of resistance (Woods, 1990). Student roles and coping mechanisms are not fixed but can change over time—for example, from being an excited and conforming elementary school student to being a bored or withdrawn high school student. Furthermore, students come to understand the framework laid out by teachers and the institutions and learn to navigate and strategize. Students will cheat on tests and copy homework when they feel they can get away with it, but show conformity and compliance with other teachers.

School subcultures

Starting in the 1950s, schooling became a process that kept young people away from the formal world of adults until a substantially older age. Longer periods of schooling, which is largely age specific (i.e., you are grouped by age as you move through elementary and secondary school), create conditions for the formation of various peer subcultures with separate norms, expectations, and coping strategies.

Furthermore, this prolonged period of youth allows relative amounts of freedom to experiment with social interactions and roles. One of the most interesting elements of peer and school subcultures is that they generally do not place high value on being bright or academically oriented. Research has shown that some students try to detract from their academic achievements for fear of losing peer group approval. For example, a study on school peer culture and race in the United States has documented how African American students who are high achievers in school have to deal with the double disadvantage of being rejected as being too white by their black peers, while also not being accepted by white mainstream students (Fordham and Ogbu, 1986). Finding a peer group to negotiate the potentially alienating culture of schools seems rather important: it helps to have people with whom to sit at lunch, walk to and from school, and attend activities. Eder (1995)

The prolonged period of youth and the central role of schools during this period allow relative amounts of freedom to experiment with social interactions and roles, which are often expressed in school subcultures.

investigated how peer group formation in a U.S. middle school (junior high; Grades 7–9) is related to who is popular and unpopular. Although being athletic and good looking may have been the most outwardly obvious markers of popularity, Eder found that popularity was also strongly related to social class. Most of the popular kids came from the more affluent student body. The poor kids would sit elsewhere in the cafeteria and be referred to as "grits" (a reference to being "tough and gritty"). Despite the importance of social class as a subconscious marker of peer groups, a small minority of students at each grade were perceived as being at the lowest end of the hierarchy. These students most dramatically felt the negative impact of school peer culture as everybody wanted to avoid being associated with them. The reasons for their marginal status were atypical gender behaviour and perceived unattractiveness, the latter being more common for girls. Special education students were very likely candidates for social isolation. Eder concluded that creating a group of "isolates" at the bottom of the hierarchy gives most students at least the assurance

that there is somebody below them. Much of the ridicule these students experienced was in the form of sexual insults. Being called "queer," a "faggot" or otherwise labelled homosexual was a common occurrence for this group of social outcasts. This is an important finding as it shows how homosexuality becomes associated with social rejection at an early age, which explains the continuing *homophobia* in schools.

Eder found that peer subcultures in high schools were less rigid and more open to debate. Those in lower status peer groups or subcultures become increasingly vocal about their disdain for the popular kids in high school and peer group hierarchies become more complex. This complexity of high school peer groups has been explored in movies and TV shows throughout the decades, from 1950s rock 'n' roll high school dramas, to the 1980s "brat pack" movies such as *The Breakfast Club*, and more recent movies such as *Mean Girls*, *Napoleon Dynamite*, or *Elephant*, a fictional account of the Columbine school shootings.

[Research Focus]

Jocks

At least in the U.S. high school context, the dominance of the jock in the school hierarchy has led to studies that investigate how the jock status is also a representation of dominant forms of gender identity, masculinity, and heterosexuality. It has been argued that the high status of the jock reflects a dominant image of masculinity characterized by a strong and muscular physical appearance and by an aggressive and competitive personality. Sociologist Donald Sabo (1994: 84–86), who now conducts research on sports, health, and gender, wrote this about his own, former experience playing football in the NCAA (National Collegiate Athletic Association):

> I learned to be an animal. Coaches took notice of animals. Animals made first team. Being an animal meant being fanatically aggressive and ruthlessly competitive. If I saw an arm in front of me, I trampled

it. Whenever blood was spilled, I nodded approval. The coaches taught me to punish the other man and to secretly see my opponents' broken bones as little victories within the bigger struggle.

Lesko (2001) argues that the celebration of these forms of overt aggression and the need to win at all costs helps us make sense of the overall violent nature of U.S. society, the types of management behaviour that have led to corporate scandals like that at Enron and WorldCom, or the aggression that has come to characterize past and present U.S. governments and their military interventions around the world.

Finally, the jock subculture is also characterized by an aggressive heterosexuality, which has been used to explain the jock's apparent advantage with girls, but also the trivialization of date rape and other forms of sexual violence.

Is the jock an important character in Canadian high schools?
Do you agree with Nancy Lesko's argument that there is a relationship between the high status of jocks in schools and larger social problems?

Bullying

The Canadian Public Health Association (2004) defines bullying as the act of bothering, making fun of, troubling, and attacking somebody on a repeated basis and with the explicit intention of hurting that person. It can take the form of physical bullying (hitting, shoving, kicking, spitting on, beating up, or stealing and damaging somebody's property), and verbal bullying (name-calling, hurtful teasing, embarrassing others, or threatening), social bullying (exclusion, gossiping, or spreading rumours). In recent years, bullying has also become electronic and digital, through the use of computers, e-mail, cellphones, camera phones, and text messaging.

According to the Canadian Public Health Association, bullying incidents are neither isolated nor rare incidents, but are part of many students' everyday experiences at school. Important to our understanding of bullying is that we cannot exclusively focus on the roles of the bullies and victims, but also need to consider those of peer groups and bystanders. A group of Canadian researchers observed and filmed playground bullying incidents (physical and verbal) at elementary schools and came to the following conclusion: peer presence was positively related to the persistence of playground bullying episodes (O'Connell, Pepler, and Craig, 1999). In 21 percent of the bullying episodes the researchers observed, peers would actively join the bully in the abuse of the victim. Older children, particularly boys, are significantly more likely to join with the bully. Two potential explanations are offered: (1) joiners can share in the bully's powerful status by joining, and (2) due to more exposure to violent TV, movies, and computer games, some might become desensitized to acts of violence. In 54 percent of the episodes, peers stood by and watched. They did not join, but also did not help the victim. The researchers found that passive peer attention also reinforces and encourages the bully, as drawing an audience is in itself a rewarde for the bully. Only in 25 percent of the episodes did peers intervene on behalf of the victim. The conclusion to be drawn from these findings is that

Research has found that we need to consider the roles of peer groups and bystanders in bullying activities.

anti-bullying strategies need to take into consideration the role of peers and bystanders and that a successful anti-bullying strategy needs to go beyond punitive measures against the bully to include strategies and programs aimed at peers and the overall school culture (Canadian Public Health Association, 2004).

Sexual harassment in schools

One specific form of bullying is sexual harassment, which we could define as gendered bullying. Statistical research in the U.S. has shown that there are significant differences in how boys and girls experience sexual harassment at school (Hand and Sanchez, 2000). Boys are more likely to commit sexual harassment than girls. Girls perceive it as more harmful than boys. Girls are more likely to be the target of sexual harassment and they experience more severe and physical forms of sexual harassment. As a result, girls are left more traumatized whereas boys are more likely to see it as part of a "natural" dominance game among peers. Interview-based qualitative studies have also shown how schools and teachers don't do enough to investigate and prevent sexual harassment. Stein (1995), a researcher and activist specializing in issues of gendered violence, argued that too often school, peer, and popular cultures trivialize or perpetuate gender inequalities and violence. Instead, she called for a normalization of discourses on sexual harassment and gendered violence by inserting age-appropriate material into class discussion and curriculum. In her opinion, it is necessary to change school culture to one that is more focused on equity and social justice, rather than competition and authority. Only then will students learn to be critical about sexism and homophobia and be able to recognize when gendered violence does take place. This, Stein argued, will change the perception of students as victims, perpetrators, and spectators toward an understanding of themselves as "justice makers" (Stein, 1995: 159).

Severe forms of violence in schools

We all still have vivid memories of the horrific school shootings that took place in Columbine in 1999. While some of us have come to expect this form of gun-related violence in the United States, school shootings have also taken place elsewhere. Later the same year, a student in Taber, Alberta, brought a gun to school and shot a classmate. In 2002, a heavily-armed student killed thirteen

teachers, two students, one policeman and eventually himself in Erfurt, Germany. On December 6, 1989, a gunman killed fourteen female engineering students at a Montreal college. On September 1, 2004, 344 civilians, at least 172 of them children, were killed in Beslan, Russia, after their elementary school was taken hostage during the first day of classes and government troops eventually stormed the school with disastrous results. And on September 13, 2006, a lone gunman entered Dawson College, a large *CEGEP* (Collège d'enseignement général et professionnel or College of General and Vocational Education) in downtown Montreal, killed one young woman and critically injured several other students, before turning the gun on himself.

These incidents have left many of us with an exaggerated sense of vulnerability at schools. In reality, it is exceedingly unlikely to be harmed while at school. Experts on crime and violence agree that most young people are safer at schools than they are in their respective neighbourhoods, the park, on the street, and in their homes. Noguera (1995) has argued that school violence and the threat of school violence affect us so strongly because we expect schools to be completely and absolutely safe. There is an unspoken assumption that schools are public spaces and controlled institutions offering children the opportunity to learn. Violence at schools thus not only offers a threat to personal safety, but also to the social contract among schools, the community and, in a sense, the state (or province). Schools have certainly responded to this perceived threat of violence. Particularly in the U.S., inner-city schools appear more like fortresses now than schools. Schools use metal detectors, police officers, and security guards to control the student population. Increasingly, violent acts at school are treated as criminal offences and delegated to the criminal justice system, rather than dealt with at school. More rigid rules, zero-tolerance policies, and severe forms of punishment are put in place to enforce order in the school. Most researchers and educators concerned with violence at school, however, agree that turning schools into high-security fortresses creates a siege mentality that treats violence as a normal occurrence against which we have to protect ourselves, rather than something to be proactively prevented (McEvoy and Welker, 2000; Noguera, 1995). Getting a handle on violence at schools is difficult because what it means is ill defined and it is often fraught with assumptions about race, class, and gender. Some researchers have documented that the acts of poor black students are more harshly dealt with than those of middle-class white students (Noguera, 1995). Clearly,

[Applied Sociology]

Code Red

Schools are responding to the perceived threat of increasing violence with a variety of measures. In the fall of 2004, *The Globe and Mail* reported on two different initiatives. In a September 27, 2004, article, the newspaper reported that several hundred school districts in the United States now feature police officers patrolling school corridors armed with taser guns, high-voltage stun guns. When shot with a taser, an electrical current capable of passing through two inches of clothing interrupts the body's central nervous system, temporarily cutting off the ability of muscles to function. Steve Tuttle, director of communications for the company that manufactures taser guns, describes being shot with a taser as "like having your funny bone banged 17 times a second for five seconds." Although school board officials in the U.S. who use police officers armed with tasers appear to be enthusiastic, Canadian schools have not yet followed suit. Terry Price, president of the Canadian Teachers' Federation, says that Canada's schools advocate non-violent conflict resolution.

Rather than having armed police officers patrol school corridors, some Canadian schools have turned to code red drills intended to prepare students for violent attacks. Here is how an October 18, 2004, article in *The Globe and Mail* reported about such a drill in a small rural school. "Suddenly over the public address system comes the warning: 'Emergency. Code Red. Code Red.' Without missing a beat, the children spring to their feet and run to a corner of the room to huddle behind the teacher's desk. A girl rushes to the window and closes a blind. OPP Inspector Mark Allen supports these drills: 'We do fire drills all the time, and a child hasn't died in a school fire in North America in 25 years. But since 1996, 44 students and seven principals and teachers have been killed in shootings. ... There is no such thing as a safe school, but there's a prepared school. It can make the difference between one child being shot or 10 being shot, if the school is prepared.' Others have questioned these practices in the light of statistics that show no increases in violence in schools'." (Philp, 2004)

Are these initiatives to prevent school violence justified? Is using armed police officers a better method of violence prevention in schools than code red drills?
Are schools doing more harm than good with code red drills and the use of armed police officers that could undermine children's sense of security and actually create more fears?

violence in schools is related to both the community and the larger culture. For instance, gang membership has an influence on who brings guns to school, and bringing guns to school seems to be in response to escalating conflicts, both inside and outside schools. Our popular culture seems to teach us that guns and violence are the most effective way of resolving conflict. Although an exceedingly violent popular culture clearly affects our attitude toward using violent means for conflict resolution, it has also been argued that we need to put school violence into a context of *state violence* and *symbolic violence*. State violence means that budget cuts have reduced welfare provisions and programs that mostly affect already disadvantaged communities. Symbolic violence means that schools are alienating

places that do not reflect the community's struggle and can therefore not support more positive responses to conflict.

Looking to the Future

Much has changed since the late 1960s and early 1970s, when educational reformers and activists tried to imagine a future education that was at once democratic and liberating. Educational reform efforts during this period were strongly influenced by countercultural movements (e.g., the student, anti-authoritarian, and ecological movements), the emergence of feminism and anti-racism as serious challenges to orthodox knowledge, and debates around critical and liberation pedagogy.

Free and alternative schools experimented with collective decision making about curriculum, behaviour, dress code, grading, and discipline by parents, administrators, teachers, and students. Their focus on exploration, open learning, intrinsic motivation, and giving students a measure of control over what and how they learned has now given way to an approach to education that is framed around individual and national competitiveness in a global economy. Integrated into a larger *neo-liberal* framework, educational reform in recent years has been marked by a "back-to-basics" ideology and concerns around accountability (Sears, 2003). Given pressures to reduce government debts and an aging population, federal and provincial governments in Canada have been struggling to find a balance between saving and spending, and where to put their money (e.g., education vs. health care). Furthermore, neo-liberal policies generally are focused on reducing the role of government and seeking free-market-based solutions to social issues. In the context of education, neo-liberal pundits have promoted the use of charter schools and school vouchers as opposed to Canada's current system of public, comprehensive education. Instead of investing in school boards, provincial governments would give parents an education credit (school voucher) to enable them and their children to select schools best fit for their educational need. This would involve a radical rethinking of schools as commercial enterprises and parents and students as customers. Neo-liberals argue that this would make schools more accountable and responsive to the demands of parents, students, and communities, as the schools need to compete for their educational dollars. Critics argue that such a market-based solution rests on a complete misunderstanding of the role of education and would lead to undemocratic and unfair outcomes. As with the discussions about the privatization of health care in Canada, critics of such market-based solutions to education fear a two-tier education system in which affluent Canadians will gain access to very good schools and solidify their privileged status, while low-income Canadians living in poor neighbourhoods will see the quality of their schools decline.

Although Canada is still strongly committed to public education, and neo-liberal solutions have made very few inroads into the educational landscape, fiscal accountability has become a preoccupation for provinces, school boards, and schools. Increasingly, proof of successful investment in education is sought in supposedly objective measures of educational performance, such as those found in standardized provincial, national, and international tests. Examples of such international tests are found in the Program for

Table 13.4	Mean Scores of 15-year-old Students by Reading Proficiency on the PISA Combined Reading Literacy Scale, Canada, Provinces, and Selected Countries, 2000
Country/Province	**Mean Score**
Alberta	550
Finland	546
British Columbia	538
Quebec	536
Canada	534
Ontario	533
Manitoba	529
Saskatchewan	529
New Zealand	529
Australia	528
United Kingdom	523
Japan	522
Nova Scotia	521
Newfoundland and Labrador	517
Prince Edward Island	517
Sweden	516
France	505
United States	504
New Brunswick	501
Average score of all countries	**500**
Italy	487
Germany	484
Poland	479
Greece	474
Mexico	422
Brazil	396

Source: Adapted from Table C6.1: "Mean Scores, Standard Errors and Distribution of 15-year-old Students by Reading Proficiency on the PISA Combined Reading Literacy Scale, Canada, Provinces and Selected Countries, 2000", Statistics Canada publication *Education Indicators in Canada: Report of the Pan-Canadian Education Indicators Program, 2005*, Catalogue 81-582, Chapter C, page 325, Released April 12, 2006.

International Student Assessment (PISA), discussed earlier in this chapter. In 2000, PISA administered tests in forty-three countries, covering anywhere from 5000 to 10 000 students per country, to measure the reading proficiency of 15-year-old students. The scores of Canadian students put them in second place. Only students in Finland scored higher on average in this test. When broken down by provinces, the results for Canadian students are even more impressive. Students in Alberta achieved the highest scores and nearly all Canadian provinces placed above the international average (see Table 13.4).

These results are in stark contrast to the arguments made by conservative education critics that students in Canada are not learning the skills necessary in a modern, knowledge-based economy. Although these remarkable test results for Canadian students may silence conservative critics and offer cause for celebration, not everybody sees this as a positive development for education. Critics from the left, teachers, and teacher federations are concerned that curriculum content and teaching are increasingly driven by the demands of standardized testing. This means that what happens at schools could be reduced to learning hard facts and preparing for successful test-taking. Yet, we can only test a small portion of what we are to learn in schools. We cannot test, for instance, if education makes us into more compassionate citizens who will work toward a society based on diversity, social justice, and sustainability.

Schools and universities are increasingly turning to private companies for funding, just as companies perceive students as an irresistible target audience to create brand loyalty.

Open for Business

Students are an irresistible market. University campuses turn into virtual malls throughout the academic year, particularly in the first few weeks of classes. Most everything is offered for purchase, from the ubiquitous poster sales, to designer clothes and perfumes. Marketing professionals agree that the earlier you can get an individual to start consuming your products, the more likely he or she will continue to be a loyal customer. In this context, brand recognition appears to be a key principle. Corporations try to get

their products featured in textbooks or offer schools promotional materials, thinly disguised as educational. It has become a widespread practice for schools and universities to sign exclusive contracts with soft drink makers. In exchange for selling only their products at school or on campus, these corporations donate money to the schools and universities for events or equipment. Does this financial support come at too high a cost? Does it turn students into hapless consumers and automatons? One

(continued)

controversial initiative in the United States is Channel One, a commercial company that broadcasts daily TV programs to schools. Schools that sign up for the Channel One program receive from the company, free of charge, a dedicated satellite dish as well as TV and VCR sets for each classroom. In exchange, the participating school agrees to show the twelve-minute Channel One program once a day in each classroom, during class time. The twelve-minute program is divided into ten minutes of fast-paced, MTV-style news reporting of headline stories and human interest stories, interrupted by a total of two minutes of commercials. Unlike watching TV at home, Channel One does not allow for the channel to be changed when the commercials come on. Researchers have also found that students are more

likely to recall the content of the commercials they have seen than the actual news stories featured on the program. Critics have argued that despite providing schools with equipment (which can be used for purposes other than watching the Channel One program) and exposing students to news, Channel One does not belong in schools; they argue that it misuses the compulsory attendance laws to force children to watch commercial advertising, wastes school time, promotes violent entertainment, promotes television instead of reading, trivializes rather than promotes an in-depth understanding of news events, and ultimately corrupts the integrity of public education. Various efforts to bring programs like Channel One to Canadian schools have so far been unsuccessful.

Are these criticisms of programs like Channel One fair? Are students who fight exclusive school and university deals with Coca Cola or Pepsi doing the right thing? Or is this a fair deal? After all, schools, universities, and students do receive equipment and services in exchange for watching a few minutes of commercials and being restricted to buying only one brand of cola. What do you think?

Summary

We began this chapter by identifying socialization and employment preparation as two central functions of education and schooling. Through the formal curriculum, schools are essential in helping young people learn about and understand the world around them. Through the hidden curriculum they are socialized to accept a range of social conventions, such as respect for authority, discipline, and punctuality.

More concretely, schools play an important role in transferring not only cultural knowledge, norms, and values, but also employment-specific knowledge and skills. From a functionalist perspective, schools are important as they provide a fair and meritocratic basis on which individuals are selected for adult roles and responsibilities. In contrast, conflict theorists have argued that schools may achieve the exact opposite. Rather than providing a fair and level playing field, education stacks the deck in favour of those who are already in advantaged positions.

School curriculum is based on middle- and upper-middle-class culture and knowledge, which gives students from these backgrounds an advantage at school and shapes how individuals experience schooling. Research has shown, for instance, that placement in specific tracks or streams at school corresponds to social class background. White middle- and upper-middle-class students are more likely to be placed in advanced, academic streams. Not only does stream placement determine what and how students learn, but it also affects longer-term educational and occupational aspirations. It may also affect how individuals engage with the education system, which can range from being enthusiastic and committed learners to resentment, resistance, and deviance.

Deviant behaviour at school has received a fair share of attention in recent years due to high-profile cases of bullying, sexual harassment, and weapons-related violence. Although the threat of extreme violence at schools is relatively minor and tends to be exaggerated in the public media, bullying and sexual harassment are far more pervasive. This chapter discussed various research findings that try to make sense of these forms of aggression and determine effective ways of combating them.

The chapter closed with a brief look at educational reform challenges, which have seen a seismic shift in recent decades. The 1960s and 1970s were dominated by reform initiatives characteristic of inclusive practices and holistic learning principles. In the spirit of feminism, anti-racism, and critical pedagogy, educators and activists sought for an inclusive education system founded on principles of social justice. More recently, educational reform debates are dominated by a "back-to-basics" agenda that views education largely in terms of its contribution to giving Canadians and Canada a competitive edge in a global economy. Added to this view of education are concerns of fiscal accountability and a belief in market-based solutions to educational problems. Although market-based solutions like school vouchers and charter schools have found little support in Canada so far, these debates will continue as we struggle to understand education as fostering social justice, reproducing social inequalities, or preparing students for success in a post-industrial knowledge economy.

Questions for Review and Critical Thinking

1. If you think back to your own time at school, what were the most important things you learned? What function did education fulfill for you?

2. In this chapter, we discussed problems around streaming and tracking students. What are the alternatives?

3. Critics of schooling have argued that curriculum in Canada continues to be dominated by a male, middle-class, white perspective. Is that your own experience?

4. Research consistently shows that young people from working-class backgrounds are far less likely to go to university than their peers from middle- and upper-class backgrounds. What could schools do to change this form of inequality?

5. Canada is an immigrant society. Should it be the role of education to reflect the multitude of students' cultural backgrounds, or should the main function of education be to promote a common Canadian identity?

6. Young women are now outperforming young men in almost all areas of education. Girls do better at secondary school, and more women graduate from university than men in nearly all disciplines, including medicine and law. Is this a problem?

Key Terms

correspondence theory, p. 308
credential inflation, p. 303
critical pedagogy, p. 305
cultural capital, p. 308
formal curriculum, p. 299
habitus, p. 308

hidden curriculum, p. 300
human capital, p. 302
lifelong learning, p. 301
meritocracy, p. 302
rational choice theory, p. 307
resistance theory, p. 307
streaming, p. 311
symbolic violence, p. 309
underemployment, p. 303

Suggested Readings

Ballantine, Jeanne H., and Joan Z. Spade (eds.)
2004 *Schools and Society: A Sociological Approach to Education* (2nd ed.). Belmont, CA: Wadsworth Thomson.
This reader provides an excellent range of classic and contemporary readings from diverse theoretical perspectives. Included are pieces on the cultural construction of adolescence, the social construction of curriculum knowledge, international comparisons of educational inequality, and the development of alternatives for non-university-bound students.

Barakett, Joyce and Allie Cleghorn
2000 *Sociology of Education: An Introductory View from Canada.* Scarborough, ON: Prentice Hall.
A short yet comprehensive introduction to theoretical perspectives in the sociology of education and key policy issues related to education in Canada, with an emphasis on feminist and critical pedagogy.

Davies, Scott and Neil Guppy
2006 *The Schooled Society: An Introduction to the Sociology of Education.* Don Mills, ON: Oxford University Press.
A thorough Canadian textbook providing an excellent introduction to various theoretical and empirical debates in the sociology of education, including discussions of the socialization function of schools, school subcultures and the organizational-institutional context of schooling in Canada.

Feinberg, Walter and Jonas F. Soltis
2004 *School and Society* (4th ed.). New York: Teachers College Press.
This book offers a very accessible introduction to the major theoretical traditions in the sociology of work. The theoretical discussions are complemented with case studies and open-ended discussion questions, which makes it particularly useful for students interested in a teaching career.

Wotherspoon, Terry

2004 *The Sociology of Education in Canada: Critical Perspectives* (2nd ed.). Don Mills, ON: Oxford University Press.

A comprehensive introduction to education in Canada, from a critical sociological perspective. Wotherspoon provides both a historical account of the development of education in Canada as well as a critical and theoretical analysis of current issues.

Websites

www.jobfutures.ca
Job Futures
This Canadian government website offers job-related resources and has detailed information on all occupations that are part of Canada's National Occupational Classification (NOC) system, including employment prospects, average salaries, gender composition, and educational requirements.

www.cpha.ca/antibullying
Assessment Toolkit for Bullying Harassment and Peer Relations at School
This useful website maintained by the Canadian Public Health Association provides definitions of bullying, as well as tools to identify, deal with, and prevent bullying in schools.

www.otffeo.on.ca
Ontario Teachers' Federation
All provincial teacher federations maintain websites with information on their organizations and issues pertaining to teaching and being a teacher in their province. The Ontario Teachers' Federation is the largest teachers' federation in the country.

Key Search Terms

Cultural capital
Curriculum
Human capital
Meritocracy
Schools
Socialization
Streaming

For more study tools to help you with your next exam, be sure to check out the Companion Website at **www.pearsoned.ca/hewitt**, as well as Chapter 13 in your Study Guide.

part five

Social Organization

This last section of this text focuses on social organization in its various aspects. Types of organizations, their sources, and their impact on society are discussed in Chapter 14, Organizations and Work. Special attention is paid here to the world of work, where people spend much of their lives. As we shall see, organizations, whether they be formally (bureaucratically) structured—as in the case of religious institutions or even the media—or based upon a more informal structure—like families—have an especially important influence on human behaviour.

Chapter 15 examines social movements. Their origins are attributed to various sources, including subcultural groups wanting a better position in society, religions trying to create a different social order, political groups seeking power, or members of certain social strata hoping to change the distribution of power and privileges. Collectively, however, social movements share a desire to achieve their goals through change. If successful, most will end up looking like the bureaucracies described in Chapter 14. Some may even become conservative oligarchies, with leaders more interested in maintaining their power than in achieving the original goals of the movement. In both instances, newer social movements may emerge and the process may be repeated once more.

Chapter 16, on demography and urbanization, looks at the factors that determine the size and composition of the population of a society, including social institutions, social differentiation, even cultural values. For instance, religious

and political values have been important in Quebec's encouragement of population growth, which is seen as a means of maintaining the size of the francophone population in Canada. Population variables, in turn, affect most other areas of society. As an example, population size partly determines stratification patterns, since it influences chances for mobility. Probably the most obvious consequence of population growth is increased urbanization. The distinctions between city, town, and rural areas are many and they affect a whole range of social phenomena, from crime to longevity.

Despite their seeming permanence, all forms of social organization are subject to change, the topic of our last chapter. The sources and patterns of change in social systems throughout history have been the subject of much study and debate. As you will see, there are many ways to understand change, with theorists focusing on differing spheres and levels of change. In this last chapter, emphasis is placed on broad changes in economics and politics. By understanding how societies change in these fundamental areas of social organization, we may be better equipped to predict the future.

This examination of social organization completes your introduction to sociology with a Canadian focus. Although presented last, it is a most important area of concern. As you read the chapters, note how the forces discussed are important determinants of the social structure, which, in turn, influences and shapes the behaviour of individuals.

[14]

organizations and work

jerry p. white and tracey l. adams

Introduction

Looking at the many societies in the world, past and present, we see a striking commonality. From the very complex to the very basic, all societies expend a majority of their creative and intellectual energy sustaining themselves in their natural environments. This chapter explores this basic social process, commonly defined as *work* and its organization. It will consider the evolution of work, and review how the organization of work is intertwined with other forms of social organization. Further, it will explore the meanings that work has for workers, and the ways in which work experiences and opportunities vary by gender, ethnicity, and age. Finally, it will look at several current issues and trends in work.

What Is Work?

If a person came across a stream by chance and drank some water from it, that act would not be considered work. If, however, that person were searching for water, dug a well, and then purified the water to take a drink, this would involve work. **Work** then may be defined as activity that makes physical materials (manual work), services (service work), or mental constructs/ideas (intellectual work) more useful.

Many animals, such as beavers, bears, or bees, can be seen working, transforming something in order to live. Although an ant can construct with a precision that may shame an engineer, human work is different in two ways from animal work. To begin with, humans conceptualize the end product before they even pick up a tool. Cabinetmakers see their cabinets in their minds before a single nail is pounded into the wood. If asked to build something they have never seen, they would be able to listen to a description and create from it an image or set of ideas for this new object to guide their building of it. This is conceptualization.

Secondly, human work is purposive and conscious. It is not performed by instinct. *Instincts* are genetically programmed, coded at birth, and relatively inflexible patterns of activity triggered by a stimulus and designed to satisfy certain needs. Human beings create things not by instinct, but through thought, which is in turn based upon learning. Braverman (1974b: 47) cited an experiment in which scientists studied the behaviour of the South African weaverbird, which builds a complicated nest of sticks and hair. Five generations of the birds were bred from eggs initially taken from the wild, and the generations were kept away from the traditional nesting materials and other weaverbirds. There was no way the sixth generation of birds could have learned how to make the nest. Yet when these pairs were released, they immediately went in search of sticks and hair and constructed a typical weaver nest. The only explanation is that the birds must have had a pattern etched in their brains acquired with the genetic material passed on in the reproductive process.

As animals evolve, we do see more evidence of an ability to learn complex tasks. Dolphins and apes, for instance, perform many very difficult tasks. It has not been demonstrated, however, that the higher-order mammals, except humans, are able to conceptualize.

Rather, it appears that our close relatives still have a major portion of their lives determined by instinctive responses. Human work is conscious, purposive, and directed by conceptual thought. Our ability to communicate symbolically through language enables this difference. Indeed many scientists argue that language, tool use, and brain size develop together, reinforcing and increasing one another.

While work done by humans is distinguishable from that performed by animals, it is nonetheless quite varied. Most of us, when we consider work, focus on activity that we do for pay, generally when employed by someone else. Work, however, can take many forms. Writing an essay and studying for exams can be a form of work—through these activities students make ideas and knowledge more useful to

[Social Trends]

Transforming Nature, Transforming Ourselves

Apes have a similar posture to humans and hands they can use much as we do. But the parts of our brain that control fine motor skills and conceptualization are larger. Humans are also one of the few animal groups that use tools to make tools, an ability closely tied to brain capacity. Washburn's thesis (1960) argues that the creation of tools led to our greater evolution. He further hypothesized that it is the labour process that develops the human capacity of conceptualization, and that this ability to conceptualize led to more work with tools, which led, in turn, to a further growth of abilities (1960: 61–72). Thus, as we transform nature, we transform ourselves. Let us look at an example of how the process may have worked.

In ancient China there was a marginally self-sufficient village. The villagers had few contacts with others down river, except for purposes of intermarriage. Each year, there were droughts in late summer and floods in the spring. To stop the flood-then-drought cycle that plagued the area, the villagers eventually built a dam on a local river. This prevented flooding and saved water for the dry

season, a transformation of nature. What were the accompanying social changes that took place in the society of the village?

First there were health improvements, which translated into a dramatic drop in infant mortality. Also, each year, larger numbers of the elderly survived. There was also a surplus of food, which eventually led to trade with surrounding villages, more sharing of experiences, and wider intermarriage. The existence of a surplus forced the village to develop laws to decide who would get the extra food and laws to determine disputes over the surplus. New skills and jobs were developed, as carts had to be built to haul the surplus, and distribution of food had to be organized to feed these small industry workers who were no longer engaged directly in agriculture. A police (army) was then drawn from the population to guard trade goods en route. We could continue, but as you can see, the transformation of the natural state—that is, the diversion of the river—led to many social changes and the growth of human potential. (For more on Social Change, see Chapter 17.)

Is it possible to forecast all of the social changes that can arise when we make changes to our physical environment? Why would this ability prove useful?

themselves. Making meals and doing laundry are also forms of work, generally referred to as domestic labour. Many people earn an income through illegal activity such as stealing, drug dealing, and prostitution. These can also be forms of work in our society. Others do legal work, but are self-employed. Many people combine different types of work each day, and across their lifetimes. Although throughout most of this chapter we focus on paid work, it is important to remember that work is variable, and is done in many different contexts.

Now let's look more closely at how work has changed and developed over time.

The Evolution of Modern Work

The development of human work has been a long and complex process, but it is possible to identify patterns and key trends over time. The transition from simple agricultural production to complex industrial production and the accompanying increase in the division of labour have been of particular interest to sociologists (see also Chapter 17, Social Change).

The division of labour

Virtually every society has a division of labour—an ordered way of determining who does what. In Chapter 1, you read of Durkheim's attempts to understand this process. In the earliest human societies, there were **social divisions of labour** shaped by gender and age. For instance, in many communities, young and middle-aged women would leave their settlements daily to gather food and other needed materials, while young and middle-aged men would leave for longer periods of time to hunt. Older villagers would be placed in charge of those too young to gather or hunt. This is what we call the social division of labour. As humans moved from hunter-gatherer societies to more complex societies, the division of labour became more complex as well, although divisions by age and gender have remained common.

In many agrarian societies—those based around farming—divisions of labour were more complex, shaped not only by age and gender, but by class and social status as well. For instance, for much of the Middle Ages in Europe, the feudal system was common.

Land was farmed by peasants, most of whom did not own the land they lived and worked on. Under the feudal system, large tracts of farm land were owned by noblemen. Peasants, called serfs, worked the land, both for themselves and their families, and for the lords who owned the land. These peasants were largely unfree: they could not leave the manor or nobleman to which they were attached without permission. They owed service to the lord of the manor and were subject to all manner of restrictions and fines established by the lord and others in the local community. In these societies the division of labour was shaped by class: serfs did the bulk of the hard labour, while lords were much less actively involved in farming (they were involved in managing estates and in the military quite often). Labour was also divided by gender and age: adult men farmed the land with the help of older children and sometimes women; women concentrated on tasks such as keeping a garden, maintaining livestock, and making clothes and other items for household consumption; young children would be cared for by older children and the elderly and infirm. Some workers in the village would concentrate their labour on providing other community needs, for instance, baking bread, brewing ale, or practising a trade. Households and communities were largely self-sufficient and through a division of labour provided for their own needs. While the social division of labour was more complex in these societies, it was still pretty straightforward.

In contrast, in industrial societies, individuals have become much more dependent on each other, and the division of labour has become more advanced. We are no longer like the self-sufficient farm families who would grow their own food and make their own clothes. We purchase food and other goods and services produced by others. Production now is rarely the result of a few individuals specializing, but involves a very **detailed division of labour**. For instance, shoes used to be made by cobblers, skilled workers who made shoes from start to finish. Today, the production of a shoe is divided among dozens people: some plan and design, some cut, some glue, some sew, others dye, finish, and package. Gender, class, and age still shape who does what in such systems, but people within the same social categories can do widely different tasks. While all known societies are characterized by some kind of social division of labour, the detailed division of labour has developed only in the modern, industrial era, and it is often viewed as harmful.

Industrialization

Between the mid-eighteenth and mid-nineteenth centuries, the traditional type of society in Europe and North America, dependent on a majority of its people producing for their own use, declined, and in its place grew industrialized society and techniques of mass production of goods (see Chapter 17, Social Change). This was a period of great uncertainty and change. People's ways of living and working changed dramatically. Whereas in the past people often had some say over what work they did, and how they did it, this declined with the expansion of industrial employment. Many contemporaries were concerned about the impact of these changes, and the striking social inequality that accompanied them. Karl Marx warned that one effect would be social discontent, which in turn would lead to the working class taking

By the turn of the century, in Europe and North America, industrialization was replacing the traditional type of society that depended on a majority of its people producing only for their own use.

control of the entire social system (see Chapter 6, Social Inequality). Durkheim (1965 [1895]) studied the division of labour and wrote that it would lead to *anomie*, a social problem where people would feel atomized and experience a sense of normlessness. In the early twentieth century, Weber and others argued that problems could arise due to the organizational changes that accompanied industrialism. We will examine some of these issues later in the chapter.

The rise of scientific management and Fordism

By the end of the nineteenth century, industrialization was expanding rapidly, and with it came further changes in the organization of work. Organizations and production facilities grew larger, and as a result, there was a greater emphasis on controlling and coordinating the work of the many different groups of workers gathered, increasingly, under one roof. **Scientific management**, sometimes called Taylorism after its inventor Fredrick Taylor, involved eliminating inefficiencies. Taylor made a detailed study of the industrial production process and then broke it down into smaller and simpler tasks, meaning that workers could be more easily trained, were easier to supervise, and their output could be measured and translated into steps, procedures, and formulae. His study led to a system of management that forced workers to perform in set, repetitive ways. Scientific management, as a system of organization, did not aim to enhance the well-being of those who did the work, but was aimed at controlling their actions in order to maximize output. Although Taylor actually introduced his program into only one steel plant in the U.S., his method influenced many areas of mass production, in particular, auto production. Henry Ford adapted Taylor's ideas to create the assembly-line work system when he designed his auto plants. **Fordism** (Wood, 1994) simply means mass production for a mass market using these assembly-line methods.

Responses to Ford and Taylor

In their early days, Taylorist principles and the Fordist system were seen by the captains of industry as the wave of the future. However, as productive as Fordist mass production was, it only worked when products were standardized—that is, made uniform. If products had to be made in small numbers (small-batch production), perhaps due to changes demanded by consumers, then the process was not very efficient. Consequently, in the latter part of the twentieth century, we saw a move to such small-batch production where manufacturers make smaller quantities, altering sizes or colours (or other characteristics) to capture niches in a more specialized consumer market.

Another problem industrialists faced came from their workers. Unions and individual workers resisted these new systems. Forced to work under scientific management, workers were absent more often than individuals working under other management systems. The problem was that scientific management tried to make people into machines, and people rebelled. Monotonous, repetitive work, with no creativity or input from workers, caused resentment. Recall that humans are conceptual beings whose unique attribute is the ability to think and plan in a purposive way and then to produce that which they have planned. These new systems thus challenged a central feature of workers' humanity by taking much of the thinking and conceptualizing out of the work process. Indeed, Taylor stated in his book *The Principles of Scientific Management* (1906) that all "brainwork" must be removed from the shop floor and placed in the hands of management. An emergent resistance to these new systems—through strikes and absenteeism and even sabotage—may, in large part, have been the result of the fact that these systems were not geared to the needs and abilities of the participants. Rather they created work environments that forced workers to do as they were told, and not to think.

Still another response to Fordism was the growing belief that workers should be better rewarded for their contribution to the "common good." In post–World War II society, particularly in Canada and the U.S., an understanding developed among those who owned business and industry, those who worked in those businesses and industries, and the state (government). This **social contract** was based on the economics of John Maynard Keynes. Essentially, the socially accepted understanding was that if one works hard and produces more goods and services each year, the economy will grow. Such growth means an increasing return on investments to the owners of capital, and increases in the standard of living for the people who work and create this production. Government would ensure stability in the social, political, and economic system by creating policies to move toward full employment. And finally, those who

earn their living from wages or salaries would not need to fear unemployment, because their jobs would be secure so long as the economy grew, or at least maintained itself.

The Great Depression of the 1930s was the impetus for such a social contract and post-World War II prosperity in North America delivered some of its promises. Standards of living rose and unemployment stayed relatively low in the 1950s and 1960s as the productivity of industry climbed substantially. This rosy situation was not without significant problems, however, nor did it last forever. Before we pursue what happened to the social contract in the 1990s, let us take a brief look at other significant developments during the twentieth century, and in particular, changes in the contexts in which we work.

Where We Work: The Many Faces of Organizations

Whether out in a field cultivating with their fellow tribespeople in Namibia or on an assembly line in Windsor, Ontario, human work is organized. Organizations come in two main types: formal and informal, with some important differences between them.

Formal organizations expanded with the rise of industrial capitalism, and by and large, the organizations we inhabit and interact with today are a product of the late nineteenth and early twentieth centuries. Formal organizations are established to make work more efficient, although they may not succeed at this task. They have a division of labour (larger organizations have very detailed divisions of labour) and are set up to achieve goals—there is a whole branch of sociology dedicated to the study of how formal organizations achieve their goals. Corporations, schools, government agencies, and even political parties are examples of formal organizations. They are common and run some of the most complex of human activities. A hospital, for example, is responsible for providing care to the ill, not a simple task. It involves more than admitting people, feeding them, and facilitating the diagnosis and treatment of their medical problems. The hospital is also a place where health-care professionals are trained, where technology is tested, and where education of patients and families is undertaken, involving coordination and communication among its many employees and the outside world.

Is the Rule of the Few Inevitable?

Michels, in his book *Political Parties* (1915), argued against Marx's prediction of a communist state where all would give according to their abilities and take according to their needs. He prophesied an **iron law of oligarchy**: in all organizations, even in democratic organizations, rule by the many will inevitably become rule by the few who will serve their own needs first.

This occurs through the bureaucratic division of labour; those at the top tend to develop a monopoly on the knowledge and skills required to oversee the bureaucracy. Wilfredo Pareto, a contemporary of Michels, came up with a different idea, but it too was critical of the possibility of a communist world. He wrote in *Circulation of Elites* about lions and foxes. *Foxes* are the challengers to the established *lions* in authority. They are clever and often act in stealth, eventually overcoming the lions that,

after years of power, have become complacent and even lazy. Eventually the foxes become the new lions and a new set of foxes starts the cycle again. The communist state never succeeds against this process.

Michels proved to be correct. Communist oligarchies in countries such as the former Soviet Union arose when party members formed an elite and took privileges for themselves that they did not give to others. These ideas also find support in studies of various labour unions. Many union leaders do not want to step down and tend to remain in office for long periods of time. Their continued leadership can then take precedence over the needs of the rank-and-file workers.

On the other hand, where the job vacated to lead the union is of a high status, stepping down is more frequent, as might be found in medical and legal associations.

Limiting the number of terms can counteract this tendency for entrenched leadership. How do oligarchs subvert this check to their continued power?

Many formal organizations function like *bureaucracies*, with rigid rules and plans (see the box "Why Is There Always So Much 'Red Tape'?"). For Max Weber, and others, the spread of bureaucracies and formal organizations more broadly, was linked to a social trend he called **rationalization,** the overriding concern within capitalist societies for constantly increasing efficiency. Highly detailed divisions of labour and rigid rules and plans have been developed to enhance efficiency and to ensure that more is done (more customers served, more objects produced), in a shorter period of time, with fewer resources. Nevertheless, rules and plans cannot anticipate every problem, nor can they always enable workers to adapt to every work situation that arises. Hence, alongside formal organization exists **informal organization,** consisting of the informal rules and interactions that enable workers to meet the challenges of complex day-to-day life.

This informal structure of an organization is made up of the activities that people engage in that are not

prescribed by the rules but that they find necessary to carry out their tasks. The informal organization thus arises within the formal one as the need arises. If we think back to our hospital example, we know that nurses are supposed to record at the nursing station all the information that they discover about a patient. However, given their frantic work environment, nurses can rarely get to all their "charting." Nurses thus rely on word of mouth to convey information to the next shift. They also may pass on information about doctors who are particularly ill-tempered or new ways of doing work that have proven effective. The communications system of the hospital, therefore, has a formal organizational side, including charting and computers, as well as an informal side, one of personal communications.

Informal networks, as in the case of the example of nursing, can be very positive, but informal structures can be dysfunctional as well. Rumour mills can target individuals or new management programs and cause harm through false information and accusations. But

Why Is There Always So Much "Red Tape"?

The study of organizations has been a specialized part of sociology since its inception as a social science. Early sociologists like Weber (1921) spent a great deal of energy trying to understand organizations and particularly something he called **bureaucracy**, a special type of complex organization. According to Weber, every bureaucracy, whether a church or a political party, shares these common characteristics:

1. *Specialization and a division of labour.* Bureaucracies employ experts with job titles and job descriptions that indicate what they do in the organization. The members of the organization specialize and are responsible for carrying out their duties in an effective manner.

2. *Hierarchy of authority.* We might think of this as the power structure or chain of command. The members of the bureaucracy report to people who have "higher" positions than they, and who in turn, supervise others "below" them.

3. *Rules and regulations.* Written rules and regulations establish authority within the organization, and the fact that they are standardized ensures that activities become more standardized as well. This allows new members to learn what to do and how to do it more efficiently and ensures that people in the organization know both what is expected and what is not allowed.

4. *Impersonality.* Interactions in a bureaucracy are supposed to be based on the rules not personal feelings or attitudes. Officials are expected to interact with subordinates based on the office they hold not on how they might feel about them.

5. *Technical competence, careers, and tenure in the office.* Candidates for a job are to be evaluated based on their ability to do the job they are being hired to do. There should be set qualifications that are considered for all candidates, and favouritism, family connections, and other subjective factors should have no effect on the hiring process. Once hired, a person should progress through a *career*, based on job performance and seniority in the job.

6. *Communications should be formal and written.* This provides a clear record of what has been done and who made the decisions. This record helps a bureaucracy to avoid repeating errors as well as the proliferation of verbal commands that can be misunderstood, misinterpreted, or even denied if there are problems that develop.

Obviously, bureaucracy represents quite a difference from informal organization. The ideal bureaucracy seems to regulate everything in a very rational way. It is important to keep in mind that in real life the people in the bureaucracy often subvert this perfection, bringing in their personal biases and ideas. As in all formal organizations, an informal organization develops alongside the formal one. Nonetheless, Weber did see the development of these forms of organization as marking the growth of *legal-rational* society, one based on law and reason.

Would modern families, busy with two careers and children, benefit from a bit of bureaucratization? Not a hierarchy of authority, but perhaps a clearer division of labour and a few written rules? If not, why not?

informal systems are also more flexible and easily transformed than formal ones, and thus generally functional. A symbolic interactionist approach, *negotiated order theory*, developed by Corwin (1987: 107), argues that organizational structures emerge from meaningful interpersonal interaction and that individuals create temporary agreements and informal understandings with co-workers to facilitate the completion of their job or even to make their work more pleasant. This again means that any organization is not a static, set pattern but rather a temporary, ever-changing body developed through the negotiation of its members.

Driving organizational change in recent years has also been the ongoing trend of *rationalization*. Companies appear to have accelerated their efforts to achieve more with less, and the drive for efficiency that used to characterize manufacturing facilities has come to be generalized to more and more sectors of the economy. Ritzer (1996: 1) argued that what we are experiencing is **McDonalidization**: a process where the principles and organization of fast-food restaurants are coming to permeate society more generally. Ritzer explained that *McDonald's* (and by extension McDonalidization) emphasizes four principles. First is *efficiency*, finding the best way to achieve a goal. Through offering only a limited menu, and mass producing standardized goods through the use of technology and tight labour control, fast-food restaurants have achieved a great deal of efficiency. Making customers do some work (carry their own trays, get their own napkins, and so on) also enhances efficiency, from the organization's point of view. Second is *calculability*, an emphasis on quantity over quality. Fast-food restaurants emphasize numbers—they emphasize the size of their sandwiches and drinks, how many they have sold, and the low cost of their services. They do not emphasize quality. Third is *predictability*: many of us like the fact that when we go into a McDonald's or similar restaurant, no matter where it is located, we know what we will get. There is comfort in knowing that the burger is familiar, even if we are in an unfamiliar town; the décor will be the same, and the place relatively clean. Fourth is *control*: workers and customers at restaurants like McDonald's are tightly controlled (sometimes in subtle ways). As Ritzer explained (1988: 11), "lines, limited menus, few options, and uncomfortable seats all lead diners to do what management wishes them to do—eat quickly and leave." Control is even more substantial for the people who work in these environments; they have little say over how they do their work, but are closely directed by machinery and supervision to do and say precisely what management wants them to.

There are advantages to McDonaldization: predictability can be comforting, and through their efficiency, fast-food restaurants can be convenient and fairly inexpensive. There is a downside, though, Ritzer warned, in that it provides us with less variety, little quality, and controls us as both workers and consumers. Given these negatives, Ritzer was concerned about the spread of McDonaldization to other sectors of society: standardization (to increase efficiency), calculability, predictability, and control are evident in the chain stores in the retail sector, the increasingly prefabricated construction sector, in banking and entertainment, as well as the education and health-care system. For instance, in the latter sector, there is evidence of attempts to increase efficiency through standardization and simplifying products— hospitals are coming to "specialize" in terms of the health services they provide, and new management techniques attempt to streamline the delivery of health-care services. Customers—patients and their families—are asked to do more work toward their own care while in hospital, and outside, as patients are released sooner than was common in the past. Moreover, there is an increased emphasis on calculability, on emphasizing how many patients can be processed through the system, by a limited staff, rather than on the quality of care provided. Workers in these environments report feeling more controlled and have higher levels of stress than in the past. These trends are positive for neither workers nor patients.

For Ritzer and others, McDonalidization is potentially "dehumanizing" and harmful to us. The tight control and emphasis on numbers and predictability removes a lot of the variability and autonomy that are so valuable to us as humans. There is concern that with the emphasis on quantity, quality of service and product is decreasing. The spread of rationalization throughout society may increasingly limit diversity and meaning in human experience.

Inequalities in Organizations and Workplaces

Organizations almost always entail hierarchical structures. There are a few at the top of the hierarchy—like executives and top managers—who run organizations and direct the labour of those underneath them, and many at the bottom whose labour is directed to meet organizational goals. Inequalities are inherent in such environments: some workers have more power and influence than others. One's job shapes one's opportunities, lifestyle, and social status (as discussed in Chapter 6, Social Inequality). It is also the case, though, that one's social position and social characteristics can influence the kind of job one is able to obtain. Just as traits like gender, age, and class shaped the division of labour historically, they continue to do so today. In our multicultural society, race and ethnicity can shape work opportunities as well.

Occupational segregation is the term used to describe the fact that people in different social categories tend to do different types of work. Although occupational segregation could be identified on the basis of a number of different characteristics, including age, studies have tended to focus on sex segregation, and to a lesser extent racial segregation, at work. *Sex segregation* occurs when men and women work in different occupations, jobs, and/or workplaces. Similarly, *race and ethnic segregation* occurs when people from different racial or ethnic backgrounds work in different jobs, occupations, and/or workplaces. Work in our society is both race- and sex-segregated. Studies suggest that sex segregation is a little more extensive than race and ethnic segregation, although there has been lit-

tle research on race segregation at work in the Canadian context.

Although it is not always easy to determine the extent of segregation, recent studies suggest that about 50 percent of Canadian women would have to change jobs to have an occupational distribution similar to men's (Brooks et al., 2003). Table 14.1 provides a list of some of the most common jobs for men and for women in Canada, according to the 2001 Census. You can see that there is little overlap on these lists. Men and women tend to work in different types of jobs. Even in those jobs where they do similar types of work—for instance in cleaning and retail trade—there are hidden internal differences. Women are more likely to work as "light duty cleaners" while men are more likely to work as "janitors." Moreover, women are more likely to work in retail stores aimed at female customers, while men

Table 14.1   The Most Common Jobs for Women and Men, Canada, 2001

Rank	Women	Number of Workers	Rank	Men	Number of Workers
1	Childcare and home support workers	373 705	1	Motor vehicle and transit drivers	426 845
2	Clerical occupations, general office	373 120	2	Computer and information systems occupations	296 620
3	Secretaries, court recorders and transcribers	357 870	3	Retail salespersons and clerks	235 595
4	Retail salespersons and clerks	355 465	4	Cleaners	227 570
5	Finance and insurance clerks	301 280	5	Managers in retail trade	204 435
6	Secondary and elementary school teachers	294 760	6	Occupations in agriculture and horticulture	201 065
7	Cashiers	237 560	7	Processing, manufacturing, and utilities labourers	178 660
8	Nurse supervisors and registered nurses	227 700	8	Motor vehicle mechanics	159 825
9	Administrative occupations	215 750	9	Machining, metalworking, and woodworking	158 030
10	Food and beverage service occupations	213 835	10	Recording, scheduling, and distribution occupations	156 440
11	Cleaners	197 560	11	Machinery and other (non-motor vehicle) mechanics	151 625
12	Food counter attendants	188 220	12	Longshore workers and materials handlers	151 250

Source: Data from the 2001Census. Employment figures based on occupational categories at the two-digit level of aggregation.

are more likely to be employed in those that predominantly serve men.

The extent of race and ethnic segregation is harder to assess, since there are so many different ethnic groups in Canadian society. Nonetheless, most recent estimates suggest that 20 percent to 25 percent of people would have to change jobs to have an occupational distribution that was not ethnically segregated (Lautard and Guppy, 1990). Although the picture of ethnic segregation is a complex one, studies have been fairly consistent in showing that Aboriginals and African Canadians are particularly disadvantaged in the labour force compared to other groups of workers. On the other hand, rates of both sex- and race-segregation have decreased over time.

These employment differences are significant because they have implications for inequality. That is, not only are the occupations in which men and women, minority and majority people work, different, but so are their rewards, opportunities for promotion, job security, and so on. Traditionally, white women, and men and women from minority backgrounds have had fewer opportunities for good-paying, meaningful work, leading to promotions than have majority men. Recall from Chapter 7, Gender Relations, that some of the wage gap between men and women is explained by the fact that they have different jobs with different responsibilities. Men's jobs are often more likely to offer opportunities for promotion, and to exercise authority. Although there has been a recent influx of women into management, men have traditionally occupied the top spots in organizations. Income differences among ethnic groups are also partly the result of occupational segregation.

How and why does occupational segregation occur? There have been many explanations put forward, but no single explanation will suffice. Rather, a number of factors appear to contribute to it. One of the most common explanations holds that men and women are in different jobs because they have different interests and make different choices. Some argue that men and women have been socialized differently. Since little girls play with dolls and little boys drive trucks, perhaps we should not be surprised when girls grow up to be child-care workers and teachers and boys grow up to be truck drivers. However, while personal choice may explain some of the differences it cannot account for all of them. It is hard to see how childhood socialization might lead women to become secretaries, finance clerks, and cashiers, while men are distribution employees, retail

managers, and manufacturing employees. It is even less clear how personal choice can explain the poor labour market position of many visible minorities. We must recognize that while our personal choices are important in shaping the kind of work that we do, the choices that we make are shaped by social structure, and, especially, the options and opportunities open to us.

Also influencing segregation are differences in education, traditional patterns of working (as we have seen divisions of labour have historically been structured around gender and other characteristics), and ideological beliefs about gender and racial difference. The hiring decisions and personal biases of employers appear to play a particularly strong role, as, at times, do the opinions and actions of other workers. Some employers may believe that women's responsibility for domestic labour and childrearing makes them less committed and successful workers, and, therefore, less worthy of promotion. For these reasons, men still predominate at the top of organizational hierarchies.

Occupational segregation has proven to be an enduring characteristic of the labour market; one that has persisted despite some substantial economic and social changes. Although societal beliefs more supportive of gender and racial equality have helped to diminish segregation over time, experts suggest it will remain a characteristic of the labour market for many years to come.

Youth and the Labour Market

Just as gender and race shape people's experiences of working, so does age. We have seen that in the past, social divisions of labour were structured by age. The same remains relatively true today. Currently, there is social concern about workers at both the beginning and the end of their working lives. In this section we focus on those problems experienced by recent generations of young workers as they enter the labour force.

Youth or young workers are generally defined as those aged 15 to 24. The recent trends in youth employment are striking. Unemployment rates for youth are high: they are generally just less than twice the national average, and in early 2006 roughly 11 percent of young workers were unemployed. More dramatic are trends in youth employment rates, a measure of the percentage of youth in paid employment. During the 1990s, full-time employment rates for youth dropped 27 percent, while there was a 3.3 percent increase for the labour force as a whole (Lowe, 2000). Only a bit of this decrease was offset by a 6 percent increase in part-time employment among youth (compared to an 18.5 percent increase for the entire labour force). Fewer youth are employed outside the home. Many of those who are working report that their skills and knowledge are not being used. Moreover, young workers are more likely to experience injury and death on the job, than older groups of workers. Also troubling is the fact that youth wages have experienced a substantial drop over the past 30 years or so. Betcherman and Leckie (1997) found a growing gap between the earnings of youth and other adult workers. The trend of stagnant and declining wages has hit young men more than young women.

Together, these trends suggest that young workers' experiences of working are increasingly negative ones. Many of these trends are related to the growing tendency of young adults to stay in school longer. The fact that more youth are pursuing postsecondary education helps to explain why youth employment is dropping. At the same time, a lack of opportunities in the labour market appears to encourage young workers to return to school, in the hopes of improving their labour-market opportunities. The result of all of these trends, many suggest, is delayed adulthood. Canadians are pushing back the age at which they marry, have children, and establish independent residences. Most youth under the age of 25 live with a parent, as do a large proportion of those in their late twenties. It is taking youth longer to get established in the labour market and get their careers under way. The prospects for young workers without education appear to be shrinking, and such workers may have even greater difficulty achieving independence. Researchers disagree over whether the problems experienced by youth are merely temporary—related to recent economic and demographic trends—or an emerging trend that will continue to affect this cohort of workers as they age. Many feel the problems will wither away soon as the baby boom generation (born in the years following World War II) nears retirement, thereby opening up more job opportunities for new workers.

Nevertheless, younger workers today are more educated than the many generations of workers that preceded them into the labour force. Whether they will find the fulfillment and security they seek in work remains an open question.

Work: Satisfying or Alienating?

In the previous sections, we established that work is linked with social inequality, and noted that some have raised concerns about the quality of work and work opportunities in our increasingly McDonaldized society. How do workers feel about working in these environments?

Karl Marx was the first sociologist to explore systematically the problems of work. He wrote in his *Economic and Philosophic Manuscripts of 1844* (1975 [1844]) that a detailed division of labour would destroy the creativity of work. It was not just the repetitive nature of the work process, but also the loss of control over work that was the key problem for Marx. He pointed out that although the workers and peasants in traditional societies worked long, hard hours and their life was difficult, they were in control of *how* they worked. They had skills and controlled the use of them, making decisions over how to employ their abilities. This gave workers a measure of satisfaction and well-being concerning their place in, and their contribution to, society. By contrast, with industrialization, workers were increasingly directed in their tasks, leading to what Marx termed **alienation**. Alienation, in this sense, is not simply a psychological problem but a structural one, rooted in the relationships between the managers and the managed, the "deciders" and the "doers." The purposive and conceptual nature of human work is lost, causing workers to feel alienated or separated from their "humanity" (White, 1990, 1993).

While, for Marx, the problem with work in modern society is the lack of control over that work, Durkheim (1965) saw anomie (normlessness) and the breakup of integrated communities as the distinguishing feature and problem in the emerging industrial society (see Chapter 1, What Is Sociology?). Durkheim saw the strikes, sabotage, and public protests as reflections of the lack of commitment to the norms of the new society, this one marked not by a collective sameness, which characterized traditional societies, but by a modern division of labour that made each person's life so separate and different from others in their society.

Both theorists join many other writers in arguing that the organization and experience of work in our society is problematic. How do workers respond to these problems?

Marx argued that alienation of the worker is endemic in capitalist society.

Instrumentalism

Many workers in modern society see work as simply a means to an end. How often have we heard "Thank God it's Friday" or found others saying they do not like their job, but can't quit because they have to pay the bills? Working only to earn money to enjoy non-work life represents a problematic relation to one's work. Goldthorpe (1969) found in his classic studies that some workers respond to the alienating aspects of work in an **instrumentalist** fashion. People often think that if they have to work under monotonous and undesirable conditions, then they had better be paid well so they can enjoy their leisure time. This is a problem because work is supposed to be fulfilling and represent an aspect of what makes us human, as we discussed above. Yet the reality of some work is that it is simply a means to an end, and an onerous activity.

Other social scientists find that many workers resist undesired aspects of work, and would like to change the organization of work to make it more fulfilling.

Thompson (1989), summarizing a wide range of sociological research, concluded that most people actively resist anti-conceptual work and control systems (see also Rinehart, 2006). White (1993) found, in Canada, that even professionals with a high dedication to their jobs, such as nurses, often exhibit resistance behaviours, striking or quitting their jobs to oppose the degradation of external control over their own work activities. Let us look closer at this aspect of work.

Resistance and consent work

In every work relationship, those who carry out the tasks have consented in one way or another to do their job. Yet, except in the most ideal circumstances, these same workers harbour some level of discontent with the safety conditions, the pay, the supervision, or a thousand other things, and will act on that discontent in minor or major ways. We call this **resistance**, action(s) aimed at passively or actively slowing, reversing, avoiding, or protesting management directions or strategies in the workplace. Resistance can manifest itself on any scale, from millions of workers launching general strikes to gain political change, to small groups protesting a supervisor's order, to individual acts.

Some workers resist unpleasant work through a variety of personal strategies. For instance, workers faced with unpleasant work might delay doing it until the last possible moment, or "play dumb" to avoid unpleasant work. Absenteeism, petty theft, and gossip can also be individual forms of resistance (Hodson, 1991). At times, individuals may engage in **sabotage**—activities aimed at destroying employers' property or otherwise disrupting the flow of production. Sabotage can help workers reduce their work-generated tension and frustration, and can grant them a break from unpleasant work.

Unhappy workers may also band together with others and engage in various forms of group resistance. The workgroup and its members formulate the conditions under which they will comply based on how, over time, they perceive the gains and/or losses involved in that decision. Salaman (1986) noted that the rewards different groups of workers expect vary based on what the workers share in terms of norms, values, and knowledge. In the same way that a society develops a culture, workers in a workplace develop a work culture.

When will workers decide to resist openly? In the simplest utilitarian terms, it is when the rewards for consenting to a situation are insufficient and the losses

[Applied Sociology]

Nursing: A Radical Profession?

In the late 1980s, nurses in Canada were leaving the profession, opting for part-time work and/or going on strike. A sociological study of the attitudes of nurses and a review of the relevant documents (White, 1993) revealed dramatic changes in the kinds of work nurses were doing and in their workplace. The drive to cut costs in hospitals was leading to a change in the time, the place, and the content of the nursing work. White concluded that the expectations of the nurses had been challenged. Nurses told the researcher that they were no longer allowed to do the job they were trained and wanted to do. Their response, according to White, was to resist the changes through strikes, quitting, or moving to part-time work. As one of the nurses interviewed for the study said, "We have felt powerless to make changes in our hospitals. When you want to deliver a first-rate service and feel good that you have really helped make people well or more comfortable but you cannot because someone or something is stopping you then … you have to take action" (White, 1993: 119).

In 2003 Canada experienced an even more dramatic "shortage" of nurses. To meet the growing demand, nursing schools have expanded enrolment across the country. How might these schools better prepare nurses to deal with the challenges they face in the workplace?

attached to resistance (loss of pay during a strike for example) are not too great in comparison to the problems they will experience by not changing the situation. Put another way, as Willmott (1990: 56) said, "the potential for resistance arises when subjects are constituted whose experience and self-understanding are denied or undermined by the demands being placed upon them." In addition, workers are more likely to resist if they do not understand what is going on in their workplace, when changes reduce feelings of job security, and when practices are forced upon them.

The key to reducing conflict and resistance in the workplace is to reduce insecurity and increase education and information, giving workers a stake in the changed systems. The Taylorist systems aimed to take all decisions from the worker and put them in the hands of the manager. Thus scientific management almost guaranteed that there would be resistance.

Since Taylor's time, newer types of management approaches have been developed that claim to give more power to the people who do the work. These approaches have many names, such as Total Quality Management and Continuous Quality Improvement. However, the success of such programs is doubtful, and analysts are already indicating that the new systems are not functioning as well as had been claimed. Too often,

the promise of involving employees in the decision-making process gives way to hidden plans to cut labour or seek other efficiencies (Armstrong et al., 1996). Although successful in Japan, where they originated, they have not been successful in North America (Rinehart et al., 1998), partly because Japanese society is more collectivist and open to managers and workers sitting down together and sharing ideas. In North America there has been a long tradition of mistrust between management and labour.

Unions and resistance

One way in which workers band together to resist managerial directives, and protect their interests, is through unionization. Legally, **unions** represent the collective group of workers in negotiations with the employer to get a contract. The behaviour of both the union and management is circumscribed by labour laws, sometimes called trade-union acts, determined separately in each province in Canada.

Unions legally won the right to exist in the workplace by the end of the nineteenth century. The growth of unions in Canada since that time can be linked to a series of conditions. The new management systems we discussed above, such as Taylorism, job insecurity, and the history of poor working conditions with long hours, all contributed to an increase in union membership. There are many complicated reasons why workers may choose to unionize their workplace. The simplest way to understand the growth of unions, sociologically, is to think of them as a response to the powerlessness experienced by the individual worker. A single worker has very little power to negotiate with a company. If there are common and very important problems, there is a greater chance that employees will unionize. Where working conditions are better, then unionization is less likely.

The End of the Social Contract and the Changing Nature of Work

In the 1990s, the social contract described earlier ceased to operate as both business and government adopted new attitudes concerning job security and full employment.

The term **downsizing** is now commonplace, and describes the process by which a firm reduces the number of employees, while trying to keep returns on invested capital at the same level or, preferably, higher. Downsizing obviously creates higher unemployment rates in Canada and makes employees nervous about job security. All levels of government, too, have laid off civil servants, claiming that a debt crisis is forcing cuts in programs. Gone, then, is the job security that comes with working hard.

It is not that Canadian workers have not been productive. Canada started the 1980s with one of the most productive workforces in the world, and maintained its productivity over the years. In 1996, the Canadian Auto Workers (CAW) went on strike against General Motors (GM). The CAW argued that its workers had been working faster and more productively and that autoworkers had been increasing profits at GM. It asked GM to agree that so long as the CAW workers remained productive and so long as GM remained profitable GM would not lay off workers. GM,

The Matsushita Electric Company is guided by collective values that transform Japan's industries into communities.

however, wanted to increase profits by outsourcing jobs—hiring outside companies, who pay their workers less, to do some of the jobs normally performed by their own employees.

Bond-rating agencies and mutual-fund stock organizations have also chipped away at the social contract. Bond-rating agencies have demanded that governments cut social programs and stay away from full-employment policies if they want a good credit rating for their borrowing of money. For their part, mutual-fund managers have tended to invest more heavily in companies that downsize, even though there is no firm evidence that downsizing is profitable. In fact, if an organization downsizes too quickly, there can be no benefits at all.

As a result of these and other factors, we have also seen a general flattening of wages and salaries in Canada. Many analysts now conclude that there has been a decrease in the standard of living for a majority of the population. Despite the change to two-income families, which may well be linked to the decline in employment and the work restructuring that has proceeded since the end of the social contract (Kerstetter, 2002), most Canadians are less well-off than before. Recall from Chapter 6, Social Inequality, however, that the rich are still getting richer.

The globalization of production

Outside of Canada, other changes have affected the world of work. Perhaps most importantly, there has been a **globalization of production**, which means that companies now look worldwide for the most profitable place to set up production (see Chapter 17, Social Change). Before, companies produced primarily in their home nations. Today, however, with the new social and economic order, companies are less nationalistic, and more freely locate to emerging areas of the world where labour is cheaper or government "red tape" for things like environmental protection is minimal. These new production sites create competition, and companies looking to invest in Canada can demand that Canadian workers be willing to work for lower wages than those to which they are accustomed.

Canada has experienced other changes in this globalized work environment. For example, changing labour laws have generally made unionization more difficult (Haiven et al., 1992). Free-trade agreements with the United States and Mexico have forced Canada

to drop some of the programs that protected workers' jobs and to change how we regulate some workplaces. Moreover, rapid reduction in government spending has resulted in a loss of jobs in the public sector and a decline in social programming like Employment Insurance.

The decline of the social contract and the globalization of production have thus had quite an effect on the world of work. We asked the question earlier about whether a new kind of social contract was being negotiated to take the place of the old. The answer to that question appears to be no. Essentially, the promises of the old social contract are gone and nothing has emerged to take their place.

Unemployment

Several interrelated changes are creating higher than perhaps necessary unemployment in Canada, including: (1) an increase in small-batch production; (2) the movement of jobs to developing countries the where labour costs are lower; (3) a reduction in governmental provisions for a safety net and a shrinking civil service; and (4) technological change.

Unemployment has gone up in industrialized countries since the end of the social contract. During the late 1980s and 1990s there was close to 10 percent unemployment. In the early years of the twenty-first century, this has levelled off or declined slightly. However, it should be noted that official figures do not count all those who want a job but cannot find one. If people give up—because they have to go on social assistance, for example—they are not counted in the official figures.

Unemployment is a negative phenomenon from several vantage points. It is very costly to a society like Canada. The need to give families and individuals living assistance is an obvious expense of unemployment, but we also lose these people's contributions in terms of work and taxes. Additionally, the health costs of the unemployed are generally higher than for those employed, and the emotional problems that plague those excluded from work can lead to family violence as well as drug and alcohol abuse.

The Future

As we enter the third millennium living in a society where technological innovation occurs so quickly, it is sometimes difficult for us to adapt. We are living in a time when technology means that one worker can produce the large numbers of goods and services that it used to take many people to produce. Yet this capacity is somehow turning into a real problem. How can we have all this ability, yet find insufficient work for our highly motivated, highly educated workers? This exclusion from work costs society billions of dollars in social assistance, lost productivity, and lost tax revenue. Thus it is the "lack of work" problem that is foremost on the agenda for the study of work in the new millennium.

But we will also have to face two other major issues that will profoundly affect our society. The first will be the imbalance between resistance and consent. The current economic situation makes it possible that we will face many serious workplace problems that generate great dissatisfaction, but where the resistance does not lead to an overt action. People fear the loss of their jobs, and in many cases this fear prevents resistance from becoming overt. The lack of disruption to production and the lower numbers of strikes in the first half of the 1990s may reflect people's understanding that the potential losses of resistance outweigh the potential gains, given current rates of unemployment. But this can only be a temporary phenomenon. These pent-up problems will likely come out in new and old forms of resistance over the next decade.

A last issue that faces us is how to organize the work that has to be done. Will we move to increasing the skill of workers and their discretion to decide how work is to be carried out? Or will we embrace a system of organization where control over work by those whose profits are at stake is the number one concern? If we choose the latter, we run the risk of dehumanizing work, and creating ever more conflict that may be met with resistance. If we choose the former, those who actually do the work will gain more control in the workplace, leading to less dissatisfaction for workers. But will globalization alter many of our deeply entrenched notions of who has the right to decide workplace issues? Will those sectors of the Canadian population that now have ownership and control of the economy agree or just move away?

Summary

We began the chapter by defining work as activity that adds value to goods, services, or ideas. Unlike the work of animals, which is often instinctual, human work is conceptualized and purposive. We discussed the distinction between social and detailed divisions of labour, and examined patterns in how labour has been organized across time and place. We then considered scientific management which, on paper, may seem to be an ideal way to maximize production; however, it is associated with many costs as well, among which alienation of labour is perhaps the greatest.

We then took a closer look at the settings in which work occurs, discussing both formal bureaucratic structures and informal modes of organization. We also considered trends towards "McDonaldization" in organizations.

Further, we saw that the organization of work is related to social inequality, and we examined, in particular, challenges traditionally faced by women, ethnic minorities, and, more recently, youth in the labour market. Then we touched on workers' responses to alienating and unfulfilling labour, including resistance and union activity.

The chapter ended with a discussion of the end of the social contract and globalization of work and their multiple effects on workers in Canada, especially downsizing, unemployment, and wage reductions.

Questions for Review and Critical Thinking

1. We read that human work involves greater conceptual ability than the work of other animals. We also learned that the scientific management system tried to remove the conceptual "thinking" from work. Is this counterproductive? Might the scientific management system have stimulated worker resistance; or do workers really care?

2. How instrumental are you about the job you hope to occupy most of your life? Are you most interested in money or are you looking to do a job that you love? Do you feel you have to justify your choice to others, and what does this reveal about the norms we attach to work today?

3. Data reveal that most workers now change jobs three to five times over a lifetime. Based on what you have learned in this chapter, discuss whether this will happen to you.

4. What are the main differences between Durkheim's notion of anomie and Marx's concept of alienation?

5. Do you believe that McDonaldization is spreading through society? Is McDonaldization a good thing or not? What are the implications of McDonaldization for society?

Key Terms

alienation, p. 335
bureaucracy, p. 331
detailed division of labour, p. 327
downsizing, p. 338
Fordism, p. 328
formal organizations, p. 329
globalization of production, p. 339
informal organization, p. 330
instrumentalism, p. 336
iron law of oligarchy, p. 330
occupational segregation, p. 333
McDonaldization, p. 332
rationalization, p. 330
resistance, p. 336
sabotage, p. 336
scientific management, p. 328
social contract, p. 329
social division of labour, p. 327
unions, p. 337
work, p. 325

Suggested Readings

Duffy, A., D. Glenday, and N. Pupo (eds.)
1997 *Good Jobs, Bad Jobs, No Jobs: Changing Work in a Changing North America.* Toronto: Harcourt Brace.
This edited text examines key issues in the private, service, and public sectors of work, tracing the new realities of working life in the evolving economy.

Johns, Gary
2000 *Organizational Behavior: Understanding and Managing Life at Work* (5th ed.). New York: HarperCollins.
Johns provides a good contemporary analysis of formal and informal structure in organizations.

Krahn, Harvey and Graham S. Lowe (eds.)
2002 *Work, Industry and Canadian Society* (4th ed.). Scarborough: Nelson.

A comprehensive introduction to the sociology of work and industry from a Canadian perspective.

Rinehart, James
2006 *The Tyranny of Work: Alienation and the Labour Process* (5th ed.). Toronto: Thomson Nelson.
A concise Marxist analysis of alienation in contemporary workplaces and worker attempts to assert themselves comprise its focus.

Websites

www.yorku.ca/crws/
Centre for Research on Work and Society
This site posts the latest research working papers and provides links to work-related research sites.

www.youngworker.ca
Workplace Health and Safety Board
This site is devoted to raising awareness of the potential dangers of youth employment and to teach youth about risks at work, and their rights to work in a safe environment.

http://jobfutures.ca
Service Canada
This site provides information on the world of work, job characteristics, and job trends in a wide range of occupations. If you want to find out about job opportunities, characteristics, and requirements, this is the site to visit.

Key Search Terms

Bureaucracy
Labour
Fordism
Unions
Globalization
Worker alienation

For more study tools to help you with your next exam, be sure to check out the Companion Website at **www.pearsoned.ca/hewitt**, as well as Chapter 14 in your Study Guide.

[15]

social movements

samuel clark

Introduction

When we employ the term *social movement*, we are usually referring to a large group of people trying to bring about or resist social change. They may want to make a small change, such as diverting an expressway that threatens an old residential community; or they may want to make a very large change, such as dismantling the existing political system or transforming the established economic order. They may, like pro-lifers or members of the anti-pornography movement, be concerned with values and morals; or they may, like anti-poverty groups, be concerned primarily with economic issues.

The first part of this chapter reviews the various ways in which sociologists have studied social movements and related kinds of social behaviour, using examples from both Canada and other parts of the world. In the second part, we shall turn to an analysis of several specific Canadian social movements, adopting a more descriptive and less theoretical tone.

Three Early Theoretical Approaches

Collective behaviour

Sociologists once believed that the best way to approach the subject of social movements was to include them in a broader category of human activity known as **collective behaviour**. As sociologists used this term, collective behaviour occurs when a large number of people do not accept some of the prevailing values, norms, and/or leaders in a society. They are unwilling to tolerate things the way they are, or they do not follow normal routines and may even try to persuade others not to follow them as well. They advocate or engage in activities that sociologists would call less institutionalized when compared with conventional, routine behaviour.

Sociologists differed widely over the kinds of activity that should be grouped together under the heading of collective behaviour. The most common practice, however, was to include such diverse phenomena as panics, crowds, fads, crazes, and publics, along with social movements, on the grounds that they are all relatively unconventional.

The least institutionalized are **panics**. They occur when people are overcome by fear or apprehension, and try to save themselves or their possessions by taking immediate action. Next come **crowds**. No sociologist would claim that all crowds should be placed in the category of collective behaviour. Many crowds are conventional, or casually emerge in the course of conventional behaviour—for example, people waiting for a bank to open or watching a street performer. But some crowds depart sharply from the routine, as when a fight breaks out among fans at a soccer game, or demonstrators are attacked by a group representing an opposing viewpoint. Somewhat more institutionalized are **fads**, which can be defined as unconventional practices that spread rapidly and are adopted in a short period of time by a large number of people. A fad is essentially a social norm (see Chapter 3, Culture), but one that is unusual and departs from the widely accepted norms in a particular society. A **craze**, such as streaking, is a special kind of fad, one that involves unusually intense commitment and enthusiasm, and is inevitably regarded as very strange, and perhaps offensive by other people. A **public** is a large and usually dispersed group made up of persons who share an interest in the same thing. They may hold similar views or they may sharply disagree. Those Canadians who are concerned about the dangers of nuclear energy constitute a public in Canada today, as do those interested in professional hockey, Avril Lavigne, poverty, solid waste disposal, or the health-care crisis. We can learn about the views of publics by studying such things as public opinion polls, the results of political elections, calls to phone-in shows, letters to newspapers, and media interviews.

Finally, a **social movement**, as we have said, is a large collectivity of people trying to bring about or resist social change. Sociologists generally assume that it is the best organized and most institutionalized type of collective behaviour. Whether or not this is true, social movements are certainly more likely to have associations that coordinate the activities of their supporters.

A number of different versions of the collective behaviour perspective emerged over the years, successively building on one another. We shall discuss two of the most influential theories within this tradition, taking them in order of their appearance in the literature.

A social movement is a large collectivity of people trying to bring about social change. The environmental movement is one prominent example of recent years.

Blumer and social contagion

One of the earliest proponents of the collective behaviour approach was Blumer, whose classic statement appeared in 1939. He was largely concerned with the behaviour of unconventional crowds, which he saw as driven by social contagion. In Blumer's words, **social contagion** refers to "the relatively rapid, unwitting, and non-rational dissemination of a mood, impulse or form of conduct" (1951 [1939]: 176). An idea, belief, or perception (often a fear) spreads through a group of people much like an epidemic. This usually happens when something (e.g., a natural catastrophe, such as a flood or earthquake) has disturbed the established ways in which people are accustomed to doing things. Or it may occur during those periods of history when people acquire new desires or impulses that cannot be satisfied through conventional behaviour. One of the most famous examples in history was the so-called Great Fear in France in July of 1789, when the idea spread through the countryside, carried by travellers and postal couriers, that gangs of aristocratic brigands were ravaging the countryside, a fear that led peasants not only to arm in their own defence, but also to attack aristocratic homes.

Emergent norm theory

This theory was developed by Turner and Killian (1957) and deals principally with crowd behaviour, as did Blumer's work. Unlike Blumer, however, they argued that there is a great diversity among those who participate in a crowd. Not all members of a crowd, for example, do the same thing; nor do they all think the same way. Indeed, in many cases a large portion of a crowd has serious doubts about what the crowd is doing, and some might even disagree. And yet they frequently go along, or at least stand back and let the crowd carry on. Why?

The answer, if you accept **emergent norm theory**, is that they are under the impression that most others in the crowd are in agreement. They perceive, rightly or wrongly, that a consensus exists about a specific action that should be taken—for example, that an accused rapist should be lynched, that police arresting a man should be resisted, or that a barricade shielding politicians should be stormed. As a result, they may conform to what the crowd is doing. Indeed, sanctions might even be imposed on those who fail to do so. When this happens—that is, when people start to conform to the apparent will of the crowd—then we can say that a new norm is emerging.

Legacy of the collective behaviour approach

In recent years, many sociologists have identified the weaknesses of this tradition. First, the irrationality implied in the concept of social contagion has been largely rejected. Second, sociologists now believe that this literature gives insufficient attention to social structure and the particularities of social structure. Collective behaviourists convey the impression that what is important is much the same in all societies, in any historical period, regardless of differences in social structure. Third, this theoretical interpretation pays little attention to interest groups and to conflict among such groups. Some sociologists argue that much of what is called collective behaviour is simply the activity of people in conflict; and yet the concept of conflict almost never appears in the collective behaviour literature.

And fourth, a number of critics dispute the assumption that collective behaviour is non-institutionalized. They point out that people may participate in collective behaviour in order to defend values they have held for years, and they may do so in a relatively conventional manner. This is often true of social movements, but even crowds can acquire a conventional character. Rioting can become a tradition, such as the storming of a football field after the final game of the year, clashes with police stemming from yearly marches or festivities, or protests at meetings of the leaders of the G8 or at conferences organized by the World Trade Organization. An example frequently cited by critics of the collective behaviour approach is the food riot that was common in Western Europe during the late eighteenth and early nineteenth centuries. Typically, these rioting crowds followed well-established norms and sought to defend time-honoured values (Rudé, 1964; Thompson, 1971) (see the box "Orderly Riots"). Cases such as these have led many writers to question the fundamental assumption of this approach: that the distinguishing feature of collective behaviour is its relative non-institutionalization.

Social breakdown

There is a widespread supposition in sociological writings that social unrest occurs when established institutions are disrupted or weakened. As a consequence, so the argument goes, people are left "uprooted" and become susceptible to the appeal of a social movement. This notion appears in many different theoretical approaches to our subject, including the collective behaviour tradition just discussed. But we shall treat it separately and call it the **social breakdown approach.**

This perspective owes a considerable debt to Durkheim's notion of **social integration**, the attachment of individuals to social groups or institutions. We saw in Chapter 1 how a lack of social integration could help explain suicides. Writers who make this kind of argument believe that the probability of social unrest is high during periods of rapid social change (especially during rapid industrialization and urbanization) because such change disrupts and weakens traditional institutions. These writers also believe that the people most likely to participate in social unrest are those who are relatively alienated, uprooted, or socially maladjusted. They are individuals who, for some reason, are poorly integrated into social institutions, perhaps even dismissed by others as misfits. Activists in the women's movement have been regarded this way, both in its recent and earlier phases. Cartoons in the late nineteenth and early twentieth centuries, commenting on women's early

[Research Focus]

Orderly Riots

It is now recognized that crowds are not as wild and senseless as was once thought. There is often a logical pattern to their activities, including the choice of victims for their violence. In some cases the behaviour of the crowd can be highly structured. E.P. Thompson has argued that English food rioters in the late eighteenth century were following the values and norms of a traditional "moral economy" which dictated that the food requirements of the local population be met before grain could be exported from a district. The conduct of many such crowds could be highly restrained and was often perfectly legitimate within the traditional social order.

It is the restraint, rather than the disorder, which is remarkable; and there can be no doubt that the actions were approved by an overwhelming popular consensus. There is a deeply felt conviction that prices ought, in times of dearth, to be regulated, and that the profiteer put himself outside of society. On occasion the crowd attempted to enlist, by suasion or force, a magistrate, parish constable, or some figure of authority to preside over the taxation populaire. In 1766 at Drayton (Oxon.) members of the crowd went to John Lyford's house "and asked him if he were a Constable—upon his saying 'yes' Cheer said he sho'd go with them to the Cross & receive the money for 3 sacks of flour which they had taken from one Betty Smith and which they w'd sell for 5s a Bushel"; the same crowd enlisted the constable of Abingdon for the same service. The constable of Handborough (also in Oxfordshire) was enlisted in a similar way, in 1795; the crowd set a price—and a substantial one—of 40s a sack upon a waggon of flour which had been intercepted, and the money for no fewer than fifteen sacks was paid into his hands.

It would be foolish to suggest that, when so large a breach was made in the outworks of deference, many did not take the opportunity to carry off goods without payment. But there is abundant evidence the other way, and some of it is striking. There are the Honiton laceworkers, in 1766, who, having taken corn from the farmers and sold it at the popular price in the market, brought back to the farmers not only the money but also the sacks; the Oldham crowd, in 1800, which rationed each purchaser to two pecks a head; and the many occasions when carts were stopped on the roads, their contents sold, and the money entrusted to the carter.

Source: E.P. Thompson, 1971. "The moral economy of the English crowd in the eighteenth century." *Past and Present* 50: 112–13. Reprinted by permission of Oxford University Press.

Can you think of other examples when seemingly disorderly conduct was, in fact, highly structured? Could recent riots protesting the policies of the World Trade Organization or the Organization of American States be considered orderly riots?

struggles for equality, portrayed feminists as unseemly and offensively self-assertive.

It is best to postpone some of the criticisms of this approach until we discuss the remaining theoretical perspectives. At this point we can simply offer one general remark. Although it is true that social integration can restrain rebellious behaviour, it can also promote it. Think of the role that universities, political parties, and labour unions have played in promoting the separatist movement in Quebec. Insofar as people are integrated into these institutions, social integration has strengthened rebellious behaviour.

Relative deprivation

This is the simplest and most straightforward theoretical approach to social movements, and probably comes closest to your own common-sense explanation. It says that people will turn against existing social arrangements when they are most unhappy with them. Concepts such as *discontent* and *dissatisfaction* have been used to describe popular feelings of this kind. According to this point of view, if the level of discontent rises in a society, people are more likely to rebel.

Numerous reasons can be given for increases in discontent. The most generally accepted in sociology is that they occur when people are experiencing **relative deprivation**, or a gap between what they believe they have a right to receive (their expectations) and what they actually receive (their achievements). A popular view today is that people are most likely to participate in social unrest when their expectations for advancement are frustrated. This situation is even more likely to generate unrest than one in which their welfare is actually deteriorating.

The idea of rising expectations has been around for a long time. It is probably most often associated with the French statesman and historian Alexis de Tocqueville, who wrote a famous study on the origins of the French Revolution (1955 [1856]). Tocqueville's explanation of the Revolution consisted of several different lines of argument, but he is most remembered for his claim that the Revolution occurred when economic conditions were relatively better and political repression less severe than in earlier periods. He also pointed out that support for the Revolution was greatest in comparatively prosperous parts of France. He suggested that prosperity and political freedom, far from satisfying people, simply raise their expectations further. And he then drew the conclusion so often quoted: "Thus the social order overthrown by a revolution is almost always better than the one immediately preceding it, and experience teaches us that, generally speaking, the most perilous moment for a bad government is one when it seeks to mend its ways" (1955 [1856]: 176–77).

In spite of its intuitive appeal, some serious questions can be raised about relative deprivation theory. Again you will find it easier to understand them after we have discussed the collective action approach. Nevertheless, we can make a preliminary observation here. The relative deprivation approach makes the mistake of focusing primarily on the conditions that immediately precede a social movement or a revolt. There is an assumption that, if we can identify and understand discontent just before an uprising, then we have explained the uprising itself. Relative deprivation explanations of the French Revolution concentrate on social conditions and the popular mood as they emerged in the late 1780s. But what if people had been just as dissatisfied in earlier years and yet did not rebel? If this were true, relative deprivation theory might be doing little more than identifying precipitating factors.

Collective Action Approaches

We can now turn to a number of more recent approaches that can together be referred to as collective action approaches. They conceive of social movements in a very different way. To begin with, they reject the concept of collective behaviour and the whole idea that a social movement is relatively non-institutionalized. Instead, they argue that social movements (as well as crowds and many other forms of social unrest) belong to an even broader category of human behaviour called collective action (Tilly, Tilly, and Tilly, 1975; Tilly, 1978). Second, they consider social movements to be much more rational, from the point of view of the actor, than do the traditional approaches.

It is necessary to define the term *collective action* carefully, since it can easily be confused with collective behaviour. As we know collective behaviour refers to relatively non-institutionalized conduct—that is, conduct that departs from the ordinary and routine. In contrast, **collective action** covers both institutionalized and non-institutionalized activity. It can best be defined as the pursuit of a goal or set of goals by a number of persons. Thus it includes a wide range of social phenomena. A terrorist organization kidnapping a diplomat, a group of neighbours cleaning a park, the members of a trade union seeking to raise their wages, a group of students doing a class project—all are examples of collective action.

Collective action is always occurring. Every day, people participate in collective efforts of some sort, within their family, at their place of work, or in a voluntary association. But not all collective action is the same. Its character varies tremendously, and this variation is what we should study, according to this theoretical perspective. Each of the preceding theoretical approaches was developed essentially to explain variations in the amount of social unrest. Collective action theorists suggest that we can understand much more by studying and explaining variations in the character of social unrest. How does collective action differ from one society to another? How does its character change over time within the same society?

Suppose we are doing a study of the Native peoples' movement in Canada during the 1990s. If we were to adopt one of the theoretical approaches described above, we would ask ourselves why protest among First

Table 15.1	Dominant Perspectives on Social Movements in Europe and North America, 1950s to 1990s	
	Dominant perspectives in the 1950s, 1960s, and early 1970s	Dominant perspectives in the late 1970s, 1980s, and 1990s
Europe	Collective action, especially Marxism	New social movements
North America	Collective behaviour, breakdown, and relative deprivation	Collective action, especially resource mobilization

Nations and Inuit increased during this period. We might look for rising expectations in the First Nations and Inuit population, or a breakdown in their traditional institutions, or perhaps the emergence of a new norm.

If, on the other hand, we were to adopt a collective action approach, we would be inclined to see the recent movement as part of a tradition of collective action by Native peoples in Canada. We would emphasize that this movement was by no means their first effort to defend their interests. We would insist on asking, therefore, how the recent movement differed from earlier movements. How did collective action by Native peoples change in terms of numbers and kinds of people participating, in terms of goals, and in terms of methods used to achieve those goals? In answering these questions we would discover, among other things, that a much younger and generally more educated Native population became involved in the 1990s, and that the objectives and strategy of collective action became less defensive and more offensive. We would learn that Natives developed more skilled leadership, which was able both to organize Native peoples and to defend their legal rights. And we would see that the movement became more unified across Canada, though many divisions persisted.

In addition to describing changes in the character of collective action, those who adopt this theoretical perspective also try to explain why such changes occur. To do this they examine the underlying social bonds and divisions in the society, and endeavour to understand how these structural conditions change over time. For each historical period, one needs to determine the particular combinations of people that are likely to engage in collective action. The job is to identify two kinds of factors: first, cleavage factors, which tend to separate people from one another or set them at odds; and second, integrating factors, which pull people together in social groups so that they can engage in collective action, whether or not collective action actually occurs. A basic argument of the collective action perspective is that both cleavage and integrating factors are necessary conditions for social movements to occur.

Notice in this regard that the collective action approach has borrowed a concept from the breakdown perspective—the concept of integration—but has broadened its application. When breakdown theorists talk about integration, they mean integration into established groups and institutions that support the status quo. Integration, as far as they are concerned, always impedes social unrest. Advocates of the collective action approach, however, are referring to integration into any kind of group or institution, whether or not it supports the established order. In other words, they assume that social integration forms the basis for any kind of collective action, radical or conservative, rebellious or loyalist. This assumption challenges the basic tenets of the breakdown approach.

The collective action approach also runs counter to relative deprivation theory. Collective action theorists are extremely critical of the emphasis placed on discontent as a condition for social unrest. They insist that discontent, though perhaps a necessary condition, is not a sufficient condition for social unrest. In other words, its presence alone does not ensure that social protest will occur. Discontent must be mobilized. The people who are dissatisfied have to come together and get organized to act collectively. Their goals must be defined; they must be persuaded to join forces; and their activities have to be coordinated.

Resource mobilization

An important body of literature within the collective action perspective focuses on the means by which people are mobilized in collective action. The term

Recent collective action by Canada's Native population can be interpreted in many ways. Does it relate to a breakdown in traditional Native institutions? Is it a result of rising expectations? Or is it a new adaptation in a history of collective action by Natives?

mobilization, it is essential to understand, is not meant to denote the creation of new resources but rather the transfer of resources from one kind of collective action

The Internet has provided an important means for coordinating massive protests throughout the world.

to another. We can identify some of the conditions that facilitate such a transfer. One is an appropriate **ideology**—that is, a set of beliefs that provide the basis for collective action, most of all by defining the goals of the movement. In resource mobilization theory the function of an ideology is to identify a problem, diagnose it, attribute blame, and offer a solution. An ideology also facilitates the coordination of activities and directs them toward a common goal. An ideology is often based on what sociologists call a **frame**, which consists of principles that enable people to make sense of their world and events taking place in their world. Whereas ideologies are political and specific, frames are structurally dispersed cognitive maps that help people interpret their environment (Hallgrímsdóttir, 2004). For example, opposition to globalization is an ideology that is supported by a number of frames: a preference for equality over inequality, a distrust of free-market capitalism and large corporations, compassion for human suffering, and so on.

The success of any organizational activity also depends on whether members possess an effective means of communicating with one another. People have to become aware of their common interests or goals, to agree on action to achieve these goals, and to coordinate their efforts. Discontented groups that already possess or are able to acquire channels for communication (particularly access to mass media) are more likely to become mobilized than those without such channels. Increasingly, the Internet has provided a key means for effective communication within, and far beyond, the group. Consider for example, the use of Web resources by G8 protestors, Native rights advocates, and environmental groups, which have successfully rallied support for their causes from far and wide (see also Chapter 12, Media).

A network of cooperative relationships serves a similar purpose. A cooperative relationship is a normal social relationship involving some kind of cooperative activity. Examples might be people working as a team on a job, spending free time together in a voluntary organization or social club, or participating in the same youth gang, trade union, church, or political party. If relationships of this kind already exist among discontented people, communication is greatly facilitated. Cooperative relationships can also serve as the basis for persuasion and influence.

A social movement is also easier to organize if leaders have *financial resources* to promote its activities. Money can buy media time, pay for members to travel, provide compensation for the work that members devote to the cause, and meet other expenses of collective action. Many social movements collapse simply because they run out of money. Those movements that have access to funds, particularly a relatively affluent body of supporters or potential supporters, will survive longer. In Canada, government grants have been an important source of funds for some movements, such as the women's movement and the environmental movement.

As a result of the need for an ideology, leadership, a means of communicating, cooperative relationships, and financial resources, social movements are much more likely to mobilize successfully if they can build on existing groups, organizations, or institutions. Literature on the emergence of political movements in western Canada between the wars has generally emphasized this point (Thompson and Seager, 1985: 231, 234; Finkel, 1989: 30). The organizational base of

urban movements in Montreal in the 1960s, like most other urban movements in North America, consisted of existing neighbourhood organizations (Hamel, 1991: 101–2). The women's movement that emerged in the late 1960s and early 1970s built on a range of existing or developing organizations. On the more conservative side, the movement built on established organizations, such as the National Council of Women, the Canadian Federation of Business and Professional Women's Clubs, the Canadian Federation of University Women, the National Council of Jewish Women, and the YWCA; on the more avant-garde side, the movement built on the new left movement and student radicalism, including student separatist organizations in Quebec (Prentice et al., 1988: 331–34, 346, 354–56; Adamson, Briskin, and McPhail, 1988).

Again, let us note the difference between this line of reasoning and a breakdown argument. Theories of breakdown, if you recall, assert that a social movement is most likely to occur when social institutions are weak; breakdown theories also claim that those who participate are, as a rule, socially isolated. The collective action literature, in contrast, emphasizes the need for organizational structures to furnish leadership and framing, and to provide channels for communication and a network of cooperative relationships. According to writers on collective action, the breakdown of institutional structures will decrease rather than increase the probability of social unrest, and those who are socially isolated are least likely, not most likely, to participate.

It is also interesting to see differences in the way collective action theory and relative deprivation theory explain the fact that it is not usually the most disadvantaged groups in society that engage in social movements. Relative deprivation theory solves this puzzle by saying that it is relative rather than absolute deprivation that makes people angry. Collective action theorists, in contrast, argue that only people who are better off have the resources to organize a social movement and impress their demands on authorities. This is why the poorest do not rebel.

Game theory

Some sociologists analyze crowds and social movements using game theory. Game theory is the study of optimal decision making when decision makers are assumed to be rational and when each decision maker tries to anticipate the actions and reactions of other decision makers. In contrast with collective behaviour theory, those who take a game theory approach to crowds assume that people behave rationally in crowds. Members of a crowd conduct themselves on the basis of the relative payoffs and costs of an activity. According to these writers the effect of a crowd on an individual is not that it induces an irrational hysteria or euphoria, but that it alters the payoffs and costs of certain kinds of behaviour. A crowd can make it easier to do something that is usually costly. The probability, for instance, of getting arrested for breaking into a store or for attacking an immigrant is greatly reduced if you are not the only person doing it. Indeed, it is even possible that in the presence of a crowd normally costly activity may be rewarded. One's status in a group could be raised if one were the first to charge a police blockade, or to throw a punch at an opposing demonstrator. In extreme cases, there might be penalties imposed on those who do *not* follow the crowd. We should not underestimate how often people may go along with collective behaviour out of fear that otherwise they might lose status among their friends, or perhaps even be attacked themselves (Berk, 1974a, 1974b; Granovetter, 1978).

On the other hand, the rational calculation of self-interest may, under certain conditions, persuade one not to engage in collective action. If a large number of people can benefit from a collective effort, the most rational behaviour for a self-interested individual is to abstain from participation and let others do the work. This is known as the **free-rider problem** (Olson, 1965). Why should I go on strike and walk the picket line if I can get the same increase in salary as my fellow workers without losing any income? Closely related is the "efficacy problem": in a collective effort that requires the participation of thousands of people, the single action of one person—recycling a piece of paper for example—is so small that it is not rational for a self-interested individual to expend any time on it (Kollock, 1998: 200). A large body of recent literature in game theory has sought to explain why and how collective action does in fact occur despite these collective action problems (for example, Macy, 1991; Macy and Flache, 1995; Kollock 1998; Ostrom, 1990, 2000; Vasi and Macy, 2003). Writers have identified social approval and pressures, sanctions of various kinds, guilt and shame, communication among potential participants, mutual identity and trust, reciprocity and past cooperation, and **selective incentives** as the conditions that make it more likely that rational people will engage in a collective effort rather than

choose to be free-riders. The term *selective incentive* refers to the direct benefits that a person can derive from belonging to an association or joining a social movement. Generally, the most common selective incentive in social movements is fellowship with other activists. In some cases, the prestige of a position of leadership in a social movement, and the media publicity that may go with it, can also be rewarding to participants. Additionally psychological benefits can bring people to invest resources in a social movement. Some movements are also able to offer more material rewards, such as salaries, travel expenses, insurance discounts, or appointment to government office. But non-material selective incentives have generally been shown to be the most effective in persuading people to participate actively in social movements.

Another collective action problem studied by some game theorists is known as the coordination problem: that people may want to participate, but only if other people are also going to do so. This kind of coordination can easily be achieved in small groups or bureaucratic organizations, but it is a major obstacle to large-scale collective action, particularly social movements. For example, I may be perfectly willing to bear the cost of donating money to a wildlife protection society, but I may be hesitant to do so out of concern that few others will support the society and so it will collapse, with the result that my money would be largely wasted. Writers who have sought to explain why collective action nevertheless occurs argue that humans have developed a number of tricks they use to coordinate their activities. Chew (2001) has asserted that rituals are used to create what is called "common knowledge": if we know that a large number of people have seen the same ritual, and if we know that they know that others have seen it, then people are more likely to engage in whatever activity the ritual encourages. This is one of the reasons why so many social movements hold demonstrations, marches, or parades. When we attend a large demonstration, or observe a march or parade making its way through a city, we know that others have seen or will see it, and that they know we have seen it.

Similarly, it has been suggested (Clark et al., 2006) that we are more likely to think that other people will engage in a certain action if it is promoted by a high-status person because we know that high-status people are more prominent. This is one of the reasons that those trying to organize a collective effort often ask celebrities to promote it. A good example in Canada is the way in which those opposed to the Atlantic seal hunt enlisted the support of Paul McCartney and his wife in 2006 in their effort to organize pressure on the Canadian government to ban the hunt. It was not that they believed the Canadian government was more likely to be persuaded by these two celebrities than by any one else; the hope of the organizers was that all those who found the seal hunt disgusting would get a sense that a movement was under way and that the contribution to the cause that they could make would less likely be a wasted effort.

The Marxist explanation of social movements

Some of the collective action literature has been significantly influenced by Marx and Marxist writers. Long before sociologists began to talk about collective action or resource mobilization, Marxists had taken what we would now call a collective action approach. During the period in which collective behaviour, breakdown, and relative deprivation were the dominant approaches in North America, Marxism was more influential in Europe.

Marxists have never been interested in social movements in general. They like to study revolts that could lead to major overhauls in the existing order. According to Marxists, such revolts fall into two categories. The first consists of revolts that led to the overthrow of feudalism. These are called bourgeois revolts. The major two in which Marxists have been interested are the English overthrow of Charles I in the seventeenth century and the French overthrow of Louis XVI in the eighteenth century (in which each king lost his head). Although the French revolt is, of course, called the French Revolution, the English do not like to call theirs a revolution; it is known as the English Civil War. Both revolts supposedly undermined the political power of the feudal lords and increased the political power of a rising bourgeois class. Some Marxists argue that this transfer of political power was a consequence of economic and structural changes taking place in the society, while other Marxists argue that the transfer of political power facilitated the economic structural changes. Neither argument has received much support from non-Marxist historians.

The second category of social movements includes those that Marx hoped would eventually lead to the overthrow of capitalism. These are primarily the labour and socialist movements of the nineteenth and twentieth centuries. As mentioned in Chapter 6, Social Inequality, Marx identified two underlying causes of these movements. First, the capitalist system creates increased exploitation, which intensifies discontent among the mass of the population and opposition to the capitalist system. Second, the capitalist system polarizes classes, brings workers together physically in crowded urban centres and in factories, provides improved means of communication among them, and in other ways creates better conditions for the mobilization of workers in collective action, including the development of class consciousness. It is this part of the Marxist thesis that has had considerable influence on the collective action approach.

More recently, many Marxists have been influenced by the writings of an Italian communist of the early twentieth century, Antonio Gramsci, who spent many years in prison jotting ideas down on paper, which were subsequently published as his *Prison Notebooks*. Gramsci argued that the proletariat needs, even before the fall of capitalism, to build a new order in which it establishes proletarian **hegemony**—the domination of a class or alliance of classes over others, not only economically but also politically and culturally. A precondition for the revolution of the working class, in Gramsci's view, is the replacement of bourgeois hegemony with proletarian hegemony. For example, the high value placed on profit and economic growth would have to be replaced by other values in order to undermine bourgeois hegemony. He referred to the achievement of pre-revolutionary proletarian hegemony as a "war of position," as opposed to a direct attack on the capitalist system, which he called a "war of movement." One of the significant contributions of Gramsci has been to persuade Marxists of the importance of non-economic struggles, including ideological struggles, against the existing order.

Political opportunity structure

Another collective action approach focuses on the political opportunities available to social movement leaders and participants. Social movements emerge in different political contexts, which can dramatically affect the character and success of a movement. Eisinger (1973) demonstrated how the opportunity structure in various American cities, most notably the degree of "openness," affected the results of social protest. In his study of protest sequences in Italy, Tarrow (1989) developed a theoretical framework of opportunity structure according to the degree of openness, stability, availability of allies, and elite conflict. Aminzade (1995) has shown how changes in the political structure of nineteenth-century France transformed the goals and tactics of French republicanism.

One of the strengths of the political opportunity approach is that it recognizes the way in which social movements are shaped by forces beyond the control of members. Most of the literature on social movements treats their emergence and consequences as the product of the intentional behaviour of actors. Yet most social movements owe much of their experience to unintended consequences and forces beyond their control. Even (sometimes remote) international forces can have significant effects on a social movement. This was the case with the post-World War I movement among Swedes living on the Åland Islands for independence from Finland, a movement that owed its initial success as well as its ultimate failure to international politics. In 1918 Woodrow Wilson, the U.S. president, called for a post-war settlement that endorsed the principle of self-determination. Encouraged by his statements numerous social groups throughout the world sought autonomy. The Åland Islanders, who had not before expressed much interest in self-determination, suddenly saw the opportunity to separate from Finland and pressed their case before the international community. In the end, however, the Ålander cause did not receive much support from world powers and the movement failed (Stanbridge, 2002).

Competition

Still another collective action approach, one greatly influenced by the Dutch anthropologist Barth (1969), focuses on competition among social groups, usually racial or ethnic groups. Sociologists who advocate this approach argue that the groups most likely to engage in collective action are not those that are the most segregated or oppressed, nor necessarily those that are the most united, but those in competition and conflict with other groups.

Kinship and communal collective action

Historically, collective action by different communal or kinship groups has been the most common form of inter-group competition. Kinship or communal groups can come into conflict either with one another or with the larger society. They typically control a certain territory and engage in conflict when "outsiders" encroach upon their territory.

An example of collective action based on kinship ties is provided by Scottish clans. A clan consisted of people supposedly having a common ancestor. In fact, however, the criterion for membership in a clan was not so much blood tie, as possession of a common surname, such as Campbell or Donald. At the head of each clan was a "chief," who was owed loyalty by members of a clan. Highlanders were not particularly deferential toward their chiefs, but would fight to the death for them (Smout, 1969: 27). Feuds between clans were numerous in both the Highlands and the Lowlands during the sixteenth century. Feuding between the Douglases and the Hamiltons was so extensive that it shaped the politics of Scotland for much of the century (Brown, 1986: 109–10). The percentage of the population involved and the magnitude of violence were greater in the Highlands than in the Lowlands; and feuds in the Highlands persisted into the eighteenth century, long after they had died out in the Lowlands (Brown, 1986). Indeed, a major confrontation emerged in the Highlands during the seventeenth and eighteenth centuries as a result of the steady encroachment of the Campbells on the territory and power of smaller clans. In 1692 the Campbells carried out what became a famous massacre of the MacIan MacDonalds at Glencoe. In addition to feuding and rebelling against British rule, Scottish factions based on clan ties also engaged in various forms of lawlessness during the seventeenth and eighteenth centuries (see the box "Rob Roy").

While the importance of kinship was particularly evident in Scotland, feuds and criminal activity based on kinship and communal ties were commonly found in many societies. In Ireland feuds were fought between rival "factions," such as the Caravats and Shanavests, and the Blackhens and the Magpies, in the early nineteenth century. Although some trivial dispute might be the alleged issue over which factions fought, it was typically the case that one party was seeking revenge for a defeat, insult, or injury inflicted on them by the other party, or by a member of the other party. It was also usually the case that each party was trying to demonstrate its physical superiority over the other and to establish its dominance within a certain territory. The criteria for membership in different factions was usually place of

Rob Roy

The most famous Scottish outlaw was Rob Roy (the Red) MacGregor, born in 1671 and named for his red hair. He was a man of enormous strength and unusually long arms, which he used to wield a sword with exceptional skill. Many MacGregors gained their livelihood by stealing cattle, selling protection, and extortion. At a young age Rob Roy joined what was called the Lennox Watch, a Highland force that provided protection for people living in the Lowlands in return for "blackmail."

He subsequently became a cattle raiser and dealer, but was accused of embezzlement and then outlawed. He mobilized the clan Gregor in 1715 to support the Jacobite Rebellion and was subsequently accused of high treason. In 1725 he was pardoned in return for joining a government force trying to establish royal authority in the Highlands. He died in 1734, having become renowned for his daring exploits, including spectacular escapes from captivity.

Can youth gangs in North American cities be understood in similar terms as communal collective action?

residence; and communal ties were often the basis of solidarity. The Irish also banded together in criminal gangs and secret societies, one of the most powerful of which was the Rockites of the 1820s. Most secret societies engaged in violent attacks on landlords and land agents, or on peasants who took land from which another peasant had been evicted (Clark, 1979: 66–73; Clark and Donnelly, 1983). These societies were deemed "illegal" by elites and by the government, but they enjoyed a considerable measure of legitimacy among the peasantry.

Modernization and collective action

Competition theory has yielded new views on modernization's effect on ethnic conflict. Until recently it was assumed that modernization would reduce conflict for two reasons. First, it would promote the assimilation of different ethnic groups, attenuating differences among them and the importance attached to such differences. Second, it would increase tolerance for differences by raising levels of education and instilling more universalistic values in populations. People would cease to be attached to communal groups and instead become more global and cosmopolitan in their orientations. In reality, the late twentieth century did not see the decline in ethnic conflict that was predicted, and proponents of competition theory have been quick to offer an explanation. According to them urbanization and industrialization bring groups into

greater contact and intensify competition for housing, jobs, status, and power. While modernization may raise the level of tolerance, this benefit is more than offset by the intense competition that it also creates. Hodson et al. (1994) studied the effect of modernization in former Yugoslavia and found this to be the case: quite remarkably, the inter-ethnic conflicts in former Yugoslavia were greatest in those regions where the overall level of group tolerance was highest.

Status competition

Often, competition in modern societies takes place among the "status groups" referred to in Chapter 6, Social Inequality. Examples of status groups in Canada today are women, men, Natives, students, juveniles, immigrants, WASPs, and visible minorities. A distinction has been made in sociology between **status communities** and **status blocs** (Turner, 1988: 12–13). The former term refers to enduring communities that have lived together over long periods of time, sharing language, culture, and other attributes. Native communities in Canada provide examples of status communities. Status blocs are organizations or associations in which people come together for specific purposes. Feminist organizations, organizations for the protection of refugees, pensioners' associations, and gay and lesbian organizations are all examples of status blocs in Canada today.

The collective action approaches have called attention to deficiencies in some of the earlier schools of thought. However, they are by no means safe from criticism. Not surprisingly, they have been chastised for ignoring discontent or motivation, or for taking these things for granted. It is frequently claimed that they overemphasize calculating, strategic, instrumental, rational, goal-oriented action, to the neglect of non-calculating, expressive, emotional, impulsive, or passionate human behaviour. They have been criticized for neglecting culture and psychological forces, for ignoring the role of social movements in giving people a collective identity and meaning to their lives, and for giving insufficient attention to non-political movements. More surprisingly, they have also been accused of neglecting ideology, major social changes, and structural conditions. (One or more of these criticisms can be found in Scott, 1990; Canel, 1992; Gamson, 1992; and McAdam et al., 1996b.) An important part of the collective action literature could also be accused of taking a cookbook approach to social movements; for some sociologists, studying social movements has become primarily a matter of developing a list of conditions for their emergence, continuation, spread, and success.

The Most Recent Approaches
Postmodernism and the new social movements

The three traditional approaches (collective behaviour, breakdown, and relative deprivation) sought to develop generalizations about social movements that would be valid in most times and places. The collective action perspectives generally give more attention to differences in time and place. Without rejecting generalizations altogether, the next approach we shall discuss is also more interested in understanding social movements in a particular time and place—the last half of the twentieth century in Western Europe and North America.

This approach is based on the assumption that Western society has changed significantly from what it was like in the nineteenth century and the first half of the twentieth. The earlier period is often referred to as "industrial" or "modern" society, while the more recent period is called "postindustrial" or "postmodern"

society. This new society has given rise to "new social movements"—movements that result from new conflicts, new problems, or new forces (Luke, 1989; Hamel, 1991). The major new social movements are the student, urban, feminist, environmental, anti-nuclear, anti-globalization, and gay and lesbian movements.

This approach emerged primarily in Europe in reaction to the Marxist approach. It rejected the earlier emphasis on class-based movements, or at least the Marxist emphasis on the working class as the only class that could bring about fundamental change. Thus, this literature was reacting against the previously dominant approach in Europe just as in North America the collective action approach was reacting against the previously dominant approaches—collective behaviour, breakdown, and relative deprivation theory.

The new social movement approach is based on two overlapping bodies of literature regarding the nature of late twentieth-century society: (1) the postmodern literature; and (2) the postindustrial literature.

Postmodernism means a lot of different things to different people, but in sociology it refers primarily to a rejection of all the scholarship that has sought to explain "modernity" (as evidenced in Western Europe and North America in the nineteenth and twentieth centuries). The scholarship that is rejected includes the major sociological theorists: Marx, Weber, and Durkheim—and all those who have been influenced by their work. Postmodernists focus on differences and discontinuities; they denounce positivism and stress indeterminacy; and they reject large, all-embracing theories, interpretations, or explanations—what they call "meta-narratives" or "totalistic" theory, theories that try to explain everything.

This literature is highly diverse, encompassing a large number of contradictory claims about what postmodern society is like. It is possible to find postmodern writers asserting that postmodern people are cynical, skeptical, amoral, individualistic, spontaneous, selfish, self-gratifying, relaxed, and/or lighthearted. Gone is the serious, committed, ideologically motivated class warrior of Marxism; in postmodern society we have less confidence in the superiority of our convictions. Class, some postmodernists insist, is no longer the principal basis for collective action.

In addition, people who were formerly ignored, who were "voiceless," come to be heard, or should be heard, in a postmodern society. There is a rejection of authority and of the separation that has been made between high arts and mass culture. Some postmodern writers suggest that struggles over culture have replaced the struggles over production that dominated modern or industrial society. There is general agreement that postmodern society is disconnected and fragmented (Huyssen, 1986; Connor, 1989; Rosenau, 1992).

According to the *postindustrial* literature, during the last half of the twentieth century there was a shift in the centre of production from resource extraction (agriculture, mining, lumbering, and so forth) and heavy manufacturing (building ships and trains) to light high-tech industry, communications, and information-based production. The manufacturing working class plays a less important role—white-collar workers and the middle class a more important role—in postindustrial production. Growth depends on science and other kinds of knowledge more than on capital accumulation and investment. Domination is achieved not through economic and political repression, but through hyper-consumption, technological progress, seductive integration, and mass manipulation. The mass media and the advertising industry are the major instruments of this postindustrial integration and manipulation (Marcuse, 1964; Touraine, 1971; Luke, 1989).

What all these arguments lead to is the assertion that the distinctive characteristics of postindustrial or postmodern society have created distinctive characteristics in the social movements that have emerged in this society. The new social movements are more concerned with values and culture than were the old working-class movements. The pop-art movement sought to collapse the distinction between high and low art, and between art and everyday life (Huyssen, 1986). Most new social movements are anti-authority. Although there is considerable disagreement on this point, some have argued that new social movements are less political than the old movements. There is more agreement that they are less economic. New social movements represent the formerly unrepresented, often involving a variety of groups and issues. The middle class plays a greater role than the employed working class. New social movements are characterized by spontaneity, fragmentation, decentralization, and discontinuity. These characteristics are well illustrated in the Montreal urban movements studied by Hamel (1991 and 1995).

The most common criticism of the new social movement approach is that the so-called "new social movements" are not so new. Feminist movements, youth movements, and even the environmental movement can be found in earlier periods. Many writers have pointed out, as well, that not all movements in the nineteenth and early twentieth centuries were working-class movements; there is nothing new about non-class movements. It has also been claimed that new social movements are not, in general, less political than earlier social movements. (It would be difficult to contend, for example, that the anti-globalization movement is non-political.) And the new social movement literature has been criticized for ignoring class struggle (Scott, 1990; Canel, 1992; Adam, 1993).

Culture and social movements

There is a long-standing concern in sociology with the cultural conditions necessary for the success or failure of social movements. Cultural conditions for collective action include feelings of oppression and discontent or the hostile beliefs that members of a group feel toward other groups; they also include religious convictions and transcendental beliefs; ethnic or nationalist sentiments; and the elements of culture that lead members of a group to identify with one another.

Historically, religion has been the most important cultural basis for social movements. This is not to say that most collective action in world history has been religious. On the contrary, as we have just suggested, in pre-industrial and rural societies most collective action has been based on kinship or communal ties. Yet when it does expand beyond kinship or communal structures, the basis has generally been religion. In some cases organized religion provides a basis for collective mobilization, but usually it is popular religion not organized religion. Considerable research has demonstrated the importance of religion even for outlawed secret societies. In eighteenth- and nineteenth-century China, popular religion was sometimes the principal source of the solidarity of secret societies. The largest and best-known was the Heaven and Earth Society or Tiandihui, which began in the 1760s in southern Fujian and then spread to other regions as a result of the suppression of the movement by the state. The movement was able to attract support by promising access to supernatural powers; the activities of the movement were abundant in religious ritual; and the mutual aid on which the movement was based was highly imbued with the supernatural (Ownby, 1995, 1996).

Recent literature on the role of culture in social movements has focused on how leaders of a social movement, and to a lesser extent participants, use and manipulate culture to promote their cause. Students of social movements who are interested in culture have been greatly influenced by a perspective on culture that sees it not as a set of values and norms that become internalized in people's minds, but as a stock of knowledge, a repertoire, or a "tool kit" consisting of practices—symbols, stories, rituals, world views, skills, and styles that—people can use or can be forced to use as they pursue their goals (Swidler, 1986, 1995; Johnston and Klandermans, 1995). We draw on our tool kit in our everyday life. If you were to go to a professor to ask him or her to raise your grade on an assignment, you would adopt a strategy that would consist of telling the professor how hard you worked on the essay, suggesting that he or she should have taken some criteria into consideration which he or she did not, and so forth; you would not argue that the grade should be raised because of your race or gender, your family background, your age, and so forth, because you know that drawing on these cultural tools would not get you anywhere. And you would adopt the former arguments rather than the latter regardless of what you personally believed.

In the same way, activists in social movements draw on existing cultural frames and manipulate the culture in which they are trying to operate, whether or not they have deeply internalized the beliefs. Successful movements tap into existing frameworks (Berezin, 1997). They react to the existing culture, or trends in the existing culture, as a result of which social movements that emerge in the same place and time often share cultural elements. For example, at the present time in Europe both the far-right and the anti-globalization movement draw on the same unease that many people have with the loss of national sovereignty experienced by European states as a result of the European Union and globalization, even though these two movements have support in very different segments of the population, do not directly influence one another, and make use of the public concern over lost sovereignty in very different ways.

The sociological literature on culture and social movements is vulnerable to several criticisms. Although sociologists who study culture and social movements are disparaging of resource mobilization literature, most of what they say is merely an extension of the latter: that is, the concern is largely with how activists in movements use culture to mobilize support and challenge their opposition. There is also an excessive focus on the role of culture in the success or survival of social movements, at the expense of our understanding of how collective action varies from one society to another or from one period of time to another as a result of differences or changes in culture.

Putting it all together

Like the people they study, sociologists are prone to fads and fashions. As already indicated, some of the above approaches are now out of favour. This is not to be deplored so long as their contributions are not cast aside. It would be a mistake, for example, to dismiss the abundant research carried out by students of collective behaviour just because we cannot accept certain parts of their argument. In particular, it would be a serious error to throw away the concept of institutionalization just because we find some collective behaviour that does not seem to be less institutionalized than routine behaviour. Social behaviour does in fact vary in its degree of institutionalization. Panics, crowds, and social movements may not always be less institutionalized than the behaviour we encounter daily, but most often they are. What we need to do is study the degree of institutionalization of any social activity in which we are interested, whether it has generally been classified as collective behaviour or not.

Similarly, theories that explain social movements as a result of social breakdown should not be totally rejected. This literature is not so much incorrect as incomplete. If people are well integrated into institutions that support the established order, then there is indeed less chance that they will engage in movements that challenge that order; and the likelihood that they will rebel against established institutions does increase if their integration into these institutions weakens. What breakdown theory has ignored, as we have seen, is that people have to be integrated into groups of some kind in order to be mobilized for collective action. People who are wholly disorganized, completely uprooted, and alienated may engage in antisocial behaviour, but they will not form social movements. Thus, the ideal condition for rebellious action is the integration of a large number of people into strong institutions or structures that are themselves "alienated" from the established order.

Although relative deprivation cannot alone account for the rise of a social movement, we must somehow explain motivation. Motivating factors are more diverse than most sociologists have recognized. We need to take into account not only relative deprivation, but also other factors that could motivate a person to join a movement, such as moral outrage, and selective incentives.

Many of the criticisms that have been made of the collective action perspective apply primarily to the resource mobilization approach, not to the collective action perspective as a whole. This is true of the claim that the approach overemphasizes calculating, strategic, and instrumental action; that it neglects ideology, macro processes, and structural conditions; and that it takes a cookbook approach to social movements. The collective action approach has been downgraded by most sociologists to resource mobilization, characterized as a "how" approach to social movements stressing the pragmatic, rational, and strategic aspects of social movements, to the neglect of meaning, identity, and so forth. Yet this criticism misunderstands what the collective action approach initially sought to achieve: the explanation not so much of "why people rebel" as of the character of their collective action, rebellious or otherwise. That explanation is possible only if we compare collective action from one context to another—one period of time to another, or one place to another (Clark, 1979).

A major strength of the new social movement approach is that it gives more emphasis to the uniqueness of societies than other approaches. It is true that the writers in this school have ignored movements outside Western Europe and North America, but at least they have never claimed that they are explaining all social movements. What they have wanted to do is to develop a perspective that would help them best understand the movements that were emerging in the society in which they lived. They believed this could not be done with general theories.

Canadian Social Structure and Collective Action

The remainder of this chapter is devoted to social movements in Canada and the social conditions underlying them. We shall not endeavour to apply or test the theoretical approaches discussed above. We shall, however, adopt the general framework provided by the collective action approaches. To help understand the conditions that have given rise to social movements in Canada, we shall look for sources of integration and cleavage in the social structure. A **social cleavage** is a division based on class, ethnicity, etc., that may result in the formation of distinct social groups. Although similar social cleavages

can be found in many societies, every society is unique in two ways. First, the relative importance or intensity of different types of cleavage varies from one society to another. In some societies, class cleavages are more divisive than ethnic cleavages, while in others the reverse is true. Second, the relationship among cleavages differs from one country to another. In some societies, people who belong to the same social class may be opposed to one another because they belong to different ethnic groups. In other societies, ethnicity may coincide with class divisions and serve to reinforce them. The final "topography" that emerges from these patterns will be unique to a particular society and will determine much of the character of its collective action

In Chapter 6, Social Inequality, we listed a number of patterns of differentiation that underlie Canadian social structure and give rise to unequal ranking or status hierarchies. Some of these same patterns of differentiation also divide Canadian society into identifiable groups on which collective action has been based. These include age, class, ethnicity, region, rural or urban residence, gender, and sexual orientation. All of these have formed the basis of social movements in Canada. For purposes of illustration, we shall focus on two of these: region and ethnicity.

Regional cleavage

Geographical disunity in Canada has resulted not only from the vast distances that separate people living in different parts of this country, but also from the fact that, for various reasons, regional variations have tended to coincide with other kinds of differences.

Most obviously, regional diversity coincides with economic functions. Some parts of the country are manufacturing centres; others are largely agricultural; and still others supply natural resources. In addition, and partly as a consequence, there are substantial inequalities in wealth and income from one province to another, particularly between western Canada and the Atlantic region (see Chapter 6, Social Inequality). Values and attitudes have differed from one province to another. Public opinion surveys have routinely shown significant differences among provinces on a wide range of issues. To take just one example, a poll conducted in 1992 indicated that the percentage of persons favouring a decrease in immigration ranged from 58 percent in the Atlantic provinces to 35 percent in Quebec (Canadian Institute of Public Opinion, 1992).

These and other differences among regions have had a profound impact on the character of collective action in this country. Social cleavage between regions, combined with social integration within regions, has resulted in collective action that tends to be weak and divided nationally, while often strong regionally. Canadians have considerable difficulty getting together and doing things as a nation. Most organizations to which they belong, whether political, economic, or social, are geographically disconnected. Inevitably, social movements tend to attract support from specific parts of the country. Even a national movement, such as the women's movement, can vary greatly from one province to another (Adamson, Briskin, and McPhail, 1988: 8, 28). And many social movements in Canada have directly reflected the grievances and animosities that some areas have felt toward others.

Prairie movements

The best-known regional movements in Canadian history are those that appeared primarily in the Prairie Provinces between the two world wars. They are by no means the only movements with a regional basis, but since they have received the most scholarly attention, we shall illustrate the effect of regional cleavage on collective action by briefly describing these movements.

The Prairie movements emerged on a social foundation that was formed by divisions of both class and region. A highly diversified population settled in the Prairie Provinces in the late nineteenth and early twentieth centuries; yet out of it there soon developed a remarkably unified social group loosely based on agriculture. We must be careful not to overstate this point. In addition to conflicts of interest between farmers and other sectors, there were significant divisions among farmers themselves, most notably as a consequence of differences in their ethnic origin, the size of their farms, and the type of agriculture in which they were engaged. We should also recognize that other social groups contributed to Prairie movements besides farmers. Still, farmers were crucial and, in comparison with most other groups in Canadian society, those in the Prairies possessed considerable solidarity and cohesion. They were brought together by common problems and a common position in the social structure. The majority engaged in the production of the same crop, namely wheat, and were therefore simultaneously affected by its success or failure. Their fortunes rose and fell

collectively, and this served to integrate them as a group, facilitating their political mobilization.

At the same time, other factors divided them from the rest of the country. No doubt the great physical distances that separated Prairie people from those living in other parts of Canada helped to alienate them. More important, however, was a fundamental opposition of interests. Western farmers were forced, as a result of tariffs, to buy expensive goods manufactured in eastern Canada, yet they had to sell their wheat on an unprotected international market. Furthermore, the marketing of this wheat was, in their perception at least, controlled by urban and eastern business interests, and the terms of trade were maintained in favour of the latter.

The first significant collective effort by western farmers was the struggle against the grain-elevator companies. The Territorial Grain Growers' Association was formed just after the turn of the century and became the Saskatchewan Grain Growers' Association in 1905. This body, along with other cooperative organizations established in this period, formed an effective base for increased political activity by farmers, which accelerated around 1910 and was directed primarily against tariffs. One of the most active new political associations was the United Farmers of Alberta, which in 1909 brought together two smaller bodies and the Canadian Council of Agriculture, which pressed the federal government for tariff reform.

The Progressives The war effort helped to restrain the call for tariff reductions, but Prairie residents expected that, once the war was over, substantial reductions would be legislated. When this did not occur, a new wave of agitation developed. A dissatisfied group of politicians formed the National Progressive Party, which shocked the nation in 1921 by capturing sixty-five seats in the House of Commons.

Nationally, the Progressive movement did not survive long as an independent political force, primarily because they drew their strength for the most part from the Prairie provinces. In British Columbia, Quebec, and the Maritimes, the Progressives had little support; in Ontario the movement's objectives were different from those in the west (Thompson and Seager, 1985: 31–34). They could, and in fact did, win some significant concessions from the major parties; but—given the regional distribution of their support—they could not themselves become a major national party. By 1926 the National Progressive Party had largely been absorbed into the Liberal Party.

At the provincial level, the situation was altogether different. Within certain provinces, farmers and their allies were able to dominate politics and elect governments generally committed to representing their interests. This became true in all three Prairie provinces in the 1920s: farmers' parties were elected in Alberta and Manitoba, and a Liberal government sympathetic to agrarian interests held power in Saskatchewan. As a consequence, while considerable dissatisfaction with the federal government persisted, western farmers were less discontented with their own provincial governments in this period. They remained so until the Great Depression.

Social Credit In 1935, under the leadership of former preacher William Aberhart, a new political party—the Social Credit Party—took power in the province of Alberta. It is not hard to understand why a movement of this kind should find support among self-employed farmers, particularly during a severe economic depression. Obtaining credit—always a serious problem for farmers—

was especially difficult at this time, and it was primarily this difficulty that Aberhart's movement promised to solve. The theory of social credit assumes that economic stagnation results from a shortage of credit in an economy, and that this shortage can be overcome by the distribution of monthly cash dividends to all citizens. The program appealed as well to other classes in Western society, particularly the urban working class, whose members were also suffering from the Depression (Bell, 1990).

Aberhart charged that eastern business elites were controlling and manipulating the economy to serve their interests. They tried, he claimed, to restrict the supply of money and to create a dependence on credit institutions from which they profited. As fashioned by Aberhart, social credit ideology was unmistakably anti-establishment (Finkel, 1989: 34–35).

CCF At approximately the same time as Social Credit, a very different kind of movement also appeared in the west. The Co-operative Commonwealth Federation

There is a long history of collective action on the Canadian Prairies. The general strike that shut down the city of Winnipeg for six weeks in 1919 was one of the most dramatic instances.

(CCF) was founded in the 1930s and eventually won a provincial election in Saskatchewan in 1944.

The surprising thing about the CCF is that its official platform was socialist, which seems a curious ideology with which to seek the support of self-employed farmers. And yet a socialist wing had been active within the farmers' movement in Saskatchewan well before the arrival of the CCF, so the CCF did not come to Saskatchewan as a foreign import. Moreover, the CCF carefully presented its program to appeal to farmers. It de-emphasized those parts of socialism that would offend their sense of free enterprise, while it stressed aspects that were plainly in their interest. The party was forced, for example, to moderate and eventually abandon its call for land nationalization, but most farmers were not put off by the idea of state regulation of the marketing of their produce, or by the nationalization of transportation and natural resources.

We should be careful not to attach too much weight to ideological differences between the Social Credit party and the CCF. The significance of these movements lies less in their respective ideologies than in their relationship to the social groups on which they were based. Both Social Credit and the CCF, as they took shape in western Canada, should be seen as collective efforts by members of a particular region to find political

[Social Trends]

Regina Manifesto

One of the most interesting and significant documents in Canadian history is the CCF program adopted at the First National Convention in Regina, July 1933. Here are the opening paragraphs of that declaration.

The CCF is a federation of organizations whose purpose is the establishment in Canada of a Co-operative Commonwealth in which the principle regulating production, distribution, and exchange will be the supplying of human needs and not the making of profits.

We aim to replace the present capitalist system, with its inherent injustice and inhumanity, by a social order from which the domination and exploitation of one class by another will be eliminated, in which economic planning will supersede unregulated private enterprise and competition, and in which genuine democratic self-government, based upon economic equality will be possible. The present order is marked by glaring inequalities of wealth and opportunity, by chaotic waste and instability; and in an age of plenty it condemns the great mass of the people to poverty and insecurity. Power has become more and more concentrated into the hands of a small irresponsible minority of financiers and industrialists and to their predatory interests the majority are habitually sacrificed. When private profit is the main stimulus to economic effort, our society oscillates between periods of feverish prosperity in which the main benefits go to speculators and profiteers, and of catastrophic depression, in which the common man's normal state of insecurity and hardship is accentuated. We believe that these evils can be removed only in a planned and socialized economy in which our natural resources and the principal means of production and distribution are owned, controlled, and operated by the people. . . .

This social and economic transformation can be brought about by political action, through the election of a government inspired by the ideal of a Co-operative Commonwealth and supported by a majority of the people. We do not believe in change by violence. . . . [This] is a democratic movement, a federation of farmer, labour, and socialist organizations, financed by its own members and seeking to achieve its ends solely by constitutional methods. It appeals for support to all who believe that the time has come for a far-reaching reconstruction of our economic and political institutions . . .

Source: Walter Young, 1969. *The Anatomy of a Party: The National CCF, MCMXXXII-LXI.* Toronto: University of Toronto Press (pp. 304–5).

To what social groups in Canada do you think this ideology would appeal? How closely do the aims of the New Democratic Party today resemble the original principles?

formations that represented their special needs. These needs were markedly different from those of most other Canadians and were not—at least in their eyes—being met by the national political parties. Although the CCF did eventually become a national party in the form of the New Democratic Party, its origins lay in western opposition to eastern Canada and the perceived domination of the country by eastern interests.

The Reform Party

This same sentiment was responsible for the emergence of a new political force in the west during the late 1980s. Under the leadership of Preston Manning, the Reform Party of Canada was founded to give westerners an alternative to the major political parties. As long as the Liberals under Trudeau formed the government in Ottawa, westerners could vote for the Progressive Conservatives in order to express their dissatisfaction with Ottawa. When, however, the Conservatives assumed office in Ottawa and took actions that were unpopular in the west, such as introducing the Goods and Services Tax and supporting some of the demands of Quebec, many westerners turned to the Reform Party. Its first major breakthrough was the election of Deborah Grey to the House of Commons in a March 1989 by-election, followed later in the year by the success of Stanley Waters in an Alberta poll to choose a nominee for a Senate appointment. The founders and early supporters of the movement espoused an unmistakably right-wing ideology, but the party broadened its policies in an effort to attract voters further to the left, including discontented supporters of the NDP.

Yet it remained very much a regional party. In the federal election of 1993, it won fifty-two seats, all but one of them in western Canada. In the election of 1997, it won sixty seats, but none outside western Canada. In the following years the party sought to expand its base and to unite conservatives in all parts of Canada. The Canadian Alliance Party was formed in 2000, and in the election of that year the party won sixty-six seats, but only two outside the West. In 2003 it merged with the Progressive Conservative Party to form a new Conservative Party of Canada, which in 2004 won more seats outside the West than Reform or Alliance had ever done, but still only thirty-one of the new party's ninety-nine seats. Finally, in the federal election of 2006 the party broke into eastern Canada, even winning ten seats in Quebec. Still, the losing Liberals won decidedly more seats outside the West than did the Conservatives, eighty-eight to the Conservatives' fifty-nine.

Ethnic cleavage

Ethnic diversity in Canada coincides with many other differences. We have already discussed in Chapter 6, Social Inequality, variations in socioeconomic status found among ethnic groups. We have also observed a tendency for ethnic groups to be distributed unevenly among provinces. And in Chapter 8, Race and Ethnic Relations, we saw that, even within the same city, considerable ethnic residential concentration is likely. These differences in socioeconomic status and residential patterns would alone be enough to create social distances between members of distinct ethnic groups. But additional factors, particularly dissimilarities in values, have served to intensify ethnic cleavages in Canadian society.

The consequences of ethnic divisions for the character of collective action in Canada are evident at almost every level. The country abounds in ethnic institutions—schools, religious groups, clubs, and other voluntary associations. In addition, a number of social movements in Canada have arisen from ethnic divisions. The largest and most successful are nationalist movements in the province of Quebec.

Quebec nationalism

There is a widespread misconception among English-speaking Canadians that nationalism in Quebec is something new. Unless defined very narrowly, French Canadian nationalism can be traced back to before Confederation. The movement for responsible government that emerged in Upper and Lower Canada in the first half of the nineteenth century was, for French Canadians, both a campaign for reform and a struggle against British political domination. Although Confederation tied French Canadians to the rest of British North America, it also gave them a separate province in which they constituted the majority, and in which, it was assumed, they would be able to protect their distinct culture. Indeed, the participation of francophones in Confederation can legitimately be interpreted as an expression of French Canadian nationalism, albeit a nationalism based on totally different premises than that found in Quebec today.

Confederation certainly did not mean a decline in the determination of French Canadians to protect their society from assimilation into the larger English-speaking culture.

Language, Guardian of the Faith

Henri Bourassa is widely regarded as the greatest nationalist leader in the history of French Canada. His nationalism emphasized the importance of preserving traditional Quebec culture, above all its religion. In La langue, gardienne de la foi, *he asserted that the French language embodies the Catholic religion more than does any other language and that this gives French Canadians a unique mission in the world:*

Our special mission, we French Canadians, is to carry on in America the struggle of Christian France, and to defend against all opposition, if necessary against France herself, our religious and national heritage. This heritage does not belong to us alone: it belongs to the whole of Catholic America, and constitutes a centre from which radiates inspiration and light; it belongs to the entire Church, for which it is the principal source of strength in this part of the world; it belongs to all of French civilization, for which it is the only port of refuge and mooring place in this immense sea of Saxon Americanism.

We are the only ones, let us not forget, who are capable of fulfilling this mission in America. French Canadians and Franco-Americans represent the only large group, the only nation of the French race and language outside Europe. . . .

But if we want to defend our intellectual and national heritage, which belongs to French people everywhere, we must do so without disturbing the harmonious relationship between our social duties and our divine calling.

Let us fight not merely to preserve our language, or to preserve our language and our faith; let us fight for our language in order better to preserve our faith.

Source: Henri Bourassa, 1918. *La langue, gardienne de la foi.* Montreal: Bibliothèque de l'Action française (pp. 49–51).

In Quebec today, what has replaced religion as a driving force for nationalism?

Almost throughout the period since Confederation, nationalism as an ideology has been popular among the Quebecois. It has been articulated and advanced by countless French Canadian intellectuals, and has been espoused, in a diversity of forms and with varying degrees of emphasis, by most Quebec politicians. Until the 1950s, Quebec nationalism tended to be conservative and at times oriented toward preserving the past. Although the material benefits of industrialization were welcome, *la survivance*—the survival of French Canada as a distinct society—was to be achieved primarily by keeping people loyal to traditional values. It was assumed that support of the traditional culture was the best way to maintain a distinct French Canadian society. It was also generally assumed that this survival could be guaranteed within Confederation simply by guarding the provincial rights that Confederation had granted.

Throughout this period, the majority of French Canadian nationalists hesitated to advocate separation from the rest of Canada. Many were "dual" nationalists, who stood for both provincial autonomy and the dissociation of Canada from Great Britain. The most repre-

sentative advocate of this brand of nationalism was Henri Bourassa. Although Bourassa was not opposed to the industrialization of Quebec, the underlying theme of his politics was the preservation of traditional French Canadian culture, in particular its religion. At the same time, he was an ardent Canadian. In 1903 his adherents organized the Ligue Nationaliste, with the double objective of promoting the independence of Canada and safeguarding the rights of French Canadians.

Writers such as Jules-Paul Tardivel and Lionel-Adolphe Groulx were representative of a more separatist brand of nationalism. Abbé Groulx was the most influential nationalist intellectual after Henri Bourassa. A historian at the Université de Montréal, he articulated a nationalism that was conservative and religious. He extolled the destiny of the French Canadian "race," stressing the importance of their traditional culture and calling on his people to resist the forces of modernization that were threatening them.

Yet, as Groulx himself came to realize, it was not in fact possible for French Canada to insulate itself from the forces of modernization. During the very years in which

Henri Bourassa was an ardent dual nationalist. He believed strongly in both provincial autonomy and Canadian independence from Great Britain.

he lived and wrote, the kind of society he lauded was being undermined as a rural decline and growing urbanization seriously threatened the traditional nationalist strategy. In various ways, modernization brought French Canadians into greater contact with Anglo culture. It also created monstrous pressures on them to assimilate into the English-speaking world, at least if they wanted to enjoy the material benefits of industrial society.

Although this process actually began around the turn of the century, the nationalist strategy for keeping French Canada distinct did not reflect the change until much later. Even when nationalist leaders became conscious of the seriousness of the threat—and they certainly were conscious of it by the time of the Depression, if not earlier—they were still reluctant to alter their approach to *la survivance*. In the 1930s and 1940s they experimented with various ideas, but they did not come up with a realistic solution to the danger that urbanization and industrialization posed.

The reasons for the lag in the development of their thinking are complex, but certainly a major factor was the conservatism of French Canadian elites, even while

urbanization and industrialization were taking place in their province. Members of the elite continued to look to the past for the model of the ideal society, and they generally opposed any significant expansion of the public sector, particularly if it threatened to interfere with the traditional functions of the Roman Catholic Church in spheres such as education and welfare. This "anti-statism" is most often associated with the Union Nationale government of Maurice Duplessis, premier of Quebec from 1936 to 1939 and again from 1944 to 1959. More than any other individual, Duplessis symbolizes the era of conservative nationalism in Quebec.

Meanwhile, changes in the social structure of Quebec continued to undermine the traditional culture. By 1961 the number of people of French origin who could be classified as rural had fallen to 29 percent, and only 13 percent were living on farms (Posgate and McRoberts, 1976: 48). As the economy of Quebec developed along the same lines as the economy of the rest of North America, the traditional basis for distinctiveness in Quebec was eroded. French Canadian leaders began to realize that they were going to have to fight even harder to prevent Quebec from melting into the larger society that surrounded it. At the same time, urbanization and industrialization were gradually creating a new French elite in the province, whose members rejected the basic premises of conservative nationalism. New leaders emerged who did not idealize the past and were unwilling to accept the traditional opposition to the expansion of the public sector. This new elite has appropriately been called the "bureaucratic middle class" (Guindon, 1964). It was composed of educated employees in both private and public bureaucracies, as well as educational institutions. These bodies had grown substantially in number and size after World War II to meet the needs of urban Quebec, but their power and further expansion were being frustrated by those who clung to the old nationalism. The closing years of Duplessis's premiership saw increasing ideological ferment in the province and opposition to his government (Coleman, 1984).

When Duplessis died in 1959, he was followed by premiers who were prepared to make greater concessions to this new bureaucratic middle class. Paul Sauvé, who succeeded Duplessis as leader of the Union Nationale, and Jean Lesage, who headed a Liberal government from 1960 to 1966, oversaw a dramatic shift in the orientation of politics in Quebec. They led governments that were not so reluctant to expand the role of the state in the lives of the people of the province. The educational system was reorganized to train French Canadians better for participation in an advanced industrial society and to reduce the power of the Church; the delivery of social services was rationalized and expanded, and again the power of the Church was curtailed; new institutions to define French Canadian culture were established; state control over natural resources was increased; and the labour code was overhauled.

The **Quiet Revolution**, as this new approach came to be called, had profound implications for the character of Quebec nationalism. A basic assumption of French Canadian nationalism had always been that only French Canadian leaders—be they religious or political—could be trusted to look after the interests of their people and to safeguard their distinct culture. So long as a relatively minor role was assigned to the state, the best strategy was simply to maintain tight control over the provincial government while resisting any encroachments by the federal government. This had been the course pursued by the majority of French Canadian intellectuals and politicians until the Quiet Revolution.

But when a new attitude toward the state began to win acceptance, the basic principles of *la survivance* inevitably underwent a change. Nationalists who believed in the Quiet Revolution felt it imperative to do more than just protect the existing powers of the provincial government; *la survivance* now appeared to depend on an extension of these powers. Within Quebec, the new nationalists sought to expand the powers of the provincial government at the expense of other institutions, most notably the Church. Within the larger political framework, they tried to expand these powers at the expense of the federal government. Unavoidably, the Quiet Revolution gave rise to increased conflict between the governments of Ottawa and Quebec City. During the Duplessis years, federal–provincial conflict had been largely avoided by Duplessis's simple refusal to cooperate with federal programs. Under Lesage and his successors (Johnson, Bertrand, and Bourassa) an intense struggle developed between federal and provincial politicians over the powers of their respective governments.

This new nationalist orientation also provided the basis for the rise of the separatist movement in Quebec. Indeed, it has been argued that separatism is simply a logical extension of the Quiet Revolution, carrying its philosophy a step further, to the conclusion that the expansion of the power of the state in Quebec cannot be achieved within Confederation. To obtain the powers needed to modernize Quebec—and to keep this

modernization under French control—almost complete autonomy is necessary.

As always, a stimulus for Quebec nationalism is fear of assimilation. Through educational institutions and the media, North American culture was reaching almost all parts of the province. Ironically, the very policies and programs of the Quiet Revolution contributed to this threat. They promoted the integration of the economy of Quebec with that of North America. They standardized education in Quebec so that it looked more like education elsewhere on the continent. As the reforms of the Quiet Revolution were introduced and the Church relinquished many of its traditional functions, only language remained to distinguish French-speaking society from the larger society that surrounded it. Many Québécois turned to separatism out of fear that French Canada would not survive (Coleman, 1984).

They also turned to separatism as a result of the relative deprivation they felt in the 1960s and 1970s. The Quiet Revolution raised expectations that could not be fulfilled. In particular, French Canadians resented the fact that the business elite in Quebec continued to be largely English-speaking and that, when they talked to English-speaking people, they still had to do so in English.

Although the Parti Québécois won provincial elections in 1976 and 1981, their goal of sovereignty association—which would have effectively given Quebec political independence while retaining economic and other ties with Canada—was defeated in the referendum of 1980. Subsequently, support for separatism declined until 1990, when it experienced a major revival. Many French Canadians were horrified when some municipalities in Ontario passed English-only resolutions for their jurisdictions and when members of the Association for the Preservation of English in Canada trampled on a Quebec flag. And the struggle over the Meech Lake Accord made many in Quebec feel rejected by the rest of Canada.

In the federal election of 1993, the Bloc Québécois won fifty-four seats in the House of Commons and became the Official Opposition. In 1994 the Parti Québécois once again became the provincial government of Quebec. This set the stage for the Quebec referendum on sovereignty in October 1995, in which the voters rejected sovereignty by a narrow margin: 50.6 to 49.4 percent. In other words, the 1995 referendum was a tie game. Precisely for that reason, however, it has come to mark the beginning of a new phase in the struggle over Quebec. The province is now clearly split in half. On the one side are French Canadians living outside the Montreal and

Ottawa regions; they are predominantly in favour of greater sovereignty for Quebec. On the other side are the anglophones, allophones (those of neither French nor British ancestry), and French Canadians living in the Montreal and Ottawa regions, most of whom are less committed to independence. Whether or not this means that the rural–urban cleavage in Quebec is now shaping the independence struggle, it is clear that separatism is no longer based primarily on the Quebec urban middle class.

Although nationalist sentiment in Quebec is not a new phenomenon, it has repeatedly changed in character. Its social basis, its ideology, and its objectives have gone through a number of transformations. Many francophones in Quebec no longer see themselves as an ethnic minority, but rather as a nation that, like other nations, is entitled to its own state (du Pays, 1996). "French Canadian" nationalism has given way to a more territorially based "Quebec" nationalism, in which the ideal is to build a new nation in North America embracing all who live in Quebec (Rocher, 1996).

In the 1998 provincial election, the Parti Québécois won a solid majority of seats, but received only 42.7 percent of the popular vote, slightly less than the Liberals. These results discouraged the Parti Québécois from holding another referendum on sovereignty. In 2003 it lost the provincial election to the Liberal Party, under Jean Charest, who opposes the separation of Quebec from the rest of Canada. However, the federal sponsorship scandal of 2004–6 led to a large growth in support for the Bloc Québécois, which won fifty-four of Quebec's seventy-five seats in the House of Commons in 2004, and fifty-one in 2006. The future will bring more struggles between separatist and federalist forces in Quebec, the results of which are impossible to predict.

Social movements of the future: The politics of status

In addition, what kind of social movements will the future bring us? Many sociologists believe that it will be more "new social movements." For them the environmental and anti-globalization movements, such as those active during World Trade Organization meetings, are the prototypes. We would suggest that, instead, it is more likely that status movements based on group membership, such as gender or disability, will predominate.

Until recently, status movements in Canada have been uncommon. The most significant was the suffragette movement in the early decades of the twentieth century.

During the past several decades, in most Western societies, there has been a significant increase in the number of status movements, but this is perhaps more the case in Canada than elsewhere as a result of the Charter of Rights and Freedoms of 1982. Section 15 of the Charter assures equality of rights for a variety of groups. Initially it gave protection to only a small number of groups, but it allowed the courts to add groups to the list. When Section 15 came into effect in 1985, the federal government offered funding to groups who wanted to take advantage of its provisions (Brodie, 1996: 254–55). Not surprisingly, the Charter encouraged the formation of a large number of interest-litigation groups: the Canadian Disability Rights Council, the Canadian Prisoners' Rights Network, the Equality of Rights Committee of the Canadian Ethnocultural Council, Equality of Gays and Lesbians Everywhere, the Women's Legal Education and Action Fund, and the Charter Committee on Poverty Issues (Brodie, 1996: 254; Brodie, 2002). Eventually the Supreme Court limited protected constitutional status to groups that are "discrete and insular minorities" or groups that have historically suffered social disadvantage. Yet it also determined that immigrants awaiting Canadian citizenship merit "protected" status, and homosexuals have been deemed a protected group (Brodie, 1996: 255–56). Moreover, it is not just the Supreme Court that recognizes the rights of such status groups. The legalization of same-sex marriages in Canada was initiated by decisions of provincial appeal courts before the issue ever went to the Supreme Court (see Chapter 10, Families).

These movements represent a new (though not altogether unprecedented) development in status rights. In earlier centuries, status groups claiming special treatment usually justified it on the basis of the high prestige they enjoyed or thought they should enjoy. Thus the European nobility claimed special privileges, such as exemption from taxation, on the basis of their alleged military and/or moral superiority. Property-owning males who enjoyed the exclusive right to vote in the nineteenth century claimed it on the basis of their alleged capacity for more responsible judgment. In contrast, status groups in Canada are now beginning to claim special treatment on the basis of the inferior position to which they have been assigned. Of course, they do not accept the validity of that inferior position and want their prestige to be raised. Yet they are basing their claim to special treatment on a supposed inferior, not superior, position.

Although a proliferation of protected status groups will dilute the advantages of the Charter of Rights and Freedoms for any single group (Brodie, 1996), this is not likely to discourage the formation of status blocs. If a certain status group has gained advantages, or is perceived to have gained advantages, at the expense of another status group, a possible recourse for the latter is to organize its own status movement. Thus movements have been formed by divorced men to challenge what they perceive to be the preference that the judicial and legal system has shown toward women in marital breakups, especially with regard to their respective rights and obligations toward the couple's children. A number of movements have also emerged to challenge discrimination against white males in recruitment practices. Small movements have even sprung up to protect heterosexuals from purported discrimination. Several organizations, such as the Canadian Family Action Coalition, have been formed to oppose the successes that gays and lesbians enjoyed, successes that ultimately led to the legalization of same-sex marriages. In June 2003, divorced men won a major decision before the Supreme Court, giving separated fathers the right to help name children. This decision departed, and explicitly so, from the previous tendency of the Court to favour "disadvantaged" over "advantaged" groups.

Summary

The first part of this chapter examined different theoretical approaches to the study of social movements. It began with the collective behaviour perspective, which was long the dominant theoretical school in North American sociology. This approach assumes that social movements are less institutionalized than ordinary behaviour, and it studies them along with other types of relatively less institutionalized events, such as panics, crowds, and crazes. The discussion then turned to the breakdown theory that social unrest occurs when institutions that normally control and restrain human behaviour are weakened. The third theoretical perspective presented was the relative deprivation approach. It makes the intuitively appealing argument that social unrest is most likely to erupt when a sharp increase develops in the difference between what people receive and what they think they have a right to receive. Collective action approaches take a different tack by placing social movements in a broad category of events called collective action. Most advocates of this position emphasize the need to study how social unrest—indeed, how any kind of collective action—varies from one society to another, and how it changes in character over time.

They also attempt to explain these variations in terms of the structural conditions that underlie and shape collective action, particularly those conditions that facilitate mobilization. They also study the way in which people overcome obstacles to collective action, such as the free-rider problem. This theoretical approach is critical of other perspectives for giving insufficient attention to how people acquire the capacity to act collectively.

Postmodernism and the "new social movement" approach sought to explain the particular movements that have emerged in postmodern or postindustrial society in Western Europe and North America, placing more emphasis on the importance of culture than other perspectives. Finally, we examined the way in culture contributes to and shapes collective action.

The second part of the chapter shifted to a necessarily brief examination of collective action in Canada. Movements in western Canada were described as examples of collective action built on regional cleavage, and Quebec nationalism as an example of collective action resulting from ethnic cleavage. Finally, it was suggested that status movements would predominate in Canada in the twenty-first century.

Questions for Review and Critical Thinking

1. Many studies have shown that the level of social unrest usually increases in a society during the transition from a non-industrial to an industrial social organization, and then declines thereafter. But there are a number of different explanations for this pattern. Given what you have just learned about theories of relative deprivation, breakdown, and collective action, how do you think each approach would explain this phenomenon?

2. Given what you have just learned about theories of relative deprivation, breakdown, collective action, and the postmodernist approaches, how do you think each approach would explain the nature of current social movements in Canada?

3. What types of people do you think are likely to join an anti-globalization protest? Are they really alienated, uprooted, and poorly integrated into social institutions, as the social breakdown approach suggests?

4. Some argue that hyper-consumption, technological progress, seductive advertising, and mass manipulation

have limited the ability of social movements to emerge in Canada. Do you agree with this view? Why or why not?

5. To what extent have regional social movements in Canada eclipsed national class-based movements? Will such regional movements continue to expand in future?

Key Terms

collective action, p. 346
collective behaviour, p. 342
craze, p. 343
crowd, p. 343
emergent norm theory, p. 344
fad, p. 343
frame, p. 348
free-rider problem, p. 350
hegemony, p. 351
ideology, p. 348
la survivance, p. 362
mobilization, p. 348
panic, p. 343
public, p. 343
Quiet Revolution, p. 364
relative deprivation, p. 346
selective incentives, p. 350
social breakdown approach, p. 344
social cleavage, p. 357
social contagion, p. 343
social integration, p. 344
social movement, p. 343
status bloc, p. 353
status communities, p. 353

Suggested Readings

Carroll, W.K. (ed.)
1997 *Organizing Dissent: Contemporary Social Movements in Theory and Practice: Studies in the Politics of Counter-Hegemony* (2nd ed.) Toronto: Garamond.
An excellent collection of articles on social movements. While all articles discuss social movements in general, some include an analysis of a specific Canadian movement.

Chew, Michael Suk-Young
2001 *Rational Ritual: Culture, Coordination, and Common Knowledge.* Princeton: Princeton University Press.

Game theory can be highly mathematical, but this book is easy to read and there is no math. It will give you lots of insights into both game theory and public culture.

McAdam, Doug, J.D. McCarthy, and M.N. Zald (eds.)
1996 *Comparative Perspectives on Social Movements: Political Opportunities, Mobilizing Structures, and Cultural Framings.* Cambridge and New York: Cambridge University Press.
A collection of articles representing the cutting edge of collective action theory, it includes some revisions of earlier versions.

Tilly, Charles
1978 *From Mobilization to Revolution.* Reading, MA: Addison-Wesley.
Tilly is the leading exponent of the collective action approach. This book is not easy reading, but it is important for anyone interested in the study of social movements.

Websites

www.swc-cfc.gc.ca
Status of Women Canada
Maintained by Status of Women Canada, a federal government department, this site provides a wealth of information about women's equality issues in Canada, and about the many women's organizations in Canada working to promote gender equality.

www.greenpeace.org
Greenpeace
Explore this site to see how one of the planet's major environmental lobby groups uses the Internet to garner worldwide support for its environmental campaigns.

Key Search Terms

Collective action
Collective behaviour
Social movements
Quiet Revolution
Ideology

For more study tools to help you with your next exam, be sure to check out the Companion Website at **www.pearsoned.ca/hewitt**, as well as Chapter 15 in your Study Guide.

[16]

demography and urbanization

kevin mcquillan and danièle bélanger

Introduction

Because Canada is a large country with a relatively small population, daily life here does not seem to be affected by population the way it is in countries like China and India. Yet when it comes time to seek a job, find a partner, or save for retirement, population questions turn out to be of considerable significance for Canadians. **Demography** is the study of population; it examines how the size, structure, and rate of growth are affected by rates of fertility (births), mortality (deaths), and migration (movement).

While demographic trends have far-reaching effects on most aspects of social life, they do not operate on their own. Their influence often comes about through their interaction with other social, cultural, and economic variables. In this chapter we shall briefly examine how population affects social life, and how, in turn, social factors influence population. In doing so, we shall concentrate on the population of Canada, and how demographic factors have influenced its evolution. As

part of this discussion, we also consider urbanization, the trend toward increased population concentration in cities and towns.

The course of world population growth

To put population growth in Canada in context, let us first look at the global situation. As we do so, we realize that since migration only moves people around, only two factors are relevant: the number of births and the number of deaths. Two simple demographic measures, the **crude birth rate (CBR)** and the **crude death rate (CDR)**, calculated by dividing the number of births (or deaths, in the CDR) occurring in a population in a given period of time (usually one year) by the total size of the population (best measured at the mid-point of the year), and expressed per thousand population, help us understand how births and deaths determine the rate of population growth.

Classical Views on Population

Scholars have examined population issues since the earliest times, but the beginnings of a modern approach to demography date from one piece of writing, Thomas Malthus's (1970) *An Essay on the Principle of Population*. The essay was first published in 1798 and immediately attracted considerable public interest. Malthus wanted to create a stir and thus had produced a provocative account of the role of population in human society. He was very critical of the optimistic ideas prominent among other Enlightenment scholars (see Chapter 1). In contrast to their views, he painted a deliberately bleak picture of humanity's future. Societies may experience considerable technological and social progress, he agreed, but population growth would always be a problem.

In the view of Malthus, human nature contains two basic needs or drives: the need to eat and what he termed "the passion between the sexes." As a result, he argued, an increase in the supply of food produces only a temporary improvement in the standard of living, because it also produces an increase in population size, which then reproduces and eats up any increase in food. Population growth can be contained only by what he termed **positive checks**—war, famine, and disease.

Not surprisingly, Malthus's essay drew considerable critical attention, and as a result he greatly expanded the book in later editions and softened his vision of the future. Human society, he acknowledged, could avoid the punishing effects of positive checks to population growth by taking steps to limit the number of births. For Malthus, an Anglican minister as well as a scholar, this did not mean the use of contraceptive practices, referring to them as "improper arts." Instead, he advised people to postpone marriage until they could provide for children. Only by using this **preventive check**, as he called it, could society avoid the endless cycle of population growth followed by insufficient food and rising mortality. Malthus, we might add, followed his own advice. He married in 1804 at the age of 38, and had only three children.

Malthus's ideas on population and society seem outdated today. Technological progress, at least in the industrialized world, has expanded food supplies far beyond

levels Malthus could have imagined. And the spread of modern birth control has meant that some modern societies even experience population decline. Still, for many countries in the developing world, rapid population growth continues to pose a major challenge to an improved standard of living. Moreover, in language that might have been borrowed from Malthus, modern environmentalists argue that we must stop exhausting nature's resources before nature intervenes with a new series of positive checks to growth.

Among the earliest and most forceful critics of Malthus was Marx, calling his essay "schoolboyish" and "a superficial plagiary" (Marx, 1906: 675). Marx felt Malthus blamed the poor for producing children they could not afford. But for Marx, as you read in Chapter 6, Social Inequality, the source of poverty lies not with the poor themselves but with the inherently oppressive character of capitalist societies. Capitalism needs what Marx called "a reserve army of [unemployed] labour" to restrain the wage demands of workers and prevent strikes. Thus overpopulation is a good thing for capitalists. Indeed, if workers followed the advice of Malthus and strictly limited the size of their families, capitalists would, Marx argued, replace workers with machines to maintain the reserve of unemployed workers. Only the transition to an economy built on socialist principles would eliminate unemployment and make clear that nature can provide for all.

Marx's ideas continue to influence the questions of contemporary analysts of population. Some less-developed societies, for example, argue that their economic problems lie less in the size of their populations than in the unequal relations between rich and poor countries (see Chapter 17, Social Change). The solution to poverty in the countries of Africa, Asia, and Latin America, they argue, requires not population control (though this may sometimes be helpful) but rather a fundamental global redistribution of wealth away from North America and Europe. More specifically, fairer prices for third-world exports and greater access to Western investment capital and modern technology will bring greater benefits to the developing world than will population control.

What arguments might you make to the West, apart from appeals to its decency, for a fairer distribution of world resources? What could poorer countries legitimately be asked to supply in return?

In the Western world of the nineteenth and early twentieth centuries, birth rates were approximately twice the death rates—stage two of the demographic transition.

The CBR in the world today is approximately twenty-one per thousand, while the CDR is only nine per thousand (United Nations, 2001: 38). The twelve persons per thousand difference between these two rates is a measure of how fast the population is growing per year, and known as the **rate of natural increase**. Twelve per thousand people is equal to 1.2 percent.

Prior to the seventeenth century, human populations tended to grow very slowly, or not at all, with any increase usually offset by periods of decline due to famine, disease, and war. With the eighteenth century, however, European societies experienced significant economic and technological development (see Chapter 17, Social Change), which, in turn, allowed a period of sustained population growth. With increased industrialization and even higher standards of living in the nineteenth century, the pace of demographic growth began to quicken. From one billion persons in 1800,

world population grew to two billion in 1920, three by 1960, four by 1975, five by 1987, and six billion in 1999, and now stands at approximately 6.5 billion. To understand the current pace, the world population will grow *in the next three weeks* by an amount roughly equal to the population of metropolitan Toronto.

While tracking world population growth is important, we have to remember that 1.2 percent is an average, concealing tremendous variation in population growth rates in different parts of the world. In countries like Canada, the rate of natural increase is low, 0.4 percent. In many countries of Eastern Europe, including Russia and Hungary, the rate is negative; more people die than are born. By contrast, in some countries of Asia and Africa, population is growing very rapidly. In Niger, for example, the rate of natural increase is 3.4 percent. Barring something tragic, at that pace the population will double in just twenty years (United Nations, 2005: 350).

Demographic Transition Theory

What lies behind such differences in population patterns? One answer comes from **demographic transition theory**. Built on the experience of the currently developed societies, the theory suggests that societies pass through a three-stage process of change (Notestein, 1945). In the first stage, population grows slowly because high birth rates are balanced by high, if fluctuating, death rates. In this stage, typical of pre-industrial Western societies, the average woman gives birth to five or six children. This high rate of birth is offset, however, by high mortality. As many as one in four babies does not live to see its first birthday, and others die in childhood due to famine and disease. If these societies are to survive, a high level of fertility is thus essential.

In these non-industrial societies, moreover, children are a valuable resource. From an early age, they contribute to the family by doing various household chores, and as they age their value increases. They can be particularly important as a source of support for their parents in old age. In addition, children in such societies are far less costly to raise than those in industrial societies. Schooling, if it exists at all, is limited to several years of basic training and is often confined to parts of the year when children's labour is not needed by the family. As a result, children's economic contribution to

---

[Research Focus]

Family Life and Child Mortality in Eighteenth-Century France

Demographic transition theory emphasizes the effect of high rates of infant and child mortality on fertility. Faced with the prospect of one or more of their children dying, families opted to have a large number of children, as the following example shows.

Husband: HESS, Sebastien
Birthdate: January 4, 1732 — Deathdate: October 10, 1792
Wife: MULLER, Anne Marie
Birthdate: July 3, 1729 — Deathdate: January 27, 1801
Marriage Date: January 19, 1751

Children	Birthdate	Deathdate
Anne Marie	April 2, 1755	January 6, 1761
Sebastien	April 17, 1759	February 20, 1761
Marie Marguerithe	November 22, 1761	March 26, 1762
Anne Marie	June 6, 1763	June 29, 1791
Sebastien	May 29, 1768	June 13, 1768
Catherine Marguerithe	April 20, 1770	December 23, 1845

In this example, drawn from the church records of a village located in northeastern France, the couple had six children, four of whom died in infancy or early childhood. A fifth died at age 28, and as a result only one child was alive at the death of the parents. Note also the interesting pattern of names. It was the custom to have a child named after each parent. When the child carrying that name died in childhood, the name was "reused" for subsequent children, a practice that many in today's societies might consider unacceptable.

Source: Example based on the parish registers of baptisms, marriages, and burials contained in the Archives départementales du Bas-Rhin, Strasbourg, France.

How have much lower rates of infant mortality today affected the structure of families in countries such as France?

the family quickly comes to outweigh their cost. To the average couple, then, having children makes good economic sense and, given the high childhood mortality a large number of children improves the chance that at least a few of them survive to adulthood, and thus to help their parents' in their old age.

Societies move into the second stage of the transition, one marked by a combination of high birth rates and declining death rates, as a result of industrialization and the development of a modern economy and the enormous changes in living conditions that come with them. A higher standard of living combined with improvements in sanitation and health gradually reduces death rates, especially for infants and children. But this decline in mortality rates is not immediately matched by a decline in the birth rate. Transition theorists suggest that families take some time to adapt to this new situation. Religious beliefs frequently forbid the use of birth control, and producing a large number of children is still often seen as a mark of social status. As a result, birth rates often remain high for a generation or so after mortality rates begin to decline, and thus societies experience a period of rapid population growth.

The persistence of low mortality gradually convinces couples that they do not need to have a large number of births to ensure several surviving children. Thus eventually societies pass into the third stage of the transition in which birth rates begin to decline significantly. Moreover, continuing economic and technological change greatly reduces the economic value of children while simultaneously increasing their costs. Childhood in today's industrial societies is no longer spent at work but in school, and the period of schooling has been constantly increasing, during which parents are expected to provide for their offspring. What this means for society as a whole is a new balance between birth and death rates, and a population that grows slowly or not at all. Returning to our question of why currently developing countries experience high population growth, transition theorists respond that these countries are simply further behind in the transition process. While Western countries have entered the final stage of the transition, lesser-developed societies are still in stage two. Transition theory predicts that as these societies continue to develop, they too will pass into the third stage, and the population problem will be solved.

How accurate is this view? Do populations naturally tend toward a position of zero population growth? Whether this occurs depends on the answers to two questions. First, does transition theory accurately reflect the past experience of Western societies? And second, will that Western experience be repeated in currently developing countries? Let us begin with the experience of Western countries.

There is little question that societies like Canada passed through a transition. Women in the past gave birth to far more children, and death rates have plunged dramatically over the last two centuries. There is some question, however, about the mechanisms responsible for this transition, as posited by transition theorists. Some critics, for example, pointed out that France experienced significant change in birth and death rates *before* the beginning of widespread industrialization (Knodel and Van De Walle, 1986). Others pointed to parts of Germany where the birth rate actually began to decline *before* the infant mortality rate did. Fewer children, they argued, enabled parents to provide a better standard of care, leading to lower rates of infant and childhood death.

Such issues have important consequences for social policy. If, as transition theorists claim, industrialization is a necessary condition for a decline in the birth rate, then that, and not family planning initiatives, should be the first goal for developing societies. If, on the other hand, people adopt birth control methods when they become available, as some critics of transition theory have suggested, then promoting family planning may lead to fertility decline even in the absence of economic development.

Turning to the second question, even if transition theory provides a good explanation of the experiences of past Western societies, its applicability to currently developing societies may still be limited because the situation they face is very different from the one faced by Western societies. First, their decline in mortality has been much faster than was true for societies like our own. Here the death rate fell gradually over the last century due to gradual improvements in the standard of living and advances in public health, and, more recently, medical care. In many developing societies, however, the introduction of Western-style public health programs has meant a more rapid reduction in death rates. In Mexico, for example, life expectancy increased from 39 years around 1940 to almost 75 years today; in Canada, it took more than a century to achieve a similar amount of progress.

Second, birth rates are much higher in many developing societies (particularly in sub-Saharan Africa) than those of past Western societies because in many developing societies marriage is nearly universal and occurs at a younger age than was true in the Western experience. This means that women will have a longer time period to produce children. As a consequence, while the rate of natural increase in European societies probably never surpassed 2 percent, in some developing societies today, the rate of natural increase has approached 4 percent per year, which means a doubling of population in just seventeen years.

Finally, the population of many developing societies is already much larger than was true of Western societies. For countries like Canada and the United States and even some European societies, land and resources were abundant and the spur of population growth probably encouraged more rapid development. But can Bangladesh, for example, with a population of 142 million living in an area less than half of the size of Newfoundland, deal with a doubling of its population over the next generation, while birth rates gradually fall into line with reduced death rates?

The points raised in the preceding paragraphs suggest that currently developing societies face more acute population problems than did currently industrialized societies. It needs to be pointed out, however, that the resources available to devote to these problems are greater as well (Caldwell et al., 1997). While the decline of fertility in Western societies occurred before the development of modern, efficient means of contraception, and usually in the face of pro-natalist opposition from major social institutions such as government and religion, in contrast, in countries such as China, Singapore, and Thailand, governments have been enthusiastic supporters of birth control. The most striking example is the case of China, where the government has used coercive means to try to bring about the spread of the "one-child family" (Johnson et al., 1998). In Thailand, also, in the 1960s, women had, on average, more than six children. Today, they have fewer than two. Thus just as death rates frequently declined more rapidly in developing societies, in several cases birth rates have fallen more dramatically as well.

In sum, then, transition theory is a flawed explanation of population trends. Its model, designed for currently developed countries, is less applicable to societies still in the process of development. Still it can be a guide to factors that must be considered when examining long-term changes in population patterns, factors discussed in the sections that follow.

Factors Affecting Population Growth
Fertility
Fertility measurement

We have already discussed the crude birth rate (CBR), a general measure of the rate of childbearing in a population. Useful as it is, the CBR has a major limitation. It considers childbearing in relation to the entire population (including men, infants, and the aged) and not in relation to those capable of having children. If women of childbearing age decline as a proportion of the total population, perhaps because a society is aging, the crude birth rate will decline even if the average woman continues to have exactly the same number of children.

To avoid this problem, demographers have developed some simple alternatives to the CBR. One is an **age-specific fertility rate**, obtained by dividing the number of births to women of a given age by the total number of women of that age in the population. Since only women of childbearing age are included, the problem of changes in the makeup of the total population is avoided. These rates have two additional benefits. One is that we can observe changes in the age pattern of fertility. For example, although the overall level of fertility may not be changing, fertility rates may be decreasing among younger women but increasing among older women. Second, if we add up the age-specific rates for women across the childbearing years, we arrive at an estimate of the average number of children a woman will bear in her lifetime if she experiences the current age-specific rates of fertility. This measure, which is of great importance in demography, is called the **total fertility rate** (TFR), and may be expressed per woman (e.g., 1.7 children per woman).

Before leaving the question of measurement, one further distinction is worth introducing. The measures discussed so far—the CBR, age-specific fertility rates, and the TFR—are all based on information gathered at one point in time. For example, the TFR for 2004 is computed by relating the number of births in the year 2004 to the number of women of childbearing age in 2004. Such measures are referred to as **period measures** because they refer to a particular period of time. But what if, for some reason, 2004 produces an unusually small crop of babies. The age-specific rate will correctly inform us of this slowdown in births, but if we attempt to use it as an indicator of future fertility, we may be misled.

To deal with this problem, demographers developed the *cohort approach* (Ryder, 1965), the basic principle of which is very simple. All people who share a common year of birth belong to a particular cohort, like the 1985 birth cohort. The cohort can then be observed over time and its behaviour recorded, in what we call a **cohort measure**. For example, we could calculate a *cohort total fertility rate* for women born in 1955. Unlike period measures, it is unaffected by year-to-year fluctuations in births. It shows the number of children the women ultimately produced, whether they had them early in life or delayed them until later. In that sense, it is a truer picture of fertility. This does not mean that cohort measures are necessarily better than period measures, however. For some purposes (e.g., the need for temporary portable classrooms) it is more important to know about year-to-year changes in fertility.

Social and biological factors affecting fertility

The term *fecundity* refers to the biological potential to bear children. Demographers use the term *fertility* to refer to the actual childbearing of a woman or group of women. Thus, a woman may be fecund (able to give birth to a child) but not fertile (she has not yet given birth to a child). For a variety of reasons fertility rates tend to fall well below the biological maximum and not only in industrialized societies. First, most societies have customs that, often unintentionally, tend to limit fertility (Weeks, 2005: 207). In Western societies, for example, until recently, childbearing outside of marriage was uncommon. And since marriage usually occurs well after the beginning of a woman's childbearing years, many years of potential childbearing were thus "lost." From a biological viewpoint, later marriage was once the biggest limit on fertility. Other practices that also unintentionally reduce fertility levels well below their biological maximum include breast-feeding, a natural contraceptive that suppresses ovulation. Indeed the World Health Organization promotes intensive breast-feeding of infants for six months as a way to enhance the child's and mother's health, and as a means to space births and reduce family size. In the Philippines, for example, where the Catholic Church discourages the use of modern contraception, efforts are made to promote breast-feeding,

as a socially acceptable way to prevent pregnancy (Mangahas, 1994).

In our society, the most important fertility-reducing practice is contraception. While significant historical differences existed among women from different religious and ethnic backgrounds in their use of contraception, contraception use today is almost universal among married couples in Canada (Wu and Martin, 1999). Sterilization is now the most popular method of contraception among married couples, with sterilization rates in Canada significantly higher than in other societies with similar population structures. Unmarried women are most likely to use birth control pills while condoms have gained in popularity with increasing concern about sexually transmitted diseases.

Finally, an important factor affecting fertility is abortion. The use of abortion varies among countries, reflecting differences in laws, population policies, reproductive health services, as well as social attitudes toward voluntary pregnancy termination. Generally speaking, where abortion is legal, available, and socially acceptable, rates are higher. Socialist countries, for instance, have a tradition of providing wide access to legal abortion services at low cost. In Russia, it is estimated that one-half of all pregnancies end in abortion (Henshaw et al., 1999). Asian countries, such as Japan and Korea, also have very high rates, partly because of fewer moral and religious objections to abortion than in countries such as the United States and Canada. In other countries, like Vietnam, abortion rates may be higher partly because women have few other options available to them to avoid conception (Bélanger and Khuat, 1998).

In sum, marriage patterns, breast-feeding practices, contraceptive use, and abortion are four very important and measurable factors explaining variations in fertility across time and among societies. Demographers commonly refer to them as *proximate determinants* because they act *directly* on fertility. Depending on social, cultural, and economic factors as well as population policies, a country may achieve a decline in fertility with different combinations of the four proximate determinants. In contrast, other factors such as the level of education or income indirectly affect the number of children families have. More educated women, for instance, have fewer children not because they are more educated *per se*, but because they tend to marry later and use contraceptive methods more effectively.

Fertility in developed societies

Table 16.1 shows period total fertility rates for a number of industrial societies. Not surprisingly, the data indicate that their fertility rates are relatively low. Since a total fertility rate of slightly more than two children per woman is necessary to avoid population decline, we can see that most advanced societies now face the prospect of a natural decrease of population and, in the absence of immigration, a decline in their total population.

If we compare the evolution of birth rates in the various societies, we see that while all now experience relatively low fertility, there are nevertheless important differences among them. Some countries, such as Italy and Germany, experienced a fairly steady downward drift of their fertility rate. In other cases, France, for example, the fertility rate has increased. Fertility rates in the U.S. and Canada were relatively high in the period following World War II, producing the "baby boom." Rates then plunged dramatically during the 1970s. But, in recent years, the two countries have followed different paths. Since the late 1990s, the Canadian rate has hovered around 1.5 children per woman (Statistics Canada, *Report on the Demographic Situation in Canada 2001*. Catalogue No. 91-209-XIE2001), while the American rate has increased, and, in 2000, stood at 2.04 (Centers for Disease Control, www.cdc.gov/nchs/data/nvsr/nvsr54/nvsr54_02.pdf [accessed 3 October 2006]), the highest total fertility rate in the Western world.

Among the factors influencing recent Canadian fertility patterns is the changed timing of childbearing. The postwar period saw a shift toward younger childbearing. Couples married younger, and this usually meant earlier childbearing. Recently, however, age at marriage has been rising, and there is an increasingly long delay between marriage and the birth of the first child. Thus, in 2003, 36 percent of first-time mothers were over 30 years of age (Statistics Canada, 2005a: 20). The increasing presence of women in higher education and their growing involvement in the labour force lie behind this shift to later childbearing. Many women probably feel it is better to become established in a career before taking on the commitments involved in having children. Some will be disappointed to find out that pregnancy at a later age is more difficult. All will find out that the empty nest described in Chapter 10, Families, will be a long time coming.

Another significant trend is the weakening of the link between marriage and childbearing (Heuveline et al., 2003). In Canada, for example, as late as 1960, only 4.3 percent of children were born to unmarried mothers, with a large proportion of these children given up for adoption shortly after birth. In recent decades, however, the proportion of children born to unmarried women has risen sharply. In 2003, 30 percent of births in Canada as a whole, and almost 60 percent of births in Quebec, occurred to unmarried women (Statistics Canada, 2005a: 17). The circumstances surrounding these births may vary greatly, of course. In some cases, the child may be born to a couple in a stable cohabiting relationship, while in others the birth may occur to a woman on her own, with no support, financial or otherwise, from the father. Data from the 2001 Census show that 43 percent Canada's lone-mother families lived below the poverty line (Galarneau, 2006).

Table 16.1	Total Fertility Rates for Selected Industrialized Nations, 1950–2005					
Country	**1950–55**	**1960–65**	**1970–75**	**1980–85**	**1990–95**	**2000–05**
Canada	3.72	3.61	1.97	1.71	1.74	1.51
U.S.A.	3.45	3.31	2.02	1.92	2.05	2.04
Sweden	2.21	2.33	1.89	1.68	2.01	1.72
Italy	2.32	2.55	2.28	1.64	1.24	1.28
Germany	2.16	2.49	1.64	1.43	1.30	1.32
France	2.73	2.85	2.31	1.80	1.70	1.87

Source: United Nations, *World Population Prospects: The 2002 Revision*, New York: United Nations, 2003; United Nations, Department of Economic and Social Affairs, Population Division, *World Population Prospects: The 2004 Revision*, http://esa.un.org/unpp (accessed 31 March 2006); United Nations, *World Urbanization Prospects: The 2003 Revision*, New York: United Nations, 2004.

Canadian Population Growth: Who Is Counting?

The British North America Act, Canada's basic constitutional document, requires a census of the country to be taken every ten years. In 1966, however, the federal government decided that a decennial census was insufficient for keeping track of Canada's rapidly changing population and decided to hold a census every five years. The information contained in these censuses provides a detailed portrait of our national population, not simply a count of the number of people in the country but also data on a wide variety of characteristics, including ethnicity, occupation, education, and income. A census was conducted on May 15, 2001. It showed that the total population of the country reached 30 007 094 in 2001, an increase of 4 percent over the 1996 total of 28 846 761.

Canada's most recent census was conducted on May 16, 2006, and the first results will be released in the spring of 2007.

Not surprisingly, the rate of growth varied significantly across the country. Alberta was the fastest-growing province with an increase of 10.3 percent, followed by Ontario at 6.1 percent; Newfoundland, Nova Scotia, New Brunswick, and Saskatchewan lost population in the five-year period. These trends reflect a long-term pattern of movement toward the west. While the Atlantic Provinces' share of Canada's population declined from 11.6 percent in 1951 to 7.6 percent in 2001, the proportion of the population in Alberta and British Columbia rose from 15 percent in 1951 to 22.9 percent in 2001.

Why is Canada's population growing in the west and declining in the east? What might account for Ontario's relatively high growth rate?

Fertility in developing societies

Few topics have attracted as much attention from demographers as fertility patterns in developing societies. In reviewing this research, the first thing that becomes apparent is the great variability in behaviour among developing countries. While it may have made sense to speak of a common Third World high fertility pattern in the 1960s, as the data in Figure 16.1 make clear, over the last generation these countries have followed a variety of paths. Let us look at a few of them to gain some clues as to the sources of fertility decline in the developing world.

South Korea is perhaps the most outstanding example of a society that experienced both rapid economic growth and rapid fertility decline. Indeed, most argue that it makes little sense any more to speak of it as a developing country. A rising standard of living, growing urbanization, and industrialization have transformed it and brought about a shift to a fertility pattern like ours. It is a nearly perfect example of the kind of change predicted by demographic transition theory.

Thailand provides a somewhat different pattern showing the importance of cultural factors in fertility decline. Thailand, by some accounts, had one of the fastest growing economies in the world during the 1980s (World Bank, 1992). Yet fertility decline sometimes leaped ahead of (not followed) economic development and, according to some analysts, particular features of the Thai culture played an important role as well. The majority of the population is Buddhist, a religion that raises no objections to contraceptive use. Moreover, women in Thai culture have considerable autonomy, particularly in comparison with women in many other developing societies (Knodel et al., 1987). Thus the Thai case demonstrates that when a culture is open to fertility control, birth rates may decline significantly, even before the society achieves a high level of economic development.

The third example of large-scale fertility decline, China, presents another strikingly different pattern. In this case, the impetus to fertility decline came from the government. Beginning in the 1970s, the Chinese government

Figure 16.1 Total Fertility Rates for Selected Developing Countries, 1960–65 and 2000–05

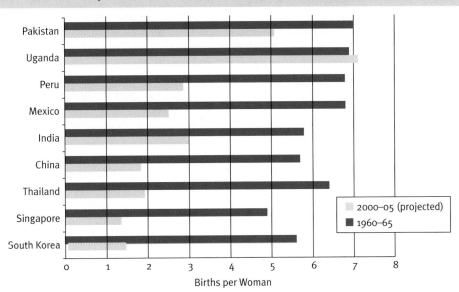

Births per Woman

2000–05 (projected)
1960–65

Sources: United Nations, 1998. *World Population Prospects: The 1996 Revision.* New York: United Nations (pp. 274–76); United Nations, 2001. *World Population Prospects: The 2000 Revision.* New York: United Nations (pp. 616–43).

introduced a series of ever more stringent fertility policies involving incentives and penalties to induce couples to have fewer children, culminating in the introduction of the one-child family policy in 1979. The policy, while generally effective, raises important ethical questions. Also, it has not been uniformly successful. While in urban areas the policy was strictly enforced, in some rural areas many families got permission to have a second or third child (Li, 1995), especially if there were no son. In fact, in 1989, the policy was revised to allow rural families whose first-born child was a daughter to have a second child. While the press has given much attention to abortion of female fetuses and to the abandonment and infanticide of female infants, data reveal that some of the missing girls were born and are alive, but that families have simply not registered their birth in order to avoid consequences (Yi et al., 1993).

Fertility has been below replacement level in China since 1992 and, in 2001, policy makers passed a law shifting from population control to a more comprehensive approach to reproductive health, the reduction of coercive measures, and a more indirect approach to limiting births (Winkler, 2002). Once fertility was low for a decade, coercive measures to limit childbearing became less necessary, and most young parents desired a small family. In fact, recent research shows how the one-child policy has become almost irrelevant because young

generations, particularly in large urban areas, have internalized the idea that having one child only is preferable, logical, and normal (Yilin and Wyman, 2005).

A second group of countries, including Mexico, Peru, and India, demonstrates a pattern of a more moderate fertility decline. As the data in Figure 16.1 show, fertility rates indicate continuing population growth. Indeed, given the relatively low mortality rates in many of these nations and the large numbers of young people entering their childbearing years, their populations will grow for some time.

The remaining nations in Figure 16.1 reflect a pattern of continuing high fertility. Although there is considerable diversity in the group of high-fertility countries, most are located in Africa and in the Islamic world, and their high fertility rates are not the simple result of lack of access to contraception. Women in these countries demonstrate knowledge of contraception and often indicate they have at times used various contraceptive methods. At the same time, they express a desire to have what we would consider a large number of children. Analysts point to a combination of economic and sociocultural factors as leading to this pattern. In many parts of Africa where families are engaged in subsistence farming, children continue to be economically useful to their parents, much as they used to be in Western societies (Weeks, 1996: 135).

Even in urban areas, children can contribute to family income from an early age through unskilled work or by providing childcare for younger siblings.

Cultural factors appear to contribute to the persistence of high fertility as well. In societies where a woman's role centres largely on her family, a large number of children adds to her stature within her family and community. For men as well, being the father of a large family may be seen as both adding to their prestige and augmenting the power of their family or lineage within the community. Having at least one son may be especially important, and this may influence decisions about having more children. Often these views are reinforced by religious values that either support high fertility or oppose the use of fertility control. Where such a powerful combination of economic and social supports for high fertility exist, birth rates may remain high despite the influx of Western ideas and official attempts to limit childbearing. Given this diversity of experience among developing countries, are there any definite conclusions we can draw about the course of fertility? Many analysts would suggest two. First, while the link between economic development and fertility decline is not a simple one, it does appear that once a society achieves a high level of economic development, birth rates decline to near or below replacement level (Watkins, 1986). Second, on an individual level, there appears to be a strong connection between education for women and lower fertility (Weeks, 1996: 146). A variety of studies have shown that women in developing countries with at least a high-school education have significantly smaller families, pointing again to the significance of economic development for population change.

Mortality

Mortality measurement

As with fertility, we shall briefly consider the problem of measuring mortality, before discussing the factors associated with mortality change. Since death, unlike childbirth, is a certainty for all of us, one might think that measuring mortality would be an easier task. Unfortunately, this is not so, and in this chapter we can only introduce some important aspects of the problem. We have already discussed the crude death rate (CDR), which relates the total number of deaths to the total size of the population. As is obvious, however, the risk of dying varies greatly by age. For example, the likelihood of a death in any year among a group of nursing-home residents is far greater than the

likelihood among a group of university students. As we saw in Chapter 9, Aging, the proportion of Canada's population in the older, high-risk age categories is growing, and this will raise the CDR. This does not mean, of course, that health conditions are deteriorating; just the opposite, it means that health conditions continue to improve. As a result, other measures are needed to understand the changes in the risk of mortality at various ages.

As was true with fertility, the first are **age-specific death rates**, calculated by dividing the number of deaths to persons of a given age by the total number of persons in that age group. Such rates can be used to construct what demographers call a **life table**, a statistical model estimating the years a person of a given age can expect to live. One specific by-product of the life table is called the **expectation of life at birth**, the average number of years a group of newborns can expect to live if current mortality risks prevail throughout their lifetime.

Table 16.2 provides data on expectation of life at birth for a number of developed and developing societies. Note that in all developed societies, life expectancy is now well above 70 and, for women, surpasses 80 years. Developing countries too have experienced considerable progress in recent years. For most countries in Asia and Latin America,

Table 16.2	Expectation of Life at Birth for Males and Females, Selected Countries, 2000–2005	
Country	**Male**	**Female**
Canada	77.3	82.4
United States	74.6	80.0
France	75.8	83.0
Italy	76.8	83.0
Switzerland	77.6	83.1
Mexico	72.4	77.4
Chile	74.8	80.8
Bolivia	61.8	66.0
China	69.8	73.3
South Korea	73.2	80.5
Bangladesh	61.8	63.4
Nigeria	43.1	43.5
Ethiopia	46.5	48.6

Source: United Nations, Department of Economic and Social Affairs, Population Division, *World Population Prospects: The 2004 Revision*, http://esa.un.org/unpp (accessed 31 March 2006).

expectation of life at birth is now more than 60 years. The lowest levels tend to be found in the less developed societies of sub-Saharan Africa, where life expectancies below 50 years are not uncommon. Worse, high rates of HIV infection in a number of these countries have caused life expectancy to decline in recent years. The United Nations estimates that the AIDS epidemic has driven expectation of life at birth in countries such as Botswana, Malawi, and Zambia to less than 40 years (United Nations, 2001: 13). (See the box "The Effect of HIV/AIDS on Life Expectancy.")

[Social Trends]

The Effect of HIV/AIDS on Life Expectancy

Given the poor quality of the data, particularly in the countries most affected by the virus, until recently the demographic impact of AIDS was difficult to estimate. But in the 1990s, the commitment of many governments to monitor the disease, combined with the work of international and non-governmental organizations, greatly increased our knowledge of this devastating pandemic. As the epidemic enters its third decade of its history, the demographic impact of HIV/AIDS is taking on unprecedented proportions.

The United Nations estimates that in 2005 over 40 million people were living with HIV/AIDS, twice as many as ten years ago. To date, an estimated total number of 25 million people have died of the disease. (UNAIDS/WHO, 2005). In sub-Saharan Africa, where some of the most affected countries are located, up to 7 percent of the adult population carries the HIV virus. In some of the most affected countries such as Botswana, Zambia, Zimbabwe, and South Africa, HIV prevalence is 20 percent or greater. In 2005, five million people were infected with HIV, which represents 14 000 new infections per day. Among these 14 000 newly infected persons, 95 percent lived in low- and middle-income countries, 2000 were children under 15, and 12 000 were adults aged 15 to 49 (of which 50 percent were 15 to 24, and 50 percent were women) (UNAIDS/WHO, 2005). The impact on mortality is dramatic. In Botswana, for instance, life expectancy at birth was only 34 in 2002, but would have been over 72 without AIDS. In Kenya, life expectancy was reduced by 20 years due to AIDS. Much of this is attributable to the large number of deaths among infants and children under age 5. In Zimbabwe, for example, the risk of dying under age 5 more than doubled in 2002 because of AIDS (101/1000 instead of 47/1000) (Stanecki, 2002). To name only a few, Cameroon, Ethiopia, Nigeria, South Africa, and Malawi also suffer important demographic losses due to AIDS. In other parts of the developing world, AIDS will seriously affect life expectancies at birth in Brazil, Guyana, Haiti, Honduras, Burma, Cambodia, and Thailand. High mortality levels due to AIDS have also begun to affect population growth. In 2002, Botswana was experiencing negative growth while other countries were experiencing substantially lower growth rates than expected without AIDS. While countries of Asia and the Pacific generally have lower prevalence rates than African countries, large countries such as India and China will experience large increases in numbers of people living with HIV/AIDS over the next decade. For the year 2003, China is estimated to have had one million people infected, and India, five million (UNAIDS/WHO, 2005). In spite of a worsening AIDS situation in some countries, declining prevalence rates in Uganda and Thailand represent notable success stories bringing hope to efforts to halt the pandemic (Stanecki, 2002).

The most recent development in the HIV/AIDS epidemic is the provision of antiretroviral treatment to people living in the developing world. While only one person in ten has access to treatment in sub-Saharan Africa, coverage now reaches 80 percent in countries such as Brazil, Argentina, Cuba, and Chile. Overall, prevention and treatment efforts have increased substantially since the year 2000 but remain largely insufficient to contain the rapid spread of the deadly virus.

In Canada, HIV/AIDS does not affect enough people to substantially affect life expectancy at birth. Since 2001, the annual number of new cases has levelled off, with approximately 2500 new cases per year, while the total number of cases keeps increasing. As of December 2005, a total of 60 000 positive HIV tests had been officially reported since 1985 (Public Health Agency of Canada, 2005). Approximately 20 000 individuals had been

(continued)

diagnosed with AIDS in Canada by the end of 2004 (Government of Canada, 2005). The number of people who died of AIDS peaked in 1995 with 1477 deaths, declined steadily, and was under 200 in 2001 (Health Canada, 2002). That is not to say that the epidemic is under control in Canada; prevention, monitoring, and awareness continue to be of crucial importance. In fact, the Canadian Government in its latest reports on HIV/AIDS is talking about "troubling trends in the Canadian epidemic." These trends include greater proportions of women and heterosexuals being infected and an increase in the total number of HIV-infected persons (Government of Canada, 2005). It is also estimated that about 17 000 Canadians do not know that they have contracted the HIV virus.

What responsibility should Canada adopt for the devastating situation of AIDS in Africa? Should it concentrate on getting medicine to those afflicted, attempt to ease religious barriers to contraception, improve the status of women, or reduce the widespread malnutrition and poverty that also lead to a lowered life expectancy?

Mortality change

As we saw earlier, past Western societies experienced very high mortality rates. In some cases, expectation of life at birth was as low as 25 years. Remember that this is an average figure; it does not mean that the majority of the population died in their early adult years. On the contrary, then as now, the early adult years were among the safest in life. Indeed, the risk of death is highest in infancy and early childhood, declines throughout later childhood and adolescence, and then gradually rises throughout the adult years to again reach high levels in older age.

Probably the first reason for mortality decline, you might think, is the growth of quality medical care. As is often true in demography, however, the obvious cause is not the right one, for mortality rates were already falling in most Western countries in the last half of the nineteenth century when medical knowledge was modest, to say the least, and only a small proportion of the population had any contact with doctors or hospitals. For example, the death rate from tuberculosis declined steadily throughout the late nineteenth and early twentieth century although no effective medical treatment was devised until the 1930s. What, then, caused the initial fall of mortality in Western societies? Most observers point to a variety of causes, but chief among them are an improving standard of living, including better nutrition, and the growth of effective public health and sanitation measures. Better nutrition allowed people to survive once-fatal diseases, and in the process, they often developed immunity to further outbreaks of the same disease. In recent generations, medical advances have produced further progress in the fight against mortality but, in most Western societies, life expectancy had already reached 60 or higher before medical care began to exert a real influence.

While medicine's contribution to lower mortality in Western countries has been modest, this is not true for developing countries. What is striking about the data in Table 16.2 is that the figures are relatively high even for countries that remain very poor. In Bangladesh, for example, where Gross National Product per capita is only $370, compared to $21 340 in Canada (World Bank, 2001), life expectancy is estimated to be 62, a figure attained in Canada only in the 1920s. One reason is that many developing countries imported all at once the advances in medical care and public health that occurred over a longer time in places like Canada. As a result, death rates have fallen rapidly, even in the absence of widespread economic development.

Differential mortality

Differences in fertility levels among various groups in Canada have been declining over time, and we might have expected to discover the same situation when studying mortality. Yet recent research on mortality patterns in Canada and other industrial countries show not only the persistence of differences in life expectancy between social groups, but in some cases, a widening of those differences. Here we briefly note some of the most significant differences uncovered:

1. Undoubtedly the most significant is the difference in expectation of life between males and females. As the data in Table 16.2 demonstrate, in all industrialized societies (and in most developing ones as well), women outlive men, often by a significant amount. A variety of factors explain the difference. In one way or another, most centre on the different social roles and behaviour of men and women. Some touch on differences in

exposure to risk. Women, for example, have historically been employed (inside or outside the home) in situations that entail lower risks of mortality whether through accident, stress, or environmental factors.

Other explanations focus on coping strategies. Studies in Canada and elsewhere, for instance, reveal a greater tendency for women when ill to seek medical help. As women's roles change and become more similar to traditionally male roles, will the advantage held by women in life expectancy shrink or even disappear? The most recent data available suggest that, in recent years, life expectancy for men has been growing faster than for women, though a gap of 5.1 years still remains. Only the future will tell us whether this is the beginning of a shift toward greater equality in the risk of dying.

2. A second difference concerns variation in expectation of life by marital status. Again, studies from a variety of nations show that married persons enjoy a significant advantage over single, divorced, or widowed persons (Waite and Gallagher, 2000). The difference is larger for males (Wilkins, 2003), but most studies show that marriage provides some advantage to women as well. One possible explanation for this situation centres on what is called a *selection hypothesis*. What this means is that the difference between the married and unmarried may be a result not of what happens after marriage, but a result of differences in the characteristics of those who marry and stay married versus those who do not. To take an obvious example, if alcoholics are more likely to divorce than non-alcoholics, the alcohol abuse and not divorce may then cause their earlier death. In general, though, while selection factors cannot be ruled out as contributing to the advantage enjoyed by the married, most research seems to point to lifestyle differences between the married and non-married as carrying the most weight. The married state is characterized by a more orderly, stable style of living, entailing fewer health risks and perhaps better care when problems occur.

On average, women in Canada outlive men by more than five years, and female rates of mortality are lower than male rates for virtually every age category.

3. There are also important class and ethnic variations in mortality. Even with our universal medical insurance, differences in life expectancy by social class, although decreasing, remain. The difference in life expectancy between the richest and poorest neighbourhoods is still five years for men and 1.6 years for women (Wilkins et al., 2002). Similarly, ethnic group membership also is associated with differences in life expectancy. French-English differences, once marked, have largely disappeared (Nault, 1997: 39), but Native peoples in Canada continue to suffer significantly higher death rates, despite some progress in recent years (MacMillan et al., 1996). No one factor is responsible for these differences. Economic and social deprivation—including poorer-quality housing and nutrition, greater environmental risks of disease and accidents, and including poorer-quality medical care—is part of the answer. But members of disadvantaged groups are also more likely to engage in behaviours that carry high health risks. Rates of smoking and drug use tend to be higher among the less affluent (Millar, 1996; Health Canada, 1998). Taken together, these factors create an enduring pattern of difference in the health and mortality of different segments of our population.

Migration

Defining migration

When we examine national or regional patterns of population growth we need to consider not only births and deaths but also the movement of people into or out of these regions. Demographers call any movement across legally defined boundaries **migration**. **International migration** involves crossing a national boundary; it is almost always regulated by law and governments typically collect statistics on the number of persons entering (and sometimes the number leaving) the country. Such data, however, generally miss illegal immigrants and, as with many issues in sociology, we need to remind ourselves that official statistics present only a partial view of the topic under study. **Internal migration** then refers to movement across boundaries within countries as when a person from Nova Scotia takes a job in British Columbia and establishes permanent residence there. Since most nations allow people to move about freely within their borders, studying internal migration can be even more difficult as often there is no legal record of the move.

International migration

Since the seventeenth century, immigrants from Europe and elsewhere have poured into Canada, the United States, and indeed all the Western Hemisphere, transforming forever the character of these lands long inhabited by a variety of Native peoples. Relative to the small size of the population, the numbers arriving were huge. Given Canada's colonial links, it is not surprising that the earliest immigrants to Canada came from France and Great Britain (see also Chapter 8, Race and Ethnic Relations). As political and economic changes occurred, however, the origins of immigrants to Canada changed, and very often newcomers were not welcomed by the host population. When thousands of Irish immigrants fled to Canada in the nineteenth century, for example, many were met with open hostility. Later, as the number of immigrants from the British Isles declined, Canada began to turn to Central Europe as a new source of people. Land-hungry immigrants from Central Europe settled in Manitoba, Saskatchewan, and Alberta. Again, there was a reaction against people who spoke a different language and were seen as too different to fit into Canadian society. According to the 1911 Census, Canada's population totalled just over seven million people, but in the years 1911–1913 more than one million, mostly European, immigrants arrived (Beaujot, 1991: 105). Many quickly moved on, most to the United States, but the many who stayed helped swell the populations of the country's still small cities and towns (see Chapter 8, Race and Ethnic Relations).

The period between World Wars I and II, including the Great Depression, was marked by much lower levels of immigration, but after 1945 immigration to Canada again increased. Thousands of Europeans uprooted by war and the economic chaos that accompanied it looked here for the chance to start a new life. And though the origins of the persons coming have changed, Canada continues today to be a country open to immigration. In no year since World War II has Canada accepted fewer than 70 000 immigrants, and in 2004, 235 000 new immigrants arrived (www.cic.gc.ca/english/pub/facts2004/permanent/1.html). Proportionate to the size of its population, Canada continues to be one of the leading recipients of immigrants in the world, with its newest immigrants increasingly likely to come from countries in the developing world, particularly Asia.

An important concern of Canadian immigration policy is the distribution of these immigrants across the regions of the country. Despite Canada's large territory, our population is largely urban and quite concentrated;

more than half of Canada's population lives in the Windsor–Quebec City corridor alone. Government efforts to direct immigrants to less populated regions of the country have generally not been successful. While immigration did help to settle the Prairies when land-hungry immigrants from Central Europe came in the nineteenth century, today's immigrants do not want to go to the less populated areas of the country. The majority are drawn to the economic and commercial centres of the country, with more than 60 percent saying they hope to settle in Toronto, Vancouver, or Montreal (Statistics Canada, *Report on the Demographic Situation in Canada 2001*. Catalogue No. 91-209-XIE2001).

Canadian interest in international migration tends to concentrate on the inflow of people to our country. But for the developing countries that today send us immigrants, migration is also a source of concern. In the nineteenth century, the outflow of European emigrants to the Americas was almost certainly a benefit for both the send-ing and receiving countries. Emigration eased the population pressures of the European countries experiencing rapid growth and industrialization and drawing ever-larger numbers of migrants to their cities. For the developing world today, however, the benefits of international migration are not so clear. Given the rate of population growth in the developing world, the number of migrants who leave is too small to make much of a difference. The population of India grows by about fifteen million people per year, or roughly twenty times the number of immigrants admitted by Canada and the U.S. in recent years. Moreover, the tendency of industrialized countries to admit only those with a high level of skill and education often means that the developing countries are robbed of the skilled persons most needed for their own development. The balance, of course, is not completely negative. Immigrants often send money to help relatives back home, and this inflow of funds can be valuable for the economy of these countries. Nevertheless, it is not

The 2001 Census showed that 18.4 percent of the Canadian population is foreign-born.

surprising that developing countries have raised the question of international migration when arguing for better treatment in their dealings with the industrialized world.

Internal migration

Canada, like all highly developed societies, has a very mobile population. Almost half of Canadians change their residence at least once during the five-year period between censuses, though only about 5 percent change their home province (Che-Alford and Stevenson, 1998: 15). While individuals move for a variety of reasons, economic factors play a primary role. In Canada, this has made Ontario, Alberta, and British Columbia the greatest recipients of internal migrants. Examining migration data for the period from 1972 to 2000, Bélanger (2002: 51) showed British Columbia to be the largest gainer of population through internal migration, while Quebec has been the largest loser. Combined with the lower fertility rate in Quebec, the province's share of the national population total declined from 28.9 percent in 1951, to 24.1 percent in 2001 (www12.statcan.ca/english/ census01/products/ standard/popdwell/Table-CMA.cfm).

Urbanization

One of the most extraordinary developments of the last century has been the increasing concentration of human populations in cities. Why this has occurred and the limits to urban growth are questions that have intrigued demographers and geographers.

The essential prerequisite for the growth of cities is society's ability to produce an agricultural surplus that would allow city-dwellers to spend their time on other types of work. For most of human history, the limited capacity to produce sufficient food and to transport it to the cities before it spoiled limited the growth of urban areas, with even the great cities of the past relatively small by present-day standards. As late as 1700, London and Paris, the largest cities in Europe, likely had populations of just over 500 000 residents, smaller than Calgary is today. Indeed, until at least 1950, more than three-quarters of the human population lived in rural areas (Davis, 1972). In 2007, more than half of the world population will live in an urban area, a major turning point in the world population history (United Nations, 2004).

[Social Trends]

"You're Moving Where?"

While mobility is an important feature of the Canadian population, not all groups in the population are equally likely to move. Demographers note that the decision to migrate normally involves a calculation about the likely rewards balanced against the costs involved in the move. Young adults are the most likely to make the decision to set off for another province. At younger ages, the rewards available in the form of better jobs and higher incomes are especially attractive. Just as important, young people are not encumbered by some of the obligations that may discourage others to move. For example, they are less likely to own homes or have children who will complain about changing schools or leaving friends. As people reach age 30 and begin to settle down, the likelihood of

moving declines. At this stage of life, a variety of commitments means that people will think carefully before pulling up stakes for a new community. Migration rates continue to decline with age, though a slight increase is noticeable around the age of retirement. Freed from the obligations of work, some of the newly retired will look for a new setting in which to spend their later years. While economic conditions are usually most important in the selection of a destination, older migrants are often lured by other factors such as climate or a move to be closer to children. The attraction of places like Vancouver Island or the southern United States for older migrants has important implications for a variety of social services such as health care.

How many times have you moved in your life?
What factors were important to you or your family in making the decision to move?

Pre-nineteenth-century cities were, to put it mildly, unappetizing places to live. Before dramatic improvements in sanitation occurred, cities struggled with problems of sewage and garbage disposal. Human waste was often dumped into the streets and left to be washed away by the rains, ending up in the streams and rivers that were the source of water for drinking, cooking, and washing. Garbage was left to rot, attracting vermin and insects that, in turn, spread disease. Such appalling conditions meant that death rates were very high and sometimes reached catastrophic levels. The great plague that struck London in 1665 killed 100 000 people or some 25 percent of the city's population at the time (Wrigley and Schofield, 1981: 82). In light of these conditions, death rates often exceeded birth rates in urban populations, and cities would have grown slowly or even declined were it not for the flow of people moving to the urban areas from the countryside.

Urbanization in developed societies

Demographers distinguish between the growth of cities and *urbanization*, the proportion of a society's population that resides in urban areas. In countries like Canada and the United States, not only have cities continued to grow rapidly throughout the twentieth century, but the share of the total Canadian population living in cities has continued to increase as well. Stone (1967: 14) estimated that approximately 7 percent of the Canadian population lived in cities of 20 000 or more in the middle of the nineteenth century. Today, more than three-quarters of the population of Canada count an urban area as their usual place of residence.

The continuing urbanization of the population is an experience Canada shares with other highly developed societies. Where Canada differs is in the dominant role played by its largest metropolitan areas. The "big three" Canadian cities—Toronto, Montreal, and Vancouver—account for an astounding 33.6 percent of the national population. That is far greater than in most other advanced societies. New York, Los Angeles, and Chicago, the three largest American cities, hold just 16 percent of the U.S. population, while Paris, Lyon, and Marseilles account for less than 20 percent of France's population. Moreover, the largest Canadian cities have continued to grow rapidly. As Table 16.3 demonstrates, though Montreal has grown slowly in recent years, Toronto and Vancouver continue to be among the fastest-growing areas in the country.

The period since the end of World War II has seen dramatic growth of Canadian cities, both in the size of

Table 16.3	Population of the Ten Largest Canadian Cities, 1976 and 2001		
City	**1976**	**2001**	**% Change**
Toronto	2 803 101	4 682 897	67.1
Montreal	2 802 485	3 426 350	22.3
Vancouver	1 166 348	1 986 965	70.3
Ottawa-Hull	693 288	1 063 664	53.4
Calgary	469 717	951 395	102.8
Edmonton	554 228	937 845	69.2
Quebec	542 158	682 757	25.8
Winnipeg	578 217	671 274	16.1
Hamilton	529 371	662 401	25.1
London	270 383	432 451	60.0

Note: Figures refer to the Census Metropolitan Area.

Sources: 1976: *Census of Canada* (Catalogue No. 92-806), Table 6; 2001: www12.statcan.ca/english/census01/products/standard/popdwell/Table-CMA.cfm.

their populations and the amount of land they cover. The period has also seen the development of a new form of settlement that we commonly refer to as *suburbanization*. The improvement of transportation systems and the growth of automobile ownership allow large numbers of urban residents to live far away from their place of work. This, in turn, leads to the development of new communities on the fringe of cities where families seek more living space and privacy while still retaining the economic and cultural advantages of city life. And although some disadvantaged urban neighbourhoods have been revitalized by young professional couples attracted to the downtown core, the fastest growth continues to occur on the urban fringe. In the period 1996–2001, the population of Toronto's core areas grew by only 4 percent, while the suburban communities of Markham and Richmond Hill increased by 20.3 percent and 29.8 percent respectively.

Urbanization in the developing world

In 1950, most urban dwellers lived in Europe and North America. But today, about two-thirds of the world's urban population lives in cities of developing countries in Asia, Africa, and Latin America. According to U.N. projections, over 80 percent of all urban dwellers will live in developing countries in the year 2030 (United Nations, 2002). Not only are cities of the developing world growing rapidly and accounting for more and more of the total urban population, but their sizes have also reached levels unimaginable a few decades ago. In 1950, only New York City had more than ten million people; in the year 2000, sixteen cities of the world have passed the ten million mark and twelve of them are located in the developing world (see Table 16.4).

Why have the cities of Asia, Africa, and Latin America grown so fast and reached such large populations? While natural increase remains important, it is not the driving force it used to be. For many cities, migration has become the most important factor behind rapid growth. In China, where fertility is now below the replacement level, migration accounts for most of the growth of cities such as Shanghai, Beijing, and Tianjin (Jones and Visaria, 1997). The same holds true for Mexico City, now the second largest city in the world.

Massive migration from rural to urban areas results from rural poverty and people's desire to have a better life for themselves and their children. Cities offer better access to basic services such as water and electricity;

Table 16.4	Population of Urban Agglomerations with 10 million inhabitants or more in 1975 and 2003	
City	**1975**	**2003**
Tokyo, Japan	26.6	35.0
Mexico City, Mexico	10.7	18.7
New York, USA	15.9	18.3
São Paulo, Brazil	9.6	17.9
Mumbai (Bombay), India	7.3	17.4
Delhi, India	4.4	14.1
Calcutta, India	7.9	13.8
Buenos Aires, Argentina	9.1	13.0
Shanghai, China	11.4	12.8
Jakarta, Indonesia	4.8	12.3
Los Angeles, USA	8.9	12.0
Dhaka, Bangladesh	2.2	11.6
Osaka-Kobe, Japan	9.8	11.2
Rio de Janiero, Brazil	7.6	11.2
Karachi, Pakistan	4.0	11.1
Beijing, China	8.5	10.8
Cairo, Egypt	6.4	10.8
Moscow, Russian Fed.	7.6	10.5
Metro Manila, Philippines	5.0	10.4
Lagos, Nigeria	1.9	10.1

Source: United Nations, *World Urbanization Prospects, The 2003 Revision, Highlights and Tables.* New York: United Nations: 2004: 8. The United Nations is the author of the original material.

urban citizens also enjoy better prospects for education, health care, and employment. Overall, city dwellers in developing nations enjoy better lives than their rural counterparts (United Nations Development Program, 1997). If, from your perspective, people's lives in a slum in Calcutta seem unbearable, to them it may seem an improvement from the quality of life in the rural villages of India. On the other hand, this migration to urban areas can also create new problems for rural areas. Migrants are often younger and more educated than non-migrants, and their departure reduces the talent pool needed to promote economic and social development there, thus increasing pressures to leave, in a bad circle.

While urbanization may entail economic development and improvement in the well-being of rural migrants, there is a consensus that policies to slow city growth are crucial. City-dwellers face acute problems, many the same problems that cities of the developed world faced over the past few hundred years. Given the very large size of these cities, however, these problems affect more people, and their solutions become more complex. Providing even the basics of urban infrastructure remains difficult for most cities of the developing world. Urban transport poses a particular problem. There has been an unprecedented increase in private vehicles and paratransit transportation, such as minibuses and microbuses, leading to congestion and contributing to pollution. Water and sanitation are two other critical problems facing most large cities in the developing world. The city of Cairo, for instance, has a population of ten million people, but its water and sanitation system is designed to serve two million (Todaro, 1997). While waste removal and recycling are certainly major issues, many cities are struggling with problems of garbage collection. The average amount of garbage not collected ranges between 30 to 50 percent for some cities (United Nations, 1995).

Urban areas in the developing world also display great disparities in income. Extreme poverty is found in slums of most cities, while the centres often look like any other large city of the world, with international hotels renting rooms in American dollars. Buying an apartment in downtown Mumbai (Bombay) in India would cost you as much as buying one in Toronto (*The Economist*, 1995). Today, slum settlements represent more than one-third of the urban population in developing countries, in many cases more than 60 percent. Better urban planning as well as sustainable rural development are the approaches local governments and international agencies are promoting for dealing with some of these daunting problems (Jones and Visaria, 1997). Keeping fertility low in rural areas to reduce migration streams from the countryside to cities is also a priority.

Malthus felt that, if population always increases to the ultimate point of subsistence, progress can have no lasting effects.

Age–Sex Structure

The fertility, mortality, and migration experienced by a population combine to shape not only its size and growth rates but also its age–sex structure. The simplest and most commonly used demographic tool for examining this issue is the **population pyramid**, a graphic representation of the composition of a population at a particular point in time. By drawing to scale bars representing the number of persons in each age and sex category (for example, males 30–34 years of age), we get an image of the overall distribution of a population and can tell at a glance some of its important characteristics. In populations with a high rate of fertility, for example, the graph will look like a real pyramid, with a broad base and narrowing gradually as we move up to the older age categories. Such populations are said to be "young," since a large proportion of the population is in the childhood and adolescent years. In some African countries today, for example, 50 percent of the population is under age 15. In many Western societies, which have been aging rapidly in recent years, less than 20 percent of the population will be under age 15.

Figure 16.2 shows the population pyramids for Canada for 1981, 1991, and 2002. The pyramids do not neatly fit the image of a young or old population, because Canada's population has been passing through a period of dramatic change. Look at the size of the bars representing those between ages 15 and 35 in 1981. These groups were born during the baby boom and constitute a bulge in the age distribution. By 2002, the baby-boom generation had entered middle age. Very soon, the first members of this unusually large generation will retire, aging the population and placing additional pressure on our pension and health systems. The dramatic decline in the birth rate that began in the late 1960s produced the relatively small cohorts who were between the ages of 21 and 36 in 2002. However, as the baby boomers began having children of their own, we saw the appearance of what has been called the "echo generation." These children were born during the 1980s and early 1990s and are, for the most part, still in the school system. Given the tremendous impact the baby boom had on Canada, the echo, while noticeable, appears rather faint. As the lowest bars on the pyramid indicate, with the baby boomers reaching the end of their childbearing years, the number of births in Canada has again declined. If fertility rates continue at their current low level, the base of the population pyramid will be narrow indeed in the years ahead (See also Chapter 9, Aging).

Figure 16.2   Age Pyramid of the Population of Canada, July 1, 1981, 1991, and 2002

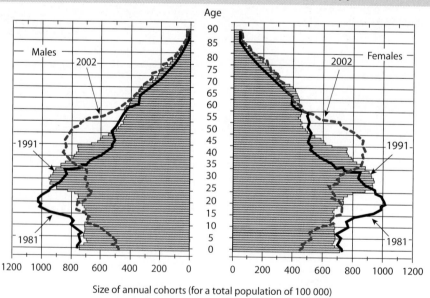

Size of annual cohorts (for a total population of 100 000)

Source: Statistics Canada, 2003. *Annual Demographic Statistics, 2002.* Catalogue No. 91-213, Statistical Table 1.4, page 13.

Population and Resources: Is Malthus Now Right?

Predictions about the dire effects of overpopulation have been articulated by many writers but none more convincingly than American ecologist Paul Ehrlich. In 1968, he wrote *The Population Bomb*, probably the most widely discussed book on population since Malthus's original essay. He predicted a global crisis involving starvation, rising mortality levels, and environmental disaster as a result of the unprecedented population growth of the late 1960s.

Twenty years later, he and his wife Anne wrote a second book, *The Population Explosion* (Ehrlich and Ehrlich, 1990), which argued that the catastrophic events he earlier predicted have already arrived. Hundreds of millions have perished through starvation and malnutrition, world grain production is falling, and quality agricultural land and water supplies are diminishing. Underlying these problems, according to the Ehrlichs, is the rapid population growth in developing countries, which places an unsustainable burden on the ecosystem, on top of the very high level of consumption in rich countries, whose even slower rate of population growth contributes daily to a coming environmental disaster. The world needs not only a halt to growth but, in their view, a population decline. If each of us does not voluntarily have only one or at most two children, they suggested, governments will eventually move toward the kind of coercive population policy that exists in China.

The Ehrlichs' position is a somewhat more extreme and popularized version of what most demographers would support. Indeed finding someone on the other side of the issue was not easy until the appearance of a book entitled *The Ultimate Resource*, published in 1981 by an American economist (Simon, 1981). Is there a population crisis? Are there too many people? Are resources being used up? Is pollution getting worse? Simon's answer to all these questions is no. For him, scarcity can be measured in only one way—by looking at the price of goods. If the world's scarce resources are being exhausted, their prices

will go up. But, he argued, the real price of most resources has been going steadily down. In relation to our salaries, items such as food, oil, and other energy supplies, and the minerals needed to produce consumer goods, are cheaper now than ever before. Concerning pollution, for Simon, things have never been better. Cities today are far cleaner than the cities of the past, and the environments of industrialized societies are often cleaner than those of developing societies. Indeed it is their higher standard of living that makes them more sensitive to pollution and to demand stronger action on the environment. People, Simon said, are the "ultimate resource," the source of new ideas that have led to the steady improvement in the human condition. Population pressure leads people to develop new and more efficient ways of doing things.

Can we say which side of this debate is right? Not really, but the two protagonists did engage in an interesting contest (Tierney, 1990). In 1980, Simon offered to bet that resources would be more plentiful in 1990, and thus their real price would decline during the 1980s. He challenged opponents to select resources they felt would become scarcer and thus more expensive. Ehrlich could not resist, saying he would "accept Simon's astonishing offer before other greedy people jumped in." He and his associates chose five resources—copper, chrome, nickel, tin, and tungsten—that they felt would appreciate in value over the decade. Who was the winner? Simon, by a clear margin. The real price of all five materials fell during the 1980s, and the same quantities that cost $1000 in 1980 could have been purchased in 1990 for $618. Simon offered the same wager to Ehrlich for the decade of the 1990s, but he declined, still refusing to acknowledge defeat and claiming that Simon was like a man who had just jumped off the roof of the Empire State building. Asked how he felt as he passed the tenth floor, the man replied "just fine so far."

What might Simon reply if Ehrlich had put water on his list?

One other tool demographers use to understand the effects of population age structures is the **dependency ratio**, which relates the number of persons in what are considered the dependent-age categories (under 15 and over 65) to the number in the independent or working-age categories (15–64). Developed for making international comparisons, the measure is less useful in Canada as many in their twenties are still dependent students and most Canadians leave work at an age other than 65. Moreover, it treats children and the elderly as being equivalent, although the direct cost to government for caring for the elderly is much higher than for a child. Nevertheless, the measure gives a reasonable indicator of shifts in the balance between the independent and

dependent parts of our population. The data show that the burden of dependency is relatively low in Canada right now. High fertility rates during the baby boom (many children under age 15) pushed the dependency ratio up during the 1950s and 1960s, but since then it has declined and will remain relatively low until the large baby-boom cohorts begin to swell the ranks of the elderly, around the year 2011. At the same time, the number of persons in the working-age categories will be reduced by the low fertility rates of recent decades. It is the combination of these trends that will put great pressure on governments to provide services to the elderly population, paid for with taxes collected from that diminished labour force.

[Social Trends]

Urbanization in the Developing World: Wrestling the Tiger

While cities in the developed world worry about issues such as tax increases, recycling, and core revitalization, developing world cities are concerned with much more basic dilemmas—most related to their phenomenal growth in recent years.

Consider the case of São Paulo, Brazil, the largest city in South America. Between 1961 and 2001 the municipality of São Paulo tripled in size, from 3.7 million to about ten million, while the greater São Paulo region increased from 4.7 million to over seventeen million. Such rapid growth has given risen to many social problems. One of the most serious of these is poverty. As an industrial and financial centre, São Paulo is the wealthiest city in Brazil (if not all of Latin America). Yet many of its residents survive on very meagre incomes. The median income of male wage earners, for example, is less than $3600, as compared with approximately $29 000 for larger cities in Canada. Some 35 percent of all families subsist on less than $4500, and about 10 percent on less than $1800 per year. A related problem is housing. Not only is household

occupant-density higher in São Paulo than in most Canadian cities, but substandard housing is also a serious problem in many areas. Nearly two million citizens inhabit precarious shacks in sprawling *favelas* spread throughout the city. Over 4000 are without homes altogether (PMSP, 1996: 146–48).

Basic services for the majority of the municipal population are also seriously lacking. In some areas of the city, especially on the periphery, streets are unpaved, and neighbourhoods frequently lack schools and parks. Commuting from outer areas to the city centre and industrial nuclei is also a challenge. The public transportation system is both inexpensive and extensive—well over three billion passengers ride the bus or subway in the municipality of São Paulo each year, compared with about 400 million in Toronto. Service, however, is often sporadic, uncomfortable, time-consuming, and sometimes unsafe.

The quality of policing represents still another concern. Municipal and especially state military police maintain a high visibility, but the crime rate remains

(continued)

staggering. From January to November of 1996, police registered 7171 homicides, 101 700 robberies, and 103 200 auto thefts ("Grande SP registra", 1996). In contrast, except for auto thefts (we have more cars in Canada) similar figures for all of Canada would be only a fraction of these numbers. For example, we have fewer than 1000 murders in any year.

Health care, finally, is seriously inadequate; São Paulo's infant mortality rate is thirty-one per thousand, five times the Canadian rate. Along with a general lack of free public facilities, hospitals and health centres tend to

Source: W.E. Hewitt 2004. Written for this volume.

be concentrated in the city core. A lack of sewers for sanitation in many regions compounds health problems. In the absence of septic tanks or other waste-treatment strategies, sewage on many streets simply flows down open drainage ditches and eventually into nearby streams and rivers. Often children play freely in these areas.

Currently, efforts are being made by the municipal government to improve living conditions for São Paulo's citizens. Given the city's limited resources, however, it may be some time before services and infrastructure can be brought up to developed world standards.

Greater urban density does spare agricultural land from being destroyed and reduces the environmental costs brought by cars and roads. In what other ways is the growth of cities beneficial?

Population in the Twenty-First Century

Demographers do not have a very good record of predictions. Just prior to the baby boom, many observers were convinced population decline was imminent. One of North America's leading demographers, Frank Notestein, writing in 1953, believed it would be sensible to plan for a world population of just over three billion by the year 2000. As we have seen, the true figure is six billion. Thus, it is best to be modest in any forecasts. However, as we

look ahead into the new century, it seems likely that population growth will continue to slow around the globe. All corners of the world have been touched by fertility decline, and past experience suggests that once fertility begins to decline, it seldom changes course. In the currently developed societies, like Italy, Spain, Japan, and Canada, discussion will likely turn more to the question of very low fertility. Experiencing fertility rates well below the level needed to replace the population, people will begin to ask whether this is a problem and if something can be done about it.

[Research Focus]

Your Birth Cohort and You . . .

An economist (Easterlin, 1987) argued that it is an advantage to be born into a small cohort (in other words, during a period of low fertility) and a disadvantage to be born into a large cohort. Being a member of a smaller cohort, he reasoned, means less competition and thus greater opportunity. By contrast, those born when fertility is high—for example, members of the baby-boom cohorts—face

intense competition throughout the life cycle and reduced chances of success. As a result, it may be harder to get accepted into university or a professional school and harder to find a first job. Houses are in greater demand and prices are higher. When members of large cohorts retire, they place a strain on pension systems and may have to get by with a lower pension or delay their age of

(continued)

retirement. Selling all of those houses at about the same time may reduce prices. Members of smaller cohorts, in contrast, benefit from this situation.

Although many believe Easterlin pushed his argument too far, cohort size does influence life chances. At the same time, other observers have noted that large cohort size can also work to a group's advantage by giving its members more political and economic weight within society. Businesses anxious to achieve maximum sales will often tailor their products to meet the demand of the largest group of consumers (Foot, 1998). Also, the politicians, anxious to collect votes, may be willing to support programs designed to appeal to the largest bloc of voters. If true, the "disadvantaged" members of large cohorts may be able to offset part of this disadvantage by using their greater weight in society to change the rules of the game, transferring their disadvantage to the cohorts that follow.

How have your life chances been affected by your birth cohort?

Tremendous progress has been made in the control of disease and mortality and many other important advances may lie ahead. But the saddest story in the early years of the century will be the toll taken by the spread of HIV/AIDS, especially in southern Africa. Many millions more are almost certain to die in the first decades of the century. With slowing population growth and continued population aging, immigration is likely to be the hot political topic. The declining rate of natural increase in countries like Canada means that a larger share of any future population growth will have to come from immigration. The questions of how many immigrants to admit and what types of immigrants to seek will remain on the front page in the years to come, as will questions related to urbanization and especially the unbridled growth within Canada's largest cities.

In Canada, population is now growing slowly. Most women have few children, and life expectancy is rapidly approaching 80 years of age. Demographers expect these patterns to continue, and once the baby-boom generation enters the older age groups, the number of deaths will exceed the number of births in Canada. If Canada's population is to grow in the future, then it will do so as a result of immigration. The distribution of Canada's population is also changing in two important ways. As a nation, we are gradually growing older. Continued low fertility will see this trend continue in the years ahead. And our population is becoming more concentrated in our major cities. The attractions of urban living continue to draw Canadians to the urban centres, leaving much of this very large land very thinly populated.

Summary

In this chapter we discussed the trends in population growth at both the global and national level. Our examination of population change was influenced by demographic transition theory, which sees populations moving from one of high birth and death rates to one in which birth and death rates are low. The economically privileged countries of the world have completed this transition and now experience slow population growth or even decline. In the rest of the world, the transition is continuing and rates of natural increase are beginning to fall. Nevertheless, global population is likely to continue to increase for some time to come and may eventually reach a total of more than nine billion people.

Questions for Review and Critical Thinking

1. Fertility rates are declining or have reached low levels in all major regions of the world. Is there still a role for governments in the area of population policy? Should the Canadian government consider incentives for couples to have more children?

2. With a fertility rate below replacement level, immigration will play a more important role in shaping the future population of Canada. In what ways will the Canadian population in 2050 differ from our population today?

3. Canada's major cities, especially Toronto and Vancouver, continue to grow rapidly, while some

areas, especially in the Atlantic region, are growing very slowly or not at all. What steps could be taken to deal with this uneven distribution of population?

4. If population growth rates continue to decline worldwide, will the importance of demography as a science also diminish? If not, why not?

Key Terms

age-specific death rates, p. 378
age-specific fertility rates, p. 373
cohort measures, p. 374
crude birth rate (CBR), p. 368
crude death rate (CDR), p. 368
demographic transition theory, p. 371
demography, p. 368
dependency ratio, p. 390
expectation of life at birth, p. 378
internal migration, p. 382
international migration, p. 382
life table, p. 378
migration, p. 382
period measures, p. 373
population pyramid, p. 388
positive check, p. 369
preventive check, p. 369
rate of natural increase, p. 370
total fertility rate, p. 373

Suggested Readings

Bélanger, Alain
2003 *Report on the Demographic Situation in Canada 2002.* Ottawa: Statistics Canada.
This annual series provides up-to-the-minute information on Canada's population.

Canadian Social Trends
A quarterly publication of Statistics Canada, it presents short, readable analyses of current social topics with a special focus on social policy.

Foot, David K. (with Daniel Stoffman)
1998 *Boom, Bust and Echo 2000.* Toronto: Macfarlane, Walter, and Ross.
The provocative bestseller that argues "two-thirds of everything" is explained by demographics; no book does a better job of showing the practical importance of studying demography.

McQuillan, Kevin and Zenaida Ravanera (eds.)
2006 *Canada's Changing Families: Implications for Individuals and Society.* Toronto: University of Toronto Press.
An up-to-date collection of articles on the demographic aspects of family change in Canada.

Weeks, John R.
2005 *Population: An Introduction to Concepts and Issues* (9th ed.). Belmont, CA: Wadsworth.
This readable text provides a good introduction to the field of demography while also presenting data on world population trends.

Websites

www.cities.com
Cities.Com
This site is your gateway to the urban world. Choose a city and explore.

www.prb.org
Population Reference Bureau
An excellent site for current world population data, its World Population Data Sheet can be consulted online. It provides current data on fertility, mortality, and population growth for every country in the world.

www.cip-icu.ca/English/home.htm
Canadian Institute of Planners
This site provides information on dimensions and benefits of urban planning in Canada, with links to related sites worldwide.

Key Search Terms

Fertility
Mortality
Migration
Population
Life expectancy
Urbanization

For more study tools to help you with your next exam, be sure to check out the Companion Website at **www.pearsoned.ca/hewitt**, as well as Chapter 16 in your Study Guide.

[17]

social change

edward bell

Introduction

Do you ever think about how the world has changed in the last quarter century? Young adults today may recall that when they were toddlers, parents did not ferry them about in sport-utility vehicles, talk on the telephone while driving, or watch NHL hockey in June. People did not meet in Internet "chat rooms," a majority of medical and law school students were men, and virtually every country in the world was in some sort of political or military alliance with either the United States or what was then the Soviet Union.

Ever wonder *why* things change? Sociologists certainly do. In Chapter 15, Social Movements, you saw that one way to learn about change is to examine how large groups of people try to create or prevent it. In this chapter a somewhat different approach is taken. Instead of focusing on the people and organizations involved in deliberate attempts to produce or hinder change, we shall look at the larger social forces and patterns of interaction that create change unwittingly. We will also take into consideration innovations like new technologies whose impact on change may be profound but unintended.

In Chapter 1 you learned that sociology itself came into being largely as an attempt to understand the tumultuous social changes that began in Europe and North America in the eighteenth century. When sociology was in its infancy, it seemed as if the foundations upon which human societies had been based were collapsing—a new world was being created by industrialization and the rise of popular democracy. It was in the midst of those developments that the sociological study of social change began.

Early sociologists, like their present-day counterparts, disagreed over where the changes were leading and what was causing them. In this chapter you will have a chance to consider a variety of arguments made by both classical and contemporary sociologists concerning those vast changes. You will also take a look at how sociologists make sense of changes unique to the present era. Another thing you will learn is that many of the scholarly debates about social change have not been resolved. This chapter will not attempt to settle those debates, but it will provide you with an introduction to the key issues involved and offer some insights on how to think about them *sociologically*.

You will find that the study of social change, perhaps more than any other area of sociology, requires a comparative and international orientation. For instance, although industrialization and democratization are important innovations, they are still largely absent in many parts of the world, and where present affect different cultures in different ways. You will also learn that some very important changes occurred in human societies thousands of years ago. It will be worthwhile to find out about those changes because in many ways people are still struggling to adapt to them. We use the term **cultural lag** to describe problems in this adaptation, as when particular aspects of a culture have not caught up with the changes in other parts of that same society. The extended time frame will also bring into focus the scope and pervasiveness of change in human societies and help to illustrate how certain sociological models and theories can be applied to any historical era.

We shall begin our discussion of social change by taking a look at early human society and how it evolved, over time, into today's forms. Then we shall consider some theories that seek to explain the fundamental changes that occurred over that time. We shall also discuss how Western industrialized countries like Canada have changed in recent decades, and examine the emerging relationship between those societies and less economically developed nations. Since social change is an ongoing process, we shall conclude with some thoughts on what the future may hold for Canada and other countries.

Early Societies and the Beginnings of Social Change

Our species, *Homo sapiens*, has been around in its current form for at least 40 000 years (Chirot, 1994: 1; Diamond, 1997: 35–41). Genetically and physiologically speaking, we have changed very little over those 400 centuries. It follows then, that the extensive changes in the human condition that took place over this period cannot be attributed to human genetic change—we simply do not evolve that quickly (recall Chapter 4, Socialization). Other causes must be considered to determine what happened.

Hunting and gathering societies

For most of their time on earth, humans lived in hunting and gathering societies, societies that survived by

For most of the time they have spent on earth, humans have lived in hunting and gathering societies. The !Kung San of Botswana still do.

hunting wild game and gathering edible plants. These early societies did not grow their own crops or raise livestock. It has only been since about 8000 BCE that humankind has engaged in farming to any significant degree.

What was life like in this original type of human grouping? There was a diversity of experiences and cultures among foraging peoples, much of it created in response to variations in the biophysical environment such as the climate, the animal and plant life available, and the topography. Some societies adapted to harsh environments like deserts or frigid regions, while others lived in more hospitable surroundings like tropical islands or lush rainforests. Some led desperate, precarious lives; others did not have to work very hard to survive.

Although there was considerable diversity among hunting and gathering societies, they were similar in certain ways. For instance, individual groups or bands tended to be small, on average about forty or fifty people. They were nomadic, usually following a circuitous route, moving when the food supply became depleted.

These people were deeply spiritual, and shared key resources among the entire group. Many practised abortion and infanticide, and domestic violence and homicide were not unheard of.

Hunting and gathering societies were also characterized by a division of labour based on gender. By and large, women did the gathering of plant products and the rearing of young children, men the hunting. Men tended to be dominant, although there was a rough equality between the sexes. Shostak states that among the !Kung San of Botswana:

> Women's status in the community is high and their influence considerable. They are often prominent in major family and band decisions, such as where and when to move and whom their children will marry. Many also share core leadership in a band and ownership of water holes and foraging areas. (1983 [1981]: 13)

In many ways foraging peoples were a lot like us. They were just as intelligent and curious. They had marriage ceremonies and elaborate kinship structures, loved their children, and liked to laugh, sing, and dance. A good story was appreciated, and the best storytellers enjoyed high prestige. But there were also some fundamental differences between hunting and gathering societies and our own. Some people claim that even after thousands of years of existence as non-foraging societies, modern societies still have not adequately adjusted to the "new" conditions created by their departure from a foraging life. For one thing, there are now states to contend with. The **state**, as defined by Weber, refers to the organization that has a monopoly on the legitimate use of force. Foraging peoples had no formal state. Group decisions were vigorously debated by all who cared to join in, and although the recommendations of some people carried more weight than others, little coercion was applied to dissidents. For example, those who disagreed over the timing or direction of the next migration were free to strike out on their own.

Another difference between hunting and gathering societies and our own is that in our society, certain groups may acquire more power or wealth than others, and may even exploit people. The absence of these forms of inequality and exploitation among hunter-gatherers was due in part to the fact that these societies had almost no surplus production; once everyone was fed, there was virtually no wealth left over to hoard. With no surplus production, there can be no material inequality or exploitation. Another factor was equal access to weapons, which prevented one faction from controlling another (Nolan and Lenski, 2006: 91–93).

Farming societies

Exploitation and pronounced inequalities had their origins in farming societies, first formed some 10 000 years ago. Farming created a sustained economic surplus, which in turn gave rise to the issue of who would have access to the surplus, an issue that remains with us to this day. In the first farming societies, which developed in the Middle East in places like Mesopotamia and Egypt, most of the surplus went to the state and the groups that controlled it. This was the beginning of social stratification in material possessions (economic inequality), a topic introduced in Chapter 6, Social Inequality.

Those who have surplus production at their disposal are able to use some of it to bolster their power. As farming technologies improved and the surplus increased, the people in control of the state became very powerful, usually creating a military organization to protect and further their interests. This greatly magnified a second dimension of social stratification: inequality of power. The historic role of the state in creating and maintaining inequality illustrates the pivotal role it can play in social change, a notion further explored later in this chapter.

The domination of one group by another within farming societies was made more effective once metals were produced and used to make weapons. In early farming societies, only the army had metal weapons, which made it relatively easy for rulers to dominate their people (Nolan and Lenski, 2006: 120–23). But states rarely rely on brute force alone to establish and maintain dominance; they usually make some claim to legitimacy. In early farming societies, state legitimacy derived in part from religious beliefs and ideologies that maintained that the ruler was a god or at least in some special relationship with a god or gods. In feudal Europe, monarchs maintained that they ruled by God's will.

The advent of metal weapons contributed to another kind of domination: **imperialism**, the control or exploitation of one society by another, usually by conquest. Although imperialism is often thought of as a European or American phenomenon, there were indigenous imperialists in the Middle East, Asia,

Africa, and the Americas long before Europe or the United States emerged as world powers.

The existence of imperialism sheds light on another important point. To understand social change, one must recognize that societies rarely live in isolation from one another. There have always been regional systems of societies, and for several centuries now a world system of societies has been in existence. In these systems, a change in one society often leads to a change in another. The shift to farming by some hunter-gatherers, for example, changed the local ecosystem, often causing the remaining foragers to seek new habitats. And throughout human history it has been very common for one society to absorb or annihilate another. For example, the indigenous and peaceful Arawaks of Barbados were conquered and destroyed by the warlike Caribs, who practised cannibalism. The Caribs were, in turn, driven from Barbados by the Spanish, who later enslaved them (Hoyos, 1978: 1–13). This sort of scenario has been played out countless times all over the world.

Another important change in farming societies, in particular after the invention of the plough, was a decline in the status of women. In hunting and gathering societies, women played a central role in food production, in some cases providing over half the caloric intake of the society (Lee, 1979: 262). In horticultural societies (societies that grow their own food but do not use ploughs), women were usually responsible for the planting, tending, and harvesting of crops, with men doing only the initial task of clearing the land. In both types of societies women enjoyed high status. Once the plough was invented, farming became more of a male endeavour, with men working the ploughs and taking over responsibility for other important aspects of food production. Women's status declined as their role in the productive process was marginalized. As we shall see later in this chapter, it was only with the advent of industrialization many centuries later that women's status began to improve (see Chapter 7, Gender Relations).

The pre-eminence of farming societies lasted until about 1800. The legacies of the ancient Greeks and Romans, the medieval European societies, and the farming societies of the Middle East, Asia, Africa, and the Americas are still with us today. In addition to creating new forms of inequality and dominance, they bequeathed to humanity the major world religions and the cultural and scientific foundations of the modern age.

The modern era

Machines fuelled by inanimate energy sources were first used for commercial purposes in the textile industry in Britain in the late eighteenth century. As the Industrial Revolution progressed, machine production was used for a variety of tasks in an increasing number of societies. The Revolution would eventually transform many countries from agrarian nations into industrial ones, a transformation that reshaped all aspects of their societies. Gender relations, the nature of work, the family structure, race relations, and politics, to name just a few things, would never be the same again.

Some of the foundations of modern ways of thinking can also be traced to the developments of the eighteenth century. This was the century of the **Enlightenment** wherein many of the doctrines of the agrarian age were challenged, especially those relating to the forms of domination prevalent at the time. Enlightenment thinkers viewed skepticism as a good thing, saw reason and observation as the best means to acquire knowledge, and proclaimed that people should not be persecuted for what they say or believe, ideas that are still popular today. The American and French Revolutions, inspired in part by Enlightenment philosophies, challenged the right of hereditary monarchs to rule over their subjects and championed a belief in social equality. Such ideals provided the inspiration for many of the changes that would take place in the next two centuries, although they were rarely put into practice at the time.

The advent of industrialization and modern capitalism drastically altered the world system of societies and many of the characteristics of the societies within it. By the middle of the nineteenth century, Marx and Engels were well aware of the scope and depth of the social change that had occurred in the wake of modern capitalism. In 1848 they wrote that the modern bourgeoisie

> was the first to show what man's activity can bring about. It has accomplished wonders far surpassing Egyptian pyramids, Roman aqueducts, and Gothic cathedrals; it has conducted expeditions that put in the shade all former Exoduses of nations and crusades. (Marx and Engels, 1979 [1848]: 83)

Marx and Engels also offered an influential theory of social change, which is considered in the next section.

[Research Focus]

Two Perspectives on Change in Early Societies

As in modern societies, the conflict experienced by hunting-gathering and farming societies often resulted in change. Sometimes the conflict and changes were extreme, as in the instances in which one society absorbed or conquered another. The Romans, for example, built a huge empire through conquest, which destroyed or radically altered the lives of the vanquished. Other forms of conflict led to less drastic changes, as when one hunting and gathering society drove another out of a given territory, or when clashes between medieval lords and their monarch resulted in constitutional change. When you are thinking about a social change in any society, it would be worthwhile to ask yourself, "Was this change a result of conflict? If so, what was at stake? Who were the major players? How did one side manage to prevail over the other?" A related question, one often posed by conflict sociologists, is, "Who benefits from this change?" Seeking answers to such questions is one way to think about social change sociologically, using the conflict perspective.

The functionalist perspective provides another useful way to make sense of change. Functionalists tend to view change as gradual or incremental, usually focusing on how a particular society became increasingly differentiated, and how the growing division of labour met some kind of need. For example, the transition from hunting-gathering to farming, a gradual process that may have taken thousands of years, satisfied a need for a greater food supply. Farming produced an economic surplus, which made occupational specialization possible; not everyone had to be a farmer. Artisans, military personnel, scribes, and other occupational groups emerged, which in turn contributed to the development of towns and cities. These were profound changes to human societies, changes that cannot be directly attributed to conflict. Functionalist approaches can sometimes be used in conjunction with, or in addition to, the conflict approach, as when considering which groups in society benefited most from the gradual increase in wealth in agrarian societies.

How might each of the approaches described above be applied to the issue of human cloning?

How were the complex societies of today created? What were the consequences of that transformation? In trying to answer these and other related questions, social scientists have formulated a number of formal theories of social change, to which we now turn.

Theories of Social Change

Evolutionism

Evolutionism and evolutionary theories of change have a long history in sociology, a history that pre-dates Darwin (Sztompka, 1993: 100). Herbert Spencer (1820–1903), who coined the term "survival of the fittest" and popularized the term "evolution," presented a theory of societal evolution that held sway among English-speaking social scientists from the late nineteenth century until the 1930s (Hamilton, 1996: 206). Darwin was very impressed with Spencer's sociological writings and publicly acknowledged his influence on

his own theories (Weinstein, 1997: 28), once remarking that Spencer is "about a dozen times my superior" (Carneiro, 1967: ix).

Spencer wrote that human societies evolve from small, disjointed, undifferentiated groups of people into larger entities composed of heterogeneous, interdependent parts in a manner analogous to the way in which biological organisms develop from single cells into complex organic systems. For example, he noted that hunting and gathering societies (which, as we have seen, have a minimal division of labour) may evolve into societies having specialized, interrelated institutions performing educational, political, kinship, religious, economic, or other functions. This he compared to the development of an organism from a single cell into a creature having interdependent organs such as a brain, heart, lungs, and so on.

The development of each aspect of society is explained in terms of the function it fulfills, in particular how it enhances the society's survival potential. For instance, Spencer argued that the form of marriage a particular society favours will be one that maximizes the likelihood that the society will survive (see Chapter 10, Families). Non-industrial societies that frequently engaged in war and sustained heavy losses of soldiers tended to have more women than men, which made polygyny an attractive option; it maximized the society's reproductive potential (all women could have a partner) and offered some care for widows and orphans. The monogamy now widely practised in industrial societies came into being in part because over the centuries sex ratios became relatively even. If a large number of men in industrial societies practised polygyny, many others would be unable to find a wife, a situation not conducive to social peace or societal survival.

For Spencer, the growing differentiation and integration in human societies results primarily from conflict. Initially at least, societies change and adapt to protect themselves from attack or to go on the offensive themselves. Although he loathed war and the social formations and personality traits that accompany it, Spencer believed that civilization would not have evolved without it. He argued that over the centuries societies have increased in size and complexity by conquering other societies and incorporating them into their own.

In addition to creating societies of increased size and complexity, war is said to be conducive to cooperation within a society, as under the conditions of war all must unite in order to avoid annihilation. For Spencer, it was the increased size, complexity, and internal cooperation generated by war that creates civilization. Nonetheless, he looked forward to the day when war would be no more, believing that such a day will arrive if all societies reach an advanced stage of evolution. As the foregoing discussion illustrates, Spencer's approach to social change incorporated both the functionalist and conflict perspectives.

With an eye to the future, Spencer predicted that some industrial societies would evolve to the point where engaging in the "higher activities" would be the prime focus of people's lives, a foreshadowing of the "postmaterialism" that would emerge almost a century later. These future societies will invert the industrial dogma that "life is for work" into the belief that "work is for life" (Spencer, 1898: 575). Spencer was reluctant to elaborate on this idea, but observed in the industrial-capitalist societies of his time an increasing number of organizations and institutions devoted to artistic and intellectual development. He did not have an overly optimistic outlook, however, as he believed that in addition to progress, a worsening of conditions was not only possible in any given society but was as likely to occur as progress. To minimize the chances of regress, he favoured minimal powers for the state, arguing that the greatest good would result if the natural evolutionary process were allowed to run its course without interference. He believed that there was little people could do to improve the world, but much they could do to foul it up. Spencer was thus the antithesis of the sociologist as "activist," a matter discussed below.

Classical evolutionists like Spencer have been subject to criticism. For one thing, their society-as-organism metaphor has been called into question. Critics claim that there is just too much inequality, conflict, disruption, strife, and suffering within modern societies to justify a model that assumes that the various organs or parts of society interact in a harmonious, integrated fashion. Also, the implication that some societies are superior to others is seen as offensive and ethnocentric.

Nevertheless, evolutionary theory has enjoyed a resurgence in recent decades. Often termed "neo-evolutionary theory," the contemporary version of this approach maintains that an evolutionary model can be devised to explain social change without the shortcomings of the original. Neo-evolutionists do not maintain that highly industrialized societies are morally, intellectually, or esthetically superior to any other kind of society. The new perspective is also based on far more archaeological and historical data than the nineteenth-century variant (Lenski, 1976: 560–61).

An example of a neo-evolutionary approach is Lenski's **ecological-evolutionary theory** (Lenski, 1966; Nolan and Lenski, 2006). This view maintains that a society is profoundly influenced by its *subsistence technology*, the technology it uses to acquire the basic necessities of life. The theory claims that societies evolve as their subsistence technologies become more sophisticated. For example, as a society shifts from hunting-gathering technology to horticultural technology, or from agrarian to industrial technology, societal characteristics like the status of women, population size, the level of urbanization, the degree of stratification, and kinship patterns are drastically altered. Human history is divided into four major epochs, according to the type of society politically and militarily dominant at the time: the hunting and gathering era (human origins to about 8000 BCE); the horticultural era (roughly 8000–3000 BCE); the agrarian age (about 3000 BCE–1800 CE); and the industrial age (about 1800 to the present) (Nolan and Lenski, 2006: 66).

Ecological-evolutionary theory also maintains that societies are influenced by their biophysical and social *environments* in important ways. The social environment refers to all societies that have an effect on a given society. The effect of the social environment can range from minimal to severe, the last including the destruction of one society by another. This perspective thus incorporates the idea that regional and later world systems of societies developed and had an important impact on human history. To illustrate the profound influence that systems of societies can have, Lenski pointed out that the vast majority of human societies that ever existed are now *extinct*. The extinct societies changed very little over their existence and as a result either perished as the biophysical environment changed, or were absorbed or destroyed by other societies. In keeping with the evolutionary model, in particular the idea of natural selection, he suggested that societies having large populations, complex social structures, and powerful military organizations have higher survival potential than those

lacking those traits, just as in the biotic world animals having certain characteristics—such as white fur in northerly regions—are more likely to survive.

Neo-evolutionists are careful not to take the comparison with biological evolution too far; the best spell out in detail how social evolution differs from its biological cousin. For instance, it is acknowledged that social evolution results in *fewer*, more *similar* societies, whereas biological evolution produces an *increasing number* of *highly differentiated* life forms. In biological evolution, highly complex species often coexist with the less complex, as when micro-organisms inhabit the human body. But in the social world, less complex societies usually do not fare well amid more complex ones. Also, because social change can result from **diffusion**, the adoption of an innovation by a society that did not create it, important changes can spread rather quickly. The use of computers, for example, spread rapidly from the United States to hundreds of other societies, including Canada. In nature, physical evolution involves genetic mutation, which can take a very long time. As noted above, our species has not undergone discernible genetic change in over 40 000 years.

[Research Focus]

Ecological-Evolutionary Theory: A Canadian Illustration

Many studies from different parts of the world have shown that societies relying on horticulture (the cultivation of plants without the use of the plough) have social characteristics very different from those found in hunting and gathering societies, the societal type from which they usually evolve. Horticultural societies tend to have larger populations, more permanent settlements, more material possessions, greater social stratification, and a greater propensity to engage in warfare than hunting and gathering societies. They are also more likely to be matrilineal (tracing descent through the female line).

This pattern appears to hold true for prehistoric horticulturalists in Canada. There is evidence that the

Iroquoian peoples, a matrilineal tribe that lived in an area stretching from southwestern Ontario to the St. Lawrence River valley, grew maize 1500 years ago, and several centuries later supplemented this with beans and squash. Over time, horticulture replaced hunting and gathering to become their primary mode of subsistence. As in other societies that underwent this transition, the Iroquoian population increased—the region in which they lived had the highest population density of any Aboriginal area in Canada. The Iroquois also became less nomadic, living in relatively permanent villages that sometimes contained over 2000 people. The advent of horticulture also appears to have increased the amount of warfare they waged.

Source: Entries "Iroquois," "Longhouse," and "Prehistory" in *The Canadian Encyclopedia* (2nd ed.). Edmonton: Hurtig, 1988.

This illustration suggests that people's behaviour is largely dependent on their society's subsistence technology. How will the moving of manufacturing from Canada to cheaper sites change the lives of Canadians?

A theory of Canadian development that in some ways parallels ecological-evolutionary theory, in particular its emphasis on the biophysical and social environment, is Innis's **staples thesis** (1956: 383–402; 1986 [1950]: 2–4). Innis argued that the economic, political, and cultural formation of Canada was shaped by its geography and the natural resources or "staples" available for export. The export of fish, furs, lumber, wheat, minerals, and energy products to more highly developed economies—France, then Great Britain, then the United States—formed the basis of the Canadian economy and strongly influenced settlement patterns, communications networks, and our political history. For instance, Innis maintained that "the northern half of North America remained British [after the American Revolution] because of the importance of fur as a staple product" (Innis, 1956: 391). Our economy at the time of the Revolution, he observed, was centred on the export of fur to Great Britain in exchange for manufactured goods; severing ties with Britain would have put that trading relationship in jeopardy.

"Each staple in its turn left its stamp," Innis wrote, "and the shift to new staples invariably produced periods of crisis in which adjustments in the old structure were painfully made, and a new pattern created in relation to a new staple" (1986 [1950]: 3). He was also mindful of the central role indigenous peoples played in the formation of Canada, especially through the fur trade: "We have not yet realized that the Indian and his culture were fundamental to the growth of Canadian institutions" (Innis, 1956: 392). An abiding theme of his work is that a reliance on the export of raw materials throughout our history limited Canadian development and made Canada vulnerable to the shifting needs and demands of more populous and developed foreign metropolitan centres.

Developmental theories

Another group of social scientists maintains that human societies develop through a series of stages, although they do not employ all of the arguments offered by the evolutionists. For example, Auguste Comte (1798–1857), the first person to call himself a sociologist, identified three stages that he believed all societies go through: the theological, the metaphysical, and the scientific or "positive" (Lauer, 1982: 51–55). The stages are based on the predominant way in which knowledge is sought; each approach to knowledge is said to create a certain kind of

society or social order. In the theological phase, explanations for physical and social phenomena are sought in the realm of the supernatural. In the metaphysical, people look for explanations in the natural world, using reason to formulate theories of abstract forces. Finally, in the positive period reason is coupled with the systematic observation of science to produce knowledge. Like most nineteenth-century thinkers Comte believed in *progress*, the notion that social change ultimately leads to improved social conditions. For Comte, the metaphysical and positive stages represented successively higher forms of civilization; progress occurs as societies enter a higher phase. And like most thinkers using the developmental paradigm, he maintained that social change characteristically occurs gradually and incrementally.

As you learned in Chapter 1, Comte believed that sociologists would form a sort of priesthood that would guide societies through the transition to the positive state by proposing solutions to social problems and teaching people to think scientifically. This illustrates that from the beginnings of the discipline, some sociologists not only *analyzed* social change but also viewed themselves as *agents* of change. As you study change, try to determine whether the author whose works you are reading advocates change of some sort. Most authors writing on the topic present either an implicit or explicit program for social change.

Another early sociologist using the idea of phases of social development was Tönnies, who in the 1880s introduced the concepts *Gemeinschaft* and *Gesellschaft*. **Gemeinschaft**, which means "community," refers to the old agrarian social setting in which people lived in small communities or villages close to their kin and friends, knew their neighbours well, and generally felt a sense of belonging and interdependence. In this sort of milieu, social norms are fairly clear and people tend to obey them. **Gesellschaft**, which means "society" or "association," describes the social situation that Tönnies believed characterizes large cities once capitalist development has taken place. Here things are more impersonal; relationships and exchanges outside kin groups and close friends tend to lack warmth and intimacy, and the interdependence and community spirit of traditional life are replaced with the pursuit of narrow self-interest. Not surprisingly, Tönnies held that deviance is more common in modern societies. Indeed, Tönnies was one of very few nineteenth-century thinkers who had grave misgivings about what the future would hold for members of industrial societies. Most writers, philosophers, social scientists, and natural scientists of the day believed in progress. It was not until the twentieth century that widespread disillusionment with modernity and its prospects arose (Sztompka, 1993: 24–27).

About a decade after Tönnies drew his conclusions on the effects of industrialization, Durkheim offered a somewhat similar if more optimistic assessment. In preindustrial societies, Durkheim noted, there is minimal division of labour; people's tasks in the economy tend to be similar to those of other people of the same gender. This creates strong bonds between the members of a society and near unanimity on the appropriateness

Conflict and Change in Canada

The conflict approach to social change, which maintains that change often has its origins in social conflict of some kind, is a fruitful perspective for understanding change in Canadian society. Here are some examples of how conflict led to change in Canada:

1. *The conquest of New France, 1759.* With New France's defeat by British forces, Canada embarked on a long history of cultural-linguistic dualism that is evident today in official bilingualism and the Quebec independence movement. One immediate result of the conquest was a greatly increased British presence in the higher echelons of business and government in the former French colony. Another was the marginalization of several Native peoples who after the conquest were no longer needed as allies and warriors in British-French conflicts. The conquest also influenced the American Revolution, as the withdrawal of the French army meant that the American colonies no longer needed British protection from French forces. This gave the Americans one less reason to remain loyal to Britain. Needless to say, American independence has had a profound effect on Canada over the past two centuries.

2. *World War I.* Desmond Morton, a Canadian historian, wrote that this conflict changed almost every facet of Canadian life. For example, women's voting rights, which were won at the federal level in 1918, grew out of the compelling argument that the service, sacrifice, and competence women showed during the war made them deserving of the vote. Canadian independence

from Britain was taken a step further by the war effort, as the Canadian military became increasingly autonomous and Canada was granted a seat in the League of Nations. The war worsened ethnic tensions between British Canadians and French Canadians, who disagreed over wartime policies such as conscription. World War I also saw the introduction of a new form of government revenue—income tax.

3. *Conflict between employees and employers.* The political rights, wages, working conditions, and benefits that Canadian working people have today are in many ways a result of a long series of conflicts between employees and employers (see also Chapter 14, Organizations and Work). In the nineteenth century, the Nine Hour movement fought to have the working day reduced from up to twelve hours down to nine. In 1894 the federal government established Labour Day after decades of labour unrest. By 1944, after many years of struggle, employers were required by law to recognize the union chosen by their employees. In the immediate post-war period, grievance procedures and vacation pay were instituted, another culmination of a long series of conflicts. More recent conflict has resulted in the establishment of maternity leave.

4. *The terrorist attacks of September 11, 2001.* Although the attacks did not take place in Canada, they caused Canadians to rethink their military strategies and to revise security procedures at airports. They also made crossing the border into the United States more difficult and time-consuming.

Canada fought alongside the U.S. in the Korean War of the early 1950s. Were there any significant changes after that lesser-known conflict?

of social norms, especially those rooted in religion. He called this similarity-based unity **mechanical solidarity**.

Durkheim drew attention to the changes that follow industrialization. An expanded division of labour, especially in urban areas, creates different experiences and perceptions, which tend to divide people. For example, the world-view of a nurse may be quite different from that of a stockbroker. Modern cities attract people from diverse cultural backgrounds, which also detracts from a uniform view of life. Durkheim claimed that, under these circumstances, the legitimacy of traditional norms may be challenged or the norms may become ill-defined, a condition referred to as **anomie**. Deviance, he argued, becomes more prevalent as anomic conditions set in (recall Chapter 5, Deviance).

As noted, Durkheim was less pessimistic about how Western societies were evolving than Tönnies, who viewed modernity in decidedly negative terms. For Durkheim there was always the possibility that **organic solidarity**, a solidarity based on the complementarity or interdependence of occupational positions, would hold modern societies together and lead to social progress. For instance, the stockbroker may fall ill and discover the value of the nurse, and the nurse may come to appreciate the stockbroker's contribution to the economic development needed to build and fund hospitals. Durkheim claimed that awareness of this sort of interdependence can unify a society and contribute to genuine social improvement.

Historical materialism

Another approach to social change is **historical materialism**. The name derives from the fact that its proponents maintain that material (usually economic) factors are the engine of change. Culture, ideas, spiritual forces, religious beliefs, and all other non-material phenomena are considered to be much less important influences. This view is exemplified in a famous statement made by Marx.

> The mode of production of material life conditions the general process of social, political, and intellectual life. It is not the consciousness of men that determines their existence, but their social existence determines their consciousness. (1970 [1859]: 20–21)

Marx and his collaborator Engels have been the most influential advocates of historical materialism (see also Chapter 6, Social Inequality). The approach they take is **dialectical**, one that sees in everything that exists its built-in antithesis and thus a transformation into a new thesis, which in turn has its antithesis, etc. Societies to them are constantly changing, and all societies (with the one important exception of future communist societies) contain conflicts and tensions that eventually lead to their demise. For example, they believed that capitalist society, like all previous social formations, contains the seeds of its own destruction. Their view of change also assumed that the social transformation that occurs is not random or arbitrary, but instead results in higher forms of social organization, and that each new form makes the next one possible.

Marx and Engels divided human history into several periods or epochs, defined according to the way in which economic production is conducted. For example, they described ancient, feudal, and capitalist epochs. They argued that the mode of production largely determines what form the other aspects of the society will take, and that if the mode of production changes, all the other facets of the society will change in a dramatic, fundamental way. For instance, if the agrarian mode of production characteristic of the Middle Ages is replaced by industrial capitalism, medieval culture collapses. Gone are such things as the divine right of kings, the belief that the aristocracy is the natural ruling class, and the notion that one cannot escape one's station in life. In its place comes capitalist culture: ideological support for open markets and free trade, a devotion to material things and those who acquire them, the belief that capitalist society is the best possible society, and so on. Marx and Engels explained culture as follows.

> The ideas of the ruling class are in every epoch the ruling ideas, i.e., the class that is the ruling *material* force of society, is at the same time its ruling *intellectual* force. The class that has the means of material production at its disposal, has control at the same time over the means of mental production . . . [T]he ruling ideas are nothing more than the ideal expression of the dominant material relationships. (1973 [1846]: 64)

For Marx and Engels, culture in the broad sense is not neutral, but instead justifies the wealth and power enjoyed by the dominant classes. For example, they argued that capitalist culture is deliberately uncritical of how rich people acquire their wealth and views the poor as incompetent or lazy.

The radical change that accompanies a new mode of production comes about through *revolution*. It is through revolution that a new epoch is created. Thus, unlike evolutionary or developmental theorists who claim that societal change usually occurs in a gradual, almost imperceptible way, Marx and Engels maintained that sharp, sudden breaks with the past can occur.

Revolution is said to come about through class conflict. This kind of conflict is so central to their theory of social change that they maintained that the "history of all hitherto existing society is the history of class struggles" (Marx and Engels, 1979 [1848]: 79). The clashes between classes are said to be "uninterrupted," a "now hidden, now open fight." Class conflict ends "either in a revolutionary reconstitution of society at large, or in the common ruin of the contending classes." Marx and Engels contended that to understand any era, one must examine the configuration of classes present and try to determine how the most powerful ones dominate and exploit the others, as this will provide clues about the prevailing form of class conflict and the revolution to come.

Marx and Engels claimed that class polarization would occur in modern capitalist societies (see Chapter 6, Social Inequality). While in the medieval epoch, the aristocracy, local lords, vassals, guild-masters, journeymen, serfs, and others made up the class structure, in the modern capitalist era that followed, the class system would be greatly simplified. Instead of the wide assortment of classes found in medieval times, "society as a whole is more and more splitting up into two hostile camps, into two great classes facing each other: Bourgeoisie and Proletariat" (Marx and Engels, 1979 [1848]: 80). Marx and Engels also described a lower middle class—small tradespeople, shopkeepers, peasants and so on—but this class is destined to "sink gradually into the proletariat" (Marx and Engels, 1979 [1848]: 88), leaving only an expanding, wretched proletariat and an increasingly insecure bourgeoisie to battle it out in a socialist revolution.

Marx and Engels suggested that, in the modern capitalist era, society is splitting more and more into two hostile camps—the bourgeoisie and the proletariat.

The final epoch, they believed, would be the communist epoch, a time when all productive property would be owned by society at large rather than private individuals. Although they had very little to say about what life would be like in this epoch, they implied that it would be free of major conflict, people would have an opportunity to cultivate their true selves, and the state would be very weak. Ironically, they hinted at a state of affairs that bears some resemblance to the future hoped for by Spencer. Marx and Engels also shared with Spencer the popular nineteenth-century belief that violence and struggle can have beneficial results. But unlike Spencer, Marx and Engels maintained that social activism can help to bring about better conditions. They claimed that it is not enough to understand society—one must also change it.

Many writers over the years have offered criticisms of Marx and Engels' theory of social change. Few social scientists today, for example, expect a socialist revolution in advanced capitalist countries. Critics also point out that the middle class did not sink into the proletariat, and that the collapse of communism suggests that their view of the future was somewhat misguided. Marx and Engels remain respected figures in the discipline, but most feel that some modification of their position is in order.

The Weber thesis

Perhaps the best-known challenge to historical materialism written by a sociologist is Weber's *The Protestant Ethic and the Spirit of Capitalism* (1930 [1904–5]), although confronting "the ghost of Karl Marx" was not his only motivation for writing the book (Hamilton, 1996: 104–6). According to Weber, the notion that change results primarily from economic factors does not provide a complete explanation of social transformation. A more comprehensive account would show how both material factors and culture or ideas interact to produce change. The change he sought to explain was the rise of modern capitalism, a phenomenon that, as we have seen, set in motion a wide range of developments. Weber maintained that even with the requisite technology, markets, banking system, and so on, capitalism would not have developed when and as it did had the necessary cultural characteristics not been present. Those cultural attributes, he suggested, were provided by Calvinism, a Protestant movement formed in Western Europe in the sixteenth century. Weber's argument linking Calvinism

with the development of capitalism was discussed in Chapter 11, Religion.

Although Weber's thesis enjoys wide popularity in sociological circles, a number of scholars have raised questions concerning the evidence (or lack thereof) he offered to substantiate his claims (see Hamilton, 1996: ch. 3; Stark, 2005: xi–xii, 62, 230–31). According to Hamilton, the Weber thesis is just that—a thesis—not a proven account. Hamilton showed that several of Weber's key points linking Calvinism with the development of capitalism are open to challenge.

Our discussion of historical materialism and *The Protestant Ethic* (as well as the criticism made of these positions) illustrates how sociologists can disagree about the influence that material factors and culture have on social change. When thinking about a particular social change, it would be worthwhile to keep this debate in mind.

The state theory of modernization

Another theory offered to explain the rise of capitalism and the broad social changes that accompanied its development is the **state theory of modernization**. According to this theory, the reason why some countries have become wealthy, industrialized nations and others have not is because despotic governments thwarted development in the latter. This view holds that if people are free to produce and exchange goods and services without fear of confiscation, excessive taxation, or other forms of state interference, they will, by pursuing their self-interest, increase the overall wealth of the society and produce a dynamic science and technology sector. It is claimed that the potential for such development has existed for centuries, but the norm for most farming societies since at least the early Middle Ages has been state suppression of economic and intellectual initiative (Chirot, 1986: 14–15).

Why would rulers in agrarian societies not allow people to freely produce and exchange goods, services, and ideas? First of all, it is important to recognize that agrarian rulers probably had no idea of the enormity of the changes they were preventing; it was impossible for them to envision the transformation that would have occurred over the long run had they acted differently. They were simply acting in what they perceived to be their self-interest—expropriation and high taxation produced revenues that were usually sufficient to maintain their place in society. Also, restricting economic activity prevented competing power bases from developing that might challenge their authority or even destroy their way of life. In addition, the dominant ideologies usually legitimized and supported their rule. To allow open intellectual discourse would leave the official justification for the regime open to challenge.

To illustrate the validity of the state theory of modernization, scholars adopting this perspective have compared the role of the state in various agrarian societies with what happened in Western Europe in recent centuries. McNeill (1982: 25–33) described how a number of privately owned and operated smelters producing iron and steel were constructed in the Chinese provinces of Honan and Hopei around 1000 CE. The smelters were so productive that they made more iron in the year 1078 than England and Wales did in 1788 in the early stages of the Industrial Revolution. The smelters were also quite profitable. They enriched the owners and provided employment for hundreds of workers. However, Chinese government officials tightly controlled the sale of iron weapons, had a long-standing policy of heavily taxing iron production, and in 1083 monopolized the distribution of iron tools. As a result, goods made of iron were sold at artificially high prices, which may have restricted civilian access to them and prevented a further expansion of production. By the twelfth century, iron and steel production had declined precipitously. Although the historical record is not complete enough to reveal exactly what caused either the boom in iron and steel products or its deterioration, McNeill (1982: 33) stated that

> . . . governmental policy was always critically important. The distrust and suspicion with which officials habitually viewed successful entrepreneurs meant that any undertaking risked being taken over as a state monopoly. Alternatively, it could be subject to taxes and officially imposed prices that made the maintenance of existing levels of operation impossible.

Chirot made a similar argument, claiming that if the Ming and Ch'ing Dynasties had not exerted their dominance over China, the Chinese rather than Western Europeans would have been the first to industrialize on a large scale (1986: 15).

How then was the old agrarian practice of state suppression of economic and intellectual affairs broken by the Europeans? Why were they the first to industrialize, rather than the Chinese, the Islamic empires, or some other group? According to Chirot (1986: ch. 2), geographical and political factors were crucial. Western Europe has many small river valleys, which made communication and the conquering of large empires difficult, a situation rather different from China and other non-Western European areas. Many small, independent principalities emerged and, after the eleventh century, competed with each other economically and intellectually. The principalities allowed freedom of movement such that those fleeing religious or intellectual oppression or overtaxation could go from one district to another. This gave people with innovative ideas and practices some chance of survival. In addition, conflicts among the four most powerful groups in society—the monarch, local lords, urban merchants and artisans, and the Church—were such that no single faction could completely control the other three. The urban dwellers often supported the monarch in order to escape the domination of local lords, who were prone to overtax them. To gain the favour of the urban classes, monarchs were less controlling and confiscatory toward them, awakening to the fact that it was in the crown's interests to have a well-off group of merchants from which it could draw taxes on a regular basis.

According to scholars taking this perspective, the stalemate that existed among these four contending groups in Western European societies, in particular the inability of the state to confiscate wealth, allowed for **rationalization**, a condition in which there are formalized procedures that give individual actors a measure of predictability in the outcomes of their actions. Economic rationality, for example, allows people to know what will happen when they make certain business decisions, as occurs when commercial regulations and tax laws spell out the consequences of business transactions. In a non-rational system, one is not sure of what will be allowed and what will not. Maybe one can earn money from a particular commercial enterprise, or maybe not. Maybe the monarch will disapprove and, without warning, confiscate the wealth, as apparently happened in China's Honan and Hopei provinces. Few are willing to risk time or resources under such uncertain conditions. As a result, economic development is minimal or nonexistent. According to the state theory of modernization, rationality evolved in Western Europe because of the limitation of state power that grew out of the stalemate among the four social ranks.

This explanation for the rise of capitalism and the social transformations that were thereby set in motion illustrates how significant social change may be totally *unplanned* and *unintended*. The monarchs who acquiesced, in their own interest, to a limitation of their power probably would have preferred not to. Similarly, each of the other three groups would have welcomed the chance to dominate society. They agreed to a compromise not to promote rationality, boost development, or advance the free exchange of ideas, but to salvage what they could from their position in society. The modernization that followed from the compromise was largely unintended.

Once they came into existence, industrial capitalist societies continued to change and evolve. The next section examines how they have changed in recent years. It also explores the modern relationship between industrialized and non-industrialized societies.

Social Change Since the 1960s
The "Great Disruption"

A number of significant social changes that first became evident in the mid-1960s radically transformed Western industrialized societies in the decades that followed. One constellation of these changes has been called the "Great Disruption" by Fukuyama (1999), a functionalist thinker. Crime rates jumped in many countries, the number of babies born to unwed parents increased (in some Scandinavian countries it reached almost 60 percent of all births), norms governing sexual behaviour became more permissive, and divorce rates increased dramatically. Fukuyama noted that although there were some national variations in these trends, they were clearly present in all Western industrialized countries, including Canada. To explain these changes, he searched for factors common to all of these societies.

Fukuyama suggested that these trends were caused by two broad social changes: one cultural, the other economic. With regard to the first, he maintained that since the Enlightenment there has been a growing acceptance of individual rights and freedoms and a concomitant decline in the ability of all forms of authority—church, state, and community—to set limits on people's behaviours. Previous forms of social control, he claimed, were rooted in religion, but with the Enlightenment religion started to lose its effectiveness in that regard. A series of bloody religious wars in Europe had caused various states to distance themselves from matters of religion and morality, leaving individuals and groups more freedom to decide on their own what moral precepts they would follow. But it soon became apparent that the use of reason espoused by the Enlightenment philosophers was not going to lead to any consensus on moral or religious issues.

In the nineteenth and early twentieth centuries, Western intellectuals examined a wide variety of moral rules and codes found in various non-Western cultures. Some of those intellectuals concluded, with Nietzsche, that morality is a social construction, not something based on reason or objective judgment. Others, such as Freud, Dewey, William James, and the behaviourist Watson, proclaimed that tight control over behaviour is not necessary for human development and may even be harmful. Both were arguments against a common strict morality. The messages of such intellectuals were eventually picked up by the popular media and found their way into childrearing manuals, educational practices, novels, movies, and television programs.

Fukuyama also claimed that changes in the economies and technologies of Western industrialized countries contributed to the growing individualism. By the 1960s, a significant proportion of the labour force was made up of non-manual occupations, a proportion that continues to rise. Chapter 6, Social Inequality, provides the relevant figures for Canada. As Table 6.1 (on page 133) shows, by 1981 a majority of the Canadian labour force worked in non-manual ("white-collar") occupations. The increase in non-manual jobs, Fukuyama contended, led to a rapid increase in the number of women in the paid labour force. He argued that this changed the nature of the marriage bond, as industrial-era marriages had previously been based on the assumption that the husband would provide the family's economic resources while the wife bore children and performed domestic duties. With women becoming more financially independent, marital breakup no longer meant financial devastation for women, which increased the frequency of divorce. (Changes made to divorce laws at this time were another important influence.) Fukuyama argued that women's enhanced financial independence also contributed to the increase in the number of unwed parents. If a woman can support herself or receive financial assistance from the state if she has a baby, avoiding parenthood outside of marriage becomes less of an issue for both men and women.

Fukuyama was confident that the "disruption" was only temporary. Social and moral life, he claimed, is cyclical. He maintained that human societies usually develop new norms to take the place of old, obsolete ones, and that societies usually return to a more balanced state. He noted that in many Western countries divorce, crime, and births to unwed parents are already declining, although he did not foresee a return to more conservative sexual norms or a revival of religious orthodoxy.

Although some scientific norms maintain that social scientists should not make value judgments in their work, it happens quite frequently, as it did in

Fukuyama's work. In calling the set of changes he examined the "Great Disruption," Fukuyama highlighted what he perceived to be the negative aspects of modern life. As you think about social change, you will find that you too will take a moral stand—you will welcome some changes and oppose others. When you come to make this sort of judgment, keep in mind that social scientists are not more qualified than anyone else in matters of morality. You be the judge—feel free to agree or disagree with any moral position offered by a social scientist—but try to learn as much about the topic at issue as you can.

[Social Trends]

Got the Time?

People today seem to be under intense pressure to squeeze more and more activities into their day, with little time left over for rest or leisure activities. In 1992, Statistics Canada data indicated that 52 percent of married mothers and 39 percent of married fathers felt stress resulting from trying to accomplish too much in too little time (Schachter, 1999: D2). A 1998 study found that women aged 25 to 44 who worked full-time in the paid labour force and had children at home were the group most likely to be time-stressed (Government of Canada, 1999).

People in economically developed countries are now more harried than ever. Forty-five-hour work weeks are increasingly common, with many people working over fifty hours. Cities have increased in size, as have commuting distances, further reducing time spent in leisure activities.

Many employers are demanding that more and more tasks be done per unit of time. For example, a Canadian nurse recently remarked that her job is now organized like assembly-line work. Employees who speak to customers on the telephone may be timed to ensure that they move on to the next caller quickly enough. And many people (including teachers and university professors) now spend a substantial amount of time engaged in the "hidden work" of answering work-related e-mail.

With both spouses working, which is now the norm, housework now greets the weary worker upon arrival at

home. Children's sports and recreational endeavours are now more formalized and organized than ever, which means more non-restful time spent transporting children to and from ballet lessons, hockey practices, music recitals, soccer games and the like, as well as many hours spent watching them perform. Time stress has reached the point where there is now a movement in Canada and the United States devoted to fighting "the epidemic of over-work, over-scheduling and time famine." The movement has declared October 24 as "Take Back Your Time Day" (www.timeday.org).

This sort of frenzied activity is a far cry from medieval times when almost a third of the year was devoted to holidays, which were usually a mixture of religious observance and community social activities. Time was not in the forefront of consciousness in those days—few people even owned clocks, which in any case were big and heavy and hence not portable. Today, of course, most people wear a wristwatch that gives them the time to the second, a reflection of the modern obsession with time.

As I was preparing this chapter, I had to dash off to buy a birthday present for my 7-year-old son. His request? A watch. On the way home from making the purchase, with the watch on his wrist, he repeatedly reminded me that we were late for another engagement.

Is our near obsession with time a permanent feature of modern life?

Increased tolerance, rejection of authority

There may be a positive side to the phenomenon Fukuyama described. The loosening of constraints on behaviour in Western societies in some ways has contributed to a greater tolerance of differences. This is evident in the proliferation of different lifestyles, fashions, haircuts, foods, books, movies, and other aspects of social life that were once forbidden or frowned upon, but are now accepted. For instance, there is a growing acceptance of gays and lesbians in society. In 2005, Bill C-38 was passed in the Canadian House of Commons legalizing same-sex marriage (see Chapter 10, Families). That signalled quite a change, given that homosexual behaviour was a criminal offence in Canada until 1969. There also appears to be greater tolerance and understanding between racial, ethnic, and religious groups in Canada. As noted in Chapter 8, Race and Ethnic Relations, although racism and prejudice have not disappeared, they have diminished. In 1949, for instance, the Ontario Court of Appeal pronounced that it was perfectly legal for Lake Huron cottagers to ban blacks and Jews from their beaches. Such discrimination would spark outrage today.

The set of factors outlined by Fukuyama also had an effect on gender relations, the topic of Chapter 7. As the number of non-manual jobs increased and women entered the paid workforce in larger numbers, and as fewer cultural restrictions were placed on individual behaviour, women began to enjoy more freedom and equality. A controversial spin-off of this trend is the recent rise of "raunch culture" in which mainstream women adopt overtly sexual behaviours such as stripping and imitating porn stars (Levy, 2005).

The general trend toward individualism and individual rights also has an explicitly political dimension. Newman (1995) argued that Canadians are now less deferential to authority than in years past (see also Nevitte, 1996). We are less likely to follow the lead of political elites, journalists, religious leaders, union officials, the royal family, or any other person of power or influence.

Trends in academe have in some ways mirrored the rejection of authority evident in Canada and other industrialized countries. For instance, in the 1980s and 1990s **postmodernism** and *deconstructionism* gained favour in some academic circles, as noted in the introductory chapter. Although there is no consensus on what these terms mean, one can discern certain themes expressed by writers in this genre. One is a moral and epistemological relativism, an adherence to Nietzsche's dictum that there are no facts, only interpretations (Nietzsche, 1910: 12). This is reflected in a questioning of scientific methods of inquiry and notions of truth by postmodernists; among those taking an extreme position, science is given the same truth status as magic. This is a rather radical departure from the Enlightenment philosophers' belief in reason as a means to truth. Another postmodernist theme is that the traditional canon of Western civilization—the revered books, the great works of art—serves to perpetuate existing forms of domination. Here the message echoes Marx and Engels' belief that "the ruling ideas are nothing more than the ideal expression of the dominant material relationships" (1973 [1846]: 64), with the words "power and gender" added after "material." While most of the public is largely unaware of these intellectual movements, there is a kind of mass "in your face" rejection of much of what was once considered sacred or at least beyond reproach.

Although postmodernist tendencies exist in industrial societies, their impact should not be overstated. Many reject the movement. The idea that there are objective truths about humanity and the natural world is still part of our culture. Shakespeare remains a huge draw among theatregoers, and his creations are more popular than ever in film. Science still enjoys enormous prestige among the general public and in the university. Nonetheless, there is now a greater willingness to create and examine culture from the perspective of people who traditionally have not been in positions of power and influence.

Postmaterialism

Another change in industrial societies has been a shift away from materialism among some segments of the population. Inglehart (1997) studied this phenomenon as part of a larger inquiry into social change. He adopted a general theoretical position comparable to the ecological-evolutionary and historical materialist approaches in claiming that cultural, economic, and political changes are closely related, and that once a country industrializes, a predictable pattern of change is likely to follow. For example, he maintained that regardless of which society one considers, as capitalist development proceeds, mass formal educational programs are created, women enter the paid labour force in increasing numbers, families get smaller, gender roles become more similar, and media of mass communication become widespread.

Values also change. People who grew up during periods of prolonged peace and prosperity have different attitudes and outlooks compared to those who did not. Inglehart argued that individuals born before the post-World War II economic expansion tend to have **materialist values**, which place a high priority on economic and physical security. By contrast, the post-war generations tend to take it for granted that they will not live lives of destitution or be victims of military attack. The latter are more likely to have *postmaterialist values*. **Postmaterialism** emphasizes self-expression, participation in decision making, belonging, self-esteem, and intellectual and artistic development. Postmaterialists do not reject material well-being; in fact they value it

highly. But because they feel secure physically and economically, they place an even higher priority on non-material things (Inglehart, 1997: 34–35). For example, Inglehart linked the environmental movement to the growing preponderance of postmaterialist values—many people now believe that the preservation and enjoyment of the environment are more important than economic development, a view that is far less popular in less economically developed countries. Postmaterialists also tend to place a lower value on the science and technology that make development possible, which may explain some of the postmodernist suspicion of science mentioned above. Inglehart's research indicates that the proportion of postmaterialists is fairly high in Canada. The percentage of postmaterialists minus the percentage of materialists in his 1990 sample of Canadians was 14; the same figure for the United States was 6 (Inglehart, 1997: 157).

[Research Focus]

Social Needs and Social Change in Canada

Functionalists maintain that social change may result from attempts to satisfy a society's needs. Several significant changes in Canadian society came about this way. Here are some examples:

1. *The creation of the Canadian Broadcasting Corporation (CBC).* The CBC was created in the 1930s to counter the growing influence of American programming in Canada. It was believed that there was a need for a Canadian perspective on culture and world events that was not being filled. Another influence was the need to foster Canadian unity and develop national spirit.

2. *The expansion of the university system in the 1960s and 1970s.* As the baby-boom generation began to reach adulthood, educators in Canada realized that the existing university system was inadequate to meet the needs of the rapidly increasing student population. As a result, universities expanded enormously, and eight new ones were created. In Quebec, in addition to

developing the existing universities, a large system of junior colleges (CEGEPs) was created.

The expansion of postsecondary education in Canada was also a response to a need for greater economic productivity, as it was widely believed that national education levels and economic productivity are related. Another need the expansion addressed was social justice. The universities expanded to allow greater access to education for people of limited financial means.

3. *Growth in the personal services sector.* With changing gender roles and a majority of married women of working age now in the paid labour force, many domestic tasks formerly done without remuneration are being performed by service workers. Daycare facilities, restaurants, house-cleaning businesses, catering firms, pet-care providers, bakeries, and other service operations have expanded to meet needs formerly satisfied by housewives.

How can we improve the condition of a service class that, while allowing two income earners in a family, is underpaid and provided with few benefits?

Inglehart believed that a general sense of security among postmaterialists explains the trend toward the rejection of authority. If one's survival is threatened in an economic, military, or medical way, one is inclined to follow leaders and authority figures. People in wartime, for example, tend to defer to military and political leaders. By contrast, people who are secure are less fond of orders and rigid rules. Whether current terrorist attacks lead to greater insecurity and less postmaterialism will be watched closely by researchers like Inglehart.

A similar argument is made to explain the shift away from religious orthodoxy in wealthy countries like Canada. In contemporary industrial societies— characterized by prolonged economic and military security, low infant mortality, advanced medical technology, and long life expectancy—death or disaster rarely seems imminent. As a result, religious quests are not pursued with the same sense of urgency or despair as they once were. Postmaterialists are interested in matters of spirituality, the meaning of life, figuring out who they are, and so on, but they are not in as great a rush to find final answers as people who grew up in more troubling times. Postmaterialists also differ from materialists in that they are reluctant to develop their spirituality by following absolute rules imposed by others, the standard method offered by established religions.

Having postmaterialist values has some drawbacks. Generally, people with these values have lower levels of overall life satisfaction than materialists in the same country (Inglehart, 1997: 87). It seems that it is more difficult for postmaterialists to meet their expectations with regard to self-expression, participation in government, intellectual development, and so forth than for materialists to satisfy their needs for material well-being.

Group rights

Although much of the foregoing illustrates how, since the Enlightenment, Western society has, for good or ill, been increasingly individualistic in orientation, a second somewhat contradictory propensity is also evident. It is a quest for group rights and equality of condition, goals embraced by one faction of Enlightenment thinkers and some of the leaders of the French Revolution (Fonte, 1999). In the nineteenth and twentieth centuries, socialists carried this banner. Recently, those promoting affirmative-action programs and various other group-based rights initiatives have adopted this philosophy. The current clash between the two perspectives,

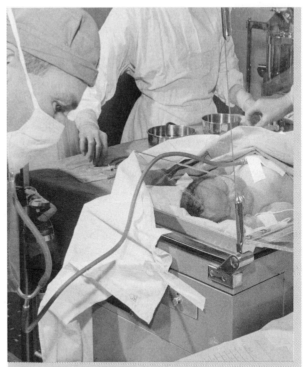

Substantial improvements in medical care since the late 1950s have helped to reduce Canada's infant mortality rate.

individual and group, can be seen in Canada in the controversies surrounding the relevance of race and gender in hiring policies, and in the conflict over language legislation in Quebec (see Chapter 15, Social Movements). Should equity among groups override individual merit or individual rights? For example, should Canada adopt hiring practices that result in even gender representation in most occupational categories, thus promoting economic equality between men and women? What if that would require different hiring criteria for the two genders? Similarly, should the government of Quebec limit the use of English and other languages on public signs in order to preserve the French language in Canada? Those who agree with these proposals tend to favour group rights over individual rights; those who disagree place a higher priority on individual rights.

Globalization and development

Another phenomenon that characterizes current times is globalization. Contemporary societies are now so closely interlinked economically, politically, and culturally that some sociologists argue that the discipline must abandon the country or single society as its primary unit of analysis and embrace "a sociology of world society" (Sztompka, 1993: 86). Economic globalization has resulted in some transnational corporations having revenues comparable to middle-sized countries; financial markets are now international in orientation and effect; and more countries are embracing free trade. Although Canada's economy has relied on international trade for centuries, the implementation of the Canada–U.S. Free Trade Agreement in 1989 and the North American Free Trade Agreement in 1994 extended the global reach of our economy.

The globalization of culture is also significant. The rich nations, especially the United States, export their culture to the poorer ones, mainly through television, movies, and popular music (recall Chapter 3, Culture, and Chapter 12, Media). For example, the U.S. news network CNN is seen around the world, as are U.S. television dramas and comedy shows. English is increasingly the international language of business, tourism, science, and the Internet. U.S.-based fast-food outlets are found around the world, as is Microsoft computer software. And more and more countries are adopting Western forms of dress. For instance, despite years of bitter war with the United States, many Vietnamese have given up their traditional conical hats in favour of American-style baseball caps (*The Globe and Mail*, 17 June 1999: A31).

The arrival of Western culture in non-Western societies can cause resentment. A dramatic illustration of this is the Iranian Revolution of 1979. The Shah, Mohammad Reza Pahlavi, who had acceded to power in the 1950s with the assistance of the American government, had for years welcomed Western investment and culture into Iran, even to the point of discouraging Iranian women from wearing the traditional Muslim head covering. Many Iranians, led by the Ayatollah Khomeini, were outraged at the extent of Western influence and drove the Shah out of power, setting up a traditional Islamic theocracy. The rejection of Western cultural and political influences also played a role in the terrorist attacks of September 11, 2001, and can be seen in the insurgency against U.S.-led forces in Iraq, although some observers see these sorts of clashes as merely the latest episodes in a history of conflict between the West and Islam that has been going on for over a thousand years (Lewis, 2003).

A related dimension of the West's relationship with the rest of the world is economic. Researchers in the area of development try to determine why some countries have a level of economic development that is far below that of the industrialized nations, and what can be done about it. Researchers are also concerned with the negative consequences of globalization and development for poorer countries. See the box "Why Are Some Countries Poor?" for a summary of the different views that have emerged on this topic.

[Research Focus]

Why Are Some Countries Poor?

Scholars disagree over the issue of why developing nations are stricken with poverty. According to **modernization theory**, limited development is a consequence of a number of characteristics of those countries (So, 1990: 58). They include: traditional cultures that may not be conducive to development; capital shortages; a lack of technological expertise; low levels of education; absence of infrastructure such as roads, bridges, and energy sources; and limited entrepreneurial skills. Advocates of modernization theory tend to view the increasing levels of contact between the industrialized nations and the Third World as favourable, as the richer countries may provide investment funds, technology transfers, field workers and, above all, the example of their own economies to emulate.

Neo-liberalism holds that international free trade, privatization, the free flow of capital and minimal government regulation provide optimal conditions for economic development in any country, wealthy or not. People adopting this perspective believe that the lack of development in poorer countries results from too much

(continued)

state ownership and intervention in the economy, along with outright corruption on the part of rulers and government officials. To back up their case, they cite examples of formerly impoverished areas like Hong Kong, Taiwan, South Korea, and Singapore, which experienced rapid economic growth by following neo-liberal principles. Mainland China and India are also seen as examples of how countries can make rapid gains through economic liberalization.

Dependency theory argues that underdevelopment in the Third World is caused by the domination and exploitation of these countries by rich industrialized nations. Used primarily to analyze Latin American development, the theory claims that the wealth required for development is usually transferred out of the region to the rich nations. For example, dependency theorists (e.g., Frank, 1967) state that Latin American countries export mainly raw materials and agricultural products to the developed world, where they are purchased at low prices. The developed nations in turn export expensive finished products to Latin America. The theory also holds that a large part of the profits acquired by foreign-owned transnational corporations in Latin America are exported to their headquarters in the developed world (So, 1990: 100). Dependency theorists argue that to foster development, the poorer countries are forced to take out loans from the wealthy nations, the interest on which constitutes another drain on their economic well-being.

They also point out that people in impoverished countries suffer at the hands of their authoritarian governments, which may form alliances with domestic and international corporations and Western governments.

World system theory, developed by Wallerstein (1974), has much in common with dependency theory as it too claims that underdevelopment is caused by the exploitation of the poorer countries by the richer ones, but its purview is the world as a whole as opposed to a particular region or country. The theory claims that all the countries of the world form a unified system, and that the social conditions in any society can be understood by examining its position in the world system. The nations of the world are divided into three groups. *Core* countries are rich and highly developed, dominating the world both economically and militarily. *Peripheral* countries are poor and weak because they are exploited by the core. *Semi-peripheral* countries are in an intermediate position, enjoying some wealth and influence but still under the domination of the core.

Many of the claims made by the theories seeking to explain global poverty continue to be debated. Critics of modernization theory and neo-liberalism argue that these theories tend to overlook or downplay the effect that colonialism has had on development. Critics of the dependency and world system theories point out that developed countries trade overwhelmingly with other developed countries, and that therefore the vast majority of their wealth is not generated at the expense of poorer countries.

Which of these theories best explains why Canada is poorer than the U.S.?
Can a combination of ideas from the four perspectives better explain this situation? If so, describe how.

Summary

In this chapter we have examined in broad outline how human societies have changed over the past, 10000 years. Their evolution from hunting and gathering bands to farming societies and finally to industrialized nations produced a number of significant changes, including new forms of inequality, altered gender relations, variations in the power of the state, and urbanization. We also examined several theories that seek to account for the changes that occurred, namely evolutionism, developmental theories, historical materialism, the Weber thesis, and the state theory of modernization. Recent changes in Western industrialized countries were discussed as well. These included increases in divorce rates and the number

of unwed parents, growing tolerance among racial and ethnic groups, a trend toward gender equality, the decline in deference to elites, and the influence of postmodernism and postmaterialism. We concluded with a discussion of globalization and development.

What will the future bring? What will the world look like years, decades, centuries from now? One thing to note in this regard is that social scientists do not have a very good record when it comes to making long-term predictions. Few anticipated the most significant changes that occurred in the past thirty years, such as the rise of feminism, the collapse of the Soviet bloc, and the increased tensions between some Muslim groups and the West. Although it is difficult to know what the world will be like in the future, one can be certain of this: in many respects it will be markedly different from the way it is today. Change is always present in human societies, and the rate of change is accelerating.

Those caveats aside, one way to make predictions is to base them on current trends. Using this method, one can expect the division of labour to continue to expand—for the most part, it shows no sign of reversing or staying constant. Likewise, the trend toward similarity in gender roles and gender equality, especially in wealthier societies, will probably continue. Liberal democracy, as Fukuyama (1989) argued, no longer has serious rivals in the economically developed world, although the form that democracy will take is open to question. Look for greater democracy in Western countries in the form of increased scrutiny of public officials and more accountability.

The individualism that has been growing over the past few centuries in Western countries will not abate. In matters of personal taste, self-expression, sexuality, spirituality, and esthetics, the range of choices that are considered acceptable will continue to grow. Developments in biotechnology in areas such as cloning, genetic engineering, and the aging process will likely create new moral dilemmas and may radically alter how we live our lives.

Greater globalization will probably occur, as more countries move away from state ownership and economic regulation toward free trade and open markets. This will likely lead to increased development in some Third World countries.

These predictions are premised on three rather flimsy assumptions. One is that warfare will continue to be localized, a condition that could change any minute. Conflicts in the former Yugoslavia, the Middle East, Kashmir, Tibet, and the Korean peninsula could draw the major powers into a larger conflagration. Particularly worrisome is the possibility of nuclear, chemical, or biological warfare. Russia, which has substantial nuclear capability, currently lingers in a state of humiliation and turmoil. China, another nuclear power, feels slighted by the rest of the world and may be seeking greater military dominance in Asia. Despite the removal of Iraqi president Saddam Hussein from power in 2003, there are about half a dozen smaller states headed by dictators who now possess or are developing nuclear and biological weapons. Recently, East-West tensions have increased as Iran appears to be creating a nuclear arsenal.

The second questionable assumption is that the world economy will not sink into depression. This premise is closely related to the first, as economic troubles often create political instability or even lead to war. Likewise, war can lead to economic disruption.

The third assumption is that the world will not be hit with a deadly international pandemic. Unfortunately, the World Health Organization has warned that a bird flu (avian influenza) pandemic "may be imminent" (World Health Organization, 2005).

Assuming that no catastrophe befalls the world, one of the most perplexing and intriguing questions in

[Debate]

What Can Be Done about Global Poverty?

An international social movement, the Global Call to Action Against Poverty, has been organized in a number of countries. In Canada, the movement is called Make Poverty History, and has been endorsed by luminaries such as musician Sarah McLachlan, Nobel laureate John Polanyi, actor Mike Myers, and author Margaret Atwood.

The movement's goals include pressuring politicians in developed countries to commit more funds to foreign aid, cancelling the debts that poor countries owe to rich nations, and introducing fair trading practices. The movement has also undertaken a number of local initiatives, such as the campaign to end child poverty in Canada.

Do movements like this ever produce fundamental social change, or is change more likely to come from larger social forces? Can social movements work in tandem with more macro social phenomena to produce change? Is poverty a violation of human rights?

the study of global social change surrounds the issue of whether non-Western countries will become culturally and politically similar to the West, especially if they experience advanced levels of economic development. Will Iraq or China become liberal democracies, or is the whole conglomeration of things that fall under the heading of Western civilization a product of historical circumstances that will never occur outside the West? Perhaps the thought that others will become similar to the West if they have comparable economies is just another example of Western ethnocentrism. Huntington (1996) made this claim. Or perhaps there is, as other social scientists have argued, a universal pattern of cultural and political change that, in the long run, follows upon capitalist development.

Questions for Review and Critical Thinking

1. What do you think was the most important social change in Canadian society in the last 100 years? How would the two general approaches to change discussed in this chapter, the functionalist and conflict perspectives, explain it?

2. What aspect of Canadian society is most in need of change? What concrete changes would you recommend? List all the positive and negative consequences of your changes, and then explain why the changes have not yet occurred.

3. Compare two different time periods in Canada, making sure to list both positive and negative aspects of each. Is there evidence of progress and improvement in the human condition?

4. Sociologists have a poor track record in making successful predictions. Should sociologists merely study society and let others determine policy?

Key Terms

anomie, p. 403
cultural lag, p. 395
dependency theory, p. 413
dialectical, p. 403
diffusion, p. 400
ecological-evolutionary theory, p. 399
Enlightenment, p. 397
evolutionism, p. 398

gemeinschaft, p. 401
gesellschaft, p. 401
historical materialism, p. 403
imperialism, p. 396
materialist values, p. 410
mechanical solidarity, p. 403
modernization theory, p. 412
neo-liberalism, p. 412
organic solidarity, p. 403
postmaterialism, p. 410
postmodernism, p. 409
rationalization, p. 406
staples thesis, p. 401
state, p. 396
state theory of modernization p. 405
world system theory, p. 413

Suggested Readings

Chirot, Daniel

1994 *How Societies Change*. Thousand Oaks, CA: Pine Forge Press.

A succinct account of how human societies have evolved from hunting and gathering groups to modern forms, it includes a very useful annotated bibliography at the end of each chapter.

Inglehart, Ronald

1997 *Modernization and Postmodernization: Cultural, Economic, and Political Change in 43 Societies*. Princeton, NJ: Princeton University Press.

Inglehart makes a compelling argument that cultural, economic, and political changes are closely related, and that once a country industrializes, a predictable pattern of changes is likely to follow. The book also offers a good discussion of postmaterialism.

Nolan, Patrick and Gerhard Lenski

2006 *Human Societies: An Introduction to Macrosociology*. Boulder, CO: Paradigm Publishers.

A thorough illustration of the ecological-evolutionary theory, from a sociological perspective.

Stark, Rodney

2005 *The Victory of Reason: How Christianity Led to Freedom, Capitalism, and Western Success*. New York: Random House.

Stark argues that Christianity, with its emphasis on the spiritual equality of all human beings and its fostering of a rational, critical theology, led to the development of science and the eventual economic and political dominance of the West. His analysis also incorporates the state theory of modernization.

Sztompka, Piotr
1993 *The Sociology of Social Change.* Oxford, UK: Blackwell.
In an excellent critical review of the theories and concepts of social change that sociologists have propounded since the birth of the discipline in the early nineteenth century, Sztompka also offers an original contribution, his "theory of social becoming."

Website

www.makepovertyhistory.ca
Make Poverty History
This website provides information on the efforts of Canadians to end global poverty.

Key Search Terms

Modernization
Dependency
Evolutionism
Developmentalism
Historical materialism

For more study tools to help you with your next exam, be sure to check out the Companion Website at **www.pearsoned.ca/hewitt**, as well as Chapter 17 in your Study Guide.

Glossary

abnormal   when something deviates from the typical patter of behavior and violates a norm. Typically implies a value judgment that the behavior is wrong. (*p. 88*)

abstinence standard   the premarital sexual standard that allows no premarital sex (*p. 235*)

acculturation   the learning of the language, values, and customs of a dominant group by an ethnic group; also called cultural assimilation (*p. 194*)

achieved status   a position in a status hierarchy attained by individual effort or accomplishment (*p. 121*)

active audience theory   the idea that audiences play an active role in interpreting or decoding media messages, often contrasted with the **hypodermic model** (*p. 283*)

activity theory   the view that the best prescription for a successful old age is to remain active and to take on new activities in later life to supplant those that have been left behind (*p. 204*)

age effects   changes that are a direct function of aging; also called **maturation** (*p. 204*)

age-graded   a system of expectations and rewards that are based on age (*p. 205*)

age-specific death rates   an alternative to the crude death rate, obtained by dividing the number of deaths to persons of a given age by the total number of persons in that age cohort (*p. 378*)

age-specific fertility rates   an alternative to the crude birth rate, obtained by dividing the number of births to women of a given age by the total number of women of that age in the population (*p. 373*)

age-stratification perspective   a macro-level approach focused primarily on two key concepts: a *stratified age structure* that favours young and middle-aged adults, and an *age cohort*, individuals who share the same age group (*p. 204*)

alienation   as developed by Marx, this concept describes the separation of the worker from the product of his labours as well as from the process of work, fellow workers, and even the basic traits of humanity (*p. 336*)

androcentrism   a bias that involves (1) seeing things from a male point of view or (2) seeing things in a way that reinforces male privilege in society (*p. 50*)

anomie   a state of normlessness caused by a large-scale breakdown of conformity to societal rules (*p. 104, 403*)

anticipatory socialization   the learning of attitudes, and behaviours for roles individuals expect to play in the future (*p. 73*)

ascetic   practising self-discipline with a view to spiritual improvement, especially by living a simple and austere life, doing without such common creature comforts as warm and soft beds, rich foods, or fancy clothing (*p. 261*)

ascribed status   a position in a status hierarchy that is inherited or assigned (*p. 120*)

assimilationism   the view that ethnic diversity gradually and inevitably declines as group members are absorbed into the general population, in the process becoming more and more like the dominant group (*p. 193*)

axiomatic logic   the making of connecting links between related statements for deriving hypotheses (*p. 20*)

bourgeoisie   the capitalist class, as defined by Marx. The petite bourgeoisie were the small property owners, destined to be swallowed by the larger capitalists. (*p. 123*)

bureaucracy   a special type of complex organization characterized by an explicit set of rules and a hierarchy of authority (*p. 331*)

calling   a purpose in life. In a religious context, it is the idea that people have been born to fulfill God's will on earth through their life's work. (*p. 261*)

chain migration   sequential movement of persons from a common place of origin to a common destination with the assistance of relatives or acquaintances already settled in the new location (*p. 173*)

church   in sociological usage, the term for religious organizations that are well established and characterized by an inclusive orientation (i.e., all people who meet certain minimal standards can belong) and involuntary membership (i.e., most members are inducted when stillinfants) (*p. 262*)

civilizing process   as defined by Norbert Elias, the historical process whereby people acquire greater capacity to control their emotions. Entails a long-term change in the structure of feelings. (*p. 95*)

class   a set of individuals sharing a similar economic status or market position (*p. 121*)

class for itself   a Marxian category including people who share the same economic position, are aware of their common class position, and who thus may become agents for social change (*p. 124*)

classical criminology   an approach that seeks to use clear laws and calibrated official sanctions to punish and deter crime. Often associated with the early work of Cesare Beccaria. (*p. 99*)

class in itself   a Marxian category including people who share the same economic position, but who may be unaware of their common class position (*p. 123*)

class, status group, party   Weber's answer to Marx concerning the bases of social inequality: class is economic, status is prestige, party is political; all three are measures of inequality (*p. 126*)

cluster sampling a series of random samples taken in units of decreasing size, such as census tracts, then streets, then houses, then residents (*p. 22*)

cofigurative cultures those in which social change brought by technological advancement, economic transformation, immigration, war and so forth makes the intergenerational linkage tenuous; as opposed to **postfigurative** and prefigurative cultures (*p. 74*)

cohort measures measuring demographic data based on segments of the population divided by year of birth (i.e., if you were born in 1985, you are a member of the 1980s birth cohort) (*p. 374*)

collaborative or role-sharing model model of task sharing in a family where both spouses spend an equal amount of time at both paid and unpaid work (*p. 240*)

collective action the pursuit of goals by more than one person. As an explanation of social movements, this perspective looks at integration and cleavage factors and seeks to explain what is dissimilar about collective action at different times and in different places. (*p. 346*)

collective behaviour activity in which a large number of people reject and/or do not conform to conventional ways of acting. Behaviour of this kind is often described as less "institutionalized" than ordinary behaviour (*p. 342*)

collective conscience the term Durkheim used to describe the sense people have while participating in religious rituals of sharing in the overall intellectual heritage and wisdom of their culture (*p. 260*)

collective effervescence the term Durkheim used to describe the sense of excitement and power people experience when participating in lively events involving relatively large crowds, like a religious revival, a rock concert, or good football game (*p. 260*)

colonialism the domination by a settler society of a native or indigenous population. The colonizing society extracts resources from the conquered land, establishes settlements there, and administers the indigenous population, frequently employing violence and a racist ideology. In time, the colonized population suffers the erosion of its traditional culture, economy, and way of life, and usually occupies a subordinate status in the pluralist society of which it has involuntarily become a part. (*p. 187*)

communications conglomerates large corporations that combine many different media holdings, or have interests both in media and other industrial sectors (*p. 280*)

complementary-roles model model of task sharing in a family where the husband spends more time at paid work and the wife more time at unpaid work (*p. 240*)

conflict theory the sociological model that portrays society as marked by competition and/or exploitation. Its three major concepts are power, disharmony, and revolution (*p. 5*)

content analysis a method of analysis that extracts themes from communications, including letters, books, and newspapers (*p. 24*)

contraculture a way of life in opposition to, not merely distinct from, the larger culture; also called counterculture (*p. 105*)

control group the group of subjects in an experiment that is not exposed to the independent variable, as opposed to the **experimental group**, which is exposed (*p. 26*)

control variables variables included in a model of behaviour that are neither independent nor dependent variables. They are controlled or held constant to check on apparent relationships between independent and dependent variables. (*p. 25*)

correlation not to be confused with cause, it is changes in one variable that coincide with changes in another variable. (*p. 31*)

correspondence theory the view that educational forms (e.g., bureaucratic schools) and processes (e.g., streaming) correspond to conditions and needs in the capitalist economy (*p. 308*)

craze an unconventional practice that is adopted by a large number of individuals but is regarded as strange by most people in the society. Crazes are generally more outlandish than fads, and therefore require greater personal commitment (*p. 343*)

credential inflation the concept that credential requirements in the labour market increase independent of the skill content of work. As individuals acquire more degrees, diplomas, and certificates, employers have increased the credentials needed to gain employment. As a result, inequalities persist (*p. 303*)

crime behavior that has been officially recognized by the state as a serious forms of antisocial behavior. Crimes are punishable through official sanctions such as prison and probation. (*p. 88*)

crime funnel the process by which the actual number of crimes is reduced through losses attributable to fear, bias, discretion, and human error (*p. 90*)

critical pedagogy a form of pedagogy that has as its central concern progressive social change, social justice, and liberation (*p. 305*)

critical school theoretical approaches that are explicitly concerned with how power operates to exclude and marginalize different segments of society (*p. 113*)

critical theory focuses on social structure in the study of power, social action, and social meanings that are part of a critique of knowledge, culture, and the economy. As related to aging, this includes examining the social construction of old age and dependency and of old-age policy. (*p. 206*)

cross-sectional research the type of research that takes place at one point in time as opposed to longitudinal research, which can detect change and demonstrate cause because it takes place over a period of time (*p. 31*)

crowd a temporary group of people in reasonably close physical proximity. Only unconventional crowds are included under the heading of collective behaviour (*p. 343*)

crude birth rate a measure devised by demographers to help us understand how births determine the rate of population growth, calculated by dividing the number of births occurring in a population in a given period of time by the total size of the population, and expressed per thousand population (*p. 368*)

crude death rate   a measure devised by demographers to help us understand how deaths determine the rate of population growth, calculated by dividing the number of deaths occurring in a population in a given period of time by the total size of the population, and expressed per thousand population (*p. 368*)

cult   a type of non-established religious organization based on voluntary membership. It is usually small and focused on the esoteric teachings of a charismatic leader (*p. 264*)

cultivation effect   the idea that heavy viewing of television leads people to perceive reality in ways consistent with the representations they see on television (*p. 289*)

cultural capital   individuals' access to and understanding of the dominant culture (*p. 308*)

cultural element   anything that (1) is shared in common by the members of some social group; (2) is passed on to new members; and (3) in some way affects their behaviour or their perceptions of the world. Three of the most important elements are values, norms, and roles. (*p. 38*)

cultural imperialism   the imposition of one nation's culture on another, not through direct occupation but by the indirect effects of media influence (*p. 290*)

cultural integration   the interrelationship of elements in a given culture such that a change in one element can lead to changes, sometimes unexpected, in other elements (*p. 47*)

cultural lag   the process of adaptation where parts of a culture catch up with other parts (also called structural lag) (*p. 395*)

cultural materialism   a theoretical perspective in which cultural elements are explained by showing how they are pragmatic and rational adaptations to the material environment (*p. 55*)

cultural studies school   a school of research that focuses on how people make meanings in everyday life, sometimes in ways that are resistant or alternative to the dominant values promoted in major media channels (*p. 281*)

cultural universals   elements of culture found in all known societies (*p. 46*)

culture   the sum total of all the cultural elements associated with a given social group (*p. 38*)

culture industry   a term originally used critically to describe the crass, conservative, and conformist tendencies of commercially organized mass entertainment, now often used approvingly to refer to business-driven media (*p. 279*)

cyberspace   the imaginary space or dimension in which we conceive of computer-mediated communication occurring (*p. 292*)

dark figure of crime   the unknown amount of crime that is not contained in official crime statistics or social science methodologies (*p. 90*)

deductive logic   the derivation of a specific statement from a set of more general statements (*p. 20*)

defective socialization   socialization attempts that have unintended outcomes or consequences (*p. 72*)

demographic transition theory   suggests that societies pass through a three-stage process of change (*p. 371*)

demography   the study of population, examining how the size, structure, and rate of growth are affected by rates of fertility, mortality, and migration (*p. 368*)

denomination   church-like religious organizations that acknowledge the legitimacy of other religious groups with which they are in competition for members (*p. 263*)

dependency ratio   relates the number of persons in what are considered the dependent-age categories to the number in the independent or working-age categories, conventionally comprising those under 15 and over 65 (*p. 390*)

dependency theory   the perspective that argues that underdevelopment in the Third World is a result of its domination and exploitation by rich industrialized nations (*p. 413*)

dependent variable   the effect in a causal statement, as opposed to the independent variable which is the cause (i.e., other things being equal, if A, then B—B is the dependent variable) (*p. 20*)

desensitization   a term applied to the alleged tendency for repeated exposure to scenes of media violence to make people increasingly indifferent to or accepting of such incidents in real-life (*p. 289*)

detailed division of labour   the division of one complete complex task into its sub-tasks. These tasks are then given to different people who can be more easily trained and often paid less in wages or salaries. (*p. 327*)

dialectical   a philosophical approach that maintains that for every thesis there is built into it its own antithesis or transformation (*p. 403*)

differential association   a theory that sees deviance as learned in small-group interaction, wherein an individual internalizes pro-deviant perspectives (*p. 109*)

diffusion   the adoption of an innovation by a society that did not create it (*p. 400*)

discrimination   the denial of opportunities, generally available to all members of society, to some people because of their membership in a social category (*p. 181*)

disengagement theory   view that the withdrawal of older persons from active social life (particularly the labour force) is functional for both the individual and the larger society (*p. 204*)

disinhibition   the idea that viewing media violence encourages people to shed their restraints against committing real-life violence (*p. 289*)

disjunctive socialization   socialization processes that lack continuity between socialization contexts, making it difficult for people to make transitions between them or to adjust to new contexts (*p. 72*)

displacement   the process whereby criminals respond to anti-crime initiatives (policing, CCTV cameras) by conducting their criminal behavior in another location (*p. 102*)

doctrine of predestination   the belief that an all-knowing and all-powerful God will have known and determined, from the dawn of creation, who is religiously saved and damned (*p. 261*)

double burden   model of task-sharing in a family where typically the wife is doing the same amount of paid work but more unpaid work (*p. 240*)

double standard   the premarital sexual standard that allows premarital sex for men only (*p. 235*)

downsizing   the process by which a company reduces its labour force to cut operating costs (*p. 338*)

dysfunctions   the occasional minor, temporary disruptions in social life, as defined by functionalists (*p. 6*)

ecclesia   a church that dominates a society or nation and considers itself, ideally at least, to be the sole legitimate religion of that society or nation (*p. 263*)

ecological-evolutionary theory   one that takes into consideration the effects of the biophysical environment, a society's subsistence technology, and interaction between societies (*p. 399*)

emergent norm theory   an explanation of crowd behaviour that stresses diversity of membership but a perception of consensus, which leads to a new norm expressing the apparent will of the crowd (*p. 344*)

employment equity   a strategy with the objectives to increase the representation of disadvantaged groups at all levels of the occupational structure, to remove barriers to their career advancement, and to create a workplace culture free of discrimination (*p. 195*)

Enlightenment   an 18th-century movement championing free speech, freedom of conscience, equal rights, empiricism, skepticism, and reason (*p. 397*)

environmental criminology   involves efforts to reduce crime and deviance by changing the physical environment in ways that make such behavior impossible or more difficult (*p. 100*)

epigenetic   in human development theory (like Erikson's), the person is likened to a flower, which has genetically preset stages of growth, the outcome of which depends on how well, or poorly, the environment nurtures it during that stage (*p. 63*)

equilibrium   envisioned by functionalist sociologists as the normal state of society, marked by interdependence of parts and by harmony and consensus (*p. 6*)

ethnic group   a people; a collectivity of persons who share an ascribed status based upon culture, religion, national origin, or shared historical experience founded upon a common ethnicity or race (*p. 176*)

ethnocentrism   seeing things from the perspective of one's own culture. It includes the belief that one's own culture is superior to others and the belief that what is true of one's culture is true of others. Two of its major variants as they affect the study of culture are androcentrism and Eurocentrism. (*p. 48*)

ethnography   see **participant obervation**

Eurocentrism   a bias shaped by the values and experiences of the white, middle class in Western industrialized societies, assuming that these values and experiences are universally shared (*p. 48*)

evolutionism   a theoretical perspective maintaining that social change is in some ways comparable to biological evolution. Change is explained by making reference to societal characteristics that promote survival and help societies reproduce themselves, such as complex social structures, powerful armed forces, and large populations. (*p. 398*)

exchange theory   focuses on the relatively weak bargaining position of older persons in their exchanges with younger ones (*p. 205*)

expectation of life at birth   the average number of years a group of newborns can expect to live if current mortality risks prevail throughout their lifetime (*p. 378*)

experimental group   the group of subjects in an experiment that is exposed to the independent variable, as opposed to the control group, which is not exposed (*p. 26*)

expressive exchanges   the emotional dimension of marriage, including sexual gratification, companionship, and empathy (*p. 226*)

external validity   the ability to generalize research results beyond the artificial laboratory experimental situation to the real world (*p. 27*)

fad   an unconventional practice that spreads rapidly and is adopted in a short period of time by a large number of people. Fads are generally less outlandish than crazes, and therefore require less personal commitment. (*p. 343*)

family   two or more people related by blood, adoption, some form of extended commitment (e.g., individuals who care for each other), and who reside together (*p. 226*)

folkways   those norms that when violated do not provoke a strong reaction on the part of group members (*p. 40*)

Fordism   a process developed by Henry Ford, designed to effect production of mass quantities of goods to facilitate mass consumption. The assembly line is often the centrepiece of Fordist production. (*p. 328*)

formal curriculum   the overt content of schooling, related to cognitive skill acquisition (*p. 299*)

formal organizations   organizations with a clear division of labour and goals. Corporations, schools, government agencies, and political parties are examples (*p. 329*)

formal social control mechanisms   the official practices used by the state to ensure conformity and lawful behavior, including policing, courts and prison (*p. 95*)

frame   a set of beliefs that helps people to interpret and explain their world and that provides the basis for collective action (*p. 348*)

free-rider problem   when self-interested individuals abstain from participation and let others do the work (*p. 350*)

fun standard   the premarital sexual standard that approves of premarital sex for either gender, even without love (*p. 236*)

functionalism (a) applied to culture, the theoretical perspective that explains cultural elements by showing how they contribute to societal stability; (b) the sociological model that portrays society as harmonious and as based on consensus. Its three major concepts are function, equilibrium, and development. (*p. 5, 52*)

functionalist definition of religion any definition that uses what religion does (not what it is) as its primary criterion (*p. 256*)

gemeinschaft a term used by Tönnies meaning "community," to describe the warm, intimate social relations that he claimed characterized agrarian communities before the advent of industrialization (*p. 401*)

gender a *social* construct based on definitions of masculinity and femininity, and norms and behavioural expectations for each gender category (*p. 154*)

gendered division of labour system in which males and females, in both the unpaid and paid labour arenas, take on what are deemed "sex appropriate" tasks (*p. 155*)

gendered norms standards of behavior that differ between men and women (*p. 106*)

gendered order the part of social structure that makes social life gendered, directing how males and females *should* act, including norms, roles, and ideology (*p. 155*)

gender identity one's perception of self as male or female, not to be confused with sexual orientation, and not necessarily consistent with a person's sex (*p. 155*)

generalized other an individual's conception of what is expected, providing a unified basis for self-reference (*p. 69*)

geriatrics the study of the physiological aspects of aging and the unique health concerns of older persons (*p. 202*)

gerontology an interdisciplinary study of aging that involves the physical, psychological, and social processes related to growing older and being an older person (*p. 202*)

gesellschaft a term used by Tönnies, meaning "society" or "association," to describe what he believed to be the cold, impersonal, and self-interested social relations typical of industrial cities (*p. 401*)

globalization of production the trend of companies looking worldwide for the most profitable place to set up production (*p. 339*)

grounded theory explanations that arise from the data collected and which are thus grounded in reality rather than in deductive logic (*p. 27*)

habitus individuals' sense of self within the social structure, informed by their social class background. Habitus creates dispositions to understand the world and act in certain ways (*p. 308*)

hedonistic calculus the philosophical assumption that people behave in light of conscious considerations of the anticipated costs and benefits of their actions (*p. 99*)

hegemony the domination of a class or classes over others, not only economically but politically and culturally (*p. 351*)

heterogamy marriage between persons who are dissimilar in some important regard such as religion, ethnic background, social class, personality, or age (*p. 238*)

hidden curriculum the unspoken norms, values, and routines that socialize students and shape their behaviour (*p. 300*)

historical materialism a perspective claiming that fundamental social change results primarily from material, in particular economic, factors. It is often associated with Marx and Engels' theory of social change. (*p. 403*)

homogamy marriage of persons with similar physical, psychological, or social characteristics. This is the tendency for like to marry like. (*p. 238*)

horizontal mobility movement by an individual from one status to another of similar rank within the same status hierarchy (*p. 121*)

human capital an individual's skills, knowledge, and experience and the value of this for economic growth (*p. 302*)

hybridization the tendency of international communication flows to create cultural mixes or crossovers between previously distinct national and ethnic groups (*p. 291*)

hypodermic model the belief that media shoot powerful messages into weak, passive audiences, thus directly controlling their behaviour (*p. 281*)

hypothesis a statement of a presumed relationship between two or more variables (*p. 20*)

I and me the two aspects of Mead's conception of the self. The *I* is the impulsive, creative aspect; the *me* is more deliberative and cautious than the *I* (*p. 69*)

ideology a set of beliefs that provides the basis for collective action, most of all by defining the goals of the movement (*p. 348*)

imperialism the control or exploitation of one country by another, often by conquest (*p. 396*)

inadequate socialization incomplete socialization, occurring when a person is not exposed to all experiences necessary to function in certain roles (*p. 72*)

independent variable the cause in a causal statement, as opposed to the **dependent variable** which is the effect (i.e., other things being equal, if A, then B—A is the independent variable) (*p. 20*)

individualization the process by which life course paths are based on individual preferences (*p. 75*)

inductive logic the construction of a generalization from a set of specific statements (*p. 27*)

infantilization the tendency to systematically associate people from other cultures with traits that we associate with children (*p. 48*)

informal organization the informal rules and groups of people that arise to meet the challenges of complex day-to-day life (*p. 330*)

informal social control mechanisms   actions by individuals or groups designed to alter the behavior of others that do not entail the use of official criminal justice system. These can include such things as shaming, gossip, ridicule or ostracizing individuals. (*p. 95*)

information imbalance   the disparity between the capacities of the developed and less-developed world to produce and distribute information (*p. 290*)

information society   a new stage of civilization supposedly being brought into being by computers and telecommunications, succeeding the old industrial society (*p. 276*)

innovation   for Merton, this refers to the situation when individuals facing social strain use deviant means to achieve broadly accepted social goals (*p. 104*)

institution   a specific set of norms and values that the members of a society use to regulate some broad area of social life (*p. 42*)

institutional completeness   the development of a full set of institutions in an ethnic community that parallels those in the larger society (*p. 175*)

institutionalized power   sometimes called domination, power is institutionalized when it becomes a regular part of everyday human existence, usually because it is established in formal laws or accepted customs (*p. 120*)

instrumental exchanges   the task-oriented dimension of marriage, including earning a living, spending money, and maintaining a household (*p. 226*)

instrumentalism   working not for the enjoyment of the job, but for the money and/or material rewards that then translate into life enjoyment (*p. 336*)

intergenerational mobility   movement or change between parental status and a child's status in the same status hierarchy (*p. 121*)

internal migration   movement across boundaries within countries (*p. 382*)

international migration   movement across national boundaries. This type of migration is almost always regulated by law and governments typically collect statistics on the number of persons entering (and sometimes the number leaving) the country. (*p. 382*)

intragenerational mobility   movement by an individual from one status to another in the same status hierarchy during a single lifetime or career (*p. 121*)

invisible religion   the term used by the sociologist Thomas Luckmann to describe non-institutional and private expressions of religiosity in modern, largely secular societies (*p. 269*)

iron law of oligarchy   the premise that even in democratic organizations, be they socialist or capitalist, rule by the many will inevitably become rule by the few (*p. 330*)

la survivance   survival of French Canada as a distinct society (*p. 362*)

learning theory   the microsociological argument that individuals act and interact based on their past history of associations, rewards and punishments, and observing and being instructed by others (*p. 10*)

liberal feminism   argues that gender inequality can be remedied by greater opportunity being given to women, such as pay equity, day care, affirmative action (*p. 160*)

liberation hypothesis   the assumption that as women become more liberated and have greater job opportunities they will also engage in more crime, just like their male counterparts (*p. 107*)

life course perspective   a framework with several linking concepts, compatible with a number of theoretical approaches rather than a theory in its own right. The life course involves a series of age-related transitions that occur along a trajectory across the age structure. (*p. 206*)

lifelong learning   the idea that the skills in demand in our modern economy constantly shift and evolve and it therefore becomes necessary to engage in constant learning and upgrading of skills and knowledge (*p. 301*)

life table   a statistical model that estimates the number of years persons of a given age can expect to live (*p. 378*)

longitudinal research   research done over time, often by participant observers (*p. 31*)

looking-glass self   Cooley's idea that personality is shaped as individuals see themselves mirrored in the reactions of others (*p. 68*)

love standard   the premarital sexual standard that permits premarital sex for persons of either gender if they are in love (*p. 236*)

manners or etiquette   informal rules of interpersonal conduct (*p. 95*)

marriage   a commitment and an ongoing exchange. The commitment can include legal or contractual elements, as well as the social pressures against dissolution. The arrangement includes both instrumental and expressive exchanges. (*p. 226*)

materialist values   values that place a high priority on economic and physical security (*p. 410*)

mating gradient   the lesser power of a woman in a typical marriage, partly due to her being younger than her husband (*p. 238*)

maturation   see **age effects**

McDonaldization   the process by which the principles of fast-food restaurants are coming to dominate more sectors of American society as well as the rest of the world (*p. 332*)

mechanical solidarity   according to Durkheim, solidarity based upon unity or sameness within a social group (*p. 403*)

meritocracy   the principle that persons are selected for social positions based on merit or achievement in a fair competition (e.g., through exams and tests in school) rather than ascribed characteristics, such as social class, race, or gender (*p. 303*)

migration   movement across legally defined boundaries (*p. 382*)

minority group   a social category, usually ethnically or racially labelled, that occupies a subordinate rank in the hierarchy of a society (*p. 179*)

mobilization   the transfer of resources, particularly human resources, from the pursuit of one goal or set of goals to the pursuit of another goal or set of goals (*p. 348*)

modernization theory the approach that argues that the limited development in the Third World is a consequence of domestic factors such as traditional cultures that may not be conducive to development, capital shortages, the lack of technological expertise, or the absence of infrastructure such as roads, bridges, and energy sources (*p. 412*)

moral entrepreneurs people who seek to influence the making of rules and definitions of deviance (*p. 112*)

mores those norms that when violated provoke a relatively strong reaction on the part of group members (*p. 40*)

nature versus nurture the debate over the extent to which human behaviour is affected by genetic vs. social factors (*p. 61*)

neo-liberalism the view that holds that international free trade, privatization, the free flow of capital, and mini-mal government regulation provide optimal conditions for economic development in any country, wealthy or not (*p. 412*)

normative structure organized systems of norms that give people direction and meaning in their lives (*p. 75*)

norms relatively precise rules specifying the behaviours permitted and prohibited for group members (*p. 39, 88*)

objectification to view someone as an object, usually a sexual object, and not fully as a person (*p. 162*)

occupational segregation when people from different social categories (gender, racial, or other) hold different types of jobs (*p. 333*)

operational definition description of the actual procedures used to measure a theoretical concept, as in I.Q. scores being an operational definition of intelligence (*p. 21*)

organic solidarity according to Durkheim, solidarity based on the complementarity or interdependence of positions in modern, complex divisions of labour (*p. 403*)

Orientalism a form of ethnocentrism representing the sum total of all the theories, analyses, and interpretations developed in the nineteenth century by Western scholars to understand societies in the Middle East (*p. 49*)

panic a rapid and impulsive course of action that occurs when people are frightened and try to save themselves or their property from perceived danger (*p. 343*)

participant observation (or ethnography) a research strategy whereby a researcher becomes a member of a group in order to study it, and group members are aware that they are being observed (*p. 20*)

pathologizing the process of attributing deviant behavior to particular individual maladies (*p. 106*)

patriarchy a system of gender relations in which traits associated with men are valued more than those associated with women and thus gives men greater privilege (*p. 160*)

period effects outcomes that result from having been a certain age at a certain point in time and capture the impact of an historical time or period (*p. 204*)

period measures measures referring to a specific period of time (*p. 373*)

pluralism the view that power in modern society is shared among competing interest groups. With respect to deviance, it means that definitions of deviance arise not from consensus, nor from any one group, but from a diversity of sources. Also suggests that ethnic diversity, stratification, and conflict remain central features of modern societies, and that race and ethnicity continue to be important aspects of individual identity and group behaviour. (*p. 112, 195*)

pluralistic society a social system of coexisting and usually hierarchically ranked racial and ethnic groups, each of which to some degree maintains its own distinctive culture, social networks, and institutions, while participating with other racial and ethnic groups in common cultural, economic, and political institutions (*p. 177*)

political economy of aging perspective macro-level view of how political and economic processes create a social structure that tends to place constraints on the lives of older persons (*p. 206*)

political economy of media an approach to communication studies that focuses on the power relations governing the production, distribution, and consumption of information (*p. 278*)

popular culture those preferences and objects that are widely distributed across all social classes in a society (*p. 42*)

population pyramid a picture or graphic representation of the composition of a population at a particular point in time (*p. 388*)

positive checks events or circumstances which stop the growth of population, including war, famine, and disease (*p. 369*)

positivism the application of natural science research methods to social science (*p. 18*)

postfigurative culture those in which the relations between parents and offspring are governed by traditional norms beyond questioning of either parent or child, as opposed to **cofigurative** and prefigurative cultures (*p. 74*)

postmaterialism a set of values stressing self-expression, participation in decision-making, belonging, self-esteem, and intellectual and artistic development (*p. 410*)

postmodern perspective a skeptical, critical, and self-aware perspective that attempts to de-mystify the claims of those with power and authority. Many postmodern theorists appear to be more preoccupied with understanding what lies behind dominant assumptions and social conventions than with developing theories to explain and predict behaviour, solving social problems, or prompting social change. (*p. 199*)

postmodernism an intellectual movement advocating, among other things, moral and epistemological relativism. It also promotes the idea that science and culture are often forms of domination and control. (*p. 409*)

power a differential capacity to command resources and thereby control social situations (*p. 119*)

power-control theory a theory that focuses on how different household dynamics pertaining to gender differences in parental dynamics of power and control influence the criminal behavior of children (*p. 107*)

praxis Marx's concept that research should not be pure, conducted just for knowledge's sake, but *applied*, undertaken to improve society (*p. 32*)

prefigurative cultures those in which the social change is so great that parental life experiences are dated and thus parental guidance is not well regarded by children, as opposed to **post-figurative** and cofigurative cultures (*p. 75*)

prejudice prejudging people based upon characteristics they are assumed to share as members of a social category (*p. 183*)

premarital sexual standards standards by which people judge the acceptability of premarital sex. See also **abstinence standard**, double standard, love standard, and fun standard (*p. 235*)

preventive checks controlling population by people postponing marriage until they could provide for the children that would be born to them (*p. 369*)

primary deviance deviant behavior that occurs prior to any labelling process (*p. 111*)

primary versus secondary sources the former are records produced by contemporaries of an event, the latter interpretations of primary sources made by others not immediately present at the event (*p. 32*)

private realm the home, unpaid domestic labour, and *expressive tasks*, nurturing and providing emotional support; the domain of women in functionalist thought (*p. 156*)

profane quite literally, all that is not sacred. In most cases, the world of everyday, non-religious experience. (*p. 259*)

proletariat Marx's word for the working class, the non-owners of the means of production (*p. 123*)

public a large and dispersed group made up of persons who share an interest in the same thing. They may hold similar views or they may sharply disagree. (*p. 343*)

public realm paid labour and the *instrumental tasks* needed for survival; the domain of men in functionalist thought (*p. 156*)

Quiet Revolution a movement in the 1960s in Quebec to expand governmental powers, decrease Church power, modernize Quebec, and fight vigorously for *la survivance* (*p. 364*)

quota sample a selection of people that matches the sample to the population on the basis of certain selected characteristics (*p. 23*)

race an arbitrary social category in which membership is based upon inherited physical characteristics such as skin colour and facial features, characteristics defined as socially meaningful (*p. 179*)

race relations cycle the four stages, posited by Park, in the relationship between dominant and minority groups. The cycle involves contact, competition, accommodation, and finally assimilation. (*p. 194*)

racialization assigning people to socially constructed racial categories and behaving toward them as though these categories were real (*p. 179*)

racist ideology an ideology that rationalizes the exploitation of certain categories of human beings on the basis of inherited characteristics (*p. 179*)

radical feminism the variant with just one goal, the abolition of male supremacy; the means, women having control over biological reproduction (*p. 160*)

random sample a sample in which every member of the population is eligible for inclusion and individuals are selected by chance (*p. 22*)

rate of natural increase a measure of how fast the population is growing per year, based on the difference between the crude birth rate and the crude death rate (*p. 370*)

rational choice theory the idea that individuals make choices based on careful cost–benefit considerations, with the intention of maximizing benefits while minimizing costs (*p. 10, 307*)

rationalization a condition in which there are formalized procedures that give actors a measure of predictability in the outcomes of their actions (*p. 330, 406*)

reaction formation Cohen's name for the tendency of working class delinquents to invert middle class values as a form of protest (*p. 105*)

rebellion for Merton, this refers to the situation where individuals reject society's ultimate goals and the means to achieve those goals and instead advocate for a new social system (*p. 104*)

relative deprivation the difference between what people believe they have a right to receive (their expectations) and what they actually receive (their achievements) (*p. 346*)

relativism an academic orientation to the study of deviance that recognizes that what counts as deviance varies across cultures and through history (*p. 87*)

reliability the degree to which repeated measurements of the same variable, using the same or equivalent instruments, are equal (*p. 21*)

religion a system of beliefs and practices about transcendent things, their nature, and their consequences for humanity (*p. 256*)

replication repeating a research project in an attempt to verify earlier findings (*p. 30*)

resistance action(s) aimed at either passively or actively slowing, reversing, avoiding, or protesting management directions or strategies in the workplace. Resistance can manifest itself on any scale, from millions of workers launching general strikes to gain political change, to small groups protesting a supervisor's arbitrary order. (*p. 336*)

resistance theory based on the work of Paul Willis, the idea that working-class youth actively reject the middle-class norms and values of education in favour of working-class ideals of manual labour (*p. 307*)

retreatism for Merton, this refers to the situation where individuals reject society's ultimate goals and the means to achieve those goals and instead withdraw from society (*p. 104*)

ritualism for Merton, this refers to the situation where individuals continue to adhere to the legitimate means held out by society for securing success, irrespective of the fact that they have little prospect of becoming successful (*p. 104*)

role a cluster of behavioural expectations associated with some particular social position within a group or society (*p. 40*)

role conflict a situation in which the behavioural expectations of one role are inconsistent with those of a concurrent role (*p. 41*)

role system an interrelated set of social positions in which people share common expectations about desired outcomes as part of a division of labour (*p. 71*)

role-taking Mead's term for individuals' attempts to put themselves in others' shoes to imagine what they are thinking thus enabling them to see themselves as others see them (*p. 68*)

rule breakers those who commit deviant acts but to whom no one responds as if they have done so, either because they are not caught, or if caught, because they are excused for some reason (*p. 110*)

sabotage activities aimed at destroying employers' property or otherwise disrupting the flow of production (*p. 336*)

sacred those things set apart by society and treated with awe and respect, in many cases because of their association with gods or God (*p. 259*)

scientific management a system of management that seeks to transfer control of the work process from skilled workers to the owners and managers of production. It relies on the establishment of a detailed division of labour. (*p. 328*)

secondary analysis the examination by a researcher of someone else's data (*p. 33*)

sect a type of religious organization that is characterized by a more exclusive orientation than churches and voluntary membership, as well as a more radical social outlook and rigorous demands of practice (*p. 262*)

secularization the process by which sectors of society are removed from the domination of religious institutions and symbols (*p. 265*)

segregation the maintenance of physical distance between ethnic or racial groups. Sometimes this term is used to describe the exclusion of minorities from the facilities, institutions, or residential space used by dominant groups, as in South Africa's system of apartheid. At other times, it refers to the residential separation among ethnic or racial populations that may occur for a variety of reasons. (*p. 182*)

selective incentives the individual benefits that a person can derive from belonging to an association or joining a social movement. Selective incentives help motivate people to join social movements. (*p. 350*)

self-fulfilling prophecy the possibility that the act of predicting a particular outcome helps to bring about that outcome (*p. 111*)

self-report studies a methodology which involves asking individuals to reveal the amount of crime or deviance in which they have personally been involved (*p. 90*)

self-socialization the recognition of one's own limitations and constraints in order to create ways to live among others (*p. 73*)

sensibilities structures of feelings (*p. 95*)

sex a *biological* ascribed trait, including chromosomes and hormones, XX and more estrogen for a female and XY and more testosterone for a male (*p. 154*)

significant others persons whose attitudes and opinions affect one's life. Significant others include family and friends as well as persons of high prestige like teachers and celebrities. (*p. 70*)

social breakdown approach an approach to collective behaviour that argues that social unrest occurs when established institutions are disrupted or weakened (*p. 344*)

social category a collection of individuals who share a particular trait that is defined as socially meaningful, but who do not necessarily interact or have anything else in common (*p. 179*)

social class a category of individuals who possess similar economic position as well as group consciousness, common identity, and a tendency to act as a social unit (*p. 121*)

social cleavage a division (based on age, class, ethnicity, etc.) that may result in the formation of distinct social groups social constructionist perspective emphasizes the subjective experience of the older person and his/her ability to exercise agency in negotiations with others (*p. 357*)

social constructionist perspective an interpretive approach that emphasizes the subjective experience of older persons and their ability to exercise agency in negotiations with others, also called the symbolic interactionist perspective (*p. 206*)

social contagion the rapid and uncontrolled spread of a mood, impulse, or form of conduct through a collectivity of people (*p. 343*)

social contract the socially accepted understanding, sanctioned by government, that if people work hard and produce more goods and services each year, the economy would grow, and thus growth financially benefits both the workers and management (*p. 329*)

social differentiation the tendency toward diversification and complexity in the statuses and characteristics of social life (*p. 119*)

social division of labour the division of jobs among people in order to ensure societal survival and prosperity (*p. 327*)

social facts social sources or causes of behaviour; used by sociologists to explain rates of behaviour in groups as opposed to individual behaviour (*p. 2*)

social inequality the general pattern of inequality, or ranking, of socially differentiated characteristics (*p. 119*)

social integration the attachment of individuals to social groups or institutions. Integration depends on a set of sanctions that rewards conformity to the group and punishes nonconformity. (*p. 344*)

social movement a large collectivity of people trying to bring about or resist social change structure. The term "structure" has many meanings, but generally it refers to a stable arrangement or interconnection among parts of a whole. (*p. 343*)

social reproduction the ways in which societies reproduce themselves in terms of privilege and status (*p. 66*)

socialist feminism the variant that sees capitalism as leading to patriarchy and then gender inequality (*p. 160*)

socialization the means by which someone is made "fit" to live among other humans (*p. 62*)

socialization ratio the number of socializers, e.g., teachers or parents, to those being socialized. The lower the ratio (fewer agents), the less the context will change those being socialized. (*p. 62*)

society a group of people who reside in the same geographical area, who communicate extensively among themselves, and who share a common culture (*p. 40*)

spurious relationship the appearance that two variables are in a causal relationship, when in fact each is an effect of a common third variable (*p. 31*)

staples thesis Innis's idea that the economic, political, and cultural formation of Canada was shaped by its geography and the natural resources and raw materials ("staples") available for export. The thesis maintains that a reliance on the export of staples limited Canadian economic development and made Canada vulnerable to the shifting needs and demands of more populous and developed foreign metropolitan centres. (*p. 401*)

state the organization that has a monopoly on the legitimate use of force in a given territory (*p. 396*)

state theory of modernization the theory that modern capitalism first emerged in Western Europe because the state was relatively weak there. It claims that the state, especially in agrarian societies, has a natural tendency to stifle economic and intellectual development. (*p. 405*)

status any position occupied by an individual in a social system (*p. 120*)

status bloc an organization or association in which people come together for specific purposes (*p. 353*)

status communities enduring communities that have lived together over long periods of time, sharing language, culture, and other attributes (*p. 353*)

status consistency similarity in the ranking of an individual's statuses in a set of status hierarchies (*p. 120*)

status hierarchy any one of a set of rankings along which statuses are related in terms of their power (*p. 120*)

status inconsistency dissimilarity in the ranking of an individual's statuses in a set of status hierarchies (*p. 120*)

status set the combination of statuses that any one individual occupies (*p. 120*)

stereotypes mental images that exaggerate traits believed to be typical of members of a social group (*p. 185*)

stigma a physical or social attribute that can devalue a person's social identity (*p. 96*)

stratum a set of statuses of similar rank in any status hierarchy (*p. 120*)

streaming the process of placing students in different educational programs (e.g., academic vs. vocational), based on a combination of previous achievement, tests, teachers' assumptions, and parents' wishes (*p. 311*)

structural assimilation acceptance of a minority group by a dominant group into its intimate, primary, social relationships (*p. 194*)

subculture a subset of individuals within a society who are characterized by certain cultural elements that set them apart from others in the society (*p. 42*)

substantive definition of religion any definition that uses some conception of what religion essentially "is," some key characteristic, as its primary criterion (*p. 256*)

supernatural those things or experiences which appear to be inexplicable in terms of the laws of nature or the material universe (*p. 256*)

surrogate theory the idea that watching media violence, rather than stimulating real-life violence, provides a substitute or safety valve for aggressive feelings (*p. 287*)

symbolic interactionism the micro-sociological perspective that assumes that individuals act and interact on the basis of symbolically encoded information (*p. 5*)

symbolic violence in the sociology of education, the concept that schools neglect the everyday experiences of students outside the mainstream (e.g., working-class students or Aboriginal students) and instead enforce middle-class values and norms on everybody (*p. 309*)

syncretism the attempt to reconcile and combine different religious and philosophical views, even ones seemingly in conflict with each other (*p. 271*)

systemic or institutionalized discrimination discrimination against members of a group that occurs as a by-product of the ordinary functioning of bureaucratic institutions, rather than as a consequence of a deliberate policy to discriminate. Systemic discrimination perpetuates a social, political, and economic structure in which some groups are privileged while others are disadvantaged. (*p. 182*)

techniques of neutralization rationalizations that allow deviants to define their behaviour as acceptable (*p. 109*)

technological determinism the idea that new technologies drive social change (*p. 277*)

technologies of freedom a phrase suggesting that computers and other digital technologies empower citizens by allowing them to create and circulate information for themselves (*p. 278*)

theory a set of interrelated statements or propositions about a particular subject matter (*p. 20*)

total fertility rate an estimate of the average number of children a woman will bear in her lifetime if she experiences the current age-specific rates of fertility, expressed per woman (*p. 373*)

transgendered   the inclusion of aspects of both genders in one's gender identity (*p. 156*)

triangulation   the application of several research methods to the same topic in the hope that the weaknesses of any one method may be compensated for by the strengths of the others (*p. 31*)

underemployment   explains employment situations in which individuals have higher levels of formal education and more skills than required by the actual content of the work they perform (*p. 303*)

union   an association of people in a definable workplace or group of workplaces whose role is to represent the collective group of workers in negotiations with the employer to get a contract (*p. 337*)

universal church   the term used to characterize very large, international religious organizations seeking, ideally, to include everyone in the world in their membership (*p. 263*)

urban legends   oral stories of the recent past, which, although believed to be true, are actually false and reflect unconscious fears (*p. 44*)

validity   the degree to which a measure actually measures what it claims to (*p. 21*)

values   relatively general beliefs that define right and wrong, or indicate general preferences (*p. 38*)

variable   a characteristic, such as income or religion, that takes on different values among different individuals or groups. Causes are generally called independent variables, and effects are usually called dependent variables. (*p. 20*)

verstehen   the understanding of behaviour as opposed to the predicting of behaviour (*p. 28*)

vertical mobility   movement up and down a status hierarchy (*p. 121*)

vertical mosaic   the hierarchical ranking of ethnic populations in a society (*p. 173*)

victimization survey   a methodology which involves asking individuals to reveal the nature and amount of criminal behavior they have personally experienced, typically over the past twelve months (*p. 90*)

virtual commerce   the use of computer networks such as the Internet and the World Wide Web for business purposes, primarily by creating direct links between producers and customers (*p. 294*)

virtual community   a group of computer users separated geographically but linked together in cyberspace on the basis of shared interests and concerns (*p. 292*)

vocation   an approach to work traditionally associated with a religious calling (*p. 261*)

work   changing physical materials (manual work) or mental constructs/ideas (intellectual work) so as to make these materials and/or ideas more useful to the producer (*p. 325*)

world system theory   the approach that argues that all the countries of the world form a unified system, and that the social conditions in any society can be understood by examining its position in the world system. The nations of the world are divided into three groups: the *core, periphery*, and *semi-periphery* (*p. 413*)

Bibliography

Abramson, Bruce
2005 *Digital Phoenix: Why the Information Economy Collapsed and How It Will Rise Again*. Cambridge, MA: MIT Press.

Adam, B.A.
1993 "Post-Marxism and the new social movements." *Canadian Review of Sociology and Anthropology* 30: 316–36.

Adams, O.
1990 "Life expectancy in Canada: an overview." *Health Reports* 2: 361–76.

Adams, Gerald, James Côté, and Sheila Marshall
2001 *Parent–Adolescent Relationships and Identity Development: A Literature Review and Policy Statement*. Report to Division of Childhood and Adolescence, Health Canada, Ottawa, September 16.

Adams, Owen, Anna Brancker, and Russell Wilkins
1989 "Changes in mortality by income in urban Canada from 1971 to 1986." *Health Reports* 1(2): 137–74.

Adamson, Nancy, Linda Briskin, and Margaret McPhail
1988 *Feminist Organizing for Change: The Contemporary Women's Movement in Canada*. Toronto: Oxford University Press.

Adelberg, Ellen and Claudia Currie (eds).
1987 *Too Few to Count: Canadian Women in Conflict with the Law*. Vancouver: Press Gang.

Adler, Freda.
1975 *Sisters in Crime*. New York: McGraw-Hill.

Adorno, Theodor and Max Horkheimer
1972 *Dialectic of Enlightenment*. New York: Herder and Herder.

Agòcs, Carol (ed.)
2002 *Workplace Equality: International Perspectives on Legislation, Policy and Practice*. The Hague: Kluwer Law International.

Akass, Kim and McCab, Janet. (Eds.)
2004 *Reading Sex and the City*. New York: I.B. Tauris.

Ali, Jennifer and Edward Grabb
1998 "Ethnic origin, class origin, and educational attainment in Canada: further evidence on the mosaic thesis." *Journal of Canadian Studies* 33: 3–21.

Allahar, Anton L. and James E. Côté
1998 *Richer and Poorer: The Structure of Social Inequality in Canada*. Toronto: Lorimer.

Almey, Marcia and Normand, Josée
2002 *Youth in Canada* (3rd ed.). Ottawa: Minister of Industry.

Ambert, Anne-Marie and Maureen Baker
1988 "Marriage dissolution." In B. Fox (ed.), *Family Bonds and Gender Divisions*. Toronto: Canadian Scholar's Press.

Aminzade, Ronald
1995 "Between movement and party: the transformation of mid-nineteenth-century French Republicanism." Pp. 39–62 in J. Craig Jenkins and Bert Klandermans (eds.), *The Politics of Social Protest: Comparative Perspectives on States and Social Movements*. Minneapolis: University of Minnesota Press.

Andres, Lesley, and Harvey Krahn
1999 "Youth pathways in articulated postsecondary systems: enrolment and completion patterns of urban young women and men." *Canadian Journal of Higher Education* 29(1): 47–82.

Andres, Lesley, Paul Anisef, Harvey Krahn, Dianne Looker, and Victor Thiessen
1999 "The persistence of social structure: cohort, class and gender effects on the occupational aspirations and expectations of Canadian youth." *Journal of Youth Studies* 2(3): 261–82.

Anisef, Paul and Paul Axelrod (eds.)
1993 "Universities, graduates, and the marketplace: Canadian patterns and prospects." Chapter 6 in P. Anisef and P. Axelrod (eds.), *Transitions: Schooling and Employment in Canada*. Toronto: Thompson Educational Publishing.

Anisef, Paul, Paul Axelrod, Etta Baichman-Anisef, Carl James, and Anton Turrittin
2000 *Opportunity and Uncertainty: Life Course Experiences of the Class of '73*. Toronto: University of Toronto Press.

Anyon, Jean
1980 "Social class and the hidden curriculum of work." *Journal of Education* 162(1): 67–92.

Appadurai, A.
1990 "Disjuncture and difference in the global cultural economy." *Public Culture* 2: 1–24.

Archibald, W. Peter
1978 *Social Psychology as Political Economy*. Toronto: McGraw-Hill Ryerson.

Armstrong, P., H. Armstrong, J. Choinière, E. Mykalovskiy, and Jerry P. White
1996 *Medical Alert*. Toronto: Garamond Press.

Arnett, Jeffrey
2000 *Adolescence and Emerging Adulthood: A Cultural Approach*. Upper Saddle River: Prentice Hall.
1999 "Adolescent storm and stress reconsidered." *American Psychologist* 54: 317–26.

1996   *Metalheads: Heavy Metal Music and Adolescent Alienation.*
         Boulder, CO: Westview Press.

Arnold, Fred, Sunita Kishor, and T.K. Roy
2002   "Sex-selective abortions in India." *Population and
        Development Review* 28: 759–85.

Association of Universities and Colleges of Canada
2002   *Trends in Higher Education.* Ottawa: AUCC.

**Astin, Alexander W., W.S. Korn, K.M. Mahoney
and L.J. Sax**
1994   *The American Freshman: National Norms for Fall 1994.*
        Los Angeles: Higher Educational Research Institute,
        University of California.

Atkinson, Michael
2004   "Tattooing and civilizing processes: body modification
        as self-control." *Canadian Review of Sociology and
        Anthropology* 41: 125–46.

Avery, Donald
1995   *Reluctant Host: Canada's Response to Immigrant Workers,
        1896-1994.* Toronto: McClelland and Stewart.

Ayalon, Hanna
2003   "Women and men go to university: mathematical back-
        ground and gender differences in choice of field in
        higher education." *Sex Roles* 47: 277–90.

Babcock, Barbara
1997   "Mudwomen and whitemen: a meditation on Pueblo
        potteries and the politics of representation." In *The
        Material Culture of Gender/The Gender of Material Culture*,
        Katharine Martinez and Kenneth Ames (eds).
        Winterthur, Delaware: Henry Francis du Pont
        Winterthur Museum.

Baer, Douglas
2004   "Educational credentials and the changing occupational
        structure." Pp. 115–31 in James Curtis, Edward Grabb,
        and Neil Guppy (eds.), *Social Inequality in Canada:
        Patterns, Problems, and Policies* (4th ed.). Toronto:
        Pearson Education Canada.

Baer, Douglas, James Curtis, and Edward Grabb
2000   "Defining moments and recurring myths: comparing
        Canadians and Americans after the American
        Revolution." *Canadian Review of Sociology and
        Anthropology* 38: 373–419.

**Baer, Douglas, James Curtis, Edward Grabb, and
William Johnston**
1996   "What values do people prefer in children? A compara-
        tive analysis of survey evidence from fifteen countries."
        Pp. 299–328 in Clive Seligman, James Olson, and Mark
        Zanna (eds.), *The Psychology of Values: The Ontario
        Symposium.* Vol. 8. Mahwah, NJ: Lawrence Erlbaum
        Associates Inc.

Baer, Douglas, Edward Grabb, and William Johnston
1993   "National character, regional culture, and the values of
        Canadians and Americans." *Canadian Review of
        Sociology and Anthropology* 30: 13–36.

Babcock, Barbara
1997   "Mudwomen and whitemen: a meditation on Pueblo
        potteries and the politics of representation." Katharine
        Martinez and Kenneth Ames (eds.). *The material culture
        of gender/The gender of material culture.* Winterthur:
        Henry Francis du Pont Winterthur Museum.

Bagdikian, Ben H.
2004   *The New Media Monopoly.* Boston: Beacon.

Baker, L., S. Pearcey, and J. Dabbs
2002   "Testosterone, alcohol, and civil and rough conflict
        resolution in lesbian couples." *Journal of Homosexuality*
        42: 77–88.

Balakrishnan, T.R.
2001   "Residential segregation and socio-economic integra-
        tion of Asians in Canadian cities," *Canadian Ethnic
        Studies,* 33: 120–31.

Balakrishnan, T.R., and Feng Hou
1996   "The integration of visible minorities in contemporary
        Canadian society." *Canadian Journal of Sociology* 21: 307–26.

Balakrishnan, T.R. and Carl Grindstaff
1988   *Early Adulthood Behaviour and Later Life Course Paths.*
        Health and Welfare Canada: Report for Review of
        Demography.

**Balakrishnan, T.R., K. Krotki, and E. Lapierre-
Adamcyk**
1993   *Family and Childbearing in Canada.* Toronto: University of
        Toronto Press.

Bales, Robert F. and Talcott Parsons
1955   *Family, Socialization and Interaction Process.* New York:
        Free Press.

Bandura, Albert
1989   "Human agency in social cognitive theory." *American
        Psychologist* 44: 1175–84.

Bandura, A., D. Ross, and S. Ross
1963   "Vicarious reinforcement and imitative learning."
        Journal of Abnormal and Social Psychology 66: 3–11.

Barber, Benjamin
1995   *Jihad vs McWorld: How the Planet Is Both Falling Apart and
        Coming Together—And What This Means for Democracy.*
        New York: Times Books.

Barth, Fredrik
1969   "Introduction." Pp. 9–38 in F. Barth (ed.), *Ethnic Groups
        and Boundaries: The Social Organization of Culture
        Difference.* Bergen-Oslo: Universitets Forlaget.

Battle, K.
1997   "Pension reform in Canada." *Canadian Journal on Aging*
        16: 519–52.

Baumeister, Roy and Mark Muraven
1996   "Identity as adaptation to social, cultural, and historical
        context." *Journal of Adolescence* 19: 405–16.

Beattie, Karen
2005   *Adult Correctional Services in Canada, 2004/2005.* Ottawa:
        Statistics Canada.

Beauchesne, Eric
1994   "University degrees put women on equal footing with men." *London Free Press,* October 5: A3.

Beaujot, Roderic
2004   *Delayed Life Transitions: Trends and Implications.* Contemporary Family Trends Paper on The Modern Life Course. Ottawa: Vanier Institute of the Family. www.ivfamille.ca/library/cft/delayed_life.html
2000   *Earning and Caring in Canadian Families.* Peterborough: Broadview.
1995   "Family patterns at mid-life (marriage, parenting and working)." In Roderic Beaujot, Ellen M. Gee, Fernando Rajulton, and Zenaida Ravanera (eds.), *Family over the Life Course.* Statistics Canada, Catalogue No. 91-543. Ottawa: Minister of Supply and Services Canada.
1991   *Population Change in Canada.* Toronto: McClelland and Stewart.
1990   "The family and demographic change: economic and cultural interpretations and solutions." *Journal of Comparative Family Studies* 2l: 25–38.

Beaujot, Roderic and Don Kerr
2004   *Population Change in Canada.* Toronto: Oxford University Press.

Beaujot, R. and J. Liu
2001   *Models of Earning and Caring: Evidence from Canadian Time-Use Data.* London: University of Western Ontario, Population Studies Centre, Discussion Paper No. 01–13.
2005   "Models of time use in paid and unpaid work." *Journal of Family Issues* 26(7): 924–46.

Beaujot, Roderic, Zenaida Ravanera and Thomas Burch
2006   "Toward an SDC (Social Development Canada) Family Research Framework." Revised version of paper presented at Social Development Canada Expert Roundtable on Challenges for Canadian Families, Ottawa, 1–2 December 2005.

Beccaria, Cesare Bonesana Marguis
1819   *An Essay on Crimes and Punishments.* E.D. Ingraham (trans.). Philadelphia: Philip H. Nicklin Publishers.

Becker, Gary S.
1981   *A Treatise on the Family.* Cambridge: Harvard University Press.

Becker, Howard S.
1973   [1963] *Outsiders. Studies in the Sociology of Deviance.* New York: Free Press.

Beckstead, Desmond and W. Mark Brown
2005   *Provincial Income Disparities Through an Urban–Rural Lens: Evidence from the 2001 Census.* Statistics Canada Analytical Paper, Catalogue No. 11-624-MIE, No. 012, July.

Beisner, M. and W. Iacono
1990   "An update on the epidemiology of schizophrenia." *Canadian Journal of Psychiatry* 35: 657–68.

Béland, Francois and André Blais
1989   "Quantitative methods and contemporary sociology in francophone Quebec." *Canadian Review of Sociology and Anthropology* 26: 533–56.

Belanger, Alain
2003   *"Report on the Demographic Situation in Canada 2002."* Statistics Canada, Catalogue No. 91-209. Ottawa: Statistics Canada.

Belanger, Alain et al.
2002   "Gender differences in disability-free life expectancy for selected risk factors and chronic conditions in Canada." *Journal of Women and Aging* 14: 61–83.

Bélanger, Alain, Yves Carrière, and Stéphane Gilbert
2001   *Report on the Demographic Situation in Canada 2000.* Statistics Canada, Catalogue No. 91-209. Ottawa: Statistics Canada.

Bélanger, Alain and Jean Dumas
1998   *Report on the Demographic Situation in Canada 1997.* Statistics Canada, Catalogue No. 91-209. Ottawa: Minister of Supply and Services Canada.

Bélanger, Danièle and Thu Hong Khuat
1998   "Young single women using abortion in Vietnam." *Asia-Pacific Population Journal* 13: 3–26.

Bell, Daniel
1980   "The social framework of the information society."Pp. 500–49 in Tom Forester (ed.), *The Microelectronics Revolution: The Complete Guide to the New Technology and Its Impact on Society.* Cambridge, MA: MIT Press.
1973   *The Coming of Post-Industrial Society.* New York: Basic Books.

Bell, Edward
1990   "Class voting in the first Alberta Social Credit Election." *Canadian Journal of Political Science* 23: 3.

Bellafonte, G., D. Cray, and D. Gross
1994   "If everyone is hip . . . is anyone hip?" *Time,* August 8, pp. 48–55.

Belliveau, Jo-Anne and Ron Logan
1995   "Working mothers."*Canadian Social Trends* 36: 24–28.

Bem, Sandra
1974   "The measurement of psychological androgyny." *Journal of Consulting and Clinical Psychology* 42: 155–62.

Benedict, Ruth
1938   "Continuities and discontinuities in cultural conditioning." *Psychiatry* 1: 161–67.
1934   *Patterns of Culture.* Boston: Houghton Mifflin.

Benford, R.D., E.B. Rochford Jr., D.A. Snow, and S.K. Worden
1986   "Frame alignment processes, micromobilization, and movement participation." *American Sociological Review* 51: 464–81.

Bengtson, V.L., E.O. Burgess, and T.M. Parrott
1997   "Theory, explanation, and a third generation of theoretical development in social gerontology." *Journal of Gerontology: Social Sciences* 52B: S72-S88.

Bengtson, V.L., L.N. Richards, and R.E.L. Roberts
1991 "Intergenerational solidarity in families: untangling the ties that bind." *Marriage and Family Review* 16: 11–46.

Bennett, William J.
1994 *The Index of Leading Cultural Indicators: Facts and Figures on the State of American Society.* New York: Touchstone Books.

Berezin, Mabel
1997 "Politics and culture: a less fissured terrain." *Annual Review of Sociology* 23: 361–83.

Bergdahl, Jacqueline and Michael Norris
2002 "Sex differences in single vehicle fatal crashes: A research note." *Social Science Journal* 39: 287–93.

Berger, Peter L.
1967 *The Sacred Canopy: Elements of a Sociological Theory of Religion.* New York: Doubleday.

Berger, Peter L. and Thomas Luckmann
1966 *The Social Construction of Reality: A Treatise in the Sociology of Knowledge.* New York: Anchor Books.

Bergob, Michael, Mary Sue Devereaux, and Colin Lindsay
1994 *Youth in Canada* (2nd ed.). Ottawa: Minister of Industry, Science and Technology.

Berk, Richard A.
1974a "A gaming theory approach to crowd behavior." *American Sociological Review* 39: 355–73.
1974b *Collective Behavior.* Dubuque, IA: Brown.

Berkowitz, L.
1975 "Some effects of thoughts on anti- and prosocial influences of media events." *Psychological Bulletin* 28: 410–27.

Besser, Howard
1995 "From Internet to information superhighway." Pp. 59–71 in James Brook and Iain Boal (eds.), *Resisting the Virtual Life: The Culture and Politics of Information.* San Francisco: City Lights.

Best, Pamela
1995 "Women, men and work." *Canadian Social Trends* 36: 30–33.

Betcherman, G. and N. Leckie
1997 *Youth Employment and Education Trends in the 1980s and 1990s.* Ottawa: Canadian Policy Research Networks.

Bettelheim, Bruno
1967 *The Empty Fortress.* New York: Free Press.
1959 "Feral children and autistic children." *American Journal of Sociology* 64: 455–67.

Beyer, Peter
2000 "Modern forms of the religious life: denomination, church and invisible religion in Canada, the United States, and Europe." In David Lyon and Marguerite Van Die (eds.), *Rethinking Church, State, and Modernity: Canada Between Europe and the USA.* Toronto: University of Toronto Press.
1997 "Religious vitality in Canada: the complementarity of religious market and secularization perspectives." *Journal for the Scientific Study of Religion* 36: 272–88.

Bibby, Reginald
995 *The Bibby Report: Social Trends Canadian Style.* Toronto: Stoddart.
1993 *Unknown Gods: The Ongoing Story of Religion in Canada.* Toronto: Stoddart.
1979 "Religion in Canada." *Journal for the Scientific Study of Religion* 18: 1–17.

Bibby, Reginald W. and Donald C. Posterski
1992 *Teen Trends: A Nation in Motion.* Toronto: Stoddart.

Birns, B., R. Friend, and N. Weitzman
1985 "Traditional and nontraditional mothers' communication with their daughters and sons." *Child Development* 56: 894–96.

Blum, D.
1997 *Sex on the Brain: The Biological Differences Between Men and Women.* New York: Viking.

Blumer, Herbert
1969 *Symbolic Interactionism: Perspective and Method.* Upper Saddle River: Prentice Hall.
1951 [1939] "Collective behavior." Pp. 167–222 in A.M. Lee (ed.), *Principles of Sociology.* New York: Barnes and Noble.

Blumler, J. and E. Katz (eds.)
1975 *The Uses and Gratifications Approach to Mass Communication Research.* Beverly Hills, CA: Sage.

Boles, Sharon and Patrick Johnson
2001 "Gender weight concerns and adolescent smoking." *Journal of Addictive Diseases* 20: 5–14.

Bonvillain, Nancy
2001 *Women and Men: Cultural Constructs of Gender* (3rd ed.). Upper Saddle River: Prentice Hall.

Bordo, Susan
1993 "Reading the slender body". Pp. 185–212 in *Unbearable Weight.* Berkeley: University of California Press.

Botta, Renee A.
2003 "For your health? The relationship between magazine reading and adolescents' body image and eating disturbances." *Sex Roles: A Journal of Research*, May Issue.

Bourdieu, Pierre
1990 *The Logic of Practice.* Cambridge: Polity.
1984 *Distinction: A Social Critique of the Judgement of Taste.* R. Nice (trans.). Cambridge, MA: Harvard University Press.

Bourdieu, Pierre and Loïc J. Wacquant
1992 *An Invitation to Reflexive Sociology.* Chicago: University of Chicago Press.

Bourhis, Richard and Annie Montreuil
2003 "Exploring receiving society attitudes towards immigration and ethnocultural diversity." *Canadian Issues: Immigration* special insert, Metropolis Project Brief # 1. April: 39–41.

Bourke, Joanna
1999 *An Intimate History of Killing: Face-to-Face Killing in Twentieth-Century Warfare.* London: Granta.

Boutilier, Marie
1977 "Transformation of ideology surrounding the sexual division of labour: Canadian women during World War Two." Paper presented at the Second Conference on Blue-Collar Workers, London, Ontario, May.

Bowlby, Geoff
2000 "The school-to-work transition." *Perspectives* (Statistics Canada Catalogue No. 75-001-XPE). Spring: 43–48.

Bowles, Samuel and Herbert Gintis
1976 *Schooling in Capitalist America.* New York: Basic Books.

Boyd, Monica
1993 "Gender, visible minority and immigrant earning inequality: reassessing an employment equity premise." In Vic Satzewich (ed.), *Deconstructing a Nation: Immigration, Multiculturalism, and Racism in the '90s in Canada.* Halifax: Fernwood Publishing.

Boyd, Monica and Doug Norris
1998 "Changes in the nest: young Canadian adults living with parents, 1981–1996." Presentation at the Canadian Population Society Meetings, Ottawa, June.
1995 "Leaving the nest? Impact of family structure." *Canadian Social Trends* 38: 14–17.

Boyko, John
1998 *Last Steps to Freedom: The Evolution of Canadian Racism.* Manitoba: J. Gordon Shillingford Publishing.

Bozinoff, Lorne and André Turcotte
1993 "Canadians split over effects of working moms." *The Gallup Report,* January 24.

Brabant, S. and L. Mooney
1989 "Him, her, or either: sex of person addressed and interpersonal communication." *Sex Roles* 20: 47–48.

Braithwaite, John
1989 *Crime, Shame, and Reintegration.* New York: Cambridge University Press.

Brake, T.
1980 *The Sociology of Youth Culture and Youth Subcultures.* London: Routledge and Kegan Paul.

Brandtstädter, Jochen and Richard M. Lerner (eds.)
1999 *Action and Self-development: Theory and Research through the Life Span.* Thousand Oaks, CA: Sage Publications.

Braverman, Harry
1974a "Labor and monopoly capital: the degradation of work in the twentieth century." *Monthly Review* 26: 1–134.
1974b *Labor and Monopoly Capital.* New York: Monthly Review Press.

Breton, R., W. Isajiw, W. Kalbach, and J. Reitz
1990 *Ethnic Identity and Equality: Varieties of Experience in a Canadian City.* Toronto: University of Toronto Press.

Breton, Raymond
1990 "The ethnic group as a political resource in relation to problems of incorporation: perceptions and attitudes." Pp. 196–255 in Raymond Breton, Wsevolod Isajiw, Warren Kalbach, and Jeffrey Reitz (eds.), *Ethnic Identity and Equality.* Toronto: University of Toronto Press.
1989 "Quebec sociology: agendas from society or from sociologists?" *Canadian Review of Sociology and Anthropology* 26: 557–70.
1964 "Institutional completeness of ethnic communities and the personal relations of immigrants." *American Journal of Sociology,* 70: 193–205.

Brines, J.
1994 "Economic dependency, gender, and the division of labor at home." *American Journal of Sociology* 100(3): 652–88.

Brislin, Richard
1993 *Understanding Culture's Influence on Behavior.* Fort Worth: Harcourt Brace Jovanovich.

Britton, John H. (ed.)
1996 *Canada and the Global Economy.* Kingston: McGill Queen's University Press.

Broad, William and Nicholas Wade
1982 *Betrayers of the Truth.* New York: Touchstone Books.

Brodie, Ian
2002 *Friends of the Court: The Privileging of Interest group Litigants in Canada.* Albany: State University of New York Press.
1996 "The market for political status." *Comparative Politics* 28: 253–71.

Brown, Dan
2003 *The Da Vinci Code.* New York: Doubleday.

Brown, K.M.
1986 *Bloodfeud in Scotland, 1573-1625.* Edinburgh: John Donald.

Brown, Lynn and Carol Gilligan
1992 *Meeting at the Crossroads: Women's Psychology and Girls' Development.* Cambridge, MA: Harvard Univ. Press.

Brown, M. and B. Warner
1992 "Immigrants, urban politics, and policing in 1900." *American Sociological Review* 57: 293–305.

Brown, Phillip
1987 *Schooling Ordinary Kids: Inequality, Unemployment and the New Vocationalism.* London & New York: Tavistock Publications.

Brown, Ryan and Robert Josephs
1999 "A burden of proof: stereotype relevance and gender differences in math performances." *Journal of Personality and Social Psychology* 76: 246–57.

Brownmiller, Susan.
1976 *Against Our Will: Men, Women and Rape.* New York: Bantam.

Bruckman, Amy
1996 "Gender swapping on the Internet." Pp. 441–47 in Victor J. Vitanza (ed.), *CyberReader.* Boston: Allyn and Bacon.

Bryman, Alan and James J. Teevan
2005 *Social Research Methods.* Toronto: Oxford University Press.

Buchan, S., S. Freeman, and Neil S. Guppy
1988 "Economic background and political representation." Chapter 33 in J. Curtis, E. Grabb, N. Guppy, and S. Gilbert (eds.), *Social Inequality in Canada: Patterns, Problems, Policies.* Scarborough: Prentice Hall.

Bulcroft, Kris A. and Richard A. Bulcroft
1991 "The timing of divorce: effects on parent-child relationships in later life." *Research on Aging* 13: 226–43.

Bunge, V. P and A. Levett
1998 *Family Violence in Canada: A Statistical Profile*. Ottawa: Statistics Canada, Ministry of Industry.

Burgess, E.W., H. Locke, and M. Thomas
1963 *The Family: From Institution to Companionship*. New York: American Book Company.

Bushman, Brad and Craig Anderson
2001 "Media violence and the American public: scientific facts versus media misinformation." *American Psychologist* 56: 477–89.

Buss, David M.
1999 *Evolutionary Psychology: The New Science of the Mind*. Boston: Allyn and Bacon.

Butler, Christopher
2002 *Post-Modernism: A Very Short Introduction*. Oxford: Oxford University Press.

Butlin, George, Elaine Fournier, and Philip Giles
2004 "Intergenerational change in the education of Canadians." Pp. 165–72 in James Curtis, Edward Grabb, and Neil Guppy (eds.), *Social Inequality in Canada: Patterns, Problems, and Policies* (4th ed.). Toronto: Pearson Education Canada.

Byerly, Carolyn and Ross, Karen. (eds.)
2006 *Women And Media: A Critical Introduction*. Oxford: Blackwell.

Cairns, Alan C.
2000 *Citizens Plus. Aboriginal Peoples and the Canadian State*. Vancouver: University of British Columbia Press.

Calasanti, Toni M.
1996 "Incorporating diversity meaning, levels of research, and implications for theory." *Gerontologist* 36(2): 147–56.

Caldwell, John C.
1976 "Toward a restatement of demographic transition theory." *Population and Development Review* 2: 321–66.

Caldwell, John C. and P. Caldwell
1997 "What do we now know about fertility transition?" Pp.15–25 in G.W. Jones, R.M. Douglas, J.C. Caldwell, and R.M. D'Souza (eds.), *The Continuing Demographic Transition*. Oxford: Claredon Press.

Calzavara, Liviana
1993 "Trends and policy in employment opportunities for women." Chapter 22 in J. Curtis, E. Grabb, and N. Guppy (eds.), *Social Inequality in Canada: Patterns, Problems, Policies*. (2nd ed.) Scarborough: Prentice Hall.

Campani, Giovanna
1992 "Family, village and regional networks and Italian immigration in France and Quebec." Pp. 183–207 in Vic Satzewich (ed.), *Deconstructing a Nation: Immigration, Multiculturalism and Racism in '90s Canada*. Halifax: Fernwod Publishing.

Campbell, Douglas
1983 *Beginnings: Essays on the History of Canadian Sociology*. Port Credit: Scribbler's Press.

Campbell, L., I.A. Connidis, and L. Davies
1999 "Sibling ties in later life: a social networks analysis." *Journal of Family Issues* 20: 114–48.

Canadian Association of University Teachers
2004 *CAUT Almanac of Post-Secondary Education in Canada 2004*. Ottawa: CAUT.

Canadian Education Statistics Council
2003 *Education Indicators in Canada: Report of the Pan-Canadian Education Indicators Program 2003*. Toronto: Canadian Education Statistics Council.

Canadian Institute of Public Opinion
1992 *Gallup Report*. Toronto: CIPO.

Canadian Press
1994 "Study urged of income disparity." *London Free Press*, March 24: A10.

Canadian Public Health Association
2004 *Assessment Toolkit for Bullying, Harassment and Peer Relations at School*. Ottawa: Canadian Public Health Association.

Canel, Eduardo
1992 "New social movement theory and resource mobilization: the need for integration." Pp. 22–51 in W.K. Carroll (ed.), *Organizing Dissent: Contemporary Social Movements in Theory and Practice: Studies in the Politics of Counter-Hegemony*. Toronto: Garamond.

Caplan, Jeremy B. and Paula J. Caplan
1999 *Thinking Critically about Research on Sex and Gender* (2nd ed.). New York: Longman.

Carneiro, Robert L.
1967 Editor's introduction to *The Evolution of Society*. Chicago: University of Chicago Press.

Carroll, Michael P.
2006 "Who owns democracy; explaining the long-running debate over Canadian–American value differences." *Canadian Review of Sociology and Anthropology* 42(Aug): 267–83.
1999 *Irish Pilgrimage, Holy Wells, and Popular Catholic Devotion*. Baltimore: The Johns Hopkins University Press.

Carroll, William
2004 *Corporate Power in a Globalizing World. A Study in Elite Social Organization*. Don Mills, ON: Oxford University Press.

Carter, D.D.
1998 Employment benefits for same-sex couples: the expanding entitlement. *Canadian Public Policy* 24: 107–17.

Cashmore, Ellis
1994 *And There Was Television*. Routledge: London.

Cassidy, John
2002 *Dot.con: The Greatest Story Ever Sold*. New York: HarperCollins.

Castells, Manuel
2001   *Internet Galaxy: Reflections on the Internet, Business and Society*. Oxford: Oxford University Publishers.
1997a *The Power of Identity*. Oxford: Blackwell.
1997b *End of Millennium*. Oxford: Blackwell.
1996   *The Rise of the Network Society*. Oxford: Blackwell.

CBC News Online
2005   *Shariah law: FAQs*. www.cbc.ca/news/background/islam/shariah-law.html (posted 26 May 2005; accessed 30 May 2006).

Centres for Disease Control
2003   "Revised birth and fertility rates for the United States, 2000 and 2001." *National Vital Statistics Reports* 51–4: 3–4.

Chafetz, Janet Saltzman and Jacqueline Hagan
1996   "The gender division of labour and family change in industrial societies." *Journal of Comparative Family Studies* 27: 187–219.

Chalk, Frank and Kurt Jonassohn
1990   *The History and Sociology of Genocide*. New Haven: Yale University Press.

Chambliss, William J.
1973   "The Saints and the Roughnecks." *Society* 11(1): 24–31.

Chamratrithirong, A., N. Debavalya, and J. Knodel
1987   *Thailand's Reproductive Revolution*. Madison: University of Wisconsin Press.

Chang, Iris
1997   *The Rape of Nanking*. New York: Penguin.

Chappell, Neena L. and Margaret J. Penning
2001   "Sociology of aging in Canada: issues for the millennium." *Canadian Journal on Aging* 20 suppl. 1: 82–110.

Charles, Nickie and Emma James
2003   "Gender and work orientations in conditions of job insecurity." *British Journal of Sociology* 54: 239–57.

Chauvel, Louis
2003   "Educational inequalities: distribution of knowledge, social origins, and social outcomes." Pp. 219–49 in Yannick Lemel and Heinz-Herbert Noll (eds.), *Changing Structures of Inequality—A Comparative Perspective*. Kingston: McGill-Queens University Press.

Chaves, Mark
1993   "What the polls don't tell us: a closer look at United States church attendance." *American Sociological Review* 58: 741–52.

Chaves, Mark, C. Kirk Hadaway, and Penny Long Marler
1998   "Overreporting church attendance in America: evidence that demands the same verdict." *American Sociological Review* 63: 122–30.

Che-Alford, Janet and Kathryn Stevenson
1998   "Older Canadians on the move." *Canadian Social Trends* 48:15–18.

Cherlin, Andrew J.
1992   *Marriage, Divorce, Remarriage*. Cambridge, MA: Harvard University Press

Chesney, Robert W.
2004   *The Problem of the Media: U.S. Communication Politics in the Twenty-First Century*. New York: Monthly Review Press.

Chesney, Robert W., Russell Newman and Benott (Eds.)
2005   *The Future of Media: Resistance and Reform in the 21st Century*. New York: Seven Stories.

Chesney-Lind, Meda
1989   "Girls' crime and woman's place: toward a feminist model of female delinquency." *Crime and Delinquency* 35: 5–29.

Chesney-Lind, Meda and Noelie Rodriguez
1983   "Women under lock and key." *Prison Journal* 63: 47–65.

Chew, Michael Suk-Young
2001   *Rational Ritual: Culture, Coordination, and Common Knowledge*. Princeton: Princeton University Press.

Child, Irvin L. and Edward F. Zigler
1973   *Socialization and Personality Development*. Reading: Addison-Wesley.

Chirot, Daniel
1994   *How Societies Change*. Thousand Oaks: Pine Forge Press.
1986   *Social Change in the Modern Era*. Toronto: Harcourt Brace Jovanovich.

Chisholm, K.
1998   "A three-year follow-up of attachment and indiscriminate friendliness in children adopted from Romanian orphanages." *Child Development* 69: 1092–106.

Chisholm, Patricia
1999   "Teens under siege." *Maclean's* May 3: 22–24.

Chomsky, Noam
2002   *Media Control: The Spectacular Achievements of Propaganda* (2nd ed.). New York: Open Media.

Chomsky, Noam and Edward S Herman
1988   *Manufacturing Consent: The Political Economy of the Mass Media*. New York: Pantheon Books.

Choquette, Robert
2004   *Canada's Religions: An Historical Introduction*. Ottawa: University of Ottawa Press.

Christian, Nicole
1999   "Is smaller perhaps better?" *Time* May 31: 19.

Christie, Nils
1993   *Crime Control as Industry: Towards Gulags, Western Type?* London: Routledge.

Christofides, L.N. and R. Swidinsky
1994   "Wage determination by gender and visible minority status: evidence from the 1989 LMAS." *Canadian Public Policy* 20: 34–51.

Chui, Tina, James Curtis, and Edward Grabb
1999   "Public participation, protest, and social inequality." Pp. 371–86 in J. Curtis, E. Grabb, and N. Guppy (eds.), *Social Inequality in Canada: Patterns, Problems, Policies*. (3rd ed.). Scarborough: Prentice Hall.

Clark, C. Robert, Samuel Clark, and Mattias Polborn
2006   "Coordination and status influence." *Rationality and Society* 18: 367–91.

Clark, Danae
1995   "Commodity lesbianism." Pp. 484–501 in C.K. Creehmar and A. Doby (eds.), *Out in Culture: Gay, Lesbian and Queer Essays in Popular Culture.* Durham: Duke University Press.

Clark, P.G.
1993   "Moral discourse and public policy in aging: framing problems, seeking solutions, and 'public ethics'." *Canadian Journal on Aging* 12: 485–508.

Clark, Peter and Anthony Davis
1989   "The power of dirt: an exploration of secular defilement in Anglo-Canadian culture." *Canadian Review of Sociology and Anthropology* 26: 650–73.

Clark, S.D.
1975   "Sociology in Canada: an historical overview." *Canadian Journal of Sociology* l: 225–34.
1959   *Movements of Political Protest in Canada.* Toronto: University of Toronto Press.
1948   *Church and Sect in Canada.* Toronto: University of Toronto Press.

Clark, Samuel
1979   *Social Origins of the Irish Land War.* Princeton: Princeton University Press.

Clark, Samuel, and J.S. Donnelly, Jr. (eds.)
1983   *Irish Peasants: Violence and Political Unrest, 1780–1914.* Madison: University of Wisconsin Press.

Clark, Warren
1998   "Religious observance: marriage and family." *Canadian Social Trends* Autumn: 2–7.

Clark, Warren and Grant Schellenberg
2006   "Who's religious." *Canadian Social Trends* Summer: 2–9.

Clarke, Juanne
1990   *Health, Illness, and Medicine in Canada.* Toronto: McClelland and Stewart.

Cleaver, Harry
1994   "The Chiapas uprising." *Studies in Political Economy* 44: 141–57.

Clement, Wallace
1988   "The state and the Canadian economy." Chapter 31 in J. Curtis, E. Grabb, N. Guppy, and S. Gilbert (eds.), *Social Inequality in Canada: Patterns, Problems, Policies.* Scarborough: Prentice Hall.
1975   *The Canadian Corporate Elite.* Toronto: McClelland and Stewart.

Clement, Wallace (ed.)
1997   *Understanding Canada: Building on the New Canadian Political Economy.* Kingston: McGill-Queen's University Press.

Clinard, Marshall and P. Yeager
1980   *Corporate Crime.* New York: Free Press.

Cloud, John
1999   "Just a routine school shooting." *Maclean's* May 31: 14–19.

Cloward, Richard and L. Ohlin
1960   *Delinquency and Opportunity.* New York: Free Press.

Cohen, Albert
1955   *Delinquent Boys: The Culture of the Gang.* New York: Free Press.

Cohen, Stanley
1985   *Visions of Social Control: Crime Punishment and Classification.* Cambridge: Polity.

Coleman, James S.
1988   "Social capital in the creation of human capital." *American Journal of Sociology* 94: S95–S120.
1990   *Foundations of Social Theory.* Cambridge: Belknap Press.

Coleman, W.D.
1984   *The Independence Movement in Quebec, 1945–1980.* Toronto: University of Toronto Press.

Collins, Randall
1979   *The Credential Society: A Historical Sociology of Education and Stratification.* New York: Academic Press.

Coltrane, Scott
1998   *Gender and Families.* Thousand Oaks: Pine Forge Press.
1996   *Family Men: Fatherhood, Housework and Gender Equality.* New Kettle York: Oxford.
1990   "Birth timing and the division of labor in dual-earner families: exploratory findings and suggestions for future research." *Journal of Family Issues* 11: 157–81.

Comack, E.
1985   "The origins of Canadian drug legislation: labelling versus class analysis. Pp. 65–84 in T. Fleming (ed.), *New Criminologies in Canada: Crime State and Control.* Toronto: University of Toronto Press.

Comstock, George and Haejung Paik
1994   "The effects of television violence on antisocial behaviour: a meta-analysis." *Communications Research* 21: 516–46.

Condon, Richard
1987   *Inuit Youth: Growth and Change in the Canadian Arctic.* New Brunswick: Rutgers University Press.

Condry, J. and S. Condry
1976   "Sex differences: a study in the eye of the beholder." *Child Development* 47: 812–19.

Conger, Jane and Nancy L. Galambos
1997   *Adolescence and Youth* (5th ed.). New York: Addison Wesley Longman.

Conkey, Margaret
1997   "Men and women in prehistory: an archaeological challenge." Pp. 57–68 in Caroline B. Brettell and Carolyn F. Sargent (eds.), *Gender in Cross-cultural Perspective.* Upper Saddle River: Prentice Hall.

Connidis, I.A.
2002   "The impact of demographic and social trends on informal support for older persons." Pp. 105–32 in David

Cheal (ed.) *Aging and Demographic Change in Canadian Context*. Toronto: University of Toronto Press.
2001   *Family Ties and Aging*. Thousand Oaks: Sage.
1999   "The impact of demographic and social trends across age groups on informal supports for older persons." Paper presented at the National Seminar on Demographic Change and Population Ageing. Moncton, New Brunswick, April.
1997   "Family ties and aging in Canada: continuity and change over three decades." *Lien social et politiques/ Revue internationale d'action communautaire* 38: 133–43.
1994   "Sibling support in older age." *Journal of Gerontology: Social Sciences* 48: S309–17.
1992   "Life transitions and the adult sibling tie: a qualitative study." *Journal of Marriage and the Family* 54: 972–82.
1989a *Family Ties and Aging*. Toronto: Butterworths/Harcourt Brace.
1989b "Contact between siblings in later life." *Canadian Journal of Sociology* 14: 429–42.
1989c "Siblings as friends in later life." *American Behavioral Scientist* 33: 81–93.
1983   "Living arrangement choices of older residents: assessing quantitative results with qualitative data." *Canadian Journal of Sociology* 8: 359–75.

Connidis, I.A. and L. Campbell
1995   "Closeness, confiding, and contact among siblings in middle and late adulthood." *Journal of Family Issues* 16: 722–45.

Connidis, I.A. and L. Davies
1992   "Confidants and companions: choices in later life." *Journal of Gerontology: Social Sciences* 47: S115–22.
1990   "Confidants and companions in later life: the place of family and friends." *Journal of Gerontology: Social Sciences* 45: S141–49.

Connidis, I.A. and J.A. McMullin
2002a "Sociological ambivalence and family ties: a critical perspective." *Journal of Marriage and Family* 64(3): 558–67.
2002b "Ambivalence, Family Ties, and Doing Sociology." *Journal of Marriage and Family* 64(3): 594–601.
1999   "Permanent childlessness: perceived advantages and disadvantages among older persons." *Canadian Journal on Aging* 18: 447–65.
1996   "Reasons for and perceptions of childlessness among older persons: exploring the impact of marital status and gender." *Journal of Aging Studies* 10: 205–22.
1994   "Social support in older age: assessing the impact of marital and parent status." *Canadian Journal on Aging* 13: 510–27.
1993   "To have or have not: parent status and the subjective well-being of older men and women." *The Gerontologist* 33: 630–36.

Connidis, I. A., C. J. Rosenthal, and J. A. McMullin
1996   "The impact of family composition on providing help to older parents: a study of employed adults." *Research on Aging* 18: 402–29.

Connor, Steven
1989   *Postmodernist Culture: An Introduction to Theories of the Contemporary*. Cambridge: Blackwell.

Connors, Edward, Thomas Lundregan, Neal Miller, and Tom McEwen
1996   *Convicted by Juries, Exonerated by Science: Case Studies in the Use of DNA Evidence to Establish Innocence After Trial*. NIJ Research Report. Washington, DC: U.S. Department of Justice, Office of Justice Programs, National Institute of Justice.

Cook, Cynthia and Rod Beaujot
1996   "Labour force interruptions: the influence of marital status and the presence of young children." *The Canadian Journal of Sociology* 21: 25–42.

Cook, Scott D. N.
1995   "The structure of technological revolutions and the Gutenberg myth." Pp. 63–84 in Joseph Pitt (ed.), *New Directions in the Philosophy of Technology*. Boston: Kluwer Academic.
1992   "Support from parents over the life course: the adult child's perspective." *Social Forces* 71: 63–84.

Cooke, Martin, Dan Beavon, and Mindy McHardy
2004   "Measuring the well-being of Aboriginal people." Pp. 47–70 in J. White, P. Maxim, and D. Beavon (eds.), *Aboriginal Policy Research: Setting the Agenda for Change*. Toronto: Thomson Educational Publishing.

Cooley, Charles H.
1956   [1909] [1902] *Human Nature and the Social Order*. Chicago: Free Press.

Cooney, T.M. and P. Uhlenberg
1992   "Support from parents over the life course: the adult child's perspective." *Social Forces* 71: 63–84.

Corak, M. (ed.)
1998   *Government Finances and Generational Equity*. Ottawa: Statistics Canada and Human Resources Development Canada.

Corbella, Licia
2000   "When the rule of law replaces logic." *London Free Press*. January 22: F6.

Cormier, Jeffrey J.
1997   "Missed opportunities: the institutionalization of early Canadian sociology." *Society/Société* 21(1): 1–7.

Cortés, Carlos E.
2000   *The Children Are Watching: How the Media Teach About Diversity*. New York: Teachers College Press.

Corwin, Ronald G.
1987   *The Organization–Society Nexus: A Critical Review of Models and Metaphors*. Westport: Greenwood Press.

Coser, Lewis
1964   *The Functions of Social Conflict*. New York: Free Press of Glencoe.

Côté, James E.
2000   *Arrested Adulthood: The Changing Nature of Identity and Maturity in the Late-Modern World*. New York: New York University Press.

1994 *Adolescent Storm and Stress: An Evaluation of the Mead/ Freeman Controversy.* Hillsdale: Lawrence Erlbaum.

1992 "Was Mead wrong about coming of age in Samoa? An analysis of the Mead/Freeman controversy for scholars of adolescence and human development." *Journal of Youth and Adolescence* 21: 1–29.

Côté, James E. and Anton A. Allahar

1994 *Generation on Hold.* Toronto: Stoddart.

2006 *Critical Youth Studies: A Canadian Focus.* Toronto: Pearson Education.

Côté, James E. and Charles Levine

2002 *Identity Formation, Agency, and Culture: A Social Psychological Synthesis.* Hillsdale: Lawrence Erlbaum.

1997 "Student motivations, learning environments, and human capital acquisition: toward an integrated paradigm of student development." *Journal of College Student Development* 38: 229–43.

1987 "A formulation of Erikson's theory of ego identity formation." *Developmental Review* 9: 273–325.

Coward, R.T. and J.W. Dwyer

1990 "The association of gender, sibling network composition, and patterns of parent care by adult children." *Research on Aging* 12: 158–81.

Creese, Gillian and Brenda Beagan

2004 "Gender at work: strategies for equality in neo-liberal times." Pp. 245–57 in James Curtis, Edward Grabb, and Neil Guppy (eds.), *Social Inequality in Canada: Patterns, Problems, and Policies* (4th ed.). Toronto: Pearson Education Canada.

Crompton, Susan

2002 "I still feel overqualified for my job." *Canadian Social Trends* Winter: 23–26.

Crompton, Susan and Leslie Geran

1995 "Women as main wage-earners." *Perspective on Labour and Income* 7: 26–29.

Crosby, Faye J.

1991 *Juggling: The Unexpected Advantages of Balancing Career and Home for Women and Their Families.* New York: Free Press.

Cumming, E. and W.E. Henry

1961 *Growing Old: The Process of Disengagement.* New York: Basic Books.

Curran, Daniel J. and Claire M. Renzetti

1992 *Women, Men and Society: The Sociology of Gender* (2nd ed.). Boston: Allyn and Bacon.

Currie, Elliott P.

1998 "Crimes without criminals: witchcraft and its control in renaissance Europe." *Law and Society Review* 3(1): 7–32.

Curtis, B. et al.

1992 *Stacking the Deck.* Toronto: Our Schools/Our Selves.

Curtis, Bruce

1992 "Pre-sociological observation? Maria Edgeworth, Elizabeth Hamilton, and A.A. de Saussure Necker." *Society* 16: 10–19.

Curtis, James, Edward Grabb, and Neil Guppy

2004 "Age-based inequalities in Canadian society." Pp. 304–14 in James Curtis, Edward Grabb, and Neil Guppy (eds.), *Social Inequality in Canada: Patterns, Problems, and Policies* (4th ed.). Toronto: Pearson Education Canada.

Dabbs, James

1990 "Testosterone, social class, and antisocial behavior in a sample of 4462 men." *Psychological Science* 1: 209–11.

Dahrendorf, Ralf

1959 *Class and Class Conflict in Industrial Society.* Stanford: Stanford University Press.

Daly, Mary

1974 *Beyond God the Father.* Boston: Beacon Press.

Dannefer, D.

1987 "Aging as intracohort differentiation: accentuation, the Matthew effect, and the life course." *Sociological Focus* 2: 211–36.

Das Gupta, Tania

1996 *Racism and Paid Work.* Toronto: Garamond.

Davidson, James and Dean Knudsen

1977 "A new approach to religious commitment." *Sociological Focus* 10: 151–73.

Davie, Grace

2000 *Religion in Modern Europe: A Memory Mutates.* Oxford: Oxford University Press.

Davies, James B.

2004 "The distribution of wealth and economic inequality." Pp. 85–98 in Rinehart, James. *The Tyranny of Work* (4th ed.). Toronto: Harcourt Canada.

Davies, Scott

2004 "Stubborn Disparities: Explaining Class Inequalities in Schooling." In *Social Inequality in Canada: Patterns, Problems, and Policies*, edited by J. Curtis, E. Grabb and N. Guppy. Toronto: Pearson Prentice Hall.

1999 "Stubborn disparities: explaining class inequalities in schooling." Pp. 138–50 in J. Curtis, E. Grabb, and N. Guppy (eds.), *Social Inequality in Canada: Patterns, Problems, Policies* (3rd ed.). Scarborough: Prentice Hall.

Davies, Scott and Neil Guppy

2006 *The Schooled Society: An Introduction to the Sociology of Education.* Don Mills, ON: Oxford University Press.

1999 *Education in Canada: Recent Trends and Future Challenges.* Ottawa: Statistics Canada and Nelson Canada.

Davies, Scott, Clayton Mosher, and Bill O'Grady

1992 "Canadian sociology and anthropology graduates in the 1980s labour market." *Society*, 16: 39–46.

Davis, Arthur K.

1971 "Canadian society and history as hinterland versus metropolis." Pp. 6–32 in Richard J. Ossenberg (ed.), *Canadian Society: Pluralism, Change, and Conflict.* Scarborough: Prentice Hall.

Davis, Kingsley
1972   *World Urbanization 1950-1970. Volume 11: Analysis of Trends, Relationships, and Development.* Berkeley: Institute of International Studies.
1949   *Human Society.* New York: Macmillan.
1937   "The sociology of prostitution." *American Sociological Review* 2: 744–55.

Davis, Kingsley and Wilbert E. Moore
1945   "Some principles of stratification." *American Sociological Review* 10: 242–49.

Davis, Mike
1990   *City of Quartz.* London: Verso.

Davis, Morris and Joseph Krauter
1978   *Minority Canadians: Ethnic Groups.* Toronto: Methuen.

Davis, Nancy J. and Robert V. Robinson
2006   "The egalitarian face of Islamic Orthodoxy: support for Islamic law and economic justice in seven Muslim-majority nations." *American Sociological Review* 71: 167–90.

Dawson, Lorne L.
1998   *Comprehending Cults: The Sociology of New Religious Movements.* Toronto: Oxford University Press.
2006   *Comprehending Cults: The Sociology of New Religious Movements* (2nd ed.). London: Oxford.

de Beauvoir, Simone
1953   *The Second Sex.* New York: Knopf.

de Young, Mary
1998   "Another look at moral panics: the case of Satanic day care centers." *Deviant Behavior* 19(3): 257–78.

Dei, George, and J. Sefa
1996   *Anti-Racism Education: Theory and Practice.* Halifax: Fernwood.

DeFrain, J. and E.E. LeMasters
1989   *Parents in Modern America* (5th ed.). Belmont: Wadsworth.

DeKeseredy, Walter S.
1992   "Wife assault." Pp. 278–312 in Vincent Sacco (ed.), *Deviance: Conformity and Control in Canadian Society* (2nd ed.). Scarborough: Prentice Hall.

Delgado, Richard and Jean Stefancic
2000   *Critical Race Theory: The Cutting Edge.* Philadelphia: Temple University Press.

Demers, David.
2002   *Global Media: Menace or Messiah?* Cresskill, NJ: Hampton Press.

Demers, M.
1998   "Age differences in the rates and costs of medical procedures and hospitalization during the last year of life." *Canadian Journal on Aging* 17: 186–96.

Denton, Margaret, Steven Prus, and Vivienne Walters
2004   "Gender differences in health: a canadian study of the psychosocial, structural, and behavioural determinants of health." *Social Science and Medicine* 58: 585–600.

Desai, Sonalde and Linda J. Waite
1991   "Women's employment during pregnancy and after the first birth: occupational characteristics and work commitment." *American Sociological Review* 56: 551–66.

Desmarais, Serge and James Curtis
2001   "Gender and perceived income entitlement among full-time workers: analyses for Canadian national samples, 1984 and 1994." *Basic and Applied Social Psychology* 23: 157–68.

DeSouza, E. and A. Fansler
2003   "Contrapower sexual harassment: A survey of students and faculty members." *Sex Roles: A Journal of Research* 48: 529–42.

DeVault, Christine, Rebecca Reynolds, Bryan Strong, and Murray Suid
1983   *The Marriage and Family Experience.* St. Paul: West Publishing.

Devor, Holly
1989   *Gender Blending: Confronting the Limits of Duality.* Bloomington: Indiana University Press.

Di Leonardo, Micaela
1991   "Contingencies of value in feminist anthropology." Pp. 140–58 in Joan E. Hartman and Ellen Messer-Davidow (eds.), *(En)Gendering Knowledge.* Knoxville: University of Tennessee Press.

Diamond, Jared
1997   *Guns, Germs and Steel: The Fates of Human Societies.* New York: W.W. Norton.

Dibbell, Julian
1996   "A rape in cyberspace." Pp. 448–65 in Victor J. Vitanza, (ed.), *CyberReader.* Boston: Allyn and Bacon.

Dickason, Olive
2002   *Canada's First Nations: A History of Founding Peoples from Earliest Times.* Don Mills: Oxford University Press.

Dietz, Thomas, Linda Kalof, and Paul Stern
2002   "Gender, values, and environmentalism." *Social Science Quarterly* 83: 353–64.

Dobasch, R.E. and R.P. Dobasch
1992   *Women, Violence, and Social Change.* London: Routledge.

Don, K. and J. Hackler
1990   "Estimating system biases: crime indices that permit comparisons across provinces." *Canadian Journal of Criminology* 32: 243–64.

Dowd, J.J.
1975   "Aging as exchange: prelude to a theory." *Journal of Gerontology* 30: 584–94.

Drabman, R. and M. Thomas
1974   "Does media violence increase children's toleration of real life aggression?" *Developmental Psychology* 10: 418–21.

Driedger, L., W. Isajiw, and A. Sev'er
1993   "Ethnic identity and social mobility: a test of the drawback model." *Canadian Journal of Sociology* 18: 177–96.

Drolet, Marie
2002 "New evidence on gender pay differentials: Does measurement matter?" *Canadian Public Policy* 28: 1–16.

Drummond, Murray
2003 "The meaning of boys' bodies in physical education." *Journal of Men's Studies* 11: 131–43.
2002 "Men, body image and eating disorders." *International Journal of Men's Health* 1: 89–101.

Duffy, Jim, Margaret Walsh, and Kelly Warren
2001 "Classroom interactions: gender of teacher, gender of student, and classroom subject." *Sex Roles* 45: 579–93.

Duleep, Harriet and Seth Sanders
1992 "Discrimination at the top: American-born Asian and white men." *Industrial Relations* 31: 416–32.

Dumas, Brigitte
1987 "Philosophy and sociology in Quebec: a socio-epistemic inversion." *Canadian Journal of Sociology* 12: 111–33.

Dumas, Jean
1990 *Report on the Demographic Situation in Canada 1988.* Statistics Canada, Catalogue No. 91–209. Ottawa: Minister of Supply and Services Canada.

Dumas, Jean and Alain Bélanger
1997 *Report on the Demographic Situation in Canada 1996.* Statistics Canada, Catalogue. No. 91–209. Ottawa: Minister of Supply and Services Canada.

Dumas, Jean and Yves Péron
1992 *Marriage and Conjugal Life in Canada.* Statistics Canada, Catalogue No. 91–534. Ottawa: Minister of Supply and Services Canada.

Du Pays, John
1996 "Les lendemains qui grincent." In Marc Brière (ed.), *Le goût du Québec: l'après référendum 1995.* La Salle: Hurtubise.

Durkheim, Emile
1965 [1895] *The Division Of Labour in Society.* New York: Free Press.
1951 [1897] *Suicide: A Study in Sociology.* Translated by J. Spaulding and G. Simpson. New York: Free Press.

Eagan, Andrea, Valerie Hey, and Sophie Laws
1985 *Seeing Red: The Politics of Pre-menstrual Tension.* London: Hutchinson.

East-West Center
1995 "Evidence mounts for sex-selective abortion in Asia." *Asia-Pacific Population and Policy* 34:4

Easterlin, R.A.
1987 *Birth and Fortune* (2nd ed.). Chicago: University of Chicago Press.

Eco, Umberto
2002 *History of Beauty.* New York: Rizzoli.

Economist
1995 "The most expensive slum in the world." *The Economist* May 6.

Eder, Donna
1995 *School Talk: Gender and Adolescent Culture.* New Brunswick, NJ: Rutgers University Press.

Edgerton, Robert B.
1985 *Rules, Exceptions, and Social Order.* Berkeley: University of California Press.

Ehrenreich, Barbara and Deirdre English
1979 *For Her Own Good: 150 Years of the Experts' Advice to Women.* New York: Anchor.

Ehrlich, A. and P. Ehrlich
1990 *The Population Explosion.* New York: Simon & Schuster.

Ehrlich, P.
1968 *The Population Bomb.* New York: Ballantine.

Eichler, M. and R. Tite
1990 "Women's studies professors in Canada: a collective self-portrait." *Atlantis* 16: 6–24.

Eisinger, P.K.
1973 "The conditions of protest behavior in American cities." *American Political Science Review* 67: 11–28.

Elder, G.H.
1991 "Lives and social change." Pp. 58–86 in W.R. Heinz (ed.), *Theoretical Advances in Life Course Research: Status Passage and the Life Course,* Vol. 1. Weinheim: Deutscher Studien Verlag.

Elias, Norbert
1994 *The Civilizing Process: The History of Manners and State Formation and Civilization.* Oxford: Blackwell.

Eller, Cynthia
2000 *The Myth of Matriarchal Prehistory: Why an Invented Past Won't Give Women a Future.* Boston: Beacon Press.

Engels, Friedrich
1972 [1884] *The Origin of the Family, Private Property, and the State.* Eleanor Burke Leacock (ed.). New York: International Publishers.

Ericson, Richard V.
1982 *Reproducing Order: A Study of Police Patrol Work.* Toronto: University of Toronto Press.

Ericson, Richard V. and Kevin D. Haggerty
1997 *Policing the Risk Society.* Toronto: University of Toronto Press, and Oxford: Oxford University Press.

Erikson, Erik H.
1968 *Identity: Youth and Crisis.* New York: Norton.
1963 *Childhood and Society* (2nd ed.). New York: Norton.

Erikson, Kai
1966 *Wayward Puritans.* New York: Wiley.

Eron, L, L.R. Huesmann, M. Lefkowitz, and L.O. Waller
1972 "Does television cause aggression?" *American Psychologist* 32: 237–44.

Evans, R.G., K.M. McGrail, S.G. Morgan, M.L. Barer, and C. Hertzman
2001 "Apocalypse NO: population aging and the future of health care systems." *Canadian Journal on Aging* 20(Supp. 1): 160–91.

Fallows, James
1985 "The case against credentialism: bad for business." *The Atlantic Monthly* December: 49–67.

Farnsworth Riche, Martha
1990 "The boomerang age: don't assume 18-to-24-year-olds are adults." *American Demographics* May: 25–30, 52–53.

Fast, Janet, Judith Frederick, Nancy Zukewich, and Sandra Franke
2001 "The time of our lives." *Canadian Social Trends* Winter: 20–23.

Faurschou, Gail
1988 "Fashion and the cultural logic of postmodernity." In A. Kroker and L. Kroker (eds.), *Body Invaders: Sexuality and the Postmodern Condition*. Bassingstoke: Macmillan Educational.

Fedders, Barbara
2001 "More young women in the juvenile justice system: girls in trouble." *Guild Practitioner* 58: 103–11.

Felson, Marcus
2002 *Crime and Everyday Life* (3rd ed.). Thousand Oaks: Sage.

Finch, J.
1989 Family Obligations and Social Change. Cambridge: Polity Press.

Fine, Gary Alan
1992 Manufacturing Tales. Knoxville: University of Tennessee Press.

Finke, Roger
1997 "The consequences of religious competition:supply-side explanations for religious change." In Lawrence A. Young (ed.), Rational Choice Theory and Religion: Summary and Assessment. New York: Routledge.

Finke, Roger, A. Guest, and Rodney Stark
1996 "Mobilizing local religious markets: religious pluralism in the Empire State, 1855 to 1865." *American Sociological Review* 61: 203–18.

Finke, Roger and Rodney Stark
2003 "The dynamics of religious economies." In Michelle Dillon (ed.), Handbook of the Sociology of Religion. Cambridge: Cambridge University Press.
1992 The Churching of America, 1776–1990: Winners and Losers in our Religious Economy. New Brunswick, NJ: Rutgers University Press.

Finkel, Alvin
1989 *The Social Credit Phenomenon in Alberta*. Toronto: University of Toronto Press.

Fiske, John
1994 *Reading the Popular*. London: Routledge.

Fitzgerald, Robin
2003 "An examination of sex differences in delinquency." Statistics Canada, Catalogue No. 85-561-MIE, No. 001.

Fjortoft, Arne
1999 "Challenging the divide." Pp. 402–10 in Anne Leer (ed.), Masters of the Wired World: Cyberspace Speaks Out. London: Financial Times.

Flannery, D.J., D.L. Hussey, L. Biebelhausen and K.L. Wester
2003 Crime, delinquency, and youth gangs. Pp. 502–22 in G. R. Adams & M. Berzonsky (eds.), Blackwell Handbook of Adolescence. Malden, MA: Blackwell.

Fleras, Augie and Jean Leonard Elliott
1992 Multiculturalism in Canada: The Challenge of Diversity. Scarborough: Nelson Canada.

Fonte, John
1999 "Back to the future." National Post [Toronto]. June 19: B7.

Foot, David K.
1998 Boom Bust & Echo 2000. Toronto: Macfarlane, Walter, and Ross.

Forcese, Dennis
1997 *The Canadian Class Structure* (4th ed.). Toronto: McGraw-Hill Ryerson.

Fordham, Signithia and John U. Ogbu
1986 "Black students' school success: coping with the burden of 'acting White'." *Urban Review* 18(3): 176–206.

Form, William H.
1985 *Divided We Stand*. Urbana: University of Illinois Press.

Forman, Frieda, Mary O'Brien, Jane Haddad, Dianne Hallman, and Philinda Masters (eds.)
1990 *Feminism and Education: A Canadian Perspective*. Toronto: Centre for Women's Studies in Education.

Foucault, Michel
1991 "Questions of method." Pp. 73–86 in G. Burchell, C. Gordon and P. Miller (eds.). *The Foucault Effect: Studies in Governmentality*. Chicago: University of Chicago Press.
1977 *Discipline and Punish: The Birth of the Prison*. A. Sheridan (trans.). New York: Vintage.
1978 *The History of Sexuality, Volume 1: An Introduction*. New York: Random House.

Fournier, Elaine, George Butlin, and Philip Giles
1999 "Intergenerational change in the education of Canadians." Pp. 130–37 in J. Curtis, E. Grabb, and N. Guppy (eds.), *Social Inequality in Canada: Patterns, Problems, Policies* (3rd ed.). Scarborough, ON.: Prentice Hall.

Fournier, Marcel
2001 Quebec Sociology and Quebec Society: The Construction of a Collective Identity, *Canadian Journal of Sociology*, Summer, 26(3): 333–48.

Fournier, Suzanne and Ernie Crey
1997 *Stolen from our Embrace: The Abduction of First Nation Children and the Restoration of Aboriginal Communities*. Vancouver: Douglas and McIntyre.

Fox, John and Michael Ornstein
1993 "The Canadian state and corporate elites." Chapter 34 in J. Curtis, E. Grabb, and N. Guppy (eds.), *Social Inequality in Canada: Patterns, Problems, Policies* (2nd ed.). Scarborough: Prentice Hall.

Francis, Diane
1986 *Controlling Interest. Who Owns Canada?* Toronto: Macmillan of Canada.

Frank, Andre Gunder
1967   *Capitalism and Underdevelopment in Latin America:
        Historical Studies of Chile and Brazil.* New York: Monthly
        Review Press.

Frank, Thomas
1997a   *The Conquest of Cool: Business Culture, Counterculture,
        and the Rise of Hip Consumerism.* Chicago: University of
        Chicago Press.
1997b   "Let them eat lifestyle: from hip to hype—the ultimate
        corporate takeover." *Utne Reader* November–December:
        43–47.

**Franzoi, Stephen L., Jennifer J. Kessenich, and
Patricia A. Sugrue**
1989   "Gender differences in the experience of body awareness:
        an experiential sampling study." *Sex Roles* 21: 499–515.

Frederick, Judith and Jason Hamel
1998   "Canadian attitudes to divorce." *Canadian Social Trends*
        48: 6–11.

Freidan, Betty
1963   *The Feminine Mystique.* New York: Dell.

Freire, Paulo
1970   *Pedagogy of the Oppressed.* New York: Seabury Press.

Frenette, Marc
2000   "Overqualified? Recent graduates and the needs of
        their employers." *Education Quarterly Review* 7(1): 6–20.

Frideres, James
1988   *Native Peoples in Canada: Contemporary Conflicts*
        (3rd ed.). Scarborough: Prentice Hall.

Friend, R.A.
1991   "Older lesbian and gay people: a theory of successful
        aging." In John Alan Lee (ed.), *Gay Midlife and Maturity.*
        New York: Haworth Press.

**Frieze, I.H., P.B. Johnson, J.E. Parsons, D.N. Rubble,
and G.I. Zellman**
1978   *Women and Sex Roles.* New York: W.W. Norton.

Froese, Paul
2001   "Hungary for religion: a supply-side interpretation of
        the Hungarian religious revival." *Journal for the Scientific
        Study of Religion* 40: 251–68.

Fukuyama, Francis
1999   "The great disruption: human nature and the reconsti-
        tution of the social order." *Atlantic Monthly* May: 55–80.

Furlong, Andy and Fred Cartmel
1997   *Young People and Social Change: Individualization and Risk in
        Late Modernity.* Buckingham, UK: Open University Press.

Furstenberg, Frank F.
1995   "Family change and the welfare of children: what do
        we know and what can we do about it." In K. Mason
        and A-M. Jensen (eds.), *Gender and Family Change in
        Industrialized Countries.* Oxford: Clarendon.

Furstenberg, Frank F., T. Hershberg, and John Modell
1976   "Social change and transitions to adulthood in histori-
        cal perspective." *Journal of Family History* 1: 7–31.

Gabor, Thomas
1994   *Everybody Does It! Crime by the Public.* Toronto:
        University of Toronto Press.

Gabor, Thomas and E. Gottheil
1984   "Offender characteristics and spatial mobility: an
        empirical study and some policy implications."
        Canadian Journal of Criminology 26: 267–81.

Galambos, Nancy and Lauree Tilton-Weaver
1998   "Multiple-risk behaviour in adolescents and young
        adults." *Health Reports* 10: 9–20.

Galarneau, Diane
2006   "Education and income of lone parents." *Perspectives on
        Labour and Income* 18(1): 7–18.

Gallagher, Sally K.
2003   *Evangelical Identity and Gendered Family Life.* New
        Brunswick, NJ: Rutgers University Press.

Gallup, George
1990   *Religion in America.* Princeton: Princeton Religious
        Research Center.

Gamson, W.A.
1992   "The social psychology of collective action." Pp. 53–76
        in A.D. Morris and C.M. Mueller (eds.), *Frontiers in
        Social Movement Theory.* New Haven: Yale University
        Press.

Gamson, William and Andre Modigliani
1974   *Conceptions of Social Life.* Boston: Little Brown and
        Company.

Gannon, M. and K. Mihorean
2005   *Criminal Victimization in Canada.* Ottawa: Statistics
        Canada.

Garland, David (ed.)
2001   *Mass Imprisonment: Social Causes and Consequences.*
        London: Sage.

Garner, David
1997   "The 1997 body image survey results." *Psychology
        Today* 30: 30–44.

Gaskell, Jane and Arlene Tigar McLaren (eds.)
1991   *Women and Education.* Calgary: Detselig.

**Gaskell, Jane, Arlene Tigar McLaren, and
Myra Novogrodsky (eds.)**
1989   *Claiming an Education: Feminism and Canadian Schools.*
        Toronto: Our Schools/Our Selves.

Gates, Bill
1995   *The Road Ahead.* New York: Viking.

Gauntlett, David
2002   *Media, Gender and Identity: An Introduction.* London;
        New York: Routledge.

Gauthier, Anne Hélène
1991   "The economics of childhood." In A.R. Pence (ed.),
        Childhood as a Social Phenomenon. Vienna: European
        Centre for Social Welfare Policy and Research.

Gavigan, Shelley
1987 "Women's crime: new perspectives and old theories. Pp. 47–66 in E. Adelberg and C. Currie (eds.), *Too Few To Count: Canadian Women in Conflict with the Law*. Vancouver: Press Gang.

Gecas, Viktor
1981 "Contexts of socialization." Pp. 165–99 in Morris Rosenberg and Ralph H. Turner (eds.) *Social Psychology: Sociological Perspectives*. New York: Basic Books.

Gee, Ellen
1986 "The life course of Canadian women: an historical and demographic analysis." *Social Indicators Research* 18: 263–83.

Gee, Ellen M.
1995 "Families in later life." Pp. 77–113 in *Family Over the Life Course: Current Demographic Analysis*. Statistics Canada, Catalogue No. 91-543. Ottawa: Ministry of Industry.

Geipel, John
1969 *The Europeans*. New York: Pegasus.

Gelles, Richard J.
1983 "An exchange/social control theory." Pp. 151–65 in David Finkelhor, Richard J. Gelles, Gerald T. Hotaling, and Murray A. Strauss (eds.), *The Dark Side of Families: Current Family Violence Research*. Beverley Hills, CA.: Sage.

Gelsthorpe, Loraine and Allison Morris (eds.)
1990 *Feminist Perspectives in Criminology*. Milton Keynes: Open University Press.

Gerber, Linda
1984 "Community characteristics and out-migration from Canadian Indian reserves: path analyses." *Canadian Review of Sociology and Anthropology* 21: 145–65.

Gerbner, George, Larry Gross, Michael Morgan, and Nancy Signorielli
1987 "Charting the mainstream: television's contributions to political orientations." Pp. 441–64 in Donald Lazare (ed.), *American Media and Mass Culture: Left Perspectives*. Berkeley: University of California Press.

Gero, Joan
1991 "Genderlithics: women's role in stone tool production." Pp. 163–93 in Joan M. Gero and Margaret W. Conkey (eds.), *Engendering Archaeology: Women and Prehistory*. Cambridge: Blackwell.

Gibson, William
1984 *Necromancer*. New York: Ace Books.

Giddens, Anthony
1991 *Introduction to Sociology*. New York: Norton.
1984 *The Constitution of Society*. Cambridge: Polity Press.
1981 *A Contemporary Critique of Historical Materialism, Volume 1: Power, Property, and the State*. London: Macmillan.
1973 *The Class Structure of the Advanced Societies*. London: Hutchinson and Co.

Giffen, P.J., S. Endicott, and S. Lambert
1991 *Panic and Indifference—The Politics of Canada's Drug Laws*. Ottawa: Canadian Centre on Substance Abuse.

Gifford-Gonzales, Diane
1993 "You can hide, but you can't run." *Visual Anthropology Review* 9(1): 23–41.

Gilder, George
1994 *Life after Television*. New York: Norton.

Giles, Philip, and Drewes Torben
2001 "Liberal arts degrees and the labour market." *Perspectives on Labour and Income* Autumn: 27–33.

Giles, Wenona
2002 *Portuguese Women in Toronto: Gender, Immigration and Nationalism*. Toronto: University of Toronto Press.

Gillborn, David, and Deborah Youdell
2001 The new IQism: intelligence, "ability" and the rationing of education. Pp. 65–99 in J. Demaine (ed.), *Sociology of Education Today*. Houndmills, Basingstoke: Palgrave.

Gillis, J.R.
1996 *A World of Their Own Making: Myth, Ritual, and the Quest for Family Values*. Cambridge: Harvard University Press.

Gilmor, Dan.
2004 *We the Media: Grassroots Media By the People For the People*. New York: O'Reilly.

Glasbeek, Harry
2002 "Corporate deviance and deviants: the fancy footwork of criminal law." Pp. 118–43 in *Wealth by Stealth*. Toronto: Between the Lines.

Glenn, N.D.
1998 "The course of marital success and failure in five American 10-year cohorts." *Journal of Marriage and the Family* 60: 569–76.

Glock, Charles Y. and Rodney Stark
1965 *Religion and Society in Tension*. Chicago: Rand McNally.

Goffman, Erving
1974 *Frame Analysis: An Essay on the Organization of Experience*. New York: Harper.
1963 *Stigma: Notes on the Management of Spoiled Identity*. New Jersey: Prentice-Hall.
1959 *The Presentation of Self in Everyday Life*. Garden City: Doubleday Anchor Books.

Goldberg, David Theo
1997 "Taking stock: counting by race." Pp. 27–58 in *Racial Subjects: Writing on Race in America*. New York: Routledge.

Goldscheider, Frances K. and Linda Waite
1991 *New Families, No Families?* Berkeley: University of California Press.

Goldstein, Joshua
2001 "Conquests: sex, rape, and exploitation in wartime." Chapter 6 in *War and Gender: How Gender Shapes the War System and Vice Versa*. Cambridge: Cambridge University Press.

Goldthorpe, J.
1996 "Class analysis and the reorientation of class theory: the case of persisting differentials in educational attainment." *British Journal of Sociology of Education* 47(3): 481–505.

Goldthorpe, John
1969   *The Affluent Worker in Class Society.* New York: Cambridge University Press.

Goode, William J.
1977   "World revolution and family patterns." Pp. 47–58 in A.S. Skolnick and J.H. Skolnick (eds.), *Family in Transition.* Boston: Little, Brown.

Gordon, Milton
1964   *Assimilation in American Life: The Role of Race, Religion, and National Origin.* New York: Oxford University Press.

Gorman, Christine
1992   "Sizing up the sexes." *Time* 139(3): 36–43.

Gorz, Andre
1982   *Farewell to the Working Class.* London: Pluto.

Gough, E. Kathleen
1959   "The Nayars and the definition of marriage." *Journal of the Royal Anthropological Institute* 89: Part 1.

Gould, Stephen Jay
1981   *The Mismeasure of Man.* New York: W.W. Norton.

Gove, Walter
1990   "The effect of marriage on the well-being of adults: a theoretical analysis." *Journal of Marriage and the Family* 11: 4–35.

Government of Canada
2005   *Strengthening Leadership: Taking Action. Canada's Report on HIV/AIDS 2005.* Ottawa: Minister of Public Works and Government Services Canada.
1999   "General Social Survey: Time use." *The Daily,* November 9. Statistics Canada.

Goyder, John C. and James E. Curtis
1977   "Occupational mobility in Canada over four generations." *Canadian Review of Sociology and Anthropology* 14: 303–19.

Grabb, Edward
2004a   "Conceptual issues in the study of social inequality." Pp. 1–16 in James Curtis, Edward Grabb, and Neil Guppy (eds.), *Social Inequality in Canada: Patterns, Problems, and Policies* (4th ed.). Toronto: Pearson Education Canada.
2004b   "Economic power in Canada: corporate concentration, foreign ownership, and state involvement." Pp. 20–30 in James Curtis, Edward Grabb, and Neil Guppy (eds.), *Social Inequality in Canada: Patterns, Problems, and Policies* (4th ed.). Toronto: Pearson Education Canada.
2002   *Theories of Social Inequality: Classical and Contemporary Perspectives* (4th ed.). Toronto: Thomson Nelson.

Grabb, Edward and James Curtis
2005   *Regions Apart: The Four Societies of Canada and the United States.* Toronto: Oxford University Press.

Gracey, Harry L.
2004   "Learning the student role: kindergarten as academic boot camp. Pp. 95–100 in J.H. Ballantine and J.Z. Spade (eds.), *Schools and Society: A Sociological Approach to Education.* Belmont, CA: Wadsworth Thomson.

Graham, Katherine and Evelyn Peters
2002   "Aboriginal communities and urban sustainability," *Canadian Policy Research Networks.* Dec. (http://www.cprn.org)

Granovetter, Mark
1978   "Threshold models of collective behavior." *American Journal of Sociology* 83: 1420–43.

Grayson, J. Paul
1997   "Who gets jobs? Initial labor market experiences of York graduates." Working Paper, York University: Institute for Social Research, January.

Greeley, Andrew M.
1995   *Religion as Poetry.* New Brunswick, NJ: Transactions Publishers.

Greer, Germaine
1992   *The Change: Women, Aging, and the Menopause.* New York: Alfred A. Knopf.

Grenville, Andrew S.
2000   "'For by Him all things were created . . . visible and invisible': sketching the contours of public and private religion in North America." In David Lyon and Marguerite Van Die (eds.), *Rethinking Church, State, and Modernity: Canada Between Europe and the U.S.A.* Toronto: University of Toronto Press.

Groneman, Carol
1995   "Nymphomania: the historical construction of female sexuality." Pp. 219–49 in Jennifer Terry and Jacqueline Urla (eds.), *Deviant Bodies.* Bloomington: Indiana University Press.

Grossman, Dave
1995   *On Killing: The Psychological Cost of Learning to Kill in War and Society.* Boston: Little Brown.

Grossman, Wendy M.
1997   *net.wars.* New York: New York University Press.

Guillemard, Anne-Marie
1996   *Combatting Age Barriers in Job Recruitment and Training: France (National Report).* Dublin: European Foundation for the Improvement of Living and Working Conditions.

Guindon, Hubert
1988   *Quebec Society: Tradition, Modernity and Nationhood.* Toronto: University of Toronto Press.
1964   "Social unrest, social class and Quebec's bureaucratic revolution." *Queen's Quarterly* 71: 150–62.

Guppy, Neil and A. Bruce Arai
1993   "Who benefits from higher education? Differences by sex, social class, and ethnic background." Chapter 16 in J. Curtis, E. Grabb, and N. Guppy (eds.), *Social Inequality in Canada: Patterns, Problems, Policies* (2nd ed.). Scarborough, ON: Prentice Hall.

Guppy, Neil and Hugh Lautard
1990   "The vertical mosaic revisited: occupational differentials among Canadian ethnic groups." Pp. 189–208 in Peter Li (ed.), *Race and Ethnic Relations in Canada.* Toronto: Oxford University Press.

Guppy, Neil, and Scott Davies
1998   *Education in Canada: Recent Trends and Future Challenges.* Ottawa: Statistics Canada.

Gusfield, J.
1986   [1963] *Symbolic Crusade.* Urbana: University of Illinois Press.

Habermas, Jurgen
1989   *The Structural Transformation of the Public Sphere: An Inquiry into a Category of Bourgeois Society.* T. Burger and F. Lawrence (trans.). Cambridge: MIT Press.

Hacking, Ian
1995   "Pull the other one." *London Review of Books,* January 26, 3–5.

Hadaway, C. Kirk, Penny Long Marler, and Hagan, John
1992   "The poverty of classless criminology: the American Society of Criminology 1991 Presidential Address." *Criminology* 30: 1–19.
1991   *The Disreputable Pleasures: Crime and Deviance in Canada* (3rd ed.). Toronto: McGraw-Hill Ryerson.

Hagan, John and F. Kay
1990   "Gender and delinquency in white-collar families: a power-control perspective." *Crime and Delinquency* 36: 391–407.

Hagan, John, J. Simpson, and Ron Gillis
1987   "Class in the household: a power-control theory of gender and delinquency. *American Journal of Sociology* 92(4):788–816.
2001   *Making Crime Count.* Toronto: University of Toronto Press.

Haggerty, Kevin D. and Richard V. Ericson (eds.)
2006   *The New Politics of Surveillance and Visibility.* Toronto: University of Toronto Press.

Haiven, L., S. McBride, and G. Shields (eds.)
1992   *Regulating Labour: The State, Neo-Conservatism and Industrial Relations.* Toronto: Garamond Press.

Hall, David R.
1996   "Marriage as a pure relationship: exploring the links between pre-marital cohabitation and divorce in Canada." *Journal of Comparative Family Studies* 27: 1–12.

Hall, David R. and John Z. Zhao
1995   "Cohabitation and divorce in Canada: testing the selectivity hypothesis." *Journal of Marriage and Family* 57: 421–27.

Hall, G. Stanley
1904   *Adolescence.* Englewood Cliffs: Prentice Hall.

Hall, Edward T.
1981   *The Silent Language.* New York: Anchor Books.

Hall, Stuart
1980   "Encoding/Decoding." Pp. 128–37 in Stuart Hall, Dorothy Hobson, Andrew Lowe, and Paul Willis (eds.), *Culture, Media, Language.* London: Hutchinson.

Hallgrimsdottir, Helga
2004   "Arbitration in ideology and frame: cultural production and the collapse of the Knights of Labour."

Halli, Shiva S. and Abdolmohammad Kazemipur
2003   "Poverty experiences of immigrants." *Canadian Issues: Immigration.* Metropolis Project Brief # 1, April: 18–20.

Hamel, Pierre
1995   "Mouvements urbains et modernité: l'exemple montréalais." *Recherches sociographiques* 36: 279–305.
1991   *Action collective et démocratie locale: les mouvements urbains montréalais.* Montreal: Les presses de l'Université de Montréal.

Hamelink, Cees
1990   "Information imbalance: core and periphery." Pp. 217–28 in J. Downing, A. Mohammadi, and Annabelle Srebery-Mohammadi (eds.), *Questioning the Media: A Critical Introduction.* Newbury Park: Sage.

Hamilton, Gary (ed.)
1999   *Cosmopolitan Capitalists: Hong Kong and the Chinese Diaspora at the End of the Twentieth Century.* Seattle: University of Washington Press.

Hamilton, Richard F.
1996   *The Social Misconstruction of Reality: Validity and Verification in the Scholarly Community.* New Haven: Yale University Press.

Hand, Jeanne Z. and Laura Sanchez
2000   "Badgering or bandering? Gender differences in experiences of, and reactions to, sexual harassment among U.S. high school students." *Gender and Society* 14(6): 718–46.

Hanegraaf, Wouter J.
1996   *New Age Religion and Western Culture.* Leiden: E.J. Brill.

Hannah-Moffat, Kelly
2001   *Punishment in Disguise: Penal Governance and Federal Imprisonment of Women in Canada.* Toronto: University of Toronto Press.

Harrell, W. Andrew
1995   "Husband's involvement in housework: the effects of relative earning power and masculine orientation." *Psychological Reports* 77: 1331–37.

Harris, Judith Rich
1998   *The Nurture Assumption: Why Children Turn out the Way They Do.* New York: Free Press.

Harris, Marvin
1985   *Good to Eat: Riddles of Food and Culture.* New York: Simon and Schuster.
1968   *The Rise of Anthropological Theory: A History of Theories of Culture.* New York: Harper & Row.

Hartnagel, Timothy
2004   "Correlates of crime" Chapter 5 in R. Linden (ed.), *Criminology: A Canadian Perspective* (5th ed.). Toronto: Nelson.

Hartnagel, Timothy and Julian Tanner
1982   "Class Schooling and delinquency: a further examination." *Canadian Journal of Criminology* 24(2): 155–71.

Harvey, Pierre
1969 "Pourquoi le Québec et les Canadiens français occupent-ils une place inférieure sur le plan économique?" Pp. 113–27 in R. Durocher and P.A. Linteau (eds.), *Le "Retard" du Québec*. Quebec: Editions Boréal Express.

Hastings, Max.
2004 *Armageddon: The Battle for Germany, 1944–1945*. New York: A.A. Knopf.

Havighurst, R.J.
1943 *Human Development and Education*. New York: Longman.

Hayes, Bernadette C. and Richard A. Wanner
1996 "Intergenerational occupational mobility among men in Canada and Australia." *Canadian Journal of Sociology* 21: 43–76.

Hazel, K., S. Herman, and C. Mowbray
1992 "Gender and serious mental illness: a feminist perspective." *Psychology of Women Quarterly* 16: 107–26.

Health Canada
2002 *HIV and AIDS in Canada. Surveillance Report to June 30, 2002*. Ottawa: Division of HIV/AIDS Epidemiology and Surveillance, Centre for Infectious Disease Prevention and Control, Population and Public Health Branch, Health Canada.
1999a "Social inequality in the health of Canadians." Pp. 300–14 in J. Curtis, E. Grabb, and N. Guppy (eds.), *Social Inequality in Canada: Patterns, Problems, Policies* (3rd ed.). Scarborough: Prentice Hall.
1999b *HIV/AIDS Epi Update*. Bureau of HIV/AIDS, STD and TB Update Series. Laboratory Centre for Disease Control.
1998 *HIV/AIDS Epidemiology Among Aboriginal People in Canada*. Bureau of HIV/AIDS, STD and TB Update Series. Laboratory Centre for Disease Control.
1995 "The determinants of health." *Seniors Info Exchange* 6(Spring): 1–30.

Heckert, Teresa et al.
2002 "Gender differences in anticipated salary: role of salary estimates for others, job characteristics, career paths, and job inputs." *Sex Roles* 47: 139–51.

Heelas, Paul
1996 *The New Age Movement*. Oxford: Blackwell.

Heidensohn, Frances
1968 "The deviance of women: a critique and inquiry." *British Journal of Criminology* 19(2): 160–75.

Heinz, Walter
2002 "Self-socialization and post-traditional society." *Advances in Life Course Research* 7: 41–64.

Heisz, Andrew
2005 Ten Things to Know About Canadian Metropolitan Areas, Statistics Canada Catalog no. 89-613-MIE-0009.

Helly, Denise
2004 "Are Muslims Discriminated Against in Canada Since September 2001?" *Canadian Ethnic Studies Journal* 36(1): 24–48.

Helm, Barbara and Wendy Warren
1998 "Teenagers talk about cultural heritage and family life." *Transition Magazine* (Vanier Institute) 28(3): 1–6.

Helmes-Hayes, Richard
1994 "Canadian sociology's first textbook: C.A. Dawson and W.E. Getty's *An Introduction to Sociology* (1929)." *Canadian Journal of Sociology* 19: 461–97.

Helmes-Hayes, R. and D. Wilcox-Magill
1993 "A neglected classic: Leonard Marsh's *Canadians In and Out of Work*." *Canadian Review of Sociology and Anthropology* 30: 83–109.

Henripin, Jacques and Rejean Lachapelle
1982 *The Demolinguistic Situation in Canada*. Montreal: The Institute for Research on Public Policy.

Henry, Frances
2004 "Two studies of racial discrimination in employment." Pp. 285–94 in James Curtis, Edward Grabb, and Neil Guppy (eds.), *Social Inequality in Canada: Patterns, Problems, and Policies* (4th ed.). Toronto: Pearson Education Canada.

Henry, Frances, Winston Mattis, Tim Rees, and Carol Tator
1995 *The Colour of Democracy: Racism in Canadian Society*. Toronto: Harcourt Brace.

Henry, Frances and Carol Tator
2002 *Discourses of Domination: Racial Bias in the Canadian English Language Press*. Toronto: University of Toronto Press.

Henshaw, Stanley K., Susheela Singh, and Taylor Haas
1999 "The incidence of abortion worldwide." *International Family Planning Perspectives* 25(supplement): S30–S38.

Herrnstein, R. and J. Wilson
1985 *Crime and Human Nature*. New York: Simon and Schuster.

Hesse-Bieber, Sharlene
1996 *Am I Thin Enough Yet?* New York: Oxford University Press.

Hesse-Bieber C. and M. Yaiser
2003 *Feminist Perspectives on Social Research*. New York: Oxford University Press.

Heuveline, Patrick, Jeffrey M. Timberlake, and Frank Furstenberg, Jr.
2003 "Shifting childrearing to single mothers: results from 17 Western countries." *Population and Development Review* 29: 47–71.

Hewitt, John P.
1994 *Self and Society: A Symbolic Interactionist Social Psychology* (6th ed.). Boston: Allyn and Bacon.

Hiller, Harry H.
1982 *Society and Change: S.D. Clark and the Development of Canadian Sociology*. Toronto: University of Toronto Press.
1979 "The Canadian sociology movement: analysis and assessment." *Canadian Journal of Sociology* 4: 125–50.

Hirschi, T.
1969   *Causes of Delinquency*. Berkeley: University of California Press.

Hobart, Charles W.
1993   "Sexual behaviour." Pp. 52–72 in G.N. Ramu (ed.), *Marriage and Family in Canada Today* (2nd ed.). Scarborough: Prentice Hall.

Hobson, Dorothy.
2003   *Soap Opera*. Oxford: Polity Press.

Hodson, Randy, Garth Massey, and Dusko Sekulic
1994   "National tolerance in the former Yugoslavia." *American Journal of Sociology* 99: 1534–58.

Hoffman, Allan and Randal Summers
2001   *Teen Violence: A Global View*. Westport: Greenwood.

Hofley, John M.
1992   "Canadianization: a journey completed?" In Wm. K. Carroll et al. (eds.), *Fragile Truths: 25 Years of Sociology and Anthropology in Canada*. Ottawa: Carleton University Press.

Holmes, Thomas H. and Richard Rahe
1967   "The social readjustment rating scale." *Journal of Psychometric Research* 11: 216.

Holt, John
1964   *How Children Fail*. New York: Dell.

Homans, George C.
1950   *The Human Group*. New York: Harcourt Brace Jovanovich.

Hou, Feng and Garnett Picot
2003   *Visible Minority Neighbourhood Enclaves and Labour Market Outcomes of Immigrants*. Statistics Canada, Catalogue No. 11F0019MIE, No. 204, July.

Hoy, D. (ed.)
1986   *Foucault: A Critical Reader*. Oxford: Blackwell.

Hoyos, F.A.
1978   *Barbados: A History from the Amerindians to Independence*. London: Macmillan.

Hughes, E.C.
1943   *French Canada in Transition*. Chicago: University of Chicago Press.

Human Resources Development Canada
2000   *Profile of Canadian Youth in the Labour Market*. Ottawa: Author. www.hrdc-drhc.gc.ca/arb.

Huntington, Samuel P.
1996   *The Clash of Civilizations and the Remaking of World Order*. New York: Simon and Schuster.

Hurst, Charles E.
1996   *Social Inequality: Forms, Causes, and Consequences* (2nd ed.). Boston: Allyn and Bacon.

Huxley, Aldous
1932   *Brave New World*. London: Triad Grafton.

Huyssen, Andreas
1986   *After the Great Divide: Modernism, Mass Culture, Postmodernism*. Bloomington: Indiana University Press.

Iannaccone, Laurence and Rodney Stark
1994   "A supply-side reinterpretation of the 'secularization' of Europe." *Journal for the Scientific Study of Religion* 33: 230–52.

Inglehart, Ronald
1997   *Modernization and Postmodernization: Cultural, Economic, and Political Change in 43 Societies*. Princeton: Princeton University Press.
1977   *The Silent Revolution: Changing Values and Political Styles among Western Publics*. Princeton: Princeton University Press.

Innis, Harold A.
1986   [1950] *Empire and Communications*. David Godfrey (ed.). Victoria, BC: Press Porcépic.
1956   *The Fur Trade In Canada: An Introduction to Canadian Economic History* (Rev.ed.). Toronto: University of Toronto Press.
1950   *Empire and Communication*. Toronto: University of Toronto Press.

Ipsos-Reid
2004   *Canadians' Attitudes Towards Financing Post-Secondary Education: Who Should Pay and How?* Montreal: Canada Millennium Foundation.

Jacobs, Bruce A.
1999   *Dealing Crack: The Social World of Streetcorner Selling*. Boston: Northeast University Press.

Jain, Harish, Simaon Taggar, and Morley Gunderson
1997   "The status of employment equity in Canada: an assessment." Paper presented at the 49th Annual Conference of the Industrial Relations Research Association, January 4–6, 1997.

James, Carl E.
1998   "'Up to no good': Black on the streets and encountering police." Pp. 157–76 in Vic Satzewich (ed.). *Racism and Social Inequality in Canada*. Toronto: Thompson Educational Publishing.

Jandorski, J. and K. Ryan
1998   "The enjoyment of sexist humor, rape attitudes, and relationship aggression in college students." *Sex Roles* 38: 743–56.

Jenkins, Hensry
1994   "Star Trek rerun, reread, rewritten: fan writing as textual poaching." Pp. 448–73 in Horace Newcomb (ed.), *Television: The Critical View*. Oxford: Oxford University Press.

Jenkins, J.C. and Bert Klandermans (eds.)
1995   *The Politics of Social Protest: Comparative Perspectives on States and Social Movements*. Minneapolis: University of Minnesota Press.

Jenson, J. and R. Mahon (eds.)
1993   *The Challenge of Restructuring*. Philadelphia: Temple University Press.

Johnson, Alan G.
1997   *The Gender Knot: Unravelling Our Patriarchal Legacy*. Philadelphia: Temple University Press.

Johnston, Hank and Bert Klandermans
1995   "The cultural analysis of social movements." Pp. 3–24 in Hank Johnston and Bert Klandermans (eds.), *Social Movements and Culture*. Minneapolis: University of Minnesota Press.

Johnson, Jacqueline, Sharon Rush and Joe Feagin
2000   "Reducing inequalities: soing anti-racism: toward an egalitarian american society." *Contemporary Sociology* 29: 95–110.

Johnson, Kay, Huang Banghan, and Wang Liyao
1998   "Infant abandonment and adoption in China." *Population and Development Review* 24: 469–510.

Jones, Gavin W. and Pravin Visaria (eds.)
1997   *Urbanization in Large Developing Countries: China, Indonesia, Brazil and India*. Oxford: Clarendon Press.

Juby, Heather, Céline LeBourdais, and Nicole Marcil-Gratton
2001   "A step further in family life: the emergence of the blended family." Pp. 169–203 in *Report on the Demographic Situation in Canada 2000*. Ottawa: Statistics Canada Catalogue No. 91-209.

Juteau, Danielle and Louis Maheu
1989   "Sociology and sociologists in francophone Quebec: science and politics." *Canadian Review of Sociology and Anthropology* 26: 363–93.

Kalbach, W. and W. McVey
1995   *Canadian Population*. Toronto: Nelson.

Kalmijn, Matthijs
1991   "Status homogamy in the United States." *American Journal of Sociology* 97: 496–523.

Kaplan, Hillard S., Jane B. Lancaster, and Kermyt G. Anderson
1998   "Human parental investment and fertility: the life histories of men in Albuquerque." In A. Booth and A.C. Crouter (eds.), *Men in Families: When Do They Get Involved? What Difference Does It Make?* Mahwah, NJ: Lawrence Erlbaum.

Kaplan, Marcie
1983   "A woman's view of DSM-III." *American Psychologist* 38: 786–92.

Kates, N. and E. Krett
1988   "Socio-economic factors and mental health problems: can census-tract data predict referral patterns?" *Canadian Journal of Community Mental Health* 7: 89–98.

Katz, Jack
1988   *Seductions of Crime: Moral and Sensual Attractions of Doing Evil*. New York: Basic Books.

Katz, Jennifer, Stephanie Kuffel, and Amy Coblentz
2002   "Are there gender differences in sustaining dating violence? An examination of frequency, severity, and relationship satisfaction." *Journal of Family Violence* 17: 247–71.

Kaufman, Gayle and Peter Uhlenberg
1998   "Effects of life course transitions on the quality of relationships between adult children and their parents." *Journal of Marriage and the Family* 60: 924–38.

Kaufman, Michael (ed.)
1993   *Cracking the Armor: Power, Pain and the Lives of Men*. Toronto: Viking.

Kazantzakis, Nikos
1952   *Zorba the Greek*. Carl Wildman (trans.) New York: Simon and Schuster.

Kazemipur, Abdolmohammad and Shiva S. Halli
2000   *The New Poverty in Canada: Ethnic Groups and Ghetto Neighborhoods*, Toronto: Thompson Educational Publishing.

Keally, Greg (ed.)
1973   *Canada Investigates Industrialism: The Royal Commission on the Relations of Labor and Capital*. Toronto: University of Toronto Press.

Keane, John
1990   *Media and Democracy*. Oxford: Blackwell.

Kegan, Robert
1994   *In Over Our Heads: The Mental Demands of Modern Life*. Cambridge: Harvard University Press.

Keith, Bruce et al.
2002   "The context of scientific achievement: sex status, organizational environments, and the timing of publication on scholarship outcomes." *Social Forces* 80: 1253–82.

Kelly, Karen, Linda Howatson-Leo, and Warren Clark
1997   I feel overqualified for my job." *Canadian Social Trends*, Winter, 11–16.

Kemeny, Anna and Susan Stobert
2003   "Childfree by choice." *Canadian Social Trends* 69: 7–10.

Kendall, Kathleen
1991   "The politics of premenstrual syndrome: implications for feminist justice." *Journal of Human Justice* 2(2): 77–98.

Kennedy, L. and S. Baron
1993   "Routine activities and a subculture of violence: a study of violence on the street." *Journal of Research in Crime and Delinquency* 30: 88–112.

Kent, Stephen
1990   "Deviance labelling and normative strategies in the Canadian 'new religions/countercult' debate." *Canadian Journal of Sociology* 15: 393–416.

Kerstetter, S.
2002   *Rags and Riches: Wealth Inequality in Canada*. Ottawa: Canadian Centre for Policy Alternatives.

Kettle, John
1980   *The Big Generation*. Toronto: McClelland and Stewart.

Kiernan, Kathleen
2001   "Cohabitation in Western Europe: Trends, Issues and Implications." Pp. 3–31 in A. Booth and A.C. Crouter (eds.), *Just Living Together: Implications of Cohabitation on*

Families, Children, and Social Policy. Mahwah, NJ: Erlbaum.

Kilbourne, Jean
1999 *Deadly Persuasion: Why Women and Girls Must Fight the Addictive Power of Advertising*. New York: Free Press.

Kimmel, Michael S.
2002 "Gender symmetry in domestic violence: a substantive and methodological research review." *Violence Against Women* 8: 1332–63.

Kitsuse, John I.
1980 "Coming out all over: deviants and the politics of social problems." *Social Problems* 28(1): 1–13.

Klein, Naomi
2000 *No Logo: Taking Aim at the Brand Bullies*. Toronto: Vintage Canada.

Knodel, J. and E. Van De Walle
1986 "Lessons from the past: policy implications of historical fertility studies." Pp. 390–416 in A.J. Coale and S.C. Watkins (eds.), *The Decline of Fertility in Europe*. Princeton: Princeton University Press.

Knodel, John, Apichat Chamratrithirong, and Nibhon Debavalya
1987 *Thailand's Reproductive Revolution: Rapid Fertility Decline in a Third-World Setting*. Madison: University of Wisconsin Press.

Kohlberg, Lawrence
1984 *Essays in Moral Development: The Psychology of Moral Development*. New York: Harper and Row.

Kohn, Melvin, A. Naoi, C. Schoenbach, C. Schooler, and K. Slomczynski
1990 "Position in the class structure and psychological functioning in the United States, Japan and Poland." *American Journal of Sociology* 95: 964–1008.

Kollock, Peter
1998 "Social dilemmas: the anatomy of cooperation." *Annual Review of Sociology* 24: 183–214.

Kourany, Janet, James P. Sterba, Rosemary Tong (eds.)
1999 *Feminist Philosophies: Problems, Theories, and Applications*, 2nd ed. New York: Harvester Wheatsheaf.

Krahn, Harvey
2004 "Choose your parents carefully: social class, post-secondary education, and occupational outcomes." Pp. 187–203 in James Curtis, Edward Grabb, and Neil Guppy (eds.), *Social Inequality in Canada: Patterns, Problems, and Policies* (4th ed.). Toronto: Pearson Education Canada.

Krahn, Harvey and Jeffrey W. Bowlby
2000 *Education-jobs Skills Match: An Analysis of the 1990 and 1995 National Graduates Surveys*. Ottawa: Human Resources Development Canada and Centre for Education Statistics, Statistics Canada.

Krahn, Harvey and Graham Lowe
2002 *Work, Industry, and Canadian Society* (4th ed.). Scarborough: Thomson Nelson.

Krahn, Harvey, Graham Lowe, and Karen Hughes
2007 *Work, Industry, and Canadian Society* (5th ed.). Toronto: Thomson Nelson.

Kraut, Robert and Vicki Lundmark
1998 "The Internet paradox: a social technology that reduces social involvement and psychological well being?" *American Psychologist* 53: 1017–31.

Kroger, Jane
2000 *Identity Development: Adolescence through Adulthood*. Thousand Oaks: Sage.

Kubat, Daniel and David Thornton
1974 *A Statistical Profile of Canadian Society*. Toronto: McGraw-Hill Ryerson.

Kuczynski, L., Marshall, S., and K. Schell
1997 "Value socialization in a bi-directional context." Pp. 23–50 in J.E. Grusec and L. Kuczynski (eds.), *Parenting and the Internalization of Values: A Handbook of Contemporary Theory*. Toronto: John Wiley & Sons.

Kunz, Jean, Anne Milan, and Sylvain Schetagne
2002 *Unequal Access: A Canadian Profile of Racial Differences in Education, Employment and Income*. Toronto: Canadian Race Relations Foundation.

Kurzweil, Ray
2005 2005 *The Singularity Is Near: When Humans Transcend Biology*. New York: Viking.

La Prairie, Carol
990 "The role of sentencing in the over-representation of aboriginal people in correctional institutions." *Canadian Journal of Criminology* 32: 429–40.

Labre, Magdala
2002 "Adolescent boys and the muscular male body ideal." *Journal of Adolescent Health* 30: 233–42.

Landman, Michael
1967 *Philosophical Anthropology*. New York: Sheed and Ward.

Langford, Tom and J. Rick Ponting
1992 "Canadians' responses to aboriginal issues: the roles of prejudice, perceived group conflict, and economic conservatism." *Canadian Review of Sociology and Anthropology* 29: 140–66.

Lapierre-Adamcyk, Evelyne, Céline Le Bourdais, and Karen Lehrhaupt
1995 "Les departs du foyer parental des jeunes Canadiens nés entre 1921 et 1960." *Population* 50: 1111–35.

Lasswell, H.
1927 *Propaganda Techniques in the World War*. New York: Knopf.

Lauer, Robert H.
1982 *Perspectives on Social Change* (3rd ed.). Toronto: Allyn and Bacon.

Lawrence, Raymond
1999 "Plains indians cultural survival school." *Transition* Winter: 1, 5.

Le Bourdais, Céline, Ghyslaine Neill, and Pierre Turcotte
2000   "The changing face of conjugal relationships." *Canadian Social Trends* 56: 14–17.

Leahey, Erin and Guang Guo
2001   "Gender differences in mathematical trajectories." *Social Forces* 80: 713–32.

Le Bourdais, Celine and Evelyne Lapierre-Adamcyk
2004   "Changes in conjugal life in Canada: is cohabitation progressively replacing marriage?" *Journal of Marriage and the Family* 66: 929–42.

Leck, J.D. and D.M. Saunders
1996   "Achieving diversity in the workplace: Canada's Employment Equity Act and members of visible minorities." *International Journal of Public Administration* 19: 299–322.

Lehmann, Wolfgang
2004   "'For some reason I get a little scared': structure, agency, and risk in school–work transitions." *Journal of Youth Studies* 7(4): 379–96.
2005a   "Choosing to labour: structure and agency in school–work transitions." *Canadian Journal of Sociology* 30(3): 325–50.
2005b   "'I'm still scrubbing the floors': experiencing youth apprenticeships in Canada and Germany." *Work, Employment and Society* 19(1): 107–29.
2005c   "No regrets: individuals' reflections on dropping out of university." In *Congress 2005: Canadian Sociology and Anthropology Association*. University of Western Ontario, London, ON.

Lehmann, Wolfgang and Alison Taylor
2003   "Giving employers what they want? New vocationalism in Alberta." *Journal of Education and Work* 16(1): 45–67.

Leiss, William, Stephen Kline, and Sut Jhally
1986   *Social Communication in Advertising: Persons, Products, and Images of Well-Being*. Toronto; New york: Methuen.

Lee, Kevin
2000   *Urban Poverty in Canada: A Statistical Profile*. Ottawa: Canadian Council on Social Development, April.

Lee, Richard Borshay
1979   *The !Kung San: Men, Women, and Work in a Foraging Society*. New York: Cambridge University Press.

Lenski, Gerhard
1976   "History and social change." *American Journal of Sociology* 82: 548–64.
1966   *Power and Privilege*. New York: McGraw-Hill.

Leonhardt, David
2005   "The college dropout boom." Pp. 87–104 in Correspondents of the *New York Times* (eds.), *Class Matters*. New York: *Times* Books.

Leridon, Henri and Catherine Villeneuve-Gokalp
1994   *Constances et Inconstances de la Famille*. Paris: Presses Universitaires de la France.

Lerner, Richard M.
2002   *Concepts and Theories of Development* (3rd ed.). Mahwah: Lawrence Erlbaum.
1976   *Concepts and Theories of Human Development*. Reading: Addison-Wesley.

Lesko, Nancy
2001   *Act Your Age! A Cultural Construction of Adolescence*. New York and London: Routledge Falmer.

Lesthaegue, Ron
1995   "The second demographic transition in Western countries: an interpretation." In K. Oppenheim Mason and A-M. Jensen (eds.), *Gender and Family Change in Industrialized Countries*. Oxford: Clarendon.

Lesthaeghe, Ron and Johan Surkyn
1998   "Cultural dynamics and economic theories of fertility change." *Population and Development Review* 14(1): 1–45.

Levy, Ariel
2004   *Female Chauvinist Pigs: Women and the Rise of Raunch Culture*. New York: Free Press.

Levy, Howard
1991   *The Lotus Lovers: The Complete History of the Curious Erotic Custom of Footbinding in China*. Buffalo: Prometheus Books.

Lewis, Bernard
2003   *The Crisis of Islam: Holy War and Unholy Terror*. Toronto: Random House.

Lewontin, Richard.
1991   *Biology as Ideology: The Doctrine of DNA*. Concord: Anasi.

Li, Jiali
1995   "China's one-child policy: a case study of the Hebei Province, 1979–1988." *Population and Development Review* 21: 563–85.

Li, Peter
2003   "Understanding economic performance of immigrants." *Canadian Issues: Immigration*. Metropolis Project Brief # 1, April: 25–27.
2000   "Economic returns of immigrants' self-employment." *Canadian Journal of Sociology* 25(1): 1–34.
1998   "The market value and social value of race," Pp. 115–30 in Vic Satzwewich (ed.), *Racism and Social Inequality in Canada*. Toronto: Thompson Educational Publishing.
1988   *Ethnic Inequality in a Class Society*. Toronto: Wall and Thompson.

Li, Peter and Victor Satzewich
1987   "Immigrant labour in Canada: the cost and benefit of ethnic origin on the job market." *Canadian Journal of Sociology* 12: 229–41.

Lian, Jason and David Ralph Matthews
1998   "Does the vertical mosaic exist? Ethnicity and income in Canada, 1991." *Canadian Review of Sociology and Anthropology* 35: 461–82.

Liebes, Tamar and Elihu Katz
1993   *The Export of Meaning: Cross-Cultural Readings of Dallas*. NY: Oxford University Press.

Lillard, Lee A. and Linda J. Waite
1991 "Children and marital disruption." *American Journal of Sociology* 96: 930–53.

Lindsay, Colin
1992 *Lone-Parent Families in Canada.* Statistics Canada, Catalogue No. 89-522. Ottawa: Minister of Supply and Services Canada.

Lippman, Walter
1922 *Public Opinion.* New York: Macmillan.

Lipset, Seymour Martin
2001 "Defining moments and recurring myths: a reply." *Canadian Review of Sociology and Anthropology* 38: 97–100.
1996 *American Exceptionalism: A Double-Edged Sword.* New York: W.W. Norton.

Livingstone, David W.
2004 *The Education–Jobs Gap: Underemployment or Economic Democracy* (2nd ed.). Aurora, ON: Garamond Press.

Lombroso, Cesare and William Ferrero
1895 *The Female Offender.* London: Unwin Fisher.

Long, Elizabeth
1997 *From Sociology to Cultural Studies.* Oxford: Blackwell Publishers Ltd.

Lorber, Judith
1994 *Paradoxes of Gender.* New Haven: Yale University Press.

Lowe, Graham
2004 "Labour markets, inequality, and the future of work." Pp. 148–64 in James Curtis, Edward Grabb, and Neil Guppy (eds.), *Social Inequality in Canada: Patterns, Problems, and Policies.* Toronto: Pearson Education Canada.
2000 *The Quality of Work: A People-Centred Agenda.* New York: Oxford University Press.

Lowman, John
1992 "Street prostitution." In Vincent Sacco (ed.), *Deviance: Conformity and Control in Canadian Society* (2nd ed.). Scarborough: Prentice Hall.

Luckmann, Thomas
1967 *Invisible Religion: The Problem of Religion in Modern Society.* New York: Macmillan.

Luescher, K. and K. Pillemer
1998 "Intergenerational ambivalence: a new approach to the study of parent–child relations in later life." *Journal of Marriage and the Family* 60: 413–25.

Luhmann, Niklas
1982 *The Differentiation of Society.* Stephen Holmes and Charles Larmore (trans.). New York: Columbia University Press.

Luke, T.W.
1989 *Screens of Power: Ideology, Domination, and Resistance in Informational Society.* Urbana: University of Illinois Press.

Lust, Christine and Susan Minot
2003 "The glass escalator: hidden advantages for men in female professions." Pp. 231–49 in M. Hussey (ed.), *Masculinities: Interdisciplinary Readings.* Upper Saddle River: Prentice-Hall.

Luxton, Meg
1990 "Two hands for the clock: changing patterns in the gendered division of labour in the home." In M. Luxton, H. Rosenberg, and S. Arat-Koc (eds.), *Through the Kitchen Window: The Politics of Home and Family* (2nd ed.). Toronto: Garamond.

Lyman, Stanford M.
1972 "The sociology of deviance: nuts, sluts and perverts. *Social Problems* 20: 103–20.

Mackey, Eva
1999 *The House of Difference: Cultural Politics and National Identity in Canada.* London: Routledge.

Mackie, Marlene
1991 *Gender Relations in Canada.* Toronto: Butterworths.

MacKinnon, Catharine A.
1999 *Toward a Feminist Theory of the State.* Cambridge: Harvard University Press.

MacMillan, Harriet L., Angus MacMillan, David R. Offord, and Jennifer L. Dingle
1996 "Aboriginal health." *Canadian Medical Association Journal* 155: 1569–78.

Macy, M.W.
1991 "Learning to cooperate: stochastic and tacit collusion in social exchange." *American Journal of Sociology* 97: 808–43.

Macy, M.W. and Andreas Flache.
1995 "Beyond rationality in models of choice." *Annual Review of Sociology* 21: 73–91.

Madoo-Lengermann, P. and J. Niebrugge
2004 "Contemporary feminist theory." In G. Ritzer and D. Goodman (eds.) *Social Theory* (6th ed.). New York: McGraw-Hill.

Magill, Dennis and William Michelson
1999 *Images of Change.* Toronto: Canadian Scholars' Press.

Maguire, Mike
2002 "Crime statistics: the 'data explosion' and its implications." In M. Maguire, R. Morgan and R. Reiner (eds.), *The Oxford Handbook of Criminology.* Oxford: Oxford University Press.

Magnusson, D. and H. Stattin
1996 "Antisocial development: a holistic approach." *Development and Psychopathology* 8: 617–45

Males, Michael A.
1996 *The Scapegoat Generation: America's War on Adolescents.* Monroe: Common Courage Press.

Malinowski, Bronislaw
1954 [1925] *Magic, Science and Religion.* New York: Doubleday.

Malthus, T. R.
1970 *An Essay on the Principle of Population.* Harmondsworth: Penguin Books.

Mangahas, Malou
1994 "The oldest contraceptive: the lactional amenorrheam method and reproductive rights (Philippines)."

Pp. 57–68 in Shymala Nataraj et al. (eds), *Private Decisions, Public Debate: Women, Reproduction and Population.* London: Panos.

Marchand, Philip
1989 *Marshall McLuhan: The Medium and the Messenger, A Biography.* Toronto: Random House.

Marcil-Gratton, Nicole
1998 *Growing up with Mom and Dad? The Intricate Family Life Course of Canadian Children.* Statistics Canada, Catalogue No. 89–566. Ottawa: Minister of Supply and Services Canada.
1988 *Les Modes de Vie Nouveaux des Adultes et Leur Impact sur les Enfants au Canada.* Health and Welfare Canada: Report for Review of Demography.

Marcuse, Herbert
1964 *One-Dimensional Man: Studies in the Ideology of Advanced Industrial Society.* Boston: Beacon.

Marleau, Jacques and Jean-Francois Saucier
2002 "Preference for a first-born boy in Western societies." *Journal of Biosocial Science* 34: 13–27.

Marsh, L.
1943 *Report on Social Security for Canada.* Ottawa: King's Printer.

Marshall, Katherine
1998 "Stay-at-home dads." *Perspectives on Labour and Income* 10: 9–15.

Marshall, V.W.
1997 *The Generations: Contributions, Conflict, Equity.* Prepared for the Division of Aging and Seniors. Ottawa: Health Canada.
1996 "The state of theory in aging and the social sciences." Pp. 12–30 in R.H. Binstock and L.K. George (eds.), *Handbook of Aging and the Social Sciences* (4th ed.). San Diego: Academic Press.
1995a "The micro-macro link in the sociology of aging." Pp. 337–71 in C. Hummel and Christian Lalive D'Epinay (eds.), *Images of Aging in Western Societies.* Proceedings of the 2nd Images of Aging Conference. Centre of Interdisciplinary Gerontology. University of Geneva, Switzerland.
1995b "Social models of aging." *Canadian Journal on Aging* 14: 12–34.
1994 "A critique of Canadian aging and health policy." Pp. 232–44 in V.W. Marshall and B.D. McPherson (eds.), *Aging: Canadian Perspectives.* Peterborough: Broadview Press.

Marsiglio, William
1998 *Procreative man.* New York, NY: New York University Press.

Martin, David
2000 "Canada in comparative perspective." In David Lyon and Marguerite Van Die (eds.), *Rethinking Church, State, and Modernity: Canada Between Europe and the U.S.A.* Toronto: University of Toronto Press.

Martin-Barbero, Jesus
1993 *Communication, Culture and Hegemony: From Media to Mediation.* London: Sage.

Martin Matthews, A.
1991 *Widowhood in Later Life.* Toronto: Butterworths/Harcourt Brace.

Martin Matthews, A. and L.D. Campbell
1995 "Gender roles, employment, and informal care." Pp. 129–43 in Sara Arber and Jay Ginn (eds.), *Connecting Gender and Ageing: A Sociological Approach.* Buckingham, England: Open University Press.

Martin Matthews, A. and C. Rosenthal
1993 "Balancing work and family in an aging society: the Canadian experience." Pp. 96–122 in G. Maddox and P. Lawton (eds.), *Annual Review of Gerontology and Geriatrics* Vol. 13. New York: Springer.

Marx, Karl
1975 [1844] "Economic and philosophic manuscripts of 1844." Pp. 279–400 in R. Livingstone and G. Benton (trans.), *Karl Marx: Early Writings.* New York: Vintage Books.
1973 *Grundrisse.* Harmondsworth: Penguin.
1972 "An introduction to the critique of Hegel's *Philosophy of Right.*" In K. Marx and F. Engels. *On Religion.* Moscow: Progress Books.
1970 [1859] *A Contribution to the Critique of Political Economy.* New York: International Publishers.
1906 *Capital: A Critique of Political Economy.* New York: The Modern Library.

Marx, Karl and Friedrich Engels
1979 [1848] *The Communist Manifesto.* Markham: Penguin.
1970 [1848] *The Communist Manifesto.* New York: Washington Square Press.
1973 [1846] *The German Ideology, Part I.* C.J. Arthur (ed.). New York: International Publishers.

Matrix Information and Directory Services
1998 "More than 100 million Internet users as of January 1998 [Online]." June 29. (http://www3.mids.org/press/pr199801.html)

Matthews, R. and J. Young
1992 *Rethinking Criminology: The Realist Debate.* London: Sage.

Matthews, S.H.
2002 *Sisters and Brothers/Daughters and Sons: Meeting the Needs of Old Parents.* Bloomington: Unlimited Publishing.
1993 "Undermining stereotypes of the old through social policy analysis: tempering macro- with micro-level perspectives." Pp. 105–18 in J. Hendricks and C. Rosenthal (eds.), *The Remainder of Their Days: Domestic Policy and Older Families in the United States and Canada.* New York: Garland.
1987a "Provision of care to old parents: division of responsibility among adult children." *Research on Aging* 9: 45–60.
1987b "Perceptions of fairness in the division of responsibility for old parents." *Social Justice Review* 1: 425–37.

Matthews, S.H. and J. Heidorn
1998 "Meeting filial responsibilities in brothers-only sibling groups." *Journal of Gerontology: Social Sciences* 53B: S278–86.

Matthews, S.H. and T.T. Rosner
1988 "Shared filial responsibility: the family as the primary caregiver." *Journal of Marriage and the Family* 50: 185–95.

Maxim, Paul, Jerry White, Dan Beavon, and Paul Whitehead
2001 "Dispersion and polarization of income among Aboriginal and non-Aboriginal Canadians." *Canadian Review of Sociology and Anthropology* 38: 465–77.

McAdam, Doug, J.D. McCarthy, and M.N. Zald (eds.)
1996a *Comparative Perspectives on Social Movements: Political Opportunities, Mobilizing Structures, and Cultural Framings.* New York: Cambridge University Press.
1996b "Introduction: opportunities, mobilizing structures, and framing processes—toward a synthetic, comparative perspective on social movements." Pp. 1–40 in Doug McAdam, J.D. McCarthy, and M.N. Zald (eds.), *Comparative Perspectives on Social Movements: Political Opportunities, Mobilizing Structures, and Cultural Framings.* New York: Cambridge University Press.

McCarthy, B. and J. Hagan
1987 "Gender, delinquency and the Great Depression: a test of power-control theory." *Canadian Review of Sociology and Anthropology* 24: 153–77.

McChesney, Robert Waterman
2004 *The Problem of the Media: U.S. Communication Politics in the Twenty-First Century.* New York: Monthly Review Press.

McChesney, Robert W., Russell Newman, and Ben Scott, eds.
2005 *The Future of Media: Resistance and Reform in the 21st Century.* New York: Seven Stories Press.

McClelland, David
1961 *The Achieving Society.* New York: Free Press.

McConville, M. and D. Shepherd
1992 *Watching Police Watching Communities.* London: Routledge.

McCreary, Donald and Doris Sasse
2002 "Gender differences in high school students' eating behaviour and their correlates." *International Journal of Men's Health* 1: 195–210.

McDaniel, S.A.
1997 "Intergenerational transfers, social solidarity, and social policy: unanswered questions and policy challenges." *Canadian Public Policy/Canadian Journal on Aging.* Supplement: 1–21.

McDaniel, Susan
1994 *Family and Friends.* Statistics Canada, Catalogue No. 11-612, No. 9. Ottawa: Minister of Supply and Services Canada.

McDonald, Kevin and Ross D. Parke
1986 "Parent–child physical play: the effects of sex and age on children and parents." *Sex Roles* 15: 367–78.

McDonald, P.L. and R.A. Wanner
1990 *Retirement in Canada.* Toronto: Butterworths.

McDowell, Ramona and Lucie Nobert
1994 *Profile of Post-secondary Education in Canada, 1993 Edition.* Ottawa: Minister of Supply and Services.

McEvoy, Alan and Robert Welker
2000 "Antisocial behaviour, academic failure, and school climate: a critical review." *Journal of Emotional and Behavioral Disorders* 8(3): 130–40.

McFadden, Mark G.
1995 "Resistance to schooling and education: questions of structure and agency." *British Journal of Sociology of Education* 16(3): 293–308.

McGee, Tom
1997 "Getting inside kids' heads." *American Demographics* January: 21–24.

McGuinness, Donald, E.G Moore, and M.W. Rosenberg
1997 *Growing Old in Canada: Demographic and Geographic Perspectives.* Statistics Canada, Catalogue No. 96-321-MPE No.1. Ottawa: Minister of Supply and Services Canada.

McKie, Craig
1990 "Lifestyle risks: smoking and drinking in Canada." Pp. 86–92 in Craig McKie and Keith Thompson (eds.), *Canadian Social Trends.* Toronto: Thompson Educational Publishing.

McLaren, Peter
2002 *Life in Schools: An Introduction to Critical Pedagogy in the Foundations of Education.* Toronto: Pearson Education Canada.

McLuhan, Marshall
1964 *Understanding Media: The Extensions of Man.* New York: McGraw Hill.
1962 *The Gutenberg Galaxy: The Making of the Typographic Man.* Toronto: University of Toronto Press.

McMullin, J.
1995 "Theorizing aging and gender relations." Pp. 30–41 in Sara Arber and Jay Ginn (eds.), *Connecting Gender and Ageing: A Sociological Approach.* Philadelphia: Open University Press.

McMullin, Julie Ann and Victor W. Marshall
1996 "Family, friends, stress and well-being: does childlessness make a difference?" *Canadian Journal on Aging* 15(3): 355–73.

McNeill, William
1982 *The Pursuit of Power: Technology, Armed Force, and Society since A.D. 1000.* Oxford: Basil Blackwell.

McPherson, Barry D.
2004 *Aging as a Social Process: Canadian Perspectives* (4th ed.). Don Mills, ON: Oxford University Press

McQuillan, Kevin
1992 "Falling behind: the income of lone-mother families, 1970–1985." *Canadian Review of Sociology and Anthropology* 29: 511–23.

McQuillan, Kevin and Marilyn Belle
2004 "Who does what? Gender and the division of labour in Canadian households." Pp. 231–44 in James Curtis,

Edward Grabb, and Neil Guppy (eds.), *Social Inequality in Canada: Patterns, Problems, Policies* (4th ed.). Toronto: Pearson Education Canada.

1999 "Lone-father families in Canada, 1971–1996." Paper presented at the Annual Meeting of the Canadian Population Society, Lennoxville, Québec, June 9.

McRoberts, Kenneth
1988 *Quebec: Social Change and Political Crisis* (3rd ed.). Toronto: McClelland and Stewart.

Mead, George H.
1934 *Mind, Self and Society.* Charles Morris (ed.). Chicago: University of Chicago Press.

Mead, Margaret
1971 *The Mountain Arapesh III.* Garden City: Natural History Press.
1970 *Culture and Commitment.* Garden City: Doubleday.
1935 *Sex and Temperament in Three Primitive Societies.* New York: Morrow.
1928 *Coming of Age in Samoa: A Psychological Study of Primitive Youth for Western Civilization.* New York: Morrow Quill Paperbacks.

Meehan, Albert J.
2000 "The organizational career of gang statistics: the politics of policing gangs." *Sociological Quarterly* 41(3): 337 70.

Meehan, Eileen R. and Riordan, Ellen (Eds).
2001 *Sex & Money: Feminism and Political Economy in the Media.* Minneapolis: University of Minnesota Press.

Memmi, Albert (ed.)
2000 *Racism.* Minneapolis: University of Minnesota Press.

Menzies, Charles
2004 "First Nations, inequality, and the legacy of colonialism." Pp. 295–303 in James Curtis, Edward Grabb, and Neil Guppy (eds.), *Social Inequality in Canada: Patterns, Problems, and Policies* (4th ed.). Toronto: Pearson Education Canada.

Menzies, Robert, Dorothy E. Chun, and Christopher D. Webster
1992 "Female follies: the forensic psychiatric assessment of women defendants." *International Journal of Law and Psychiatry* 15: 179–93.

Merton, Robert K.
1968 *Social Theory and Social Policy.* New York: The Free Press.

Michels, Robert
1915 *Political Parties: A Sociological Study of the Oligarchical Tendencies of Modern Democracies.* Translated by Eden & Cedar Paul. London: Jarrold & Sons.

Miedzian, Myriam
1991 *Boys Will Be Boys: Breaking the Link Between Masculinity and Violence.* New York: Basic Books.

Milan, Anne
2000. "One Hundred Years of Families." *Canadian Social Trends*, Spring, pages 2–13. Statistics Canada Catalogue No. 11-0008.

Milan, Anne and Alice Peters
2003 "Couples living apart." *Canadian Social Trends* 69: 2–6.

Milan, Ann and Brian Hamm
2003 "Across the Generations: Grandparents and Grandchildren." *Canadian Social Trends*, Winter, pages 2–7. Statistics Canada Catalogue No. 11-008.

Millar, Wayne J.
996 "Reaching smokers with lower educational attainment." *Health Reports* 8(2): 11–19.

Miller, James Roger
1996 *Shingwauk's Vision: A History of Native Residential Schools.* Toronto: University of Toronto Press.

Mills, C. Wright
1959 *The Sociological Imagination.* New York: Oxford University Press.
1956 *The Power Elite.* Oxford: Oxford University Press.

Milner, Henry and Sheilagh Hodgins Milner
1973 *The Decolonization of Quebec.* Toronto: McClelland and Stewart.

Mitra, Aparna
2002 "Mathematics skill and male-female wages." *Journal of Socio-Economics* 31: 443–56.

Mogelonsky, Marcia
1996 "The rocky road to adulthood." *American Demographics* May: 26–35, 56.

Moghaddam, Fathali, Richard Lalonde, and Donald Taylor
1987 "Individualistic and collective integration strategies among Iranians in Canada." *International Journal of Psychology* 22: 301–13.

Montgomery, Marilyn and James Côté
2003 "The transition to university: outcomes and adjustments." In Gerald Adams and Michael Berzonsky (eds.), *The Blackwell Handbook of Adolescence.* Oxford: Blackwell.

Moore, Maureen
1987 "Women parenting alone." *Canadian Social Trends* 7: 31–36.

Morley, David
1986 *Family Television: Cultural Power and Domestic Leisure.* London: Routledge.
1980 *The Nationwide Audience: Structure and Decoding.* London: British Film Institute.

Morley, David and Kevin Robins
1995 *Spaces of Identity: Glogal Media, Electronic Landscapes and Cultural Boundaries.* London: Routledge.

Morris, Raymond
1991 "The literary conventions of sociological writing in Quebec and English Canada." *Society* 15: 10–15.

Morton, Desmond
1988 "World War I." Pp. 2341–44 in *The Canadian Encyclopedia* (2nd ed.). Edmonton: Hurtig.

Mosco, Vincent
2005 *The Digital Sublime: Myth, Power, and Cyberspace.* Cambridge, MA: MIT Press.

Mosher, Clayton J., Terance D. Miethe, and Dretha M. Phillips
2002 *The Mismeasure of Crime.* London: Sage.

Mulvey Laura
1977 "Visual pleasure and narrative cinema." In Karyn Kay and Gerald Peary (eds.), *Women and the Cinema.* New York: Dutton.

Mumme, Carla and Kate Laxer
1998 "Organizing and union membership: a Canadian profile in 1997." No. 18. Working Papers Series, Centre for Research on Work and Society, York University.

Murdock, George P.
1960 *Social Structure.* New York: Macmillan.
1957 "World ethnographic sample." *American Anthropologist* 59: 664–87.

Myles, J.
1991 "Editorial: women, the welfare state, and caregiving." *Canadian Journal on Aging* 10: 82–85.
1984 *Old Age and the Welfare State.* Boston: Little Brown.

Naffine, Ngair
1997 *Feminism and Criminology.* Sydney: Allen and Unwin.
1987 *Female Crime: The Construction of Women in Criminology.* Sydney: Allen and Unwin.

Nakhaie, Reza
1997 "Vertical mosaic among the elites: the new imagery revisited." *Canadian Review of Sociology and Anthropology* 34: 1–24.

Nakhaie, Reza and R. Arnold
1996 "Class position, class ideology and class voting: mobilization of support for the New Democratic Party in the Canadian election of 1984." *Canadian Review of Sociology and Anthropology* 33: 181–213.

Nakhaie, Reza, and James Curtis
1998 "Effects of class positions of parents on educational attainment of daughters and sons." *Canadian Review of Sociology and Anthropology* 35: 483–516.

National Advisory Council on Aging
1999 *1999 and Beyond: Challenges of an Aging Canadian Society.* (Draft) January.
1992 *The NACA Position on Managing an Aging Labour Force.* Ottawa: Minister of Supply and Services.

National Council of Welfare
1993 "Poverty in Canada." Ch. 9 in J. Curtis, E. Grabb, and N. Guppy (eds.), *Social Inequality in Canada: Patterns, Problems, Policies* (2nd ed.). Scarborough: Prentice Hall.
1990 *Women and Poverty Revisited.* Ottawa: Ministry of Supply and Services.

Nault, François
1997 "Narrowing mortality gaps, 1978–1995." *Health Reports* 9: 35–41.

Nault, Francois and Alain Belanger
1996 *The Decline in Marriage in Canada, 1981 to 1991.* Statistics Canada, Catalogue No. 84-536-XPB. Ottawa: Minister of Supply and Services Canada.

Nayyar, Seema
2001 "Inside the mind of Gen Y." *American Demographics* September: 6.

Neallani, Shelina
1992 "Women of colour in the legal profession: facing the familiar barriers of race and sex." *Canadian Journal of Women and the Law* 5: 148–65.

Neuman, W. Lawrence
2003 *Social Research Methods.* (5th ed.) Boston, MA: Allyn & Bacon.

Nevitte, Neil
1996 *The Decline of Deference: Canadian Value Change in Cross-national Perspective.* Peterborough: Broadview Press.

Newburn, Tim and Elizabeth Stanko (eds.)
1994 *Just Boys Doing Business? Men, Masculinities and Crime.* London: Routledge.

Newman, Oscar
1973 *Defensible Space: Crime Prevention Through Urban Design.* New York: Collier.

Newman, Peter C.
1995 *The Canadian Revolution 1985–1995: From Deference to Defiance.* Toronto: Viking.

Nie, Yilin and Robert J. Wyman
2005 The one-child policy in Shanghai: acceptance and internalization. *Population and Development Review.* 31: 313–36.

Niebuhr, Gustav
1997 "God therapy: putting life's trials in a sacred context." *New York Times,* February 9.

Niebuhr, H. Richard
1929 *The Social Sources of Denominationalism.* New York: Henry Holt.

Nietzsche, Friedrich
1910 *The Will To Power: An Attempted Transvaluation of All Values,* Vol. II. London: George Allen & Unwin.

Nieuwbeerta, P.
1996 "Educational expansion and educational reproduction in Central Europe, 1940–1975." Pp. 165–85 in H. van der Wusten (ed.), *Proceedings of Third Workshop on Transformation Processes in Eastern Europe, February 1996.* The Hague: NOW.

Nobert, L., R. McDowell, and D. Goulet
1992 *Profile of Higher Education in Canada: 1991 Edition.* Ottawa: Ministry of Supply and Services.

Noguera, Pedro A.
1995 "Preventing and producing violence: a critical analysis of responses to school violence." *Harvard Educational Review* 65(2): 189–212.

Nolan, Patrick and Gerhard Lenski
2006 *Human Societies: An Introduction to Macrosociology* (10th ed.). Boulder, CO: Paradigm Publishers.

Noonan, Mary C.
2001   "The impact of domestic work on men's and women's wages." *Journal of Marriage and the Family* 63: 1134–45.

Normand, Josée
1995   "Education of women in Canada." *Canadian Social Trends* Winter: 17–21.

Norris, Clive and Gary Armstrong
1999   *The Maximum Surveillance Society: The Rise of CCTV.* Oxford: Berg.

Norris, D.
1999   "Demographic outlook for Canada." Paper presented at the National Seminar on Demographic Change and Population Ageing. Moncton, New Brunswick, April.

Northcott, H.C.
1994   "Public perceptions of the population aging crisis." *Canadian Public Policy* 20: 66–77.

Notestein, F. W.
1945   "Population—the long view." Pp. 36–57 in T.W. Schultz (ed.), *Food for the World.* Chicago: University of Chicago Press.

Novak, Mark
1997   *Aging and Society: A Canadian Perspective.* Toronto: ITP Nelson.

Oakes, Jeannie
2006   *Keeping Track: How Schools Structure Inequality* (2nd ed.). Knodel.

Oakley, A.
1998   "Gender, methodology, and people's ways of knowing: some problems with feminism and the paradigm debate in social science." *Sociology* 32: 701–31.

Oberschall, Anthony
2000   "Utopian visions, engaged sociologies for the 21st century: achieving basic survival: Preventing genocide." *Contemporary Sociology* 29: 1–13.

O'Brien, M.
1991   "Never-married older women: the life experience." *Social Indicators Research* 24: 301–15.

O'Connell, Paul Debra Pepler, and Wendy Craig
1999   "Peer involvement in bullying: insights and challenges for intervention." *Journal of Adolescence* 22(4): 437–52.

O'Connor, Julia
1999   "Ownership, class, and public policy." Pp. 35–47 in J. Curtis, E. Grabb, and N. Guppy (eds.), *Social Inequality in Canada: Patterns, Problems, Policies* (3rd ed.). Scarborough: Prentice Hall.

OECD
1996   *Main Economic Indicators 1965 through 1996.* Accessed online at http://www.oecd.org/pdf/M00041000/M00041020.pdf

Ogbu, John U.
1992   "Understanding cultural diversity and learning." *Educational Researcher* 21(8): 5–14.

Ogmundson, R. and J. McLaughlin
1992   "Trends in the ethnic origins of Canadian elites: the decline of the BRITS?" *Canadian Review of Sociology and Anthropology* 29: 227–42.

Olsen, Dennis
1980   *The State Elite.* Toronto: McClelland and Stewart.

Olson, Mancur, Jr.
1965   *The Logic of Collective Action: Public Goods and the Theory of Groups.* Cambridge: Harvard University Press.

Olzak, Susan
1992   *The Dynamics of Ethnic Competition and Conflict.* Stanford: Stanford University Press.

Oppenheimer, Valerie K.
1997   "Women's employment and the gain to marriage: the specialization and trading model." *Annual Review of Sociology* 23: 431–53.
1994   "Women's rising employment and the future of the family in industrial societies." *Population and Development Review* 20: 293–342.

Ortner, Sherry
1972   "Is female to male as nature is to culture?" *Feminist Studies* 1: 5–31.

Ostrom, Elinor
1990   *Governing the Commons: the Evolution of Institutions for Collective* Action. New York: Cambridge University Press.
2000   "Collective action and the evolution of social norms." *Journal of Economic Perspectives* 14: 137–58.

O'Toole, Roger
2000   "Canadian religion: heritage and project." In David Lyon and Marguerite Van Die (eds.) *Rethinking Church, State, and Modernity: Canada Between Europe and the USA.* Toronto: University of Toronto Press.

Otto, Rudolf
1958   [1917] *The Idea of the Holy.* John W. Harvey (trans.). Oxford: Oxford University Press.

Ownby, David
1995   "The Heaven and Earth Society as popular religion." *The Journal of Asian Studies* 54: 1023–46.
1996   *Brotherhood and Secret Societies in Early Mid-Qing China: The Formation of a Tradition.* Stanford: Stanford University Press.

Palantzas, T.
1991   "A search for 'autonomy' at Canada's first sociology department." *Society/Société* 15: 10–18.

Palladino, Grace
1996   *Teenagers: An American History.* New York: Basic Books.

Palmer, Bryan
1983   *Working-Class Experience: The Rise and Reconstitution of Canadian Labour, 1800–1980.* Toronto: Butterworths.

Papillon, Martin
2002   "Immigration, diversity and social inclusion in Canada's cities." Canadian Policy Research Networks, Discussion paper F27, Dec.

Park, Robert E.
1952 *Human Communities.* New York: Free Press.
1950 *Race and Culture.* New York: Free Press.

Parkin, Frank
1979 *Marxism and Class Theory: A Bourgeois Critique.* London: Tavistock.

Parliament, Jo-Anne
1990 "Increased life expectancy, 1921-1981." Pp. 64–65 in Craig McKie and Keith Thompson (eds.), *Canadian Social Trends.* Toronto: Thompson Educational Publishing.

Parnell, A.M. and R.R. Rindfuss
1989 "The varying connection between marital status and childbearing in the United States." *Population and Development Review* 15: 447–70.

Parsons, Talcott
1959 "The school class as a social system: some of its functions in American society." *Harvard Educational Review* 29: 297–318.
1953 "A revised analytical approach to the theory of social stratification." Pp. 92–128 in Reinhard Bendix and S.M. Lipset (eds.), *Class, Status and Power.* Glencoe: The Free Press.
1951 *The Social System.* Glencoe: The Free Press.
1937 *The Structure of Social Action.* New York: Free Press.

Paul, Pamela
2001 "Getting inside Gen Y." *American Demographics* September: 42–50.

Pendakur, Krishna and Ravi Pendakur
2002 "Colour my world: have earnings gaps for Canadian-born ethnic minorities changed over time?" *Canadian Public Policy* 28(4): 489–512.

Péron, Yves, Hélène Desrosiers, Heather Juby, Evelyne Lapierre-Adamcyk, Céline Le Bourdais, Nicole Marcil-Gratton, and Jael Mongeau
1999 *Canadian Families at the Approach of the Year 2000.* Catalogue No. 96-321, No. 4. Ottawa: Statistics Canada.

Pfohl, Stephen
1994 *Images of Deviance and Social Control: A Sociological History* (2nd ed.). New York: McGraw Hill.

Phillips, Andrew
1999 "Lessons of Littleton." *MacLean's* May 3: 18–21.

Phillips, Charles
1957 *The Development of Education in Canada.* Toronto: W.J. Gage and Company Ltd.

Phillips, Ruth B. and Elizabeth Johnson
2003 "Negotiating new relationships: Canadian museums, First Nations, and cultural property." Pp. 149–67 in J. Torpey (ed.), *Politics and the Past: On Repairing Historical Injustices.* Lanham, Maryland: Rowman and Littlefield Publishers.

Philp, Margaret
2004 "Teaching a new generation to duck and cover." *Globe and Mail,* October 18: A8.

Piaget, Jean
1954 *The Construction of Reality in the Child.* New York: Basic Books.

Picot, Garnett and Feng Hou
2003 "The rise in low-income rates among immigrants in Canada," Ottawa: Statistics Canada, Research Paper, Catalogue No. 11F0019MIE - No. 198, June.

Pillemer, K. and J. Suitor
1991 "Will I ever escape my child's problems? Effects of adult children's problems on elderly parents." *Journal of Marriage and the Family* 53: 585–94.

Pinard, Maurice
1968 "Mass society and political movements: a new formulation." *American Journal of Sociology* 73: 682–90.

Pineo, Peter, John Porter, and Hugh McRoberts
1977 "The 1971 census and the socioeconomic classification of occupations." *Canadian Review of Sociology and Anthropology* 14: 91–102.

Pinker, Steven
2002 *The Blank Slate: The Modern Denial of Human Nature.* New York: Viking Penguin.

Pino, Nathan and Robert Meier
1999 "Gender differences in rape reporting." *Sex Roles* 40 (11–12): 970–90.

Platiel, Rudy
1993 "Inuit to sign deal for 'our land'." *The Globe and Mail,* May 25: 1.

Pleck, Joseph
1981 *The Myth of Masculinity.* Cambridge: MIT Press.

Polakowski, Michael
1994 "Linking self- and social control with deviance: illuminating the structure underlying a general theory of crime and its relation to deviant activity." *Journal of Quantitative Criminology* 10: 41–78.

Pollack, Otto
1961 *The Criminality of Women.* New York: A.S. Barnes.

Ponting, Rick
1998 "Racism and stereotyping of First Nations." Pp. 269–98 in V. Satzewich (ed.), *Racism and Social Inequality in Canada.* Toronto: Thompson Educational Publishers.

Popenoe, David
1998 *Disturbing the Nest: Family Change and Decline in Modern Societies.* New York: Aldine de Gruyter.

Pool, Ithiel de Sola
1983 *Technologies of Freedom.* Cambridge: Harvard University Press.

Pooley, Eric
1999 "Portrait of a deadly bond." *Time,* May 10: 14–20.

Porter, John
1980 "Canada: dilemmas and contradictions of a multi-ethnic society." Pp. 325–36 in Jay Goldstein and Rita Bienvenue (eds.), *Ethnicity and Ethnic Relations in Canada.* Toronto: Butterworths.

1965   *The Vertical Mosaic: An Analysis of Social Class and Power in Canada.* Toronto: University of Toronto Press.

Posgate, Dale and Kenneth McRoberts
1976   *Quebec: Social Change and Political Crisis.* Toronto: McClelland and Stewart.

Prentice, Alison et al.
1988   *Canadian Women: A History.* Toronto: Harcourt Brace Jovanovich.

Public Health Agency of Canada
2005   *HIV and AIDS in Canada. Surveillance Report to June 30, 2005.* Ottawa: Surveillance and Risk Assessment Division, Centre for Infectious Disease Prevention and Control, Public Health Agency of Canada.

Quart, Alicia
2002   *Branded: The Buying and Selling of Teenagers.* New York: Perseus.

Raag, Tarja and Christine Rackliffe
1998   "Preschoolers' awareness of social expectations of gender: relationships to toy choices." *Sex Roles* 38: 685–700.

Rafter, Nicole Hann
1990   *Partial Justice: Women in State Prisons, 1800–1935* (2nd ed.). Boston: Northeastern University Press.

Ravanera, Zcnaida and Fernando Rajulton
1996   "Stability and crisis in the family life course: findings from the 1990 General Social Survey, Canada." *Canadian Studies in Population* 23: 165–84.

Ravanera, Zenaida, Fernando Rajulton, and Thomas Burch
1998a "Trends and variations in the early life courses of Canadian men." University of Western Ontario. Discussion Paper No. 98-7.
1998b "Early life transitions of Canadian women: A cohort analysis of timing, sequences, and variations." *European Journal of Population* 14: 179–204.
1995   "A cohort analysis of home leaving in Canada, 1910–1975." *Journal of Comparative Family Studies* 26: 179–94.

Reich, Robert B.
1992   *The Work of Nations: Preparing Ourselves for 21st Century Capitalism.* New York: Vintage.

Reid, G.M.
1994   "Maternal sex-stereotyping of newborns." *Psychological Reports* 75: 1443–50.

Reimer, Samuel H.
2003   *Evangelicals and the Continental Divide.* Montreal and Kingston: McGill-Queen's University Press.
1995   "A look at cultural effects on religiosity: a comparison between the United States and Canada." *Journal for the Scientific Study of Religion* 34: 445–57.

Rheingold, Howard
1993   *The Virtual Community: Homesteading on the Electronic Frontier.* Reading, Mass.; Don Mills, Ont.: Addison-Wesley.

Reinharz, Shulamit
1992   *Feminist Methods in Social Research.* New York: Oxford University Press.

Reitsma-Street, Marge
1999   "Justice for Canadian girls: a 1990s update." *Canadian Journal of Criminology* 41: 335–46.

Reitz, Jeffrey
1998   *Warmth of the Welcome: The Social Causes of Economic Success for Immigrants in Different Nations and Cities.* Boulder: Westview Press.
1990   "Ethnic concentrations in labor markets and their implications for ethnic inequality." Pp. 135–95 in Raymond Breton, Wsevolod Isajiw, Warren Kalbach, and Jeffrey Reitz (eds.), *Ethnic Identity and Equality.* Toronto: University of Toronto Press.

Reitz, Jeffrey G. and Raymond Breton
1994   *The Illusion of Difference: Realities of Ethnicity in Canada and the United States.* Toronto: C.D. Howe Institute.

Renaud, Marc, Suzanne Doré, and Deena White
1989   "Sociology and social policy: from a love–hate relationship with the state to cynicism and pragmatism." *Canadian Review of Sociology and Anthropology* 26: 426–56.

Renk, Kimberly et al.
2003   "Mothers, fathers, gender role, and time parents spend with their children." *Sex Roles* 48: 305–15.

Rheingold, Howard
2002   *Smart Mobs: The Next Social Revolution.* Boulder, CO: Perseus.

Rice, Frank P.
1998   *Human Development: A Life-span Approach* (3rd ed.). Upper Saddle River: Prentice Hall.

Rice, Patricia C.
1981   "Prehistoric Venuses: symbols of motherhood or womanhood?" *Journal of Anthropological Research* 37: 402–14.

Richer, Stephen and Pierre Laporte
1971   "Culture, cognition, and English-French competition." Pp. 141–50 in Jean L. Elliott (ed.), *Minority Canadians II: Immigrant Groups.* Scarborough, Ont.: Prentice Hall.

Riley, J.W. and M.W. Riley
1994   "Age integration and the lives of older people." *The Gerontologist* 34: 110–15.

Riley, M.W., M. Johnson, and A. Foner (eds.)
1972   *Aging and Society, Vol. 3: A Sociology of Age Stratification.* New York: Russell Sage Foundation.

Riley, M.W., R.L. Kahn, and A. Foner
1994   *Age and Structural Lag: Society's Failure to Provide Meaningful Opportunities in Work, Family and Leisure.* New York: Wiley.

Rindfuss, Ronald R. and Audrey VandenHeuvel
1990   "Cohabitation: precursor to marriage or an alternative to being single." *Population and Development Review* 16: 703–26.

Rinehart, J., C. Huxley, and D. Robertson
1998   *Not Just Another Auto Plant.* Ithaca: Cornell University Press.

Rinehart, James W.
2006 *The Tyranny of Work: Alienation and the Labour Process* (5th ed.). Toronto: Harcourt Brace.

Rioux, Marcel
1978 *Quebec in Question.* Toronto: James Lorimer.

Rist, Ray C.
1977 "On understanding to processes of schooling: the contributions of labeling theory. In J. Karabel and A. H. Halsey (eds.), *Power and Ideology in Education.* New York: Oxford University Press.

Ritchie, Karen
1995 "Marketing to Generation X." *American Demographics* April: 34–39.

Ritzer, George
1996 *The McDonaldization of Society* (Revised ed.). Thousand Oaks: Pine Forge Press.

Roberts, Julian.
1994 "Crime and race statistics: toward a Canadian solution. *Canadian Journal of Criminology* 36: 175–85.

Roberts, Julian and Thomas Gabor
1990 "Lombrosian wine in a new bottle: research on crime and race." *Canadian Journal of Criminology* 32: 291–314.

Roberts, R.E.L., L.N. Richards, and V.L. Bengtson
1991 "Intergenerational solidarity in families: untangling the ties that bind." *Marriage and Family Review* 16: 11–46.

Robson, Karen and Jean Wallace
2001 "Gendered inequalities in earnings: a study of Canadian lawyers." *Canadian Review of Sociology and Anthropology* 38: 75–95.

Rocher, G.
1996 "Préface." In Marc Brière (ed.), *Le goût du Québec: l'après référendum 1995.* La Salle: Hurtubise.
1992 "The two solitudes between Canadian sociologists." In Wm. K. Carroll et al. (eds.), *Fragile Truths: 25 Years of Sociology and Anthropology in Canada.* Ottawa: Carleton University Press.
1977 "The future of sociology in Canada." In Christopher Beattie and Stewart Crysdale (eds.), *Sociology Canada: Readings.* Toronto: Butterworths.

Rohde-Dascher, C. and S. Price
1992 "Do we need a feminist psychoanalysis?" *Psychoanalysis and Contemporary Thought* 15: 241–59.

Romanow, Roy
2002 *Building on Values: The Future of Health Care in Canada.* Ottawa: Commission on the Future of Health Care in Canada.

Roof, Wade Clark
996 "God is in the details: reflections on religion's public presence in the United States in the mid–1990s." *Sociology of Religion* 57: 149–62.

Rosaldo, Michelle
2002 "Women, culture, and society: a theoretical overview." In Nancy McKee and Linda Stone (eds.), *Readings in Gender and Culture in America.* Upper Saddle River: Prentice Hall.

Roscoe, Paul
1996 "Incest." Pp. 631–34 in D. Levinson and M. Ember (eds.), *The Encyclopedia of Cultural Anthropology*, Vol. 2. New York: Henry Holt.

Roscoe, W.
1991 *The Zuni Man-Woman.* Albuquerque: University of New Mexico Press.

Rose, Fred
1997 "Toward a class-cultural theory of social movements: reinterpreting new social movements." *Sociological Forum* 12: 461–94.

Rosenau, P.M.
1992 *Post-modernism and the Social Sciences: Insights, Inroads, and Intrusions.* Princeton: Princeton University Press.

Rosenberg, Harriet
1990 "The home is the workplace." In M. Luxton, H. Rosenberg, and S. Arat-Koc (eds.), *Through the Kitchen Window: The Politics of Home and Family* (2nd ed.). Toronto: Garamond.

Rosenberg, M. Michael and Jack Jedwab
1992 "Institutional completeness, ethnic organizational style and the role of the state: the Jewish, Italian, and Greek communities of Montreal." *Canadian Review of Sociology and Anthropology* 29: 266–87.

Rosenfeld, Rachel A.
2002 "What do we learn about difference from the scholarship on gender?" *Social Forces* 81: 1–24.

Rossi, Alice S.
1985 *Gender and the Life Course.* New York: Aldine de Gruyter.

Roussel, Louis
1989 *La famille incertaine.* Paris: Odile Jacob.

Rowe, Kathleen
1994 "Roseanne: unruly woman as domestic goddess." Pp. 202–11 in Horace Newcomb (ed.), *Television: The Critical View.* Oxford: Oxford University Press.

Royal Commission on Aboriginal Peoples
1996 *Report.* Ottawa: Indian and Northern Affairs Canada (http://www.ainc-inac.gc.ca/ch/rcap).

Royal Commission on Bilingualism and Biculturalism
1969 *Report. Book IV: The Cultural Contribution of the Other Ethnic Groups.* Ottawa: Information Canada.
1967 *Report. Book I: The Official Languages.* Ottawa: Queen's Printer.

Rudé, George
1964 *The Crowd in History: A Study of Popular Disturbances in France and England, 1730–1848.* New York: Wiley.

Rushkoff, Douglas
1994 *Media Virus! Hidden Agendas in Popular Culture.* New York: Ballantine.

2001   *The merchants of cool* (video cassette*)*. Public
        Broadcasting System, Frontline, www.pbs.org.

Rushton, J. Philippe
2000   *Race, Evolution, and Behaviour: A Life History Perspective*
        (3rd ed.) Port Huron: Charles Darwin Research
        Institute.
1988   "Race differences in behavior: a review and evolutionary
        analysis." *Personality and Individual Differences* 9: 1009–24.

Russel, Bob
1990   *Back to Work? Labour, State and Industrial Relations in
        Canada.* Scarborough: Nelson Canada.

Ruth, Sheila
1990   *Issues in Feminism* (2nd ed.). Toronto: Mayfield.

Ryan, John and William W. Wentworth
1999   *Media and Society: The Production of Mass Media.*
        Needham Heights: Allyn and Bacon.

Ryan, K. and J. Kanjorski
1998   "The enjoyment of sexist humor, rape attitudes, and
        relationship aggression in college students." *Sex Roles* 38:
        743–56.

Ryder, N.B.
1965   "The cohort as a concept in the study of social change."
        American Sociological Review 30: 843–61.

Sabel, Charles, F.
1982   *Work and Politics: The Division of Labor in Industry.*
        New York: Cambridge University Press.

Sabo, Donald
1994   Pigskin, patriarchy and pain. Pp. 82–88 in D. Sabo and
        M. Messner (eds.), *Sex, Violence and Power in Sports:
        Rethinking Masculinity.* Freedom, CA: Crossing Press.

Sacco, V. and H. Johnson
1990   *Patterns of Criminal Victimization in Canada.* Ottawa:
        Minister of Supply and Services.

Said, Edward
1978   *Orientalism.* New York: Pantheon Press.

Salaman, Graeme
1986   *Working.* New York: Routledge, Chapman and Hall.

Salutin, Rick
1993   "Men and feminism." *This Magazine* 26: 12–18.

Sampson, R. and J. Laub
1990   "Crime and deviance over the life course: the salience
        of adult social bonds." *American Sociological Review* 55:
        609–27.

Satzewich, Victor (ed.)
1998   *Racism and Social Inequality in Canada.* Toronto:
        Thompson Educational Publishers.

Scanzoni, John and Letha Scanzoni
1988   *Men, Women and Change: A Sociology of Marriage and
        Family* (3rd ed.). New York: McGraw-Hill.

Schachter, Harvey
1999   "The hurrier we go, the behinder we get." *The Globe and
        Mail*, May 15: D1-D2.

Scheff, Thomas
1984   [1966] *Being Mentally Ill: A Sociological Theory.* Chicago:
        Aldine.

Schiller, Dan
1999   *Digital Capitalism: Networking the Global Market System.*
        Cambridge: MIT Press.

Schiller, Herbert J.
1991   "Not yet the post-imperial era." *Critical Studies in Mass
        Communication* 8: 13–28.

Schissel, Bernard
1992   "The influence of economic factors and social control
        policy on crime rate changes in Canada, 1962–1988."
        Canadian Journal of Sociology 17: 405–28.

Schlegel, Alice and Herbert Barry
1991   *Adolescence: An Anthropological Inquiry.* New York:
        Free Press.

Schor, Julliet B.
2004   *Born to Buy: The Commercialized Child and the New
        Consumer Culture.* New York: Scribner.

Schur, Edwin M.
1984   *Labeling Women Deviant: Gender, Stigma, and Social
        Control.* New York: Random House.

Scott, Alan
1990   *Ideology and the New Social Movements.* London: Unwin
        Hyman.

Sears, Alan
2003   *Retooling the Mind Factory: Education in a Lean State.*
        Aurora, ON: Garamond Press.

Seidman, Steven
1996   "Empire and knowledge: more troubles, new opportu-
        nities for sociology." *Contemporary Sociology* 25: 313–15.

Sellin, T.
1938   *Culture, Conflict and Crime.* New York: Social Science
        Research Council.

Serjak, John and Neil Swan
1993   "Analysing regional disparities." Chapter 30 in J. Curtis,
        E. Grabb, and N. Guppy (eds.), *Social Inequality in
        Canada: Patterns, Problems, Policies* (2nd ed.).
        Scarborough: Prentice Hall.

Shalinsky, Audrey and Anthony Glascock
1988   Killing infants and the aged in nonindustrial societies:
        removing the liminal. *Social Science Journal* 25(3): 277–87.

Sharma, Nandita
2001   "On being not Canadian: the social organization of
        'migrant workers' in Canada." *Canadian Review of
        Sociology and Anthropology* 38: 415–40.

Sharot, Stephen
2002   "Beyond Christianity: a critique of the rational choice
        theory of religion from a Weberian and comparative
        religions perspective." *Sociology of Religion* 63: 427–54.

Sharp, R.L.
1952   "Steel axes for stone age Australians." *Human
        Organization* 11: 17–22.

Shore, Marlene
1987 *The Science of Social Redemption: McGill, the Chicago School, and the Origins of Social Research in Canada.* Toronto: University of Toronto Press.

Shorter, Edward
1977 *The Making of the Modern Family.* New York: Basic Books.

Shostak, Marjorie
1983 [1981] *Nisa: The Life and Words of a !Kung Woman.* New York: Vintage Books.

Simon, J.
1981 *The Ultimate Resource.* Princeton: Princeton University Press.

Skolnick, Arlene S.
1996 *The Intimate Environment: Exploring Marriage and the Family.* New York: Harper Collins.
1991 *Embattled Paradise: The American Family in an Age of Uncertainty.* New York: Basic Books.

Small, Stephen
1998 "The contours of racialization: structures, representation and resistance in the United States." Pp. 69–86 in Vic Satzwewich (ed.), *Racism and Social Inequality in Canada.* Toronto: Thompson Educational Publishing.

Smith, Dorothy
1990 *The Conceptual Practices of Power: A Feminist Sociology of Knowledge.* Toronto: University of Toronto Press.
1989 "Feminist reflections on political economy." *Studies in Political Economy* 30: 37–60.
1987 *The Everyday World as Problematic.* Toronto: University of Toronto Press.

Smith, Philip (ed.)
1998 *The New American Cultural Sociology.* Cambridge: Cambridge University Press.

Smout, T.C.
1969 *A History of the Scottish People, 1560–1830.* Glasgow: Collins.

Snider, Laureen
1993 *Bad Business: Corporate Crime in Canada.* Toronto: Nelson.
1992 "Commercial crime." Pp. 313–62 in Vincent Sacco (ed.), *Deviance: Conformity and Control in Canadian Society* (2nd ed.). Scarborough: Prentice Hall.

Sniderman, P., D. Northrup, J. Fletcher, P. Russell, and P. Tetlock
1993 "Psychological and cultural foundations of prejudice: the case of anti-Semitism in Quebec." *Canadian Review of Sociology and Anthropology* 30: 242–70.

So, Alvin
1990 *Social Change and Development: Modernization, Dependency, and World-System Theories.* Newbury Park: Sage Publications.

Solomon, R. and T. Madison
1986 "The evolution of non-medical drug use in Canada." In Robert Silverman and James Teevan (eds.), *Crime in Canadian Society* (3rd ed.). Toronto: Butterworths.

"Spanker spanked."
1995 *Globe and Mail* February 9: A2.

Sparks, Allister
1995 *Tomorrow Is Another Country: The Inside Story of South Africa's Road to Change.* Chicago: University of Chicago Press.

Speer, Tibbett L.
1998 "College come-ons." *American Demographics* March: 41–45.

Spencer, Herbert
1898 *The Principles of Sociology,* Vol. II-2. New York: D. Appleton.
1897 *The Principles of Sociology,* Vol. I-2. New York: D. Appleton.

Spitzer, S.
1975 "Toward a Marxian theory of deviance." *Social Problems* 22: 638–51.

Stanbridge, Karen
2002 "Master frames, political opportunities, and self-determination: the Åland Islands in the post-WWI period." *The Sociological Quarterly* 43(4): 527–52.

Stanecki, Karen
2002 *The AIDS Pandemic in the 21st Century.* U.S. Census Bureau.

Stark, Rodney
2005 *The Victory of Reason: How Christianity Led to Freedom, Capitalism, and Western Success.* New York: Random House.
1996 *The Rise of Christianity.* Princeton: Princeton University Press.

Stark, Rodney and Roger Finke
2000 *Acts of Faith: Explaining the Human Side of Religion.* Berkeley, CA: University of California Press.

Statistics Canada
2006 CANSIM Table 202-0403 and Catalogue No. 75-202-X1E.
2005a *Births 2003.* Catalogue No. 84F0210XIE. Ottawa: Statistics Canada.
2005b *Labour Force Historical Review 2004.* Catalogue No. 71F0004XCB. Ottawa: Statistics Canada.
2003a *Report on the Demographic Situation in Canada 2002.* Catalogue No. 91-209-XPE
2003a *Marriages 2000.* Catalogue No. 84F0212XPB. Ottawa: Statistics Canada.
2003b *Income of Canadian Families.* Catalogue No. 96F0030XIE2001014. Ottawa: Statistics Canada.
2003c *Canada's Ethnocultural Portrait: The Changing Mosaic, 2001 Census.* (2001 Census: Analysis Series). Catalogue No. 96F0030XIE2001008. Ottawa: Statistics Canada.
2003d *2001 Census Table.* Catalogue No. 97F0019XCB2001060. Ottawa: Statistics Canada.
2002a *Profile of Canadian Families and Households: Diversification Continues.* Catalogue No. 6F0030XIE2001003. Ottawa: Statistics Canada.
2002b *Changing Conjugal Life in Canada.* Catalogue No. 89-576. Ottawa: Statistics Canada.

Steering Committee on Cancer Statistics
2001 *Canadian Cancer Statistics 2001.* Toronto: National Cancer Institute of Canada.

Steffensmeier, D. and C. Streifel
1991 "Age, gender, and crime across three historical periods: 1935, 1960, and 1985." *Social Forces* 69: 869–94.

Stein, Nan
1995 "Sexual harassment in school: the public performance of gendered violence." *Harvard Educational Review* 65(2): 145–62.

Steinberg, Laurence
2001 "We know some things: parent-adolescent relationships in retrospect and prospect." *Journal of Research on Adolescence* 11: 1–19.

Stobert, Susan and Kelly Cranswick
2004 "Looking after seniors: Who does what for whom?" *Canadian Social Trends* Autumn: 2–6.

Stone, L.O., C.J. Rosenthal, and I.A. Connidis
1998 *Parent-Child Exchanges of Supports and Intergenerational Equity.* Ottawa: Statistics Canada.

Stone, Leroy O.
1988 *Family and Friendship Ties among Canada's Seniors.* Statistics Canada, Catalogue No. 89-508. Ottawa: Minister of Supply and Services Canada.
1967 *Urban Development in Canada.* Ottawa: Dominion Bureau of Statistics.

Strain, Laurel A.
1990 "Receiving and providing care: the experiences of never-married elderly Canadians." Presentation, XII World Congress of Sociology, Madrid, July.

Strasburger, Victor C. and Edward Donnerstein
1999 "Children, adolescents, and the media: issues and solutions." *Pediatrics* 103: 129–39.

Street, Debra and Ingrid Connidis
2001 "Creeping selectivity in Canadian women's pensions." Pp. 158–78 in Jay Ginn, Debra Street and Sara Arber (eds.), *Women, Work and Pensions.* Buckingham, England: Open University Press.

Sumner, William G.
1940 *Folkways.* Boston: Ginn.

Sunahara, Ann
1981 *The Politics of Racism: The Uprooting of Japanese Canadians During the Second World War.* Toronto: James Lorimer.

Sutherland, Edwin
1939 *Principles of Criminology* (3rd ed.). Philadelphia: Lippincott.

Swedlund, Alan C. and Jacqueline Urla
1996 "The anthropology of Barbie: unsettling ideas of the feminine body in popular culture." Pp. 277–313 in Jennifer Terry and Jacqueline Urla (eds.), *Deviant Bodies.* Bloomington: Indiana University Press.

Sweeney, Megan
2002 "Two decades of family change: the shifting economic foundations of marriage." *American Sociological Review* 67: 132–47.
1997 "Women, men and changing families: the shifting economic foundations of marriage." University of Wisconsin-Madison: Center for Demography and Ecology, Working Paper No. 97-14.

Swidler, Ann
1986 "Culture in action." *American Sociological Review* 51: 273–86.
1995 "Cultural power and social movements." Pp. 3–24 in Hank Johnston and Bert Klandermans (eds.), *Social Movements and Culture.* Minneapolis: University of Minnesota Press.

Sykes, G. and D. Matza
1957 "Techniques of neutralization: a theory of delinquency." *American Sociological Review* 22: 664–70.

Symons, Thomas H.B.
1976 *To Know Ourselves, the Report of the Commission on Canadian Studies.* Vol. 1 and 2. Ottawa: Association of Universities and Colleges of Canada.

Sztompka, Piotr
1993 *The Sociology of Social Change.* Oxford: Blackwell.

Tabutin, D. and B. Schoumaker
2004 "The demography of sub-Saharan Africa from the 1950s to the 2000s. A survey of changes and a statistical assessment." *Population* 59(3/4): 457–555.

Tannen, Deborah
1990 *You Just Don't Understand: Women and Men in Conversation.* New York: Ballantine Books.

Tanner, J. and H. Krahn
1991 "Part-time work and deviance among high school seniors." *Canadian Journal of Sociology* 16: 281–302.

Tarde, Gabriel
1903 [1962] *The Laws of Imitation.* Elsie Clews Parsons (trans.). New York: Henry Holt & Company.

Tarrow, Sidney
1989 *Democracy and Disorder: Protest and Politics in Italy, 1965–1975.* Oxford: Clarendon.

Tastsoglou, E. and B. Miedema
2003 "Immigrant women and community development in the Canadian Maritimes: outsiders within?" *Canadian Journal of Sociology* 28: 203–34.

Taylor, F.W.
1906 *The Principles of Scientific Management.* New York: Harper Bros.

Teixeira, Carlos
2000 "Community resources and opportunities in ethnic economies: a case study of portuguese and black entrepreneurs in Toronto." *Urban Studies* 38: 2055–78.

Templeton, Alan R.
1999   "Human races: a genetic and evolutionary perspective." *American Anthropologist* 100: 632–50.

Tessler, Richard, Robert Rosenheck, and Gail Gamache
2001   "Gender differences in self-reported reasons for homelessness." *Journal of Social Distress and the Homeless* 10: 243–54.

Thomas, W.I.
1923   *The Unadjusted Girl.* Boston: Little Brown.

Thompson, E.P.
1971   "The moral economy of the English crowd in the eighteenth century." *Past and Present* 50: 76–136.

Thompson, J.H. and Allen Seager
1985   *Canada, 1922–1939: Decades of Discord.* Toronto: McClelland and Stewart.

Thompson, Paul
1989   *The Nature of Work.* Basingstoke: Macmillan.

Thussu, Daya Kishan
1998   "Localising the global: Zee TV in India." Pp. 273–94 in Daya Kishan Thussu (ed.), *Electronic Empires: Global Media and Local Resistance.* London: Arnold.

Tierney, J.
1990   "Betting the planet." *New York Times Magazine,* December, p. 52.

Tilly, Charles
1978   *From Mobilization to Revolution.* Reading: Addison-Wesley.

Tilly, Charles, Louise Tilly, and Richard Tilly
1975   *The Rebellious Century, 1830–1930.* Cambridge: Harvard University Press.

Tocqueville, Alexis de
1955   [1856] *The Old Regime and the French Revolution.* New York: Doubleday.

Todaro, Michael
1997   *Urbanization, Unemployment, and Migration in Africa: Theory and Policy.* New York: The Population Council.

Tomlinson, John
1991   *Cultural Imperialism.* Baltimore: John Hopkins University Press.

Touraine, Alain
1971   *The Post-Industrial Society: Tomorrow's Social History: Classes, Conflicts and Culture in the Programmed Society.* L.F.X. Mayhew (trans.). New York: Random House.

Townsend, Joan B.
1990   "The goddess: fact, fallacy and revitalization movement." Pp. 179–203 in Larry W. Hurtado (ed.), *Goddesses in Religions and Modern Debate.* Atlanta: Scholars Press.

Troeltsch, Ernst
1931   *The Social Teachings of the Christian Churches,* Vol. 2. Olive Wyon (trans.). New York: Macmillan.

Trost, S.
1986   "What holds marriage together." In J. Veevers (ed.), *Continuity and Change in Marriage and Family.* Toronto: Holt, Rinehart and Winston.

Trovato, Frank
1991   "Sex, marital status, and suicide in Canada: 1951–1981." *Sociological Perspectives* 34: 427–45.

Turcotte, Pierre and Alain Bélanger
1998   "The dynamics of formation and dissolution of first common-law unions in Canada." Ottawa: Statistics Canada.

Turkle, Sherry
1995   *Life on the Screen: Identity in the Age of the Internet.* New York: Simon and Schuster.

Turner, B.S.
1988   *Status.* Minneapolis: University of Minnesota Press.

Turner, R. and L.M. Killian
1957   *Collective Behavior.* Englewood Cliffs: Prentice Hall.

Tylor, Edward
1871   *Primitive Culture: Researches into the Development of Mythology, Philosophy, Religion, Language, Art, and Custom,* Vol. 1. London: John Murphy.

Underwood, T.
1999   "Are your kids driving you crazy?" *The Globe and Mail,* April 17: D1.

United Nations
2005   *World Population Prospects: The 2004 Revision.* New York: United Nations, Department of Economic and Social Affairs, Population Division, http://esa.un.org/unpp (accessed 31 March 2006).
2004   *World Urbanization Prospects: The 2003 Revision, Highlights and Tables.* New York: United Nations.
2003   *World Population Prospects: The 2002 Revision.* New York: United Nations.
2002   *World Urbanization Prospects: The 2001 Revision.* Estimates and Projections of Urban and Rural Populations and of Urban Agglomerations. Dept. of Economic and Social Affairs. New York: United Nations.
2001   *World Population Prospects: The 2000 Revision.* New York: United Nations.
1998   *World Population Prospects: The 1996 Revision.* New York: United Nations
1997   *1997 Demographic Yearbook.* New York: United Nations.
1995   *Challenge of Urbanization: The World's Large Cities.* Dept. of Economic and Social Information and Policy Analysis. Population Division. New York: United Nations.

UNAIDS/WHO
2005   *AIDS Epidemic Update: December 2005.* UNAIDS Joint United Nations Program on HIV/AIDS.

United Nations Development Program/World Health Organization
2002   *AIDS Epidemic Update.*

United Nations Development Program
2002   *Report on the Global HIV/AIDS Epidemic.*

1997   *Human Development Report 1997.* New York: Oxford University Press.

U.S. Bureau of the Census
1998   *Statistical Abstract of the United States 1998.* Washington: U.S. Government Printing Office.

Urla, Jacqueline and Alan C. Swedlund
1995   "The anthropometry of Barbie: unsettling ideals of the feminine body in popular culture." In J. Terry and J. Urla (eds.), *Deviant Bodies.* Bloomington: Indiana University Press.

Urmetzer, Peter and Neil Guppy
2004   "Changing income inequality in Canada." Pp. 75–84 in James Curtis, Edward Grabb, and Neil Guppy (eds.), *Social Inequality in Canada: Patterns, Problems, and Policies* (4th ed.). Toronto: Pearson Education Canada.

Usher, Alex
2005   *A Little Knowledge Is a Dangerous Thing: How Perceptions of Costs and Benefits Affect Access to Education.* Washington, Toronto, and Melbourne: Educational Policy Institute.

Vaillant, C. and G.E. Vaillant
1993   "Is the U-curve of marital satisfaction an illusion? A 40-year study of marriage." *Journal of Marriage and the Family* 55: 230–39.

Van den Berghe, Pierre
1967   *Race and Racism: A Comparative Perspective.* New York: Wiley.

van Poppel, F. and L. Day
1996   "A test of Durkheim's theory of suicide." *American Sociological Review* 61: 500–07.

Vasi, I.B. and Michael Macy
2003   "The mobilizer's dilemma: crisis, empowerment, and collective action." *Social Forces* 81: 979–98.

Waddell, Eric
1986   "State, language and society: the vicissitudes of French in Quebec and Canada." Pp. 67–110 in Alan Cairns and Cynthia Williams (eds.), *The Politics of Gender, Ethnicity, and Language in Canada.* Toronto: University of Toronto Press.

Wadhera, Surinder and Wayne Millar
1997   "Teenage pregnancies, 1974 to 1994." *Health Reports* 9: 9–17.

Waite, Linda J. and Maggie Gallagher
2000   *The Case for Marriage.* New York: Doubleday.

Walkowitz, J.
1980   "The politics of prostitution." *Signs: Journal of Women in Culture and Society* 6(1): 123–35.

Walker, A.
1991   "The relationship between the family and the state in the care of older people." *Canadian Journal on Aging* 10: 94–112.

Waller, Willard
1937   "The rating and dating complex." *American Sociological Review* 2: 727–34.

Wallerstein, Immanuel
1974   *The Modern World System.* New York: Academic Press.

Wallis, Roger and Krister Malm
1984   *Big Sounds from Small Peoples: The Music Industry in Small Countries.* New York: Pendragon.

Wanner, Richard A.
2004   "Social mobility in Canada: concepts, patterns, and trends." Pp. 131–47 in James Curtis, Edward Grabb, and Neil Guppy (eds.), *Social Inequality in Canada: Patterns, Problems, and Policies* (4th ed.). Toronto: Pearson Education Canada.
1999   "Expansion and ascription: trends in educational opportunity in Canada." *Canadian Review of Sociology and Anthropology* 36: 409–42.

Wanner, Richard and Bernadette Hayes.
1996   "Intergenerational occupational mobility among men in Canada and Australia." *Canadian Journal of Sociology* 21: 43–76.

Ward, Martha C. and Monica Edelstein
2006.   *A World Full of Women* (4th ed.). Boston: Pearson.

Washburn, Sherman
1960   "Tools and human evolution." *Scientific American.* September: 61–74.

Waterman, Peter
1998   *Globalization, Social Movements and the New Internationalism.* London: Mansell.

Watkins, S. C.
1986   "Conclusions." Pp. 420–49 in A.J. Coale and S.C. Watkins (eds.), *The Decline of Fertility in Europe.* Princeton, NJ: Princeton University Press.

Watson, James L.
2000   "China's Big Mac attack." *Foreign Affairs* 79: 120–34.

Weber, Max
1978   [1958] *From Max Weber: Essays in Sociology.* Translated by H.H. Gerth and C. Wright Mills. New York: Oxford University Press.
1930   [1904–05] *The Protestant Ethic and the Spirit of Capitalism.* London: Allen and Unwin.
1921   *Economy and Society: An Outline of Interpretive Sociology,* Vols. 1 and 2. G. Roth and C. Wittich (eds). Berkeley: University of California Press.

Weeks, John R.
2005   *Population: An Introduction to Concepts and Issues* (9th ed.). Belmont CA: Wadsworth Thomson Learning.
1996   *Population: An Introduction to Concepts and Issues* (6th ed.). Belmont: Wadsworth Publishing Company.

Weinstein, Jay
1997   *Social and Cultural Change: Social Science for a Dynamic World.* Toronto: Allyn and Bacon.

Wells, L. Edward and Joseph H. Rankin
1991   "Families and delinquency: a meta-analysis of the impact of broken homes." *Social Problems* 38: 71–93.

White, Jerry P.
1993   "Changing labour process and the nursing crisis in Canadian hospitals." *Studies in Political Economy,* 40(Spring): 103–34.
1992   "The state and industrial relations in a neo-conservative era." Pp. 198–221 in L. Haiven, S. McBride, and G. Shields (eds.) *Regulating Labour: The State, Neo-Conservatism and Industrial Relations.* Toronto: Garamond Press.
1990   *Hospital Strike: Women, Unions and Public Sector Conflict.* Toronto: Thompson Educational Press.

White, Jerry P. and Norene Pupo
1994   "Union leaders and the economic crisis: responses to restructuring." *Industrial Relations* 49: 821–45.

White, Jerry P., Dan Beavon, and Paul Maxim
2003   *Aboriginal Conditions: The Research Foundations for Public Policy.* Vancouver: University of British Columbia Press.

White, Lynn
1994   "Coresidence and leaving home: young adults and their parents." *Annual Review of Sociology* 20: 81–102.

White, Pamela
1986   *Census of Canada: Ethnic Diversity in Canada.* Ottawa: Minister of Supply and Services Canada.

Whyte, William Foote (ed.)
1991   *Participatory Action Research.* Newbury Park: Sage.

Wien, Fred and Catherine Corrigall-Brown
2004   "Regional inequality: explanations and policy issues." Pp. 325–50 in James Curtis, Edward Grabb, and Neil Guppy (eds.), *Social Inequality in Canada: Patterns, Problems, and Policies* (4th ed.). Toronto: Pearson Education Canada.

Wilhelm, Anthony G.
2006   *Digital Nation: Toward an Inclusive Information Society.* Cambridge, MA: MIT Press.

Wilkins, Kathryn
2003   "Social support and mortality in seniors." *Health Reports* 14: 21–34.

Wilkins, Russell, Jean-Marie Berthelot, and Edward Ng
2002   "Trends in mortality by neighbourhood in urban Canada from 1971 to 1996." *Health Reports* 13(Supp.): 1–28.

Williams, Raymond
1983   *Keywords.* Oxford: Oxford University Press.
1980   *Problems in Materialism and Culture.* London: Verso.

Williams, Thomas Rhys
1972   *Introduction to Socialization.* St. Louis: C.V. Mosby.

Willis, Paul
1977   *Learning to Labour: How Working Class Kids Get Working Class Jobs.* Farnborough: Saxon House.

Willmott, Hugh (ed.).
1990   *Labour Process Theory.* Hampshire: Macmillan.

Wilson, Bryan
1982   *Religion in Sociological Perspective.* Oxford: Oxford University Press.
1966   *Religion in Secular Society.* London: Watts.

Wilson, Edward O.
2000   *The Future of Life.* New York: Alfred A. Knopf.
1975   *Sociobiology: The New Synthesis.* Cambridge: Harvard University Press.

Wilson, Paul, Robyn Lincoln, and Duncan Chappell
1986   "Physician fraud and abuse in Canada: a preliminary examination." *Canadian Journal of Criminology* 28: 129–46.

Winkler, Edwin A.
2002   "Chinese reproductive policy at the turn of the millenium." *Population and Development Review* 28: 379–418.

Wister, Andrew, Barbara A. Mitchell, and Ellen M. Gee
1997   "Does money matter? Parental income and living arrangement satisfaction among 'Boomerang' children during coresidence." *Canadian Studies in Population* 24: 125–45.

Wister, A. and C. Moore
1998   "First Nations elders in Canada: issues, problems and successes in health care policy." In Andrew Wister and Gloria Gutman (eds.), *Health Systems and Aging in Selected Pacific Rim Countries: Cultural Diversity and Change.* Vancouver: Gerontology Research Centre, Simon Fraser University.

Wolf, Naomi
1997   *Promiscuities: The Secret Struggle for Womanhood.* Toronto: Random House.
1990   *The Beauty Myth.* Toronto: Random House.

Wolff, K. (ed.)
1950   *The Sociology of Georg Simmel.* New York: The Free Press.

Wolff, Lee
1991   "Drug crimes." *Canadian Social Trends* 20: 26–29.

Wood, A.
1994   *North–South Trade, Employment and Inequality.* Oxford: Oxford University Press.

Wood, David (ed)
1996   *Torture Garden: A Photographic Archive of the New Flesh.* London: Creation Books.

Woods, Peter
1990   *The Happiest Days? How Pupils Cope With School.* London and New York: Falmer Press.

World Bank
2001   *World Devleopment Indicators,* www.worldbank.org/data/wdi2001
1999   *Knowledge for Development: 1998/99 World Development Report.* New York: Oxford University Press.
1992   *World Development Report 1992.* New York: Oxford University Press.

World Health Organization
2005   *Avian influenza: assessing the pandemic threat* , January, www.who.int/csr/disease/influenza/WHO_CDS_2005_29/en/index.html

Wotherspoon, Terry
2004   *The Sociology of Education in Canada: Critical Perspectives* (2nd ed.). Toronto: Oxford University Press.

Wotherspoon, Terry and Vic Satzewich
1993   *First Nations: Race, Class, and Gender Relations.* Scarborough: Nelson Canada.

Wrigley, E.A. and R.S. Schofield
1981   *The Population History of England, 1541–1871.* Cambridge: Cambridge University Press.

Wrong, Dennis
1961   "The oversocialized conception of man in modern sociology." *American Sociological Review* 26: 183–93.

Wu, Zheng and Kelly Martin
1999   "Contraceptive choice in Canada." Paper presented at the Annual Meeting of the Canadian Population Society, Lennoxville, Quebec.

Wuthnow, Ro bert (ed.)
1994   *"I Come Away Stronger": How Small Groups Are Shaping American Religion.* Grand Rapids: Eerdmans.

Yi, Sun-Kyung
1991   "Crime statistics based on race promote hatred, board told." *The Globe and Mail*, Aug. 23.

Yi, Zeng, T. Ping, G. Baochang, X. Yi, L. Bohau, and L. Yongping
1993   "Causes and implications of the recent increase in the reported sex ratio at birth in China." *Population and Development Review* 19: 283–301.

Yinger, J. Milton
1970   *The Scientific Study of Religion.* New York: Macmillan.

Young, Jock and Roger Matthews (eds.)
1992   *Rethinking Criminology: The Realist Debate.* London: Sage.

Zavitz-Gocan, Amanda
2003   "The politics of race, ideology and media: the portrayal of First Nations capacity for self government in Canadian newspapers." Paper presented at the Congress of the Social Sciences and Humanities held in Halifax, Nova Scotia, May 28–June 4.

Ziman, John M.
2000   *Real Science: What It Is and What It Means.* Cambridge: Cambridge Univ. Press.

Zollo, Peter
1995   "Talking to teens: the teenage market is free-spending and loaded with untapped potential." *American Demographics* November: 22–28.

Subject Index

1984 (Orwell), 278

A

abnormal behaviour, 88
Aboriginal Canadians, 172
  see also First Nations, Iroquois
    Indians
  and colonialism, 187–189
  and education, 304, 305, 306
  high arrest and incarceration
    rates of, 92
  high mortality rates of, 382
  segregation of children, 178, 305–306
  social inequality and discrimination
    against, 140–141, 173, 181, 304–305
abortion, 374
abstinence standard, 235
accidental sampling, 23
acculturation, 194
achieved status, 121
active audience theory, 283
activity theory, 204
adolescents
  see also youth(s)
  impact of nurture on, 70
  influence of parenting styles on, 77
  socialization in Western society, 70
adultery, 228, 247
advertising, 283–284
affirmative action, 195, 411
Africa
  high fertility rates, 377–378
  HIV/AIDs epidemic, 379
  population growth, 370
African Americans, 305
African Canadians, 306
age effects, 204
age pyramid, 388
age-specific death rates, 378
age-specific fertility rate, 373
age-stratification perspective,
  204–205
aggression, 103
aging
  critical theory, 206
  future directions and
    challenges of, 221
  government income and, 216
  and health, 214
  and health care, 214–216
  and mental illness, 102
  and migration, 384

  personalizing, 202–203
  population of Canada, 202,
    206–207, 221
  and retirement, 216–218
  senior discounts, 168
  and social inequality, 143–144
  and social policy, 219–220
  stereotypes of, 203
  study of, 203–204, 205
  summary of, 221–222
  theoretical approaches to,
    204–205, 206
aging and family
  childless older persons, 213
  impact of caring, 209
  intergenerational ties, 211
  intimate ties, 208
  marriage in the later years, 208–209
  parent–child relationship, 211–212
  qualitative data, 205
  same-sex relationships, 211
  siblings, 213–214
  single people (never-married), 210
  widowhood and divorce, 209–210
aging theory
  activity theory, 204
  age-stratification perspective, 204–205
  critical theory, 206
  disengagement theory, 204
  exchange theory, 205
  feminist theories, 206
  life course perspective, 206
  political economy of aging
    perspective, 206
  social constructionist perspective, 206
AIDs. *See* HIV/ AIDs
Aland Islands, 352
Al Qaeda, 294
alienation, 335
altruistic suicide, 3
Amazons, 46
American Revolution, 45, 397, 401, 402
analysis
  in experimentation, 26
  micro and macro, 204
  in participant observation, 29
  in survey research, 24–27
androcentrism, 50
Anglican Church, 268
  adverse effects of Aboriginal
    mission, 47–48
  influence on English Canada, 46

Anglo-Saxons, economic dominance of,
  138–140
anomic suicides, 3
anomie, 328, 335, 403
anomie theory, 104–105
anthropology, 3
anticipatory socialization, 73
apartheid, 182
appearance. *See* body image; body
  transformations
Apprentice, 283
Arabs. *See* Islam
Arapesh, 43, 154, 229
Arawak Indians, 397
Arunta, 259–260
ascetic, 261
ascribed status, 120–121
Asia
  fertility control, 373
  HIV/AIDs epidemic, 379
  mobile technology adoption in, 276
assimilationism, 193–195
  background of, 193–194
  criticisms of, 194–195
  defined, 193
Atanarjurat: The Fast Runner, 188
Athena, 51
Aum Shinrikyo, 262
Australian Aboriginals, 47–48, 259–260
authoritative parenting, 77, 78
axiomatic logic, 20

B

baby boomers, 221
Bangladesh, 108, 276
Barbados, 397
Barbie, as a cultural icon, 51
Baywatch, 286
behaviour
  see also culture
  genetics and, 103
  impact of social forces on, 2–3
  and social action, 19
Beslan, Russia, 317
bias
  see also stereotypes
  among police force, 110
  androcentrism, 50
  ethnocentrism, 48
  Eurocentrism, 48, 50
  infantalization, 48
  orientalism, 49

Photography Credits